P9-CJY-618

Primate Functional Morphology and Evolution

World Anthropology

General Editor

SOL TAX

Patrons

CLAUDE LÉVI-STRAUSS
MARGARET MEAD
LAILA SHUKRY EL HAMAMSY
M. N. SRINIVAS

MOUTON PUBLISHERS · THE HAGUE · PARIS
DISTRIBUTED IN THE USA AND CANADA BY ALDINE, CHICAGO

Primate Functional Morphology and Evolution

Editor

RUSSELL H. TUTTLE

MOUTON PUBLISHERS · THE HAGUE · PARIS

DISTRIBUTED IN THE USA AND CANADA BY ALDINE, CHICAGO

Distributed in the United States of America and Canada
by Aldine Publishing Company, Chicago, Illinois
ISBN 90-279-7689-9 (Mouton)
0-202-02016-9 (Aldine)
Jacket photo: Chicago Zoological Society by Leland La France
Indexes by John Jennings
Cover and jacket design by Jurriaan Schrofer
Printed in the Netherlands

to

Sir Wilfrid E. LeGros Clark

General Editor's Preface

This book presents and discusses new research on the origin and evolution of primates, from molecular structures to anatomical correlates of their feeding behaviors, means of locomotion, and communication leading to language in hominids. Studies of primates have developed so rapidly in this generation—and include so large a variety of disciplines — that only journals can maintain the pace. Each journal necessarily confines itself to a particular subject and puts limits as well on style and length. The present book and its two companion volumes therefore offer a unique variety of new information and ideas, often by younger people from different continents writing freely for discussions which were then also published. This book required both the creative energy of the brilliant young paleoanthropologist who organized the meetings and edited the results, and also the inspiration of an unusual international Congress.

Like most contemporary sciences, anthropology is a product of the European tradition. Some argue that it is a product of colonialism, with one small and self-interested part of the species dominating the study of the whole. If we are to understand the species, our science needs substantial input from scholars who represent a variety of the world's cultures. It was a deliberate purpose of the IXth International Congress of Anthropological and Ethnological Sciences to provide impetus in this direction. The *World Anthropology* volumes, therefore, offer a first glimpse of a human science in which members from all societies have played an active role. Each of the books is designed to be self-contained; each is an attempt to update its particular sector of scientific knowledge and is written by specialists from all parts of the world. Each volume should be read and reviewed individually as a separate volume on its own given subject. The set as a whole will indicate what changes are in store for anthropology as scholars from the developing countries join in studying the species of which we are all a part.

The IXth Congress was planned from the beginning not only to include as many of the scholars from every part of the world as possible, but also with a view toward the eventual publication of the papers in high-quality volumes. At previous Congresses scholars were invited to bring papers which were then read out loud. They were necessarily limited in length; many were only summarized; there was little time for discussion; and the sparse discussion could only be in one language. The IXth Congress was an experiment aimed at changing this. Papers were written with the intention of exchanging them before the Congress, particularly in extensive pre-Congress sessions; they were not intended to be read at the Congress, that time being devoted to discussions — discussions which were simultaneously and professionally translated into five languages. The method for eliciting the papers was structured to make as representative a sample as was allowable when scholarly creativity — hence self-selection — was critically important. Scholars were asked both to propose papers of their own and to suggest topics for sessions of the Congress which they might edit into volumes. All were then informed of the suggestions and encouraged to re-think their own papers and the topics. The process, therefore, was a continuous one of feedback and exchange and it has continued to be so even after the Congress. The some two thousand papers comprising *World Anthropology* certainly then offer a substantial sample of world anthropology. It has been said that anthropology is at a turning point; if this is so, these volumes will be the historical direction-markers.

As might have been foreseen in the first post-colonial generation, the large majority of the Congress papers (82 percent) are the work of scholars identified with the industrialized world which fathered our traditional discipline and the institution of the Congress itself: Eastern Europe (15 percent); Western Europe (16 percent); North America (47 percent); Japan, South Africa, Australia, and New Zealand (4 percent). Only 18 percent of the papers are from developing areas: Africa (4 percent); Asia-Oceania (9 percent); Latin America (5 percent). Aside from the substantial representation from the U.S.S.R. and the nations of Eastern Europe, a significant difference between this corpus of written material and that of other Congresses is the addition of the large proportion of contributions from Africa, Asia, and Latin America. "Only 18 percent" is two to four times as great a proportion as that of other Congresses; moreover, 18 percent of 2,000 papers is 360 papers, 10 times the number of "Third World" papers presented at previous Congresses. In fact, these 360 papers are more than the total of ALL papers published after the last International Congress of Anthropological and Ethnological Sciences which was held in the United States (Philadelphia, 1956).

The significance of the increase is not simply quantitative. The input of scholars from areas which have until recently been no more than subject matter for anthropology represents both feedback and also long-awaited theoretical contributions from the perspectives of very different cultural, social, and historical traditions. Many who attended the IXth Congress were convinced that anthropology would not be the same in the future. The fact that the next Congress (India, 1978) will be our first in the "Third World" may be symbolic of the change. Meanwhile, sober consideration of the present set of books will show how much, and just where and how, our discipline is being revolutionized.

In addition to its two companion volumes, *Paleoanthropology: morphology and paleoecology* and *Socioecology and psychology of primates*, readers of this book will be particularly interested in others of this series on *World Anthropology* which deal with archeology and with biological, psychological, and linguistic anthropology, and with particular geographic areas of the Old World.

Chicago, Illinois
August 25, 1975

SOL TAX

Preface

This volume contains papers that were prepared for discussion in Session 211 at the IXth International Congress of Anthropological and Ethnological Sciences. The session was convened on September 2, 1973, at the Conrad Hilton Hotel in Chicago, Illinois.

Although a few papers were volunteered in response to the initial call for papers from the conference office, I solicited most of them with the intention of focusing discussion on a limited number of problem areas in evolutionary primatology that are characterized by current intensive research and thecretic ferment. Small subsets of papers and two or three topics were discussed by three panels which included authors of papers in the session, other experts on one or more subjects treated in the papers, and reputable raconteurs.

Becky Sigmon and Phillip Tobias served with me as co-chairpersons and discussants during the entire session.

The first panel included Susan Cachel, Brunetto Chiarelli, Robert Eckhardt, Morris Goodman, C. Owen Lovejoy, Peter Murray, Frederick Szalay, and Phillip Walker. They were principal discussants of papers in Sections I, II, and III of this volume.

The second panel included John V. Basmajian, Morris Goodman, Farish Jenkins, Jr., Adriaan Kortlandt, Benno Kummer, Gabriel Lasker, and C. Owen Lovejoy. They were principal discussants of papers in Sections IV and V herein.

The third panel included Robert Eckhardt, Morris Goodman, Hannibal Hamlin, Philip Lieberman, George Sacher, Christian Vogel, and Milford Wolpoff. They were principal discussants of papers in Section VI.

The format of discussion varied considerably during the session. But generally panelists were asked to summarize their own papers and to comment on related papers of other symposiasts. The topics and papers were then opened for discussion by the panel and the audience. In some instances the briefs were illustrated with slides.

The arrangement of this volume does not faithfully reflect the chronology of events in Session 211. Some panelists continued into the next session under my chairmanship (where closely related topics were discussed); and conversations occurred that I believe more properly belong in this volume than in another. Further, the order in which the topics and papers were discussed is not exactly represented in the arrangement of chapters herein.

I prepared and edited typescripts of all discussions in the session and mailed them to the commentators for further editing, brief augmentation, and permission to publish. Summaries of papers were deleted from the typescript. So we have here a greatly condensed (but I hope no less mentally nutritious) rendering of the conference discussions.

Many persons contributed to the success of this adventure. Preeminent among them is Sol Tax, who was encouraging, challenging, and insightful about every aspect of the session and volume. His staff, especially Roberta MacGowan and Gay Neuberger, and my secretaries, June Ford and Susan Kurth, greatly expedited the preparation of manuscripts and correspondence with the contributors. It was also delightful to work with Jean Block and other staff members of the Midway Editorial Service and Karen Tkach and Peter Zoutendijk of Mouton Publishers.

Marlene Tuttle contributed in many ways to the development and completion of the project, especially assisting with typescripts of the discussions and the index. We are grateful to Nicole and Matthew Tuttle for their cooperation which permitted us to work together on the project.

The good cheer, cooperation, and communicativeness of the participants were overwhelming. We are very grateful for their colleagueship.

University of Chicago
Chicago, Illinois
May 25, 1974

RUSSELL H. TUTTLE

Table of Contents

SECTION THREE: ANATOMICAL CORRELATES OF FEEDING BEHAVIOR IN MONKEYS, APES, AND MAN

SECTION FOUR: KNUCKLE-WALKING AND HOMINOID EVOLUTION

SECTION FIVE: MECHANISMS AND EVOLUTION OF BIPEDALISM IN THE HOMINOIDEA

SECTION SIX: BRAIN EVOLUTION IN THE HOMINOIDEA AND THE EVOLUTION OF HUMAN LANGUAGE

SECTION ONE

New Perspectives on the Origin and Deployment of Catarrhine Primates

Haplorhine Phylogeny and the Status of the Anthropoidea

F. S. SZALAY

INTRODUCTION

Although the name Haplorhini, encompassing the Tarsiiformes, Platyrrhini, and Catarrhini, dates back to Pocock (1918), the hypothesis that tarsiers were more closely related to the Anthropoidea (Mivart 1864) than to the lemurs had been suggested several times prior to that date. In recent years, both the concept and the name Haplorhini as a subordinal category have found increasing acceptance (Hill 1955; Luckett 1971; Martin 1972).

Evidence suggests the Haplorhini to be a monophyletic category, and the common ancestors of platyrrhines and catarrhines probably share a more recent common ancestor with tarsiiforms than with any other primates. There are several views on the direction of dispersal for the ancestral platyrrhine and catarrhine primates. As fossil evidence for the route of deployment is lacking, some of these suggestions merely attempt to give an alternative to the one which states that the ancestral platyrrhines arrived in South America as a colonizing stock from Africa.

I shall briefly discuss (1) the origins and the degree of relationships of haplorhine primates (Tarsiiformes, Platyrrhini, and Catarrhini) among themselves, (2) the problem of the monophyly of the Anthropoidea, and (3) some aspects of the catarrhine radiation. It is perhaps advisable first to briefly review some concepts and practices used in systematics to determine phylogenetic relationships.

A recent lucid and thorough review of methods of phylogenetic inference has been provided by Schaeffer, Hecht, and Eldredge (1972).

Research for this paper was supported by National Science Foundation Grant GS 32315. Figures were drawn by Anita J. Cleary, and technical assistance with the manuscript was rendered by Miriam Siroky.

For Plates, see pp. ii–iii, between pp. 560–561

These authors review such crucial concepts as homology versus convergence and morphocline polarity (i.e. the estimation of what is primitive and what is advanced in a series of homologous characters) and advocate an essentially sound cladistic methodology, rooted in both the contributions of the school of evolutionary systematics and those of Hennig (1965, 1966) and other cladists.

Schaeffer, Hecht, and Eldredge advance a position which they believe paleontologists should have in regard to cladistic phylogenetics, but I believe that they may underrate the relative importance of the temporal dimensions of fossil taxa for phyletic studies. They state (1972: 43) that "biostratigraphy is rarely relevant to the problem of working out relationships because it may add a distorting bias, and . . . identification of an actual fossil taxon with an ancestral morphotype is unnecessary for the delimitation of relationships." As Hennig's cladistic methodology, which they advocate, is an essentially workable one, I would like to point out that the temporal position of taxa may be relevant more often than they suggest. Most paleontologists probably would agree that exact common ancestors in the fossil record on the species level are rarities. A cladistic analysis of all (fossil and extant) known taxa, however, can yield morphotypes whose relationships to known species of fossil taxa can be stated with some certainty. The result is usually a phylogenetic hypothesis, clearly more useful and closer to reality than a view that it is impossible to find common ancestors. Thus, the fossil record will continue to be used in phylogenetic analysis, the very nature of which is biological history. The fossils are the only key to this history.

Today paleogeography, via plate tectonics, and paleozoogeography, as revealed by the fossil record, are coming into their own for systematic biology. Knowledge of whether corridors, barriers, filter bridges, and sweepstakes routes (Simpson's extremely useful concepts) existed between moving land masses at a given time is increasingly important. The spatial and temporal position of fossil taxa can add a crucial dimension to the analysis of their morphology. Often, polarity cannot be inferred with the clarity that the crispness of the concept implies; equally often, the addition of geographical information may make a given taxon useful in the construction of a theory of relationships.

Biostratigraphical information, therefore, is as much a part of the evolutionary biology of taxa, hence of their phylogenetic characters, as their more tangible phenotypic attributes. In addition, the time dimension supplied by those fossils which either are or closely resemble a morphotype allows the only tangible approximations of the actual phylogeny of a group, in contrast to necessarily less sophisticated assessments offered by cladograms when the available time dimension is not considered. It is obvious, but worth restating, that only the fossil record offers the solutions to problems of the "whens" and "wheres" of evolutionary inquiries, problems often tied to genealogical questions.

In their assessment of phylogenetic analysis conducted by paleontologists, Schaeffer, Hecht, and Eldredge (1972) do not mention the use of functional studies in systematics. In most of the paleontological literature on mammals, it is perhaps silently implied or supposed that morphocline polarity and the homologies of derived states of static patterns alone are sufficient to infer phylogeny. Systematists often maintain that the reliability of their phylogenetic hypotheses is largely dependent on the diversity and abundance of usable characters. The fossil record and living forms of some groups are often said to be inadequate bases for phylogenetic inferences at even gross levels of resolution. As perhaps all biologists who have done some functional research on the meaning of given character complexes could testify, studying mechanical function in both fossil and living taxa and the biological role (Bock and von Wahlert 1965) of these character complexes in living forms yields surprisingly great "numbers" of new characters or new, more profound appreciation of "known" ones. This increase in the available and analyzable paleontological and neontological information often allows a more convincing arrangement of morphocline polarity and more clearly established homologies (including homologous functions [Bock 1969: 72]), hence it often permits construction of more reliable phylogenetic hypotheses where the evidence, prior to a functional study, was judged to be inadequate. Yet, as functional anatomical studies often ignore the polarity of characters studied and thus deprive the work of the phyletic meaning of the very functional explanations they seek, so systematic studies can greatly weaken their power of resolution in analyzing character states when basic functional considerations are set aside.

Most primatologists and human biologists have little opportunity to judge various phylogenies, let alone work on problems of phylogeny. Unfortunately, it is customary in textbooks, in introductory chapters of books on primates, and often in journal articles also, to refer to taxonomies and classifications when authors should be discussing phylogeny. Although the differences between a phylogenetic hypothesis and its taxonomic expression have been thoroughly discussed by Simpson (1961) and Mayr (1969), the most articulate proponents of evolutionary systematics, two vocal schools of systematics—the pheneticists and the pure cladists (see in particular Mayr's 1965 discussion of the former) — have advocated methods and practices for the construction of classifications different from those of evolutionary systematists. Pure cladists such as the founder of this school of systematics (Hennig 1950, 1965, 1966) would base classifications entirely on inferred recency of common ancestry, so that classifications would reflect nothing but genealogy. Most evolutionary systematists feel that sole reliance on phylogeny would rob classifications of their usefulness because such classifications (a) would not provide for the nonspecialist the extremely useful "biological common denominators" of the taxa included in a given group, (b) would lessen stability of classifications, and (c) would still remain inadequate in expressing the multidimensional nature of evolutionary descent (consult Simpson 1961, 1963; Mayr 1969; and recent issues of *Systematic Zoology* for enlightening and sometimes exasperating debates on the subject).

It should be added here that it has become an increasingly common practice for evolutionary systematists to include in taxa of any level those subordinate taxa which make the higher category monophyletic. In other words, a genus, family, or higher category usually contains the most recent alleged common ancestor of all the descendants included in that group (see Ashlock 1972). This does not mean, however, as the pure cladistic school of systematics would have it, that all the descendants of a common ancestor must be included in that group.

Figure 1 presents a phylogeny of the primates and Table 1 is a classification based on that phylogenetic hypothesis. Note that the Cheirogaleidae are shown to be derived from taxa included in the Lemurinae, and the Lorisidae are subsequently shown to have originated from cheirogaleids. The platyrrhines are shown to be derived from some of the Omomyinae, and the catarrhines in turn are alleged to have been derived from taxa which are stated to be platyrrhines. The tarsiiformes are shown to have been derived possibly from Paleocene forms which were very similar to or were the earliest strepsirhines. This latter ancestral stock was derived from taxa which, were they known, would probably be allocated to the Paromomyiformes.

HAPLORHINE RELATIONSHIPS

I will first examine some of the evidence for the hypothesis that there is a more recent common ancestry between tarsiiforms, platyrrhines, and catarrhines than between these three groups and any of the strepsirhine or paromomyiform primates. Perhaps one of the more convincing character complexes which allows the best use of fossils for phylogenetic inference on the level of mammalian higher categories is the morphology of the basicranium. It is complex and conservative within family groups, yet often divergent enough between families and superfamilies.

A recent survey of adult basicranial morphology of living and fossil primates reaffirmed a dichotomy at least in a number of closely interwoven characters such as the nature of the bulla and the relative size and path of the branches of the internal carotid artery and the various orifices associated with them. Character analysis of the bony morphology of the basicranium as it reflects the internal carotid circulation of living and fossil primates easily lends itself to an arrangement in a morphocline, the polarity of which appears very convincing. The inferred primitive condition as well as the prevailing pattern of both the predominantly Paleocene Paromomyiformes (Szalay 1972, 1973) and the Strepsirhini appears to indicate that the promontory branch of the internal carotid artery was relatively tiny, as in most primitive Eutheria, whereas the stapedial artery, at least in the primitive lemuriform strepsirhines, was of considerable importance (Szalay and Katz 1973). The presence of an ex-

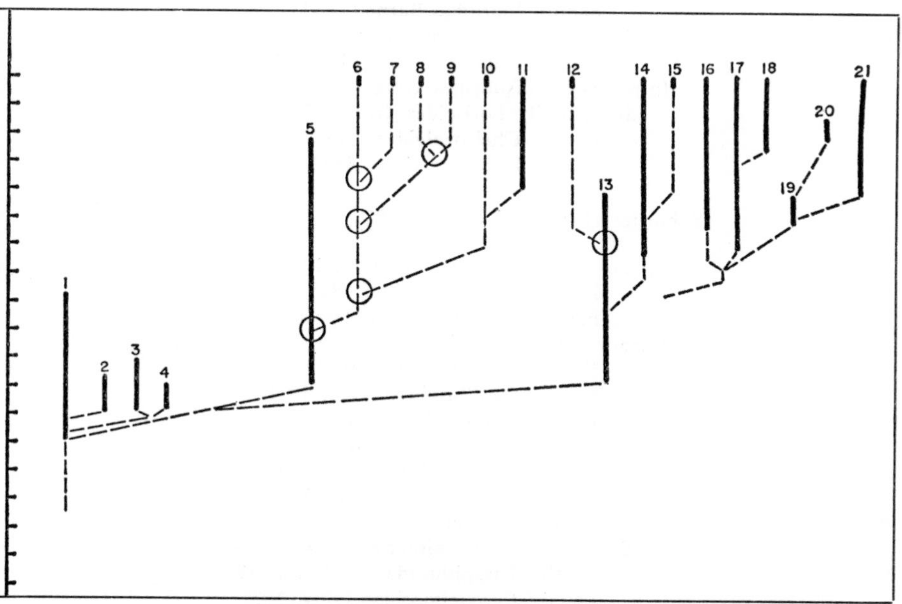

Figure 1. Phylogeny of the recognized families of primates. Heavy solid lines represent known ranges and broken lines depict recency of relationships. 1. Paromomyidae; 2. Picrodontidae; 3. Plesiadapidae; 4. Carpolestidae; 5. Adapidae; 6. Lemuridae; 7. Megaladapidae; 8. Indriidae; 9. Daubentoniidae; 10. Cheirogalidae; 11. Lorisidae; 12. Tarsiidae; 13. Omomyidae; 14. Cebidae; 15. Callithricidae; 16. Hylobatidae; 17. Pongidae; 18. Hominidae; 19. Parapithecidae; 20. Oreopithecidae; 21. Cercopithecidae. Circles represent uncertainty as to even an approximate time of divergence

Table 1. An evolutionary classification of primates based on the phylogenetic hypothesis presented in Figure 1 and on the compromise judgment of structurally (and presumably biologically) most significant changes

Order Primates Linnaeus, 1758

Suborder Paromomyiformes Szalay, 1973

Superfamily Paromomyoidea Simpson, 1940
Family Paromomyidae Simpson, 1940
Family Picrodontidae Simpson, 1937
Superfamily Plesiadapoidea Trouessart, 1897
Family Plesiadapidae Trouessart, 1897
Family Carpolestidae Simpson, 1935

Suborder Strepsirhini E. Geoffroy, 1812

Infraorder Lemuriformes Gregory, 1915
Superfamily Lemuroidea Gray, 1821
Family Adapidae Trouessart, 1879
Family Lemuridae Gray, 1821
Family Megaladapidae Flower and Lydekker, 1891
Family Indriidae Burnett, 1828
Superfamily Daubentonoidea Gray, 1821
Family Daubentoniidae Gray, 1821
Infraorder Lorisiformes Gregory, 1915
Superfamily Lorisoidea Gray, 1821
Family Cheirogaleidae Gray, 1870
Family Lorisidae Gray, 1821

Suborder Haplorhini Pocock, 1818

Infraorder Tarsiiformes Gregory, 1915
Family Tarsiidae Gray, 1825
Family Omomyidae Trouessart, 1879
Infraorder Platyrrhini Hemprick, 1820
Family Cebidae Bonaparte, 1831
Family Callithricidae Gray, 1821
Infraorder Catarrhini Hemprick, 1820
Superfamily Hominoidea Gray, 1825
Family Hylobatidae Gray, 1870
Family Pongidae Elliot, 1913
Family Hominidae Gray, 1825
Superfamily Cercopithecoidea Gray, 1821
Family Parapithecidae Schlosser, 1911
Family Cercopithecidae Gray, 1821
Family Oreopithecidae Schwalbe, 1915

trabullar anterior carotid artery in cheirogaleids and the latter condition coupled with petromastoid inflation in the lorisids does not alter the interpretation that the primitive strepsirhine pattern is displayed by the lemuriforms, as the former conditions are certainly derived character states.

The tarsiiforms, platyrrhines, and catarrhines, in contrast to the strepsirhines, share a distinctly enlarged promontory artery, along with the possibly primitively extrabullar ectotympanic. The enlarged promontory artery is certainly a derived character in all three higher categories, and it is most likely a shared derived condition from a common ancestry rather than a convergent one. In addition to the basicranial morphology, the morphocline polarity of the early development of the fetal membranes of primates (Luckett 1971) is equally convincing in showing that *Tarsius* shares derived developmental patterns with platyrrhines and catarrhines but not with strepsirhines.

Although the subject could be pursued further, I state with confidence that the total evidence of numerous shared derived character states appears very convincing for haplorhine monophyly (see Jones's [1929] stimulating review, which remains modern in many ways). Another question is whether or not the Anthropoidea may be considered a natural higher category.

Among the Haplorhini the inferred common ancestor, the morphotype, of the Tarsiiformes is distinctly more primitive than those of either the Platyrrhini or the Catarrhini. The European early Eocene anaptomorphine *Teilhardina* is perhaps not unlike this hypothetical morphotype (Plates 1 and 2). In addition to the poor representation of the extant Tarsiidae (? one species), a great diversity of primate genera, unequivocally tarsiiforms, is known from the North American Eocene-Miocene and the European Eocene and Oligocene. As a result of a current revision I believe that separation of the Anaptomorphidae Cope, 1883, from the Omomyidae Trouessart, 1879, on the family level (Gazin 1962) is not warranted on either the dental or particularly the postcranial evidence. They share a common ancestor, exclusive of other families, somewhere in the Paleocene, and the degree of divergence for the Eocene genera does not allow family rank separation. The known differences between these Tertiary omomyids is best expressed by the subfamily separation of the omomyines from the anaptomorphines, a conclusion strongly supported by the analysis of the total available evidence.

As detailed elsewhere, the Microchoerinae share some distinct, probably homologous, specializations with some Anaptomorphinae, but they possess specializations not shared with the Tarsiidae. Because microchoerines probably share a more recent common ancestor with either omomyines or anaptomorphines and because basicranially and dentally they are quite distinct from tarsiids (the convergence of *Pseudoloris* and *Tarsius* is shown in Szalay 1974), their classification within the Omomyidae is now preferred to their allocation to the Tarsiidae by Simons (1961). Tibiofibular fusion in *Tarsius* and in known microchoerines is a feature of some importance in tarsiiform phylogenetics. I know of no tibia or fibula which may belong to any of the Omomyidae other than the microchoerines. Because of these derived character states, eventual separation of the Microchoerinae as a distinct family from the Omomyidae is plausible and is under investigation at the present. Thus, perhaps a combination of tibiofibular fusion and extreme inflation of the petromastoid, a unique complex among the known tarsiiforms, might be the grounds for this systematic action.

The nature of the genealogical relationships of the Platyrrhini and Catarrhini and the biogeographical aspect of their evolutionary history are still unresolved. Hoffstetter (1972; see also Hershkovitz 1969) has argued, with remarkably little basis in morphological evidence, not only that the two groups shared a more recent common ancestor than did either of them with tarsiiforms (a plausible hypothesis), but that platyrrhines were derived from an African anthropoid stock. In other words, the alleged "simian grade of organization" was not independently derived but instead was inherited from a common ancestry, and dispersal was in the noted direction.

Some questions on the validity of the Anthropoidea may be asked. Are the morphotypes of known platyrrhines and catarrhines more recently related to each other than is either of them to taxa that we would classify as tarsiiforms? Are the primitive platyrrhine and primitive catarrhine character states shared derived features, or were they convergently (= parallelly) derived from a tarsiiform level of organization, one perhaps akin to that displayed by the omomyid *Rooneyia* (Figure 2)? In other words, was there a stock of primates which possessed the "simian grade of organization," the characters listed below, and were these common ancestors of the platyrrhines and catarrhines? Stated this way, the problem is perhaps a little clearer than the usual question of whether South American "monkeys" are "true" monkeys or not.

There is no space here to examine what this simian grade might be, but it may be summarized as a combination of convergent, perhaps frontated orbits; incipient orbital funnels (i.e. postorbital closure); frontal suture fusion at an early age; synostosed mandibular symphysis; an enlarged brain with specific sulcal patterns; a pneumatized bulla; and a

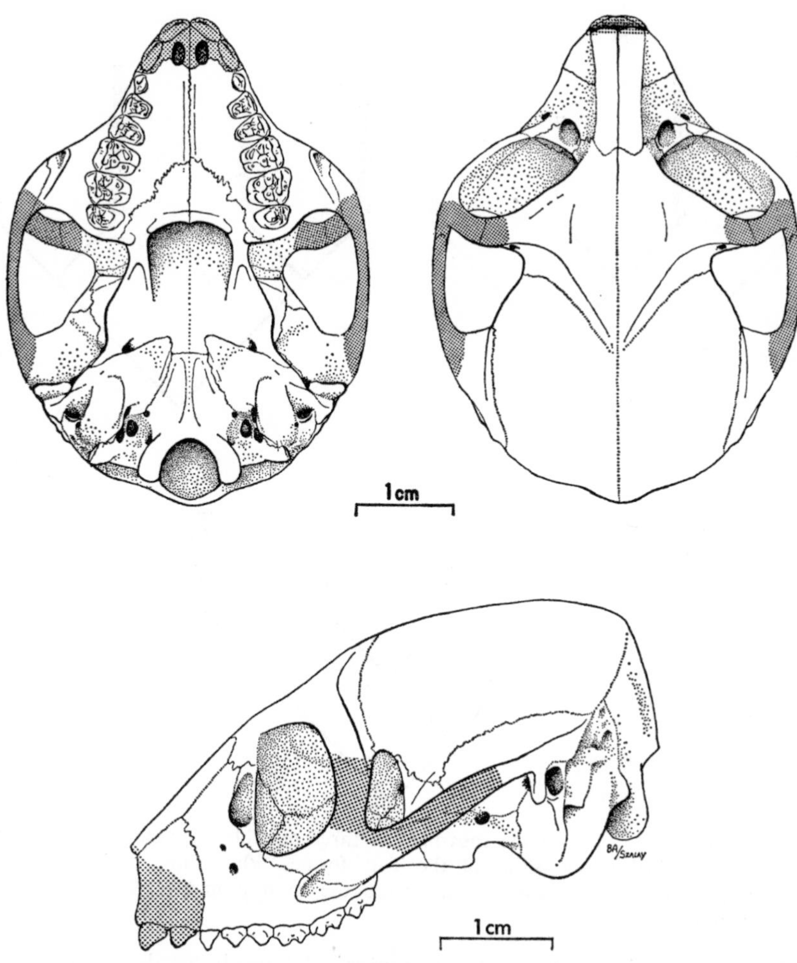

Figure 2. *Rooneyia viejaensis*, early Oligocene of Texas. Ventral (above left), dorsal (above right), and lateral below), views. Stippled areas are reconstructed

very large promontory branch of the internal carotid.

This primarily phylogenetic problem may be broken down into two general ones, the first dealing with the nature of genealogical relationships between the known Haplorhini and the second with the facts needed to determine these relationships. The aim is, clearly, to determine which of the three phylogenetic hypotheses presented in Figure 3 is the most plausible. Given a common ancestry of the Hominoidea and Cercopithecoidea more recent than that of either with any of the other known haplorhines, the three cladograms cover all the possibilities of genealogical ties among the three infraordinal categories of the Haplorhini.

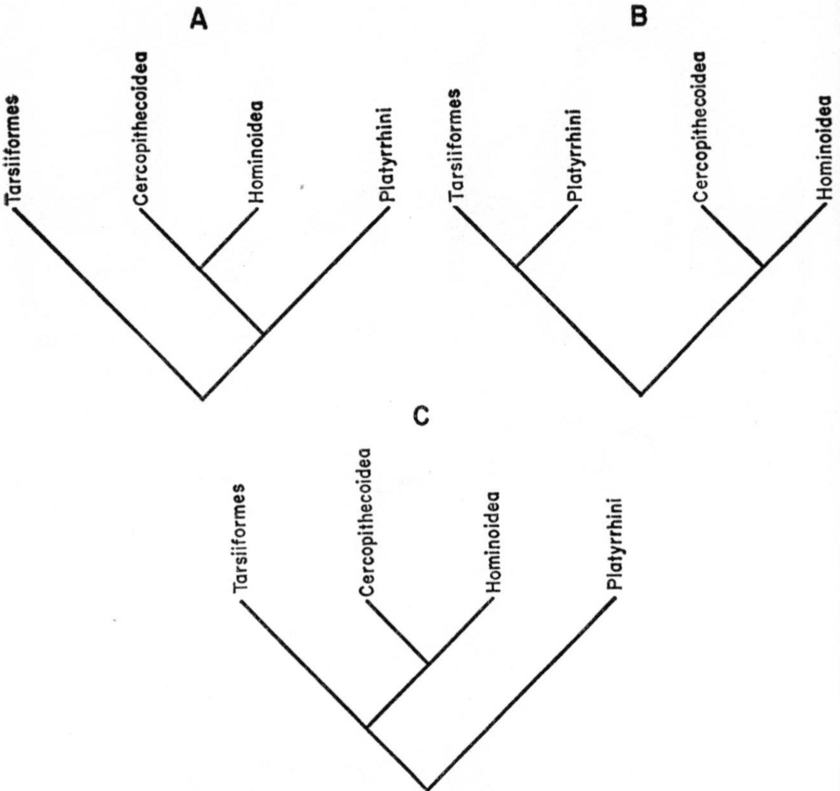

Figure 3. Three cladograms showing the three possible hypotheses concerning the genealogical relationships of the Tarsiiformes, Platyrrhini, and Catarrhini (Cercopithecoidea and Hominoidea), from the most probable (A) to the least likely (C)

The presentation of the three genealogical hypotheses does not imply three different judgments of anagenesis but merely states the recency of relationships. Figure 3A shows the Anthropoidea (*sensu* Mivart 1873, and Simpson 1945) as a monophyletic category, whereas Figures 3B and 3C do not. The three hypotheses differ from each other in the relative recency of a common ancestor between the Tarsiiformes, Platyrrhini, and Catarrhini. The evidence perhaps favors A; B is possible; and C is rather unlikely.

Considerations advanced here are tied to osteological evidence of the haplorhines because comparative analysis of the fossil groups is restricted to the skeletal system. Lack of Tertiary tarsiiform soft anatomy or biochemical attributes makes it difficult to judge which states of these characters in living haplorhines are primitive haplorhine, platyrrhine, catarrhine, or truly anthropoid in nature. Clearly, however, careful and broadly comparative studies on all living primates can surmount some of these obstacles.

Let us now briefly examine one character which would suggest the validity of the Anthropoidea. Perhaps the most convincing, probably a shared derived osteological character state between platyrrhines and catarrhines[1], but not (to my knowledge) present in any known tarsiiforms, is the pneumatized nature of the bulla cover, the petrosal and part of the squamosal. This cancellous condition may be distinguished from that of lorisid basicrania in which, adjacent to the highly partitioned middle ear cavity, the petromastoid portion is inflated, containing numerous larger cavities which are partly continuous with the middle ear cavity.

The conformation of the ectotympanic itself is different in platyrrhines and catarrhines, although the homology of extant catarrhine uniformity in this respect is uncertain in light of the reported ectotympanic condition of *Aegyptopithecus* (Simons 1969, 1972).

In both of these haplorhine groups, coupled with the condition of the cancellous bullar floor is the uniform manner of entry of the carotid artery (i.e. promontory branch of the carotid) into the circle of Willis. In all known primates this artery is either exposed or housed in a canal going though the middle ear cavity on the surface of the promontorium of the petrosal. In living anthropoids, however, the very large promontory artery is slightly displaced medially on the promontorium. This displacement is perhaps best explained as the result of the expanded brain, which dictates the manner of conformation of surrounding bony morphology.

In order to answer the important question of whether platyrrhine bulla pneumatization and carotid entry are convergent or homologous with those of the catarrhines, some correlation must be found between the cancellous nature of this area and the mechanical requirements of the muscles and tendons attached there. As a working hypothesis, one might consider the shift in the basicranially attached muscles as the result either of changes in carriage of the skull due to the phyletic hypertrophy of the brain or of some other causes such as the changing relationship of the facial and neural skulls brought about by the evolution of the feeding mechanism. Some of these changes may have occurred either in the common anthropoid stock or independently in platyrrhine and catarrhine ancestry. The fossil record will eventually prove or disprove this sugges-

[1] I do not know whether *Aegyptopithecus* has a pneumatized bulla.

tion by providing evidence on the homologous or convergent nature of these characters.

Whatever might have been its exact origin or biological role, pneumatization of the bullar part of the petrosal in platyrrhines and catarrhines may represent a necessity for spatial separation of the inside and outside of the bulla cover. The inner layer clearly retained the original function of protecting the middle ear, whereas the outside is now utilized for some musculoskeletal function involving stress resistance. These requirements may have also brought about the derived condition displayed by the entry of the promontory artery.

To conclude this somewhat involved treatment of a single character, I firmly believe that understanding the physiological causes of the morphology as well as its biological role would go a long way in helping to decide whether the pneumatized bulla is a shared derived or convergent character state in these two major groups of primates. From this it should follow that a thorough mechanical-functional evaluation of many characters of the skeletal system, along with such phyletically important organ systems as the nervous system, and a clear delineation of the biological roles of new characters would help immeasurably in understanding haplorhine phylogeny.

Paleogeography and paleozoogeography are clearly relevant to this problem, and we can now ask whether paleogeography is helpful in determining the phylogeny and the history of dispersal of the haplorhines. However, in spite of Hoffstetter's assertions, the plate tectonic evidence and the lack of an adequate South American fossil record[2] render the paleogeographic evidence secondary, as yet, to the morphological analysis.

If platyrrhines and catarrhines are specially related, then known morphological evidence is still ambiguous and inadequate to allow the inference that primitive catarrhines colonized South America and gave rise to the platyrrhine radiation. The opposite, i.e. that primates with platyrrhine characters radiated into the Catarrhini upon reaching Africa, is equally unsubstantiated but nevertheless just as possible.

The geological stories of the origins of hystricomorphan rodents and anthropoid primates are probably tied together, as is well argued by both Lavocat (1971) and Hoffstetter (1972). Late Eocene rodents with a clearly hystricognathous lower jaw from the late Eocene of Texas (Wood 1972) represent tantalizing evidence which might be invoked hastily as

[2] The molar morphology of the Peruvian Oligocene *Branisella* is clearly platyrrhine, yet the nearly completely reduced P^2 shows this genus not to be ancestral to any platyrrhine known.

an argument for the Nearctic origins of the Hystricomorpha and their subsequent spread to South America and then Africa. Yet the possibility is equally likely that African arrivals in South America found their way to the northern hemisphere through sweepstakes dispersal.

I conclude that although the Anthropoidea and Hystricomorpha are natural taxa, the morphological, biostratigraphical, and geographical facts supporting an African origin for these categories are not as self-evident and as convincing as Hoffstetter's and Lavocat's arguments would make us believe.

ASPECTS OF THE CATARRHINE DIVERGENCE

I will not give a detailed analysis of the early catarrhine fossil record (for some of this see Kälin 1961; Simons 1961, 1965). I merely comment on aspects of this fossil record which are relevant to the nature of early catarrhine diversity.

Although we have known for half a century that at least since medial Oligocene times a diversity of catarrhines existed in Africa, there is only negative evidence (the lack of record) for the absence of other African penecontemporaneous primates. Is this lack real, an artifact of preservation, or merely a local absence of contemporaneous African noncatarrhine primates? As our understanding of the complexities of plate tectonics and primate phylogeny grows, simplistic explanations of primate paleozoogeography based on assumptions of what ought or ought not to be at certain locations no longer suffice. It is clear that lorisiforms are not slightly modified representatives of ancestral primates (*contra* Martin 1972) but highly derived descendants of lemuroid lemuriforms (Szalay and Katz 1973). Because Miocene lorisiforms are known from East Africa, their early Tertiary presence has been tacitly assumed or stated as fact (Martin 1972). Yet in many ways, the inferred phylogeny of strepsirhines and the lack of Fayum noncatarrhines suggest otherwise. The three distinct time levels represented by the Fayum fossils have failed to yield primates other than cercopithecoids and hominoids. These three distinct horizons span several million years, perhaps the first half and the medial portion of Oligocene time, and the deposits represent forest environments. This makes absence of noncatarrhines especially important as, over that long period, one would expect influx of other primates (if they were present) from other parts of the continent. Thus, the Miocene presence of lorisiforms in Africa is not an unequivocal proof of their residence there during the Oligocene.

Another significant feature to be considered while seeking reconstruction of the beginning of the catarrhines is the relative diversity displayed by the Fayum primates. By itself, without cranial and postcranial morphology, the relatively restricted diversity of dental morphology is not very significant. Yet there is a suggestion in this evidence that the common ancestor of the known taxa lived not too many million years earlier, sometime in the late Eocene, prior to the earliest known African primate fossils.

Three important problems remain unresolved: (1) What kinds of primates were in Africa when the first catarrhines, by definition the common ancestors of known ones, reached or evolved there? (2) Was the beginning of the known catarrhine divergence sometime during the late Eocene? (3) Were taxa of either anthropoid or catarrhine level of organization present in any part of the world prior to this time?

Each of the two major groups of catarrhines, the cercopithecoids and the hominoids, has a large number of derived character states, which makes the task of inferring the ancestral catarrhine morphology difficult. I shall briefly consider three areas of skeletal morphology, those most often represented in the fossil record — dentition, basicranium, and aspects of the postcranial anatomy. I should add here that Catarrhini is clearly a monophyletic group. Thus, for example, the catarrhine nose condition is derived compared with the platyrrhine one, and therefore cercopithecoids and hominoids clearly shared a common ancestor more recently than did either of these with the platyrrhines. The possibility that either cercopithecoids or hominoids might share a more recent ancestor with platyrrhines or tarsiiforms is highly unlikely.

The Oligocene Fayum catarrhines, along with other Tertiary catarrhine fossils, give us a moderate sweep of morphologically divergent dentitions. Although the various Oligocene groups are well differentiated, it can be easily observed (see Kälin 1961; Simons 1969) that divergence has not been as great as, for example, between living monkeys and apes. Studying the dental morphology of catarrhines, particularly the relatively unmodified Oligocene evidence, reveals a number of character states which were likely to have been present in the most recent common ancestor of all catarrhines. Some of the most outstanding of these primitive catarrhine (but not haplorhine and probably not anthropoid) characters concern the morphology of the molar talonids, although the effects are also manifested on some premolars. In *Oligopithecus, Parapithecus, Apidium, Aegyptopithecus*, and *Propliopithecus*, irrespective of the more recent affinities among some of them, the plan of the talonid construction is the same (Szalay 1970, 1972). The well-defined, cuspate hypoconulid is found in all catarrhines except in such dentally advanced forms as the colobine and cercopithecine monkeys, but it is extremely rare among noncatarrhine primates. Thus one might conclude with some assurance that the inferred primitive catarrhines had this structure. Furthermore, this ancestral catarrhine character is at the same time an advanced feature of the catarrhine morphotype when the latter is compared with other known primates, particularly with Eocene forms and with the living and the few known fossil platyrrhines. It is in this respect that the dental characters of early catarrhines are significant in the evaluation of the phyletic ties of extra-African Eocene fossil primates.[3]

A glance at the basicranial morphology of living catarrhines reveals a high degree of uniformity. The external ear is covered by an osseous auditory tube, and the shallow middle ear cavity is covered by a bulla with small sinus cavities, as in platyrrhines, as noted above. The very large promontory branch of the carotid circulation, a probable homologue of the eutherian promontory artery, is the dominant branch of the internal carotid artery, as in other haplorhines.

In spite of this uniformity in virtually all known catarrhines, the question of the basicranial morphology of the pongid *Aegyptopithecus* appears puzzling. Simons (1969, 1972) briefly reported that an ectotympanic ring external to the edge of the bulla proper (rather than a tube) characterizes this genus. If his observation is correct, then it appears that the osseous tube of other catarrhines may be not a shared but rather a convergent derived feature. One might get around this conclusion by stating either that *Aegyptopithecus* is an aberrant pongid rather than one representing the ancestral pongid structural organization in this respect or that it is the common ancestor of cercopithecoids and hominoids; neither of these appears very probable to me. At present, however, we must at least admit that there is reasonable doubt that the uniform ectotympanic pattern of most cercopithecoids, on the one hand, and hominoids, on the other, is a shared derived feature. The bony tube may be a convergent trait from an ancestor with a narrower external band. The latter condition is, of course, displayed by all known platyrrhines.

A survey of the tarsus in catarrhines reveals an interesting dichotomy in the lower ankle joint (Decker, personal communication). Unlike the primitive primate condition in pongids, platyrrhines, tarsiiforms, strepsi-

[3] Based on the dental evidence, the allocation of the late Eocene Burmese *Amphipithecus* to the Anthropoidea is not warranted. This form, perhaps a lemuriform, as noted elsewhere (Szalay 1970), does not share the only presently identifiable homologous specializations that appear to be present in the primitive condition of the earliest catarrhines: the accentuated hypoconulid of Fayum catarrhines is clearly lacking in *Amphipithecus*.

rhines, and paromomyiforms, a screwlike lower ankle joint is not present in most cercopithecoids. In some colobines in which helical movements at this joint are possible, the joint morphology shows a secondary modification. What is the significance of either the presence or the absence of a screw-type lower ankle joint? Work by Szalay and Decker (1974) and Decker and Szalay (1974) indicates that the lower ankle joint of primates was modified to facilitate habitual inversion and to increase the range of inversion from an ancestry that was primarily adapted to habitual eversion. Part of the osteological modifications in response to the structural needs of the astragalocalcaneal complex for increased inversion involved the enlargement and posterior extension of posterior astragalocalcaneal

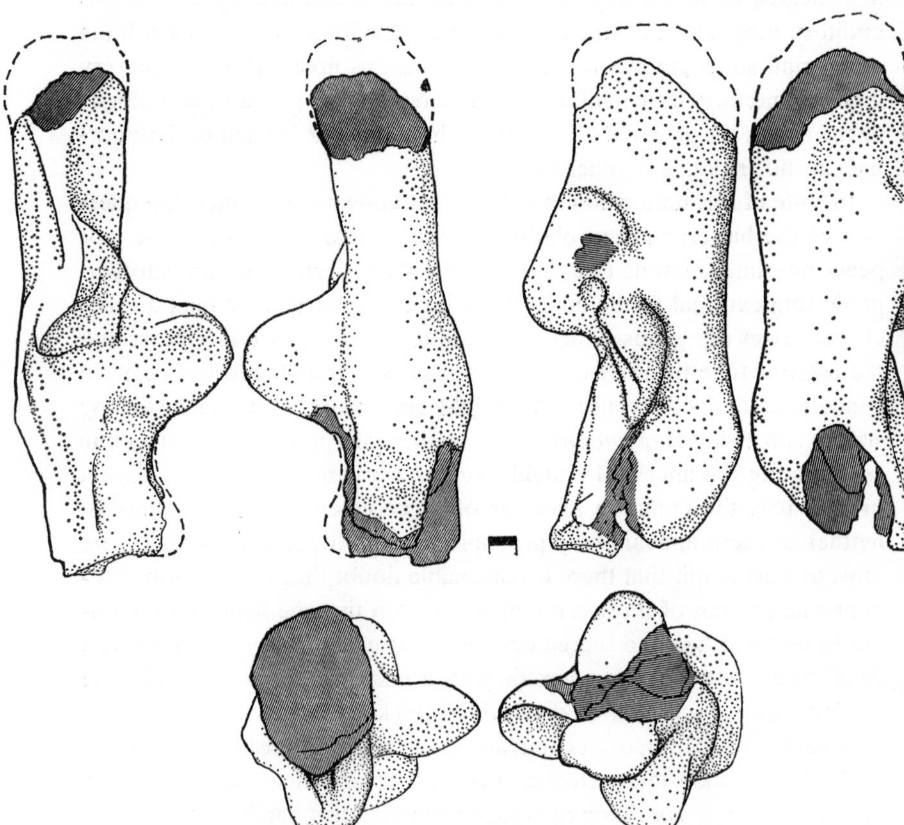

Figure 4. Right calcaneum of catarrhine primate from the Oligocene of the Fayum, North Africa (AMNH 14607). Note, in particular, the shape of the posterior astragalocalcaneal facet which indicates a screw-type joint with helical movements between the astragalus and calcaneum (the manner primitive for the primates). This is unlike the independently acquired advanced conditions displayed in cercopithecoids and in Plio-Pleistocene hominids

and the calcaneoastragalar facets of the calcaneum and astragalus, respectively. As a result of these modifications, the movements in the lower ankle joint between the astragalus and calcaneum became helical (screwlike) from the primitive eutherian condition in which they were simple rotations.

Considering both the widespread occurrence of the screw joint and its ubiquitous presence in the most ancient primates, the condition in cercopithecoids is most likely a derived one. As in the latter, but to a greater degree, the known hominid lower ankle joint has also lost its ability for movements in a helical path. There is little doubt that these character states in cercopithecoids and hominids are convergent. It may be noted, incidentally, as one of the many pieces of supporting evidence for the phylogeny of *Oreopithecus* shown in Figure 1, that the lower ankle joint of this genus shares the derived state of cercopithecoids, and it is most likely homologous with it rather than convergent; it is apparently a retention from a primitive cercopithecoid level of tarsal organization. A Fayum primate calcaneum (AMNH 14607[4]; Figure 4) clearly shows, however, that the primitive catarrhine condition of the lower ankle joint was like that in most other primates, i.e. a screw-joint.

Clearly much evolutionary morphological research is necessary to judge the merits of any hypothesis, but it is important that we systematists strive for some causal explanations of the origins of the higher categories we delineate.

SUMMARY AND CONCLUSIONS

The suborder Haplorhini, including the Tarsiiformes, Platyrrhini, and Catarrhini, represents a monophyletic category of the primates. Taxa included in it are more recently related to one another than to any other nonhaplorhines. Whether or not the Anthropoidea, including the Platyrrhini and Catarrhini, represent a monophyletic grouping depends on the homology or convergence (including parallelism) of those characters which allegedly characterized the common "simian grade of organization." The monophyly of the Anthropoidea is still not satisfactorily established, as most of the alleged diagnostic character states of this group can be compared primarily to *Tarsius*, a single survivor of a once extremely varied tarsiiform radiation. This fact should caution all students of biochemistry and soft anatomy, as well as students of the skeleton.

[4] The exact stratigraphic provenance of this specimen collected in 1909 was not recorded.

When claiming characters to be anthropoid, they should keep in mind the possibility that these might be haplorhine features, altered to a derived state in *Tarsius*, and thus perhaps unrepresentative of their homologues in the bulk of the tarsiiform radiation.

Given the hypothetical sweepstakes dispersal of omomyids into South America from the distant North American continent, if the Anthropoidea are monophyletic, then the hypothetical origins of the catarrhines from primates crossing from South America to Africa should be as plausible as the hypothesis stating that the ancestors of the platyrrhines arrived from Africa. Because exact relative continental positions during the Tertiary are still poorly understood and because much of the mid-Atlantic Ocean was probably open to the Pacific, prevailing Atlantic currents of today do not necessarily reflect those of the Eocene.

The patterns shown by the Fayum catarrhine dentitions suggest not too great a divergence from a common ancestor. This might indicate, as has been remarked for the penecontemporaneous Rodentia, that the ancestors might have reached Africa not much earlier than the latest Eocene.

REFERENCES

ASHLOCK, P. D.
1972 Monophyly again. *Systematic Zoology* 21(4):430–438.

BOCK, W. J.
1969 Discussion: the concept of homology. *Annals of the New York Academy of Sciences* 167(1):71–73.

BOCK, W. J., G. VON WAHLERT
1965 Adaptation and the form-function complex. *Evolution* 19:269–299.

DECKER, R. L., F. S. SZALAY
1974 "Origins and function of the pes in the Eocene Adapidae (Lemuriformes, Primates)," in *Primate locomotion.* Edited by F. A. Jenkins, Jr., 261–291. New York: Academic Press.

GAZIN, C. L.
1962 A further study of the lower Eocene mammalian faunas of southwestern Wyoming. *Smithsonian Miscellaneous Collections* 144(1): 1–98.

HENNIG, W.
1950 *Grundzüge einer Theorie der phylogenetischen Systematik.* Berlin: Deutscher Zentralverlag.
1965 Phylogenetic systematics. *Annual Review of Entomology* 10:97–115.
1966 *Phylogenetic systematics.* Urbana: University of Illinois Press.

HERSHKOVITZ, P.

1969 VI. The recent mammals of the neotropical region: a zoogeographic and ecological review. *Quarterly Review of Biology* 44(1): 1–70.

HILL, W. C. O.

1955 *Primates. 2. Haplorhini, Tarsioidea.* Edinburgh: University of Edinburgh Press.

HOFFSTETTER, R.

1972 "Relationships, origins, and history of the ceboid monkeys and caviomorph rodents: a modern reinterpretation," in *Evolutionary biology,* volume six. Edited by T. Dobzhansky, M. K. Hecht, and W. C. Steere, 323–347. New York: Appleton-Century-Crofts.

JONES, F. W.

1929 *Man's place among the mammals.* London: Edward Arnold.

KÄLIN, J.

1961 Sur les Primates de l'Oligocène inférieur d'Égypte (morphologie comparée et interprétation évolutive de *Parapithecus fraasi* Schlosser, *Propliopithecus haeckeli* Schlosser, et *Moeripithecus markgrafi* Schlosser). *Annales de Paléontologie* 47:3–48.

LAVOCAT, R.

1971 Affinités systématiques des caviomorphes et des phiomorphes et origine Africaine des caviomorphes. *Annales Academia brasileira de ciêncas* 43:515–522.

LUCKETT, W. P.

1971 A comparison of the early development of the fetal membranes of Tupaiidae, Lorisidae and *Tarsius,* and its bearing on the evolutionary relationships of the prosimian primates. *Proceedings of the Third International Congress of Primatology,* Zurich 1970, 1:238–245.

MARTIN, R. D.

1972 Adaptive radiation and behavior of the Malagasy lemurs. *Philosophical Transactions of the Royal Society, London* 264:295–352.

MAYR, E.

1965 Numerical phenetics and taxonomic theory. *Systematic Zoology* 14:73–97.

1969 *Principles of systematic zoology.* New York: McGraw Hill.

MIVART, ST. GEORGE

1864 Notes on crania and dentition of the Lemvridae. London.

1873 Man and apes, an exposition of structural resemblances and differences bearing upon questions of affinity and origin. London: Museum of Natural History.

POCOCK, R. I.

1918 On the external characters of the lemurs and of *Tarsius. Proceedings of the Zoological Society of London,* 19–53.

SCHAEFFER, B., M. K. HECHT, N. ELDREDGE

1972 "Phylogeny and paleontology," in *Evolutionary biology,* volume six. Edited by T. Dobzhansky, M. K. Hecht, and W. C. Steere, 31–46. New York: Appleton-Century-Crofts.

SIMONS, E. L.

1961 Notes on Eocene tarsioids and a revision of some Necrolemurinae. *Bulletin of the British Museum (Natural History), Geology* 5(3):43–69.

1965 New fossil apes from Egypt and the initial differentiation of Hominoidea. *Nature* 205:135–139.

1967 The earliest apes. *Scientific American* 217(6):28–35.

1969 The origin and radiation of the primates. *Annals of the New York Academy of Science* 167:319–331.

1972 *Primate evolution.* New York: Macmillan.

SIMPSON, G. G.

1945 *The principles of classification and a classification of mammals.* Bulletin of the American Museum of Natural History 85.

1961 *Principles of animal taxonomy.* New York: Columbia University Press.

1963 *The meaning of taxonomic statements.* Chicago: Aldine.

SZALAY, F. S.

1970 *Amphipithecus* and the origin of catarrhine primates. *Nature* 227 (5256):355–357.

1972 *Amphipithecus* revisited. *Nature* 236(5343):179.

1973 New Paleocene primates and a diagnosis of the new suborder Paromomyiformes. *Folia Primatologica* 19:73–87.

SZALAY, F. S., R. L. DECKER

1974 "Origins, evolution, and function of the tarsus in late Cretaceous eutherians and Paleocene primates," in *Primate locomotion.* Edited by F. A. Jenkins, Jr., 223–259. New York: Academic Press.

SZALAY, F. S., C. C. KATZ

1973 Phylogeny of lemurs, galagos, and lorises. *Folia Primatologica* 19:88–103.

WOOD, A. E.

1972 An Eocene hystricognathous rodent from Texas: its significance in interpretations of continental drift. *Science* 175:1250–1251.

The Beginnings of the Catarrhini

SUSAN CACHEL

Revelation of the development and pattern of catarrhine evolution hinges upon investigation and interpretation of the earliest catarrhines. Investigation necessitates study of continental drift, of morphological, behavioral, and ecological comparisons with New World primates, and of paleoecological reconstruction of fossil sites. This paper will deal only with the beginnings of catarrhine evolution, specifically as evidenced by the Fayum fossil finds, leaving aside questions of continental drift and platyrrhine comparisons. A morphological examination of these fossil finds will stress their basic similarity, particularly with regard to the morphology of the molar crown surfaces — with one exception, all finds show a common "Fayum pattern" which is hypothesized to be a hallmark of the catarrhine grade. Special emphasis will fall on the nature of the parapithecids and their position within a uniform array of early catarrhines. Because the environment influencing the development of early catarrhines is important, a rather detailed analysis will be made of Oligocene deposits in the Egyptian Fayum. Following this, a discussion of the evolutionary interpretation of the fossil primates will integrate both morphological and paleoecological findings.

I wish to thank Dr. K. W. Butzer for advising me on reconstruction of the Fayum paleoenvironments and Dr. Albert Dahlberg for advice on the dental research upon which this article is based. Dr. C. F. Vondra kindly supplied unpublished manuscripts dealing with geological investigations of the Fayum formations. I especially wish to thank R. H. Tuttle for discussions of the article.

I am currently receiving financial support from a National Science Foundation Graduate Fellowship.

FOSSIL PRIMATES FROM THE OLIGOCENE FAYUM

Extinct primates from the Jebel el Qatrani formation have been well described in many places (Schlosser 1911; Simons 1963, 1969, 1971, 1972) and do not need further delineation. The following attempt to explicate traits and relationships of the fossil forms is based on personal examination of fossil casts.

Oligopithecus

In the original description of the type and only specimen of *Oligopithecus,* Simons (1962) debated whether it might be the remains of a cercopithecoid forerunner or a hominoid. Evidence favoring the former alternative can be found in the partial posterior loph lying parallel to the anterior (protoconid-metaconid) loph. Evidence that Simons (1963) thinks definitive for inclusion of *Oligopithecus* among the Hominoidea lies in robust canine morphology and associated anterior-posterior elongation of P_3 — features that distinguish it from the later, undoubted hominoid *Propliopithecus.*

The extreme primitiveness of molar crown patterns in *Oligopithecus* (CGM 29627), however, leads one to suspect that the find can be classed neither as ancestral cercopithecoid nor as ancestral hominoid. In opposition to all other Fayum primates yet discovered, the molar crowns of *Oligopithecus* are unintegrated, the trigonid and talonid remaining distinct, and the posterior part far exceeding the trigonid in length and width. This is true neither of the undoubted hominoids *Propliopithecus* and *Aegyptopithecus* nor of the parapithecids *Apidium* and *Parapithecus.* So marked is the difference in molar crown patterns between *Oligopithecus* and all other Fayum primates that one measures talonid height in *Oligopithecus*, looking for signs of elemental, primitive shear. Although both parts of the tooth are equal in height, it is clear that crest functions, as opposed to the bulbous cusp functions of other Fayum primates, are emphasized. Szalay (1970) considers *Oligopithecus* to bear the closest resemblance to *Amphipithecus* from the upper Eocene Pondaung beds of Burma. The approach of these two forms is seen in the clear trigonid/talonid separation and in the fact that the talonids are transversely broader than the trigonids. Doubt thrown on the anthropoid status of *Amphipithecus* then renders suspect the characterization of *Oligopithecus* as the earliest catarrhine (Szalay 1970). Yet, however the debate over *Amphipith-*

ecus is resolved, *Oligopithecus* is clearly distinguishable from later Fayum forms, and phylogenetic relationships between this find and the remainder of the Jebel el Qatrani primates remain ambiguous.

The Parapithecids

The parapithecids *(Apidium* and *Parapithecus),* like the undoubted Fayum hominoids, and distinguished from *Oligopithecus,* possess well-integrated and compact molar crown surfaces. In the case of *Apidium phiomense* (AMNH 13370), this surface becomes remarkably bunodont — the multicuspidate nature of the molar crowns leads to the creation of a nine-cusped tooth. The four principal cusps stand in two opposed pairs, and the topography of the molar crown surface is complicated by other cusps (paraconid, centroconid) and accessory cuspules flanking the hypoconulid. The discovery of an earlier species, *Apidium moustafai* (YPM 20911), reveals that evolutionary trends within the genus were confined to size increase through time and perhaps a greater emphasis on bunodonty (Simons 1962). Further finds demonstrate the existence of a closed postorbital septum in *Apidium* and the presence of central maxillary incisors that are clearly rather large (see restorations, Simons 1971, 1972). The horizontal mandibular ramus in this genus is robust, although its shallow form in the juvenile type specimen led to long misrepresentation (see Simons 1972).

Concentration on features unique to the *Apidium* dentition (such as the existence of a centroconid and the flanking of the hypoconulid by lateral cuspules) tends to obscure the basic similarity in molar crown patterns which characterizes all the Fayum fossil forms with the exception of *Oligopithecus*. The Fayum pattern is developed on well-integrated molar crowns whose trigonid/talonid division is not distinct. Bulbous cusp functions are emphasized and sometimes exaggerated (as in *Apidium*). Paired relationships exist between protoconid/metaconid and hypoconid/entoconid such that two sets of opposing cusps are found on the occlusal surface. The median paraconid degenerates to an anterior ridge, and a large, median hypoconulid follows the two paired sets of cusps. The pattern of this basically five-cusped tooth is found in all the Fayum primates except *Oligopithecus* and may serve as a unifying trait for the whole group. It is possible that future research could reveal a functional explanation for the origin of this pattern.

It was noted by Schlosser (1911) that *Parapithecus fraasi* — YPM 13120 (cast of SMN 12639a)—most closely approaches *Propliopithecus* in the composition of its premolars and molars. *Parapithecus* resembles *Apidium* in its dental formula and the extreme bunodonty of molar crown surfaces, although, unlike *Apidium,* the tendency to develop multicuspidate teeth is lacking. The horizontal ramus of the mandible is perhaps more shallow than in adult *Apidium,* but because the ascending ramus is very high and wide, masticatory forces generated within this form may also have been notable.

A second species, *Parapithecus grangeri* — YPM 23954 (composite of YPM 23954 and CGM 26912) — whose only distinction from the earlier (?) *P. fraasi* lies in its greater size, is the latest of the Fayum primates to enjoy the status of ancestral cercopithecoid (Simons 1969, 1972). Loss of the cusped hypoconulid and P_2, and the development of cresting are assumed to have taken place within *P. grangeri,* eventually leading to a cercopithecoid resembling *Miopithecus talapoin.* Realizing that any attempt to settle the phylogeny of the catarrhines from a given body of evidence will seem forced does not enhance the approach of *P. grangeri* to a cercopithecoid condition. The most telling argument against this approach is the lack of any special crest development in *P. grangeri.* Furthermore, it appears that the deciduous dentition of this primate (Simons 1969: Figure 3) is very different from the deciduous dentition of cercopithecoids. Studies of trends in the deciduous dentition (e.g. von Koenigswald 1967) show that the cercopithecoid deciduous dentition is "progressive," foreshadowing features of the permanent dentition. The hominoids, however, possess a "conservative" deciduous dentition, whose traits reflect ancestral conditions in the molars. The deciduous premolars of cercopithecoids — particularly dP_4 — are bilophodont; the dP_4 of *P. grangeri* shows a clear trigonid/talonid separation, with a hypoconulid and good paraconid. The dP_4 of *P. grangeri* therefore follows the "conservative" hominoid trend. Cercopithecoid bilophodonty surely developed from a more hominoid-like condition (Gregory 1922; Remane 1951). For this reason, it is difficult to judge to which lineage a primitive catarrhine belongs when only parts of the masticatory apparatus are preserved. Militating against inclusion of *Apidium* or *Parapithecus* in the cercopithecoid lineage, however, is the steadfastly bunodont nature of their teeth. Although size increases occur in both lineages, the emphasis on bulbous cusps, as opposed to cresting, still remains.

The Undoubted Hominoids

Propliopithecus — YPM 13122 (cast of SMN 12639b) and SMN 12638 — (including "Moeripithecus") is an undoubted hominoid with a dental formula of 2:1:2:3, small canines, and a simple lower third premolar associated occlusally with a small upper canine. The molar crowns show the well-integrated surface and bulbous cusp arrangement that I designate the Fayum pattern, although the median paraconid has degenerated further than among the parapithecids. *Propliopithecus* is the first of the Fayum forms (except for *Oligopithecus*) to show unequivocal development of an anterior crest joining protoconid and metaconid.

Aegyptopithecus zeuxis — YPM 21032, YPM 24204 (cast of CGM 26901), YPM 21535 (cast of AMNH 13389), and composite reconstruction YPM 24006 — has been advanced as the connecting form between *Propliopithecus* and the dryopithecine apes of the Miocene. *Aegyptopithecus* differs from *Propliopithecus* in having greater canine development and associated lower premolar heteromorphy. Molar crown surfaces in this form demonstrate the Fayum pattern, but, as in *Propliopithecus,* a slight anterior crest joins protoconid and metaconid; there is even a suggestion of a crest joining hypoconulid and entoconid. Bunodonty still prevails, but greater crest formation occurs than among the parapithecids. As in *Propliopithecus haeckeli,* M_3 narrows posteriorly — the result of a large median hypoconulid set distally. A nearly complete skull of *Aegyptopithecus* (YPM 23975) has been found in Quarry M of the Jebel el Qatrani formation. The snout is rather pronounced, postorbital closure is less complete than in other known catarrhines, and there is no external tubular bony auditory meatus.

The *Aeolopithecus* find (YPM 26923) is difficult to interpret because of the degree of weathering. Recovered postcranial material also remains ambiguous because of the lack of association between postcranial and dental material, along with an inability to determine specific locomotor adaptations from fragmentary pieces.

PALEOENVIRONMENTS AT THE EGYPTIAN FAYUM

The Fayum, an Egyptian province approximately sixty miles southwest of Cairo, is a closed desert depression created by Pleistocene wind working on material affected by salt action and desultory wash.

The lowest portion of this depression is occupied by a shallow lake, Birket el-Qurun, which has had a complex history during the Pleistocene and Holocene. The great importance of the Fayum is established by the evidence which this depression supplies that Africa was an important center of mammalian evolution and a source for diffusion of indigenous forms into Eurasia.

In 1898, H.J.L. Beadnell of the Egyptian Survey discovered certain Eocene strata with prolific vertebrate remains; in 1901 he re-examined some of these Fayum bone-bearing localities and uncovered the first well-preserved terrestrial vertebrate remains from the early Tertiary of Africa (Beadnell 1901, 1905). Beadnell's definition of the formations and description of the Fayum topography can be summarized as follows. To the north of Lake Qurun, the land rises in a series of escarpments separated by terraces of varying width. The summit of the rim surrounding the depression is reached at 340 meters, and a rolling, stony desert upland stretches north from here. The Jebel el Qatrani escarpment, basalt-capped for the most part, and dating from Oligocene times, ascends from a lower escarpment provided by the late Eocene Qasr el-Sagha formation. The Birket el-Qurun formation creates the third escarpment, so that three lines of cliff represent the three great lithological stages which form the northern part of the Fayum. The separating terraces are mostly dip-slope plains formed of hard rock resistant to erosion. Below these main divisions lie two further divisions, less spectacularly exposed, the Ravine Beds — which Simons (1968) holds is not lithologically different from the Birket el-Qurun formation — and the Wadi Rayan formation, which contains the oldest beds found in the depression. The Widan el Faras basalt which caps the Jebel el Qatrani formation after a period of erosion is dated by the potassium-argon method to twenty-five million years B.P. The Jebel el Qatrani itself is thought to cover the span of time from approximately twenty-seven million years B.P. to the beginning of the Oligocene. Conformably underlying this formation is the Qasr el-Sagha and Birket el-Qurun/Ravine Beds sequence of the late Eocene. The Wadi Rayan formation is thought to date from the mid-Eocene and forms the limit of strata recognized in the Fayum.

Two formations have been studied by recent Yale expeditions. The Qasr el-Sagha formation is best seen in the northern part of the depression, where it is exposed as a long escarpment. Vondra (n.d.). has recently concluded that transitional and near-shore marine environments are represented among the sediments of this formation.

Specifically, four distinct facies are represented here: an "arenaceous bioclastic carbonate" facies, deposited along offshore bars and barrier beaches of the late Eocene Tethys Sea; a "gypsiferous and carbonaceous laminated claystone and siltstone" facies, deposited in open and restricted lagoonal areas; an "interbedded claystone, siltstone and quartz sandstone" facies, deposited along a prograding delta front; and a quartz sandstone facies, deposited by distributary channels behind the actual delta mouth.

Climatic inferences are not as striking as the reconstructed topography of this region during the late Eocene, but such inferences can be made. For example, the second facies, representing deposition in open and restricted lagoonal areas, is very carbonaceous, with excellent preservation of broad leaves: not only is a nearby source of plant material indicated, but so is a low-energy area of deposition. Great amounts of gypsum are present, occurring either as thin sheets or as wedges filling polygonal shrinkage cracks. Microcrystalline halite is also present. A restricted lagoonal facies is therefore inferred, one with a very high rate of evaporation. Because lagoonal evaporites are a standard element for reconstruction of arid and semiarid environments, at least some seasonal aridity is indicated. Vondra (n.d.) reconstructs lobate deltas building up across the lagoons, impeding circulation, and thus creating hypersaline waters.

The third facies, representing deposition along a prograding delta front, consists of foreset units 10 to 35 centimeters thick which cyclically fine upward. A periodic influx of sediments (representing periodic flooding of some kind) is probably the cause of such cyclicity. This is another sign pointing to seasonal aridity during the time of deposition of the Qasr el-Sagha formation. Because modern Nile hydrology was established only during the Middle Pleistocene and involved the capturing of a number of separate drainage basins (Butzer and Hansen 1968), the late Eocene/Oligocene proto-Nile was a completely Egyptian river whose water was supplied by no exotic sources, although it received considerable influx from the east, up to and across the area now covered by the Red Sea. Seasonal aridity within the immediate environment can therefore be inferred.

The Jebel el Qatrani formation conformably overlies the Qasr el-Sagha and, according to recent studies (Bowen and Vondra n.d.), represents an entirely terrestrial deltaic plain deposit consisting of 110 to 270 meters of quartz sandstone, chert pebble conglomerate, siltstone, claystone, and some carbonate lenses. Bowen and Vondra believe that a complex of channel, floodplain, and transitional alluvial deposits characterizes the Jebel el Qatrani formation. Although Vondra had once considered that two complete cycles of stream evolution might be represented in this formation (Simons 1968), he now believes that only one such cycle is actually represented here.

The lower portion of the Jebel el Qatrani (basal 100 meters) consists of a great lateral extent of channel deposits, point bar complexes, and a general absence of floodplain indications. A braiding, loosely sinuous stream which remained constant through time is therefore reconstructed. The upper portion of the Jebel el Qatrani was apparently laid down by a more fixed stream, meandering and carrying a significant amount of suspended load. Hence, crevasse-splay, transitional channel fill, floodplain deposits can be found in these younger sediments. Lenticular carbonates in the upper Jebel el Qatrani are apparently the vestiges of floodbasin lakes. Evidence of dolomitic caliche formed by alternating dry and wet periods in a subaerial environment can be discovered not only in the upper, floodplain portion of the formation, but throughout the Jebel el Qatrani.

Faunal evidence for the Jebel el Qatrani environment is bound to be problematical, considering that animals are not fixed to certain areas. Environmental reconstruction on the basis of sedimentological evidence is therefore better founded. Furthermore, the tropical rain forest traditionally reconstructed for the Oligocene Fayum is not a necessary environment for early primates, because gallery forests along the banks of the Oligocene Jebel el Qatrani river could just as well have provided arboreal niches for these primates.

RECONSTRUCTION OF THE JEBEL EL QATRANI ENVIRONMENT

Bowen and Vondra (n.d.) believe that a savanna environment with gallery forest along river banks is probably the best reconstruction to be made from Jebel el Qatrani sedimentological evidence. Certainly nothing can be said for the estuarine or fluvio-marine conditions which Beadnell (1905) thought were present. A terrestrial environment is therefore irrefragable, although the nature of the climate governing this environment can be disputed. Tropical rain forest conditions can be reconstructed on no sure evidence, and some contraindications are present. Bowen and Vondra (n.d.) believe that seasonal aridity is clearly demonstrable, probably most clearly from the caliche remains occurring through the formation. This interpretation is the more favorable for the existence of extensive evaporites through the underlying Birket el-Qurun and Qasr el-Sagha formations. A continuing climatic pattern of at least seasonal aridity is then indicated. Furthermore, there is a distinct possibility that the cyclic deltaic deposits of the Qasr el-Sagha are the remains of seasonal floods.

The term "savanna" need mean nothing more than rather open, or lightly wooded country. As grasses had not spread during the Oligocene, this open country behind the river could have had some other type of herbaceous covering, alternating with shrubbery and copses. Cut-off lakes and backswamps would provide water for local tree concentrations. Altogether, this environment could well have been more complex than Bowen and Vondra have envisioned it to be.

In an attempt to understand Plio/Pleistocene sediments and the preservation of associated faunal remains from the Omo Basin, Butzer (1970) studied depositional environments in the modern Omo River delta. Present evidence from this semiarid, tropical region shows significant parallels to conditions reconstructed from the Jebel el Qatrani. In fact, the lower Jebel el Qatrani appears almost directly comparable to deltaic depositional environments in the Omo, the upper portion of this formation being comparable to the Omo floodplain environment. These parallels can probably also be extended to the underlying Qasr el-Sagha and Birket el-Qurun formations — the environments represented here are deltaic fringe and prodeltaic zones. Thus, in the same area a progressive terrestriality can be traced through time (see Table 1).

Table 1. Comparison of depositional environments

Formation		Omo delta analogs
Jebel el Qatrani upper	Floodplain	Meanders, natural levees, pointbars, floodbasins, backswamps, abandoned channels, ox-bow lakes, etc.
lower	Deltaic	Repeated bifurcations of channel, multiple distributary channels, interdistributary floodbasins, etc.
Qasr el-Sagha	Delta fringe	Lobate delta patterns, distributaries, lagoonal mud-flats, barrier bars, spits, etc.
Birket el-Qurun	Prodeltaic zone	Active fluvio-marine sedimentation, waterlogged wood, etc.

The complexity of environments in the modern Omo delta certainly argues against highly reductionist interpretations of depositional environments at the Egyptian Fayum. A corollary to this complexity is that no single environment can be viewed as the setting for early catarrhine evolution. Rather, a mosaic of environments was the probable backdrop for catarrhine emergence, and explanations of this emergence must take environmental diversity into account.

DISCUSSION

Fayum primates from the Jebel el Qatrani, with the exception of *Oligopithecus*, form a rather unified array which seems to exclude the presence of unequivocal cercopithecoids. *Parapithecus* and *Apidium* emerge as members of a very early group of hominoids. Without more evidence, it cannot be said that either of the known parapithecid genera are ancestral to the later, undoubted hominoids (although the resemblance of *Parapithecus* to *Propliopithecus* is suggestive); but the known parapithecids are probably remnants of a group that gave rise to the undoubted hominoids.

The presence of a common, identifiable configuration on the molar crown surfaces of all these primates with the exception of *Oligopithecus* argues that this Fayum pattern is functionally associated with the rise of the catarrhines. The bulbous cusped teeth indicate that crushing functions were emphasized in the molars, but details of the cusp arrangement may prove important for understanding occlusal advantages.

The rise of the parapithecids, here considered to be the earliest discovered hominoids, can be hypothesized from examination of the more completely known *Apidium*. The presence of a full postorbital septum in this form is remarkable in view of the incomplete septal closure found in the undoubted hominoid *Aegyptopithecus*. Recent analysis of vertebrate jaw mechanics in terms of variables which maximize the moment arm of the mandible (DeMar and Barghusen 1972) reveals that the moment arm can be most efficiently increased by moving forward the origin and insertion of the adductor jaw musculature. Morphological consequences of this movement are anterior displacement of the orbits and anterior increments to the temporal fossa. The end result would be the creation of an orbital septum. Given the presence of a well-developed coronoid process (as is true of all mammals), such selection for increasing efficiency can come about only with anterior rotation of the line of muscle action. The temporalis musculature, especially the anterior temporalis, would be emphasized. EMG studies reported by Basmajian (1967: 327, 329) indicate that the anterior temporalis in man is primarily active in incisor bite. Extrapolation from the condition in man suggests that the anterior temporalis and incisor bite must have been important in *Apidium*. Reconstructions of *Apidium* (Simons 1971, 1972) show the presence of transversely broad central maxillary incisors. Such a dental configuration and emphasis on incisor bite would take place if fruit eating, particularly eating of relatively large, fleshy fruits, was important. Perhaps seasonal aridity at the Fayum during the time of deposition of the Qasr el-Sagha and Jebel el Qatrani formations led to great synchronicity of fruiting, which would have placed greater selective pressure on developing dental specializations for processing fruit than would the irregular fruiting schedules occurring in more favorable tropical climates. Later hominoids, shortening the tooth row by losing the second premolar, would continue maximizing the moment arm — a process thought to have begun in the parapithecids by anterior migration of the temporalis.

The hypothetical parapithecid ancestor of later hominoids would possess a complete or very nearly complete postorbital septum. Size increases seen in *Propliopithecus* and *Aegyptopithecus* would mean that a relatively small brain case would provide attachment for masticatory musculature. Size increase may have led to the development (or accentuation) of fissures in the orbital septum. Change of size would necessitate some change in structure to retain a previous function. The hypothetical parapithecid ancestor of later hominoids, besides possessing a complete or nearly complete postorbital septum and a size equal to *Parapithecus* and *Apidium,* would have no bony tubular auditory meatus; a brain whose olfactory bulbs were still of prosimian size; a foreshortened snout; a broad ascending mandibular ramus; a dental formula of 2:1:3:3; transversely broad central maxillary incisors; a "conservative" deciduous dentition; small canines with no P_3 elongation; and a molar pattern of the Fayum type (with perhaps a tendency toward cresting).

The Fayum pattern might be thought of as a phylogenetic trait corresponding to the dryopithecine Y5 pattern. The Fayum pattern, however, gave rise both to the Y5 pattern and to cercopithecoid bilophodonty. The dryopithecine Y5 pattern was created with a buccal shift of the hypoconulid, so that primitive catarrhine cusp pairing was lost. Although a functional explanation of the Fayum pattern has not yet been found, the Y5 pattern presents three cusps on the buccal or occlusal portion of the lower molars and would thus enjoy the advantage of greater occlusal surface. Only with the arrival of the Y5 pattern can cercopithecoid bilophodonty be thought impossible to develop from a hominoid condition. Later hominoids *(Propliopithecus, Aegyptopithecus, Limnopithecus, Pliopithecus)* gave rise to the cercopithecoids, especially as some cresting (particularly anterior cresting) can be seen in these later forms. *Victoriapithecus leakeyi* from Rusinga Island, dated at about eighteen million years B.P., and the younger *V. macinnesi* from Maboko, the earliest known cercopithecoids, clearly show derivation from an ancestor that possessed the Fayum molar pattern. The opposition of cusps seen in the primitive catarrhine pattern would not be sufficient to cause crest formation without selective factors influencing such formation. Walker and Murray (this volume) suggest that a shift from frugivory toward leaf eating was responsible for the creation of cercopithecoid bilophodonty. Such a shift would enable cercopithecoids to survive and expand in areas not exploitable by frugivores or during environmental crises.

The parapithecids which are so abundant in the upper quarries of the Jebel el Qatrani would be driven to extinction by their descendants — later hominoids more specialized for frugivory and cercopithecoids more specialized for leaf eating. The parapithecids would be left no niche in which to compete successfully.

SUMMARY

Paleoenvironments at the Egyptian Fayum are shown to have been extremely complex within a seasonally arid or semiarid climatic regime. The Fayum fossil finds are found to have been, with the exception of *Oligopithecus,* a unified group showing a basic dental pattern called the Fayum pattern. The parapithecids emerge as an early hominoid group giving rise to *Propliopithecus, Aegyptopithecus,* and all later hominoids. The rise of the parapithecids is conditioned by frugivory, whose selective advantage may have been enhanced by synchronic fruiting in a seasonally arid environment. The cercopithecoids evolve from a later hominoid which had not yet developed a Y5 molar pattern. This is possible because the later hominoids show cresting tendencies in the Fayum pattern which could emerge as cercopithecoid bilophodonty for processing leaves. The parapithecids are then driven to extinction by their descendants, which are more specialized for processing food resources.

REFERENCES

BASMAJIAN, J. V.
1967 *Muscles alive* (second edition). Baltimore: Williams and Wilkins.

BEADNELL, H. J. L.
1901 The Fayum depression: a preliminary notice of the geology of a district in Egypt containing a new Palaeogene vertebrate fauna. *Geological Magazine* 8:540–546.
1905 *The topography and geology of the Fayum Province of Egypt.* Survey Department, Egypt.

BOWEN, B. E., C. F. VONDRA
n.d. "Paleoenvironmental interpretations of the Oligocene Jebel el Qatrani Formation, Fayum Depression, Egypt, United Arab Republic." Unpublished manuscript.

BUTZER, K. W.
1970 Contemporary depositional environments of the Omo Delta. *Nature* 226:425–430.

BUTZER, K. W., C. L. HANSEN
1968 *Desert and river in Nubia.* Madison: University of Wisconsin Press.

DE MAR, R., H. R. BARGHUSEN
1972 Mechanics and the evolution of the synapsid jaw. *Evolution* 26:622–637.

GREGORY, W. K.
1922 *The origin and evolution of the human dentition.* Baltimore: Williams and Wilkins.

REMANE, A.
1951 Die Entstehung der Bilophodontie bei den Cercopithecidae. *Anatomischer Anzeiger* 98:161–165.

SCHLOSSER, M.
1911 Beiträge zur Kenntnis der Oligozänen Landsäugetiere aus dem Fayum: Aegypten. *Beiträge zur Paläontologie und Geologie Österreich-Ungarns und des Orients* 24:51–167.

SIMONS, E.
1962 *Two new primate species from the African Oligocene.* Postilla Yale Peabody Museum 64.
1963 "A critical reappraisal of Tertiary primates," in *Evolutionary and genetic biology of primates*, volume one. Edited by J. Buettner-Janusch, 65–129. New York: Academic Press.
1968 *Early Cenozoic mammalian faunas, Fayum Province, Egypt.* Volume one: *African Oligocene mammals: introduction, history of study, and faunal succession.* Peabody Museum Bulletin 28.
1969 The origin and radiation of the primates. *Annals of the New York Academy of Sciences* 167:319–331.
1971 "A current review of the interrelationships of Oligocene and Miocene Catarrhini," in *Dental morphology and evolution.* Edited by A. A. Dahlberg, 193–208. Chicago: University of Chicago Press.
1972 *Primate evolution.* New York: Macmillan.

SZALAY, F. S.
1970 Late Eocene *Amphipithecus* and the origins of catarrhine primates. *Nature* 227:355–357.

VONDRA, C. F.
n.d. "The upper Eocene transitional and near-shore marine Qasr el-Sagha Formation Fayum Depression, Egypt, United Arab Republic." Unpublished manuscript.

VON KOENIGSWALD, G. H. R.
1967 Evolutionary trends in the deciduous molars of the Hominidea. *Journal of Dental Research* 46:779–786.

Paleoecology and Zoogeography of the Old World Monkeys

E. DELSON

The Cercopithecidae are perhaps the most successful family of living primates, as measured either by the number of species or by their tolerance of ecological-environmental situations, which is surpassed only by *Homo*. Moreover, the ecology and behavior of this family have been well studied, with at least some investigation of almost every genus or species-group. This quantity of data provides an excellent source for comparison and elucidation of the paleobiology of the extinct cercopithecids, while the latter can provide some interesting additions to the present diversity of the family as well as throw light on the history of its adaptations. In this paper, the dispersal and environmental history of the Cercopithecidae will be discussed in terms of the fossil record, and some types of ecoethological data useful in paleobiological reconstruction will be considered.

The analysis of mammalian paleoecology is still in its earliest developmental stages. Despite some attempts by Shotwell (1958, 1964), among others, the understanding of community relationships among fossil mammal species is far behind that for many invertebrates and even some Mesozoic vertebrates (see Olson 1952). In fact, the present state of the art for mammalian paleoecology is better considered as paleoenvironmental study, an attempt to determine the regional climate and/or ecotype by comparing the species known from a series of fossil assemblages or local faunas in the region with the ecological/environmental preferences of their nearest living relative or functional cor-

The research reported here was supported in part by funds from Columbia University, the National Geographic Society, and the Wenner-Gren Foundation for Anthropological Research (Grant number 2810). I thank them once again.

relate. Paleobotanical (including palynological) data associated with fossil mammals are rare, but such associations, or even plant remains of similar age and distribution as mammal fossils, provide the best source of paleoenvironmental baseline information. In either case (faunal or floral), a relatively firm stratigraphic framework is a necessary prerequisite for the development of an environmental history.

THE NEOGENE TIME-SCALE

Fossil cercopithecids are known from the Miocene through Pleistocene epochs of the Tertiary, and only this time span (the Neogene "subperiod") need be considered here.[1] The most recent summaries of the correlation and calibration of time and rock units of this age are those of Berggren (1971, 1972) and Van Couvering (1972; see also Delson 1973). Only areas of conflict among these published time-scales or with my interpretations shall be discussed here. The Neogene epochs were originally defined by Lyell (1833) on the basis of aquatic (essentially marine) Euro-Mediterranean invertebrate faunas, and modern re-evaluations of the epochs and their boundaries must be based similarly on marine organisms in the type regions. Planktonic micro-organisms such as foraminifera and radiolaria have proved most useful in this endeavor, and local sequences based on assemblages of fossils and/or the evolutionary stages deduced for given lineages have been developed in or correlated to these areas of southwestern France and Italy. Several parallel sets of regional chronostratigraphic[2] units of lower rank than epoch have also been reinterpreted; among these stages most correlation usually is determined.

Although world-wide definition and correlation are based on these marine units, continental mammalian assemblages are more common-

[1] The Fayum catarrhines (Oligocene of Egypt) have been intentionally left out of further consideration here. The special relevance of certain of these species to cercopithecid ancestry has been argued by Simons (e.g. 1967, 1970, 1972), but I question such a relationship for *Parapithecus* (Delson 1973, i.p.b). The environment inhabited by these animals is well reconstructed by Simons and Pilbeam (1972) as gallery forest alongside broad, sluggish, tropical rivers.

[2] Chronostratigraphy may be defined (see the American Code of Stratigraphic Nomenclature) as dealing with subdivisions of rocks considered solely as the record of a specific interval of geologic time; such subdivisions are tied closely to specific rock units known as stratotypes. Biostratigraphy deals with rock units as delineated by the fossils they contain and may be as formal and strictly defined as the preceding. Biochronological units, however, as presently understood for mammals at least, are less strict and may be considered as the record of geologic time as represented by organisms existing at that time.

ly considered in terms of regional sequences of biochronologic (or biostratigraphic) units known as Land Mammal Ages (Tedford 1970; Wood et al. 1941). For Europe, earlier authors usually employed the name of the supposedly time-equivalent marine stage in similar sense, but Thaler (1965) proposed a set of semiformal "biochronologic zones," based essentially on the ranges of single rodent taxa, and most recently a distinct set of terms has been employed in a manner analogous to that followed in North America (Azzaroli 1972; Tobien 1972).

In Table 1, I attempt to correlate the marine sequence with several continental and local parallels, with major fossil faunas included as reference points. As Berggren (1971: 755) has noted, the tendency to subdivide "things and events into a three-fold division on a linear scale" is a "propensity of scientists" and not necessarily a reflection of nature. The use of Early, Middle, and Late segments of the Miocene has come to imply rather specific division for modern authors, and this usage is followed in the marine ("standard") scale. The Pliocene is less certainly split into two portions, whose names are lowercased to reflect this informality; the "Astian" of many authors is probably a facies occurring throughout the epoch.

Subdivisions of the Pleistocene have previously been made by workers interested in such continental events as glaciation and mammalian or botanical evolution, with little regard for the marine sequence (Adam 1964; Butzer 1971; van der Hammen, Wijmstra, and Zagwijn 1971; Howell 1966). In order to bring the correlation of this last Tertiary epoch into balance with that of earlier ones, I suggest the equation of the beginnings of the Middle and Late Pleistocene with the bases of the Sicilian and Neotyrrhenian stages, respectively. This subdivision seems more reasonable than one based either on nonbiological events (e.g. magnetic reversals) without links to paleontology or on continental evidence. Gradstein (1970) has recently shown that the early (type) Sicilian represents a relatively warm period, and although there is as yet no direct evidence, this time may be roughly correlated with the interval of warmer climate known in the Netherlands as the Waalian; the paleomagnetic work of von Montfrans (1971) suggests an age of about one million years for the beginning of the Middle Pleistocene by this definition. Much of the Sicilian has been thought correlative with the so-called Cromerian mammalian faunal interval, but the use of this term for paleontologic, lithologic, and climato-stratigraphic units is confusing. It may be replaced by the term Biharian Land Mammal Age (see Kretzoi 1969; Jánossy 1970), which begins with the first widespread presence in western Europe of eastern steppe mammals circa one million years ago, spans the Brunhes-Matuyama magnetic reversal at 0.7 million years, and extends to the end of the Mindel glacial. The Biharian as here understood closely equates not only to the Cromerian and St. Prestian of these authors but also to the Galerian of Ambrosetti et al. (1972). For the most part, the division of the Pleistocene in this way closely approximates the accepted divisions of the authors cited above.

The dates and some of the stage/age assignments of Table 1 may not be familiar to those accustomed to the correlations of North American (and in fact most English- and German-speaking) vertebrate paleontologists (for example, Thenius 1958, 1959; Evernden et al. 1964; Simons 1972) and who have not followed recent developments. This time-scale does not imply changes in the "absolute" or radiometric ages assigned to such events as the appearance of *Hipparion* or the beginning of the Villafranchian Land Mammal Age; it merely reflects better understanding of the position of these continental events in a sequence based on marine fossils. Recently, deep drilling has clarified the most important event in the Mediterranean marine realm — namely, the closing of the straits of Gibraltar by tectonic activity related to the drifting of northwestern Africa into contact with Europe at a time that corresponds to the gap between Lyell's Miocene and Pliocene. Following this, the Mediterranean basin became completely desiccated several times, to depths of more than 10,000 feet (3,000+ meters) below present sealevel, until Atlantic water cut first a waterfall and then a deep contact through the straits and renewed oceanic circulation (Ryan et al. 1970; Hsü 1972; Cita and Ryan 1972; Hsü, Ryan, and Cita 1973).

This event, cataclysmic in terms of its effect on marine faunas, certainly merits recognition as the cause of a stratigraphic gap at the Miocene–Pliocene boundary, and thus the first sediment deposited by the refilling Atlantic water may be considered earliest Pliocene in age; the salt deposits formed subaerially by Late Miocene evaporation compose much of the rocks assigned to the Messinian stage, which is thus assigned to the end of the Late Miocene. Note that the first appearance of *Hipparion* has nothing whatsoever to do with this boundary redefinition but must instead be correlated to the marine sequence somehow.

This correlation is in fact quite important, because it aids in determining and calibrating another marine boundary. *Hipparion* first occurs in the late Barstovian Mammal Age in North America before 12 million years ago, but it is morphologically distinct (having less complex cheek teeth and a different facial structure) from the oldest Eurasian forms, known from the Vallesian Mammal Age of Europe (and apparently the lower part of the Nagri Formation in the Siwaliks [Hussain 1971, personal communication]). It is generally assumed that *Hipparion* of Old World type did evolve in North America (possibly in the Pacific Northwest) and upon crossing a Bering "filter-bridge" migrated rapidly across Eurasia, reaching all available regions within a geological "instant." Van Couvering and Miller (1969) noted that a date of 12.4 million years has been reported in close association with a very early *Hipparion*-including assemblage at Höwenegg, Germany, and they suggested a date of some 12.5 million years for the first appearance of this genus in Eurasia and thus the beginning of the Vallesian. However, they neither note the 1.1 million-year error range provided for this date by Lippolt, Gentner, and Wimmenauer (1963) nor consider that although this may be a technically "good" or accurate date, it is still a single determination at the top of a concordant series of ages (and thus could conceivably be too old). There is by definition a 33 percent chance that the actual date is within the range 12.4 to 11.3 million years (or, of course, between 12.4 and 13.5, but this is negated by other data), and the younger range agrees better with North American results. I thus suggest an age of 12.0 to 11.5 million years for the first widespread occurrence of *Hipparion* and the base of the Vallesian.

Few correlations exist between assemblages of mammals and marine fossils well placed with regard to their respective relative-age sequences, but two have recently been reported from Crete. De Bruijn, Sondaar, and Zachariasse (1971) recorded the association of very early Tortonian foraminifera and rodents of late Vallesian age (at Kastellios Hill), while de Bruijn and Meulenkamp (1972) noted that the Plakia assemblage of late pre-Vallesian rodents was found in rocks of late pre-Tortonian age (greater precision is not yet possible). These observations would seem to indicate a rather close concordance between the beginnings of the Tortonian stage and the Vallesian Mammal Age. Similar but less precise intercalations have been reported in France between mammals and molluscs: Mein and Truc (1966) recorded late Vallesian contemporaneous with "middle" Tortonian, while Guérin et al. (1972) reported *Hipparion* teeth in seemingly pre-Tortonian rocks, although both of these marine placements are questionable. From these data and in conjunction with published (and personal) communications from Berggren and Van Couvering, I would estimate that the Vallesian may have begun slightly before the Tortonian (on present definitions), and thus I assign an age of about 11 million years to the base of the Late Miocene (Tortonian).

The locality of Hauterives, southern France, yields a mammalian assemblage of probably earliest Ruscinian age (Guérin and Mein 1971) and has been shown by Ballesio (1971) to postdate the deep cutting of the Rhone valley brought on by the drop in Mediterranean baselevel at the end of the Miocene. It may thus be suggested that the base of the Ruscinian as here understood closely corresponds to the base of the Pliocene. This also agrees well with eastern and central European (Paratethys) evidence, for the type Pontian is generally equated roughly with part of the Messinian (e.g. Cicha and Senes 1972), and the immediately post-Pontian or latest Pontian local faunas of Baltavar and Polgardi in Hungary (Kretzoi 1969; Kertai 1968) may be of early Ruscinian age (Mein and Michaux 1970; Mein, personal communication). Interpretations of the Villafranchian in terms of the epoch time-scale have varied greatly, but it is now generally agreed that its position must be determined with respect to marine stages, not defined *a priori* (e.g. as earliest Pleistocene). Radiometric dates and marine correlations (Savage and Curtiss 1970) indicate that the type (earliest) Villafranchian is of mid-Pliocene age (approximately 4 million years), while latest Villafranchian and latest Calabrian appear contemporaneous (Azzaroli and Ambrosetti 1970; Azzaroli and Berzi 1971). Dates and paleomagnetic results from Senèze (Prévot and Dalrymple 1970), a crater lake at whose top is a late Villafranchian mammal fauna, suggest that the middle/late Villafranchian "boundary" approximates that between the Pliocene and the Pleistocene at about 1.9 million years (Delson 1973). Given these independent calibrations of the mammalian sequence, it is possible to consider environmental evidence from the continental record and to correlate this with other events.

CERCOPITHECID PALEOENVIRONMENT AND DISPERSAL

In the discussion that follows, all Old World monkeys are considered to belong to a single family, Cercopithecidae, of the "infraorder" Catarrhini. The leaf-eating monkeys may be separated as the subfamily Colobinae, while the nominate subfamily may be further divided into tribes: Cercopithecini for *Cercopithecus* and its allies (*"Miopithecus," Allenopithecus,* and *Erythrocebus)* and Papionini for the baboon/macaque/mangabey/gelada group and their extinct relatives. Geladas (*Theropithecus*) are clearly members of this tribe, although their "specialized" dentition tends to isolate them somewhat.

The Earliest Monkeys

The oldest fossils that can undoubtedly be allocated to Cercopithecidae are known from the East African Early Miocene. Pilbeam and Walker (1968) have reported an upper molar of cercopithecine aspect and a partial frontal bone said to be most similar to those of platyrrhines or juvenile colobines. On the basis of this association (at Napak, Uganda, dated to about 19 million years), they suggested a prior separation of the two modern subfamilies. In fact, however, the specimens merely reflect the expected ancestral cercopithecid conditions for the known parts; that is, on the basis of comparative morphology irrespective of geologic age (see Schaeffer, Hecht, and Eldredge 1972), the ancestral cercopithecid would be expected to have cercopithecine-like molars and a colobine-gibbon type of facial skull (Delson 1973, 1975).

More complete remains from the probably Middle Miocene Maboko Island local fauna suggest the presence of more than one "morph," although the distinction of two species of *Victoriapithecus* in this material by von Koenigswald (1969) is mostly based on incorrect interpretation of a portion of the sample. Further study in progress suggests that both colobine and cercopithecine specializations, as well as moderate adaptation to terrestrial life on the part of some cercopithecids (?early cercopithecines), had been developed by this time. No undoubted monkeys are known from Fort Ternan (L. Leakey 1968, to the contrary), but Hooijer (1963, 1970) reported a tooth of cercopithecine form from Ongoliba (Zaïre, previously Congo) and Simons (1969) discussed *Prohylobates* from Wadi Moghara, Egypt; the latter is possibly close to *Victoriapithecus*. Little is known about the environment of the last two Miocene localities (Simons and Pilbeam 1972).

No complete study has yet been made of the main East African Early and Middle Miocene assemblages either, but rather more is known of the probable environment, especially for Rusinga Island. Much of the Lake Victoria region was dominated by large volcanoes rising 2,000 to 4,000 feet (about 1,000 meters) above the lake. The floral remains were interpreted by Chesters (1957) as indicative of gallery forest along streams, with more open country farther back, but Andrews and Van Couvering (1975) suggest that denser forest is more likely in light of both fauna and topography, as nearby volcanoes are heavily forested today. The majority of the cercopithecid fossils are from Maboko, whose fauna is poorly known but appears somewhat distinct from Rusinga on the one hand and Fort Ternan on the other. It may be intermediate in age, but the dominance (among primates) of monkeys suggests a different local environment, possibly drier lowland savanna with deciduous groves.

Circum-Mediterranean Province

During the Late Miocene, further differentiation and dispersal of cercopithecids may have occurred in sub-Saharan Africa (see below), but the record is essentially restricted to the circum-Mediterranean region (Delson 1973). The best-known fossil cercopithecid is *Mesopithecus pentelici,* hundreds of specimens of which have been recovered from the early Turolian locality of Pikermi, near Athens. Local faunas of similar age in Macedonia (Greek, Bulgarian, and Yugoslavian) and the Ukraine have also yielded *M. pentelici,* and single individuals are known from the possibly late Turolian assemblage at Maragha, Iran, and the possibly late Vallesian local faunas at Wissberg, Germany, and Baccinello, Italy (youngest vertebrate horizon). This species is clearly a colobine in terms of cranio-dental morphology, which suggests at least beginning development of the colobine digestive tract specializations for processing leaves; the postcranial remains indicate a habitus as terrestrial as that of *Presbytis entellus.*

Two different colobine species characterize the European Pliocene: the larger and even more terrestrial *Dolichopithecus ruscinensis* and the slightly smaller and probably more arboreal *?Mesopithecus monspessulanus.* These two often occur in the same assemblages, spread across southern Europe from northern Spain to the Crimea; neither is found after the early Villafranchian, except for one tooth referred to *?M. monspessulanus* from the probably middle Villafranchian Red Crag of England.

In northern Africa, two further colobine species are known in Late Miocene deposits, both associated with cercopithecines. At Marceau, Algeria, a small local fauna is dominated by cercopithecid teeth: most are cercopithecine (macaquelike, but not clearly referable to *Macaca),* but the type of Arambourg's *Macaca flandrini* (1959) and some other teeth are in fact colobine, of apparently African affinity. The latest Turolian, (about 6 million years old, Cooke and Maglio 1972) assemblage from Wadi Natrun, Egypt, contains the skull and one isolated tooth of *Libypithecus markgrafi,* an African-type colobine, as well as numerous dental remains of a macaque (named *M. libyca).*

The slightly younger early Ruscinian local faunas of Europe contain the first cercopithecines outside Africa, which also seem to be identifiably *Macaca.* This group gains in importance with time, becoming the only cercopithecid in Europe during most of the Pleistocene and persisting apparently until the last interglacial (? Borgio, Italy), perhaps into the "postglacial" *(M. majori,* a small form at Capo Figari,

Sardinia). European fossil macaques ranged from England to the Caucasus and probably are closely linked phyletically to the modern populations of *Macaca sylvanus* of the Maghreb. A larger more terrestrial form *(Paradolichopithecus)* is known in France and Romania during the late Villafranchian; possible early members of this lineage occur in the same areas during the early Villafranchian (Delson 1971). More complete locality data on all circum-Mediterranean occurrences are given by Delson (1973, i.p.a.).

The climate record of the later Neogene in Europe is relatively well-known, at least on a large scale. The Middle Miocene would appear to have been characterized in general by a well-watered woodland environment (except perhaps at the end of this interval, in the typical Sarmatian of north-central Europe, where Thenius [1960] reported drier elements of flora and fauna). The typical Vallesian and Turolian succeed one another in two Spanish local basins, in which the former assemblage reflects continuity with the preceding Middle Miocene (with the addition of *Hipparion* and then murid rodents), while the latter evidences drying and replacement of "forest" by "steppe" mammals.

Tobien (1970b) has questioned whether this picture is typical of all of Europe or whether these two facies could have coexisted throughout the Late Miocene (his "Pontian") in different regions. He noted that most southern European assemblages (e.g. Pikermi) were of predominantly open-country type and thus associated with the Turolian, but that at least some North African "steppe-savanna" local faunas (e.g. Oued el Hammam; no monkeys) were of Vallesian-equivalent age on the basis of mammalian stage-of-evolution. Tobien further suggested that most central European local faunas were of woodland or Vallesian aspect, but that if some could be shown to be Turolian in age, this would suggest that the two facies were time-successive all over the Mediterranean region.

Various small pieces of evidence do imply both earlier woodland assemblages in the south and later steppe/parkland in the north along with woodland. Thenius (1955) reported a forest-dwelling suid (Hünermann 1969) from central Greece; Hünermann (1968) indicated that some German sites (Wissberg) contain a suid indicative of more open country; and the latest vertebrate horizon (V–3) at Baccinello may be interpreted best as a late Vallesian intermediate environment. Both of the last two assemblages contain isolated teeth attributed to *Mesopithecus pentelici*, associated in the Balkans with an open-country fauna. Moreover, Kretzoi (1969) has reported late Turolian Hungarian assemblages with a woodland character but late mammalian and invertebrate species. Finally, the Austrian local fauna of Eichkogel is interstratified with molluscs of latest Pannonian (late Pontian, latest Turolian) age but includes many mammalian species similar to those of the Franco-Spanish early Turolian as well as more "advanced" ones (Daxner-Hock and Rabeder 1971; Daxner-Hock 1972); this seems best understood as a mixture of evidence from age and ecology, the latter leading to similarities with older environmental equivalents to the south and west, despite a younger actual age.

Taken together, the mammalian evidence indicates that the Vallesian was characterized throughout Europe by a continuation of faunas adapted to rather well-watered and well-wooded environments, but during the Turolian the climate generally became drier, as was the case in Spain (and as had been the situation in North Africa during at least part of the Vallesian). In northern and central Europe, however, woodland faunas persisted nearly to the end of the Miocene. At any given time, therefore, there would have been a gradient from well-watered deciduous (or even evergreen) woodland in the north, through parkland, scrub, and into a steppelike vegetation similar to that of the western Soviet Union, but more thermophilous and with gallery forests along watercourses; the dominant factor was probably a relative decrease in moisture (Butzer 1971: 71–75).

This suggestion from mammalian evidence is supported by the rarer paleobotanical results available. Grassland with moderately developed coniferous forest has been reported from the Turolian of Macedonia (Gillet and Faugères 1970), while a picture of progressive decrease in hygrophilous plants but retention of some evergreen forest on higher slopes has been painted for central Europe (see Knobloch 1970; Nagy 1970; Planderova 1971). On the other hand, the apparently late Turolian local fauna from Marceau (Algeria) was recovered from lignite deposits indicating relatively humid woodlands. It may finally be suggested that the tectonically controlled Mediterranean desiccation at the end of the Miocene accentuated the independent dehumidification of southern Europe (which had gone on for some time already) through removal of the potential evaporation source for precipitation.

At the beginning of the Pliocene, the situation reversed somewhat, with the peri-Mediterranean lands becoming much more humid, while the drying trend may have persisted longer in the north. Kretzoi (1969) has suggested that the mammal fauna of the Ruscinian (and the early Villafranchian, following Tobien [1970a]) is of monsoon-forest aspect. Michaux (1971) also considered that the great abundance of murid rodents in Spain and southern France at this time was due to high humidity, and that a drying during the Pleistocene led to the reduction of this group in Europe; although this seems to have been the case, it leaves unexplained the great increase of murids during the equally dry later Turolian. Furthermore, Lobreau-Callen and Suc (1972) have been able to determine a pollen spectrum closely analogous to that of the monsoon/dry season climate of North Vietnam, at a middle Ruscinian locality (Celleneuve/Montpellier) where *Macaca, ?Mesopithecus,* and *Dolichopithecus* have been recovered.[3] The earliest Villafranchian locality of Vialette (with "*Paradolichopithecus*" and dated to earlier than 3.8 million years) has recently yielded a pollen flora of more modern aspect than earlier sites, indicating a relatively open forest with pine, juniper, and beech, perhaps on neighboring slopes (Meon-Vilain 1972). Levels above and below the mammal-bearing horizon were more densely wooded, but grasses were quite common (35 percent) in the matrix surrounding the bones, despite the quantities of forest-dwelling tapir, deer, and mastodont recovered (Viret 1954; Guérin 1972). Finally, both *Dolichopithecus ruscinensis* and *?Mesopithecus monspessulanus* have been found in the contemporaneous lignites of Baraolt-Capeni (Romania), further suggesting a forest facies at this time.

As Tobien (1970a), Azzaroli (1970), and Kretzoi (1969), among others, have noted, the major environmental break in the Villafranchian is neither at its beginning nor at the middle/late transition which approximates the Plio–Pleistocene boundary, but at the early/middle transition when the humid forest retreated again to allow the spread of holarctic open-country environments. At this time, also, it becomes feasible to attempt correlation with the Netherlands pollen sequences most recently summarized by van der Hammen, Wijmstra, and Zagwijn (1971). They noted that the first important cooling in the paleobotanical record occurred during the Pretiglian (roughly middle Villafranchian), at which time many of the older, southeast Asian forms disappear from Europe for the last time. There may also have been tundra in the North Sea–Baltic region at this time, but mammal faunas do not clearly reflect such conditions. The Tiglian of the Netherlands is essentially the late Villafranchian of this scheme, as Tegelen also yields mammals of that age, including macaque. Floras from Tegelen and from Senèze (Elhaï 1969) indicate relatively warm climate and de-

[3] On the other hand, Heintz (1971) has reported the strongly open-country gazelle from the same locality. More complete review of the total mammalian assemblage at some Ruscinian localities might indicate which animals were most common, at least in the vicinity of the recovered death assemblages.

ciduous forest, with periods of open-country parkland ("steppe").

During the Pleistocene in Europe, macaque (the only cercopithecid known) is widespread in relatively warm, interglacial or "interstadial" times but never present in faunas of distinctly cold aspect. This feature has been especially discussed by Bartolomei (1969)[4], as well as by Hinton (1908), Bernsen (1930), and Viret (1954). The corresponding assumption made by Kurtén (1963) and Forsten (1968) that the presence of monkeys also implies forest or woodland is not supported by faunal evidence. The mammals associated with macaque, as with earlier monkeys in Europe, may be of forest or steppe type, and the latter seems more common during the Pleistocene (as well as the Late Miocene).

Asia

An essentially similar climatic history seems to have characterized much of Asia, although details differed. This region is treated more specifically by Prasad (1975), but a few comments may be made here. Comparison of *Hipparion* stage-of-evolution in particular and of total faunal aspect in general (Hussain i.p.) suggests that the Vallesian is closely time-equivalent with the Nagri "age" in the Siwalik region. The subsequent Dhok Pathan probably equates not only to the Turolian, but to the Ruscinian and possibly part of the Villafranchian as well (Maglio, personal communication). Tattersall (1969a 1969b; Leakey and Bazett 1969) has indicated that the Nagri mammals are of woodland type, as are those of the Chinji; moreover, he noted lithological evidence (from Krynine 1937) for seasonal rainfall in a forested environment during Nagri time, with development of prairie and aridification during Dhok Pathan time. Prasad (1971) has confirmed these results with paleobotanical evidence. It must be recalled, however, that the Siwalik "faunas" each derive from units of rock thousands of feet (more than 1,000 meters) thick, as opposed to the relatively brief spans sampled by isolated European localities. On the one hand, it is possible to speak of "Nagri time," represented by a continuous sequence of rock and a faunal assemblage, but on the other hand, direct associations between specimens or taxa are usually not certain.

[4] Bartolomei's paper is a useful contribution reviewing the distribution of macaque and porcupine (*Hystrix*) in the European Plio-Pleistocene and concluding that both forms are good indicators of a relatively warm climate. Two minor errors in his distribution list for macaques may be corrected here: neither Villany-3 nor Sutto (both Hungary) have yielded any cercopithecid. Other taxonomic errors in terms of Ruscinian and older localities and a more complete listing may be found in Delson (i.p.a).

The earliest known cercopithecid fossils from the Siwalik sequence are of Dhok Pathan age, subsequent to any certainly placed hominoids. Although these few specimens have been variously assigned to *Macaca, Semnopithecus,* and *Cercopithecus,* Simons (1970, 1972) correctly identified several of them as colobine. All specimens from the Dhok Pathan published or known to me can be referred to a single colobine species, which may be termed *?Presbytis sivalensis* (Lydekker). This form may have been quite similar to *Mesopithecus pentelici,* of equivalent age and (probably) environment in Europe, but as yet only dental fragments are known. The two partial mandibles from the next younger Tatrot Formation have previously been identified as colobines (or ignored, as by Simons [1970, 1972]), but they in fact represent the oldest cercopithecine in Asia, *Macaca paleindicus* (Lydekker). Without further study and revision of both the mammal species and their relative stratigraphic placement, little can be said about the environments of either the Tatrot or the succeeding Pinjor.

Younger Asian cercopithecid fossils are known from India, China, Vietnam, Laos, Indonesia, and Japan. The most interesting of these are a maxilla from the Pinjor and some dental and postcranial specimens from China which may be referred to the genus *Procynocephalus.* Jolly (1967) has shown that the long bones and foot indicate a highly terrestrial adaptation, while the dentition is clearly cercopithecine. This form may have evolved locally from *Macaca* in parallel with *Paradolichopithecus* of similar age, or the two lineages may be specially related (Simons 1970, 1972). From the same horizons and also from Tung-Lang, North Vietnam, the Chou-Kou-Tien caves, and the *Gigantopithecus* caves come specimens of one or more large species of *Macaca* which seem closest to the modern *M. thibetana-M. assamensis* group (of Fooden 1971), possibly indicating a wider range for this type than today. Most other specimens are smaller and appear closely related to the modern inhabitants of the local regions.

Africa

Although *Libypithecus* and the Marceau colobine *(?Colobus flandrini)* are apparently of African aspect and relationship, sub-Saharan Africa is as yet nearly barren of cercopithecids from the Middle Miocene until the Pliocene (one tooth has been reported from the early Late Miocene of Ngorora by Bishop and Chapman [1970] and the isolated cercopithecine tooth from Ongoliba may also be of Late Miocene age).

Moreover, very little can yet be discussed about the paleoenvironments of the regions producing fossil monkeys in the Pliocene and Pleistocene, in part because many East African localities are still being worked intensively and no complete faunal lists are available and in part because of the lack of comprehensive studies of the long-known southern African cave sites. The few papers reviewing the fossil mammals of the latter area (e.g. Sampson 1971) have not attempted specific environmental reconstructions, but most do tend to agree with the granulometric-petrographic work of Brain (1967) in suggesting a ranking of relative aridity of the major sites from Taung (dry) through Sterkfontein, Makapan, Swartkrans, and Kromdraai (see also Peabody 1954). This is also approximately a time order, with Sterkfontein or Makapan the oldest, but it is unlikely (although possible) that a single drying trend occurred through the time span represented (perhaps 3 to 1.5 million years [Cooke and Maglio 1972]).

As at most African localities, the dominant groups of cercopithecids at these sites are the baboons and geladas – the large Papionini. The moderately large, probably (semi-) arboreal colobine *Cercopithecoides*, however, is represented in almost all of the caves. Several taxa allocated to the genus *Parapapio* are most common at the older localities, where a range of sizes has been divided into three "species" (Freedman and Stenhouse 1972). Animals with more typically *Papio*-like facial morphology are more abundant at the three younger sites (and at several others of less certain age, e.g. Bolts Farm), ranging from small species to the very large forms with baboon- (not gelada-) type teeth, *Dinopithecus* and *"Gorgopithecus."* True geladas, *Theropithecus* (*Simopithecus*) species, have been reported only from Makapan and Swartkrans as yet.

In eastern Africa, the same taxonomic dominance occurs. Small monkeys, both cercopithecines of the *Cercopithecus* or true *Cercocebus* type and colobines *(?Colobus* sp.) have been noted from East Rudolf (Cooke and Maglio 1972), Omo (Eck and Howell 1972), and Kanam (Delson 1975). *Theropithecus* species are common (only or most abundant form) at most East African localities; the majority of these are of waterside environment (Jolly 1972), with the exception of the two sites lacking gelada, Kanam and Laetotil (Delson 1975). As yet no very large baboons have been reported, but *Papio* or *Parapapio* spp. are known from many localities, spanning an age range from Lothagam (latest Miocene or earliest Pliocene) to the present. The possible replacement of gelada-like forms by *Papio* baboons has been discussed by Jolly (1970, 1972) in an environmental framework for East Africa and may be reflected in the more sketchy South African evidence as well. Large colobines are also present at some eastern localities: *?Cercopithecoides* in the Omo and the probably related *Paracolobus* in the upper Chemeron Formation and probably at Laetolil and East Rudolf (R. Leakey 1969; M. Leakey, personal communication; Delson 1975).

The distinction between the moister, possibly more open environments favored by the early *Theropithecus* and the drier mixed parkland in which fossil *Papio* and *Parapapio* are found is interesting but may reflect only part of the story. The African Papionini today include mangabeys and mandrills of denser woodland as well, and all four of these "types" are distinct both geographically and morphologically from the more adaptable Asian (and northwest African) macaques. The latter, it will be recalled, first appeared in North Africa during the latest Miocene, then in Europe in the early Pliocene, and in Asia in the late Pliocene, or Pleistocene. Possibly at the same time that the peri-Mediterranean lands suffered great aridity as a result of the combination of tectonically caused Mediterranean desiccation and the previously begun Late Miocene deterioration of climate, the region of the present Sahara also suffered a drying, perhaps to the extent of forming a temporary barrier to migration between northern and east-central Africa. The Sahara has generally been considered to be of much younger age (Moreau 1963; Monod 1963), but there is little evidence for its earlier condition; Beucher (1967) described a flora of "Pliocene" age in the northwest Sahara that included elements of both tropical and circum-Mediterranean affinity but was dominated by desertic types. A hypothesis of an ecological barrier across the region of the present Sahara in the Late Miocene would explain the differentiation of African and Eurasian cercopithecines at approximately this date and could be tested by comparison with other groups.

Historical Zoogeography

The dispersal pattern of cercopithecids has been discussed briefly by Napier (1970), who has suggested that the early cercopithecids were essentially colobines, one group of which gave rise to cercopithecines in Eurasia during the early Miocene. This hypothesis appears to be based mostly on the view that "colobines are essentially arboreally adapted in locomotion and diet and it is well-nigh inconceivable, on anatomical and physiological grounds alone, that they should have evolved from a ground-living stock" (Napier 1970: 79). This argument agrees neither with the fossil evidence nor with morphological considerations suggesting that colobine teeth (and related digestive tract features) are more "specialized" than those of cercopithecines. Moreover, because of their behaviorally linked plasticity, postcranial elements are notoriously dangerous to use in studying relationship or ancestry. Finally, there is nothing to require that the common ancestor of colobines and cercopithecines had to be effectively one or the other already.

A more realistic approach to the historical pattern of Old World monkey deployment might begin with Napier's (1970) suggestion that the eating of leaves as well as fruits in a deciduous forest environment would prolong the time during which food was plentifully available, thus conferring a selective advantage. Ancestral (as yet unknown) monkeys that occupied this mixed leaf-and-fruit niche in the early Miocene might by the mid-Miocene have diverged into the source groups for the two subfamilies: early colobines concentrating on leaves and developing specialized dentitions and digestive tracts, and early cercopithecines retaining the earlier food preferences or re-emphasizing fruits, as well as concentrating on development of terrestrial locomotion with concomitant evolution of longer faces and cheek pouches.

As partly discussed by Van Couvering (1972, personal communication) and others, it is possible to envisage the dispersal of catarrhines in general as a series of sequentially replacing migrations out of Africa. The small apes such as *Pliopithecus* (and *Limnopithecus)* first occur in the earliest Miocene of Africa and appear in Europe by the early Middle Miocene, becoming most common late in this period, before waning to a last occurrence in the late Vallesian. *Dryopithecus* species are first found late in the African Early Miocene, entering Europe by mid-Middle Miocene, and having a widest Eurasian distribution in the late Middle and early Late Miocene (Chinji–Nagri), but probably not lasting into the Turolian/Dhok Pathan of temperate regions. Both of these genera were basically forest-adapted, *Dryopithecus* possibly semiarboreal to as terrestrial as chimpanzees; the presence of *Ramapithecus* at this time implies that it may not have been closely linked to the still rare open country.

By the later Vallesian, semiarboreal colobines had entered Eurasia, developing further terrestrial adaptations in Europe during the Turolian *(M. pentelici)* and present but of uncertain habit in Asia during Dhok Pathan time. It was probably the most terrestrial colobines that departed Africa, leaving more arboreal types to radiate as an African natural group, still connected across the Sahara region. Drying on both sides of the Mediterranean at the end of the Miocene may have led to a tripartite division of the Papionini, which had already diverged from the more arboreal Cercopithecini.

The ancestral macaques were able to enter Europe by the earliest Pliocene, reaching Asia late in the epoch. Ancestral *Theropithecus* (first known as fossils in eastern and northern Africa by 4 million years ago) may have diverged from other African Papionini as a wet-lowland adaptation, leaving *Parapapio*-like forms to diversify into the several living and extinct dentally typical genera. The late exit of papionins suggests that they may have been too terrestrially committed by the Vallesian to follow the colobines across a semiforested Afro-Asian corridor at that time, while cercopithecines were too arboreal.

Finally, a fifth catarrhine group, early man (already *Homo* cf. *erectus?*), may not have been able to depart Africa until the earliest Pleistocene because of the return of wooded conditions in western Asia during the Pliocene.

PROGNOSIS FOR PALEOBIOLOGY

Research of the type summarized here obviously draws upon, but also may contribute to, studies of modern relatives. The comparative anatomical study of joint surfaces and limb-element proportions provides quantifiable data that may indicate similarities between fossil forms and living analogues in terms of postcranial adaptations and the possible range of movements and thus behaviors of which the animals were capable.

Five fossil cercopithecid species are sufficiently represented by postcranial specimens to suggest something of their way of life. The European Late Miocene (Turolian) *Mesopithecus pentelici* is best known in this respect, and preliminary studies of its limbs indicate not only colobine affinities, but terrestrial adaptations as pronounced as in the most terrestrial living colobine, *Presbytis entellus* (Delson 1973; Gaudry 1862; Gabis 1960). Its occurrence at Pikermi and elsewhere in association with a fauna and flora of open parkland type suggests that *Mesopithecus* may have slept in gallery forests, traveling terrestrially between isolated stands of deciduous feeding-trees and foraging on ground products as well. The analogy with *Presbytis entellus* as studied by Beck and Tuttle (1972) and others (reviewed by Dolhinow 1972) may be rather close.

The larger European colobine *Dolichopithecus ruscinensis*, of the

Pliocene (Ruscinian and early Villafranchian), was even more terrestrially adapted (Delson 1973). Although the mosaic of character states seen in this form is not the same as that found in any known cercopithecine, it might have been as agile terrestrially as a mandrill or Barbary ape. Its presence in the "monsoon forest" of the Ruscinian suggests further ecological similarity with large semiterrestrial cercopithecines. On the other hand, an even larger extinct colobine, East African *Paracolobus chemeroni,* shows a few morphological parallels with terrestrial forms, but its feet and limb proportions indicate a fully arboreal habitus, although more complete study is required to draw further analogies.

Two fossil cercopithecines have also been studied (Jolly 1967, 1972) in terms of postcranial adaptations: Asian *Procynocephalus* and African *"Simopithecus."* The former genus is represented by limb bones published by Teilhard de Chardin (1938) from locality 12 of Chou-Kou-Tien, which Jolly interpreted as being about as terrestrially inclined as those of *Papio* species. *"Simopithecus"* includes the most ground-adapted species of cercopithecid yet known, especially the late large forms of East Africa with massive limbs and lengthened humerus. These animals went well beyond the modern gelada in their morphological adjustments to terrestrial life and probably represent the mainstream of *Theropithecus* evolution, as opposed to the relict-refuge distribution of *T. gelada* today.

It is clear that none of these observations on the habits of fossil animals could be made without study of the skeletons of modern forms by both paleontologists and anatomists. But the right sorts of observations on the activity patterns of living, behaving primates are also of great importance, especially as they cannot usually be made by the paleontologist himself. Studies of cineradiographic films of monkeys chewing or locomoting are also useful, but they do not necessarily reflect an animal's natural range of actions in its own habitat. For that information, we must rely on ecoethologists (in the widest sense).

Among the types of observations that might be most useful in interpreting fossils and their anatomy (as well as relationships and taxonomy of both living and extinct species) we can list:

1. Percentages of time spent by animals in different locomotory modes — either typical classes (e.g. terrestrial quadrupedalism, branch-walking, arm-support stance, etc.) or species-specific modes employed by the animals as observed and delimited *a posteriori.*
2. The activities that employ these modes — feeding, travel, play, sleep, etc. Observation of the use of the thumb or other body elements,

such as those made by Lorenz (1971), could be of great use in deciphering relationships, as of colobines with differentially reduced thumbs (*Mesopithecus,* for example, has an ancestrally long thumb, intermediate between those of *Nasalis* and macaques, at the extremes of their respective subfamilies).

3. Inter- and intraspecific differences in feeding behavior (e.g. in mastication time and concentration of effort for different food items); food preferences among differing consistencies; types of food preparation (husking, shelling, stripping) required; the use of fingers, teeth, etc., in holding, preparing, and transporting food objects.

4. Especially important, the range of activities and variations observed. The ecological variability found in *Presbytis entellus* (or *Papio* of the *cynocephalus* group), for example, has been shown to be reflected in its behavior, yet it would appear that its morphology is constant. On the other hand, even that statement needs to be checked, for although Simons (1970: 110) states that *P. entellus* is "fully arboreally adapted," my examination of a limited number of skeletons suggests that it is certainly more terrestrially adapted than any other living colobine, as in fact has been observed of its behavior. The interaction, feedback, and reinforcement of paleontological-anatomical observations and ethological ones will eventually allow for a true understanding of primate paleobiology.

REFERENCES

ADAM, KARL D.

1964 Die Grossgliederung des Pleistozäns in Mitteleuropa. *Stuttgarter Beiträge zur Naturkunde* 132:1–12.

AMBROSETTI, P., A. AZZAROLI, F. P. BONNADONNA, M. FOLLIERI

1972 A scheme of Pleistocene chronology for the Tyrrhenian side of central Italy. *Bolletino della Societa Geologica Italiana* 91:169–190.

AMERICAN COMMISSION ON STRATIGRAPHIC NOMENCLATURE

1961 Code of stratigraphic nomenclature. *American Association of Petroleum Geologists Bulletin* 45:645–665.

ANDREWS, PETER, JUDY VAN COUVERING

1975 "Palaeoenvironments in the East African Miocene," in *Approaches to primate paleobiology*. Edited by Frederick S. Szalay. New York: Karger.

ARAMBOURG, CAMILLE

1959 Vertébrés continentaux du Miocène supérieur de l'Afrique du nord. *Publications du Service de la Carte Géologique de l'Algérie. Paléontologie*, n.s. *(mémoire)* 4:5–159.

AZZAROLI, AUGUSTO

1970 Villafranchian correlations based on large mammals. *Giornale di Geologia* serie 2 35:1–21.

1972 *Villafranchien et Pliocène/Quaternaire*. Committee on Mediterranean Neogene Stratigraphy Circular 1, Appendix, 10–11.

AZZAROLI, AUGUSTO, P. AMBROSETTI

1970 Late Villafranchian and early mid-Pleistocene faunas in Italy. *Palaeogeography, Palaeoclimatology and Palaeoecology* 8:107–111.

AZZAROLI, AUGUSTO, ANNALISA BERZI

1971 On an upper Villafranchian fauna at Imola, northern Italy, and its correlation with the marine Pleistocene sequence of the Po Plain. *Palaeontologica Italica* 66:1–12.

BALLESIO, R.

1971 Le pliocène rhodanien. *Documents des Laboratoires de Géologie de la Faculté des Sciences de Lyon, hors série* 1:201–239.

BARTOLOMEI, GIORGIO

1969 Considerazioni ecologiche sulle faune Pleistoceniche dell'Europa contenenti scimmie ed istrichi. *Scritti sul Quaternario in onore di Angelo Pasa, Museo Civico di Storia Naturale, Verona*, 39–52.

BECK, BENJAMIN B., RUSSELL TUTTLE

1972 "The behavior of gray langurs at a Ceylonese waterhole," in *The functional and evolutionary biology of primates*. Edited by Russell Tuttle, 351–377. Chicago: Aldine-Atherton.

BERGGREN, WILLIAM A.

1971 "Tertiary boundaries and correlations," in *Micropaleontology of oceans*. Edited by B. F. Funnel and W. R. Riedel, 693–809. Cambridge: Cambridge University Press.

1972 A Cenozoic time-scale — some implications for regional geology and paleobiogeography. *Lethaia* 5:195–215.

BERNSEN, J. J. A.

1930 On a fossil monkey found in the Netherlands (*Macacus* cf. *florentina* Cocchi). *Proceedings of the Royal Academy of Sciences, Amsterdam* 33:771–778.

BEUCHER, FRANCOISE

1967 Quelques éléments de flore pliocène au Sahara. *Comptes Rendus Hebdomadaires de l'Académie des Sciences, Paris*, série D, 265: 1117–1120.

BISHOP, WALTER WILLIAM, G. R. CHAPMAN

1970 Early Pliocene sediments and fossils from the northern Kenya Rift Valley. *Nature* 226:914–918.

BRAIN, C. K.

1967 "Procedures and some results in the study of Quaternary cave fillings," in *Background to evolution in Africa*. Edited by W. W. Bishop and J. D. Clark, 285–301. Chicago: University of Chicago Press.

BUTZER, KARL W.

1971 *Environment and archeology* (second edition). Chicago: Aldine.

CHALINE, JEAN

1973 Biogéographie et fluctuations climatiques au Quaternaire d'après les faunes de rongeurs. *Acta Zoologica Cracoviensia* 18:141–165.

CHESTERS, K. I. M.

1957 The Miocene flora of Rusinga Island, Lake Victoria, Kenya. *Palaeontographica* 101:30–71.

CICHA, IVAN, JAN SENES

1972 Probleme der Beziehung zwischen Bio- und Chronostratigraphie des jüngeren Tertiärs. *Geologicky Zbornik — Geologica Carpathica* 22:209–227.

CITA, MARIA B., WILLIAM B. F. RYAN

1972 "Time scale and general synthesis," in *Initial reports of the Deep Sea Drilling Project*, volume thirteen. Edited by W. B. F. Ryan, K. J. Hsü, et al., 1405–1415. Washington, D.C.: United States Government Printing Office.

COOKE, H. B. S., VINCENT MAGLIO

1972 "Plio-Pleistocene stratigraphy in East Africa in relation to proboscidean and suid evolution," in *Calibration of hominoid evolution*. Edited by W. W. Bishop and J. A. Miller, 303–329. Toronto: University of Toronto Press.

DAXNER-HOCK, GUDRUN

1972 Cricetinae aus dem Alt-Pliozän vom Eichkogel bei Mödling (Niederösterreich) und von Vösendorf bei Wien. *Paläontologisches Zeitschrift* 46:133–150.

DAXNER-HOCK, GUDRUN, GERNOT RABEDER

1971 Vorläufige Ergebnisse der paläontologischen Grabung 1968 im Altpliozän (O-Pannon) des Eichkogels (N.Ö.). *Anzeiger der Österreichischen Akademie von Wissenschaften, Mathematisch-Naturwissenschaftliche Klasse* 107(2):47–50.

DE BRUIJN, HANS, J. E. MEULENKAMP

1972 Late Miocene rodents from the Pandanassa Formation (Prov. Rethymnon), Crete, Greece. *Proceedings of the Nederlandse Akademie van Wetenschappen, Amsterdam*, series B, 75:53–60.

DE BRUIJN, HANS, PAUL SONDAAR, W. J. ZACHARIASSE

1971 Mammalia and Foraminifera from the Neogene of Kastellios Hill (Crete), a correlation of continental and marine biozones. *Proceedings of the Nederlandse Akademie van Wetenschappen, Amsterdam*, series B, 74:1–22.

DELSON, ERIC

1971 Estudio preliminar de unos restos de simios pliocénicos procedentes de "Cova Bonica" (Gava) (Prov. Barcelona). *Acta Geológica Hispánica* 6:54–57.

1973 "Fossil colobine monkeys of the circum-Mediterranean region and the evolutionary history of the Cercopithecidae (Primates, Mammalia)." Unpublished doctoral dissertation.

1975 "Evolutionary history of the Old World monkeys," in *Approaches to primate paleobiology*. Edited by Frederick S. Szalay, 167–217. New York: Karger.

i.p.a Preliminary review of cercopithecid distribution in the circum-

Mediterranean region. *Mémoires du Bureau de Recherches Géologiques et Minières de France* 78.

i.p.b "Toward the origin of the Old World monkeys," in *Problèmes actuels de paléontologie: évolution des vertébrés.* Colloques Internationaux du Centre National des Recherches Scientifiques 218. Paris: Centre National des Recherches Scientifiques.

DOLHINOW, PHYLLIS JAY

1972 "The north Indian langur," in *Primate patterns.* Edited by P. J. Dolhinow, 181–238. New York: Holt, Rinehart and Winston.

ECK, GERALD G., F. C. HOWELL

1972 New fossil *Cercopithecus* material from the Lower Omo Basin, Ethiopia. *Folia Primatologica* 18:325–355.

ELHAÏ, HENRI

1969 La flore sporo-pollinique du gisement villafranchien de Senèze (Massif Central, France). *Pollen et Spores* 11:127–140.

EVERNDEN, J. F., D. E. SAVAGE, G. H. CURTIS, G. T. JAMES

1964 Potassium-argon dates and the Cenozoic mammalian chronology of North America. *American Journal of Science* 262:145–198.

FOODEN, JACK

1971 Female genitalia and taxonomic relationships of *Macaca assamensis. Primates* 12:63–73.

FORSTEN, ANN-MARIE

1968 Revision of the Palearctic *Hipparion. Acta Zoologica Fennica* 119:1–134.

FREEDMAN, LEONARD, N S. STENHOUSE

1972 The *Parapapio* species of Sterkfontein, Transvaal, South Africa. *Palaeontologica Africana* 14:93–111.

GABIS, RENÉE V.

1960 Les os des membres chez les singes cynomorphes. *Mammalia* 24: 577–602.

GAUDRY, ALBERT

1862 *Animaux fossiles et géologie de l'Attique.* Paris: F. Savy.

GILLET, SUZETTE, L. FAUGÈRES

1970 Contribution à l'étude du Pontien de Macédoine — analyse géologique et sédimentologique des dépôts de Trilophos (SW de Salonique). *Revue de Géographie Physique et de Géologie Dynamique* 12:9–24.

GRADSTEIN, F. M.

1970 Foraminifera from the type Sicilian at Ficarazzi, Sicily (Lower Pleistocene). *Proceedings of the Nederlandse Akademie van Wetenschappen, Amsterdam,* series B, 73:305–333.

GUÉRIN, CLAUDE

1972 Une nouvelle espèce de rhinoceros (Mammalia, Perissodactyla) à Vialette (Haute-Loire, France) et dans d'autres gisements du Villafranchien inférieur européen: *Dicerorhinus jeanvireti* n. sp. *Documents des Laboratoires de Géologie de la Faculté des Sciences de Lyon* 49:53–150.

GUÉRIN, CLAUDE, PIERRE MEIN
1971 Les pincipaux gisements de mammifères miocènes et pliocènes du domaine rhodanien. *Documents des Laboratoires de Géologie de la Faculté des Sciences de Lyon,* hors série 1:131–170.

GUÉRIN, CLAUDE, *et al.*
1972 Découverte d'*Hipparions* ante-Tortoniens dans le bassin de Vaison-la-Romaine (Vaucluse, sud-est de la France). *Comptes Rendus Hebdomadaires de l'Académie des Sciences, Paris,* série D, 274: 1276–1279.

HEINTZ, EMILE
1971 Présence de *Gazella* (Bovidae, Artiodactyla, Mammalia) dans les sables marins Pliocènes de Montpellier, Hérault, France. *Bulletin du Muséum National d'Histoire Naturelle, Paris,* série 2, 46: 1334–1336.

HINTON, MARTIN A. C.
1908 Monkey's bone in the Norfolk "Forest-Bed." *Geological Magazine,* n.s. (decade V) 5:440–444.

HOOIJER, DIRK ALBERT
1963 Miocene Mammalia of Congo. *Annales du Musée Royale de l'Afrique Centrale,* série in 8vo, *Sciences Géologiques* 46:1–77.
1970 Miocene Mammalia of Congo, a correction. *Annales du Musée Royale de l'Afrique Centrale,* série in 8vo, *Sciences Géologiques* 67:163–167.

HOWELL, F. CLARK
1966 Observations on the earlier phases of the European Lower Paleolithic. *American Anthropologist* 68 (2, part two): 88-201.

HSÜ KENNETH J.
1972 When the Mediterranean dried up. *Scientific American* 227(6): 27–36.

HSÜ, KENNETH J., WILLIAM B. F. RYAN, MARIA B. CITA
1973 Late Miocene desiccation of the Mediterranean. *Nature* 242:240–244.

HÜNERMANN, KARL ALBAN
1968 Die Suidae (Mammalia, Artiodactyla) aus den Dinotheriensanden (Unterpliozän-Pontian) Rheinhessens (Südwestdeutschland). *Mémoires Suisses de Paléontologie* 86:1–96.
1969 Über die Leitwert der Suidae im europäischen Neogen. *Eclogae Geologicae Helveticae* 62:715–730.

HUSSAIN, S. TASEER
1971 Revision of *Hipparion* (Equidae, Mammalia) from the Siwalik Hills of Pakistan and India. *Bayerische Akademie der Wissenschaften, Mathematisch-Naturwissenschaftliche Klasse, Abhandlungen,* n.s. 147:1–68.
i.p. Rejection of "Meotian" and "Pontian" as mammalian time terms: correlation of *Hipparion* of the Siwaliks within Holarctica. *Mémoires du Bureau de Recherches Géologiques et Minières de France* 78.

JÁNOSSY, DÉNES

1970 The boundary of Lower-Middle Pleistocene on the basis of microvertebrates in Hungary. *Palaeogeography, Palaeoclimatology and Palaeoecology* 8:147–152.

1972 Middle pliocene microvertebrate fauna from the Osztramos Loc. 1. (Northern Hungary). *Annales Historico-naturales musei Nationalis Hungarici* 64:24–52.

JOLLY, CLIFFORD J.

1967 "The evolution of the baboons," in *The baboon in medical research*, volume two. Edited by H. Vagtborg, 24–50. Austin: University of Texas Press.

1970 "The large African monkeys as an adaptive array," in *Old World monkeys*. Edited by John R. Napier and P. H. Napier, 141–174. New York: Academic Press.

1972 The classification and natural history of *Theropithecus (Simopithecus)* (Andrews, 1916), baboons of the African Plio-Pleistocene. *Bulletin of the British Museum (Natural History), Geology* 22:1–123.

KERTAI, G.

1968 Geology of the Pannonicum. *Hungarian Academy of Sciences, Guide to Excursion 42C, International Geological Congress, Twenty-third Session, Prague.*

KNOBLOCH, E.

1970 The Tertiary flora of Moravia (Czechoslovakia). *Giornale de Geologia*, serie 2, 35:77–83.

KRETZOI, MIKLOS

1969 Sketch of the Late Cenozoic (Pliocene and Quaternary) terrestrial stratigraphy of Hungary. *Foldrajzi Kozlemenyek* 176:198–204.

KRYNINE, P. D.

1937 Petrography and genesis of the Siwalik series. *American Journal of Science*, series 5, 34:422–440

KURTÉN, BJORN

1963 Villafranchian faunal evolution. *Societas Scientifica Fennica, Commentationes Biologicae* 26(3):3–13.

LEAKEY, LOUIS, SEYMOUR BAZETT

1968 Upper Miocene primates from Kenya. *Nature* 218:527–530.

1969 Ecology of north Indian *Ramapithecus*. *Nature* 223:1075–1076.

LEAKEY, RICHARD E. F.

1969 New Cercopithecidae from the Chemeron beds of Lake Baringo, Kenya. *Fossil Vertebrates of Africa* 1:53–69.

LIPPOLT, H. J., W. GENTNER, W. WIMMENAUER

1963 Alterbestimmungen nach der Kalium-Argon-Methode an tertiären Eruptivgesteinen Südwestdeutschlands. *Jahreshefte des geologischen Landesamtes* 6:507–538.

LOBREAU-CALLEN, DANIELLE, JEAN-PIERRE SUC

1972 Présence de pollens de *Microtropis fallax* (Celastraceae) dans le Pleistocène inférieur de Celleneuve (Hérault). *Comptes Rendus Hebdomadaires de l'Académie des Sciences, Paris*, série D, 275: 1351–1354.

LORENZ, RAINER
1971 The functional interpretation of the thumb in the Hylobatidae. *Proceedings of the Third International Congress of Primatology* 1:130–136. Basel: Karger.

LYELL, CHARLES
1833 *Principles of geology*, volume three. London: Murray.

MAGLIO, VINCENT J.
1972 Vertebrate faunas and chronology of hominid-bearing sediments east of Lake Rudolf, Kenya. *Nature* 239:379–384.

MEIN, PIERRE, JAQUES MICHAUX
1970 Un nouveau stade dans l'évolution des rongeurs pliocènes de l'Europe sud-occidentale. *Comptes Rendus Hebdomadaires de l'Académie des Sciences, Paris*, série D, 270:2780–2783.

MEIN, PIERRE, GEORGES TRUC
1966 Facies et association faunique dans le Miocène supérieur continental du Haut-Comtat Venaissain. *Travaux des Laboratoires de Géologie de la Faculté des Sciences de Lyon*, n.s. 13:273–276.

MEON-VILAIN, HENRIETTE
1972 Analyse palynologique de la flore du gisement villafranchien de Vialette (Haute-Loire). *Documents des Laboratoires de Géologie de la Faculté des Sciences de Lyon*, n.s. 49: 151–156.

MICHAUX, JACQUES
1971 Evolution et signification des peuplements de murides (Rodentia) en Europe sud-occidentale au Neogène supérieur. *Comptes Rendus Hebdomadaires de l'Académie des Sciences, Paris*, série D, 273:314–317.

MONOD, T.
1963 "The Late Tertiary and Pleistocene in the Sahara," in *African ecology and human evolution*. Edited by F. C. Howell and F. Bourlière, 117–229. Chicago: Aldine.

MOREAU, R. E.
1963 "The distribution of tropical African birds in relation to past climatic changes," in *African ecology and human evolution*. Edited by Fa C. Howell and F. Bourlière, 28–42. Chicago: Aldine.

OLSON, E. C.
1952 The evolution of a Permian vertebrate chronofauna. *Evolution* 6:181–196.

NAGY, ESTHER
1970 Hungary's Neogene climate on the basis of palynological researches. *Giornale di Geologia*, series 2, 35:91–104.

NAPIER, JOHN R.
1970 "Paleoecology and catarrhine evolution," in *Old World monkeys*. Edited by J. R. Napier and P. H. Napier, 55–95. New York: Academic Press.

PEABODY, FRANK E.
1954 Travertines and cave deposits of the Kaap Escarpment of South Africa, at the type locality of *Australopithecus africanus* Dart. *Geological Society of America Bulletin* 65:671–706.

PILBEAM, DAVID R., ALAN WALKER

1968 Fossil monkeys from the Miocene of Napak, northeast Uganda. *Nature* 220:657–660.

PLANDEROVA, EVA

1971 The problem of floristic boundary between Pliocene-Pleistocene in western Carpathian Mts. on the basis of palynological examination. *Geologicky Zbornik — Geologica Carpathica* 22:229–241.

PRASAD, K. N.

1971 Ecology of the fossil Hominoidea from the Siwaliks of India. *Nature* 232:413–414.

1975 "Observations on the paleoecology of South Asian tertiary primates," in *Paleoanthropology: morphology and paleoecology*. Edited by Russell H. Tuttle. World Anthropology. The Hague: Mouton.

PRÉVOT, MICHEL, G. BRENT DALRYMPLE

1970 Un bref épisode de polarité géomagnetique normale en cours de l'époque inverse Matuyama. *Comptes Rendus Hebdomadaires de l'Académie des Sciences, Paris,* série D, 271:2221–2224.

RYAN, WILLIAM B. F., *et al.*

1970 Deep-sea drilling project, leg XIII. *Geotimes* 15(10):12–16.

SAMPSON, C. GARTH

1971 "Sequential dating of the South African australopithecine-bearing breccias." Paper presented to the Seventieth Annual Meeting, American Anthropological Association, New York, 1971.

SAVAGE, DONALD E., GARNISS H. CURTISS

1970 The Villafranchian stage-age and its radiometric dating. *Geological Society of America, Special Papers* 124:207–231.

SCHAEFFER, BOBB, MAX K. HECHT, NILES ELDREDGE

1972 "Phylogeny and paleontology," in *Evolutionary biology*, volume six. Edited by T. Dobchansky, M. K. Hecht, and W. C. Steere, 31–46. New York: Appelton-Century-Crofts.

SHOTWELL, J. ARNOLD

1958 Intercommunity relationships in Hemphillian (mid-Pliocene) mammals. *Ecology* 39:271–282.

1964 "Community successions in mammals of the Late Tertiary," in *Approaches to paleoecology*. Edited by John Imbrie and Norman D. Newell, 135–150. New York: Wiley.

SIMONS, ELWYN L.

1967 The significance of primate paleontology for anthropological studies. *American Journal of Physical Anthropology*, n.s. 27:307–325.

1969 Miocene monkey (*Prohylobates*) from northern Egypt. *Nature* 223:687–689.

1970 "The deployment and history of Old World monkeys (Cercopithecidae, Primates)," in *Old World monkeys*. Edited by John R. Napier and P. H. Napier, 97–139. New York: Academic Press.

1972 *Primate evolution: an introduction to man's place in nature*. New York: Macmillan.

SIMONS, ELWYN L., DAVID R. PILBEAM

1972 "Hominoid paleoprimatology," in *The functional and evolutionary biology of primates.* Edited by Russell Tuttle, 36–62. Chicago: Aldine.

TATTERSALL, IAN

1969a Ecology of north Indian *Ramapithecus. Nature* 221:451–452.

1969b More on the ecology of north Indian *Ramapithecus. Nature* 224:821–822.

TEDFORD, RICHARD H.

1970 Principles and practices of mammalian geochronology in North America. *Proceedings of the North American Paleontological Convention,* Part F:666–703.

TEILHARD DE CHARDIN, PIERRE

1938 The fossils from locality 12 of Choukoutien. *Palaeontologica Sinica,* n.s. C, 5:2–46.

THALER, LOUIS

1965 Une échelle des zones biochronologiques pour les mammifères du Tertiaire d'Europe. *Comptes Rendus Sommaires des Séances de la Société Géologique de France* 1965(4):18.

THENIUS, ERICH

1955 *Sus antiquus* aus ligniten von Sophades (Thessalien) und die Altersstellung der Fundschichten. *Annales Géologiques des Pays Helléniques* 6:199–205.

1958 Tertiärstratigraphie und tertiäre Hominoidenfunde. *Anthropologischer Anzeiger* 22:66–77.

1959 *Tertiär,* volume two: *Wirbeltierfaunen.* Stuttgart: Enke.

1960 Die Jungtertiären Wirbeltierfaunen und Landfloren des Wiener Beckens und ihre Bedeutung fur die Neogenstratigraphie. *Mitteilung der Geologischen Gesellschaft in Wien* 52:203–209.

TOBIEN, HEINZ

1970a Subdivision of Pontian mammalian faunas. *Giornale di Geologia,* serie 2, 35:1–5.

1970b Biostratigraphy of the mammalian faunas at the Pliocene-Pleistocene boundary in middle and western Europe. *Palaeogeography, Palaeoclimatology and Palaeoecology* 8:77–93.

1972 *Méotian/Pontien.* Committee on Mediterranean Neogene Stratigraphy Circular 1, Appendix, 7–10.

VAN COUVERING, JOHN A.

1972 "Radiometric calibration of the European Neogene," in *Calibration of human evolution.* Edited by W. W. Bishop and J. A. Miller, 247–271. Toronto: University of Toronto Press.

VAN COUVERING, JOHN A., JACK A. MILLER

1969 Late Miocene marine and non-marine time scale in Europe. *Nature* 230:559–563.

VAN DER HAMMEN, T., T. A. WIJMSTRA, W. H. ZAGWIJN

1971 "The floral record of the Late Cenozoic of Europe," in *Late Cenozoic glacial ages.* Edited by K. K. Turekian, 392–424. New Haven: Yale University Press.

VIRET, JEAN
1954 Le loess à bancs durcis de Saint-Vallier (Drôme) et sa faune de mammifères villafranchiens. *Nouvelles Archives du Muséum d'Histoire Naturelle de Lyon* 4:1–200.

VON KOENIGSWALD, G. H. R.
1969 Miocene Cercopithecoidea and Oreopithecoidea from the Miocene of East Africa. *Fossil Vertebrates of Africa* 1:39–51.

VON MONTFRANS, H.
1971 Paleomagnetic dating in the North Sea basin. *Earth and Planetary Science Letters* 11:226–235.

WOOD, HORACE ELMER II, *et al.*
1941 Nomenclature and correlation of the North American continental Tertiary. *Geological Society of America Bulletin* 52:1–48.

Discussion

SZALAY: Miss Cachel, why do you refer to the parapithecids, i.e. *Parapithecus* and *Apidium*, as hominoids?

CACHEL: As explained in my paper, viewing all of the characteristics of the parapithecids and of the undoubted hominoids I did not observe any significant differences that would distinguish the parapithecids as a major independent group, i.e. one different from the undoubted hominoids like *Propliopithecus* and *Aegyptopithecus*.

SZALAY: Did you examine both upper and lower teeth of *Parapithecus?*

CACHEL: I only studied available casts of lower dentitions.

SZALAY: The upper teeth of *Parapithecus* spp. clearly exhibit incipient bilophodonty, thereby evidencing an evolutionary trend whether it be an independent one or part of the primitive reservoir precedent to later Cercopithecoidea. In showing this alignment of the cusps on upper molar teeth *Parapithecus* spp. are very different from *Aegyptopithecus*.

CACHEL: Does this show a trend through time?

SZALAY: Well, no, there are only three or four taxa. But my point here is simply that since there are apparently a number of shared advanced similarities between cercopithecoids and the *Parapithecus-Apidium* group it might not be wise to consider these fossils to be hominoids on the basis of primitive similarities with the Fayum apes. I believe that the advanced features of the parapithecids outweigh the primitive melange of similarities to all other early catarrhines.

CACHEL: I see what you mean. I notice that in your paper you dwell quite heavily on phylogenetic systematics. And in that respect I can see that if indeed the parapithecids possessed advanced traits I would be creating a paraphyletic group. I would hope to study the original specimens when they are available.

ECKHARDT: I would like to direct a question to both Sue Cachel and to Fred Szalay. I think that we have a larger question opened up here with regard to what Fred and others before him have called the Oligocene apes. There is a question in my mind as to where taxonomy comes in here. On the basis of dental characteristics it seems entirely possible to consider *Parapithecus* and/or *Aegyptopithecus* as ancestors of the later dryopithecines. You may disagree with *Parapithecus*, but for my point that is irrelevant. There is a difference between calling *Aegyptopithecus* an ancestor of the later dryopithecines and necessarily considering *Aegyptopithecus* itself as an ape. There is something of a contrast between dental characteristics and a question that one might pose on the basis of overall body size. Fred, you have spoken of body size as an important ecological characteristic. It seems to me that we might be dealing here with something which is perhaps an ancestor of the later apes although itself not occupying the ecological position of a later dryopithecine ape.

SZALAY: In many features the Fayum hominoids are clearly more primitive than the "pre-monkeys" which I consider *Parapithecus-Apidium* to be. And if we begin to discuss what a pongid level of organization is we will wind up talking a lot about primitive catarrhine characteristics. I think that the evidence for that is so scanty that perhaps we should talk about it in private.

TUTTLE: But this is very private!

GOODMAN: Mr. Eckhardt's question implies an attack on the concept of pongid. It may actually be answered more fully when we discuss molecular evidence. But now I would ask is there any need to have a separate family, the Pongidae, in the Hominoidea when it appears cladistically that the bulk of the living apes, the two African apes — chimpanzee and gorilla — are much closer to man than to the orangutan and the gibbon, and the orang in turn is closer to the two African apes and man than they are to the gibbon? I wonder if we might not want to dispense with the "pongids" and just have "hylobatids" and "hominids" in the classification of hominoid primates?

SZALAY: I believe that taxonomic philosophies that are premised on molecular evidence of living primates will always be very insufficient because the overwhelming majority of taxa are and will be represented by fossils. So you must have a system, old fashioned as it might seem to be, that accommodates the osteological evidence.

GOODMAN: Yes, but would it not be easier for the osteologists to sort out all of these fossils if they did not overrate the pongids and instead made more use of the hominids.

SZALAY: This is really a matter of taste. There should be little debate on the issue. We could argue about the recency of relationships between all forms considered to be hominoids. But this would not settle questions of evolutionary classification. I prefer a scheme, like that of Simpson and Mayr, that attempts to take into account overall selective breakthroughs, levels of organization, etc., in other words, something that reflects natural selection *in toto* as opposed to features that only reflect recency of phylogenetic relationships.

ECKHARDT: To keep the discussion between Fred Szalay and Morris Goodman going, and perhaps to bring in Professor Chiarelli, I will ask Fred what he meant by the statement in his paper that in phylogenetic analysis we are dealing with biological history and the fossils are the only key to this history. It strikes me that perhaps there are other locks because we have other keys.

SZALAY: Cladistic analysis is simply a way of determining which state of a given character is more primitive than others among taxa. This is different from evolutionary history. A whole series of cladistic analyses must be combined in order to reflect our best reconstruction of a phylogeny. Because history is time, the elements that played a role in time, viz. the fossils, are the ultimate materials for testing evolutionary hypotheses. In this sense the fossils are the only true key of history *per se*. Cladistic analysis is not.

GOODMAN: I would ask my paleontologist friends what time dimensions they can give for the key branching points in the Catarrhini. I think that this is relevant to the evolutionary clock discussion that may or may not get going later. For example when would they place the split between the Cercopithecoidea and Hominoidea?

SZALAY: There are three different fossil levels in the Fayum representing successive and presumably continuous occupation by catarrhines in North Africa. I would guess that the common ancestor of the Cercopithecoidea and Hominoidea occurred perhaps five or six million years before the earliest Fayum catarrhines, i.e. *Oligopithecus*, possibly also in Africa.

CHIARELLI: Coming back to the discussion on the pongid-hylobatid division, I think that here is a matter of the different weight we give to different characters in taxonomy. From my point of view if we use the chromosomes, and I have some reason to believe them to be good structures for studies of evolution, we are aware that the chromosomes of gibbons have nothing to do with the chromosomes of the real apes — the orangutan, chimpanzee, gorilla — and man. The gibbon chromosomes are very similar to those of the Colobinae. If we take this character into account, I think we have a major division between these two groups. I agree with Morris Goodman about the possibility of devising a classification that at some level keeps the orangutan, chimpanzee, gorilla, and man on one side along with a second division which keeps the chimpanzee, gorilla, and man separate from the orangutan.

SECTION TWO

Biomolecular Perspectives on Primate Evolution

Molecular Evidence as to Man's Place in Nature

MORRIS GOODMAN and GABRIEL W. LASKER

From interspecific comparisons of proteins and DNA a variety of data now exists on the genetic distances among primate lineages. In this paper we assemble tables of these distances from the different types of molecular data. We then compare the data of these tables to each other and, to the extent that seems justified from the assumptions underlying each set of distances, combine results into generalized scores. Furthermore, these distance scores provide a measure of evolutionary relationships among primates independent of traditional morphologically based views. We therefore note some of the special features of traditional taxonomic classification of man and other primates in the light of the molecular evidence.

ANTIGENIC DISTANCES AMONG PRIMATE LINEAGES

The serum proteins provide numerous and soluble, hence accessible, material for study; this allows the approximate distances between other animals and man to be measured by the number of differences in serum proteins. A rough measure of these differences is the extent of nonshared antigenic sites reflected in spur size in trefoil Ouchterlony plates (Moore and Goodman 1968; Goodman and Moore 1971) The antigenic sites are shaped by amino acid groups at the protein surfaces. Thus if one compares two related proteins with antisera to one of them (the homologous antigen), the length of the spur of this homologous antigen against

This research was supported by National Science Foundation grant GB-36157.

For Plates, see iv–v, between pp. 560–561

Table 1. Antigenic distance ×10 using rabbit antisera to primates, tree shrews, and elephant shrews

	Anti-*Homo*	Anti-*Pan*	Anti-*Gorilla*	Anti-*Hylobates*	Anti-*Macaca*	Anti-*Papio*	Anti-*Erythrocebus*	Anti-*Presbytis*	Anti-*Saimiri*	Anti-*Aotes*	Anti-*Tarsius*	Anti-*Galago*	Anti-*Nycticebus*	Anti-*Loris*	Anti-*Urogale*	Anti-*Tupaia*	Anti-*Nasilio*	Ant *Elephantulus*
Homo		6	8	21	42	35	33	36	59	61	94	104	111	99	113	120	141	129
Pan	10		8	25	39	36	44	39			86			112				
Gorilla	8	4		22	36			36			86			111				
Pongo	20	11	16	21	39	48	37	39	59	61	86							
Hylobates	26	22	19		31	41	39	36	53	61	86			117				
Symphalangus	25	21		2														
Macaca	36	34	28	35		1	2	21	56	65	92			108	111	117	166	
Papio	42	37	26		2		0	20			86			108				
Theropithecus	44	31	28	35	2		4	19			85							
Cercocebus	36	29	29	35	6	1	0	18			86							
Cercopithecus	40	25	26	30	9	5	0	15			86							
Erythrocebus	38	29	28	35	1	4		18			86			110				
Presbytis	40	32	29	29	10	19	18		62	65	84			118				
Nasalis				38				2										
Pygathrix								2										
Colobus	44	32	26	36	15	11	14	5										
Ateles	76		71		52		75		37	22	104			104				
Lagothrix	66		71		54		72		33	23								
Alouatta	73				61		72		29	12								
Saimiri	76	76	67	65	64	60	57	65		26	99	107	112	91				
Cebus	71	73	68		58		74		30	30	102							
Chiropotes	67	71	63		56	35	62		33	29								

Callimico									28	10								
Saguinus	64		67		60		69		31	11								
Tarsius	88		95		84		92		98							110		
Galago	105	119	105	113	93	103	95	109	107	118	108		39	41	102	115	140	158
Galagoides												7		39				
Nycticebus	104	122	102	113	106	104	98		113	120	115	34		27		129	175	
Loris	100	119	107	114	116	111	97	109	109	118	114	45	19		102			
Perodicticus	106	116	105	122	110		95		107	123	111	37	48	51	122	123		
Arctocebus	124											40	45					
Lemuroidea	112	119	96	107	100	103	98	109			111	96	107	88	95	117	166	
Urogale	122															16		
Tupaia	126	127	117	110	108	104	106		118	123	109	115	123	125	42		149	144
Erinaceidae	136	152	131	142			122	140			141			137	128	150	143	160
Soricidae				154			118	151								154	146	160
Scapanas															130	150		
Tenrec				153			118								121	140	179	
Rhynchocyon	122							142								143	105	113
Petrodromus	128		120								137				120	137	57	43
Nasilio				150			117									149		33
Elephantulus i.																	33	19
Elephantulus m.															137		33	
Eptesicus															140	151		
Dasypus	134	141	115	123			113				125			144	114	135	166	
Bradypus	156	150	121	120				137			137			144		120	137	160
Myrmecophaga	156	141	121	125				137								144	146	
Rodentia	150	123	114	138		89	119	135			125			129	126	140	175	
Carnivora	128	152	119	129			116	140						125	115	130	179	
Ungulata	115	141	111	125		92	107	135			130			134			179	
Elephantinae	143			125			118									121		
Marsupialia	164			153														

the other (the heterologous antigen) will be longer as the dissimilarity between the two proteins in their surface configurations of amino acid groups becomes greater. If two heterologous antigens are compared, the one which bears the closer relationships to the homologous antigen will yield the longer spur against the other, i.e., a positive net spur size. On the basis of set theory logic (Moore, Goodman 1968; Goodman, Moore 1971), a computer program translates these spur sizes in a series of plate comparisons into a table of antigenic distances.

Table 2. A summary of antigenic distance data of Table 1. Genera have been grouped starting with the smallest antigenic distances and then going to more inclusive groupings. All applicable comparisons between members of the two groups have been averaged. Man's place in nature in terms of his serum proteins is represented by his membership in the hierarchical groupings of the left-hand column (cf. Table 19)

			Average Antigenic distance
Homo	versus	*Pan, Gorilla*	0.80
Homo, Pan, Gorilla	versus	*Pongo*	1.60
Homo, Pan, Gorilla, Pongo	versus	Hylobatinae	2.23
Hominoidea	versus	Cercopithecoidea	3.47
Catarrhini	versus	Platyrrhini	6.49
Anthropoidea	versus	*Tarsius*	9.16
Haplorhini	versus	Strepsirhini	10.89
Haplorhini, Strepsirhini	versus	Tupaioidea	11.46
Primates	versus	Other Eutheria	12.11–14.91
Eutheria	versus	Marsupialia	15.83

Such antigenic distances from tests, whether on the same or different proteins, are averaged to yield general antigenic distances between a pair of species. When the plates in these tests show multiple precipitin lines representing different protein antigens in whole serum, each line is counted as a separate reaction in the calculation of average distances from antisera to antigens of either species. This procedure for adjusting the scales of the antigenic distance scores obtained with antisera to whole serum or to specific purified proteins of different species makes the scores of various species comparisons more nearly equivalent. Our colleague, Dr. G. William Moore, developed the method and will present a detailed description of it elsewhere.

Table 1 shows the mean distance between different species from over 3,000 Ouchterlony plate comparisons with a wide variety of rabbit antisera to whole blood serum or to specific serum proteins of eighteen species. Table 2, calculated from the data in Table 1, shows in terms of increasing average antigenic distance the degrees of relationship of man to other primates and mammals. The African apes (chimpanzee and gorilla) are closest to man; they are followed in succession by orangutan, gibbons, cercopithecoids (Old World monkeys), ceboids (New World monkeys and marmosets), tarsier, strepsirhines (lemuroids and lorisoids), tree shrews, other eutherian mammals, and marsupials. Thus, except for the grouping of African apes with man rather than with orangutan, this whole array is very similar to the traditional morphological taxonomy of the primates.

The close relationship of the African apes to man and the other relationships among the major primate groups indicated by the rabbit antisera (Tables 1 and 2) have been confirmed in over 3,000 additional Ouchterlony plate comparisons using cercopithecoid (vervet and rhesus) and ceboid (spider, woolly, and capuchin monkey) antisera to hominoid serum proteins and using chicken antisera to serum proteins of various primate species (Goodman and Moore 1971; Goodman, et al. 1974). Moreover the albumin antigenic distance values among species of Anthropoidea, gained by Sarich (1970) using the microcomplement fixation test, also depict the close relationship between the African apes and man, the hominoid affinities of the gibbons, and the subdivision of Anthropoidea into Platyrrhini (Ceboidea) and Catarrhini (Hominoidea and Cercopithecoidea).

AMINO ACID AND CODON SEQUENCE DISTANCES AMONG PRIMATE LINEAGES

The distances calculated by immunological methods compare antigens (such as serum proteins) only indirectly and are therefore a relatively crude measure of genetic distances among species. Antibodies only react to the surface configuration of a molecule, and it is not possible to know how many of the amino acid residues need differ to cause a given difference in immunological reaction. More refined measures of genetic distance can be obtained when the actual amino acid sequences of homologous peptide chains of the species are known from biochemical analyses of the proteins under comparison. A growing amount of this data on the sequential order of amino acids in peptide chains, much of it reviewed in Dayhoff (1972), now exists. The sequences within each collection of homologous chains have been aligned by matching amino acid residue positions so as to maximize homologies. A simple count of amino acid differences (AAD) can then be taken for each pair of species.

A still more refined measure of genetic distance from these sequence differences is obtained by calculating the minimum mutation distance (MMD) for each pair of aligned protein chains. The calculations use a conversion table (Fitch and Margoliash 1967) based on the genetic code (Crick 1966) to determine at each alignment position for each amino acid pair the minimum number of nucleotides that would need to be changed in order to convert a codon for one amino acid into a codon for the other. Because there are three nucleotide positions in each codon, up to three nucleotide substitutions can be detected over each pair of amino acids; however, multiple substitutions at the same nucleotide positions and substitutions producing synonymous codons for the same amino acid cannot be detected.

A further refinement in measuring genetic distance from amino acid sequences depends on the fact that living species are related through common ancestors and that the amino acid sequences of these ancestral species can be reconstructed from our knowledge of the sequences in the living species (Moore, Barnabas, Goodman 1973). Although the actual course of evolution for these sequences may have been more tortuous, the best estimation one can make of their phylogeny is the evolutionary tree (dendrogram) which *in toto* has the fewest mutations. This ensures that the maximum number of amino acid identities in the descendant sequences are due to inheritance from common ancestors and, conversely, the fewest number to parallel or back mutations. Indeed the analysis is extended to the nucleotide level of the sixty-one codons which specify the twenty different amino acids in such a way that often different codons for the same amino acid can be distinguished; a leucine, e.g. in one region of the tree at an alignment position may have to be specified, due to the configuration of amino acids in surrounding species, by a different codon from that used for a leucine in another region of the tree to yield *in toto* the minimum number of mutations. Considering the many permutations in amino acids, and the even greater number in codons, which are possible due to mutations, a probabilistic argument can be used to justify a procedure based on the parsimony principle. This priciple seeks that tree for the amino acid sequences of living species that has the maximum number of codon identities based on inheritance from common ancestors. Such trees are theoretically best because it seems more probable that the identities in codon sequences observed between related species are due to common inheritance.

A combination of computer programs, developed by Dr. Moore, is used to construct these maximum parsimony trees. When more than a few species are compared, the number of possible trees is very large indeed and it is not practicable to consider them all even by computer. Instead, the search for the parsimony tree is carried out by an iterative procedure, in which mutational tree lengths are determined for many alternative tree topologies. The search is directed by those changes in topology, which lower the mutational length the most and stops when the tree of the shortest length appears to have been discovered. Usually there are alternative solutions for the maximum parsimony ancestral codons on this tree. A computer program then selects the solution which minimizes the number of times a mutation is counted among lineages between the most ancestral point on the tree and each contemporary species. The distance between two species, in terms of the number of mutations calculated through intervening branch points in this way, is the maximum parsimony distance (MPD). The MPD can include more than one mutation between two species at the same nucleotide position if the most parsimonious tree dictates such multiple (or even reverse) mutations, but the MPD can never be less than the minimum mutation distance (MMD), which does not take such past intermediate branch points into consideration and merely counts the minimum differences between the extant species.

As information on additional related species is added, maximum parsimony distances increase, so that the maximum parsimony length calculated on a sparsely studied evolutionary branch is not equivalent to that of one in which many subsequent branchings have occurred and have been studied. This, plus the fact that a new tree must be calculated every time data on additional species or on additional sequences becomes known, makes it prudent to retain the simpler counts of amino acid substitution (AAD) and minimum mutation distances (MMD) for most comparisons of protein composition with molecular data of other types and with gross morphological information, even though the Maximum Parsimony Method would theoretically yield the best estimate of evolutionary distances in a more or less equally branching group of interrelated organisms, whose homologous proteins have been well studied. Unfortunately it takes much work to sequence even a single protein of a species; therefore, none of the distance calculations from amino acid sequences can yet be applied to more than a limited array of data.

Examples of the three types of genetic distances AAD, MMD, and MPD within the primates and between primates and nonprimate mammals from amino acid sequences of myoglobins, alpha and beta hemoglobin chains, fibrinopeptides, cytochrome Cs, and carbonic anhydrases I and II are given in Tables 3-15.

In addition, in all cases in which at least two protein chains and over 150

Table 3. Amino acid differences (AAD) of hemoglobin alpha chains within primates and between primates and other mammals

	Man	Chi	Gor	Lan	Mac	Gal	Slo	Lem	Sif	Tre
Man										
Chimpanzee	0									
Gorilla	1	1								
Langur	3	3	4							
Macaque	4	4	5	5						
Galago	13	13	12	13	12					
Slow Loris	9	9	8	10	11	8				
Lemur	15	15	16	15	16	16	14			
Sifaka	19	19	20	20	19	21	19	13		
Tree Shrew	24	24	25	24	21	24	22	25	26	
Horse	18	18	18	18	16	22	18	22	29	25
Pig	18	18	19	20	18	24	20	21	27	26
Bovine	17	17	18	17	16	23	20	22	27	26
Sheep	21	21	21	21	18	24	22	26	31	23
Mouse	18	18	19	18	17	22	20	23	23	20
Dog	23	23	22	23	24	23	21	20	25	26
Rabbit	25	25	26	24	25	29	25	25	28	28
Kangaroo	27	27	28	27	26	32	30	32	35	32

The sequences for many of these alpha chains are given in Dayhoff (1972); those which are not are from langur and slow loris (G. Matsuda, unpublished data) and from galago, lemur, sifaka, and tree shrew (Hill 1968). The distances were calculated for 141 shared amino acid positions.

Table 4. Minimum mutation distances (MMD) of hemoglobin alpha chains within primates and between primates and other mammals

	Man	Chi	Gor	Lan	Mac	Gal	Slo	Lem	Sif	Tre
Man										
Chimpanzee	0									
Gorilla	1	1								
Langur	3	3	4							
Macaque	5	5	6	6						
Galago	14	14	13	15	14					
Slow Loris	11	11	10	13	14	8				
Lemur	18	18	18	18	20	19	17			
Sifaka	23	23	24	25	24	25	22	18		
Tree Shrew	31	31	31	32	29	30	29	31	33	
Horse	22	22	21	22	19	27	23	29	37	33
Pig	20	20	20	22	21	25	22	24	32	31
Bovine	20	20	20	20	19	25	24	28	34	29
Sheep	26	26	25	26	24	27	26	29	38	28
Mouse	21	21	21	21	21	24	23	27	29	27
Dog	25	25	23	25	27	24	22	22	29	33
Rabbit	28	28	28	27	29	32	28	30	34	37
Kangaroo	34	34	34	34	31	39	39	41	41	42

Table 5. Maximum parsimony distances (MPD) of hemoglobin alpha chains within primates and between primates and other mammals

	Man	Chi	Gor	Lan	Mac	Gal	Slo	Lem	Sif	Tre
Man										
Chimpanzee	0									
Gorilla	1	1								
Langur	3	3	4							
Macaque	5	5	6	6						
Galago	15	15	16	16	18					
Slow Loris	13	13	14	14	16	8				
Lemur	20	20	21	21	23	23	21			
Sifaka	29	29	30	30	32	32	30	19		
Tree Shrew	36	36	37	37	39	39	37	36	45	
Horse	34	34	35	35	37	37	35	34	43	42
Pig	37	37	38	38	40	40	38	37	46	45
Bovine	37	37	38	38	40	40	38	37	46	45
Sheep	41	41	42	42	44	44	42	41	50	49
Mouse	29	29	30	30	32	32	30	29	38	29
Dog	25	25	26	26	28	28	26	25	34	39
Rabbit	42	42	43	43	45	45	43	42	51	50
Kangaroo	47	47	48	48	50	50	48	47	56	55

The maximum parsimony tree of alpha sequences from which these MPD values were calculated is presented elsewhere (Goodman et al. 1974).

Table 6. Amino acid differences (AAD) of hemoglobin beta chains within primates and between primates and other mammals

	Man	Chi	Gor	Gib	Lan	Mac	Mar	Nig	Spi	Squ	Slo
Man											
Chimpanzee	0										
Gorilla	1	1									
Gibbon	3	3	4								
Langur	4	4	5	4							
Macaque	8	8	7	8	5						
Marmoset	7	7	8	7	5	7					
Night Monkey	7	7	8	7	3	8	4				
Spider Monkey	6	6	7	6	4	9	6	4			
Squirrel Monkey	9	9	10	9	7	11	6	6	6		
Slow Loris	11	11	12	10	10	12	11	11	12	12	
Horse	25	25	26	26	24	28	25	23	23	25	25
Pig	24	24	25	23	23	26	26	25	23	27	25
Bovine	24	24	23	23	24	26	27	25	22	26	29
Sheep	26	26	27	26	23	26	24	23	23	26	29
Mouse	26	26	27	27	24	26	27	25	26	28	26
Dog	15	15	14	14	16	15	16	15	15	18	19
Rabbit	14	14	15	13	13	16	11	13	15	14	14
Kangaroo	38	38	37	38	38	36	37	37	38	38	38

The sequences for most of these beta chains are given in Dayhoff (1972); those which are not are from langur and slow loris (G. Matsuda, unpublished data). The distances were calculated for 146 shared amino acid positions, except in the comparisons with bovine and sheep sequences in which the calculations were for 145 positions.

Table 7. Minimum mutation distances (MMD) of hemoglobin beta chains within primates and between primates and other mammals

	Man	Chi	Gor	Gib	Lan	Mac	Mar	Nig	Spi	Squ	Slo
Man											
Chimpanzee	0										
Gorilla	1	1									
Gibbon	3	3	3								
Langur	5	5	6	4							
Macaque	10	10	9	9	7						
Marmoset	10	10	11	9	7	10					
Night Monkey	10	10	11	9	5	12	4				
Spider Monkey	8	8	9	7	5	12	6	4			
Squirrel Monkey	12	12	13	11	9	14	6	6	6		
Slow Loris	15	15	16	14	14	15	15	15	15	15	
Horse	31	31	32	32	30	34	31	29	28	31	28
Pig	28	28	29	27	27	31	32	30	27	31	27
Bovine	27	27	26	27	28	30	31	29	27	29	33
Sheep	33	33	34	32	29	35	30	28	28	32	35
Mouse	33	33	34	36	33	35	36	34	35	36	33
Dog	18	18	17	17	19	18	20	18	18	20	22
Rabbit	16	16	17	15	15	18	12	14	16	15	16
Kangaroo	53	53	52	53	54	50	53	54	54	55	55

Table 8. Maximum parsimony distances (MPD) of hemoglobin beta chains within primates and between primates and other mammals

	Man	Chi	Gor	Gib	Lan	Mac	Mar	Nig	Spi	Squ	Slo
Man											
Chimpanzee	0										
Gorilla	1	1									
Gibbon	3	3	4								
Langur	5	5	6	4							
Macaque	11	11	12	10	8						
Marmoset	13	13	14	12	10	16					
Night Monkey	10	10	11	9	7	13	4				
Spider Monkey	10	10	11	9	7	13	6	4			
Squirrel Monkey	14	14	15	13	11	17	6	6	8		
Slow Loris	17	17	18	16	14	20	19	17	17	21	
Horse	41	41	42	40	38	44	43	41	41	45	42
Pig	35	35	36	34	32	38	37	35	35	39	36
Bovine	44	44	45	43	41	47	46	44	44	48	45
Sheep	46	46	47	45	43	49	48	46	46	50	47
Mouse	43	43	44	42	40	46	45	43	43	47	44
Dog	23	23	24	22	20	26	25	23	23	27	24
Rabbit	21	21	22	20	18	24	23	21	21	25	22
Kangaroo	73	73	74	72	70	76	75	73	73	77	74

The maximum parsimony tree of alpha sequences from which these MPD values were calculated is presented elsewhere (Goodman et al. 1974).

Table 9. Distances of myoglobin chains within primates and between primates and other mammals

	Man			Chimpanzee			Gibbon			Macaque			Baboon		
	AAD	MMD	MPD	AAD	MMD	MPD	AAD	MMD	MPD	AAD	MMD	MPD	AAD	MMD	MPD
Man															
Chimpanzee	1	1	1												
Gibbon	1	1	1	2	2	2									
Macaque	7	7	7	8	8	8	6	6	8						
Baboon	6	6	6	7	7	7	5	5	7	1	1	1			
Horse	19	21	25	18	20	26	20	22	26	18	20	24	18	19	23
Bovine	29	34	35	28	33	36	30	35	36	29	32	34	29	32	33
Sheep	25	28	29	24	27	30	26	29	30	25	26	28	25	26	27
Seal	24	27	28	23	26	29	25	28	29	23	25	27	23	25	26
Porpoise	20	23	27	19	22	28	21	24	28	22	24	26	22	24	25
Dolphin	23	25	29	22	24	30	24	26	30	24	25	28	24	25	27
Sperm Whale	25	26	37	24	25	38	26	27	38	25	25	36	26	26	35
Kangaroo	22	29	29	23	30	30	23	30	30	22	26	28	22	27	27

The sequences for many of these myoglobin chains are given in Dayhoff (1972); those which are not are from man, chimpanzee, gibbon, macaque, and baboon (Romero Herrera and Lehmann 1971a, 1971b; 1972a, 1972b) and from sheep (Han et al. 1972). The maximum parsimony tree of myoglobin sequences from which the MPD values were calculated is presented elsewhere (Goodman et al. 1974). The distances were calculated for 153 shared amino acid positions.

Table 10. Amino acid differences (AAD) of fibrinopeptides A and B within primates and between primates and other mammals

	Man	Chi	Gor	Ora	Gib	Sia	Mac	Dri	Cer	Spi	Cap	Slo
Man												
Chimpanzee	0											
Gorilla	0	0										
Orangutan	2	2	2									
Gibbon	4	4	4	2								
Siamang Gibbon	3	3	3	1	1							
Macaque	4	4	4	5	5	4						
Drill	8	8	8	6	6	5	6					
Cercopithecus	5	5	5	3	3	2	3	3				
Spider Monkey	9	9	9	8	8	7	9	12	9			
Capuchin Monkey	10	10	10	8	8	7	9	11	8	3		
Slow Loris	16	16	16	15	14	14	14	19	16	13	13	
Horse	11	11	11	11	8	10	10	14	12	12	14	13
Pig	14	14	14	14	12	14	13	13	16	17	18	17
Bovine	15	15	15	14	14	14	13	16	16	15	16	21
Sheep	14	14	14	14	12	14	12	18	16	15	16	17
Rat	17	17	17	18	15	17	14	18	19	17	18	19
Dog	14	14	14	14	13	15	13	17	16	16	17	16
Rabbit	17	17	17	16	15	16	16	17	17	17	17	14
Kangaroo	15	15	15	15	11	14	10	14	14	14	15	16

The sequences for the primate fibrinopeptides A and B are given in Wooding and Doolittle (1972) and for the other fibrinopeptides A and B in Dayhoff (1972). The alignment employed for these sequences is that of Wooding and Doolittle (1972). Within the primates in most cases, there are twenty-five shared amino acid positions in comparisons involving macaque fibrinopeptides A and B, twenty-nine positions in gibbon comparisons, and thirty in the other primate to primate comparisons. Between these primates and the other mammals in most cases there are twenty-five shared positions in the comparisons to horse and kangaroo and twenty-seven positions in comparisons to pig, bovine, sheep, rat, dog, and rabbit

amino acid residue positions of both members of a pair of primate species could be compared, the total AAD value as a percentage (number of amino acid differences per 100 amino acid residues) was calculated. Table 16 designates for each species involved in these comparisons the different protein chains on which AAD values were obtained, and Table 17 presents the AAD results for the species pairs. In addition to the more extensively compared protein chains of Tables 3–15, delta hemoglobin chains were also compared in hominoids (Boyer et al. 1971) as were ^{A}gamma and ^{G}gamma hemoglobin chains in chimpanzee and man (DeJong 1971). The amino acid distances of Table 17 are from a different selection of proteins than are the antigenic distances of Table 2, but both sets of distances involve the same primate groups. Thus it is of interest to

Table 11. Minimum mutation distances (MMD) of fibrinopeptides A and B within primates and between primates and other mammals

	Man	Chi	Gor	Ora	Gib	Sia	Mac	Dri	Cer	Spi	Cap	Slo
Man												
Chimpanzee	0											
Gorilla	0	0										
Orangutan	2	2	2									
Gibbon	4	4	4	2								
Siamang Gibbon	3	3	3	1	1							
Macaque	5	5	5	5	5	4						
Drill	8	8	8	6	6	5	6					
Cercopithecus	5	5	5	3	3	2	3	3				
Spider Monkey	10	10	10	9	9	8	11	13	10			
Capuchin Monkey	10	10	10	8	8	7	9	11	8	3		
Slow Loris	17	17	17	15	14	14	15	19	16	15	15	
Horse	16	16	16	15	12	14	14	18	16	14	17	18
Pig	19	19	19	17	14	17	18	22	19	20	21	22
Bovine	21	21	21	20	19	20	18	22	22	20	22	30
Sheep	19	19	19	17	15	17	13	21	19	19	20	20
Rat	19	19	19	20	17	19	17	21	21	20	21	25
Dog	19	19	19	18	17	19	17	22	21	17	20	19
Rabbit	21	21	21	19	18	19	21	21	20	22	22	19
Kangaroo	18	18	18	17	13	16	13	17	17	18	19	19

Table 12. Maximum parsimony distances (MPD) of fibrinopeptides A and B within primates and between primates and other mammals

	Man	Chi	Gor	Ora	Gib	Sia	Mac	Dri	Cer	Spi	Cap	Slo
Man												
Chimpanzee	0											
Gorilla	0	0										
Orangutan	2	2	2									
Gibbon	4	4	4	2								
Siamang Gibbon	3	3	3	1	1							
Macaque	7	7	7	5	5	4						
Drill	8	8	8	6	6	5	7					
Cercopithecus	5	5	5	3	3	2	4	3				
Spider Monkey	10	10	10	8	8	7	11	12	9			
Capuchin Monkey	9	9	9	7	7	6	10	11	8	3		
Slow Loris	17	17	17	15	15	14	18	19	16	19	18	
Horse	23	23	23	21	21	20	24	25	22	25	24	24
Pig	25	25	25	23	23	22	26	27	24	27	26	26
Bovine	36	36	36	34	34	33	37	38	35	38	37	37
Sheep	30	30	30	28	28	27	31	32	29	32	31	31
Rat	24	24	24	22	22	21	25	26	23	26	25	25
Dog	24	24	24	22	22	21	25	26	23	26	25	25
Rabbit	26	26	26	24	24	23	27	28	25	28	27	27
Kangaroo	21	21	21	19	19	18	22	23	20	23	22	22

The maximum parsimony tree of fibrinopeptides A and B from which these MPD values were calculated is shown in Figure 2.

Table 13. Distances of cytochrome C within primates and between primates and other mammals

	Man			Chimpanzee			Macaque		
	AAD	MMD	MPD	AAD	MMD	MPD	AAD	MMD	MPD
Man									
Chimpanzee	0	0	0						
Macaque	1	1	1	1	1	1			
Horse	12	15	18	12	15	18	11	14	17
Pig	10	11	12	10	11	12	9	10	11
Bovine	10	11	12	10	11	12	9	10	11
Sheep	10	11	12	10	11	12	9	10	11
Dog	11	12	13	11	12	13	10	11	12
Whale	10	12	13	10	12	13	9	11	12
Rabbit	9	11	15	9	11	15	8	10	14
Kangaroo	10	11	14	10	11	14	11	12	13

The sequences for these cytochrome C's are given in Dayhoff. The maximum parsimony tree from which the MPD values were calculated is from unpublished data of M. Goodman, C. Callahan, and G. W. Moore. The distances were calculated for 104 shared amino acid positions.

Table 14. Distances of carbonic anhydrase I within primates

	Man			Chimpanzee			Orangutan			*Cercopithecus*			Baboon		
	AAD	MMD	MPD	AAD	MMD	MPD	AAD	MMD	MPD	AAD	MMD	MPD	AAD	MMD	MPD
Man															
Chimpanzee	1	1	1												
Orangutan	4	4	4	3	3	3									
Cercopithecus	4	4	6	3	3	5	4	4	4						
Baboon	6	6	8	7	7	7	6	6	6	4	4	4			
Macaque	5	5	7	6	6	6	5	5	5	3	3	3	1	1	1

These distances, from the data in Tashian et al. (1972), were calculated for 115 shared amino acid positions.

Table 15. Distances of carbonic anhydrase II within primates and between primates and sheep

	Man			*Cercopithecus*			Macaque		
	AAD	MMD	MPD	AAD	MMD	MPD	AAD	MMD	MPD
Man									
Cercopithecus	0	0	0						
Macaque	2	2	2	2	2	2			
Sheep	36	46	49	36	46	49	36	46	49

The distances, from the data in Tashian et al. (1972), were calculated for 115 shared amino acid positions.

Table 16. Protein substances compared for amino acid differences between primates

Man	αHb	βHb	δHb*	$^{G}\gamma$Hb	$^{A}\gamma$Hb	Myo	Fib A–B	Cyt C	CaI	CaII
Chimpanzee	αHb*	βHb*	δHb*	$^{G}\gamma$Hb*	$^{A}\gamma$Hb*	Myo*	Fib A–B	Cyt C	CaI*	
Gorilla	αHb*	βHb*	δHb*				Fib A–B			
Orangutan	αHb†	βHb†					Fib A–B		CaI*	
Gibbon	pαHb‡	βHb*	δHb*			Myo*	Fib A–B			
Macaque	αHb	βHb				Myo*	Fib A–B	Cyt C	CaI*	CaII*
Baboon						Myo*	Fib A–B		CaI*	
Cercopithecus							Fib A–B		CaI*	CaII*
Langur	αHb	βHb								
Spider Monkey	pαHb‡	βHb*					Fib A–B			
Slow Loris	αHb	βHb					Fib A–B			

* Sequence largely inferred from amino acid composition of peptide fragments by homology with known sequences.
† Amino acid composition (Buettner-Janusch et al. 1969).
‡ Sequence on the first thirty-one positions from the N-terminal end of the alpha hemoglobin chain (Boyer et al. 1972).

Table 17. The amino acid difference matrix for primates

Upper half of matrix: number of differing amino acids per number of shared amino acid positions
Lower half of matrix: percent of differing amino acids

	Man	Chi	Gor	Ora*	Gib	Mac	Bab	Cer	Lan	Spi	Slo
Man		3/1127	3/463	12/432	12/505	31/799	20/293	9/260	7/287	18/207	36/317
Chimpanzee	0.27		2/463	11/432	12/505	31/684	22/298	X	7/287	18/207	36/317
Gorilla	0.65	0.43		7/322	10/352	16/312	X	X	9/287	18/207	36/317
Orangutan*	2.78	2.54	2.17		5/175	X	X	X	X	X	X
Gibbon	2.38	2.38	2.84	2.85		19/323	11/182	X	8/177	17/206	27/206
Macaque	3.89	4.54	5.13	X	5.88		8/293	8/255	10/287	19/202	37/312
Baboon	6.83	7.39	X	X	6.06	2.73		X	X	X	X
Cercopithecus	3.45	X	X	X	X	3.13	X		X	X	X
Langur	2.44	2.44	3.18	X	4.52	3.48	X	X		7/177	20/287
Spider Monkey	8.69	8.69	8.69	X	8.25	9.32	X	X	3.95		28/207
Slow Loris	11.36	11.36	11.36	X	13.10	11.85	X	X	7.00	13.51	

* The amino acid composition data of orangutan alpha and beta hemoglobin chains were used in the estimations of amino acid differences in the comparisons of the orangutan to other hominoids but not in those of orangutan to phylogenetically more distant primates because amino acid composition data could only be expected to yield correct or nearly correct AAD values between closely related species.

X Comparisons not done due to insufficient data.

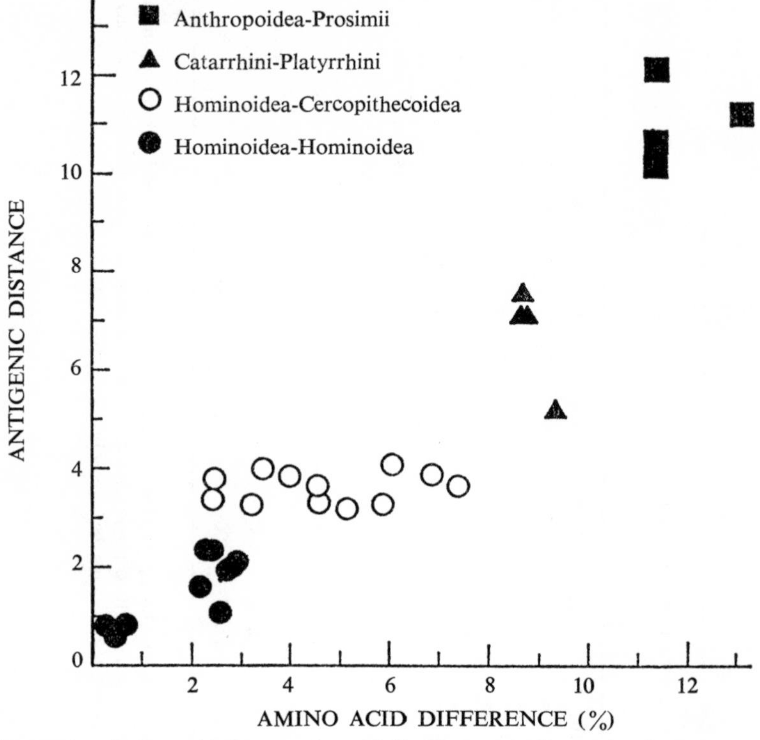

Figure 1. Amino acid distances from Table 17 compared to antigenic distances from Table 1 for corresponding species comparisons

plot the two sets of genetic distances together (Figure 1). This figure shows that the amino acid distance values are, in general, similar to the antigenic distance values, but the two kinds of distances are not completely proportional. Probably because of the relatively small number of homologous peptides so far sequenced and the fact that different proteins are involved in different pairs of species, the amino acid differences of each taxonomic group show considerable variability, are not linearly related to the immunological differences, and fail to separate the Hominoidea from the Cercopithecidae.

The maximum parsimony trees of the various globin chains, fibrinopeptides, cytochrome Cs, and carbonic anhydrases I and II, from which the maximum parsimony distances of Tables 5, 8, 9, and 12–15 were derived, provide information about the interrelationships of the species, from which the sequences came. The maximum parsimony tree for the fibrinopeptides is shown in Figure 2, and those for the other proteins have been or are being presented elsewhere (see legends of the Tables for references). The main cladistic conclusions can be briefly summarized

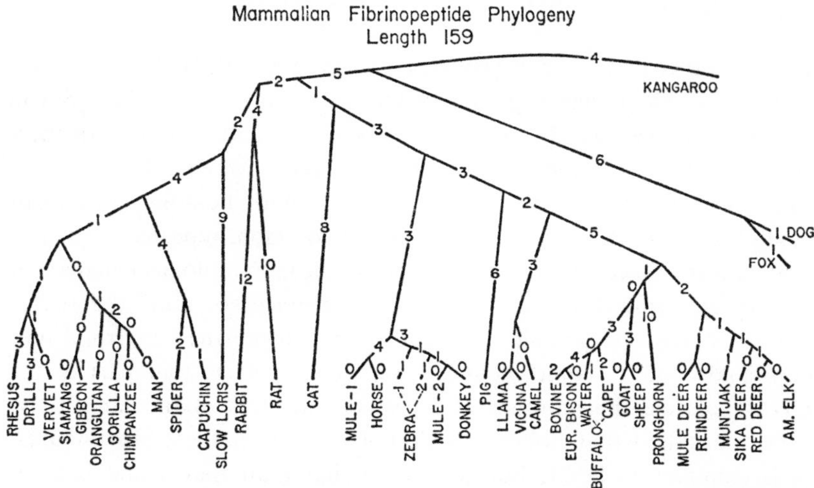

Figure 2. Maximum parsimony tree of mammalian fibrinopeptide A and B sequences. In the alignment employed, that of Wooding and Doolittle (1972), twenty-seven amino acid residue positions are shared by most species, and the numbers of nucleotide replacements recorded on the branches are for these twenty-seven positions except on the terminal branches to kangaroo, horse and mule-1, cape buffalo, and rhesus monkey, in which the numbers are for twenty-five, twenty-five, twenty-three, and twenty-five residue positions respectively. This tree was first prepared for the Elliot Smith symposium (Goodman 1973)

here. The African apes and man are closer to each other than to other primates; the gibbon group is closer to hominoids than to Old World monkeys; and Old World monkeys and hominoids group together into the catarrhine branch, which is then joined by the platyrrhine branch (New World monkeys and marmosets) to constitute the Anthropoidea. Lorisoids are closer to these higher primates than to nonprimates and, in the case of alpha hemoglobin sequences, lemuroids are also closer. This is not true for beta hemoglobin sequences, but the evidence suggests that the betalike sequences of the lemuroids descend from a different ancestral gene locus than the ancestral locus for typical eutherian mammal beta chains. Most of these conclusions from the maximum parsimony trees on the cladistic relationships of the primates are also apparent from simply inspecting the amino acid and minimum mutation distances (AAD and MMD values in Tables 3–17), which are not biased as are the maximum parsimony distances by a predetermined phylogeny. For example in the man-chimpanzee, chimpanzee-gorilla, and man-gorilla comparisons, distances range (AAD values in Table 17) from 0.27 to 0.65 as compared to distances ranging from 2.17 to 2.84 in the comparisons of orangutan and gibbon.

DNA DISTANCE AMONG PRIMATE LINEAGES

DNA distance data have largely been gained by Dr. B. H. Hoyer and his colleagues. The earlier experiments focused on the part of the DNA in primate genomes which consists of repeated polynucleotide sequences (Hoyer et al. 1964; 1965; Hoyer, Roberts 1967; Martin, Hoyer 1967). The degree of complementarity between DNA of homologous and of heterologous species due to the sharing of common, repeated sequences was measured in comparisons analogous to the immunological analysis of protein antigenic distances. The results obtained for man and rhesus monkey agree with protein data in that they divide the Catarrhini into hominoids and cercopithecoids. Tests which analyze that part of the DNA molecule that consists of repeated sequences of the same polynucleotides show that gibbon DNA is not quite as similar to human DNA as is chimpanzee DNA, but is more similar than rhesus and baboon repeated DNAs. Rhesus DNA is more similar to that of baboon than to that of man, chimpanzee, or gibbon. The DNA of each catarrhine group is more similar to that of the others than to the DNA of New World monkeys (capuchin and night monkey repeated DNAs). Likewise the DNA of catarrhines is more similar to platyrrhine DNA than to repeated DNAs from animals outside the Anthropoidea. The order of divergence after New World monkeys is: *Tarsius*, lorisoids (galago, slow loris, and potto), lemur, tree shrew, mouse, hedgehog and chicken.

More recently DNA reassociation experiments have focused on the nonrepeating polynucleotide sequences in primate genomes (Kohne et al. 1972; Hoyer et al. 1972). This DNA fraction is the best suited for phylogenetic comparisons because it yields measures of species divergence, in which the ancestral separation of a sequence in one species from its homolog in another is more likely to have coincided with the ancestral separation of the two species, i.e. the most recent common ancestor of the two species probably had only one form of sequence for unique parts of the DNA molecule but may have had several forms of the repeated part and have transmitted different ones (or different proportions) to different descendants. The experiments of Kohne et al. (1972) were carried out (by using homologous DNA) on man and the green monkey *Cercopithecus aethiops*; those of Hoyer et al. (1972) were on man and the orangutan. The results from the two studies are combined and presented as distance scores in Table 18. These scores provide further evidence that the chimpanzee and gorilla are cladistically closer to man than to the orangutan and other primates. The scores also suggest that gorilla DNA may have diverged slightly more than chimpanzee or human

Table 18. Distances of nonrepeated DNA sequences within primates from the data of Kohne et al. (1972) and Hoyer et al. (1972)

	Man	Orangutan	*Cercopithecus*
Man	0	4.9	9.6
Chimpanzee	1.8*	4.7	9.6
Gorilla	2.3	5.8	
Orangutan	4.9	0	
Gibbon	4.9*	6.2	9.6
Cercopithecus	9.5*	11.0	0
Macaque			3.5
Capuchin Monkey	15.8		16.5
Galago	42.0		42.0

* Average of data from Kohne et al. (1972) and weighted data from Hoyer et al. (1972).

In putting together these data first the distances from the standpoint of orangutan were weighted to those from standpoint of man in Hoyer et al. (1972) and then the two scales were weighted to match the distances from the standpoints of *Cercopithecus* and man in Kohne et al. (1972).

DNA from the ancestral state because the orangutan does not diverge as much from the chimpanzee or from man as it does from the gorilla. Although the present molecular evidence leaves little doubt that the African apes and man constitute a monophyletic branch within the Hominoidea, the question as to whether the gorilla is cladistically closer to the chimpanzee or to man still remains; but this one item of information tends to place the chimpanzee cladistically closer to man even than to the gorilla. A more decisive answer to this question will be forthcoming when DNA comparisons of the chimpanzee and gorilla are complete and when more protein chains are sequenced in the gorilla as well as in the chimpanzee and man.

THE MOLECULAR EVIDENCE COMPARED TO MORPHOLOGICALLY BASED VIEWS ON PRIMATE RELATIONSHIPS

To evaluate the protein and DNA distances and see what they should mean for taxonomy, one can take a traditional classification of the extant primates, for instance that recently used by one of us (Table 19), and look for deviations from it in the molecular record. One can then determine if there are consistent patterns in the discrepancies and, if so, what characterizes the traditional taxonomy in respect to just those features of it

Table 19. Comparison of a traditional classification of some primate genera (Lasker 1973) with their molecular relationships

Traditional classification						Molecular relationships					
Sub-order	Infra-order	Super-family	Family	Sub-family	Genus	Sub-family	Family	Super-family	Infra-order	Sub-order	Grade
Prosimii	Tupaiiformes				*Tupaia*				Tupaiiformes		(unnamed)
					Urogale						
	Lemuriformes				*Lemur*				Lemuriformes		Strepsirhini
	Lorisiformes			Lorisinae	*Loris*	Lorisinae			Lorisiformes		
					Nycticebus						
					Arctocebus	(unnamed)					
					Perodicticus						
				Galaginae	*Galago*	Galaginae					
	Tarsiiformes								Tarsiiformes		Haplorhini
Anthropoidea	Platyrrhini		Callithricidae		*Saguinus*				Platyrrhini	Anthropoidea	
			Cebidae		*Aotus*						
					Callicebus						
					Cacajao						
					Chiropotes						
					Alouatta						
					Ateles	Atelinae					
					Lagothrix						
					Cebus						
					Saimiri						

Catarrhini	Cercopithecoidea		Cercopithecinae	*Cercopithecus*	Cercopithecinae		Cercopithecoidea	Catarrhini
				Cercocebus				
				Theropithecus				
				Macaca				
				Papio				
				Erythrocebus				
			Colobinae	*Colobus*	Colobinae			
				Presbytis				
				Nasalis				
				Pygathrix				
	Hominoidea	Hylobatidae		*Hylobates*	Hylobatinae	Hylobatidae	Hominoidea	
				Symphalangus				
		Pongidae		*Pongo*		Pongidae		
				Gorilla	Homininae	Hominidae		
				Pan				
		Hominidae		*Homo*				

which separate taxa known to be similar in molecular configurations or combine taxa known to differ in molecular respects.

In traditional taxonomy, the primates are usually divided into two suborders, Prosimii and Anthropoidea. The molecular data that yield suitable distances (serum proteins, fibrinopeptides A and B, the various globins, and DNA) agree with this subdivision placing all the tested species of Anthropoidea closer to one another than to any species outside the Anthropoidea.

The traditional division of the Prosimii into four infraorders is not well sustained in the molecular data, however. The four "infraorders" are well represented in serum protein tests, and amino acid sequences of alpha globin chains from three of them are available. Virtually all comparisons, Tarsiiformes-Lorisiformes, Tarsiiformes-Lemuriformes, Tarsiiformes-Tupaiiformes (in respect to serum proteins), and Lorisiformes-Lemuriformes, Lorisiformes-Tupaiiformes, and Lemuriformes-Tupaiiformes (in respect to both serum proteins and alpha globin) have distances of about the same or greater magnitude than the distances of these taxa from various Anthropoidea. The antigenic distances between Lorisiformes and Lemuriformes are somewhat smaller than the others, however, and therefore justify use of the term Strepsirhini as a grade which groups them together (Hill 1953). This molecular evidence suggests that from the perspective of the Anthropoidea, these four "infraorders" can be considered as equivalent to suborders. The serum proteins place them all closer to each other and to the Anthropoidea than to nonprimate animals so there is no challenge to their status as primates. The Tupaioidea, however, are borderline primates on the basis of this as well as morphology — about which debate continues (see, for example, Van Valen 1965). The elephant shrews (*Elephantulus* and *Nasalio*) show no special affinity to the primates in serum proteins. Except for the elongated proboscislike snout, they resemble tree shrews in general morphology (Plate 1,2) but elephant shrews cannot be allocated to the same monophyletic order.

The alpha globin amino acid sequences do not decisively identify Tupaiiformes as primates. Although the maximum parsimony tree of alpha sequences (Goodman et al., 1974) places Lemuriformes in the primates, this is not obvious from simply inspecting the AAD and MMD values. The hemoglobin comparisons, however, make the tested Lorisiformes appear more similar to Anthropoidea than to any other animals. The tarsier proteins have been studied only by immunological methods. According to these, tarsier is closer to the Anthropoidea than to any other "Prosimii" or nonprimate with which it has been compared. Its repeated DNA also diverges less from human DNA than does the DNA of lorisoids, lemur, and tree shrew.

The suborder "Prosimii" is thus established on the basis of its general level of organization. Its infraorders are molecularly heterogeneous, however; this suggests that level of organization does not lead to natural taxa which have retained common, genetically determined forms of proteins.

Tarsius is rather peculiar in its habits and habitus. It has been placed in the grade Haplorhini by Hill (1953) as well as some others. The term "grade" is used purely as a taxonomic category and does not mean "level." In fact it is precisely its level of organization and the presumed antiquity of its fossil lineage that have justified the inclusion of the Tarsiiformes in the suborder "Prosimii," but the details of anatomy and the molecular evidence, place it in the Haplorhini grade.

Various Platyrrhini (Ceboidea) species that have been studied are more similar to each other than to any other taxa in fibrinopeptides and serum proteins. The long separation of a continental group, as reflected in the traditional classification, is confirmed by the molecular evidence despite considerable adaptive radiation of the New World monkeys.

All the Catarrhini species studied are more closely related to each other than to Platyrrhini with respect to their serum proteins (including prealbumin, albumin, $alpha_2$ macroglobulin, thyroglobulin, transferrin, ceruloplasmin, and gamma globulin; Goodman, Moore 1971), their fibrinopeptides A and B, and DNA. That the beta globins do not distinguish them well from Platyrrhini is therefore of little moment in respect to classification. Traditional taxonomy groups the Catarrhini together because of common dental formula and geographic confinement to the Old World. The wide adaptive radiation into different ecological niches is not considered to bar them from the same infraorder.

The Catarrhini are traditionally divided into two superfamilies, Cercopithecoidea and Hominoidea, on the basis of a marked difference in molar tooth patterns as well as locomotor and other differences. They are, in addition, distinct with respect to serum proteins (prealbumin, $alpha_2$ macroglobin, and gamma globulin tests do not show this unequivocally, but it is clear from other purified proteins and from general serum and plasma immunological tests; Goodman and Moore 1971). The Hominoidea are similar to each other in amino acid sequences of hemoglobins, myoglobin, fibrinopeptides, carbonic anhydrase, and cytochrome C and also in DNA. The Cercopithecoidea do not adhere quite so well to each other despite very similar dental and locomotor adaptations. Every series of tests with antiserum to cercopithecine or colobine plasma, sera, or albumin indicates that the two subfamilies,

Cercopithecinae and Colobinae — so similar in the anatomy of their limbs, face, and teeth, but markedly different in their digestive systems — are distinctly separate groups; no amino acid sequence data bear on the point.

The Hominoidea are frequently divided into three families: Hylobatidae, Pongidae, and Hominidae. Locomotor differences support this division as do sexual dimorphism (little in man and gibbon) and other adaptive traits, such as nest-building by pongids and language and culture in man. The immunological and sequence data as well as DNA data clearly support the separate position within the Hominoidea of the Hylobatidae. Except for those involving a comparison of a few antisera to purified proteins (prealbumin and cerulopasmin), immunological tests distinguish the Hylobatidae from Pongidae and *Homo sapiens*. In beta hemoglobin, myoglobin, and fibrinopeptide amino acid sequences and in DNA reassociation the same classification is supported.

On the other hand, the Pongidae, as traditionally constituted, do not appear as a natural group in molecular perspective. They have much in common (brachiation, knuckle-walking, laryngeal sacs, etc.), but the orangutan is distinct from the chimpanzee and the gorilla and, in turn, the chimpanzee and the gorilla are more similar to man in virtually all types of immunological tests than either is to the orangutan. In carbonic anhydrase *Pan* and *Homo* differ from each other in one amino acid residue, but they differ from *Pongo* by three and four respectively. In fibrinopeptides A and B *Homo*, *Pan*, and *Gorilla* do not differ in any amino acid residues, but *Pongo* differs from them in two. Man and the chimpanzee do not differ in either alpha or beta hemoglobin, and the gorilla differs from them in only one amino acid residue in each chain. Man and the chimpanzee differ in only one amino acid residue of myoglobin and in none in cytochrome C. Chimpanzee and gorilla DNA differ more from orangutan DNA than from human DNA. Thus the African apes and man constitute a natural group in molecular perspective despite the enormous differences in behavioral patterns and the associated anatomical differences in brains, jaws, limbs, hair, and other adaptive structures. Because of the very close genetic and cladistic relationship of the African apes to man, demonstrated by the molecular data, one of us (Goodman 1962, 1963a, 1963b) has suggested that the African apes be removed from the Pongidae and placed in the Hominidae, indeed even in the Homininae (Goodman, Moore 1971).

The chief differences, then, between a molecular and a traditional taxonomy are in the placement of those taxa, in which the traditional classification emphasizes highly adaptive behavioral and anatomical specializations. Le Gros Clark (1955) stresses the use of adaptive characters in the assessment of phylogenetic relations because they would be stable, in a given environment, whereas a character with no apparent selective advantage is subject to rapid change. On the other hand, as new adaptive niches open, evolutionary "distance" is covered rapidly in just such traits as the locomotor adaptations; the basic molecular pattern, much as (among primates) the basic dental pattern, however, behaves conservatively and continues to show genetic relationships. How one constructs his taxonomy will depend on the purpose for which it is to be used. Because one of the usual uses is communication among biologists about given sets of animals, only very persuasive arguments should lead to a change in well-known formal taxonomic designations with well-established meanings. As Simpson (1963) has shown, if one accepts the traditional classification but also accepts the molecular evidence as re-

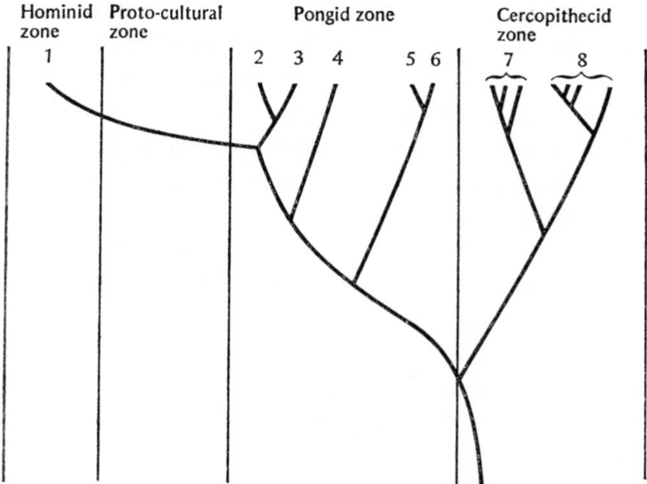

Figure 3. Adaptive and molecular relationships between the Old World monkeys, apes, and man. The distance between the numbers shows the relative closeness to each other of living species in respect to structural and functional adaptation. The depths of the branches show the relative antiquity of common origins as inferred from similarities in response to rabbit anticatarrhine antibodies of blood serum from the various species. Compared with the apes (Pongidae) the designation of the Old World monkeys as a separate family (Cercopithecidae) is justified by molecular differences. The designation of the Hominidae as a separate family is, however, justified only by the wide adaptive differences and lack of any surviving species with an intermediate proto-cultural adaptation. 1, man; 2, chimpanzee; 3, gorilla; 4, orangutan; 5, siamang; 6, gibbon; 7, Colobinae; 8, Cercopithecinae. From *Physical anthropology* by Gabriel Ward Lasker. Copyright © 1973 by Holt, Rinehart and Winston, Inc. Reprinted by permission of Holt, Rinehart and Winston, Inc.

presenting the relative depths of actual branchings into different adaptive zones, the primate dendrogram will have some long horizontal branches. Figure 3 shows this for the Catarrhini. The depths of the branchings represent the extent of relative immunological differences. Other molecular evidence would place the chimpanzee and its branch further to the left, and some would even suggest a short common trunk with man. The distances between the terminal twigs represent in a crude one-dimensional way the extent of anatomical and behavioral differences.

Unfortunately there is no satisfactory method for scoring the extent of morphological differences with anything like the precision that can now be applied to the molecular dimensions. For essentially all the kinds of distinctions that can be made on traits of fossil and recent bones, some adaptive significance can be inferred. There is also, no doubt, some degree of adaptive significance in the molecular differences (the notions of non-Darwinian evolution and a constant molecular clock to the contrary notwithstanding). The mere fact that we do not see any adaptive significance in some biological differences does not mean that nature is blind to it.

How one classifies the primates will vary depending on what weight is given to different characters. The weights chosen will depend on what one wishes to accomplish with the taxonomy, Those who are concerned only with relative antiquity of common origins should weight the molecular evidence very heavily because it comes close to measuring overall genetic similarities. Others, more concerned with ecological considerations, might deliberately emphasize adaptive morphological traits because they are the traceable products of known kinds of natural selection. The nature of the environmental impact through natural selection can best be studied if one examines distances between the same groups of animals with respect to different kinds of traits and compares the different classifications that would be inferred. Such a comparison may itself lead to interesting insight into the mode of radiation of the primates.

REFERENCES

BOYER, S. H., G. F. FULLER, S. E. LESLIE, L. J. DONALDSON, G. R. VRABLIK, E. W. SCHAEFER, JR., T. F. THURMON

1971 Primate hemoglobins: some sequences and some proposals concerning the character of evolution and mutation. *Biochemical Genetics* 5:405–448.

BOYER, S. H., A. N. NOYES, C. F. TIMMONS, R. A. YOUNG

1972 Primate hemoglobins: polymorphisms and evolutionary patterns. *Journal of Human Evolution* 1:515–543.

BUETTNER-JANUSCH, J., V. BUETTNER-JANUSCH, G. A. MASON

1969 Amino acid compositions and amino-terminal end groups of alpha and beta chains from polymorphic hemoglobins of *Pongo pygmaeus*. *Archives of Biochemical Biophysics* 133:164–170.

CRICK, F. H. C.

1966 The genetic code. *Cold Spring Harbor Symposia on Quantitative Biology, Proceedings* 31:1.

DAYHOFF, M. O.

1972 *Atlas of protein sequence and structure*, volume five. Silver Spring, Maryland: National Biomedical Research Foundation.

DE JONG, W. W. W.

1971 Chimpanzee foetal haemoglobin: structure and heterogeneity of the gamma chain. *Biochemica et Biophysica Acta* 251:217–226.

FITCH, W. M., E. MARGOLIASH

1967 Construction of phylogenetic trees. *Science* 155:279–284.

GOODMAN, M.

1962 Immunochemistry of the primates and primate evolution. *Annals of the New York Academy of Science* 102:219–234.

1963a "Man's place in the phylogeny of the primates as reflected in serum proteins," in *Classification and human evolution*. Edited by S. L. Washburn, 204–234. Chicago: Aldine.

1963b Serological analysis of the systematics of recent hominoids. *Human Biology* 35:377–436.

1973 "The chronicle of primate phylogeny contained in proteins." Symposium of the Zoological Society of London 33.

GOODMAN, M., G. W. MOORE

1971 Immunodiffusion systematics of the primates. I. The Catarrhini. *Systematic Zoology* 20:19–62.

GOODMAN, M., G. W. MOORE, J. BARNABAS, G. MATSUDA

1974 The phylogeny of human globin genes investigated by the maximum parsimony method. *Journal of Molecular Evolution* 3:1–48.

GOODMAN, M., W. FARRIS, JR., G. W. MOORE, W. PRYCHODKO, E. POULIK, M. W. SORENSON

i.p. "Immunodiffusion systematics of the primates. II. Findings on *Tarsius*, Lorisidae and Tupaiidae," in *Prosimian biology*. Edited by R. D. Martin, G. A. Doyle, and A. C. Walker. London: Duckworth.

HAN, K., D. TETAERT, Y. MOSCHETTO, M. DAUTREVAUX, C. KOPEYAN

1972 The covalent structure of sheep heart myoglobin. *European Journal of Biochemistry* 27:585–592.

HILL, R. L.

1968 "Unpublished results," in *Handbook of biochemistry*. Edited by H. A. Sober, C-174–C-176. Chicago: The Chemical Rubber Company.

HILL, W. C. OSMAN

1953 *Primates: comparative anatomy and taxonomy*, volume one: *Strepsirhini*. Edinburgh: University Press.

HOYER, B. H., B. J. MC CARTHY, E. T. BOLTON

1964 A molecular approach in the systematics of higher organisms. *Science* 144:959–967.

HOYER, B. H., E. T. BOLTON, B. J. MC CARTHY, R. B. ROBERTS
1965 "The evolution of polynucleotides," in *Evolving genes and proteins.* Edited by V. Bryson, H. J. Vogel, 581–590. New York: Academic Press.

HOYER, B. H., R. B. ROBERTS
1967 "Studies of nucleic acid interactions using DNA-agar," in *Molecular genetics*, part two. Edited by H. Taylor, 425–479. New York: Academic Press.

HOYER, B. H., N. W. VAN DE VELDE, M. GOODMAN, R. B. ROBERTS
1972 Examination of hominid evolution by DNA sequence homology. *Journal of Human Evolution* 1:645–649.

KOHNE, D. E., J. A. CHISCON, B. H. HOYER
1972 Evolution of primate DNA sequences. *Journal of Human Evolution.* 1:627–644.

LASKER, G. W.
1973 *Physical anthropology*. New York: Holt, Rinehart and Winston.

LE GROS CLARK, W. E.
1955 *The fossil evidence for human evolution.* Chicago: University of Chicago Press.

MARTIN, M. A., B. H. HOYER
1967 Adenine plus thymine and guanine plus cytosine enriched fractions of animal DNA's as indicators of polynucleotide homologies. *Journal of Molecular Biology* 27:113–129.

MOORE, G. W., M. GOODMAN
1968 A set theoretical approach to immunotaxonomy: analysis of species comparisons in modified Ouchterlony plates. *Bulletin of Mathematical Biophysics* 30:279–289.

MOORE, G. W., J. BARNABAS, M. GOODMAN
1973 A method for constructing maximum parsimony ancestral amino acid sequences on a given network. *Journal of Theoretical Biology* 38:459–485.

ROMERO HERRERA, A. E., H. LEHMANN
1971a Primary structure of human myoglobin. *Nature*, *New Biology* 232: 149–152.
1971b The myoglobin of primates. I. *Hylobates agilis* (gibbon). *Biochemica et Biophysica. Acta* 251:482–487.
1972a The myoglobin of primates. II. *Pan troglodytes* (chimpanzee). *Biochemica et Biophysica Acta* 278:62–67.
1972b The myoglobin of primates. III. Cercopithecidae (Old World monkeys): *Papio anubis* (olive baboon) and *Macaca fascicularis* (=irus, crab-eating monkey). *Biochemica et Biophysica Acta* 278:465–481.

SARICH, V. M.
1970 "Primate systematics with special reference to Old World monkeys: a protein perspective," in *Old World monkeys: evolution, systematics, and behavior*. Edited by J. R. Napier, P. H. Napier, 175–226. London: Academic Press.

SIMPSON, G. G.
1963 "The meaning of taxonomic statements," in *Classification and human evolution.* Edited by S. L. Washburn, 1–31. Chicago: Aldine.

TASHIAN, R. E., R. J. TANIS, R. E. FERRELL, S. K. STROUP, M. GOODMAN
1972 Differential rates of evolution in the carbonic anhydrase isozymes of catarrhine primates. *Journal of Human Evolution* 1:545–552.

VAN VALEN, LEIGH
1965 Treeshrews, primates, and fossils. *Evolution* 19:137–151.

WOODING, G. L., R. F. DOOLITTLE
1972 Primate fibrinopeptides: evolutionary significance. *Journal of Human Evolution* 1:553–563.

The Study of Primate Chromosomes

B. CHIARELLI

THE IMPORTANCE OF THE CHROMOSOMES IN TAXONOMIC AND PHYLOGENETIC STUDIES

Recently acquired knowledge on number and morphology of the chromosomes in many animal groups has furnished important data for reconstructing their evolution and has provided us with one more criterion for taxonomic organization (Chiarelli and Capanna 1973).

Knowledge of the chromosomes is important to the study of phyletic evolution and taxonomy because these structures are the direct carriers of genetic information. For each species of Eukaryota the structural affinity between homologous chromosomes is consistently controlled by their pairing at meiosis in each individual. Incomplete chromosome pairing at meiosis suggests the presence of structural changes in the organization of the genetic information that is linearly distributed along the chromosomes. Unlimited structural change is incompatible with the functional organization of the genetic information; it results in the inability of homologous chromosomes to pair at meiosis and consequently the failing of the meiotic process. As a consequence the formation of gametes will not be accomplished.

Homologous chromosome pairing at meiosis acts as a filter through which only a functionally patterned genetic system can pass. Furthermore, in native populations meiosis represents a barrier which prevents exchange between diverging genetic systems. It therefore has to be considered as a basic step in diversifying populations for separation into new species.

The constancy of features of the karyotype in each species is therefore

For Plates, see pp. vi–vii, between pp. 560–561

a consequence of the meiotic filter. On the other hand, the existing differences between karyotypes of different species are due to the variations in the chromosomes of the germinal cell line which could filter through the meiotic sieve and establish themselves if selectively advantageous.

By studying and hypothesizing the possible steps by which the chromosomes of two related species differentiated, one can construct a phyletic line connecting different species and can establish their taxonomic affinities.

However, before one can establish chromosome identity between individuals of different species, it is important to be sure of their homologous genetic content. The only control we can have at the moment is the observation of the behavior of chromosomes during meiosis (especially diakinesis) in individuals derived from crossbreeding two related species (Plate 1). In cytotaxonomic research, therefore, data from hybrids are of considerable importance.

HOW CHROMOSOMES MAY CHANGE IN NUMBER AND MORPHOLOGY

Several mechanisms are capable of altering the karyotype of individuals or groups of individuals to the point of isolating them reproductively from other representatives of their species. In regard to numerical variation, polyploidy has certainly played a very important role in the evolution of many vegetal species and some lower animals. In mammals, this mechanism may be disregarded because of the complication interposed by well-differentiated sex chromosomes. Single chromosomes may be increased in number by meiotic or mitotic nondisjunction. Another theoretical means of increasing the number of chromosomes is the asynchronous reduplication of some of them in a cell. If this duplication occurred during the first mitotic division of the germinal line it could be important in the evolution of a species. Another mechanism which can increase the number of chromosomes, without any variation in the genetic material, is the transverse misdivision of the centromeres. In this case the centromere divides transversely rather than longitudinally during mitosis, so that the chromosome divides into two chromosomes each with a functional centromere.

The chromosomes can also be reduced in number. Centric fusion can cause reduction in the number of chromosomes without grave damage to the genome. In this mechanism two chromosomes having the centromere in the terminal position (acrocentric) unite forming a new metacentric

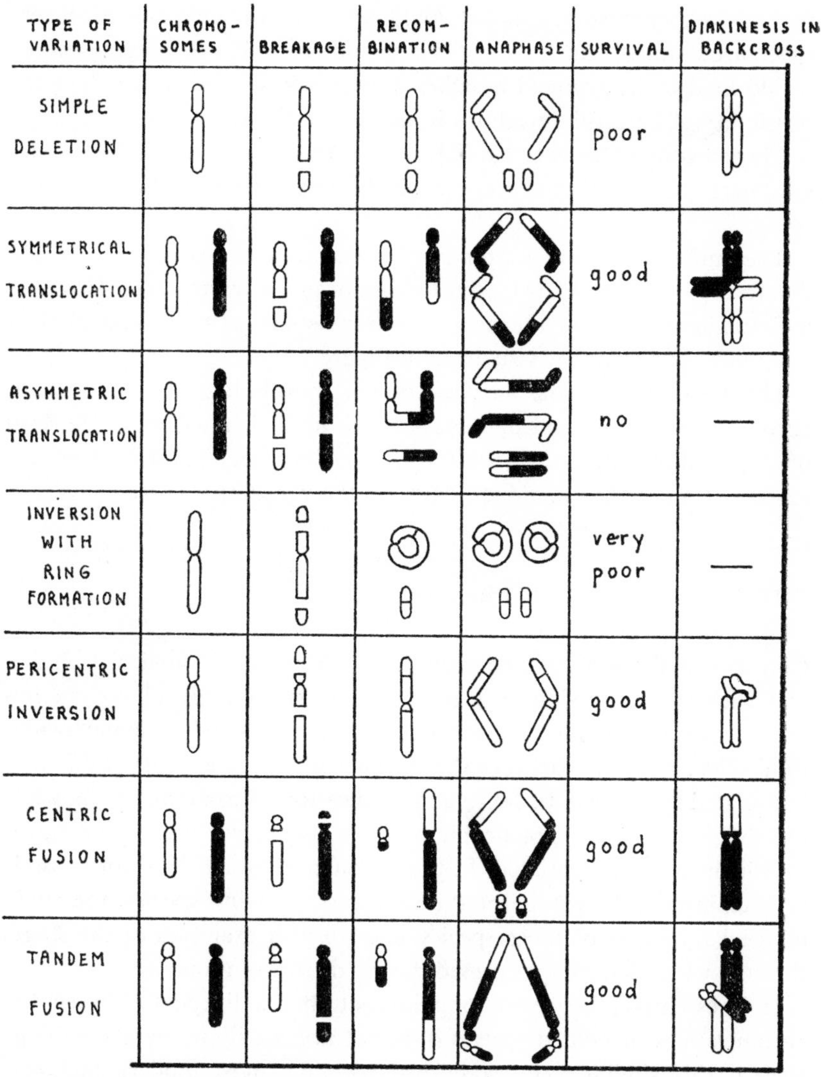

TYPE OF VARIATION	CHROMOSOMES	BREAKAGE	RECOMBINATION	ANAPHASE	SURVIVAL	DIAKINESIS IN BACKCROSS
SIMPLE DELETION					poor	
SYMMETRICAL TRANSLOCATION					good	
ASYMMETRIC TRANSLOCATION					no	—
INVERSION WITH RING FORMATION					very poor	—
PERICENTRIC INVERSION					good	
CENTRIC FUSION					good	
TANDEM FUSION					good	

Figure 1. Graphic representation of possible mechanisms of chromosomal variations in number (centric and tandem fusion) and morphology

chromosome. This phenomenon is thus the opposite of "misdivision" of the centromere. The reduction of the number of chromosomes by means of centric fusion has been demonstrated in the most diverse organisms. The number of chromosomes undoubtedly has some evolutionary importance, and yet it is difficult to determine the reason. Probably it corresponds to particular requisites of ecological nature. In fact it is possible that a low chromosome number could represent an advantage for a very specialized animal. Such a condition would create blocks of genes which would tend to be grouped together during meiosis and thus reduce the possibility of harmful deviations in the descendants.

Chromosomes may vary not only in number but also in their morphology. There are a number of ways in which these variations may come into being.

The entire process of chromosomal mutation is now under revision due to the increased knowledge of chromosome ultrastructure. However a simplified scheme of the possible chromosomal changes and of their possibility of survival is visualized in Figure 1.

The possibility of the survival of the morphological mutations of chromosomes is lessened by factors which limit them either at the level of cell multiplication (e.g. dicentric chromosomes) or at that of the reproduction of the individuals carrying the variation.

THE KARYOTYPE OF PRIMATES

Chromosomal variations, concomitant with special ecological isolation and with the succession of generations, have certainly played an important role in the differentiation of primate species and in human evolution. The similarities between the chromosome complements of different but related species can be taken as an indication of common origin, while the differences make practicable a rough reconstruction of the stages by which they differentiated. In this manner, although it is not possible to examine the karyotype of the ancestors of living species, the study of the karyotypes of those species may furnish examples of the stages through which karyotypes passed during their evolution.

It is essential, however, to point out that a likeness between the chromosomes of related species does not necessarily imply a homology even if this similarity is established with the most modern and new techniques of chromosome banding. Only the study of the meiotic chromosomes of interspecific hybrids will permit the establishment of possible homologies between apparently similar chromosome complements.

Even with this limitation, data collected on primate chromosomes can well be used for taxonomic and phylogenetic purposes and serve as a basis for further studies with the new techniques of chromosome banding.

THE CHROMOSOMES OF PROSIMIANS

The phylogeny of the Prosimiae, a group characterized by heterogeneity, remote evolutionary history, and geographic isolation, seems to be particularly suitable for a karyological approach. Prosimian phylogenetic organization has been the object of continuous discussion, notably with respect to classificatory order at a suprafamilial level.

A synthesis of available information for the chromosomes of the species that have been studied to date is presented in Table 1. Data on the content of the DNA per nucleus are reported in Table 3. From Table 1 it can easily be seen:

1. The absence of karyological information for the genera: *Dendrogale*, *Ptilocercus*.
2. The incompleteness of data for other genera, for which only preliminary information is available (*Phaner*, *Daubentonia*.)
3. The variability in the number of chromosomes in all the genera that have been more extensively studied (*Galago* and *Lemur*).

Information on the diploid number of somatic chromosomes overlooks one of the most common chromosome mutations, namely, centric fusion. This difficulty is partially overcome by using Matthey's fundamental number, which considers solely the number of arms. Use of the fundamental number is based on the assumption that centric fusion (or misdivision of the centromere) is one of the more successful mutations to pass through the sieve of meiosis. This mutation would not interfere with the organization of the genetic information on the chromosomes. The only resulting change would be the reduction or increase in the random distribution of the genetic information in the offspring.

The reduction or increase of chromosome units certainly presents an adaptative advantage to an organism, reducing or increasing the potential variability in a population. Moreover, a relation between chromosome morphology and the chiasma frequencies must exist although we do not have enough information to define the exact relationship.

These types of data are shown in the fourth column of Table 2.

The karyological data elaborated in this way lend themselves more safely to analysis and yield more reliable results on taxonomic grounds.

Matthey's fundamental number is 70 to 84 in Tupaiidae; 87 to 102 in Lorisidae; 61 to 94 in Galagidae; 36 to 70 in Lemuridae; 66 to 78 in Indriidae, 94 in Tarsiidae and 54 in Daubentoniidae.

No problem exists with regard to the taxonomic, and hence phylo-

Table 1. Numerical data and morphological information on the chromosomes of Prosimiae

Taxa*	2*n*	S–M	A	X	Y
1. Tupaiidae					
1.1. *Tupaia glis*	60–62	14–12	44–48	M–S	A
1.2. *T. montana*	52–68			M	A
1.5. *T. minor*	66				
3.1. *Urogale everetti*	44				
2. Lorisidae					
1.1. *Loris tardigradus*	62	34–38	26–22	S	S–A
2.1. *Nycticebus coucang*	50–52	48		S	S
2.2. *N. pygmaeus*	50				
3.1. *Arctocebus calabarensis*	52	50		S	
4.1. *Perodicticus potto*	62	24	36	S	A
3. Galagidae					
1.1. *Galago senegalensis*	36–38	22–24–30	14–12–6	S	S–A
1.2. *G. crassicaudatus*	62	6–30	54–30	S	A–S
1.3. *G. alleni*	40				
1.4. *G. demidovii*	58				
4. Lemuridae					
1.1. *Microcebus murinus*	66		64	A	A
2.1. *Cheirogaleus major*	66		64	A	A
2.2. *C. medius*	66		64	S–M	?
3.1. *Phaner furcifer*	48				
4.1. *Hapalemur griseus*	54–58	10–6	42–50	A	A
4.2. *H. simus*	60	4	54	M	A
5.1. *Lemur catta*	56	10–14	44–50	S–A	A
5.2. *L. variegatus*	46	18	26	S	A
5.3. *L. macaco*	44	20	22	A	A
5.4. *L. fulvus*	48–52–58–60	16–4	30–52–54		
5.5. *L. mongoz*	58–60	4	52–54	A	A
6.1. *Lepilemur mustelinus*	34–38	2–6	26–32	M	A
5. Indriidae					
1.1. *Propithecus diadema*	42	32	8	M	A
1.2. *P. verreauxi*	48	30	16	M	A
2.1. *Avahi laniger*	64	2	60	M	A
3.1. *Indri indri*	40	32	8	M	A
6. Daubentoniidae					
1.6 *Daubentonia madagascariensis*	30				
7. Tarsiidae					
1.2. *Tarsius syrichta*	80				
1.3. *T. bancanus*	80	14	66		

* The code numbers for species are those used in Chiarelli (1972b).

Table 2. Information on the fundamental number (N.F.) in Prosimiae chromosomes*

Genera	Known/studied	2n	N.F.	
Tupaia	11/6	52–60–62–66–68	70–72–74–76	70
Dendrogale	2/0			↓
Urogale	1/1	44	84–80	↓
Ptilocercus	1/0			84
Loris	1/1	62	98–101	87
Nycticebus	2/2	50	100	↓
Arctocebus	1/1	52	102	↓
Perodicticus	1/1	62	87	102
Galago	6/4	36–62	61–64–69–75–94	61–94
Microcebus	2/1	66	68	36
Cheirogaleus	2/2	66	68	↓
Phaner	1/1	48	62	↓
Hapalemur	2/2	54–60	64	↓
Lemur	6/6	44–46–48–52–56–58–60	62–64–66–70	↓
Lepilemur	1/1	22–38	36–42	70
Propithecus	2/2	42–48	74–78	66
Avahi	1/1	64	66	↓
Indri	1/1	40	72	78
Daubentonia	1/1	30	54	54
Tarsius	3/2	80	94	94

* In calculating N.F. metacentrics and submetacentrics are counted as 2 and acrocentrics and subacrocentrics are counted as 1.

genetic, separation between Tupaiidae in respect to Daubentoniidae, Tarsiidae and Indriidae among themselves and in respect to the other Prosimiae superfamilies. However, difficulties do arise for the Lorisidae and Lemuridae families, concerning which some controversial opinions exist. The fundamental number available for their chromosomes can provide some clear support for their separation. Lorisidae and Lemuridae can, in fact, be sharply distinguished from each other because their fundamental numbers are different and can be in no way superimposed (87 to 102, 62 to 70, respectively).

The taxonomic position of the Galagidae whose fundamental number represents in some way a bridge between the Lemuridae and Lorisidae — it varies between 61 and 94 — is of particular interest. The large, striking variation in the diploid chromosome in the *Galago* species (*G. senegalensis* [2n=36] and *G. crassicaudatus* [2n=62]) was an attractive basis for speculation on the possibility of a polyploid mechanism in the origin of this variation.

However, the recent findings of (1) chromosomal polymorphism in

Table 3. Nuclear DNA content and area of primate lymphocytes (courtesy M. G. Manfredi-Romanini 1972)

Species	DNA ± S.D. (arbitrary units)	DNA (pg)
Lemur catta	12.18 ± 0.11	5.91
Lemur fulvus	12.80 ± 0.16	6.21
Lemur macaco	12.68 ± 0.16	6.15
Lemur mongoz	12.07 ± 0.10	5.85
Galago senegalensis	13.97 ± 0.09	6.78
Tarsius syrichta	18.95 ± 0.77	9.19
Cebuella pygmaea	12.31 ± 0.12	5.97
Cebus albifrons	14.07 ± 0.13	6.83
Cebus apella	13.01 ± 4.19	6.34
Cebus capucinus	13.45 ± 4.27	6.52
Cebus nigrovittatus	12.02 ± 0.19	5.83
Saimiri sciureus	11.66 ± 0.13	5.65
Alouatta caraya	13.59 ± 3.05	6.59
Alouatta palliata	12.82 ± 0.70	6.22
Ateles belzebuth	12.82 ± 0.15	6.22
Ateles geoffroyi	11.48 ± 0.12	5.57
Ateles paniscus	12.26 ± 0.20	5.95
Cercopithecus aethiops	10.42 ± 0.35	5.05
Cercopithecus cephus	12.49 ± 0.57	6.06
Cercopithecus patas	12.43 ± 0.29	6.03
Cercocebus galeritus	16.72 ± 0.29	8.11
Cercocebus torquatus	17.31 ± 0.29	8.40
Macaca mulatta	11.11 ± 0.26	5.39
Macaca silenus	11.24 ± 0.18	5.45
Papio hamadryas	12.48 ± 0.48	6.05
Colobus satanas	12.75 ± 0.13	6.18
Nasalis larvatus	15.27 ± 0.19	7.41
Pongo pygmaeus	14.50 ± 8.40	7.03
Pan troglodytes	13.60 ± 4.60	6.60
Gorilla gorilla	12.62 ± 7.30	6.12
Hylobates agilis	9.80 ± 0.12	4.75
Hylobates lar	10.35 ± 0.16	5.02
Symphalangus syndactylus	10.54.± 0.22	5.11
Homo sapiens	12.36 ± 0.11	6.00

S.D. = standard deviation

the chromosome number of *G. senegalensis* due to centric fusion (Ying and Butler 1971); (2) a diploid chromosomal number of 58 in *G. demidovii* and of 40 in *G. alleni* (De Boer 1972a, b, 1973); and (3) identical DNA content in the two *Galago* species (7.54±0.17 in *G. senegalensis* and 7.26±0.09 in *G. crassicaudatus* in a.u.) by Manfredi-Romanini et al. (1972) have definitively negated this possibility. These data support a stricter taxonomic relation of the Galagidae to the Lorisidae and open the field to extensive speculation on the adaptive advantages for such a chromosomal polymorphism in the Galagidae.

The fact that *Lemur* (see Table 2) also exhibits extensive polymorphism due to centric fusion and resulting in karyological subspecies (Rumpler and Albignac 1969) enormously increases our interest in the adaptive advantage of these variations and this peculiar mechanism of speciation.

THE CHROMOSOMES OF THE NEW WORLD MONKEYS

The diploid number of chromosomes of the platyrrhine monkeys studied to date varies from 2n=20 to 2n=62 (Table 4).

The various species of the family Callithricidae present a natural uniformity in the number (from 44 to 46) and in the morphology of the chromosomes. Therefore they represent a particularly close group of species. The variations which have led to the diversification of the number of chromosomes can all be brought back to mechanisms of centric fusion.

The family Cebidae presents instead a greater range of variability. The chromosome number in the different genera, ranges from 34 in *Ateles* to 62 in *Lagothrix* with 44 in the different species of *Saimiri* and 54 in the ones of *Cebus*. The computation of their fundamental number (N.F.) does not help much in the search for common origin. The recent re-evaluation of Wegener's theory of the continental drift on the other hand reopens under a new and stimulating light the phylogenetic status of the South American monkeys. The study of their chromosomes, and especially of their possible homologous regions, with the new available techniques of chromosome banding, is expected to provide new data for assessing their phylogenetic interrelations and their position in respect to the Old World primates and the different groups of Prosimiae.

THE CHROMOSOMES OF THE OLD WORLD MONKEYS

The number of chromosomes in the Old World primates varies from 2n=42 to 2n=72, (Table 5). In all the species of the genera *Macaca*, *Papio*, *Theropithecus*, and *Cercocebus* the diploid number of chromosomes is 42. The differences between the karyotypes of the different species are of little importance and can be reconciled with structural rearrangements of the inversion or translocation types.

In all species of *Macaca*, *Papio*, *Cercocebus*, and *Theropithecus* the X chromosome appears to be of average size with the centromere more or less in the middle. The Y chromosome is very small and, when it is

Table 4. Numerical data and morphological information on the chromosomes of New World primates

Taxa	2*n*	M	S	A	X	Y
Callithricidae						
Callithrix chrysoleuca	46	4	26	14	S	S
C. jacchus	46	4	28	12	S	A
C. argentata	44	4	28	10	S	M
C. humeralifer	44	4	28	10	S	A
Cebuella pygmaea	44	4	28	10	S	A
Saguinus oedipus	46	4	26	14	S	M
S. fuscicollis	46	4	26	14	S	M
S. nigricollis	46	4	26	14	S	M
S. mystax	46	4	26	14	S	M
S. leucopus	46	–	–	–	–	–
S. tamarin	46	–	–	–	–	–
Leontideus rosalia	46	4	28	12	S	M
Callimiconidae						
Callimico goeldii	48	4	24	18	S	A
Cebidae						
Alouatta seniculus	44	4	12	26	A	S
A. villosa	52	–	–	–	–	–
A. caraya	52	4	16	30	S	A
Aotus trivirgatus	54 (52)	4	16	32	S	S
Cebus albifrons	54	4	16	32	S	A
C. capucinus	54	4	14	34	S	A
C. apella	54	4	20	28	A	A
Callicebus moloch	46	4	16	24	S	A, M
Callicebus torquatus	20	–	10	10	–	–
Cacajao rubicundus	46	4	16	24	S	–
Pithecia pithecia	46	–	–	–	–	–
Saimiri sciureus	44	4	26	12	S	A
Saimiri madeirae	44	4	28	10	S	A
Saimiri boliviensis	44	4	28	10	S	A
Lagothrix ubericola	62	–	–	–	–	–
Ateles arachnoides	34	–	–	–	–	–
A. paniscus	34	–	30	2	S	A
A. belzebuth	34	–	30	2	S	A
A. geoffroyi	34	–	30	2	S	A, S

possible to distinguish the centromere, it seems to be metacentric. Further a common characteristic of these species, is the occurrence of one chromosome of medium size with an achromatic region on one arm surmounted by a linear satellite (Figure 2).

This shared endowment of chromosomes lends support to the theory that these four genera of the family Cercopithecidae had a recent common origin. Later geographical and ecological isolation would have led to the differentiation of the karyotypes and to the formation of groups of individuals, each group reproductively isolated from the others, which

Table 5. Numerical data on the chromosomes of Old World anthropoid primates

Taxa	2*n*	S–M	A	X	Y
1.1. Macaca					
1. *M. silenus*	42	40	–	S	S,A
2. *M. nigra*	42	40	–	S	S
3. *M. sylvana*	42	40	–	S	S
4. *M. arctoides*	42	40	–	S	S
5. *M. maura*	42	40	–	S	S
6. *M. sinica*	42	40	–	S	S
7. *M. radiata*	42	40	–	S	S
8. *M. cyclopis*	42	40	–	S	S
9. *M. mulatta*	42	40	–	S	S
10. *M. fuscata*	42	40	–	S	S
11. *M. nemestrina*	42	40	–	S	S
12. *M. fascicularis*	42	40	–	S	S
13. *M. assamensis*	42	40	–	S	S
1.2. Papio					
1. *P. hamadryas*	42	40	–	S	S
2. *P. ursinus*	42	40	–	S	S
3. *P. anubis*	42	40	–	S	S
4. *P. cynocephalus*	42	40	–	S	S
5. *P. papio*	42	40	–	S	S
6. *P. sphinx*	42	40	–	S	S
7. *P. leucophaeus*	42	40	–	S	S
1.3. Theropithecus					
1. *T. gelada*	42	40	–	S	S
1.4. Cercocebus					
1. *C. galeritus*	42	40	–	S	S
3. *C. torquatus*	42	40	–	S	S
4. *C. aterrimus*	42	40	–	S	S
5. *C. albigena*	42	40	–	S	S
1.5. Cercopithecus					
1. *C. aethiops*	60	34	24	S	A
2. *C. cynosuros*	60	36	22	S	A
3. *C. sabaeus*	60				
4. *C. cephus*	66	46	18	S	A
5. *C. diana*	58	42	14	S	A
6. *C. l'hoesti*	58–60	48	14–16	S	A
7. *C. preussi*	66				
9. *C. mona*	66–68	46	18–20	S	S,A
10. *C. campbelli*	66–68	46	18–20	S	S,A
13. *C. denti*	66				
14. *C. petaurista*	66				
15. *C. neglectus*	58–62	44–46	12–14	S	S
16. *C. nictitans*	66–70	46	18–22	S	A
17. *C. ascanius*	66				
20. *C. mitis*	72	44–52	22	S	A,S
21. *C. nigroviridis*	48	46	–	S	A
22. *C. talapoin*	54	38	14	S	A
23. *C. hamlyni*	64	50	12	S	–

Table 5. *continued*

Taxa	2*n*	S-M	A	X	Y
1.6. Erythrocebus					
1. *E. patas*	54	36	16	S	A,S
2.1. Presbytis					
1. *P. entellus*	44	40	2	S	A
2. *P. senex*	44	40	2	S	A
10. *P. obscurus*	44	40	2	S	A
2.2. Pygathrix					
1. *P. nemaeus*	44	42	–	S	A
2.5. Nasalis					
1. *N. larvatus*	48	46	–	S	?
2.6. Colobus					
1. *C. polykomos*	44	42	–	S	?
4. *C. badius*	44	42			
5. *C. kirkii*	44	42	–	S	A
3.1. Hylobates					
1. *H. lar*	44	42	–	S	S
2. *H. agilis*	44	42	–	S	S
3. *H. moloch*	44	42	–	S	S
4. *H.* (*Nomascus*)*concolor*	52	44	6	S	A
5. *H. hoolock*	44	42	–	S	S
3.2. Symphalangus					
1. *S. syndactylus*	50	46	2	S	S
4.1. Pongo					
1. *P. pygmaeus*	48	26	20	S	S
4.2. Pan					
1. *P. troglodytes*	48	34	12	S	A
2. *P. paniscus*	48	34	12	S	A
4.3. Gorilla					
1. *G. gorilla*	48	30	16	S	S
5.1. Homo					
1. *H. sapiens*	46	34	10	S	A

became the ancestors of many species belonging to these four genera. Comparative analysis of the morphology of individual chromosomes, demonstrates closer similarity between species of these genera.

These karyological similarities are validated by the idioplasmatic continuity still evident among the various species of these genera. Data on hybrids reveal, in fact, a remarkable frequency of chance hybridization between individuals of different species of this group, whereas this does not happen among the others (Figure 3).

The species of *Cercopithecus* (including *Erythrocebus*) present a variable

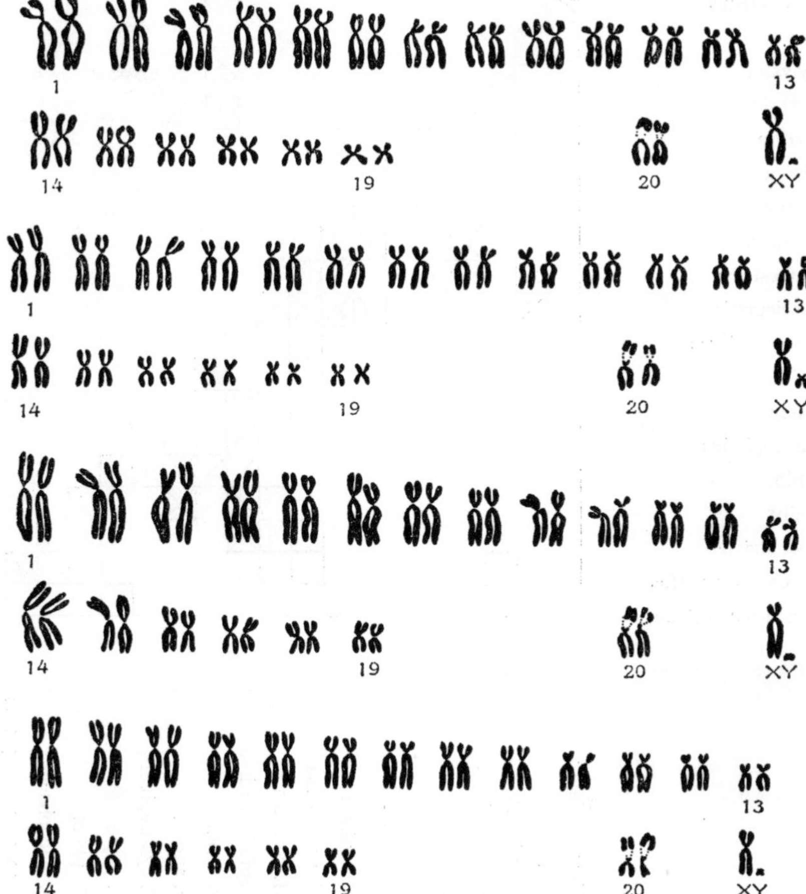

Figure 2. The chromosomes of *Macaca*, *Papio*, *Cercocebus*, and *Theropithecus*

number of chromosomes ranging between 48 and 72 and more than one chromosome number may sometimes be found in the same species (see Table 5). The cause of this variation in the chromosome number among the species of a single genus is still mysterious, and different hypotheses have been proposed to explain it. Research is now in progress to find the mechanism of this variation (Figure 4).

No data are available for *Rhinopithecus* and *Simias*, which are now extremely rare and which could furnish important karyological information.

The karyotype of *Colobus polykomos* (2n=44) appears to have many characteristics in common with that of *Presbytis* (*P. obscurus*). They

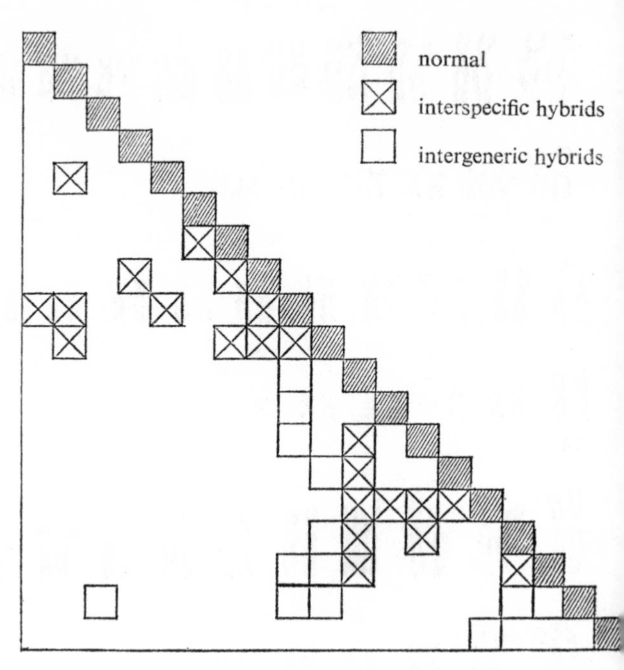

Figure 3. Known hybrids among species of Old World monkeys

share a large number of morphologically similar chromosomes (Figure 5a). *Nasalis* has a diploid number of 2n=48 chromosomes; the chromosomes are morphologically similar to those of *Colobus* and *Presbytis* (Figure 5a).

The available species of *Hylobates* (Figure 5b) have diploid numbers of 2n=44, 50 and 52 chromosomes. Their chromosomes have many morphological characteristics in common with or identical to those of *Colobus polykomos*, *Presbytis obscurus*, and *Nasalis larvatus*.

These and other data challenge the traditional taxonomic organization which places the Colobinae among the Cercopithecoidea, and the Hylobatinae among the Hominoidea.

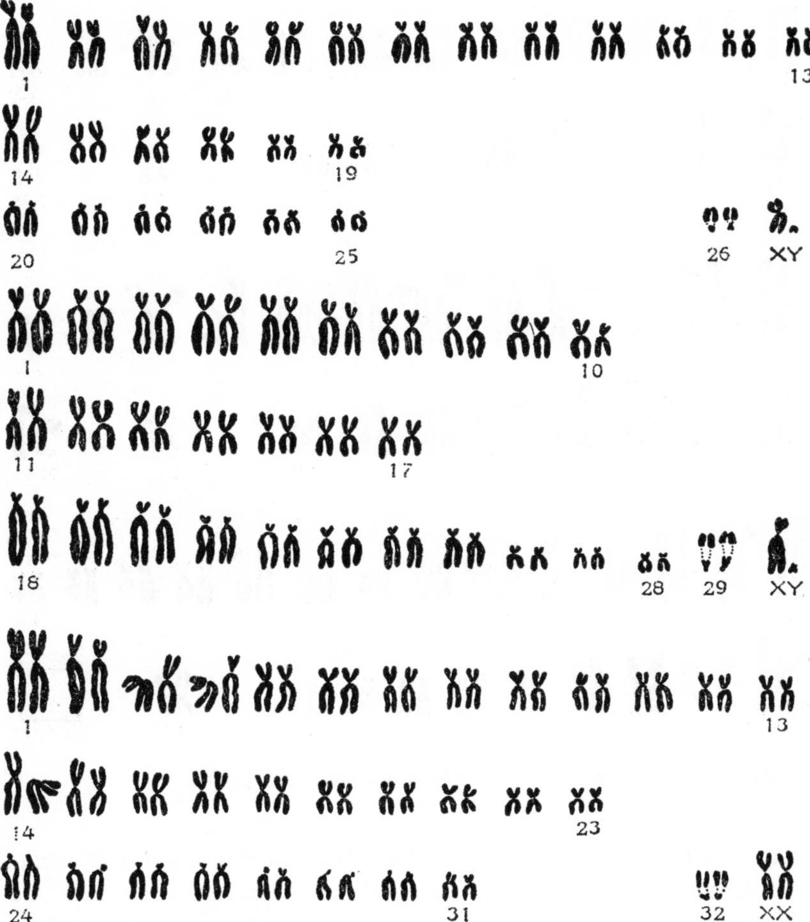

Figure 4. The chromosomes of three different species of the genus *Cercopithecus*

THE CHROMOSOMES OF THE ANTHROPOID APES AND THE ORIGIN OF THE HUMAN KARYOTYPE

The number and morphology of the chromosomes of the true large-bodied apes (orangutan, gorilla, and chimpanzee) and man are by now known in detail (Figure 6). The diploid chromosome complement of the three species of great apes is 48. Man has 46 chromosomes. The possible homologies of these structures between the great apes and man can be tested in different ways. A strictly morphological comparison gives

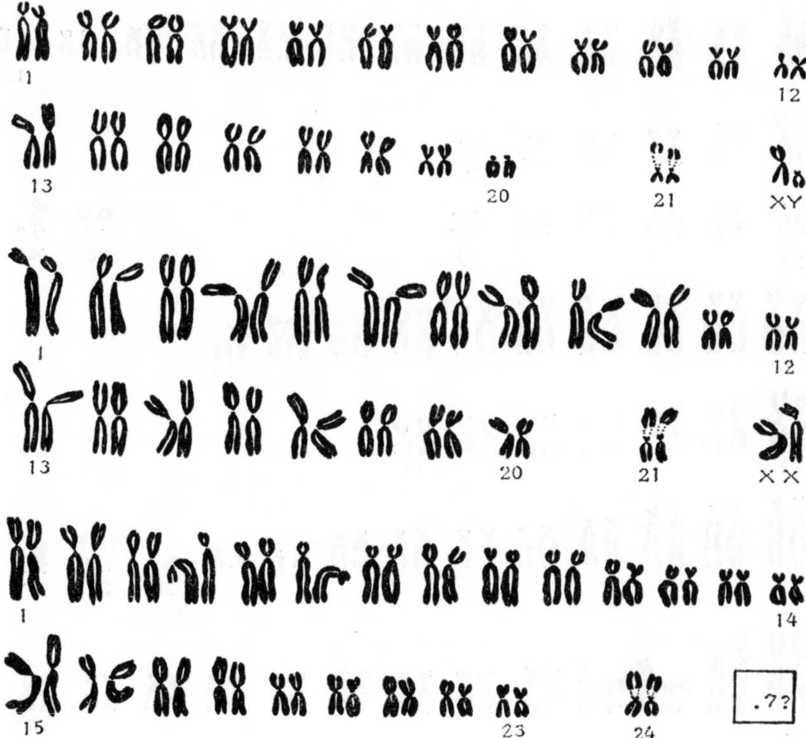

Figure 5a. The chromosomes of *Presbytis*, *Colobus*, and *Nasalis*

an approximate idea of gross variations (i.e. different number of metacentric, submetacentric, or acrocentric; different size; etc.). However, the recently available techniques of chromosome banding can, with caution, help in identifying homologies among different karyotypes. Various attempts have been made during the last few years to identify homologies between the chromosomes of different apes and man (de Grouchy et al. 1972a; Khudr et al. 1973; Lin et al. 1973). Among these the most extensive study is certainly the one done by Turleau and de Grouchy. However, the results obtained with quinacrine seem to be more constant and in any case they seem to detect some real structural heterogeneity among the chromosomes. For this and other reasons we give our preference to this method and for avoiding heterogeneity in the treatment we prepared mixed cultures of human and ape chromosomes.

In general it appears that chromosomes 1, 3, 11 12, 14, and the X of the chimpanzee possess banding patterns similar to the corresponding human chromosomes. Chromosomes 6, 8, 10, and 13 of the chimpanzee

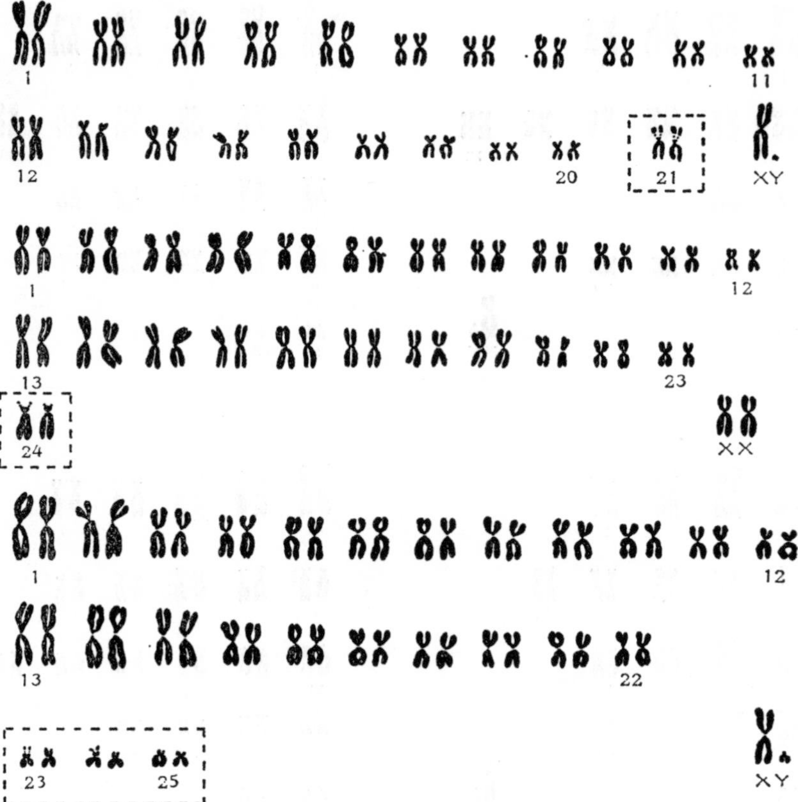

Figure 5b. The chromosomes of *Hylobates*, *Symphalangus* and *Nomascus*

also have banding patterns, particularly in the long arms, closely resembling the human chromosome of the same number (Plate 2).

Morphologically the chimpanzee chromosome 2 appears similar to the human one, but the banding patterns are distinctly different. The same holds for chromosomes 4, 5, 15, 16, 17, 18, 19, and for the Y. They seem to have no apparent human counterpart. It is possible that some structural change might have occurred in these chromosomes during the divergence of man from the chimpanzee line.

The main difference, however, between the karyotypes of man and the apes remains in the number. A centric fusion might account for a reduction of the chromosome number from 48 to 46 in an ancestor of man, which realized an important distinction between the karyotypes of the anthropoid apes and man as we hypothesized in 1962.

The similarity of the banding patterns of two chromosomes of the

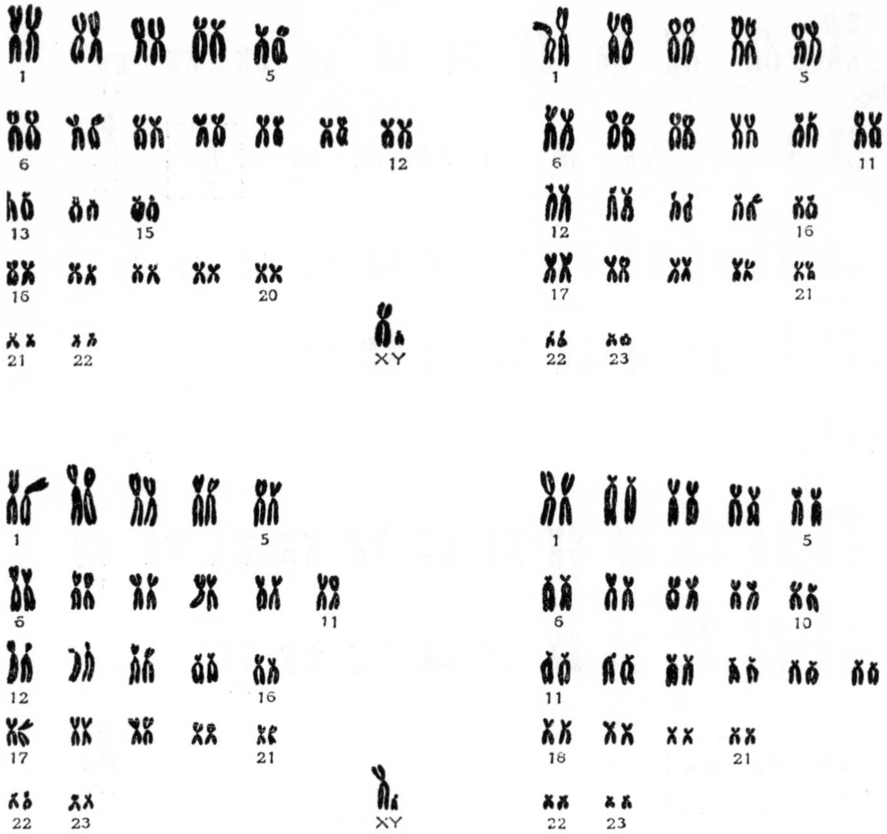

Figure 6. The chromosomes of apes and man

G group in the chimpanzee to the human n. 2 led some authors to propose that this chromosome in man originated from the centric fusion of two chromosomes of the G group type in the ancestry of man.

The study made up to now concerns the comparison of the chromosomes of thirty different chimpanzees with the human chromosomes. The results obtained are in large part already published (Lin et al. 1973).

Apart from some variable features in the chromosomes of the different chimpanzees studied, some chromosomes appear to be almost identical in the two species whereas others appear to be absolutely different.

The other important differences between chimpanzee and man, could be due to translocations or inversions which occurred during the long period of phyletic diversification between the two species. A similar study with the other two apes (especially the gorilla) will probably tell us which of these variations are unique to the chimpanzee and which are unique to the human line.

When and how could a transformation from 48 to 46 chromosomes have occurred? Such mutations are not very rare. Study of the karyotype of present-day human populations has uncovered cases of previous fusions between two acrocentric chromosomes resulting in a karyotype of 45 chromosomes. If two such individuals were to mate, offspring having 44 chromosomes would be produced, and would probably be perfectly normal. It is unlikely that this would happen in an actual population. Individuals with a karyotype of 45 chromosomes produced by centric fusion are fairly rare, and a mutation of this sort can easily be lost.

In order to understand how this could have occurred in an ancestral prehominid, we must consider the demographic dimensions of the populations at that time. Group size could not have exceeded twenty individuals. The groups were family clans, very often dominated by a single male who enjoyed absolute dominion over the females of the group. The mating of some of the males with their own daughters must have happened fairly frequently. Indeed, it appears that the "leadership" of a group of chimpanzees may last more than ten years; the females reach sexual maturity at eight years.

A male with such a mutation, that is with a karyotype of 47 chromosomes, therefore had two possibilities of establishing the new karyotype of 46 chromosomes: (1) mating with the various females of the resulting offspring, half would have had 47 chromosomes, so that the reduction could have been completed in the successive generation; and (2) mating with his daughters in a sort of backcross. In this case the reduction of the karyotype would have been even more rapid and could have taken only two generations — at the most therefore thirty years, considering the shorter time necessary for sexual maturity in our monkeylike ancestors.

The chances of establishing such a mutation obviously are conditioned not only by the existence of small reproductive communities but also by the intrinsic power of survival of this mutation. Clearly, little can be said on this point, yet the loss of a larger number of genes in the same chromosome may have represented some selective advantage at a certain moment in the evolution of the Hominidae.

When did this event occur? As yet it is impossible to say, but as knowledge of the karyotypes of the anthropoid apes increases, a means of attempting a calculation based both on the frequencies of chromosomal mutations in natural populations and the length of generations may be discovered.

A REVISION OF THE CLASSIFICATION OF CATARRHINE PRIMATES AND AN INTERPRETATION OF THEIR PHYLOGENESIS ON THE BASIS OF KARYOLOGICAL DATA

The data on the number and morphology of the chromosomes of catarrhine monkeys led to an attempt to revise the taxonomic groupings, especially at the supergeneric level. Undoubtedly, it is at this level that karyological studies are most useful.

Macaca, *Papio*, *Theropithecus*, and *Cercocebus* must be separated from species of *Cercopithecus* and placed in a different subfamily, to which the name Papinae could be assigned, leaving the name Cercopithecinae to the species of *Cercopithecus* only.

Symphalangus must be separated from the various species of *Hylobates* and *H. concolor* should be placed in the genus *Nomascus*. These three genera should be removed from the superfamily Hominoidea. They could be included in the superfamily Cercopithecoidea and constitute a family by themselves.

A detailed discussion of the Colobinae is not yet possible, although they appear to be a fairly homogeneous group.

The superfamily Hominoidea should be restricted to the great apes (*Pongo*, *Gorilla*, and *Pan*) and to man. Among these, man is clearly distinguished by the number of chromosomes and must be classified in the subfamily Homininae while the true apes constitute the subfamily Ponginae.

In the Ponginae the karyotype of the orangutan can be distinguished clearly from those of the gorilla and the chimpanzee. This difference could be taken into consideration at a supergeneric level to distinguish the orangutan from the African apes. The anthropoid ape with the karyotype most similar to the human one is the chimpanzee.

The morphological variations in the chromosomes of different species of Old World primates may be the result of different mechanisms, the most common of which are inversion and translocation. Nevertheless, from a phyletic point of view, the variation in the number of chromosomes is of greater interest. The mechanisms that lead to these numerical variations, as we have shown, are centric fusion, centric fission, polyploidy, and polysomy.

Which of these mechanisms is responsible for the numerical variations in this group of species? What was the original chromosome number of the ancestor common to all the Old World primates, accepting that we had a single common ancestor? The chromosome number in the somatic cells in the living species of Old World primates varies from 42 to 72, but the greater part of this variability (from 48 to 72) can be attributed to the diverse species of the genus *Cercopithecus*. Extremely discordant opinions exist concerning the mechanisms that have led to such a wide variation among the different species of a single genus. Moreover, these species are very homogeneous from an anatomical-physiological standpoint. It is therefore impossible to hypothesize about when this group was separated from the other species of Old World primates, or to which group of Cercopithecoidea they are most closely related.

In the other species of Old World primates the number of chromosomes varies from 42 to 52. The original number of chromosomes in the possible ancestor of the Old World primates probably must be sought within the limits of these eight pairs. The fact that such groups of taxonomically diverse and phylogenetically ancient species as *Presbytis*, *Colobus*, and many species of *Hylobates* have 44 chromosomes suggests that this number of chromosomes characterized the ancestor of the Old World primates in the middle Eocene, about fifty million years ago.

A centric fusion between two pairs of acrocentric chromosomes or a double translocation could have been responsible for the reduction from 44 to 42. For an interpretation of the chromosome number 48 in *Nasalis*, 50 in *Symphalangus*, and 52 in *Hylobates* (*Nomascus*) *concolor*, recourse must be had to mechanisms of centric fission or polysomy.

Probably the number and morphology of the chromosomes of the great apes are not directly connected with the primate forms mentioned above. The general morphology of the chromosomes is very different, and if there was a common ancestor, it must be sought in the very remote past.

Thus from the karyological point of view, we can recognize three distinct lines of evolution in the catarrhine monkeys as schematized in Figure 7: (1) the species of *Cercopithecus*; (2) the various genera *Macaca*, *Papio*, *Theropithecus*, *Cercocebus*, *Presbytis*, *Colobus*, *Symphalangus*, *Hylobates* and *Nasalis*; and (3) the three great apes and man. The connections between these three karyological lines of evolution as yet seem indistinct and controversial.

Could the marked chromosome serve as a key for the correlation of the three lines?

The physiological homology of the achromatic portion of this chromosome in different species is suggested because this is the nucleolus organizing region (Huang et al. 1969; Chiarelli 1971). As I (Chiarelli 1966 a,b) have shown, a chromosome pair with an achromatic region is present in all the species of Cercopithecinae, Papinae, Colobinae and almost all the Hylobatinae, but it is absent in the Ponginae and in man.

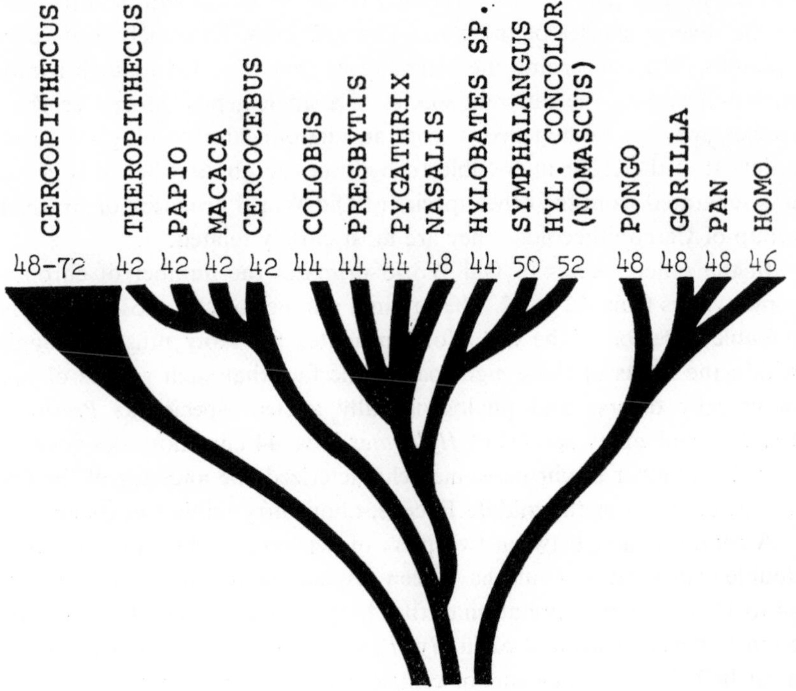

Figure 7. Possible phylogenetic relationship among the diverse genera of the Old World Primates

The fact that this achromatic region plays the role of nucleolus organizer, and therefore must be a constant feature of the cell, stimulates the search for its possible location in the species that apparently do not possess it and therefore the establishment of possible homologies among the chromosomes involved.

The nucleolus organizing region in the human karyotype seems to be situated in the achromatic appendages, bearing satellites in the short arms of acrocentric chromosomes 13, 15, and 21 (Levan and Hsu 1959; Slizynski 1964; Valencia 1964). Direct comparison of these chromosomes to nucleolus-organizing chromosome pairs of Papinae is hazardous. However, when these two chromosomes are joined together in man or in the great apes, their likeness to the marked chromosomes of macaque or a baboon, in both size and shape is remarkable.

Apart from the physiological interest of this region, the perspective of such a homology in different species provides a means to confront the question of the connections between the three different chromosomal lines that have been distinguished among the Old World primates. This is, of course, primarily a matter of speculation. However, it could serve as a working hypothesis to develop further research.

REFERENCES

ARRIGHI, F. E., M. W. SORENSON, L. R. SHIRLEY

1969 Chromosomes of the tree shrews (Tupaiidae). *Cytogenetics* 8: 199–208.

BENDER M. A., E. H. Y. CHU

1963 "The chromosomes of primates," in *Evolutionary and genetic biology of primates*, volume one. Edited by J. Buettner-Janusch, 261–310. New York: Academic Press.

BENDER M. A., L. E. METTLER

1958 Chromosome studies of primates. *Science* 128: 186–190.

CHIARELLI, B.

1961a Ibridologia e sistematica in Primati. I. Raccolta di dati. *Atti Associazione Genetica Italiana* 6: 213–220.

1961b Some chromosome numbers in primates. *Mammalian Chromosome Newsletter* 6: 3–5.

1962a Comparative morphometric analysis of primate chromosomes, I: The chromosomes of anthropoid apes and of man. *Caryologia* 15: 99–121

1962b Comparative morphometric analysis of primate chromosomes, II: The chromosomes of the genera *Macaca*, *Papio*, *Theropithecus* and *Cercocebus*. *Caryologia* 15: 401–420

1963 Comparative morphometric analysis of primate chromosomes, III: The chromosomes of the genera *Hylobates*, *Colobus* and *Presbytis*. *Caryologia* 16: 637–648.

1966a Marked chromosomes in Catarrhine monkeys. *Folia Primatologica* 4: 74–80.

1966b Caryology and taxomony of the Catarrhine monkeys. *American Journal of Physical Anthropology* 24: 155–169.

1968a Chromosome polymorphism in the species of the genus *Cercopithecus*. *Cytologia* 33: 1–16.

1968b From the karyotype of the apes to the human karyotype. *South African Journal of Science* 64: 72–80.

1971 New data for one comparison of the karyotype of the anthropoid apes with that of man. *Proceedings of the Third International Congress of Primatology, Zurich, 1970*, 2:104–109. Basel: Karger.

1972a "The karyotypes of the gibbons," in *Gibbon and Siamang*, volume one. Edited by D. M. Rumbaugh, 90-102. Basel: Karger.

1972b *Taxonomic atlas of living primates*. London: Academic Press.

CHIARELLI, B., C. C. LIN

1972 Comparative fluorescent patterns in human and chimpanzee chromosomes. *Genen en Phaenen* 15:2–3.

CHIARELLI, B., E. CAPANNA, *editors*

1973 *Cytotaxonomy and evolution of vertebrates*. London: Academic Press.

CHU, E. H. Y., M. A. BENDER
1961 Chromosome cytology and evolution in primates. *Science* 133: 1399–1405.
1962 Cytogenetics and evolution of primates. *Annals of the New York Academy of Sciences* 102: 253–266.

CHU, E. H. Y., B. A. SWOMLEY
1961 Chromosomes of Lemurine lemurs. *Science* 133: 1925–1926.

DE BOER, L. E. M.
1972a The karyotype of *Galago alleni* Waterhouse 1837 (2n = 40) compared with that of *Galago senegalensis* Geoffroy 1796 (2n = 38). (Primates, Prosimii: *Galagidae*). *Genetica* 43: 183–189.
1972b The karyotype of *Galago demidovii* Fischer 1808 (2n = 58). (Primates, Prosimii: *Galagidae*). *Genen en Phaenen* 15: 19–22.
1973 Studies on the genetics of Prosimians. *Journal of Human Evolution* 2:271–278.

DE GROUCHY, J. C., C. TURLEAU, M. ROUBIN, M. KLEIN
1972a Evolutions caryotypiques de l'homme et du chimpanzé. Etude comparative des topographies de bandes après denaturation menagée. *Ann. Genet.* 15:79–84.
1972b The chromosomes of lemurs. *Folia Primatologica.* 17: 171–176.

ECKHARDT R. B.
1969 A chromosome arm number index and its application to the phylogeny and classification of lemurs. *American Journal of Physical Anthropology* 31: 85–88.

EGOZCUE J.
1967 Chromosome variability in the Lemuridae. *American Journal of Physical Anthropology* 26: 341–348.
1969 "Primates," in *Comparative mammalian cytogenetics.* Edited by K. Benirschke, 357-389. New York: Springer-Verlag.
1970 The chromosomes of the lesser bushbaby (*Galago senegalensis*) and the greater bushbaby (*Galago crassicaudatus*). *Folia Primatologica* 12: 236–240.

EGOZCUE J., B. CHIARELLI
1967 The idiogram of the lowland gorilla (*Gorilla gorilla gorilla*). *Folia Primatologica* 5: 237–240

EGOZCUE J., B. CHIARELLI, M. SARTI-CHIARELLI, F. HAGEMENAS
1968 Chromosome polymorphism in the tree shrew (*Tupaia glis*). *Folia Primatologica* 8:150–158.

EGOZCUE J., M. VILARASAU DE EGOZCUE
1967 The chromosome complement of the slow loris (*Nycticebus coucang*). *Primates* 7: 423–432.

HUANG, C. C., H. HABBITT, J. L. AMBRUS
1969 Chromosomes and DNA synthesis in the stumptail monkey (*Macaca speciosa*) with special regard to marker and sex chromosomes. *Folia Primatologica* 11:28–34.

KHUDR, G., K. BENIRSCHKE, C. J. SEDGWICK
1973 Man and *Pan paniscus*: a karyologic comparison. *Journal of Human Evolution.* 2: 323–331.

LEVAN A., T. C. HSU

1959 The human idiogram. *Hereditas* 45: 665.

LIN, C. C., B. CHIARELLI, L. E. M. DE BOER , M. M. COHEN

1973 A comparison of the fluorescent karyotypes of the chimpanzee (*Pan troglodytes*) and man. *Journal of Human Evolution* 2: 311–321.

MANFREDI-ROMANINI, M. G.

1972 Nuclear DNA content and area of primate lymphocytes as a cytotaxonomical tool. *Journal of Human Evolution* 1:23–40.

MANFREDI-ROMANINI M. G., L. E. M. DE BOER, B. CHIARELLI, S. TINOZZI MASSARI

1972 DNA content and cytotaxonomy of *Galago senegalensis* and *Galago crassicaudatus*. *Journal of Human Evolution* 1: 473–476.

RUMPLER Y.

1970 Etude cytogénétique du *Lemur catta*. *Cytogenetics* 9:239.

RUMPLER Y., R. ALBIGNAC

1969 Etude cytogénétique de deux Lémuriens, *Lemur macaco macaco*, Linné 1766, et *Lemur fulvus rufus* (Audebert 1800) et d'un hybride *macaco macaco/fulvus rufus*. *C. R. Soc. Biol.* 163: 1247–1250.

1969 Existence d'une variabilité chromosomique intraspécifique chez certains Lémuriens. *C. R. Soc. Biol.* 163:1989.

1971 Cytogenetic studies of the endemic Malagasy Lemurs subfamily Cheirogalinae Geoffroy 1915. *American Journal of Physical Anthropology* 38: 261–269.

1972 Etude cytogénétique du *Varecia variegata* et du *Lemur rubriventer*. *C. R. Soc. Biol.* 165:741–745.

RUMPLER, Y., R. ALBIGNAC, N. RUMPLER-RANDRIAMONTA

i.p. "Variabilité chromosomique chez un Lémurien du Nord de Madagascar, *Lepilemur septentrionalis*."

SLIZYNSKI, B. M.

1964 "On human pachytene chromosomes." in *Mammalian cytogenetics and related problems in radiobiology*. Edited by Pevan et al., 171–186. Oxford: Pergamon Press.

VALENCIA, J. I.

1964 Discussion on the B. M. Slizynski paper. "On human pachytene chromosomes," in *Mammalian cytogenetics and related problems in radiobiology*. Edited by Pevan et al., 186–187. London: Pergamon Press.

YING K. L., H. BUTLER

1971 Chromosomal polymorphism in the lesser bush babies (*Galago senegalensis*). *Can. J. Genet. Cytol.* 13:793–800.

Discussion

TUTTLE: I would encourage a discussion on the utility of the various biomolecular methods that are now available and ask what sort of consensus is developing out of the combination of the inferences from these various methods.

GOODMAN: Well, there are three or four major approaches. The immunological approach is directed at serum protein and other protein antigens. Closely related to this, because it deals with proteins (but much more precisely), is the amino acid sequencing work. This is providing the most elegant data but at the same time only on a relatively small sample of the genomic measures because of the great amount of labor involved in working out the amino acid sequence of a protein. Finally there are the polynucleotide hybridization techniques. These are directed at the chromosomal DNA. They deal with the actual genetic material itself, but procedurally are comparable to immunological techniques rather than to amino acid sequencing techniques. Now, with respect to the correspondence regarding phylogenetic relationships among these three major methods which I just outlined, the most salient observation is that the two African apes are much closer to man, who may perhaps be considered the third African ape, than to the orangutan or gibbon. This was first observed immunologically and now all amino acid sequence data point in this direction. Further, the polynucleotide or DNA hybridization data strongly back up this point of view. So moving back in time we would have perhaps the following order of relationships. The orangutan seems somewhat closer to the African apes and man than to any other group. And almost as close would be the gibbon, although the degree of similarity varies according to which of the three methods is employed. Somewhat more divergent but by some methods practically as closely related would be the Old World monkeys. Perhaps here I should point out that the molecular data do not quite agree with the chromosome data. But we can reconcile the two sets of data. Chiarelli would place the hylobatids or gibbons with the Old World monkeys. The molecular data are fairly strong in placing the hylobatids cladistically with the hominoids, that is with the large-sized apes and man. However, they obviously do descend as an ancient branch in the Catarrhini and it may be that the chromosome features are retentions of primitive morphological chromosome features rather than indicative of more recent common ancestry with Old World monkeys. Perhaps Brunetto Chiarelli would wish to comment on this.

CHIARELLI: In fact some recent data, especially on *Nomascus* (cf. *Hylobates concolor*) places some of the gibbons nearer to the apes. However, I am still inclined to envisage their relationship with the Colobinae thereby stressing their differences from the Hominoidea. Moreover, I can view the gibbons as a branch by themselves, the Hylobatidae. There is a real difference between the karyotypes of all the Hylobatidae, including *H. symphalangus* and *Nomascus*, and those of the real apes. It is a big difference and maybe represents an ancient division.

ECKHARDT: Again I think that it is necessary to differentiate between phylogeny and taxonomy. It is entirely possible to have one taxonomy which is consistent with several different phylogenies and vice versa. We have to realize that higher taxonomic categories, genera and so forth, up to families like Pongidae and Hominidae, are relatively arbitrary categories and there is going to be a high degree of disagreement about them. I think that it is much more important to agree on the phylogenies underlying these. With regard to the contrast between the molecular evidence and the chromosome evidence, it is something of a commonplace, but still often lost sight of, that different character complexes can evolve at quite different rates. Thus, even though the chromosomal evidence and the molecular evidence may seem to be in contradiction, perhaps we can make something out of this by asking not what does chromosomal evidence and what does molecular evidence tell us about the sequence of evolution, but what can we infer from sequence of evolution, as deduced from other characteristics, about rates of evolution in the chromosomal complex as opposed to the molecular complex. Perhaps we can infer that changes occur more rapidly at the molecular level than at the chromosome level, or perhaps the reverse, or perhaps something more complex than either of these simple alternatives.

GOODMAN: The next major relationship, which will be no surprise, is that the platyrrhines would join the catarrhines in the molecular phylogenetic tree. Then after a fair jump with respect to antigenetic distance would come the tarsiers. The tarsier branch would join the Anthropoidea. This supports Szalay's concept of Haplorhini as distinct from the Strepsirhini. Next we have the lorisoids and lemuroids joining together as a branch for which we use the term Strepsirhini. This branch then joins the Haplorhini. Finally, as borderline primates and as a group at least quite close with respect to our antigenic data are the tree shrews. There are certain points of interpretation with respect to the Strepsirhines which I wish to discuss with Fred Szalay. In his paper he speculates that the lorisoids evolved out of a particular branch of the lemuroids, the Cheirogaleinae. Now although we do not have strong evidence against this notion (and we never would because we are dealing with different kinds of data), I did want to point out that the lorisoids seem to diverge less from catarrhines and platyrrhines at the molecular level than the lemuroids do. I would interpret this to mean that the lorisoids have strayed less from the ancestral stock than the lemuroids. I would add that within the lorisoids we would relate the African Lorisinae, the potto and *Arctocebus*, slightly closer to other African lorisoids, the galago group, than to the Asiatic lorisoids, the slender loris and the slow loris.

[Frederick Szalay summarized and illustrated his paper with slides.]

SECTION THREE

Anatomical Correlates of Feeding Behavior in Monkeys, Apes, and Man

An Assessment of Masticatory Efficiency in a Series of Anthropoid Primates with Special Reference to the Colobinae and Cercopithecinae

PHILLIP WALKER and PETER MURRAY

INTRODUCTION

This is a preliminary investigation of the functional differences in dentitions that may exist among various anthropoids. Hypotheses having considerable impact on theoretical assessments of fossil anthropoids have been based on assumed functional differences in the dentition (Jolly 1970). Because little is actually known about the biomechanical aspects of cusp morphology and because practically no empirical work has been done to determine whether or not these rather slight morphological differences are indeed functionally significant, we have attempted to provide such a contribution. Empirical assessments have been made on ruminant masticatory efficiency by recording the number of jaw movements in various ways (Stobbs and Cowper 1972), and attempts to assess the extent to which the food has been orally processed have been accomplished by esophageal fistulation.

While the latter technique would have been more satisfactory for our purposes, it has been impractical as yet for us to use it. We have instead substituted an analysis of the stomach contents of a large series of wild-shot anthropoids for the fistula-derived sampling technique. We suggest that our findings closely approximate the work done on ruminants because we have added a variety of procedures that verify one another in a convincing manner and lead to firm conclusions. If

We wish to thank Dr. Jack Fooden for allowing us to examine the stomach contents of primates he collected in Thailand. We are greatful to Dr. Benjamin Beck for the assistance he gave us during our experimentation with living primates. Drs. Albert Dahlberg, Russell Tuttle and Leonard Radinsky read the manuscript and offered helpful criticism.

For Plates, see pp. viii–ix, between pp. 560–561

differences in the masticatory efficiency of morphologically similar dentitions can be demonstrated experimentally, we are approaching the point of being able to define specific functionally significant attributes of teeth. These attributes can be associated with the diets of living forms and then applied to fossil species with a high probability of being correct. The ability to assess accurately the dietary proclivities of a fossil form is extremely useful for reconstructing aspects of its ecology and behavior. The acquisition of this information on living forms is equally important in assessing the energetics of the organism, an area that has been scarcely dealt with by primate biologists.

We have employed *Macaca* and *Presbytis* as representative Cercopithecidae and have compared them with *Hylobates* because these forms are known to have markedly different dietary requirements and presumably budget their energy in accordingly different ways. *Macaca* and *Presbytis* are ideal forms for comparison because their dentitions are morphologically alike in most respects. Slight differences in the shape of the dentitions of colobines and cercopithecines are well known, but their actual efficacy in handling specific diets has only been suggested and has remained until now unverified. *Hylobates* has the least-specialized dental morphology and thus serves well for comparison with the cercopithecoids.

METHODS AND MATERIALS

Food materials examined in the investigation were removed from *Presbytis, Macaca,* and *Hylobates* stomachs from wild specimens shot in northern Thailand (Fooden 1971). The stomachs were preserved whole, as removed from the specimen, in ethyl alcohol (Table 1).

Table 1. Specimens employed in the analysis of stomach contents

Species	Common name	Total
Presbytis cristatus	Silver leaf langur	8
Presbytis phayrei	Dusky leaf monkey	2
Macaca assamensis	Assamese macaque	10
Macaca fascicularis	Crab-eating macaque	3
Macaca nemestrina	Pigtailed macaque	3
Hylobates lar	White-handed gibbon	11

Living primates representing these genera were observed at the Chicago Zoological Park (Table 2). Dental specimens for illustration of occlusal contact areas were obtained from the Field Museum of Natural History collection in Chicago, Illinois.

Several procedures were employed in obtaining the data. The contents of the stomachs of eleven specimens of *Presbytis* spp., sixteen specimens of *Macaca* spp. and eleven specimens of *Hylobates lar* were sorted into different particle size categories by passing the material through a graduated series of screens having diminishing mesh diameters. The four mesh sizes used ranged from 1.0 to 0.125 square centimeters, while the very small residual particles were collected in a final layer of doubled surgical gauze.

Table 2. Living cercopithecine and colobine subjects observed at Chicago Zoological Park

Species	Common name	Males	Females	Total
Presbytis obscurus	Spectacled langur		1	1
Colobus polykomos	Black colobus	1	2	3
Colobus guereza	Black-and-white colobus		2	2
Macaca nemestrina	Pigtailed macaque	1	1	2

Unequal quantities of food contained in the stomachs led to the adoption of the following technique: food materials were removed from the stomach of each individual and mixed with a beaker of water. The particles were put in suspension by agitating the beaker, then the mixture was poured into the stacked series of screens, so that the largest particles were trapped in the first screen and the smallest in the gauze. Approximately 2 or 3 percent loss of material occurred in *Presbytis* samples because of the presence of minute, partially digested particles of leaves. The contents of each screen was then transferred to a graduated cylinder containing fifty millimeters of water and was quantified according to the amount of resulting displacement.

Individual fragments of leaves were extracted from recombined screen samples of *Presbytis* and *Macaca*. Additional leaf fragment samples were obtained from *Cercopithecus ascanius* specimens but were not employed because observations of living guenons were not made. Leaf fragments were not present in *Hylobates* stomachs. Randomly selected leaf fragments were measured with vernier calipers and a calibrated binocular microscope. Measurements were made on undigested leaf fragments only. These could be distinguished from digested fragments by their clearly severed edges and sharply demarcated or angled projections. The leaf fragments were also examined microscopically for evidence of mechanical action of the dentition.

Living specimens of *Macaca, Presbytis,* and *Colobus* were given measured quantities of various food types in order to determine the number of chews required to process the food before swallowing (Tables 4, 5). Squares of escarole lettuce measuring 2 x 2 centimeters and apple pieces having dimensions of 1 x 1 x 2 centimeters were administered to each subject. The number of chews required to process the food prior to swallowing was recorded with the aid of an automatic blood cell counter.

The data were treated statistically by employing the University of Wisconsin SSRF computer program for analysis of variance (NWAY-1).

Observations on dental morphology were made on primarily unworn upper and lower second molars in order to assess the functionally significant aspects of cusp shape among the various genera. Worn dentitions were examined for patterns of wear and striations.

RESULTS

Assessment of the Stomach Contents by Screening

The texture of food in all genera reflected the predominance of particles between 0.125 and 0.5 centimeters. Relatively few coarsely chewed or whole food items (diameters exceeding 0.5 centimeters) were recovered from the entire sample (7.2 percent). Only 9.5 percent of the food particles were less than 0.125 centimeters (Figure 1).

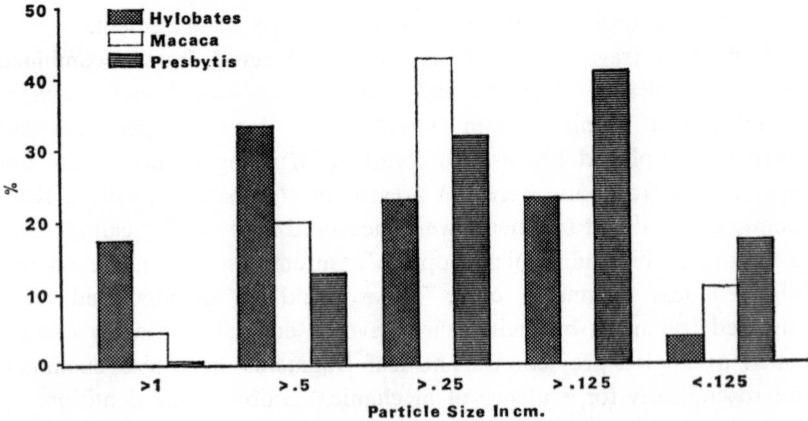

Figure 1. Histogram depicting the proportions of food particles of differing dimensions collected by means of a series of graduated screens

Hylobates lar stomachs contained the highest percentage of food items larger than 1.0 centimeter. Cross-generic comparison shows that approximately 80 percent of the food items greater than 1.0 centimeter in diameter were recovered from the stomachs of this genus, while *Macaca* had 18.8 percent and *Presbytis* the remaining 1.2 percent. Food items larger than 1.0 centimeter in diameter consisted of moderate-sized whole and partially chewed fruits and very large (greater than 2.0 centimeters) seeds or pits (Plate 1). Numbers of partially chewed wild figs also formed a modest proportion of the gibbon stomach contents that were collected in the first screen.

Figs, seeds, and leaf fragments formed the majority of large food particles in *Macaca* stomachs. These items comprised, however, a rather low percentage (4.0 percent) of the total range of particle sizes obtained from within-genus samples when compared with that of *Hylobates* (17 percent). Only a trace of material (0.2 percent) was present in *Presbytis* screen-one samples.

Particles less than 1.0 but greater than 0.5 centimeters comprised 21.8 percent of the combined samples of anthropoid genera. Cross-generic comparison demonstrated that *Hylobates* stomachs contained over 50 percent of the total screen-two materials. *Macaca* samples account for nearly one-third, while *Presbytis* increased to 18 percent of the total. Within-genera assessment demonstrated that *Macaca* stomachs were comprised of 19 percent particles of screen-two size. About one-third of *Hylobates* stomach contents were from this category, as were 12 percent of *Presbytis* stomach contents.

Macaca accounted for 44 percent of the screen-three sample of particles greater than 0.25 centimeters in diameter. Gibbon stomachs contributed 23 percent of the total screen-three sample, and *Presbytis* made up the remaining proportion of nearly one-third.

For the combined genera only 29 percent of the stomach contents were comprised of particles less than 0.25 but greater than 0.125 centimeters. *Presbytis* stomachs contained the largest proportion of this size category (47 percent). Gibbons and macaques contributed approximately equal proportions (slightly less than one-fourth each) of screen-four particles. Screen-four particles thus represent a very large proportion of the total *Presbytis* sample (40 percent).

Screen five (gauze) showed that extremely small food particles were considerably more abundant in the stomachs of *Presbytis* (53 percent); macaques contributed the remaining 11.0 percent. However, even in *Presbytis*, particles of less than 0.125 centimeters in diameter account for only 15 percent of the stomach contents. The fact that food particles of this size are primarily the result of the digestive process and not of mechanical action adds an additional complication.

The major differences in food particle size can be characterized by the manner in which each genus occupies an area of a normal curve. *Hylobates* stomachs containing the highest proportion of large food particles, comprise the ascending limb. *Macaca* samples dominate the central area, and *Presbytis* contributes more generously to the descending small-particle limb.

The assessment of the size of particles of food obtained from the stomachs of this anthropoid series clearly suggests that materials of initially comparable dimensions and texture are processed by the dentition less in gibbons than in either macaques or langurs. Langurs appear to have the most thoroughly masticated stomach contents, as would be expected for folivorous forms having food-fermenting forestomachs. While these differences are easy to demonstrate, the mechanism responsible is yet to be isolated and explained. More thorough mastication can be achieved by an increase in the number of chews or by an actual increase in the efficiency of the dentition for a particular food type. Leaves were therefore extracted from the stomachs and measured to control for food type.

Examination of Leaf Fragments from Macaque and Langur Stomachs

Examination of undigested leaf fragments provides a control for otherwise varied food items contained in the stomachs of the genera considered. *Hylobates* samples contained no leaves or remotely comparable plant materials and have been eliminated from this aspect of the study. Because the stomach contents of *Presbytis* consisted almost entirely of small leaf fragments, smears were prepared for examination under the microscope. *Macaca* leaf specimens were measured directly. Microscopic examination of undigested leaves contained in the stomachs of both genera demonstrated close comparability in their texture, thickness, and relative density of fibrous supportive networks. Although the screens were useful in revealing general differences in the texture of ingested food, the measurement of comparable food items permits statistical verification of the differences. Maximum and minimum primary dimensions of leaf fragments extracted from four macaque and six langur specimens yielded highly significant differences (Table 3).

Table 3. Analysis of variance table comparing maximum and minimum primary dimensions of leaf fragments (undigested) in macaques and langurs. Figures for maximum are above, minimum below. Both parameters are significantly different

Genus	N	X	$\sqrt{F} = t$	df	p
Macaca	4	3.2			
		2.5	3.71		
Presbytis	6	1.9	3.52	87	< 0.001
		1.6			

These data appear to verify the hypothesis that comparable food materials are treated differently before they reach the stomach. Leaves removed from *Cercopithecus ascanius* cheek pouches and stomachs were comparable to those of *Macaca,* which further suggests that the members of the Cercopithecinae are basically similar in their masticatory pattern.

Assessment of the Amount of Oral Processing

Systematic evaluation of the extent of masticatory action stimulated by measured amounts of differing foods was accomplished in a series of feeding experiments. A leafy material having two primary dimensions (escarole lettuce) and a homogeneous compact food substance having three primary dimensions (apple) were administered to captive subjects. Forty-nine separate feedings of pieces of lettuce 2 x 2 centimeters in size to five individuals of two colobine species and to two individuals of a macaque species yielded no demonstrable differences.

Colobine species chewed each piece of lettuce fewer times than did the macaque subjects (Table 4).

Table 4. Analysis of variance table comparing number of chews for lettuce

Genus	N	Trials	$\bar{x}$ N chews	$\sqrt{F} = t$	df	p
Macaca	2	16	11.6			
Colobus	5	23	7.9	1.9	49	< 0.100
Presbytis	1	10	10.6			

A more pronounced difference occurred between *Macaca* and *Colobus* than between *Macaca* and *Presbytis,* which suggests that the langurs are perhaps less efficient in handling leafy materials than are their African relatives. Both colobine genera, however, appear to be able to process leafy foods more readily than do the cercopithecine representatives if the differences in food particle size from the stomachs indicate the extent to which living representatives have processed the food offered in the experiment. This is the major uncertainty in our assessment.

Differences in the extent to which apple pieces were dentally processed are equally interesting. The analysis of the results of counting apple chews in fact produced a more highly significant difference among the genera (Table 5).

Table 5. Analysis of variance table comparing number of chews for apple pieces in three cercopithecoid genera

Genus	N	Trials	$\bar{x}$ N chews	$\sqrt{F} = t$	df	p
Macaca	2	18	27.2			
Colobus	5	40	23.6	6.34	109	<0.001
Presbytis	6	10	15.3			

The treatment of apple required considerably fewer masticatory strokes per unit weight in all three genera. This corresponding and relatively proportioned reduction in the number of chews associated with a different food type points out the high responsiveness of the chewing mechanism to varying textures and toughness of materials. The assessment strongly suggests that the major factor responsible for the differences in food particle size in the stomachs of the various genera under consideration is not the number of chews but the morphology of the dentition.

Qualitative Assessment of Leaf Fragments

Microscopic examination of leaf fragments recovered from the stomachs of cercopithecines and colobines supports the hypothesis that differences in dental morphology are sufficient to account for the ability to finely comminute leafy food materials. Chewed leaves from *Macaca* samples have on their surfaces cuts, punctures, and crushed areas that clearly correspond to the morphology of the molar cusps. The majority of these markings suggest that the dentition lacks sufficient shearing action to cut all the way through the leaf body. Instead, many criss-crossing partial cuts are produced along with evidence of tearing (Plate 3).

Leaf fragments obtained from *Presbytis* are less elongated and only rarely bear the marks of cusps on their interior. Instead, they are sheared cleanly along the edges into confettilike fragments. The mechanism responsible for these differences can be isolated by examining the teeth of the respective genera.

Functional Differences in Cercopithecoid Molar Morphology

Cercopithecoid molars are characterized by four well-developed main cusps which are separated into two lophs by a buccolingual groove. When viewed from the side, the molar cusps of the Colobinae are pointed and high relative to the buccolingual groove. Those of the Cercopithecinae are more rounded and relatively low.

One way to elucidate the functional significance of these differences in morphology is through the examination of occlusal contact areas (the area of the crown that comes in contact with the teeth of the opposing arch when the teeth are in occlusion). The contact area of the tooth can be measured by placing a thin sheet of wax between opposing teeth and applying pressure. This produces a thinned, translucent area in the wax where the opposing teeth come in direct contact. In *Macaca* the articulation between the cusps of M_1 and their maxillary foveae form round, circumscribed contacts (Figure 2). This type of contact produces a mortar-and-pestle action in which the occlusal fovea holds the food while the opposing cusp tip places compressive forces on it.

The contact areas formed between the molars of colobines differ considerably from those of *Macaca* (Figure 2). Articulation of the

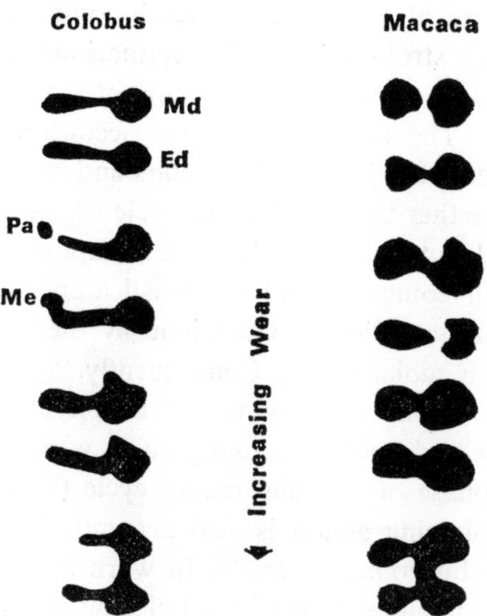

Figure 2. Contact areas between maxillary first molar and mandibular first and second molars of *Macaca fascicularis* and *Colobus badius* arranged in order of increasing wear. Md, Ed, Pa, and Me mark the points of contact of the metaconid, entoconid, paracone, and metacone respectively.

unworn metaconid and entoconid with the maxillary teeth produces rounded occlusal contacts, similar to those found in *Macaca*. Colobines differ from cercopithecines, however, in that the crests between protoconid and metaconid and between hypoconid and entoconid make a continuous, well-defined contact with the occlusal and interproximal grooves of the upper teeth in unworn specimens. This suggests that the buccolingual crests of the colobine teeth may perform a shearing action. This interpretation is strengthened by examination of microscopic patterns of occlusal abrasion. In the molars of the Colobinae, wear striations are concentrated along the sides of the buccolingual crest (Plate 2D). This suggests forceful contact between the sides of the crests during mastication. The molars of the Cercopithecinae contrast with those of the colobines in that heavy concentrations of wear striations are present on the wear facets at the tips of the cusps (Plate 2C), indicating that much of the triturating action of cercopithecine teeth is produced while food is stabilized in the occlusal fovea and crushed with the tip of the cusp. In both the Colobinae and the Cercopithecinae, wear decreases the integrity of the buccolingual crests because of the disproportionate amount of wear on the lingual maxillary cusps and buccal mandibular cusps (Plate 2A, B). In the Colobinae and to a lesser extent the Cercopithecinae, the wear differential between the buccal and lingual cusps would tend to reduce the amount of vertical shear that the teeth could potentially produce. If the masticatory stroke of the Cercopithecinae were limited to an orthal closing movement, the efficiency of worn teeth would be severely reduced. The analysis of molar occlusion (Mills 1963) and the analysis of wear striations on the molars and incisors (Walker 1973) suggests, however that the masticatory cycle of the Cercopithecidae is not purely orthal but has a considerable component of lateral movement. The lateral component of the masticatory stroke seems to be particularly accentuated in the Colobinae by the channeling effect of the relatively high molar cusps. Consequently, a leaf placed between the teeth of a *Colobus* monkey would be pierced by sharp lingual mandibular cusps and buccal maxillary cusps when the jaw was closed during the first phase of the masticatory cycle (Figures 2,4A). In unworn teeth the piercing action is also accompanied by vertical shear produced by the buccolingual crests. In worn teeth this type of shear is of reduced significance. If the initial closing movement of the mandible is followed by or synchronous with a medial movement of the mandible (on the working side), the cusps that initially pierced the leaf would produce considerable shredding action that would be of value to a leaf-eating animal (Figure 3). The low, rounded cusps of the Cercopithecinae therefore differ considerably in function from those of the Colobinae. They do not possess the potential for efficient shredding of leafy materials during mediolateral excursions of the mandible.

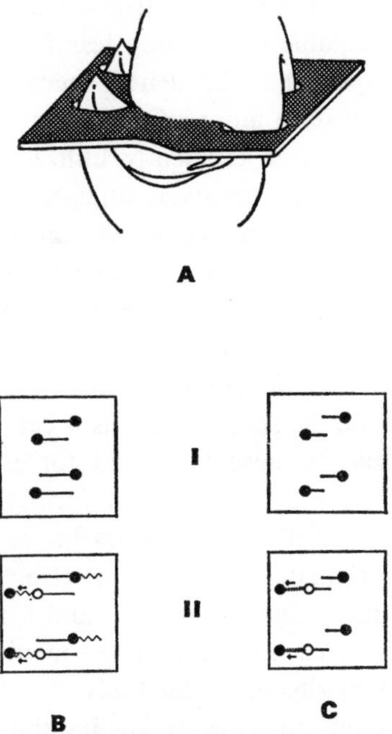

Figure 3. (A) Diagrammatic drawing of occluded left mandibular and maxillary second molars of *Presbytis*, depicting the manner of piercing an object with two primary dimensions (leaf) with the apical portions of the buccal cusps of M^2 and lingual cusps of M_2. Schematic representation of the manner in which the cusps of *Presbytis* (B) sever and tear leaves compared with *Macaca* (C). In phase I the teeth are occluded as depicted in A. Phase II shows the results of lateral excursion of the mandible. Circles depict pre-excursion position of lingual cusps of lower molar. Zig-zag lines represent tearing of the leaf tissue by the puncturing apical portions of the cusps. In *Macaca* (C) hachures represent crushing during lateral excursion because cusp tips typically do not puncture the leaf. Unbroken lines represent primary loph shearing which occurs during occlusal phase I

DISCUSSION

The results of this series of procedures provide convincing evidence for the existence of pronounced differences in function that would be difficult, if not impossible, to discern employing standard odontometrics (measurement of crown length and breadth and cusp height). In the case of fossils, variance in the metrical attributes of teeth alone may not be valid grounds for taxonomic differentiation or inclusion. The definition of functional attributes that connote adaptive shifts provides a more meaningful basis for classification (Szalay 1968). The size of teeth expressed in terms of total occlusal surface area is an important consideration only when functional attributes are taken into account. Small mammals are capable of exerting less force on foods than are large ones. This suggests that the dental mechanisms for processing a given type of food must be more refined in small forms because less available force must be more efficiently utilized in order to perform the same masticatory task. Moreover, enamel can withstand only a certain amount of stress (Yamada 1970). Small mammals exerting less force on the enamel have the potential to develop high, narrow cusps which serve to concentrate forces at their apexes. Within a given lineage larger forms having more powerful masticatory muscles will sometimes show less specific response to a given dietary specialty because of limitations on the shapes that cusps can assume under higher compressive forces and because increased forces by themselves are sufficient for processing the food without further functional elaboration. Consequently, the dietary differences between chimpanzees and gorillas and between siamangs and gibbons (Chivers 1972) are probably expressed in terms of increased body and tooth size of the more vegetarian species within each lineage. In the medium-sized cercopithecines, colobines, and hylobatines, the body size factor is sufficiently similar so that functional attributes expressing their dietary proclivities are anticipated even though standard odontometric techniques are not particularly effective for describing these differences. This is because overall dimensions of teeth are only secondarily related to the biomechanical differences between the dentitions of the cercopithecines and colobines.

The analysis of contact areas and wear striations in conjunction with the examination of stomach contents implicates several features of cusp morphology that determine the differences in the molar efficiency of the Cercopithecinae and the Colobinae in processing food materials with two primary dimensions:

1. The height of the buccal maxillary cusp pairs (lingual mandibular cusp pairs) relative to the distance between cusp tips is related to the ability to pierce and also produce vertical shear (Figure 4).
2. The angle produced by the two planes that form the lingual surface of the buccal maxillary cusp pairs (buccal surface of the lingual mandibular cusp pairs) tends to shred thin, broad food objects

when the mandible is moved laterally on the working side (Figure 4).

The principles that we have illustrated for defining functionally significant attributes of teeth could be of considerable importance when properly applied to the highly confused systematics of Tertiary pongids, hylobatids, cercopithecids, and perhaps oreopithecids. Forms within a lineage having approximately similar body and tooth dimensions should be examined for subtle qualitative differences in cusp shape. Likewise, forms having similar tooth morphologies but differing significantly in body and tooth size may represent a primary adaptive shift. Our anthropoid series serves to demonstrate this potential. However, it is necessary to consider the difference between a culminated evolutionary sequence and one that is commencing differentiation. An understanding of the functionally significant aspects of dental morphology should permit apprehension of an adaptive shift because even incipient (but consistently present) manifestations of a fully developed characteristic found in modern forms can be employed to indicate a divergent trend. Understanding of the mechanical principles responsible for dental morphology will permit clarification of the function of dentitions for which analogous culminated or modern lineages are absent.

Our data suggest that selective pressures acting on the masticatory

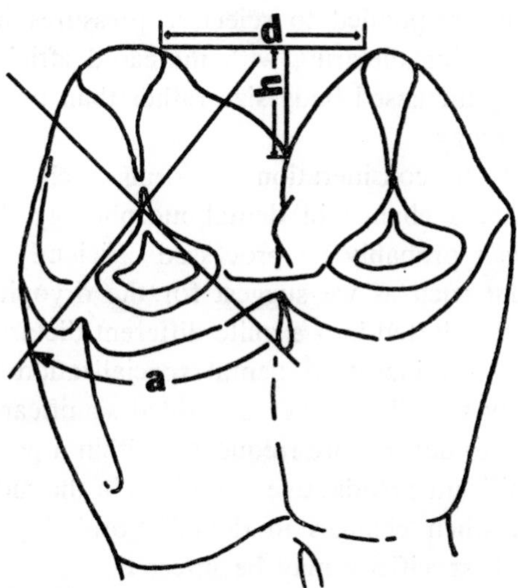

Figure 4. Illustration of mandibular first molar of *Macaca* showing measurements of functionally significant features of cusp morphology. Relative cusp height equals distance between cusp tips (d) divided by height of cusp tips relative to buccal lingual groove (h). Angle (a) is produced by the two planes that form the lingual surface of the buccal maxilary cusps (buccal surface of the lingual mandibular cusps)

apparatus are directly related to the relative difficulty of transforming food into energy. Foods with a high fiber content (mature leaves, stems, etc.) must be processed by the dentition to a much higher degree of refinement than those with a low fiber content. Studies of ruminant digestion have demonstrated that foods having high fiber content are processed longer by the digestive tract and are masticated more thoroughly (Stobbs and Cowper 1972). Food removed from the stomachs of *Hylobates* exemplify the lesser importance of mastication of high energy potential, low fiber content diets. Whole or scarcely chewed fruits in gibbon stomachs attest to the rapidity of ingestion and the probable lack of stringent selective pressure acting on the dentition. This may account for the high degree of dental variability reported for gibbons by Frisch (1965).

The siamang's proclivity for young leaves and shoots (Chivers 1972) is probably indicated by increase in body size, a feature that can incur two major advantages for the animal: (1) increased size of the masticatory muscles supplying more power to the dentition for the processing of slightly tougher foods, and (2) more efficient maintenance of metabolic heat than in the smaller, active forms. Because leaves are abundant compared to fruit, the high energy expenditure of moving rapidly from one food source to another is avoided. Perhaps the dryopithecines responded to selective pressures in an analogous manner, differentiating dietarily, with increased efficiency being supplied primarily by increased body size rather than by marked changes in dental morphology.

This brings us to consideration of forms such as *Ramapithecus* which do indicate a change in dental morphology. Because a wide range of diets can probably be processed efficiently by simple allometric adjustment such as we suggest for the dryopithecines, *Ramapithecus* must have shifted into a quite different dietary adaptive zone, one that selected for increased dental specialization rather than for alteration of body size. This takes on added significance because size variation appears to occur more frequently within a population than do functionally significant preadaptive variations in the morphology of the dentition. Thus, when changes in dental morphology occur, dietary changes of a high specificity may be inferred.

Functional analysis of cercopithecoid molar morphology suggests that an adaptive shift away from frugivory toward leaf eating must have occurred. This divergence may be exemplified by considering *Parapithecus,* which has low, rounded cusps and narrow, laniary incisors, as a possible stem form. As has been suggested, the inclusion of leaves and shoots in the diet could be accomplished by increase in body size. In fact, size differences do occur in *Parapithecus* and Simons (1970) has suggested such a trend. However, forms that began to include mature leaves and other browse in their diets and that were also relatively small would have required dental specializations. Selective pressures refined the dentitions of stem Colobinae for more efficient browsing, while the Cercopithecidae apparently did not develop a regime exclusively of leaves. It appears that certain members of the typically omnivorous cercopithecines, particularly *Cercopithecus*, have reinvaded the primarily frugivorous adaptive zone. *Cercopithecus* species reflect this in their loss of the hypoconulid on the M_3 and in the presence of low cusps with broad lophs and rather poorly defined shearing crests. Simons (1970) points to the similarities between the talapoin monkey (*Cercopithecus talapoin*) and *Parapithecus*, implying that the molars of *Cercopithecus* reflect the primitive cercopithecine condition. We suggest that these similarities are functional ones and should not be taken as an indication of a direct phylogenetic relationship between this small species of guenon and *Parapithecus*. Fossil evidence suggests that the molar specializations of *Cercopithecus* evolved after macaquelike five-cusped dentitions represented by *Victoriapithecus* of the African Vindobonian appeared.

SUMMARY AND CONCLUSIONS

The primary objective of this paper was to present evidence for significant differences in dental efficiency between two closely related anthropoids having similar molar morphology. The assessments of food particle sizes, leaf fragments, and numbers of masticatory strokes characteristic of each genus indicate that important functional differences exist. Examination of the dentitions of cercopithecines and colobines permitted definition in each genus of the important functional attributes which can account for marked differences in the ability to chew coarse, fibrous foods having two primary dimensions. Definition of the mechanical principles that are closely associated with specific dietary requirements permits more accurate assessment of fossil lineages than do standard odontometric techniques which do not take into account subtle angles, facets, and planes of the teeth responsible for translating forces to food materials.

REFERENCES

CHIVERS, D.
1972 The siamang and gibbon in the Malay Peninsula. *Gibbon and Siamang* 1:103–135.

FOODEN, J.
1971 Report on the primates collected in western Thailand, January-April 1969. *Fieldiana Zoology* 59:1–62.

FRISCH, J.
1965 Trends in the evolution of hominid dentitions. *Bibliotheca Primatologica* 3:1–30.

JOLLY, C.
1970 The seed eaters: a new model of hominid differentiation. *Man* 5:5–26.

MILLS, J.
1963 "Occlusion and malocclusion of the teeth of primates," in *Dental anthropology*. Edited by D. R. Brothwell, 29–54. New York: Pergamon Press.

SIMONS, E.
1970 "The deployment and history of Old World monkeys (Cercopithecidae, Primates)," in *Old World monkeys*. Edited by J. R. Napier and P. H. Napier. New York: Academic Press.

STOBBS, T., L. COWPER
1972 Automatic measurement of the jaw movements of dairy cows during grazing and rumination. *Tropical grasslands* 6:107–111.

SZALAY, F.
1968 The beginnings of primates. *Evolution* 22:19–36.

WALKER, P.
1973 "Wear striations on the incisors of the Cercopithecidae." *American Journal of Physical Anthropology* 40:155.

YAMADA, H.
1970 *Strength of biological materials*. Baltimore: Williams and Wilkins.

The Role of Cheek Pouches in Cercopithecine Monkey Adaptive Strategy

PETER MURRAY

Members of the subfamily Cercopithecinae can be differentiated from other Cercopithecoidea by the presence of cheek pouches and by the lack of gastrointestinal specializations characteristic of the Colobinae. This article deals explicitly with the ecological and behavioral correlates of cheek pouch function. The reader can acquire further anatomical information in Fahrenholz (1937), Geist (1931), Gregory and McGregor (1914), Hanel (1932), Hill (1966, 1969), Huber (1931b), Lightoller (1928), Ruge (1887), Schneider (1958), and Stanley, Moor-Jankowski, and Grayowski (1965). A detailed assessment of the structure of the cheek pouches is given in Murray (1973).

Determination of the level of biological activity in which a structure plays an active role is a prerequisite for assessing its value for phylogenetic and taxonomic purposes. Because the cheek pouches have been mployed for many years to denote cercopithecine monkey separation from the Colobinae, elucidation of the adaptive meaning of

I thank many individuals and the several Institutions who made this study possible. Dr. Russell Tuttle of the University of Chicago was my primary source of guidance. I am indebted to him for a model for creative scientific inquiry and as the source for many of the approaches applied in this article. Much valuable information was acquired during a visit to the Southwestern Foundation for Research and Education in San Antonio, Texas. Dr. Hummer permitted me to work freely with the animals and placed me in contact with those persons who could further my research. Among the many persons who assisted me were Dr. Nancy Campbell, Dr. Andrew Hendrickx, Dr. Eby and Mr. Cornelio Celaya. The excellent facilities of the Chicago Zoological Park, Brookfield, Illinois, and an especially creative and helpful member of their staff, Dr. Benjamin Beck, are also thanked for their substantial contributions to this investigation.

Support for this study was provided by an NDEA Title IV Fellowship and the Committee on Evolutionary Biology (Hines Fund), The University of Chicago.

these organs should provide insights into the phylogenetic background of the stem Cercopithecoidea. Moreover, the ubiquitous presence of cheek pouches within the Cercopithecinae links the entire adaptive array to a fundamental adaptive zone that is otherwise obfuscated by numerous minor specializations and adaptive radiations. An understanding of the fundamental adaptive zone of the cercopithecine monkey lineage can facilitate the reconstruction of major events in the evolution of the subfamily. The major difficulties in pinpointing the derivation of each living cercopithecine monkey genus stem from their considerable morphological homogeneity, combined with a paucity of fossil materials and a lack of paleoecological evidence.

Careful analysis of the anatomical and behavioral data derived from the study of cercopithecine monkey cheek pouches provides a basis for inferring the pattern of adaptive radiation of the group that no other structure seems to imply. This is due primarily to the complex interrelationship of the organs with the animal's biology. The cheek pouches are an interface between behavior and morphology, and as such require an examination of the total biology of the organism for their explanation.

Differences in the degree of development and extent of employment of the cheek pouches among various cercopithecine monkey genera appear to be accurate indications of specializations leading away from the fundamental cercopithecine adaptive zone. Consequently, it has been possible to suggest which of the living genera are closest behaviorally, ecologically, and presumably, morphologically to the stem Cercopithecinae, and which are the farthest removed.

METHODS AND MATERIALS

The facial region and cheek pouches of forty-five cercopithecine monkey cadavers, representing all currently accepted living genera, were dissected and measured (Table 1). The technique for measuring the cheek pouches is based on that of Jones (1970) and Fooden (1964), who measured the area of stomachs and other portions of the gastrointestinal tracts of various anthropoids. The cheek pouches were measured in the collapsed and fixed condition by removing them from the cadaver, slitting them down the posterior crease, and laying over them an acetate grid marked off at five-millimeter intervals. Measurements were defined dorsally at the level of the orific, and in other primary dimensions by the natural contours of the pouch. The total area of both cheek pouches was then compared with the total body weight

ble 1. Specimens measured and described (cadaveric)

cies	Number	Age	Sex	Source
caca				
rctoides	UC-SF1	Adult	Female	University of Chicago primate lab
rctoides	UC-SF4	Adult	Female	University of Chicago primate lab
ulatta	UC-RF2	Adult	Female	University of Chicago primate lab
ulatta	UC-RF3	Adult	Female	University of Chicago primate lab
ulatta	UC-RF5	Adult	Female	University of Chicago primate lab
ulatta	UC-RF9	Adult	Female	University of Chicago primate lab
ulatta	UC-RF6	Immature	Female	University of Chicago primate lab
ulatta	UC-RM2	Immature	Male	University of Chicago primate lab
ascicularis	-IM4	Immature	Male	University of Chicago primate lab
ascicularis	-IF4	Adult	Female	University of Chicago primate lab
emestrina	UC-NM4	Adult	Male	University of Chicago primate lab
emestrina	UC-NM5	Adult	Male	University of Chicago primate lab
emestrina	UC-NM3	Immature	Male	University of Chicago primate lab
copithecus				
eglectus	UC-444	Adult	Male	University of Chicago primate lab
eglectus	UC-105	Adult	Male	University of Chicago primate lab
iana	UC-643	Adult	Female	University of Chicago primate lab
iana	UW-F31	Adult	Female	University of Wisconsin primate lab
ethiops	UC-AE1	Adult	—	University of Chicago primate lab
ethiops	UC-AE3	Adult	—	University of Chicago primate lab
ethiops	UC-AE4	Adult	—	University of Chicago primate lab
scanius	UC-SP6	Adult	Male	University of Chicago primate lab
scanius	UW-F31	Adult	Female	University of Wisconsin primate lab
scanius	UW-F32	Adult	Female	University of Wisconsin primate lab
scanius	UW-F33	Adult	Female	University of Wisconsin primate lab
scanius	UW-M34	Adult	Male	University of Wisconsin primate lab
scanius	UW-M35	Adult	Male	University of Wisconsin primate lab
throcebus				
atas	UC-PA1	Adult	Female	University of Chicago primate lab
atas	UC-903	Immature	Female	University of Chicago primate lab
cocebus				
lbigena	UW-F31	Adult	Female	University of Wisconsin primate lab
lbigena	UW-F32	Adult	Female	University of Wisconsin primate lab
lbigena	UW-M35	Adult	Male	University of Wisconsin primate lab
lbigena	UW-M36	Adult	Male	University of Wisconsin primate lab
lbigena	UW-M38	Adult	Male	University of Wisconsin primate lab
orquatus	UW-F33	Adult	Female	University of Wisconsin primate lab
orquatus	UW-M34	Adult	Male	University of Wisconsin primate lab
orquatus	UW-M37	Adult	Male	University of Wisconsin primate lab
io				
nubis	UC-166	Immature	Male	University of Chicago primate lab
nubis	UC-PO7	Adult	Male	University of Chicago primate lab
p.	UC-POM	Immature	Male	University of Chicago primate lab
p.	SWF-3	Adult	Female	Southwestern Foundation
amadryas	UC-HA1	Immature	Male	University of Chicago primate lab
apio	UW-M21	Adult	Male	University of Wisconsin primate lab
eropithecus				
elada	UC-GM1	Adult	Male	University of Chicago primate lab
elada	UC-GM2	Adult	Male	University of Chicago primate lab
elada	UC-GM3	Immature	Male	University of Chicago primate lab

of each individual. In order to render the measurements equivalent, the resulting ratio between cheek pouch area and body weight was corrected by the formula $\frac{\sqrt{A}}{\sqrt[3]{W}} \times 100$.

A "scatterplot" program run on the Univac 1108 computer processed the data statistically. Fitted scatter diagrams, correlation coefficients, and regressions were calculated.

The behavioral studies were made at Lincoln Park Zoo, Chicago; Chicago Zoological Park; The Southwestern Foundation for Research and Education, San Antonio; the University of Chicago; and the University of Wisconsin-Milwaukee. Film footage of free-ranging baboons was also employed in the analysis.

CERCOPITHECINE CHEEK POUCH STRUCTURE

The cheek pouches of cercopithecine monkeys are bilateral, oblong sacculations formed in the inferior portion of the buccinator pocket (Figure 1 A, C). Each cheek pouch is provided with a slitlike orifice capable of considerable lateral distension in accordance with the varying sizes of food objects. In most species, the orifice of the cheek pouch extends from interproximal P_4-M_1 to interproximal M_2-M_3. The interior of the cheek pouches is lined with typical mucous membrane. Concentrations of mucous and in some cases seromucous glands are located in the anterior and posterior creases of the pouch and around the orifice. These glandular tracts are aligned with the passage of food in and out of the cheek pouches and are presumed important for lubrication of the mucous membrane (Figure 1 D).

A functional relationship between the parotid duct and the orifice of the cheek pouches occurs in all genera. The parotid duct pierces the buccinator muscle at its extreme posterosuperior aspect on the lateral side, to open internally at the level of the gingival junction of interproximal M^1 and M^2, directly above the posterior portion of the cheek pouch orifice (Figure 1 D).

The size and position of the cheek pouches in the various genera are among the more important differences applicable to the interpretation of function. The general uniformity in the musculature and the wide range of variation in the distribution and density of buccal glands negate their usefulness in the reconstruction of phylogenesis. Size and position of the cheek pouches, however, appear to be fairly constant features (Figures 1 C, 2–6).

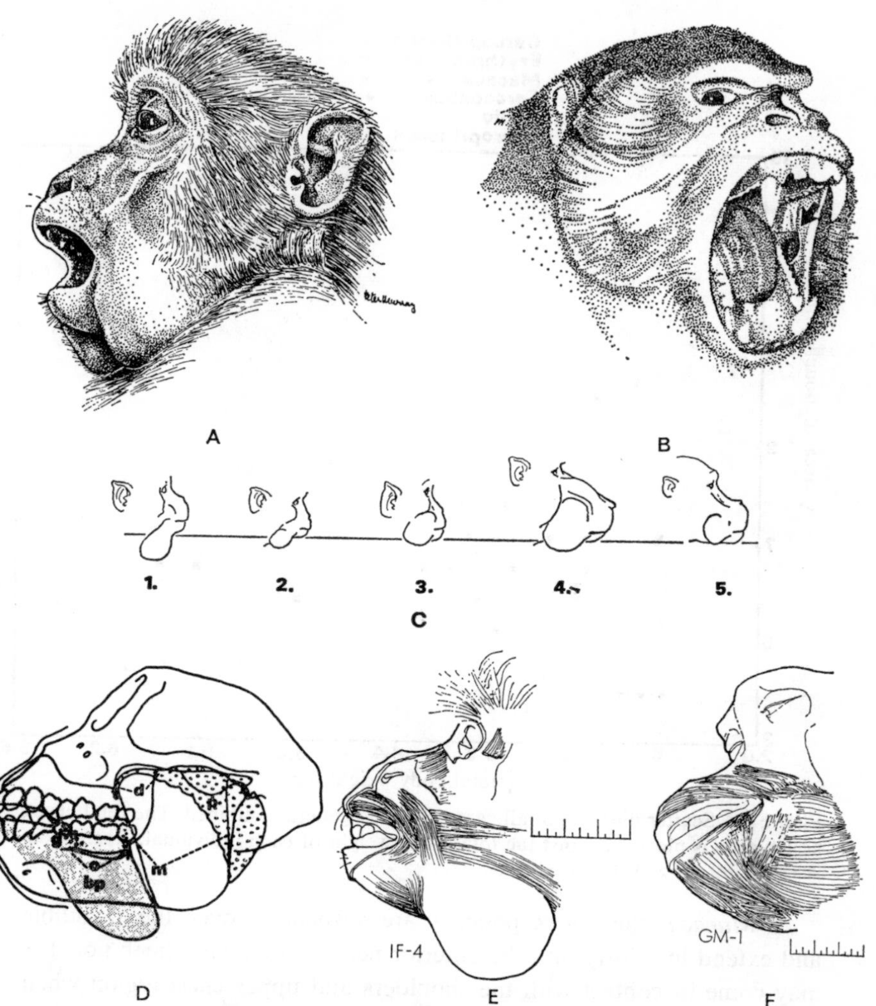

Figure 1. (A) External view of buccal pouch of a rhesus monkey (*Macaca mulatta*) filled to capacity (drawn from a cadaver). (B) Drawing of a pig-tailed macaque (*Macaca nemestrina*) showing the position of the orifice of the buccal pouch (arrow) on the left side of the cavum oris. Drawn from a photograph in Napier and Napier (1967). (C) Positions and relative sizes of the cheek pouches of a series of cercopithecine monkeys; horizontal line represents the level of the inferior border of the mandible. (1) *Macaca*; (2) *Cercopithecus*; (3) *Cercocebus*; (4) *Papio*; and (5) *Theropithecus*. (D) Diagrammatic drawing showing major relationships of the cheek pouches and adnexal structures: g, buccal glands; o, orifice; bp, buccal pouch (stipple shows buccinator-orbicularis oris complex); d, parotid duct; p, parotid gland; m, masseter muscle. (E) Dissection of a crab-eating macaque (*Macaca fascicularis*) displaying the facial muscles associated with the buccal pouches; scale in millimeters. (F) Dissection of a gelada adult male (*Theropithecus gelada*) showing anomalous unilateral absence of the cheek pouch on the left side. Compare with E; scale in millimeters

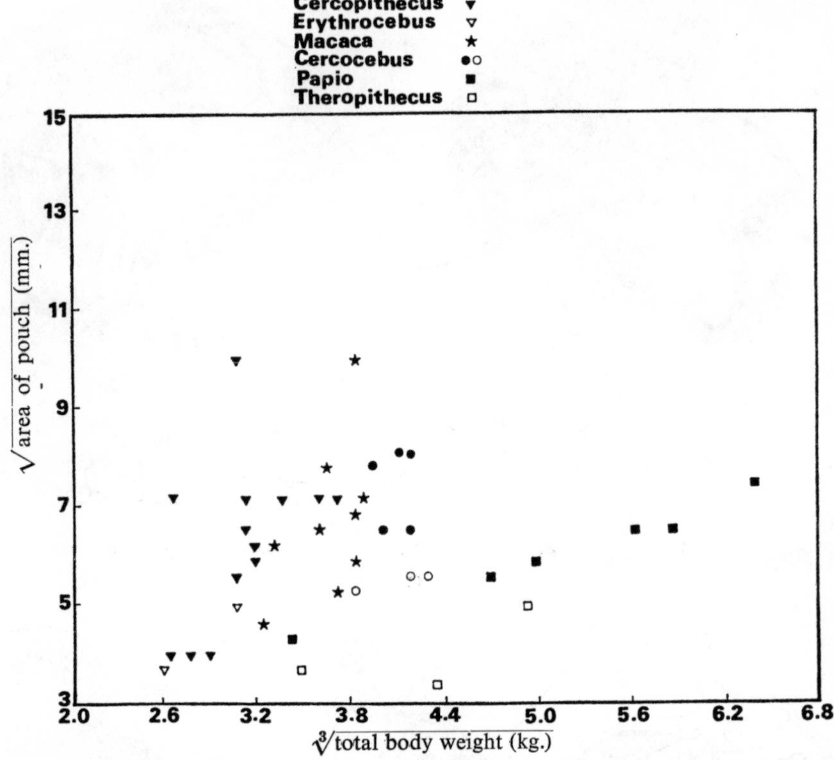

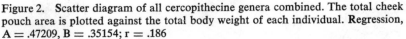

Figure 2. Scatter diagram of all cercopithecine genera combined. The total cheek pouch area is plotted against the total body weight of each individual. Regression, A = .47209, B = .35154; r = .186

In *Macaca*, the cheek pouches are suspended over the mandible and extend inferiorly into the anterior neck region. The cheek pouches may come in contact with the shoulders and upper chest region when filled to capacity. The body of the cheek pouch expands to its maximum dimension at or below the level of the inferior border of the mandible. Macaques possess the largest cheek pouches of the subfamily absolutely, as well as relatively, on the basis of the ratio of cheek pouch area to total body weight. The mean ratio calculated for macaques is .40. Members of the genus *Cercopithecus* are morphologically similar to macaques with regard to the cheek pouches, which tend to be slightly smaller, however, having a mean ratio for the genus of .37. The mean ratio for closely related *Erythrocebus* is .31, which is near the lowest range recorded for *Cercopithecus* (.29 in *Cercopithecus aethiops*). *Cercocebus* cheek pouches are slightly less elongated and tend to have their maximum diameter at, or slightly above,

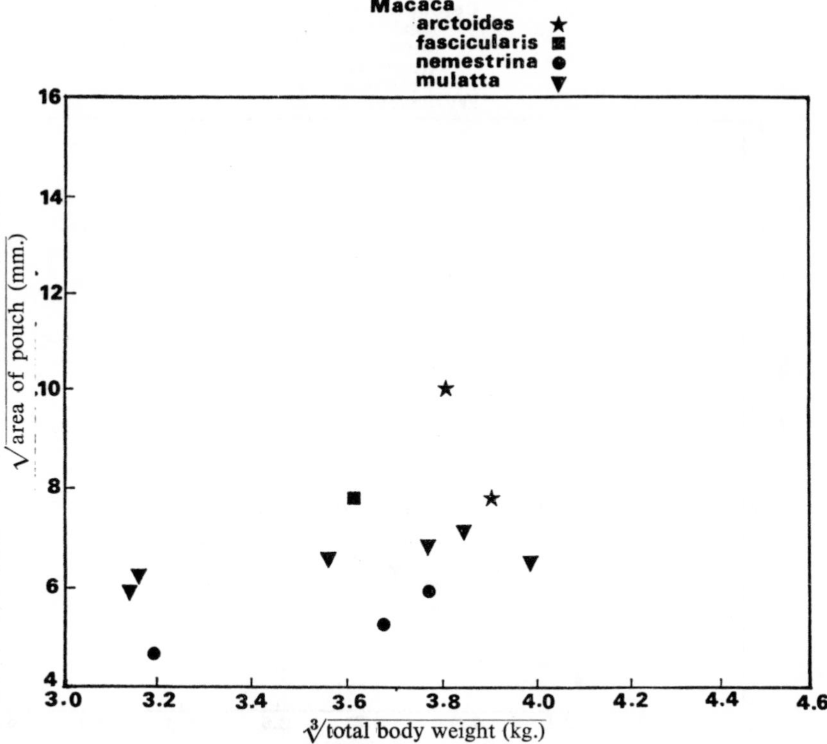

Figure 3. Scatter diagram of the area of the cheek pouches of *Macaca* spp. plotted against the body weight of each individual. Regression, A = —.22372, B = .24353; r = .516

the level of the inferior border of the mandible. The cheek pouches of *Cercocebus* are comparable to those of *Cercopithecus* and *Macaca* in being quite large (mean ratio of .37).

Smaller cheek pouches are characteristic of *Papio*, which has a mean ratio of cheek pouch area to body weight of .25. The cheek pouches tend to develop their maximum diameter above the inferior border of the mandible, and food may be held in the superior buccinator sulcus, so that the cheek pouches occasionally appear to protrude into the animal's visual field. *Theropithecus* has the smallest cheek pouches, both absolutely and relatively, of the entire series. The computed cheek pouch area–body weight ratio for this genus is .19, less than half the proportional area found in *Macaca*. In addition, the cheek pouches of *Theropithecus* are shallow and poorly expressed. Unilateral development of the cheek pouches was encountered in one adult specimen.

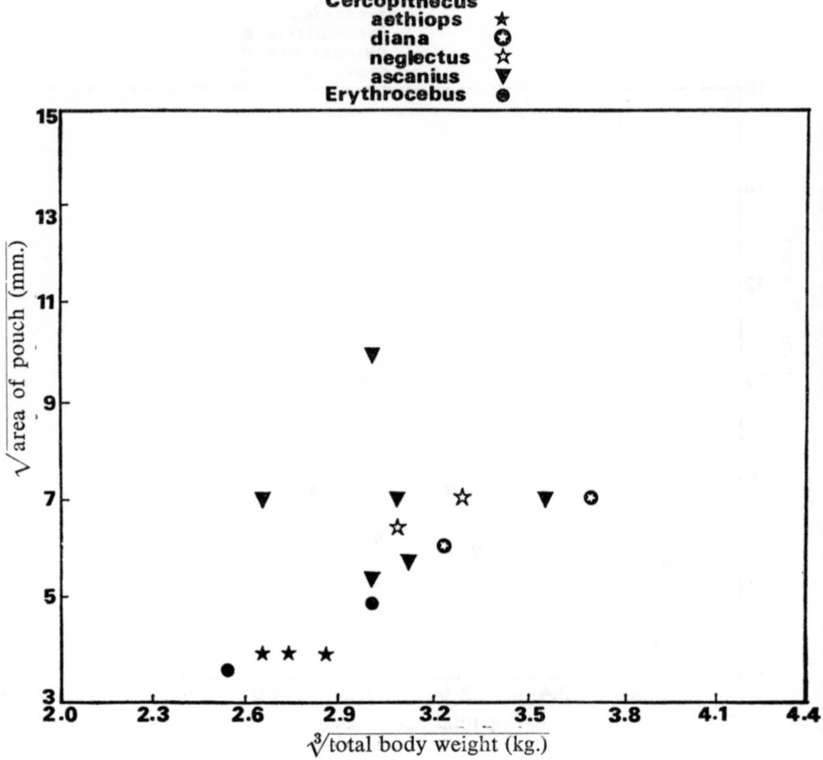

Figure 4. Scatter diagram of the area of the cheek pouches of *Cercopithecus* spp. and *Erythrocebus patas* plotted against the body weight of each individual. Regression, A = .28154, B = .28739; r = .527

The differences in cheek pouch size appear to be related to a combination of factors. At the extreme ends of the continuum, selection appears to operate on size, while the series also expresses an apparent allometric relationship in which the larger animals tend to have smaller cheek pouches. In addition to these variables, a third element, the relative frequency of employment of the cheek pouches, adds a measurable degree of ontogenetic influence.

Theropithecus gelada expresses qualitative as well as quantitative differences in the degree of development of the cheek pouches. The musculature is sparse and thin, and the cheek pouches are shallow and occasionally difficult to locate. Unilateral development of the pouches strongly suggests that the structure is trending toward becoming vestigial (Figure 1 F). Had I been unable to observe the gelada employ its cheek pouches or had I missed Crook and Aldrich-Blake's

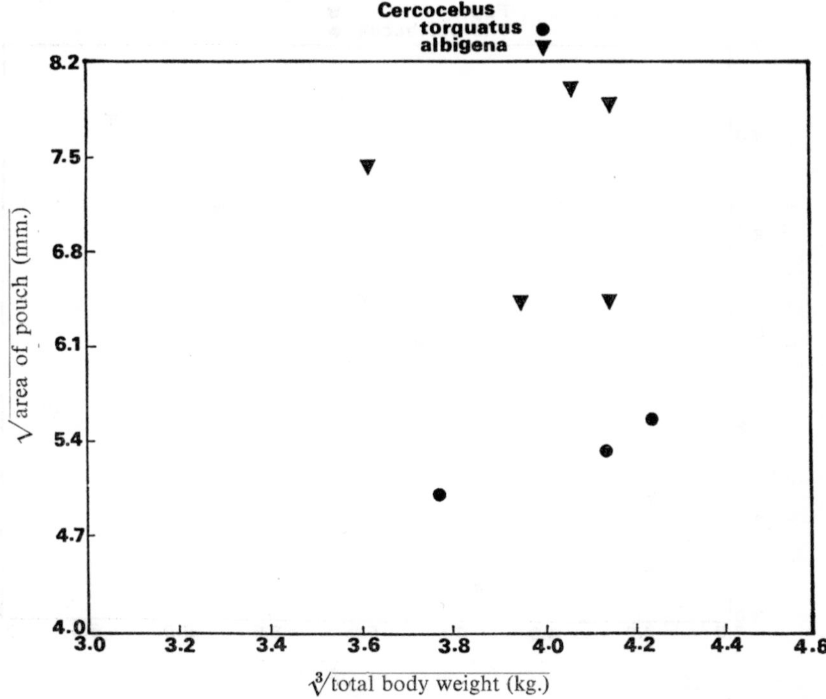

Figure 5. Scatter diagram of the area of the cheek pouches of *Cercocebus torquatus* and *Cercocebus albigena* plotted against the total body weight of each individual. Regression, A = .83292, B = .45502; r = —.082 (*C. torquatus* tends to be more terrestrial than the *albigena* mangabeys)

(1968) observation of their use, I would have considered them vestigial structures. In *Macaca* the cheek pouches tend to be enormous, and they have associated structural features that accommodate their considerable expansion into the gular region. In most species of *Macaca,* conspicuous, loose, skin folds originate at the angles of the mandible and continue inferiorly into the medial upper chest region. These expand with underlying tissues as the pouch is being filled.

The extent to which allometry can be implicated is unclear. The ideal allometric relationship is one in which the entire series expresses a highly correlated size relationship between the structure in question and the total body weight, length, or some other expression of body size. In the cercopithecine monkey sequence, the macaques are larger than the guenons, yet they do not have correspondingly smaller cheek pouches. The samples of *Cercocebus albigena* and *Cercocebus torquatus* have similar body sizes, yet the cheek pouches were consist-

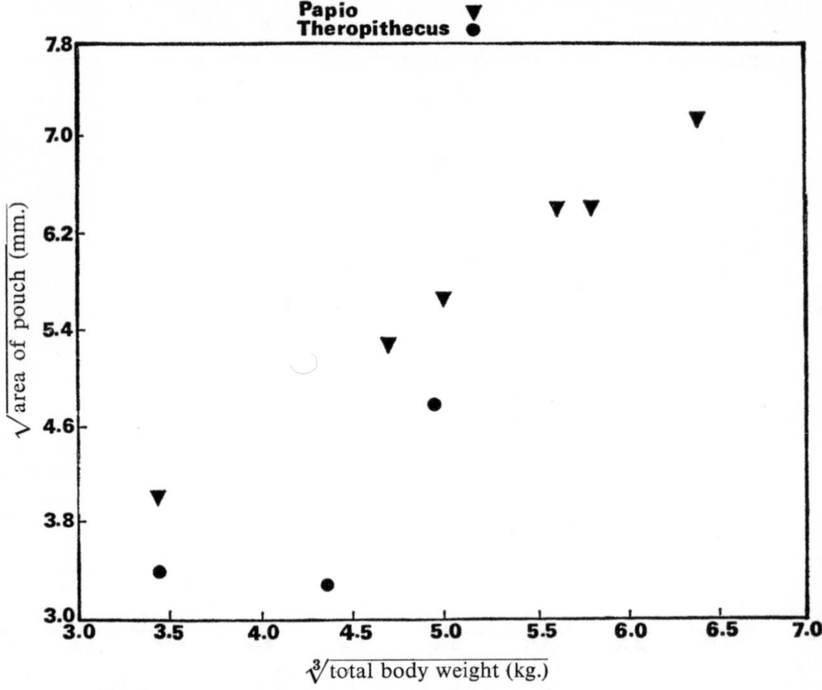

Figure 6. Scatter diagram of the area of the cheek pouches of *Papio* and *Theropithecus* plotted against the body weight of each individual. Regression, A = –.11555, B = .12929; r = .922 (for combined genera)

ently smaller in the *torquatus* form. Finally, the *Papio* samples as compared with *Theropithecus* show a comparable reversal of the trend: *Papio* is larger, yet has more cheek pouch area than smaller *Theropithecus*. Thus, if negative allometry is a factor, it is certainly being obscured by other variables. Statistical assessment of this problem further suggests that allometry is not the only variable being expressed. Correlation coefficients between body weight and cheek pouch size on the entire series should be high if an allometric relationship is entirely responsible. This is not the case since the r for all species combined was .19. Conversely, much higher correlation coefficients were obtained on samples grouped by genus, ranging from .52 in *Macaca* to .98 in *Papio*. This clearly implies that the size of the cheek pouches is highly correlated with the body weight within a given genus, but other factors, presumably reflecting adaptive differences, are strongly influencing an apparent allometric trend.

An ontogenetic factor influencing cheek pouch dimension was detected by examining the cheek pouch tissues. In *Cercopithecus* and

Macaca, mature individuals have developed a "set" in the cheek pouches that renders them more or less permanently expanded. The thickness of the tissues of the lateral wall of the pouches diminishes as well. In very old individuals, enormous, very thin-walled cheek pouches were encountered. Some of these had formed adhesions with overlying and underlying tissues and could not be removed without taking the skin and facial muscles as well. The tendency to develop permanently stretched cheek pouches is believed to be an expression of the frequency of employment and the extent to which the cheek pouches are filled to their maximum capacity. The cheek pouches of adult *Papio*, for example, tend to be thick walled and relatively shallow.

FUNCTION OF CERCOPITHECINE MONKEY CHEEK POUCHES

Two general hypotheses for cheek pouch function in the Cercopithecinae have been discussed in previous literature. The most obvious function of the cheek pouches is to "separate intake and digestion of food and to assign each of these actions a special locality" (Hediger 1964). Several suggestions in the primate literature have been to this effect. Hill (1966) notes the advantages of the cheek pouches in crop-raiding forays by *Cercopithecus* monkeys. Napier and Napier (1967) and Napier (1970) recognize the value of cheek pouches in the exploitation of terrestrial resources and imply a terrestrial heritage for the entire subfamily. Gautier-Hion (1971) suggests that the cheek pouches are important assets for the talapoin (*Cercopithecus talapoin*) in making terrestrial forays and in conspecific competition for food.

Gautier-Hion (1971) also suggests that the cheek pouches are important in salivary predigestion of foods. This exemplifies the second group of hypotheses of cheek pouch function — the implication of a physiological contribution. Owen (1835, 1841) opened this line of speculation in his investigation of the stomachs of colobine monkeys. He suggested that the cheek pouches may perform a food-fermenting function analogous to that of the stomachs of the leaf-eating forms. F. W. Jones (1929) adhered to this notion by alluding to the fact that cercopithecines eructate food from the stomach into the cheek pouches, where it is held and then reswallowed. Schneider (1958) follows Owen (1835, 1841) in his appraisal of cheek pouch function.

Cheek Pouches as Predigestive or Food-Fermenting Organs

The cheek pouches of cercopithecine monkeys differ from those of most other cheek-pouched mammals in their possession of adnexal and intrinsic glandular structures. Rodents for example, have keratinized, glandless cheek pouch linings, apparently suited for keeping food and other materials to be stored dry and unmodified by parotid and submandibular gland enzymes. Involvement of the cheek pouches in food fermentation or salivary predigestion was tested in three ways: (1) examination of the food removed from the cheek pouches and stomachs of cercopithecines for evidence of bacterial or enzymatic attack; (2) observation of the employment of cheek pouches under controlled conditions with selected administered food objects; and (3) assessment of the efficacy of the cheek pouches as catchments and reservoirs for salivary secretions.

EVIDENCE FOR FOOD FERMENTATION All lines of investigation failed to substantiate claims of food fermentation in the cheek pouches of cercopithecine monkeys. In several hundred hours of observation of captive *Macaca mulatta*, only one occurrence of eructation of food into the cheek pouches from the stomach was recorded. A single occurrence was also observed in *Papio cynocephalus*. Lindburg (1971) reported regurgitation of food into the mouth and oral cavity in twelve different individuals in his FRI group. Regurgitation was not seen in the forest groups. This inconsistency in the pattern of regurgitation is not as suggestive of food fermentation as it is of either extremely rapid engorgement of food, with the subsequent and rather expectable gastric reaction of vomiting, or simply poor quality food materials. Either of these explanations would fit the situation at FRI, where conspecific competition and the presence of man would hasten feeding and where the general quality of the food is probably poor.

The length of time that the food is held in the cheek pouches is variable and quite short compared to the length of time that it is held in the food-fermenting forestomachs of colobines. Bauchop and Martucci (1968) report that volatile fatty acids are produced by fermentation in the stomach for up to six-and-a-half hours. In *Macaca*, the mean length of time that a maximum load of monkey chow was held in the cheek pouches was 45.5 minutes, and in these cases the food was simultaneously being processed by the dentition, so that most food was held for a fraction of the duration documented for colobines (Figure 7 A). Food samples removed from the cheek pouches and

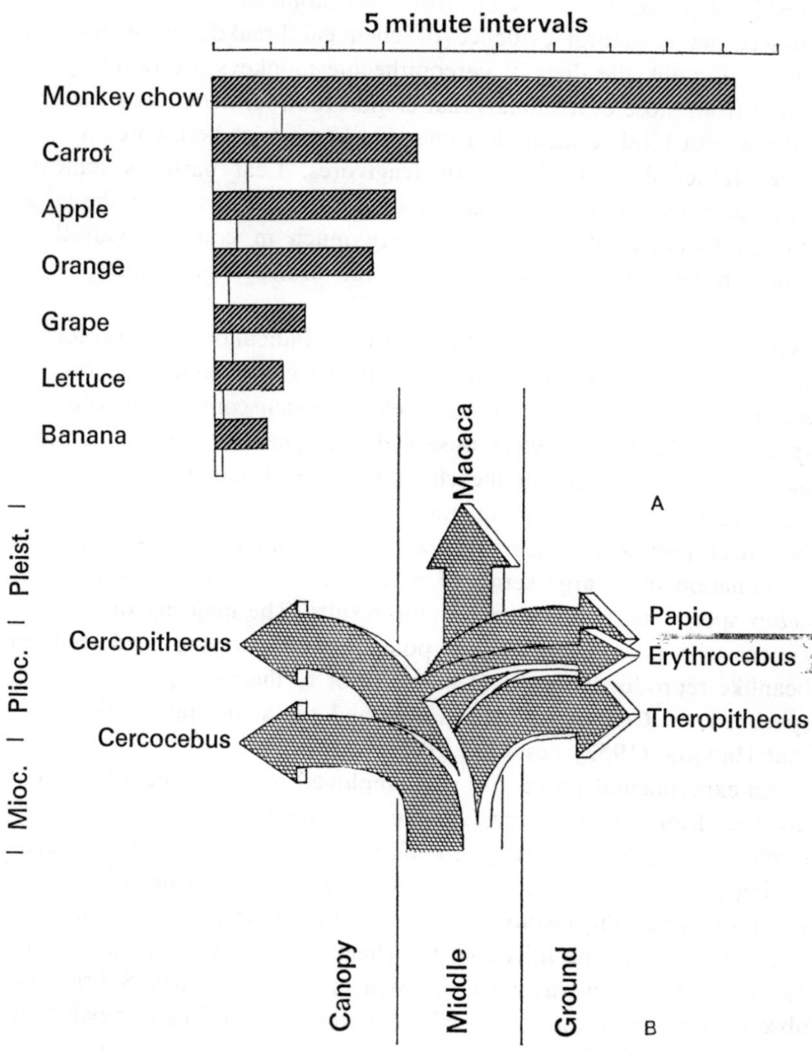

Figure 7. (A) Histogram depicting the length of time equal quantities of various types of foods are held in the cheek pouches until swallowed by *Macaca mulatta*. Hachured bar represents the mean length of time 200 milliliters of food was held; open bars represent a twenty-five milliliter sample of the same food type. Foods were selected for varying degrees of dryness, coarseness, and fiber content. (B) Diagram depicting a possible pattern for the differentiation of major cercopithecine taxa into their respective adaptive zones

freshly ingested leaves taken from the stomach of cercopithecines showed no structural evidence of chemical breakdown or bacterial attack. Finally, the diets of cercopithecine monkeys are radically different from those of mammals that exhibit food fermentative structures. Forms with food fermentation chambers are strict herbivores or folivores rather than omnivores or frugivores. Leaf particles removed from colobine stomachs frequently demonstrated erosion of the edges due to biochemical activity and were much in contrast with those found in cercopithecines (see Walker and Murray, this volume).

EVIDENCE FOR SALIVARY PREDIGESTION Indications of prolonged withholding of certain types of foods in the cheek pouches is derived indirectly from the examination of cheek pouch contents in wild-shot specimens. Haddow (1952) observed that guenons sometimes carry hard, nutmeglike seeds in the cheek pouches. Fooden (1971) reports that beanlike seeds and other hard materials appear to be retained in the cheek pouches, often to the exclusion of other materials. My own examination of a large series of wild-shot *Cercopithecus* and *Cercocebus* specimens yielded comparable results. The majority of the specimens with food in their cheek pouches were carrying hard seeds or beanlike reproductive parts of plants prior to their being shot. Several specimens of *Cercopithecus ascanius* had the same nutmeglike seeds that Haddow (1952) describes (Table 2).

An experimental procedure was employed to determine whether or not the cheek pouches serve as reservoirs for parotid fluid. An adult *Papio cynocephalus* was given pilocarpine hydrochloride, a drug having pronounced sudoriferous effects. The animal's head was held in a normal upright position while the drug took effect. Approximately five minutes after the injection, the cheek pouches were examined for parotid fluid, which was indeed present in large quantities. Subsequent observations of anesthetized *Macaca mulatta* specimens verify the same relationship between the parotid duct and the cheek pouch orifice. The cheek pouches have been observed to fill, up to one-third of their relaxed dimension, with parotid and mucous secretions.

A further line of evidence for salivary predigestion is the presence of high levels of alpha-amylase in the parotid glands of two cercopithecine monkey species tested by Jacobsen (1970). Samples of food removed from the cheek pouches of living subjects are generally well inundated in this seromucous secretion. While these data suggest that some predigestive advantages are offered by the cheek pouches, the usual interval of time that most kinds of food are held is still

Table 2. Observations on apparently inedible or unusual contents of cheek pouches not present in stomach contents[1]

Species	Material or "food"	Context of observation	Observer
Cercopithecus ascanius	Hard, woody, inedible, aromatic kernels; hard, possibly inedible seeds	Wild shot	Haddow (1952) Murray (1973)
Macaca mulatta	Large, flat, beanlike seeds	Wild shot	Fooden (1971)
Macaca mulatta	Cage litter (inorganic gritty material)	Captive	Watson (personal communication)
Macaca fascicularis	Small, unidentified snails	Wild shot	Fooden (1971)
Macaca assamensis	Head of agamid lizard (*Japulara*)	Wild shot	Fooden (1971)
Cercocebus albigena	Hard, beanlike seeds	Wild shot	Murray (1972)
Various Cercopithecinae	Corks, wood chips, and other foreign matter	Captive	Clarkson et al. (1971)

[1] Regarding this phenomenon, Jones (1970: 109) "observed that food from a known source contained in the cheeks of monkeys was not always identifiable in the stomach contents."

rather short. It may be sufficient, however, for producing highly efficient amylization of the food. This would seem to correspond well to the high carbohydrate intake characteristic of most cercopithecine monkeys (Hladik and Hladik 1972).

In the case of retention of hard seeds and kernels, the possibility that these are softened in the cheek pouches by remaining in contact with the salivary and mucous secretions cannot be ignored. Many of the beanlike seeds are extremely good sources of protein (Watt and Merrill 1950; Martin, Zim, and Nelson 1951), and the cheek pouches may facilitate efficient use of these materials by softening and processing them before ingestion. It is possible, of course, that these are residual products of fruits or legumes that were to be discarded, but their frequency of occurrence renders this explanation improbable. The seeds of red grapes were retained by captive individuals of *Macaca mulatta* and eaten subsequently. Whole wheat grains are also stored in the cheek pouches by captive rhesus monkeys and eaten a few minutes later. These patterns are variable, however, and require further investigation before final conclusions can be offered.

Cheek Pouch Convergence and Functional Analogies

Cheek pouches are present in seventeen mammalian families, with species representing volant, aquatic, arboreal, and terrestrial adaptive zones (Figure 8). Patterns of cheek pouch employment among these species can be divided into three categories: (1) motile feeding carnivorous forms, including the duckbill platypus, water opossum, and fishing bat; (2) motile feeding vegetarian mammals, including semi-arboreal and primarily terrestrial rodents, and (3) a sedentary, folivorous form, the koala (*Phascolarctos*).

The cheek pouches of the motile carnivorous mammals are associated with an aquatic foraging pattern. The duckbill platypus (*Ornithorhynchus*) feeds on small aquatic life forms including crustaceans, nymphs of insects, and other active food objects (Walker 1964). The cheek pouches permit the duckbill to forage actively for food without interruption by trituration and swallowing. Because several of the food organisms may be encountered when a suitable habitat is invaded by the platypus, the cheek pouches probably permit the animal to gather numbers of its prey rapidly, before they can seek protective cover. Huber (1931a) notes that the cheek pouches of *Ornithorhynchus* are filled with grit which may aid in breaking down the food. The water opossum (*Chironectes*) feeds on similar types of aquatic organisms, and presumably employs the cheek pouches to advantage in much the same manner as the platypus, except for the suggested additional food-preparing function. A similar case can be made for the fishing bat (*Noctilio*). *Noctilio* feeds on schools of small surface-feeding fish. These fish are caught by the bat's specialized claws, which are trailed through a placid water surface while the bat is in flight. Having impaled a fish, the bat transfers its prey to the mouth, where it is stored in the cheek pouches, allowing the bat to continue feeding. This is highly advantageous to the bat in permitting it to stay with the school of fish as it feeds. Considerable time and energy would be wasted in relocating its resource if each time it had to pause to chew and swallow a large piece of food. After filling the cheek pouches, the bat returns to its roost and processes its food (Walker 1964).

A variety of rodents have evolved cheek pouches. These have apparently arisen independently in no fewer than five different lineages. In certain families, the presence of cheek pouches can certainly be associated with hoarding. In addition to food, materials for nest lining and even infants may be carried in the cheek pouches (Witte 1971). The cheek pouches are also advantageous in permitting the

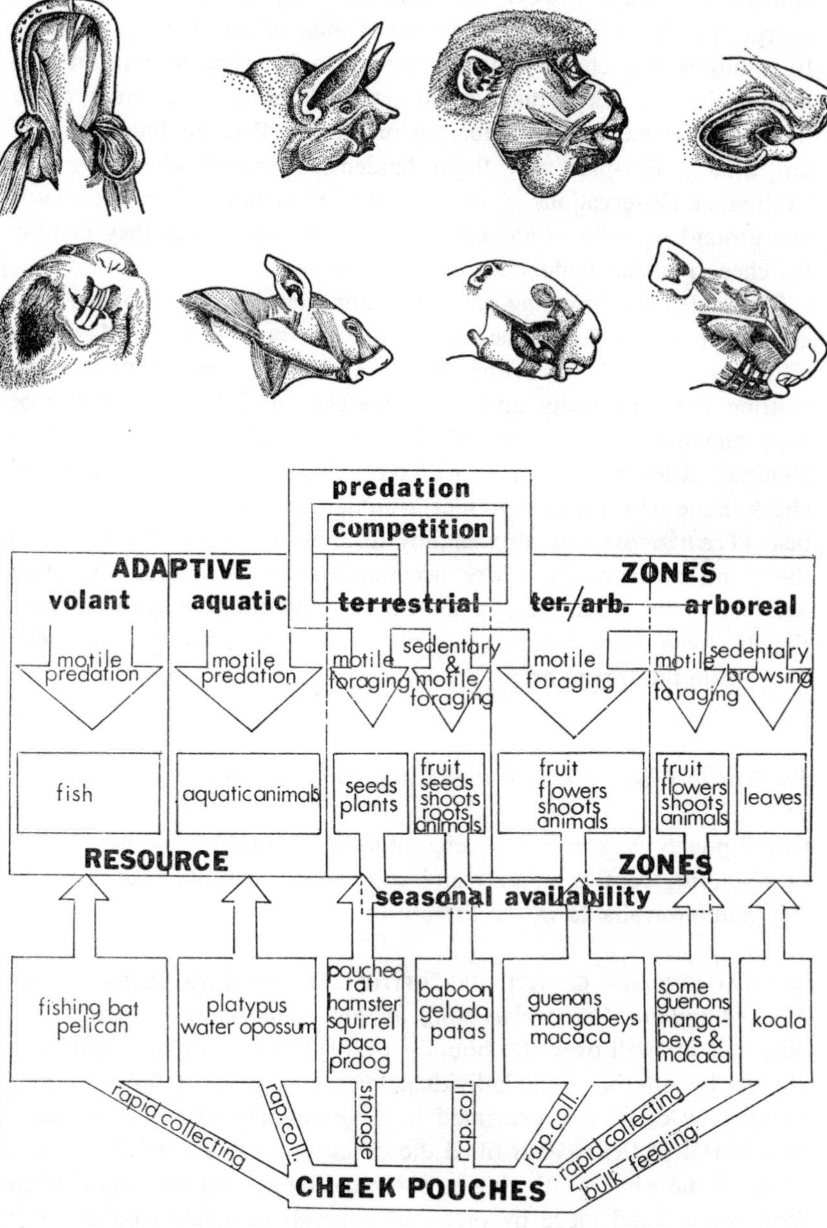

Figure 8. Representative cheek-pouched mammals. Top left to right: duckbill platypus (*Ornithorhynchus*), fishing bat (*Noctilio*), guenon (*Cercopithecus*), pouched rat (*Saccostomys*). Below left to right: pocket gopher (*Geomys*), hamster (*Mesocricetus*), prairie dog (*Cynomys*), paca (*Agouti*). Diagram below depicts the major factors in cheek pouch function for a variety of vertebrates

animals to forage rapidly and efficiently by conserving time and energy, which results in an extension of their effective foraging range. In addition, the cheek pouches appear to be advantageous in permitting the animals to make rapid retrievals of foods in areas where they may be particularly liable to predation. Rodents have variable but usually low-proximity flight tendencies, except where they are habituated. Observations of nonhabituated chipmunks (*Tamias striatus*) and ground squirrels (*Eutamias townsendii*) suggest that they employ the cheek pouches under these circumstances.

The sedentary browsing pattern exemplified by *Phascolarctos* suggests that its cheek pouches are related to bulk feeding. Maximum efficiency in food processing and procurement may be attained by stuffing the oral cavity and cheek pouches with large quantities of leafy material which can be held in excess, as chewing and collecting continue. Kangaroos (*Macropus*) have loose folds of buccinator-lined cheek tissue which may represent a similar adaptation. The spectacled bear (*Tremarctos*) may also employ its pouched buccinator region in the same manner. These are accommodations for processing large amounts of food that must be thoroughly masticated; they differ functionally from cheek pouches that are employed for transporting foods away from the forage area.

Patterns of Cheek Pouch Use in Cercopithecine Monkeys

Cheek pouch use patterns in cercopithecine monkeys were investigated by observing captive animals and comparing these observations with information available in the literature.

OBSERVATIONS ON CAPTIVE CERCOPITHECINE MONKEYS Singly caged *Macaca mulatta*, *Cercocebus albigena*, and *Cercocebus torquatus* were observed for well over 300 hours. In all species, hoarding behavior is elicited by offering each individual large quantities of food. Lettuce or monkey chow was presented in large amounts or piece by piece. Individuals of *Cercocebus* filled the cheek pouches as rapidly as possible, all the while continuing to chew and reach for more food. When food was offered piece by piece, at intervals of a few seconds, they placed the food in the cheek pouches and waited for the next piece. With the cheek pouches filled, they continued to hold food items in the hands and feet, often to the point of frustration with their overload. *Macaca* subjects were more difficult to observe because of their low-proximity flight tendency. The approach of an observer offering food to the animals led to their clinging to the highest, most remote portion of their small cages. As the observer backed away or gave the impression that he was not watching, the subjects dropped to the cage floor and retrieved their food as rapidly as possible. Habituated subjects showed the same hoarding pattern described for *Cercocebus*. Paired caged individuals of *M. mulatta* demonstrated no overt antagonism toward each other for food, but the rapidity of collection and extent to which the cheek pouches were filled appeared to be intensified. Singly caged individuals were more leisurely about filling their pouches with excess food lying on the cage floor. The paired subjects observed were very young animals (2.5–3.5 kilograms) and may give a misleading impression of the extent of agonistic interaction over food.

Captive, bisexual, multiple-age, multiple-social-status baboon groups (*Papio cynocephalus*) were observed during feeding time for approximately a month. The animals were supplied with sufficient food to last most of the day. By morning, however, the food supply in the feeder was depleted, and intensive feeding took place at the time of refilling. Few overt agonistic displays were noted. Threatening of low to moderate intensity was directed toward the observer and occasionally toward conspecifics near the feeder. Because the feeder unit was placed several feet from the floor of the cage, individuals had to climb the side of the cage in order to retrieve food. Orderly successions of animals approached the feeder and filled the cheek pouches to capacity. Once acquired, the food was often carried a considerable distance from the feeder to a "resting platform" on one of the concrete "rocks," where it could be processed by the dentition in a leisurely manner.

Representatives of all cercopithecine monkey genera employed the cheek pouches during feeding in zoo contexts. *Cercopithecus*, *Cercocebus*, and *Macaca* all displayed a retrieve-and-retreat pattern with the aid of the cheek pouches. Once the cheek pouches were filled with selected food items, the animals departed to a high perch or some remote portion of the cage to finish processing the food. Presumed dominant animals appeared to control the food supply during initial feeding. Feeding by all individuals was rapid and involved the use of the pouches. Terrestrial feeding forms, particularly *Papio*, tended to displace conspecifics on the cage floor. Retreat to upper cage platforms was less frequent among baboons than in the smaller arboreal forms.

Cheek Pouch Employment in Free-Ranging Cercopithecine Monkeys

Representative first-hand observations of cheek pouch use are infrequent in the literature. The following includes the more complete and contextually meaningful reports I was able to find.

Haddow (1952: 343, 351) observed *Cercopithecus ascanius* feeding in the middle and lower canopy to "cram the mouth and cheek pouches with [*Markhamia*] flowers." He noted that "redtail monkeys surprised while feeding on some favorite food [fruits of *Morsopsis*] may be seen to stuff their cheek pouches before moving off," and that a solitary monkey feeding quietly and shot before it has any realization of danger may similarly have its cheek pouches crammed with food. Fruits, flowers, and *Pycanthus* kernels, but rarely greens, were stuffed in the cheek pouches.

Cercopithecus aethiops feeding in open grassland were observed to fill their cheek pouches, then ascend termite nests to "improve vision" (Jackson and Gartlan 1965). Vervets were noted to ascend sleeping trees at dusk with the cheek pouches filled (Glen Hausfater, personal communication).

Four contexts of cheek pouch use were recorded by Gautier-Hion (1971) for *Cercopithecus talapoin*. The cheek pouches were employed to hold live prey (insects); when feeding on large pieces of pulpy food (salivary predigestion); when there was potential danger, as near villages; and when competing with conspecifics for food.

For *Macaca mulatta* Lindburg (1971: 20, 34) reports that "consumption of food [small berries and fruit] occurred at the time of foraging [in fringe areas of forest edge], but monkeys also filled their cheek pouches and sat in a safe and alert position." In ground level food sources (fruit of low shrubs of *Zysyphus jujaba*), "cheek pouches were quickly filled before retirement to a position of good visibility, often a few feet off the ground." In an exposed resource area, the following behavior was recorded:

> Once a group was observed to move in relays of two or three individuals to a fruit tree in an exposed erosion bed then return to the safety of the tree line with filled cheek pouches. Undoubtedly, cheek pouches provide some protective advantage feeding under these conditions.

Lindburg further suggests that in addition to their use for temporary storage of food, cheek pouches permit the animal to continue feeding while engaging in social activities and nursing the young.

Some observations are available for *Papio*. Figure 2 in Dart (1963) shows a baboon stuffing steinbok flesh into its cheek pouches. Washburn and Devore (1963) describe and figure a similar incident. Altmann and Altmann (1970) figure a baboon with its cheek pouches stuffed with rhizomes. Hausfater and Stuart Altmann both communicated to me that the *Papio* groups observed by them use their cheek pouches only rarely.

Crook and Aldrich-Blake (1968: 213) report that:

T. gelada were seen feeding on grass seeds picked up from the ground, dry grass blades and stems, dried turf roots and small bulbs dug up with the hands, and when visiting the forest near the cliff-edge dried olive seeds were collected below the trees and stuffed into the cheek pouches.

Recent observations on the gelada suggest that they also rarely employ their cheek pouches (Altmann, personal communication).

Careful scrutiny of film sequences of feeding free-ranging baboons revealed no definite employment of the cheek pouches. It is equally informative that Hall (1966) observed only one sequence of food carrying by *Erythrocebus*. This occurred during a low-intensity competitive bout over a cluster of large mushrooms. The food objects were carried in the hands rather than the cheek pouches. The behavior suggests that the pattern of cheek pouch employment may be less well developed in *Erythrocebus* than in *Cercopithecus*, *Cercocebus*, or *Macaca*.

Certain aspects of cheek pouch use are remarkably similar in free-ranging and captive cercopithecine monkeys. Where patterns appear to differ, it is possible to isolate the more influential factors as comparison of the animal's behavior in both captive and free-ranging situations imposes a certain amount of control.

Similar behavior patterns include the tendency for retrieval and retreat with food, hoarding when large quantities of food are concentrated in a small area, reflection of a low-proximity flight tendency in *Macaca*, and the peculiar retention of a variety of hard, apparently inedible items in the cheek pouches (Table 2).

The primary difference between captive and free-ranging species in cheek pouch use is the tendency for all forms to employ the cheek pouches consistently in captivity, whereas in free-ranging circumstances, the use of cheek pouches appears to be infrequent in *Papio*, *Theropithecus*, and possibly *Erythrocebus*. This suggests that the spacing of the animals is an important variable. Conspecific competition for food apparently facilitates the employment of the cheek pouches in captive representatives of those species which use them infrequently in natural surroundings.

This suggests that the retrieve-and-retreat pattern (moving to high perches or remote cage areas or ascending termite nests, trees, shrubs, or rocks with sequestered food) may be as much a spacing maneuver as it is a defense against predation.

The function of the cheek pouches in nonprimates can be associated with certain specific feeding patterns. Cercopithecine monkeys approximate the potential range of cheek pouch function except for food fermentation, infant and nesting material transportation, and trituration. Some degree of salivary predigestion is implicated, the use of cheek pouches in potentially dangerous foraging areas is documented, the use of cheek pouches in rapid feeding on active prey is reported for the talapoin, and finally, the cheek pouches appear to be of value in conspecific competition for food. The cheek pouches of cercopithecine monkeys therefore serve multiple functions, as do many adaptations. While a variety of selective pressures is probably responsible for the evolution of the cheek pouches in the Cercopithecinae, it is possible to suggest a behavioral-ecological common denominator which aids in clarifying the pattern of cercopithecine differentiation.

CHEEK POUCHES AND THE ELUCIDATION OF THE CERCOPITHECINE MONKEY ADAPTIVE ZONE

A general hypothesis of cheek pouch function in cercopithecine monkeys has been formulated on the basis of close correspondence between behavior and ecology and the observed differences in the degree of development of the cheek pouches in various genera. Cheek pouch employment appears to be related to a complex set of factors (Figure 2). The paucity of evidence for heavy predator pressure on cercopithecines (Jolly 1972), suggests that conspecific and to some extent extraspecific competition for food are major variables in the use of cheek pouches. However, the fact that few animals have been observed being caught and eaten by predators should not be taken as a positive indication that predator pressure is not high. More important here is the context of predation, i.e. whether cercopithecine monkeys are captured primarily during feeding or during other activities.

The intensity of conspecific competition for food is dependent upon the food grain, number of individuals in a given social unit, degree of dominance, and extent of competive pressure for the same resources exerted by extraspecifics (other primates, birds, vegetarian and frugivorous nonprimate mammals, insects, etc.). Predation and extraspecific competition may be viewed as influencing to some extent the structure and numbers of the social unit (Denham 1971). The maintenance of high populations may be advantageous in displacing extraspecifics from the community, but it will concomitantly increase the intensity of competition for food within the social unit. Although it is difficult to generalize about patterns of predation, large local populations of prey species can actually be advantageous to predators, whose chances of acquiring game are thereby increased, especially in the case of nocturnal predators or predators that select young, injured, or sick animals (Klopfer 1962). The more arboreal species of cercopithecines do not employ large numbers of conspecifics for predator encounter but instead exhibit a highly developed flight tendency. An important function served by having large numbers of individuals within the social unit is to give warning of the presence of predators. This flight tendency is less developed among terrestrial Cercopithecinae such as baboons and *Theropithecus*, but *Erythrocebus* can be likened to the arboreal or forest-adapted species in having a well-developed low-proximity flight tendency (Hall 1966). These variables can be demonstrated to impinge on various genera differentially in such a manner as to either increase or diminish the importance of the cheek pouches. Each genus is considered in relation to its cheek pouch size, diet, ecological factors, and social organization (Tables 3, 4, 5).

In *Macaca* high conspecific competition for food appears to be related to the maintenance of moderate- to large-sized troops in habitats having a discontinuous food grain. Macaque species feed selectively on a large number of relatively high-energy food sources. A considerable number of diverse resource units are employed in acquiring such foods. In addition, these units contain clusters of food items which may be insufficient for feeding all members of the troop at any given time (but see exceptions in Hladik and Hladik 1972). Lindburg (1971) reported that 48.5 percent of the agonistic encounters in *M. mulatta* were over provisioned food. Bertrand (1969) reported similar behavior in captive *M. speciosa* but noted that this was not so apparent in free-ranging animals. These observations do, however, attest to the potential for conspecific competition for circumscribed food clusters. It is suggested that forms feeding in discontinuous food grain situations, where many resources are employed, incur several advantages through the maintenance of larger troop size. First, the animals are better able to locate dispersed food clusters; second, predator warning is more efficient; and third, high local populations

Table 3. Diets of the dissected species, as reported in the literature

Species	pods	fruits	nuts	petioles	leaves	buds	flowers	bark	twigs	roots	rhizomes	tubers	shoots	mushrooms	seeds	berries	vertebrates	invertebrates	cultivated crops	grass	References
Presbytis cristatus		—		+	+		+	—													Furuya (1961–1962)
Colobus abyssinicus		—			+														—		Booth (1954)
Macaca arctoides		+		+	—	+	—		+						+	+	—	+	+		Bertrand (1969)
Macaca mulatta		+	(+)	+	—	+	—	—	—				+	+	+	+	—	+	+		Lindburg (1971)
Macaca fascicularis		+	(+)	+	—	+	—	—	—						+	+	—	+	+		Fooden (1971) Furuya (1962)
Macaca nemestrina		+	(+)	+	—	+	—	—	—				+		+	+	—	+	+		Bernstein (1967)
Erythrocebus patas	+	+		+										+	+	+	—	+		—	Hall (1966)
Cercopithecus neglectus		+		—	—													+	+		Booth (1962)
Cercopithecus diana		+																			Tappen (1960)
Cercopithecus aethiops	+	+		+	—	+	+		—				—		+	+	—	+	+	—	Struhsaker (1967)
Cercopithecus ascanius		+		+	—		+								+			—	+	—	Haddow (1952)
Cercocebus albigena		+	+		—			—							+		(—)	(—)			Jones and Sabator Pi (1968)
Papio anubis	+	+			—	+			+	+	+	+	+		+	+	—	+	+	+	Crook and Aldrich-Blake (1968)
Papio hamadryas		+								+	+	+	+		+	+	—	+	+	+	Kummer (1968) Crook (1966),
Theropithecus gelada		+								+	+	+	+		+	(+)		+	+	+	Crook and Aldrich-Blake (1968)

\+ = preferred
— = occasionally eaten
( ) = no report but presumably eaten

Species described and dissected	(Tropical hardwood or mature temperate) Canopy High Terminal	High Middle	Middle Terminal	Middle Middle	Low Terminal	Low Middle	Shrub	Litter zone	Meadow	Soil	Riparian-littoral	(Gallery and scrub) Branches	Shrub	Litter zone	Riparian-littoral	Soil	Nonarbo-rescent (Savanna) Grassland-highland meadow	Riparian-littoral	Soil	Total zones	References
Presbytis cristatus	+	—	+																	3	Furuya (1961–62)
Colobus abyssinicus	+	—	+																	3	Booth (1954)
Macaca arctoides						—	+	+	+			+	+	+			+			8	Tappen (1960) Bertrand (1969)
Macaca mulatta				+	—	+	+	+	—			+	+	+						9	Lindburg (1971)
Macaca fascicularis				+	—	+	+	+			+									6	Furuya (1962)
Macaca nemestrina				+	—	+	+	+				+	+	+						8	Bernstein (1970)
Erythrocebus patas												+	+	+	—		+			5	Hall (1966)
Cercopithecus neglectus	—	+	—	+																4	Haddow (1952)
Cercopithecus diana	—	+	—	+																4	Tappen (1960)
Cercopithecus aethiops											—	+	+	+	—	—	+			7	Struhsaker (1967)
Cercopithecus ascanius			—	+	—	+	+													5	Haddow (1952)
Cercocebus albigena		+	—	+	—	+														5	Jones and Sabator Pi (1965)
Papio anubis												+	+	+	+	+	+	+	+	8	Crook and Aldrich-Blake (1968)
Papio hamadryas													+	+	+	+	+	+	+	7	Kummer (1968)
Theropithecus gelada													—	+	—	+	+	—	+	7	Crook and Aldrich-Blake (1968)

Table 5. Comparative summary of ecological and behavioral factors relating to the employment of cheek pouches

	Colobus (3, 21, 24)	*Presbytis* (11, 12, 17, 22, 26)	*Macaca* (2, 10, 11, 12, 20)	*Cercopithecus* (4, 5, 9, 13, 14, 16, 24)
Diet	Vegetarian	Vegetarian	Omnivorous	Frugivorous-omnivorous
Distribution of food	Locally uniform	Locally uniform	Dispersed, small and large concentrations	Dispersed, small and large concentrations
Home range	Small, well-defined	Moderate to small (3.5×10^3 sq.m. *P. cristatus*; 1.5–3.5 sq.m. *P. entellus*)	Large (10×10^5 sq.m. *M. fuscata*; 15 sq.km. *M. mulatta*)	Moderate or none (e.g. 1.3 sq.km. *C. ascanius*)
Daily range	—	Limited (e.g. 200 m. *P. cristatus*)	Large (2 km *M. fuscata*; 2,820 m. *M. mulatta*)	Large (but varies: 500 m to 17.6 km. for *C. aethiops*)
Time utilization	More time feeding than traveling	More time feeding than traveling	Move frequently (maximum time spent feeding in one area was 3 hours for *M. fascicularis*)	Move frequently, spend considerable time traveling
Troop size	Small (2–8 *C. abyssinicus*; 2–8 *C. satanus*)	Medium (22–48 *P. cristatus*; 16–54 *P. entellus*)	Large to small (3–600 *M. fuscata*; 8–98 *M. mulatta*; 6–58 *M. assamensis*; 6–30 *M. fascicularis*)	Large to small (usually one-male bands; 3–50 *Cercopithecus* sp.; 82–158 *Miopithecus*
Social relations within troop	Agonistic frequency and intensity low	Agonistic frequency and intensity low to rather severe (low in *P. cristatus*; high in *P. entellus*)	Agonistic frequency and intensity high	Moderate to low rate of agonistic encounters?
Social relations between troops or with other species	Conspecific agonistic reactivity, stratification of genera	Agonistic frequency and intensity high to low (*P. cristatus*, low; *P. entellus*, high and aggressive)	High frequency and intensity of agonistic behavior, aggressive species displacement	Moderate to low rate of agonistic encounters (*C. aethiops* is highly reactive and territorial)

Altmann and Altmann (1970); Bernstein (1967); Booth (1954); Booth (1956); Bourliere et a (1970); Chalmers (1968); Crook (1966); Crook and Aldrich-Blake (1968); Crook and Aldric Blake (1970); Fooden (1971); Furuya (1961–1962); Furuya (1962); Gautier-Hion (1971); Ha dow (1952); Hall (1966); Jackson and Gartlan (1965); Jay (1965); Jones and Sabator Pi (1968 Kummer (1968); Lindburg (1971); Napier and Napier (1967); Poirier (1969); Struhsaker (1969 Tappen (1960); Yoshiba (1968).

rcocebus 18, 24)	*Erythrocebus* (15)	*Papio* (1, 8, 15, 19)	*Theropithecus* (7, 8)
ugivorous- nivorous	Omnivorous	Omnivorous (more varied than patas?)	Omnivorous (more varied than patas?)
spersed, small and ge concentrations	Dispersed, small concentrations	Dispersed, small concentrations	Dispersed, large concentrations, locally uniform
oderate to large *. albigena* 00×400 m *torquatus* larger dry season	Large (up to 82 sq.km)	Large (8.4 km)	Moderate (within 1 mile of sleeping cliffs)
oderate to large pproximately 00 m. *C. albigena* d *C. torquatus*)	Moderate to large (500–12,000 m)	Moderate to large (more than 5 miles to approximately same as *Erythrocebus*)	Moderate (less than 5 miles; usually stay near sleeping cliffs)
ove frequently, end considerable ne traveling	Move frequently, spend considerable time traveling	More frequently, more time traveling or sitting than feeding (feeding occupies 20 percent of time)	More time feeding than traveling (feeding occupies up to 70 percent of time)
edium -11 *C. albigena*; -25 *C. torquatus*)	Small to medium (dispersed one-male bands; 5–34 individuals)	Large (200) to small (8) (80 *P. anubis*; 13–185 *P. cynocephalus*)	Large to small (300 at Debra Libanos break into 1-male bands)
me agonistic havior of high tensity	Moderate to low rate of agonistic encounters	High rate of agonistic encounters	Moderate to high, reactive display behavior
ve sympatrically th several *ercopithecus* spp.	Reactive and nervous to conspecific troops; tolerate nonpredators and nonprimates	High rate of agonistic encounters (severe reactions to conspecific troops. Displace *E. patas*, passive toward observers)	"Nervy," noisy displays toward human observers; passive toward observers (Altmann, personal communication)

pplementary references: *Cercopithecus*: Hall and Gartlan (1965); Roberts (1951); Malbrant d McClatchy (1949); Thorington (1970). *Cercocebus:* Malbrant and McClatchy (1949); Thorgton (1971). *Macaca*: Pocock (1939). *Papio*: Malbrant and McClatchy (1949); Tappen (1960). *ieropithecus*: Stuart Altmann, personal communication.

Table 6. Summary of relationships of cheek pouch size to feeding pattern, habitat, and observed frequency of use

Genus	Mean size of cadaver cheek pouches (ratio $\frac{\sqrt{A}}{\sqrt[3]{W}}$)	Feeding pattern summary	Habitat preference: Terrestrial	Arboreal	Forest	Nonforest	Observed frequency of pouch use
Macaca	Large ($\bar{x} = .40$)	Omnivorous motile feeding	—	+	+		High frequency (Lindburg 1971)
Cercocebus	Large ($\bar{x} = .37$)	Omnivorous-frugivorous motile feeding	—	+	+		No field observations on cheek pouch use
Cercopithecus	Large ($\bar{x} = .37$)	Omnivorous-frugivorous motile feeding	—	+	+	—	High frequency (Haddow 1952; Gautier-Hion 1971)
Erythrocebus	Moderate ($\bar{x} = .32$)	Omnivorous motile feeding	+			+	Infrequent (no clear field observation)[1]
Papio	Moderate ($\bar{x} = .25$)	Omnivorous motile feeding	+	—	—	+	Infrequent (Hausfater, S. Altmann, personal communication)
Theropithecus	Small ($\bar{x} = .19$)	Omnivorous sedentary feeding	+		—	+	Infrequent but observed (Crook and Aldrich-Blake 1968)

[1] Hall (1966) reported that only on the occasion when *Erythrocebus* encountered a cluster of mushrooms was this genus seen to carry food or any other object in the mouth while walking or running.

of a species tend to displace extraspecifics from the community. The marked dominance system of the macaques effectively distributes individuals of the troop over the entire foraging area. When food is encountered by an individual, a more adequate supply can be carried away from a potential conspecific competitor by filling the cheek pouches, thus diminishing the likelihood of a physical encounter. Overall, the cheek pouches in combination with the distributive force of dominance appear to increase the foraging efficiency for the entire troop. It is possible that the intensity of conspecific competitive pressure is at least partly responsible for the high degree of omnivorousness demonstrated by most macaque species, because less dominant animals are forced to subsist on other than the preferred food items. Conspecific displacement of individuals because of dominance may be implicated in the pattern of raiding potentially dangerous feeding zones, which is yet another situation in which the cheek pouches are advantageous. These elements comprise a system that can extract large amounts of energy from the community, permitting members of the genus to remain unchallenged for the occupancy of this broad fundamental niche. In consequence, well-developed cheek pouches with a high frequency of use can be taken as a reflection of this adaptative strategy in *Macaca.*

Members of the genus *Cercopithecus* also have well-developed cheek pouches. The social organization and feeding behavior of guenons differs markedly, however, from that of *Macaca.* Most, if not all, arboreal guenons have one-male band organization (Struhsaker 1969), and many feed in mixed-species groups (Booth 1956; Jones and Sabator Pi 1965; Gautier-Hion and Gautier-Hion 1969). The well-developed cheek pouches characteristic of the more arboreal members of this genus can be attributed to a markedly discontinuous food grain, perhaps even more so than that of preferred macaque habitats. This is closely related to the more specialized habitus of the *Cercopithecus* species, because they tend to be more specifically frugivorous and prefer more restrictive arboreal communities than do *Macaca.* A reasonable hypothesis for guenon speciation can be derived from the factors just enumerated. If stem guenon populations became progressively more specialized toward arboreality, increased intraspecific intolerance would result as closeness of fit to the fundamental niche was attained (Christian 1970). Territorial behavior and well-developed dominance would tend to force subordinate individuals and populations into newly "realized" niches, leading to rapid but minor adaptive radiation into included niche intersections something like Miller's (1967) "B" and "C" types. The resultant, apparently slowly evolving sympatry of *Cercopithecus* species could incur several advantages, the most important of which is to decrease the intensity of conspecific competition for food. The influence of intratroop dominance and competition for resources other than food is lessened in favor of extraspecific competition for food and space alone. Because these feeding flocks are suggested to be composed of members of realized niches of the included types, there is sufficient overlap in food and habitat preferences to support large local populations of Cercopithecini. Sympatric foraging flocks of *Cercopithecus* appear to have limited, specialized social interactions appropriate to their organization, thus elaboration of social communication to the extent of that developed in *Macaca* is apparently unnecessary. It follows that among many *Cercopithecus* species, the role of the cheek pouches is likely to be for rapid food collection under the stress of extraspecific competition. The primary advantages of the situation described for *Macaca* could be expressed in the case of sympatric *Cercopithecus* species by the maintenance of large, high-energy-utilizing local populations, which permits them to remain dominant species among moderate-sized frugivores within the community, while the advantages of social aggregates in food location are not compromised.

The two other terrestrial species of the Cercopithecini tribe, *C. aethiops* and *Erythrocebus patas*, appear to have consistently less well-represented cheek pouches, and can be seen to separate out from the remaining species (Figure 4). The small sample size may be implicated, yet within a given genus, there is a tendency for the cheek pouches to be somewhat smaller in terrestrially adapted forms. This can be seen in *Cercocebus torquatus* compared with *Cercocebus albigena* (Figure 5). Among the Cercopithecinae as a whole, the most terrestrially adapted genera, *Papio* and *Theropithecus*, have relatively the smallest cheek pouches (Figure 6). The genus *Macaca* appears to be exceptional in that no clear pattern was discernable among the more or less terrestrially adapted species (Figure 3).

Erythrocebus patas differ from the arboreal guenons in that the former forage over large ranges and are organized into small, one-male bands. It is possible, therefore, that the opportunities for more efficient forage spacing are present, diminishing the importance of the cheek pouches. Small to moderate troop size and a more uniform food grain may also be reflected by the less well-developed cheek pouches of *C. aethiops*. In the case of vervets, considerable differences in habitat and feeding behavior have been recorded. It is conceivable that some local populations may be under minimal extraspecific and conspecific competitive pressures, while others may be in situations more like those of the guenons. This would leave the possibility for rather marked variability in the ontogenetic expression of the cheek pouches.

Cercocebus also appears to conform to the proposition that discontinuous food grain and selective feeding for high-energy foods is complicated by conspecific competition for sporadically occurring food clusters. Chalmers (1968) reported agonistic behavior in *Cercocebus albigena* over *Cynometra* fruits. The smaller cheek pouches of *Cercocebus torquatus* may be related to more efficient spacing because of their terrestrial proclivities. *Cercocebus torquatus* are able to expand their feeding range during the dry season, and unlike some of the macaque species, they tend to live in more moderate-sized social aggregates. However, all of these forms have generally large, well-developed cheek pouches, and these subtle differences characteristic of species may possibly be fortuitously associated with minor ecological and social differences. The differences between the large cheek-pouched genera and the two most terrestrial cercopithecines are considerably more pronounced, and appear to be well correlated with differences in the food grain, the nature of the food, and the presence of efficient spacing mechanisms.

Members of the genus *Papio* appear to employ their cheek pouches infrequently in free-ranging conditions (Altmann and Hausfater, personal communication). Hausfater informed me that *Papio cynocephalus* feeding on a variety of grasses and roots did not use their cheek pouches during a four-month period from June to September. Evidence from the diets and feeding patterns of *Papio* species, particularly the species inhabiting sparsely forested and scrub regions (*P. anubis*, *P. hamadryas*), indicates that clusters of small food items are acquired and eaten at a more leisurely rate than observed in *Cercopithecus*, *Macaca*, and *Cercocebus*. Kummer (1971) describes hamadryas baboon feeding as follows:

> . . . flowers, young leaves and beans of many species of acacias are their most important food source in the Southern Danakil Plain. They pick them with one hand and rapidly stick them into their mouths one by one.

The probable reasons for this type of feeding pattern are: (1) most of the food is of small size and is abundant enough to feed all individuals of the foraging unit when encountered, and (2) the baboons are able to organize themselves into "single-tree foraging units" (Kummer

1968, 1971). Kummer (1971) suggests that the "single-tree foraging unit" is permitted by low predator pressure and sparse but a more or less continuous food grain: "The small foraging units of hamadryas baboons support our impression from the field that predator pressure in the semi-desert is less important than the food problem."

The pattern that emerges from *Papio* is one in which the food grain is continuous but provides a low yield per unit. The animals must therefore disperse and also move a considerable part of the time. When local clusters of food are encountered, as in the case of meat or plant concentrations, the cheek pouches are then employed by individuals in order to maximize their harvest. The pattern of "retrieve-and-retreat" under the stress of predation or conspecific competitive pressures is negated by their terrestrial feeding adaptation.

The small size of the cheek pouches of the gelada is related to differences in the food grain of their habitat and to their concomitant foraging pattern and social organization. Crook and Aldrich-Blake (1968) demonstrated that *Theropithecus* spends far more time feeding and less time traveling to food resources than do sympatric *Papio anubis*. *Theropithecus* concentrates on small areas for long periods of time, moving slowly and for minimal distances. Small food items are recovered from the soil and are picked and ingested. There is no advantage in storing food items in the cheek pouches under these circumstances, as predator pressure is light and conspecific competition for food is low. Large, sporadically encountered food items are the major stimuli for cheek pouch employment, particularly under the stress of having the food usurped by a higher status individual. Because the animals feed and move slowly, the necessity to recover food quickly in order to keep up with a rapidly moving troop is also diminished. Crook and Aldrich-Blake's (1968) observation of cheek pouch use when the animals were collecting dried olive seeds describes a situation where localized foods are concentrated, circumscribed, and limited.

Thus, the relative development of the cheek pouches is closely related to the energy budget. Forms with large cheek pouches are motile feeders that prefer habitats having a discontinuous food grain. These habitats tend to partially correspond with forested regions, and therefore, most of the monkeys with large cheek pouches are wholly or partially arboreal. These forms feed selectively on a wide variety of fruits, vegetables, and small animals; maintain rather small home ranges; and live in moderate to large aggregates consisting of sympatric or homogeneous-species social units. They tend to be motile-feeding forms that employ many resource units, including terrestrial ones in some cases, expending large amounts of energy in the process of interaction, movement, and selective feeding.

The Cercopithecinae with small cheek pouches are more terrestrially adapted and prefer to feed in continuous food grain habitats. Differences in cheek pouch development among them relate to the frequency with which circumscribed and limited food clusters are encountered, the extent of conspecific competitive pressures placed on individuals in acquiring food, and the absence of a retrieve-and-retreat feeding pattern, as they control the resource upon which they feed at any given time against predators and other conspecific social groups. These forms apparently represent energy-conserving adaptations, reaching the highest degree of development with the gelada (Table 6).

ASSESSMENT OF THE CERCOPITHECINE "FUNDAMENTAL NICHE"

We are now in a position to examine the following hypothesis of the original cercopithecine adaptive zone given by Napier (1970: 79):

> The anatomical correlates of leaf-eating, the specialized leaf-eating stomachs and salivary apparatus of *Colobus* and *Presbytis*, clearly must have evolved after the cercopithecine stock separated from the colobines in Miocene times, for the Cercopithecinae show no evidence of these adaptations. By the same token, cheek pouches, a hallmark of cercopithecine monkeys, must have been acquired since their separation from the Colobinae which show no signs of this particular specialization. The presence of cheek pouches in the genus *Cercopithecus* is one of the strongest indications that this genus is secondarily arboreal, having evolved from a ground living stock.

Two assumptions made in this statement are difficult to substantiate in light of the evidence of cheek pouch function. The first is that cercopithecine monkeys were derived from a ground-living stock, and the second is that the stem Cercopithecinae are represented by members of the genus *Cercopithecus*.

The advantages of cheek pouches have been shown to correspond with several important variables, including the food grain, nutritional value and relative abundance of food, foraging pattern, degree of dominance, local population size, and perhaps intensity of predator pressure. As previously pointed out, these variables are partially independent of whether the habitat is terrestrial or arboreal. In the case of medium-sized social omnivores or frugivores, a forested habitat offers the most complex and potentially most discontinuous food grain, particularly where high-energy requirements are placed on the community by competing extra- and conspecifics. Foods higher in nutritional value, such as fruits, are present in locally concentrated clusters which attract many animals. An efficient means of locating such food sources is through social interaction. Because the resources are potentially limited on a local basis, intraspecific competition for food is expected. The development of hierarchical systems based on dominance diminishes agonistic behavior by displacing subordinate competitors by means of social signaling alone. However, the presence of cheek pouches serves to optimize the amount of food recovered by each individual, thus permitting the social unit to extract more energy from the habitat than would an equal biomass of less efficient, slower feeding forms. The forest-adapted Cercopithecinae, whether partially or wholly arboreal, are thus well suited to dominate this fundamental niche.

Because the forms occupying this niche have the best-developed cheek pouches, and because cheek pouches are basic to the definition of the subfamily Cercopithecinae, it seems reasonable to conclude that the stem cercopithecines utilized arboreal and some terrestrial resources within forest habitats. In most cases, it can be seen that the primarily terrestrial African cercopithecines have undergone reduction of the cheek pouches or show little evidence of their use in free-ranging circumstances.

The probability that cercopithecine monkeys are secondarily terrestrially adapted corresponds well with Christian's (1970) discussion of social subordination, population density, and evolution. Christian points out that intraspecific intolerance increases in discontinuous or circumscribed habitats. Dominant members of the population tend to displace subordinates away from optimal resources, ultimately dispersing them into suboptimal habitats. The dominant forms are the most conservative evolutionarily, as they remain in the same niche. The dispersed members of the population are forced into more or less alien habitats to which they must either adapt or die. It is among these individuals that adaptive radiation is believed to take place. This model could easily be applied to the cercopithecines, if it is accepted that the most intense conspecific competition is among forest-dwelling forms and that the more terrestrial or extremely arboreal species have evolved in response to conspecific displacement.

CERCOPITHECINE MONKEY ADAPTIVE STRATEGY AND SPECIATION

Several cercopithecine monkey genera contain species that have radiated into either more terrestrial or more arboreal habitats (Tuttle 1969). The numerous minor radiations of the Cercopithecinae tend to obscure the more basic pattern of differentiation, which is characterized better at the genus level.

Several lines of evidence permit controlled speculation on the nature of the stem Cercopithecinae, including paleontology, biogeography, ecology, and comparative anatomy. Current fossil evidence indicates that the earliest Cercopithecinae appeared in the Middle Miocene (Vindobonian), as represented by *Victoriapithecus* remains recovered from Mohari, Rusinga, and Kiboko (Maier 1970). The lower third molars bear a well-developed hypoconulid unlike *Cercopithecus* and are, in most respects, more macaquelike than anything else. Biogeographic evidence suggests that early cercopithecines may have dispersed into Asia, where they were cut off from rapidly radiating African populations by Upper Miocene or Lower Pliocene times. The considerably more homogeneous *Macaca* groups suggest that this stock may have rapidly assumed control of optimum habitats and subsequently radiated more slowly than the African forms. *Macaca* show the same tendencies to radiate into terrestrial and arboreal habitats as the African Cercopithecinae but have done so on a more conservative basis. In evidence there are Asian baboon parallels such as *Macaca niger* and somewhat *Cercopithecus*-like long-tailed macaques which spend a considerable part of their lives in arboreal habitats. They have tended, however, to maintain generalized cercopithecine morphologies, even to the extent of showing no appreciable reduction in the size of the cheek pouches. It is suggested that the forest-adapted, semiarboreal macaques are better models for stem cercopithecines than are any of the more terrestrial African species or the more arboreal members of the genus *Cercopithecus*. The African Cercopithecinae represent a more archaic and certainly more specialized adaptive array than those of Asia. It is probable that the cheek-pouched monkeys filled a broad fundamental niche comprised of middle zone to forest floor resources. Social organization provided access to these varied resources, but as local populations grew, competition increased, and thus dominance functioned to force individuals into ever-widening niche inclusion, the interface for rapid evolution. Therefore, adaptive radiation in cercopithecines has proceeded from an intermediate, generalized forest adaptation to extreme arboreality, on the one hand, and extreme terrestriality, on the other (Figure 7 B). The phenomenon is repetitive at various taxonomic levels — among genera, then among species — because of the combined factors of high-energy feeding, social organization, dominance, and subsequent displacement.

CONCLUDING REMARKS

Although the cheek pouches are but one of several elements in this adaptive system, they serve as an adequate focus for its description. Examination of the function of cercopithecine monkey cheek pouches leads directly into an assessment of the fundamental adaptive strategy of the group. The unique contribution of an examination of the cheek pouches is that certain behavioral and morphological qualities of cercopithecine adaptive strategy can be roughly quantified. The degree of reliance on the cheek pouches and their relative sizes can serve as an overall gauge for the rate at which energy is extracted from the community by a given genus. Thus, the large size of the cheek pouches of *Macaca* is an expression of their high social reactivity, communicative development, intense competitiveness, and tenacious domination of their fundamental niche. The small cheek pouches of the gelada indicate that they have begun to move out of the fundamental cercopithecine niche.

A leading proponent of the cercopithecine monkey displacement hypothesis on hominid origins suggests that "the adaptive radiation leading to the African apes and man began as a result of competition in the trees by the evolving cercopithecines (today the macaques, baboons, mangabeys and guenons)" (Sarich 1971). Although I do not doubt that cercopithecine evolution influenced the differentiation of other anthropoids, I am not convinced that the process was simply one of arboreal cercopithecines driving the hominoids into terrestrial habitats. Simons (1970) is more careful to point out that other arboreal and probably frugivorous potential competitors for the presumed pongid adaptive zone were present in Africa in the Mio–Pliocene, particularly the oreopithecids and hylobatines. Working from the postulated fundamental niche of cercopithecines presented here, an alternative pattern of community interaction and evolution might be given consideration. While I will discuss only primates, it must be kept in mind that many other mammals and birds share in community succession and evolution. It is also impossible at this time to give an accurate or comprehensive description of the highly important particulars of dispersal, including times of geographic isolation or floral successions.

If it is accepted that *Parapithecus* was primarily a frugivore, as Gregory (1922) first suggested, the earliest Old World monkeys may have begun to fill an omnivorous niche in response to competition from the frugivorous stem apes (Dryopithecinae). The specialization of cercopithecoid dentitions as opposed to the relatively conservative dental evolution of the dryopithecines is offered in support of this supposition. It is also possible that the dryopithecines were in competition with frugivorous and highly arboreal hylobatines, which led to selection for the increased omnivorousness and more generalized locomotor repertoire that culminated in the chimpanzee. In Africa, the middle arboreal and forest floor zone is less well represented by cercopithecines than in Asia. It is possible, therefore, that the dryopithecines were successfully competing with the more generalized cercopithecine stock for their original niche. In contrast, the Asian primate fauna has excellent cercopithecine representation of middle arboreal and forest floor zone omnivores (*Macaca*) (Harrison 1962) and a complete absence of semiterrestrial pongids. To complete the African picture, it is not improbable that the community pressures exerted on the generalized Cercopithecinae culminated in their radiation into specialized arboreal and terrestrial niches, leaving the middle and forest floor omnivorous zone to the Dryopithecinae and only a few species of Cercopithecinae. The success of the small, active, social frugivores represented by modern *Cercopithecus* may thus account for the local demise of African hylobatines and perhaps oreopithecids, which may have become "trapped" in an included niche between the fundamental niches of the cercopithecines and the dryopithecines. While this is one of several reasonable pathways for the local demise of a species given by Miller (1967), there is as yet insufficient paleoecological or current synecological data on extraspecific competition in primate communities to aid in verifying such general postulates.

What does stand to reason is that the Dryopithecinae evolved more complex behavioral systems than did the Cercopithecinae, and the impetus for this would be more likely to have come from the more highly organized competing species, either other dryopithecines or the hylobatines and perhaps the oreopithecids.

To conclude, it appears that the adaptive strategies of the Cercopithecinae and the Hominoidea have taken different trends. The Cercopithecinae have been successful competitors by evolving a dominance-based social system leading to intraspecific competition that compels them to extract large amounts of energy from the community, thus giving them the power of extraspecific displacement, and eventual hegemony over resources. The Hominoidea have evolved more intricate social interrelationships that permit efficient extraction of energy from the community via rudimentary but effective cooperation in food locating and occasionally food sharing (Teleki 1973). Consequently, two effective means of maintaining community dominance have evolved around the opposing principles of competition and cooperation.

SUMMARY

The cheek pouches of the Cercopithecinae appear to be an aspect of a competitive, dominance-based social system which leads to increasing the efficiency of energy extraction from the community. This contributes to cercopithecine adaptive success by effectively displacing extraspecifics from their fundamental niche. It is also an important factor in displacing members of the population into suboptimal habitats where selective pressures are the most stringent, leading to numerous adaptive radiations. The size of the cheek pouches appears to be closely associated with the intensity of conspecific competition for food, which is in turn dependent upon the food grain and local population density. It has been concluded that the cheek pouches play no role in food fermentation, but their importance in "salivary predigestion" or food softening may be significant for processing beans and seeds which have high protein content. The presence of cheek pouches suggests that the fundamental niche of the Cercopithecinae is semiarboreal middle zone and forest floor omnivorousness. Extremely arboreal and extremely terrestrial species appear to be subsequent specializations of an original, probably macaquelike stock represented by the Vindobonian fossil *Victoriapithecus*. The adaptive strategy of cercopithecine monkeys contrasts with that of the hominoids in that their adaptive success is based on competition for food, while the apes, especially the chimpanzee, show a proclivity for conspecific cooperation in food location and food sharing.

REFERENCES

ALTMANN, S., J. ALTMANN

1970 Baboon ecology. *Bibliotheca Primatologica* 12:1–215.

BAUCHOP, T., R. MARTUCCI

1968 Ruminant-like digestion of the langur monkey. *Science* 161:698–700.

BERNSTEIN, I.

1967 A field study of the pig-tail monkey *Macaca nemestrina*. *Primates* 8:217–228.

BERTRAND, M.

1969 The behavioral repertoire of the stump-tailed macaque. *Bibliotheca Primatologica* 11:1–273.

BOOTH, A. H.

1954 A note on the colobus monkeys of the Gold and Ivory Coasts. *Annals of the Magazine of Natural History* 7:857–860.

1956 The Cercopithecidae of the Gold and Ivory Coasts: geographic and systematic observations. *Annals of the Magazine of Natural History* 9:476–480.

1962 Some observations on behavior of Cercopithecus monkeys. *Annals of the New York Academy of Science* 102:447–487.

1968 Taxonomic studies of *Cercopithecus mitis* Wolf. *National Geographic Society Report* (1963 projects): 37–51.

BOURLIERE, F., C. HUNKELER, M. BERTRAND

1970 "Ecology and behavior of Lowe's guenon (*Cercopithecus campbelli lowei*) in the Ivory Coast," in *Old World monkeys*. Edited by J. R. and P. H. Napier. New York: Academic Press.

CHALMERS, N. R.

1968 Group composition, ecology and daily activities of free-living mangabeys in Uganda. *Folia Primatologica* 8:247–263.

CHRISTIAN, J.

1970 Social subordination, population density and mammalian evolution. *Science* 3:84–89.

CLARKSON, T. B., B. C. BULLOCK, N. D. LEHNER, P. J. MANNING

1970 "Diseases affecting the usefulness of non-human primates for nutritional research," in *Feeding and nutrition of non-human primates*. Edited by R. S. Harris. New York: Academic Press.

CROOK, J. H.

1966 Gelada baboon herd structure and movement: a comparative report. *Symposium of the Zoological Society of London* 18:237–248.

CROOK, J. H., P. ALDRICH-BLAKE

1968 Ecological and behavioral contrasts between sympatric ground-dwelling primates in Ethiopia. *Folia Primatologica* 8:192–227.

1970 "The socio-ecology of primates," in *Social behavior in birds and mammals: essays on social ethology of man and animals*. Edited by J. H. Crook. New York: Academic Press.

DART, R.

1963 The carnivorous propensities of baboons. *Symposium of the Zoological Society of London* 10:49–56.

DENHAM, W.
1971 Energy relations and some basic properties of primate social organization. *American Anthropologist* 73:77–95.

FAHRENHOLZ, C.
1937 "Drüsen der Mundhöhle," in *Handbuch der Vergleichenden Anatomie der Wirbeltiere,* volume three. Edited by L. Balk, E. Goppert, E. Kallius, and W. Labosch. Berlin, Wien: Urban und Schwartzenberg.

FOODEN, J.
1964 Stomach contents and gastro-intestinal proportions in wild-shot Guinean monkeys. *American Journal of Physical Anthropology* 22:227–231.
1971 Report on primates collected in western Thailand. January-April, 1969. *Fieldiana Zoology* 59:1–62.

FURUYA, Y.
1961–1962 The social life of the silver leaf monkeys (*Trachypithecus cristatus*). *Primates* 3:41–60.
1962 Ecological survey of the wild crab eating monkeys in Malaya. *Primates* 3:75–76.

GAUTIER-HION, A.
1971 Comportements de talapoin. *Biologica Gabonica* 13.

GAUTIER-HION, J. P., A. GAUTIER-HION
1969 Les assciations polyspécifiques chez les Cercopithecidae du Gabon. *La Terre et la Vie* 2:164–201.

GEIST, F. D.
1931 "Nasal cavity, larynx, mouth and pharynx," in *The anatomy of the rhesus monkey*. Edited by C. G. Hartman and W. L. Straus, 189–209. New York: Hafner.

GREGORY, W. K.
1922 *The origin and evolution of human dentition*. Baltimore: Williams and Watkins.

GREGORY, W. K.; MC GREGOR
1914 "Primates." *Encyclopaedia Britannica.*

HADDOW, A. J.
1952 Field and laboratory studies on an African monkey *Cercopithecus ascanius schmidti Matschie. Proceedings of the Zoological Society of London* 145:37–56.

HALL, K. R. L.
1966 Behavior and ecology of the wild patas monkey, *Erythrocebus patas,* in Uganda. *Journal of the Zoological Society of London* 148:15–87.

HALL, K. R. L., J. S. GARTLAN
1965 Ecology and behavior of the vervet monkey *Cercopithecus aethiops,* Lolui Island, Lake Victoria. *Proceedings of the Zoological Society of London* 145:37–56.

HANEL, H.
1932 Über die Gesichtsmuskulatur der Katerrhinen Affen. *Morphologisches Jahrbuch* 71:1–76.

HARRISON, J.

1962 The distribution of feeding habits among mammals in a tropical rainforest. *Journal of Animal Ecology* 31:53–64.

HEDIGER, H.

1964 *Wild animals in captivity*. London: Butterworth Scientific Publications.

HILL, W. C. O.

1966 *Primates*, volume five: *Cercopithecoidea*; volume six: *Cercopithecinae*. Edinburgh: Edinburgh University Press.

1969 On the muscles of expression in the gelada, *Theropithecus gelada* (Ruppell) (Primates, Cercipithecoidea). *Zeitschrift für Tiermorphologie* 65:247–286.

HLADIK, C. M., A. HLADIK

1972 Disponibilités alimentaires et domains vitaux des primates à Ceylan. *La Terre et la Vie* 2:149–215.

HUBER, E.

1931a Studies on the organization of monotremes contrasted with the marsupials and placentals. *Morphologisches Jahrbuch* 66:46–64.

1931b "The facial musculature and its innervation," in *The anatomy of the rhesus monkey*. Edited by C. G. Hartman and W. L. Straus, 176–188. New York: Hafner.

JACKSON, G., J. S. GARTLAN

1965 The fauna and flora of Lolui Island. *Journal of Ecology* 53:573–597.

JACOBSEN, N.

1970 Salivary amylase, II: Alpha amylase in salivary glands of the *Macaca irus* monkey, the *Cercopithecus aethiops* monkey and man. *Caries Research* 4:200–205.

JAY, P.

1965 "The common langur of North India," in *Primate behavior: field studies of monkeys and apes*. Edited by I. DeVore, 197–249. New York: Holt, Rinehart and Winston.

JOLLY, A.

1972 *The evolution of primate behavior*. New York: Macmillan.

JONES, C.

1970 Stomach contents and gastro-intestinal relationships of monkeys collected in Rio Muni, West Africa. *Mammalia* 34:107–117.

JONES, C., J. SABATOR PI

1965 Notes on the distribution and ecology of the higher primates of Rio Muni, West Africa. *Tulane Studies in Zoology* 14:101–110.

1968 Comparative ecology of *Cercocebus albigena* and *Cercocebus torquatus* in Rio Muni, West Africa. *Folia Primatologica* 9:99–113.

JONES, F. W.

1929 *Man's place among the mammals*. London: Arnold.

KLOPFER, P.

1962 *Behavioral aspects of ecology*. Englewood Cliffs, New Jersey: Prentice-Hall.

KUMMER, H.
1968 *Social organization of hamadryas baboons, a field study.* Chicago: University of Chicago Press.
1971 *Primate societies: group techniques of ecological adaptation.* Chicago: Aldine.

LIGHTOLLER, G. S.
1928 The facial muscles of three orang-utans and Cercopithecidae. *Journal of Anatomy, London* 63:19–81.

LINDBURG, D. C.
1971 "The rhesus monkey in North India," in *Primate behavior II.* Edited by L. A. Rosenblum, 1–89. New York: Academic Press.

MAIER, W.
1970 Neue Ergebnisse der Systematik und Stammesgeschichte der Cercopithecoidea. *Zeitschrift für Säugetierkunde* 35:193–256.

MALBRANT, R., A. MC CLATCHY
1949 *Faune de l'équateur Africain Français, II. Mammifères.* Paris: Lechevalier.

MARTIN, A., H. S. ZIM, A. NELSON
1951 *American wildlife plants: a guide to wildlife food habits.* New York: Dover.

MILLER, R. S.
1967 "Pattern and process in competition," in *Advances in ecological research IV.* Edited by J. B. Cragg, 1–74. New York: Academic Press.

MURRAY, PETER F.
1973 "The anatomy and adaptive significance of cheek pouches (Bursae buccales) in Cercopithecinae, Cercopithecoidea." Unpublished doctoral dissertation, University of Chicago.

NAPIER, J. R.
1970 "Paleoecology and catarrhine evolution," in *Old World monkeys.* Edited by J. R. and P. H. Napier, 53–96. New York: Academic Press.

NAPIER, J. R., P. H. NAPIER
1967 *A handbook of living primates.* London: Academic Press.

OWEN, R.
1835 On the sacculated form of the stomach as it exists in genus Semnopithecus. *Transactions of the Zoological Society of London* 1:65.
1841 Description of the stomach of *Colobus ursinus* Ogilby. *Proceedings of the Zoological Society of London,* 84–85.
1868 *On the anatomy of the vertebrates III.* London: Longmans, Green.

POCOCK, R. I.
1939 *The fauna of British India, including Ceylon and Burma: Mammalia I.* London: Taylor and Francis.

POIRIER, F.
1969 The Nilgiri langur (*Presbytis johnii*) troop, its composition, structure and change. *Folia Primatologica* 10:20–47.
1970 The communication matrix of the Nilgiri langur (*Presbytis johnii*) of South India. *Folia Primatologica* 13:92–136.

RIPLEY, S.

1967 "Intertroop encounters among Ceylon gray langurs," in *Social communication among primates*. Edited by S. Altmann, 237–254. Chicago: University of Chicago Press.

1970 "The social organization of foraging in gray langurs *Presbytis entellus thersites*," in *Old World monkeys*. Edited by J. R. and P. H. Napier, 481–512. New York: Academic Press.

ROBERTS, A.

1951 *The mammals of South Africa*. Capetown: Central News Agency.

RUGE, G.

1887 *Untersuchungen über die Gesichtesmuskulatur der Primaten*. Leipzig: Verlag von Wm. Englemann.

SARICH, V. A.

1971 "A molecular approach to the question of human origins," in *Background for man*. Edited by P. Dolhinow and V. A. Sarich. Boston: Little, Brown.

SCHNEIDER, R.

1958 "Vestibulum Oris und Morphologie der Mundspeicheldrüsen," in *Primatologia III*. Edited by A. Hofer, A. H. Schultz and D. Stark, 5–40. New York: Karger.

SIMONDS, P. E.

1965 "The bonnet macaque in South India," in *Primate behavior: field studies of monkeys and apes*. Edited by I. DeVore, 175–196. New York: Holt, Rinehart and Winston.

SIMONS, E.

1970 "Deployment and history of Old Word monkeys, Cercopithecidae, Primates," in *Old World monkeys*. Edited by J. R. and P. H. Napier, 99–136. New York: Academic Press.

STANLEY, H. R., J. MOOR-JANKOWSKI, E. GRAYOWSKI

1965 Cheek pouches of Old World monkeys as sites for tissue transplantation experiments. *Experiments in Medical Surgery* 23:38–60.

STRUHSAKER, T.

1967 *Behavior of the vervet monkey* (Cercopithecus aethiops). University of California Publications in Zoology 82.

1969 Correlates of ecology and social organization among African cercopithecines. *Folia Primatologica* 11:80–118.

TAPPEN, N. C.

1960 Problems of distribution and adaptation of the African monkeys. *Current Anthropology* 2:91–120.

TELEKI, G.

1973 The omnivorous chimpanzee. *Scientific American* 228:33–42.

THORINGTON, R. W.

1970 "Feeding behavior of non-human primates in the wild," in *Feeding and nutrition of non-human primates*. Edited by R. S. Harris, 15–27. London: Academic Press.

TUTTLE, R. H.

1969 Terrestrial trends in the hands of the anthropoidea. *Proceedings of the Second Congress of Primatology* 2:192–200. Basel: Karger.

WALKER, E. P.
1964 *Mammals of the world.* Baltimore: Johns Hopkins.

WASHBURN, S. L., I. DE VORE
1963 "The social life of baboons and early man," in *Social life of early man.* Edited by S. L. Washburn, 91–105. London: Methuen.

WATT, B., A. MERRILL
1950 *Composition of foods — raw, processed, prepared.* United States Department of Agriculture Handbook Number 8.

WITTE, G. R.
1971 Jungentransport in den Bachentaschen beim Syrischen Goldhamster *Mesocricetus auratus. Zeitschrift für Säugetierkunde* 36:193–256.

YOSHIBA, K.
1968 "Local and intertroop variability in ecology and social behavior of common Indian langurs," in *Primates: studies in adaptation and variability.* Edited by P. Jay, 217–242. New York: Holt, Rinehart and Winston.

Discussion

TUTTLE: By way of introduction to this topic I would say that traditionally we have looked at the dental features as somewhat stable heritage features that reflect phylogeny while *per contra* the postcranial parts were considered to be much more plastic and would therefore reflect the particularities of the environments in which species live. Thus, we have relied on dental features more than postcranial features for tracing phylogeny. The paper by Walker and Murray demonstrates that there are many functionally related characteristics in the dentition as well.

GOODMAN: I would ask those who speak on this question to indicate when they think that the features which are very important functionally are useful in deriving phylogenetic relationships and when they might actually lead to the opposite by representing convergence. We should know which of them may be depicting phylogenetic relations, if any of them do, and which are apt to be similar in different primates because of similar functional adaptations on a convergent basis.

SZALAY: Pursuant of what Russ Tuttle just said, I also find that the old adages about dental features being of a heritage sort and postcranial features being mostly plastic reflections of environment are absolutely false. If you ask proper questions, you will find "primitive," "advanced," "convergent," etc., features in the postcranial skeleton as well as in the teeth. And you find functional characters in all teeth. Every biological feature has to be evaluated from phylogenetic, mechanical, and functional perspectives. You cannot neatly separate these. There are no hard and fast answers as to which are better for phylogeny.

CHIARELLI: I agree, but we have to give weight to the different characters. Morphological characters are sometimes built up by many genes and with the intervention of the environment during the development of the body. We know that there is this intervention at this level. I think that at this level, the epigenetic traits — the special traits that we can sort out in the cranium or in the total body which are in fact in large part the characters which Szalay was proposing to use for differentiation — are better than the general morphological characteristics because we know that they are directly related with some gene or genotype. We have hereditary variation in them. These can be profitably inspected in the human skeleton in family studies. I would also like to say that the phylogeny of the prosimians presented by Szalay is in large agreement with the chromosomal data if we examine not only number but also structure using the so-called fundamental number, i.e. the number of arms on the chromosomes. This data confirms the connection of the Lorisidae with the Lemuridae.

TUTTLE: Mr. Walker or Mr. Murray would you please respond to Goodman's comment that was directed to you earlier?

MURRAY: Our paper attempts to assess the closeness of fit between the dentition and specific kinds of food and to obtain measures of a particular animal's ability to handle foods of various textures. We were not really stressing phylogenetic or even taxonomic questions *per se*. It is actually more of a biomechanical and functional anatomical exercise.

SZALAY: It is a beautiful paper.

MURRAY: Thank you. The principal objective was to establish a premise from which we can interpret the fossil record.

TUTTLE: But you did find functionally related dental characters.

MURRAY: There is one further point here. We chose bilophodont dentitions because there is a lot of convergence in this particular type of dental pattern. We intend eventually to study some Australian marsupials, particularly phalangerids. We will compare them in the same manner as primates to see if we can get a broader comparative base regarding the evolution of this type of dentition.

LOVEJOY: A comment of a more general nature. With the morphological evidence we are at least in a position to decipher whether or not we are dealing with adaptive characters and the problems of convergence and divergence. The molecular evidence is still in a state of flux because of uncertainties in the protein clock and the hypothesis of non-Darwinian evolution. Therefore, we are not yet in a position to say whether we are dealing primarily with drift or whether we are in fact dealing with selective evolution and in what proportions. There is also a tendency to dichotomize "morphologic" and "protein" evolution. However, morphologic evolution is also protein evolution. In terms of establishing phylogenies based on morphological data at least we are in a position to say, and I think with greater accuracy at this point, what kind of selective mechanisms might be involved and how intense they might be.

GOODMAN: Although you can make such statements about the particular morphological features in terms of phylogeny, potentially the greatest data are the molecular data. They have led the way toward re-evaluating the relationships for example of the African apes to the Asiatic apes, on the one hand, and man, on the other. Theoretically, the molecular data are the ones closest to the genome. They are the kind of data that give you true measures of genetic distance regardless of how much of this is due to selection, drift, and so on. With proteins and the nucleic acids we are dealing with the genetic messages themselves. I will not take a back seat to any of my morphological friends with regard to the overriding importance of this kind of data.

TUTTLE: We could rearrange the seating.

LOVEJOY: On the other hand, I think that at the present time we have a very limited viewpoint of the total genome of the animal, perhaps with the exception of the DNA data, but even they are not always in accord with the antigen cross reaction and protein sequencing data. The total number of proteins versus the number that have actually been sequenced gives us a very limited viewpoint.

GOODMAN: Actually the data are much more in agreement than disagreement. As I stated earlier the key points of the three sets of data agree with each other exactly in placing the African apes with man, in placing the Old World monkeys with the Hominoidea, and placing the platyrrhines with the catarrhines in a group we can call the Anthropoidea. Thus in the suborder Anthropoidea we get a marvelous agreement in the three types of data available to us from a molecular vantage point.

LOVEJOY: I did not mean to imply that this was not the case. What I simply want to point out is that in the construction of a phylogenetic sequence I do not think that morphology is outdated. It is protein based and it is therefore equally important.

SZALAY: I am very happy to hear that morphology is not outdated. The phrases "modern methods" in systematics and "modern approaches" to systematics always amuse me. Techniques can be modern but that does not mean very much. To me it is the conceptual orientation of the questions asked that makes a study modern. In terms of functional approach and actual results obtained, for example, I consider the paper by Walker and Murray to be an ingenious study.

ECKHARDT: Since we have returned to Walker and Murray's paper I would like to address a more specific question to them. In the methods section you noted that the dietary material came from the stomachs of wild-shot specimens. There is no information on the length of time that the material had been in the stomach for digestion. What effect might this have on your results? Further, I would expect that different foods, e.g. fruit versus leaves, would have different chemical compositions, for example, the relative amount of lignin and cellulose. What effect might this have on the ultimate particle size produced in your analysis?

WALKER: We attempted to control for both of those factors by examining the stomach contents of the macaques and langurs and selecting out all leaf fragments. We studied these fragments microscopically to determine whether the edges had been subjected to digestion. The samples that we isolated in this way consisted of leaves that showed no sign of digestive erosion. We only measured these.

ECKHARDT: That is not a control for time *per se* because there might be one further variable introduced, namely the relative rates of digestion in the stomachs of the animals.

MURRAY: Ideally we would like to use esophageal fistulation to retrieve food directly from the esophaguses of the animals. But, of course, colobines are extremely valuable animals and no one would allow us to do this kind of experimentation. So we took second best and that is the primary flaw in this. We tried to be judicious about our inferences. There is evidence of corrosive action of digestion on the leaves. Almost all of them show brownish coloration, so there had been chemical activity. But the animals had taken a succession of food over a period of time and we measured only those leaves that seemed to be least damaged. These were the maximum sized leaves as well. We selected the ones which showed actual shearing of lophs on the food. Thus we think that ours is a fairly good measure, considering that we could not do fistulation experiments.

LIEBERMAN: There is a very large dental literature on chewing efficiency which Walker and Murray appear to have overlooked. The data is derived from human chewers and it comes from schools of dentistry that are interested in testing the efficiency of dentures. Now the basic conclusions of these studies is that chewing efficiency in man is entirely a function of swept tooth area. The larger the amount of tooth area that is in contact during grinding the more efficient the tooth action will be. How does this relate to your studies? Did you experiment with mechanical models that might confirm this hypothesis?

WALKER: No, we did not. We were simply trying to assess the relative efficiencies of cercopithecine and colobine teeth for processing different types of food, i.e. leafy foods with two primary dimensions, like leaf lettuce, and food with three primary dimensions, like apples.

ECKHARDT: We should distinguish here between efficiency which will have to do with the arrangement of cusps on the teeth and the more detailed structural arrangements of the muscles and so on, and the area. I think that in the human setup, most of the differences that you get will reflect different areas. But here we are dealing with rather different functional complexes viz., from species to species with respect to cusp arrangement. Walker and Murray's paper deals primarily with the effect of cusp arrangement.

LIEBERMAN: Yes, but still I object that the uncontrolled variables are so great that it would be very interesting to correlate this study with a controlled mechanical model.

SECTION FOUR

Knuckle-Walking and Hominoid Evolution

Knuckle-Walking and Knuckle-Walkers: A Commentary on Some Recent Perspectives on Hominoid Evolution

RUSSELL H. TUTTLE

In the auspicious year 1859, Sir Richard Owen designated chimpanzees, gorillas, and orangutans KNUCKLE-WALKERS in distinction from gibbons, which he termed BRACHIATORS. He did not provide descriptions of knuckle-walking and brachiation. That the African apes are knuckle-walkers has passed virtually unchallenged, though this fact seldom received proper attention in discussions of hominoid phylogeny and especially in the classic debates between disciples of the brachiationist and nonbrachiationist schools. The status of orangutans as knuckle-walkers has always been equivocal, though in conceptual models several prominent theorists have treated their terrestrial hand postures as if they were identical with the knuckle-walking of African apes (Straus 1940; Schultz 1936; Napier 1959). Several primate morphologists of the

I thank the following colleagues for their assistance in aspects of research upon which this article is based: Dr. John V. Basmajian (director), Mrs. Eleanor Regenos (director of research), G. Shine (formerly), J. Malone, and J. Perry of Emory University Regional Rehabilitation Research and Training Center; Dr. Geoffrey Bourne (director), Gen. George Duncan (assistant director), Dr. Michael Keeling, Dr. C. M. Rogers, Dr. I. Bernstein, R. Pollard, E. van Ormer, and J. Roberts of Yerkes Regional Primate Research Center; Dr. Josef Biegert (director), Professor A. Schultz, and E. Etter of the Anthropologisches Institut der Universität Zürich; Dr. James Wanner, University of Northern Colorado; Dr. Benjamin Beck and L. La France of the Chicago Zoological Park; Dr. Donald Davis (director) of Cheyenne Mountain Zoo; and R. Susman and K. Barnes, University of Chicago. This work was supported by National Science Foundation Grant GS-3209, Public Health Service Research Career Development Award 1-K04-GM16347-01 from the National Institutes of Health, the Lichtstern Fund of the University of Chicago, and the Wenner-Gren Foundation for Anthropological Research. The article was read at the Forty-second Annual Meeting of the American Association of Physical Anthropologists in Dallas, Texas, April 12, 1973.

For Plates, see pp. x–xiii, between pp. 560–561

nineteenth century (Mayer 1856; Gratiolet and Alix 1866; Broca 1869) reported that captive orangutans position their hands on the ground in a manner unlike that of chimpanzees. Further, in 1957 Kallner reported and illustrated captive orangutans engaged in non-knuckle-walking hand postures. But these isolated observations had no notable effect on models of hominoid phylogeny.

In 1967 I described a remarkable variety of terrestrial hand postures exhibited by twenty-six orangutans that had arrived recently at Yerkes Regional Primate Research Center. They evinced a spectrum of palmigrade and flexed-finger postures, the most common ones being variants of fist-walking, but none of them truly knuckle-walked in African pongid fashion (Plate 1). Subsequent cursory surveys of orangutans in zoological parks in Europe and the United States and of the subjects at the Yerkes Center revealed no instance of knuckle-walking (Tuttle 1969a, 1970).

During the 1960's, when concepts of orangutan and African pongid locomotive behavior and manual morphology were undergoing revision, a renaissance and refinement of biomolecular perspectives on hominoid evolution occurred, the upshot of which was overwhelming evidence that man, chimpanzee, and gorilla share remarkably close affinities (Goodman 1962, 1963, 1967; Chiarelli 1962; Klinger et al. 1963; Williams 1964; Sarich and Wilson 1967; Wiener, Gordon, and Moor-Jankowski 1964).

Sherwood Washburn, the imaginative champion of the Keith-Gregory brachiationist model was quick to account for the mass of novel data from these several inquiries in a manner consistent with the hypothesis that man evolved from a troglodytian ancestor that was not markedly unlike the common chimpanzee. Thus, he interposed a stage of knuckle-walking between the stages of brachiation and bipedalism in the classic Keith-Gregory model (Washburn 1967, 1968). He cited the hand bones from F. L. K. NN 1 in Olduvai Gorge as paleontological evidence for a stage of knuckle-walking, stating that they show "many of the features of a knuckle-walker" (Washburn 1967).

Washburn's new theory has been endorsed by at least two of his colleagues at the University of California at Berkeley — Clark (1970) and Sarich (1971) — and several other evolutionary anthropologists are willing to admit knuckle-walkers to man's family tree. Pilbeam (1972:48) recently confessed that the Miocene protohominids may have been "at least incipiently knuckle-walkers." Napier (1970:197) proposed that *Paranthropus* may have resorted to knuckle-walking "under duress" as its bipedal gait was inefficient and clumsy. Leakey (1971) and Kortlandt (1972:62) also accept that *Paranthropus* may have knuckle-walked. Following my suggestion of 1967, Robinson (1972: 196) argued that the hand bones from Olduvai F.L.K. NN 1 are as reasonably attributed to *Paranthropus* as to *Homo africanus*. And since the lower limb of *Paranthropus* may have been relatively short this form may have knuckle-walked (Robinson 1972:196). But later in the same work Robinson (1972:206) concluded that because of the complete absence of morphological particularities related to knuckle-walking on the second metacarpal bone from Kromdraai (TM 1517) "knuckle-walking was at best a very insignificant part of the locomotive activity of [*Paranthropus*]." In this case, I would suggest use of the term *knuckling* instead of knuckle-walking.

Consequent upon the new studies of knuckle-walking in African apes, another set of models surfaced recently. While it has several advocates (Simons and Pilbeam 1972; Simons 1972; Conroy and Fleagle 1972), its authorship is difficult to pinpoint precisely. Yale University is a major center for it though subscribers there cite a generous supply of personal communications from Alan Walker (Simons and Pilbeam 1972; Pilbeam 1972). This second new set of schemes would have all great apes, implicitly or explicitly including the orangutan, and in most cases man also, derived from terrestrial quadrupedal ancestors. Many of the features traditionally associated with "brachiation" in extant large-bodied hominoids are attributed primarily to terrestrial knuckle-walking in Miocene apes. Accordingly, knuckle-walking was precedent and prospectively adaptive for the arboreal climbing and suspensory behavior of orangutans, chimpanzees, and gorillas. Clearly this pristinely terrestrial ape model of the Yale-Walker group contrasts markedly with Washburn's brachiationist/knuckle-walking model.

Simons and Pilbeam (1972; Pilbeam 1972) posit an extensive period of parallel evolution of knuckle-walking in lineages that culminated in gorillas and chimpanzees because they recognize dentally distinct ancestors for the two lines among Miocene dryopithecine apes. Washburn (1967, 1968), Clark (1970), and Sarich (1971), per contra, stress modern biomolecular evidence that indicates quite recent divergence of chimpanzee and gorilla.

Several recent behavioral and morphological observations will probably contribute more to the current intellectual ferment surrounding hominoid phylogeny than to resolution of tensions between available models. I present them here with the hope that students of evolutionary anthropology will be stimulated to knuckle down to the kinds of comprehensive comparative and experimental studies that are essential if we are to advance assuredly toward the truth.

In 1971, Benjamin Beck, curator of research at the Brookfield Zoo, observed that Felix, a sixteen-year-old male orangutan, occasionally placed his hands in knuckle-walking postures. A subsequent pilot study that Beck and I made revealed that the subject knuckled while sitting-resting, sitting-feeding (Plate 2), and engaging in a distinctive mode of squatting orthograde progression (Tuttle and Beck 1972). He did not exhibit the degree of hyperextension of metacarpophalangeal joints II–V that is typical of adult chimpanzees and gorillas. When he progressed rapidly on dry substrates and sometimes on wet substrates, he adopted a semierect quadrupedal fist-walking posture. At other times when the floor was wet, he would slide his fists or knuckled hands forward without the load passing directly over the hand. He consistently placed his hands in fist-walking posture as he leaned over to investigate objects on the floor and to descend headfirst from his resting platforms to the floor.

Recently, Susman (1974) conducted a more thorough study of Felix's locomotion and documented circumstances wherein knuckle-walking occurred. This study confirmed observations of Tuttle and Beck and added important new information. Susman reported that when the floor of the cage was wet, the subject engaged in facultative diagonal sequence, diagonal couplets knuckle-walking in order to obtain bits of food. During these episodes, the hand was prominently load bearing (Plate 3). Susman inferred that lubrication of the floor might serve to dissipate potential stresses on the metacarpophalangeal joints, especially when the fingers initially contact the ground. Even during this mode of knuckle-walking, Felix's metacarpophalangeal joints did not hyperextend as markedly as they would have in most African apes of equivalent weight (250 pounds). Further, as distinct from African apes, in Felix the elbow joint is not fully extended during the support phase of the hand (Susman 1974).

Felix is not the only knuckle-walking orangutan. James A. Wanner of the University of Northern Colorado recently observed knuckle-walking in several subadult and adult orangutans at the Cheyenne Mountain Zoo and kindly sent me photographs of them. These subjects employ knuckled hands for crutch-walking, diagonal sequence, diagonal couplets progression, resting, and sliding. When Beck and I visited Cheyenne Mountain Zoo in August, 1972, we learned that the floor of the orangutan enclosure is kept wet because the animals enjoy sliding. The floor has become polished and even appears to be oily. Wanner and his students are undertaking a more thorough study of knuckle-walking and other knuckling behavior at the Cheyenne Mountain Zoo. This study should elucidate further the ontogeny and circumstances conducive to knuckle-walking in captive orangutans.

Finally, I should mention that the 6½-year-old orangutan (#0–38) that Basmajian and I employ in electromyographic experiments at the Yerkes Center occasionally places her hands in knuckled postures. But she has not borne notable loads on them.

In sum, recent behavioral studies demonstrate that in a single species of ape we may witness a remarkable spectrum of terrestrial hand postures, ranging from full palmigrady, through modified palmigrady and fist-walking, to facultative knuckle-walking modes that are very close counterparts to those consistently exhibited by African apes. That a highly advanced arboreal climber and arm swinger like the orangutan can develop ontogenetically into a knuckle-walker (albeit in special circumstances of captivity) suggests that ancestors of the African apes were somewhat similarly predisposed to knuckle-walking by their own arboreal heritage. It also seems reasonable to argue that if the common ancestor of chimpanzee and gorilla possessed somewhat advanced features of the hand for suspensory behavior and climbing, it could develop into a knuckle-walker quite rapidly after adopting terrestrial habits.

But we can progress only a limited distance toward the truth about phylogenetic events on the basis of inferences from extant species alone. In order to trace the evolution of knuckle-walking we must identify bony features in the hands of knuckle-walkers that discretely relate to knuckle-walking and therefore cannot be confused with other locomotive or manipulatory behaviors in fossil forms. Thus, concurrently with behavioral observations on available apes, I conducted passive arthrologic examinations and qualitative osteologic studies on pongid, hylobatid, and cercopithecoid hands (Tuttle 1969b, 1969c, 1970). These morphological investigations led me to posit that the wrist joint and the metacarpophalangeal joints of digits II–V are characterized by particular close-packed positioning mechanisms that evolved as special components of the terrestrial adaptive complex in emergent prototroglodytians and were premised on features of an arboreal heritage that included suspensory behavior (Tuttle 1969a, 1969b, 1970; Tuttle and Basmajian 1974). Basmajian and I are testing this hypothesis with electromyographic studies on gorilla, chimpanzee, and orangutan subjects at the Yerkes Center (Tuttle et al. 1972; Tuttle and Basmajian 1974). Jenkins and Fleagle (this volume) have conducted cineradiographic studies on the hands of knuckle-walking chimpanzees.

Synthesis of results of electromyographic and cineradiographic studies should go a long way toward testing the close-packing hypotheses.

On the basis of descriptive osteologic studies on the carpal bones of anthropoid primates, Lewis (1972a, 1972b, 1973) denied that knuckle-walking is discretely impressed on the wrist bones of African apes. Following Straus (1940), Lewis explained the knuckle-walking of African apes as the direct result of brachiating habits of their ancestors. Thus, limited wrist extension in chimpanzees and gorillas is a "logical consequence of aligning hand and forearm" for brachiation (Lewis 1972a:211). He further cited the relative shortness of the long digital flexor muscles as "a potent factor in limitation of wrist extension" in the great apes (1972a:211). He explains all particularities of the carpal bones that evidence close functional affinities of the two African apes and man in the context of a brachiationist model that would leave orangutans in some ways less advanced for brachiation than the other three large-bodied hominoids. He concluded that "knuckle-walking requires no especially striking modifications of the wrist joint" (1972a: 212). By implication, the search for bony hallmarks that might be employed phylogenetically will be fruitless (Tuttle and Basmajian 1974).

But the scope and emphasis of Lewis's studies are not sufficient to deny categorically the existence of bony features that are discretely related to knuckle-walking. Further, it is absurd to assume that certain features in the wrists of man and the African apes are more advanced for brachiation than that of the orangutan, which among large-bodied hominoids engages most frequently in suspensory behavior and is most progressive in features of other anatomical regions that are clearly related to suspensory behavior (Tuttle and Basmajian 1974). To cite one example from Lewis's own work: exclusion of the ulna from participation in the wrist joint, which he states is the hallmark that permitted other morphological changes in the wrist associated with brachiation (Lewis 1969, *et seq.*), is more advanced in *Pongo* than in the other Hominoidea. Other features of the carpal bones that are reasonably associated with suspensory behavior are also more conspicuously developed in *Pongo* than in *Homo* and *Pan* (Tuttle and Basmajian 1974; Jenkins and Fleagle, this volume).

The logicality of limitations of wrist extension being consequent upon the alignment of hand and forearm in "brachiators" and the potency of the relative shortness of the long digital flexor muscles to limit wrist extension are devalued by my observations on *Pongo* (Tuttle 1967 *et seq.;* Tuttle and Basmajian 1974). For instance orangutans often possess remarkable capacities to extend the wrist and fingers. This flexibility is probably of considerable advantage to them during climbing-bridging behavior in trees.

Unlike features of the carpal bones, the special set of metacarpal heads II–V and the dorsal shelving associated with them, which Napier (1959) and I (Tuttle 1967, *et seq.*; Tuttle et al. 1972; Tuttle and Basmajian 1974) related especially to knuckle-walking, have remained unchallenged by other workers. Unfortunately, the hand bones from F.L.K. NN 1 do not include these bits (Napier 1962). The other features of the Olduvai hand bones cannot be related unequivocally to knuckle-walking as opposed to other hand postures (Tuttle 1967, 1970; Tuttle and Basmajian 1974).

However, because man knuckles in certain circumstances (Tuttle and Beck 1972), and because individual orangutans may indeed knuckle-walk in captivity, it is not unreasonable to posit that the hominid (or hominids) at Olduvai also knuckled, especially while resting in squatting postures. But whether true knuckle-walking constituted a discrete stage in hominid phylogeny remains unconfirmed by fossil evidence. My current surmise (Tuttle 1969a; Tuttle and Basmajian 1974), which Simons (1972) seems to share, is that because of special arboreal circumstances, protohominids were probably predisposed to bipedalism before they ventured more or less permanently to the ground. Thus they would not have passed through a phase of knuckle-walking. Of course, they may have knuckled while resting, but only to a degree approximating that of modern man. Accordingly, we should not expect to find features related especially to knuckle-walking in the wrist and metacarpal bones of fossil hominids. Yet I would caution also that we should not be so biased that we might pass over such features that might exist. And certainly we should not close our minds to the possibility that discrete features related to knuckle-walking exist in the manual osteology of African apes and their ancestors. Indeed the recent studies of Tuttle and Basmajian (1974) and their associates (Tuttle et al. 1972) and of Jenkins and Fleagle (this volume) indicate that such particularities do exist. The considerable challenges of quantification and biomechanical explanation of these features await the application and development of innovative research strategies and techniques that will complement electromyographic and cineradiographic studies.

REFERENCES

BROCA, P.
1869 L'ordre des primates parallèle anatomique de l'homme et des singes. *Bulletins de la Société d'anthropologie de Paris* 4:228–401.

CHIARELLI, B.
1962 Comparative morphometric analysis of primate chromosomes. I. The chromosomes of anthropoid apes and of man. *Caryologia* 15:99–121.

CLARK, J. D.
1970 *The prehistory of Africa.* New York: Praeger.

CONROY, G. C., J. G. FLEAGLE
1972 Locomotor behaviour in living and fossil pongids. *Nature* 237: 103–104.

GOODMAN, M.
1962 Evolution of the immunologic species specificity of human serum proteins. *Human Biology* 34:104–150.
1963 "Man's place in the phylogeny of the primates as reflected in serum proteins," in *Classification and human evolution.* Edited by S. L. Washburn, 204–235. Chicago: Aldine.
1967 Deciphering primate phylogeny from macromolecular specificities. *American Journal of Physical Anthropology* 26:255–276.

GRATIOLET, L. P., P. H. E. ALIX
1866 Recherches sur l'anatomie du *Troglodytes Aubryi. Nouvelles Archives du Muséum d'Histoire Naturelle,* Paris 2:1–264.

KALLNER, M.
1957 Die Muskulatur und die Funktion des Schultergürtels und der Vorderextremität des Orang-Utans. *Morphologisches Jahrbuch* 97:554–665.

KLINGER, H. P., J. L. HAMERTON, D. MUTTON, E. M. LANG
1963 "The chromosomes of the Hominoidea," in *Classification and human evolution.* Edited by S. L. Washburn, 235–242. Chicago: Aldine.

KORTLANDT, A.
1972 *New perspectives on ape and human evolution.* Amsterdam: Stichting voor Psychobiologie.

LEAKEY, R. E. F.
1971 Further evidence of Lower Pleistocene hominids from East Rudolf, North Kenya. *Nature* 231:241–245.

LEWIS, O. J.
1969 The hominoid wrist joint. *American Journal of Physical Anthropology* 30:251–268.
1971a Brachiation and the early evolution of the Hominoidea. *Nature* 230:577–579.
1971b The contrasting morphology found in the wrist joints of semibrachiating monkeys and brachiating apes. *Folia Primatologica* 16:248–256.

1972a "Evolution of the hominoid wrist," in *The functional and evolutionary biology of primates*. Edited by R. H. Tuttle, 207–222. Chicago: Aldine-Atherton.

1972b Osteological features characterizing the wrist of monkeys and apes, with a reconsideration of this region in *Dryopithecus (Proconsul) africanus*. *American Journal of Physical Anthropology* 36:45–58.

1973 The hominoid os capitatum, with special reference to the fossil bones from Sterkfontein and Olduvai Gorge. *Journal of Human Evolution* 2:1–11.

MAYER, PROF.

1856 Zur Anatomie des Orangutans und des Schimpanses. *Archiv für Naturgeschichte* 22:279–304. Berlin.

NAPIER, J. R.

1959 *Fossil metacarpals from Swartkrans*. Fossil Mammals of Africa 17. London: British Museum (Natural History).

1962 Fossil hand bones from Olduvai Gorge. *Nature* 196:409–411.

1970 *The roots of mankind*. Washington, D.C.: Smithsonian Institution Press.

OWEN, R.

1859 *On the classification and geographical distribution of the Mammalia*. London: Parker.

PILBEAM, D. R.

1972 *The ascent of man*. New York: Macmillan.

ROBINSON, J. T.

1972 *Early hominid posture and locomotion*. Chicago: University of Chicago Press.

SARICH, V. M.

1971 "A molecular approach to the question of human origins," in *Background for man: readings in physical anthropology*. Edited by P. Dolhinow and V. M. Sarich, 60-81. Boston: Little, Brown.

SARICH, V. M., A. C. WILSON

1967 Immunological time scale for hominid evolution. *Science* 158: 1200–1203.

SCHULTZ, A. H.

1936 Characters common to higher primates and characters specific for man. *Quarterly Review of Biology* 11:259–283, 425–455.

SIMONS, E. L.

1972 *Primate evolution: an introduction to man's place in nature*. New York: Macmillan.

SIMONS, E. L., D. R. PILBEAM

1972 "Hominoid paleoprimatology," in *The functional and evolutionary biology of primates*. Edited by R. H. Tuttle, 36–62. Chicago: Aldine-Atherton.

STRAUS, W. L., JR.

1940 The posture of the great ape hand in locomotion, and its phylogenetic implications. *American Journal of Physical Anthropology* 27:199–207.

SUSMAN, R.

1974 Facultative terrestrial hand postures in an orangutan (*Pongo pygmaeus*) and pongid evolution. *American Journal of Physical Anthropology* 40:27–37.

TUTTLE, R. H.

1967 Knuckle-walking and the evolution of hominoid hands. *American Journal of Physical Anthropology* 26:171–206.

1969a Knuckle-walking and the problem of human origins. *Science* 166: 953–961.

1969b Quantitative and functional studies on the hands of the Anthropoidea. I. The Hominoidea. *Journal of Morphology* 128:309–364.

1969c Terrestrial trends in the hands of the Anthropoidea: a preliminary report. *Proceedings of the Second International Congress of Primatology,* Atlanta, Georgia 2:192–200. Basel/New York: Karger.

1970 "Postural, propulsive, and prehensile capabilities in the cheiridia of chimpanzees and other great apes," in *The chimpanzee*. Edited by G. H. Bourne, volume two, 167–253. Basel/New York: Karger.

TUTTLE, R. H., J. V. BASMAJIAN

1974 "Electromyography of forearm musculature in *Gorilla* and problems related to knuckle-walking," in *Primate locomotion*. Edited by F. A. Jenkins, Jr., 293–347. New York: Academic Press.

TUTTLE, R. H., J. V. BASMAJIAN, E. REGENOS, G. SHINE

1972 Electromyography of knuckle-walking: results of four experiments on the forearm of *Pan gorilla*. *American Journal of Physical Anthropology* 37:255–266.

TUTTLE, R. H., B. B. BECK

1972 Knuckle-walking hand postures in an orangutan (*Pongo pygmaeus*). *Nature* 236:33–34.

WASHBURN, S. L.

1967 Behavior and the origin of man. *Proceedings of the Royal Anthropological Society*.

1968 "The study of human evolution." Condon Lectures, Oregon State System of Higher Education, Eugene, Oregon.

WIENER, A. S., E. B. GORDON, J. MOOR-JANKOWSKI

1964 Immunological relationship between serum globulins of man and of other primates, revealed by a serological inhibition test. *Transfusion* 4:347–350.

WILLIAMS, C. A., JR.

1964 "Immunochemical analysis of serum proteins of the primates: a study in molecular evolution," in *Evolutionary and genetic biology of primates*. Edited by J. Buettner-Janusch, 2:25–74. New York: Academic Press.

Knuckle-Walking and the Functional Anatomy of the Wrists in Living Apes

FARISH A. JENKINS, JR., and JOHN G. FLEAGLE

Knuckle-walking, a characteristic mode of terrestrial progression unique to gorillas and chimpanzees, has been studied principally in an attempt to answer two fundamental questions. First, what are the major anatomical adaptations for this behavior? Second, how do such adaptations and behavior relate to the pattern of higher primate evolution, and specifically to the evolutionary divergence of pongids and hominids? Resolution of these issues will depend upon interrelating data from three sources: field studies of the naturalistic behavior of knuckle-walking species, investigations of functional anatomy, and the fossil record.

Traditionally, many of the questions concerning knuckle-walking have been posed in morphological terms. An alternate but complimentary approach is through physiological or other techniques that are designed to provide data on conditions in vivo. Notable among recent studies are those of Tuttle, Basmajian, and colleagues employing electromyography in gorillas (Tuttle et al. 1972; Tuttle and Basmajian

We thank Dr. Richard G. Naegeli (Director of Zoological Parks for the Metropolitan District Commission of Boston) for the loan of the chimpanzees used in this study, Dr. C. Richard Taylor for the resources of the Concord Field Station, and V. J. Rowntree for the treadmill training and maintenance of the animals. The technical expertise of John Klopping and the Shields Warren Radiation Laboratory provided our cineradiographic capabilities. We are grateful to Dr. Wendell H. Niemann for access to the chimpanzee, gibbon, and macaque colonies at the Laboratory for Experimental Medicine and Surgery in Primates (New York University) and to Denis Signorelli for technical assistance. Laszlo Meszoly rendered Figure 2 and A. H. Coleman photographically reproduced the radiographs in Figures 3–10. This work was supported by grants from the John Milton Fund of Harvard University and from the National Institutes of Health.

For Plates, see pp. xiv–xx, between pp. 560–561

1974), and of Taylor and Rowntree (1973) measuring the energetic cost of knuckle-walking versus bipedalism in chimpanzees.

We present here some preliminary results of an in vivo radiographic study of the chimpanzee wrist during knuckle-walking. The radiographic technique, although not yet perfected, documents carpal bone relationships and wrist excursions that cannot be positively established by other means. These data provide the basis for a more meaningful comparison of primate wrist structures.

MATERIALS AND METHODS

This study of the chimpanzee wrist is based on cineradiographic records of knuckle-walking, radiographic examination of sedated subjects, and observations on embalmed and osteological materials. Radiographic data on gibbons and macaques are also included.

For cineradiography, two three-year-old chimpanzees (*Pan troglodytes*; 17.5 kilograms average weight) were trained to move on a variable speed treadmill (Plate 1). The chimpanzees readily became habituated to the treadmill and excercised freely on it without fear or constraint for periods up to ten minutes. A 30-kilowatt, grid-controlled tube with a 0.06-millimeter focal spot and a Siemens image intensifier (Sirecon duplex image intensification system with an Eclair GV–16 16-millimeter camera run at fifty frames per second) were positioned on either side of the treadmill, and the X-ray beam was projected perpendicularly to the direction of treadmill movement.

The actual radiographic projection of the moving wrist depended on the orientation of the hand. As in the chimpanzees observed by Tuttle (1967: 177, 1970: 175), the hand varied from a perpendicular (palm facing posteriad) to an oblique (palm facing posteromediad) position. Additional variation resulted from gross changes in body orientation on the treadmill; in many sequences, the subject's median plane was turned obliquely in relation to treadmill movement. The two most commonly obtained radiographic projections of the wrist are reported here: (1) lateral projection — the wrist as seen in radioulnar (or ulnoradial) aspect and (2) anteroposterior projection — the wrist as seen in palmar aspect. Approximately 300 feet of film containing knuckle-walking sequences were analyzed with an L and W Photo-optical Data Analyzer 224A. It must be emphasized that the two radiographic projections are not different views of the same knuckle-walking position; rather, the two projections are of knuckle-walking positions that differ in orientation with respect to the direction of movement.

For radiographic examination of the stationary wrist, four adult male chimpanzees (numbers 114, 197, 209, and 250) were selected from the colony at the Laboratory for Experimental Medicine and Surgery in Primates (New York University). These subjects ranged in age from approximately 13.5 to 15 years and ranged in weight from 56 to 67 kilograms. Under sedation, each was placed in a prone position on a narrow operating table. The forelimbs hung freely from the table, which was inclined to elevate the shoulders above the pelvis. The relative height of the table was adjusted to allow the knuckles to rest on a flat surface below, thus permitting the forelimb to bear some of its own weight. The hand, in a "knuckle-walking" posture, was loaded additionally by a downward traction at the elbow provided by the investigator. In this manner, we attempted to simulate the posture of a weight-bearing wrist in a knuckle-walking stance. Radiographs were taken in lateral, anteroposterior, and oblique projections. In addition, radiographs were taken of non-weight-bearing wrists passively manipulated into maximum radial and ulnar deviation (anteroposterior projection) and into maximum flexion and extension (lateral projection). As in the simulated knuckle-walking postures, compressive stress was applied across the wrist.

Radiographic records of passively manipulated wrist postures, including pronation and supination, were taken of two more chimpanzees (numbers 1 and 16), five adult gibbons *(Hylobates lar,* numbers 1, 2, 3, and 5, and *H. agilis*, number 12), and six macaques *(Macaca mulatta,* numbers 55, 177, 564, and 568, and *M. fascicularis,* numbers 22 and 27).

Embalmed and osteological specimens of chimpanzees and other primates examined in this study are from the collections in the Museum of Comparative Zoology.

OBSERVATIONS

An understanding of certain bony features of the chimpanzee wrist is prerequisite to evaluating radiographic records of stationary and locomotor postures. Accordingly, each major joint system is reviewed with special reference to the topography and orientation of the principal articular surfaces; radiographic observations are then discussed.

Proximal Carpal Joint

MORPHOLOGY The largest weight-bearing surfaces at the proximal carpal joint are the scaphoid, lunate, and distal radius. The radial articular surface is concave and has an oblique, rather than a perpendicular, orientation to the radial shaft. The surface as a whole is inclined somewhat toward the volar and ulnar aspects (Figure 1C). This orientation is difficult to quantify precisely because of irregularities in the curvature and margins of the articular surface. As an approximation, a tangent to the dorsal and volar margins (determined from lateral radiographic projection; Plate 3B—D) intersects the proximodistal axis of the radius at approximately 70° to 75°. Thus, instead of being perpendicular to the shaft, the orientation of the articular surface has a volar component of some 15° to 20°.

The proximal articular surfaces of the scaphoid and lunate, although confluent, differ fundamentally in orientation and topography. The lunate surface is broadly convex from the volar margin, which is narrow, to the dorsal margin, which is broad. The center of this triangular-shaped, curved surface is directed proximally. However, because of the marked widening toward the dorsal margin, much of the articular surface has a dorsal orientation.

The scaphoid surface is concavo-convex. The convex part of the facet, adjacent to the volar margin, is oriented more or less proximally. The remainder of the facet is shallowly concave and is oriented dorsoproximally.

RADIOGRAPHY OF STATIONARY POSTURES Radiographs of a weight-bearing wrist in lateral projection show clearly the radio-carpal articulation (Plates 2A, 3). The dorsal half of the radial facet is engaged by the concave part of the scaphoid articular surface. The volar half is engaged by the convex part of the scaphoid, as well as by the lunate. The characteristic form of these surfaces may have specific functional implications for wrist stability. As the wrist flexes, only the lunate and the convex part of the scaphoid articulate with the distal radius (Plate 5C); the essentially rotary movement between these similarly curved surfaces simulates a hinge mechanism. At maximum extension (whether by passive manipulation or in simulated knuckle-walking postures) the radio-scaphoid articulation consistently attains the same position. Mechanically, the concave part of the proximal scaphoid surface, in contact with the distal radius, appears to limit extension at the proximal carpal joint. Hinge movement ceases

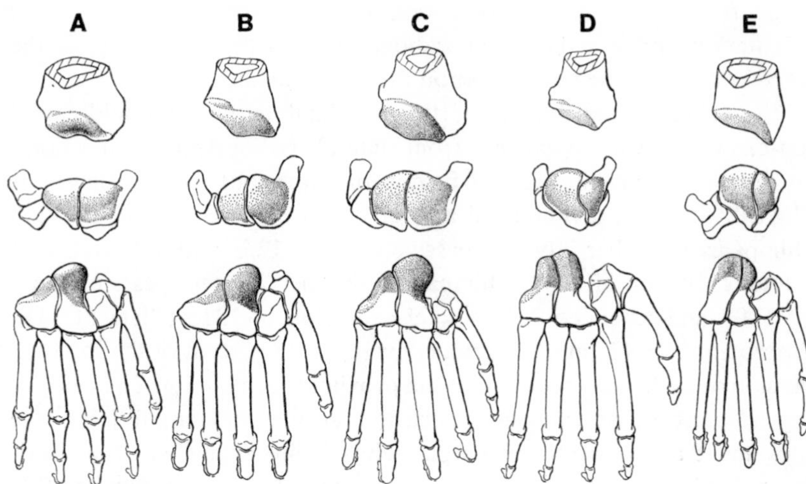

Figure 1. Proximodorsal view of articular surfaces in the wrists of (A) *Macaca mulatta*, (B) *Gorilla gorilla*, (C) *Pan troglodytes*, (D) *Pongo pygmaeus*, and (E) *Hylobates lar*. The radius (top) is depicted as if transparent in order to reveal the contours of the distal articular surface (stippled). On the proximal carpals (middle), the proximal articular surfaces of the lunate (left) and scaphoid (right) are stippled. On the distal carpals (bottom), the proximal articular surfaces of the hamate (left) and capitate (right) are stippled. In each case, the proximodorsal, rather than the conventional dorsal, view is depicted to display more fully the selected articular surfaces. Not to scale

as the radius contacts the concave part of the scaphoid. The dorsal margin of the radial articular surface never extends beyond the dorsal lip of the scaphoid. In a weight-bearing situation, no further movement is possible without disengaging the articular surfaces, which are held in apposition by body weight loading and possibly also by muscular contraction. Thus, this part of the joint achieves a "locked" or "close-packed" position.

Tuttle (1967: 189–190) described a ridge on the chimpanzee and gorilla scaphoid that lies along the dorsal aspect of the bone between the proximal and distal articular surfaces. We believe that Tuttle's interpretation of this feature correctly associates it with an extension-limiting function. However, radiographs do not show that the apex of the ridge itself acts as a "stop" that prevents further extension on the radius. Instead, the ridge partly supports the concave surface, which appears to be the significant feature in delimiting movement.

Anteroposterior radiographs of the wrist in a stationary, weight-bearing position (Plates 2B, 4) show the same relationship of the distal radius to the scaphoid and lunate observed in lateral projections. A large fraction of these articulating surfaces are dorsoproximal in orientation and are thus seen radiographically as an overlap of the dorsal margin of the radial facet on the scaphoid and lunate.

The relative contribution of the proximal carpal and mid-carpal ion-extension was estimated from lateral radiographic projections. In the neutral position (0° of flexion or extension) the metacarpus is aligned with the proximodistal axis of the forearm. From this position chimpanzee number 209 was passively flexed 125° and extended 45°, a total excursion of 170°. Chimpanzee number 250 was passively flexed 100° and extended 21°, a total excursion of 121° (Plate 5C, D). Approximately 42° and 27°, respectively, or 25 percent of the total excursion in each case, occurred at the proximal carpal joint. The remaining 75 percent of excursion occurred at the mid-carpal joint, the movement at the carpometacarpal joints being negligible. The maximum flexion-extension values obtained for chimpanzee number 209 are near the means established by Tuttle (1969: 328–329) on the basis of seventeen individuals. The values obtained for chimpanzee number 250 are not as great as even the minimum values observed by Tuttle; however, our determination in this case may not represent the true limits because of the variable degree of relaxation under sedation. It is significant that a one to three ratio of movement at the proximal carpal and mid-carpal joints occurs nevertheless in both cases.

The relative contribution of the proximal carpal and mid-carpal joints to ulnar and radial deviational movement was estimated from anteroposterior radiographic projections. The wrist of chimpanzee number 250 was moved passively from 40° of ulnar deviation to 22° of radial deviation, a total range of 62° (Plate 5A, B). The wrist of chimpanzee number 114 had a total range of 66°: 37° of ulnar deviation, 29° of radial deviation. Chimpanzee number 16 had a total range of 95°: 62° of ulnar deviation, 33° of radial deviation. In all three cases, the displacement at the proximal carpal joint was relatively small and equivalent to approximately one-third of the total deviational movement.

CINERADIOGRAPHY OF KNUCKLE-WALKING Cineradiographic records of the proximal carpal joint are in two projections: lateral (wrist seen in radioulnar aspect; hand oriented more or less perpendicularly to the direction of movement) and anteroposterior (hand oriented more or less parallel to direction of movement). Because these two projections represent different support postures, they will be discussed separately.

Lateral projection cineradiography clearly shows the relationship of the radius to the scaphoid and lunate (Plate 6A). Records of the initial part of the propulsive phase were not obtained, but during the middle and late propulsive phases, at least, the carpus and metacarpus are slightly extended; more precisely, the proximodistal axis of the carpus and metacarpus lies at 10° to 15° to that of the radius. Terminating the propulsive phase, the wrist flexes slightly and begins the swing phase in a position of about 20° of flexion. The striking feature of the extended wrist is the angular relationship between the distal radius and the scaphoid and lunate; the anterior (dorsal) third of the radial articular surface is positioned dorsally on the wrist and remains so until the wrist flexes at the end of the propulsive phase. However, considering the dorsal orientation of the scaphoid and lunate articular surfaces, together with those structural aspects of surface form related to the "close-packed" position, it is not surprising that the radiocarpal joint planes face dorsoproximally rather than strictly proximally.

Anteroposterior cineradiographic records of the wrist, taken of a knuckle-walking hand oriented in a plane parallel to the direction of movement, show relatively little movement at the proximal carpal and mid-carpal joints during flexion (see above). At the end of the swing phase, the wrist extends to a neutral position and shows no ulnar or radial deviation. Initial contact with the substrate is accompanied by slight ulnar deviation as the wrist becomes fully weight bearing. This movement occurs at both the proximal carpal and mid-carpal joints and is estimated to be a total of 10° to 20°. Throughout the swing phase the slight ulnar deviation is maintained. The intercarpal and carpometacarpal relationships remain more or less constant and appear to be the same as in the static posture depicted in Plate 4A.

With the exception of the slight ulnar deviation that occurs at the initial weight-bearing phase of knuckle-walking, the proximal carpal joint appears to remain static throughout a propulsive movement. Superposition of successive cineradiographic projections shows that forearm, carpus, and metacarpus rotate forward on the digits and about a center of rotation that lies either at the level of the metacarpophalangeal joints or slightly distal to them. The axis of rotation shifts consistently toward the radial side as the limb passes through the propulsive phase. Initially, the center lies typically between digits III and IV; as the propulsive phase is completed, the center is usually through digit or between digits II and III.

Mid-Carpal Joint

MORPHOLOGY The mid-carpal joint in the chimpanzee has a complex configuration. For purposes of comparison and radiographic study, the form and orientation of three joint planes in particular are worth noting. First, the concavo-convex triquetral-hamate articulation faces equally toward the ulnar side of the wrist as proximally. Only the ulnar half of the proximal hamate facet articulates with the triquetral. Second, the lunate occupies the radial half of the proximal hamate facet and the ulnar half of the capitate head. This articulation, like that of the radio-lunate, is hingelike and extends from volar to dorsal aspects; however, unlike the radio-lunate joint, is broadest aspect is along the volar rather than the dorsal margin. Third, the scaphoid-capitate joint consists of a shallowly concave surface on the scaphoid and a concavo-convex surface on the capitate. The capitate facet for the scaphoid is not smoothly confluent with the capitate facet for the lunate, as has been suggested in some published illustrations. The articular facet faces dorsally and to the radial side, whereas the adjacent facet for the lunate is inclined toward the ulnar side. The boundary between these two facets is therefore clearly demarcated.

RADIOGRAPHY OF STATIONARY POSTURES The mid-carpal joint may be visualized in various radiographic projections. With the hand slightly extended and in knuckle-walking posture, a characteristic feature is the position of the scaphoid on the capitate. Seen in lateral projection (Plate 3B), the long axis of the capitate is aligned with the metacarpal shafts. The scaphoid, however, lies principally on the dorsal side of this axis. In an anteroposterior projection (Plate 4), the dorsal margin of the scaphoid is again seen overlapping the dorsal aspect of the capitate head. The structural basis for this relationship is the degree of dorsal orientation of the concavo-convex capitate facet for the scaphoid (described above; Figure 1). As the wrist is brought into extension, the leading, or dorsal, edge of the scaphoid contacts the concave part of the capitate facet. The relationship between a concave proximal surface and a concavo-convex distal surface is similar to that of the radio-scaphoid articulation and represents an extension-limiting mechanism, especially in weight-bearing.

Lewis (1972: 55) described a screwlike action at the chimpanzee mid-carpal joint during wrist extension, with the distal carpal row rotating to a more supinated position relative to the proximal carpal row. In our radiographic examination of the chimpanzee wrist, we could not verify a conjunct rotation at the mid-carpal joint upon wrist extension. A modified interpretation of the mid-carpal mechanism is presented below.

CINERADIOGRAPHY OF KNUCKLE-WALKING No flexion-extention movements at the mid-carpal or carpometacarpal joints could be identified in lateral cineradiographic projection during the weight-bearing phase of knuckle-walking. If such movements ever occur, they might take place at the beginning of a propulsive phase when the forelimb is fully outstretched to effect maximum stride length; such postures were not observed in the present study.

Oblique and anteroposterior cineradiographic projections of the wrist during the terminal phase of weight-bearing and during the non-weight-bearing, swing phase confirmed other radiographic observations concerning the relative contributions of the proximal carpal and mid-carpal joints to flexion.

DISCUSSION

Having described chimpanzee carpal morphology and relationships in both static and active knuckle-walking postures, we will discuss some of the possible relationships between wrist anatomy and locomotor behavior and will attempt to evaluate hypotheses that treat functional-anatomical features as adaptations for distinctive locomotor repertoires.

A characteristic of knuckle-walking African apes that has attracted the attention of numerous workers (reviewed in Tuttle et al. 1972) is the limited degree of wrist extension. The structural basis of this phenomenon has been variably attributed to relative shortness of flexor tendons, carpal ligaments, muscular tension, or specializations of carpal architecture. Most workers have argued that one or another of these particular features provides the primary limiting mechanism. As Tuttle noted, however, there is little reason to assume that only one morphological feature is principally responsible; rather, this limited excursion is probably reflected in many aspects of wrist morphology. There is no reason to expect, for example, that cutting the flexor tendons in the chimpanzee wrist should lead to substantial freedom of extension, for other features such as joint surfaces and ligaments would also be adapted for limited extension.

Despite the repeated emphasis by various authors on the restricted wrist extension of knuckle-walking African apes, Lewis (1972: 55) was unable to identify any features in the wrists of African apes that he would consider as knuckle-walking adaptations. The features that he could distinguish he felt were "primarily responses to the anatomical demands of forelimb suspension", and he claimed "that there are no logical grounds for assuming that they are specifically correlated with knuckle-walking."

In an attempt to identify the features that might be related to knuckle-walking abilities, we compared the bony structures of the wrists of *Pan* and *Gorilla* with those of two brachiating apes, *Pongo* and *Hylobates,* and a quadrupedal cercopithecoid monkey, *Macaca mulatta* (Figure 1). These genera present a rough gradation of locomotor behavior from the predominantly terrestrial gorilla and the somewhat more arboreally inclined chimpanzee to the slow-climbing orangutan and the brachiating gibbon. Recognition of these basic differences in locomotor behavior is necessary to separate those wrist features that characterize knuckle-walkers from those that are common to all apes. We will analyze the proximal and mid-carpal joints separately, first describing major structural differences and then suggesting how these may be related to wrist function.

Proximal Carpal Joint

Tuttle (1967: 189–190) pointed out that the distal articular surface of the radius in the chimpanzee and gorilla is deeply concave in comparison to that in the orangutan (Figure 1, top). As noted above, much of this concavity is a result of the extension of the dorsal margin which gives the articular surface as a whole a distinct volar orientation. This contrasts with the more or less perpendicular positioning of the distal radial articular surface in *Pongo* and the macaque. In biomechanical terms, both the greater curvature and volar orientation may be interpreted as adaptations to increase wrist stability. Tuttle (1967: 177) observed that the excursion of the knuckle-walking chimpanzee forelimb is large — 100° to 180°. The principal movement takes place at the shoulder joint; the elbow remains extended, and cineradiography reveals no substantial movement at the wrist during most of the propulsive phase. The forelimb, therefore, may be compared to a lever powered largely by shoulder muscles. In such a situation, a shearing stress would occur across the wrist and perpendicular to the hand. If the plane of the joint were perpendicular to the forearm axis, the form of the articular surface itself would offer no intrinsic resistance to shear stress other than the close-packing arrangement described above. However, a 15° to 20° volar angulation of the radial surface ensures that the plane of the joint is oblique to shear stresses across the wrist; the posteriorly directed propulsive force acting on the limb tends to oppose, rather than separate, the joint surfaces. Therefore, in addition to a close-packed position that fixes the hand in a slightly extended posture, the joint is provided with further intrinsic stability not otherwise present in shallow hinge joints.

A clear difference in the relative size and shape of the proximal articular surfaces of the scaphoid and lunate in the proximal carpal joint can be seen in Figure 1. In the two African apes, as in the macaque, the proximal articular surfaces of the scaphoid and lunate are roughly similar in size. Together, these carpals provide an articular surface that is narrow in the volar-dorsal dimension and wide in the radioulnar dimension. In *Pongo,* the articular surface of the lunate makes a much greater contribution to the proximal carpal joint than does the scaphoid. In both *Pongo* and *Hylobates,* the scaphoid and lunate articular surfaces together form an ellipse in which the volar-dorsal and radioulnar dimensions are more nearly equal. In addition, the degree of curvature from ulnar to radial aspect is greater in these genera than in African apes. We tentatively suggest that the proximal carpal joint in *Pongo* and *Hylobates* may represent an adaptive shift toward a ball-and-socket mechanism, specifically for providing additional rotary capability. The African apes, like the cercopithecoids, retain a less specialized biaxial joint.

Mid-Carpal Joint

The capitate facet for the os centrale (this element is fused to the scaphoid in African apes) shows a distinct gradation in both form and orientation among the genera represented in Figure 1. In the macaque (Figure 1A), the proximal part of the facet is convex, the distal part concave. As a whole, the facet lies on the dorsal aspect of the bone. In the chimpanzee and gorilla (Figure 1B, C), the convex part of the facet is relatively enlarged, and the articular surface is somewhat more oblique, facing as much radially as dorsally. In the orangutan and gibbon (Figure 1D, E), the facet is entirely convex and faces almost exclusively to the radial aspect of the wrist.

Gradations are also apparent in the extent and orientation of the lunate articulation in the proximal carpal joint. In the macaque and gorilla (Figure 1A, B), the lunate articulates with the rounded head of the capitate. In the chimpanzee, the lunate articulation extends slightly onto the hamate as well as the capitate. In the orang (Figure 1D), the relatively large lunate also covers the proximal surfaces of the capitate and hamate; in the gibbon (Figure 1E), there are no distinct facets, only a continuous surface on the capitate and hamate with which the lunate can articulate.

There are also distinctive differences in the shape of the hamate and the orientation of its triquetral facet. In *Macaca* and *Gorilla* (Figure 1 A, B), the hamate is relatively broad; the triquetral facet is oriented obliquely and occupies the entire proximolateral surface. This facet is smoothly confluent with the lunate facet on the head of the capitate. In *Pan* (Figure 1C), the hamate is somewhat narrower than in *Gorilla*. The triquetral facet has a somewhat more lateral (i.e. ulnar) orientation than the lunate facet, with the result that the angulation between triquetral and lunate facets is more distinct than in *Gorilla* or *Macaca*. In *Pongo* (Figure 1D), the hamate is narrow but projects almost as far proximally as the capitate. The lunate facet on the hamate has a distinct proximal orientation, while the triquetral facet occupies the extensive lateral face of the bone. In *Hylobates* (Figure 1E), the condition is similar to that in *Pongo*. The hamate is larger than the capitate, and there is a rounded, laterally directed surface for articulation with the triquetral. However, distinct facets for triquetral and lunate do not occur on the spheroidal articular surface formed by hamate and capitate.

The differences in facet form and orientation of the capitate and hamate determine how the mid-carpal joint participates in flexion-extension, ulnoradial deviation, pronation-supination, and weight bearing. Although we have radiographic data on chimpanzee wrist movements only, the structural similarities and differences discussed above, together with Tuttle's (1969: 328–329) data, permit comparison of some basic functional relationships.

In the gibbon and orang, the proximal capitate and hamate form a narrow, knoblike process. The articular surface in the gibbon is distinctive for its sphericity and lack of discrete triquetral, lunate, and centrale facets. These features provide potential for a wide range of movements, possibly including pronation and supination (Plate 7). In the orang, the presence of discrete facets on the capitate and hamate appears to indicate more limited possibilities for pronation-supination, but in terms of facilitating other movements, the similarities with those of the gibbon are obvious.

We have been unable to show radiographically that stabilization in the chimpanzee wrist in extension is achieved by a supinating movement of the distal carpals upon the proximal carpals, as suggested by Lewis (1972: 55). However, we do find that the centrale facet of the scaphoid contacts the concave neck of the capitate during extension; this concavity reverses the curvature of the articular surface, and thus would limit further extension. Although our data are as yet insufficient to support firm conclusions on mid-carpal joint movements during extension, we wish to comment on several aspects of Lewis's view that rotational movement between triquetral and hamate is part of a close-packing mechanism limiting wrist extension.

First, the presence of a spiral facet on the hamate is not always accompanied by an extension-limiting mechanism between the centrale and capitate (contra Lewis 1972: 53; cf. *Pongo).* Second, our radiographic evidence does not demonstrate that rotational movement between triquetral and hamate is conjunct with wrist extension. In both chimpanzees and macaques, triquetral-hamate movement appears to be related to pronation and supination (Plates 8, 9). Thus, the mechanism of limiting mid-carpal extension may not be deduced from triquetral-hamate relationships.

Finally, Lewis has argued that this close-packing mechanism limiting extension and the structural features that indicate its presence (spiral hamate facet, "waisted" capitate, dorsal orientation of the centrale facet on the capitate) are adaptations for suspensory activity. However, these features are most evident not in genera that habitually exhibit suspensory behavior but in genera that move quadrupedally, including *Macaca.*

Comparison of the orientation of triquetral and lunate articular surfaces provides further evidence of structural differences between forms that are predominantly suspensory and those that are predominantly quadrupedal in forelimb use. In *Macaca, Gorilla,* and *Pan* these surfaces are relatively broad and oriented in a proximal or proximo-ulnar direction. This arrangement appears more likely to be an adaptation for weight transmission and stability in extended, weight-bearing postures than for suspensory activity. Indeed, the gibbon and orang have narrow surfaces by comparison, and little area is oriented in a proximal or proximo-ulnar direction (Figure 1).

The evolutionary significance of the locomotor repertoire of African apes has been a long-debated question. Many authorities believe that their habits represent a secondary reversion to terrestrialism and that knuckle-walking features evolved as terrestrial modifications of a suspensory hand. An alternate possibility, that the locomotor repertoire of African apes represents a relatively unspecialized version of that in early apes, is suggested by two lines of evidence. First, in many features of carpal structure the African apes bear similarities to the less specialized pattern found in cercopithecoid monkeys. Distinctive features of living hominoids, such as the exclusion of the ulna from carpal articulation by an intra-articular meniscus, need not be correlated with the extreme specializations for suspensory behavior found in the gibbon and orang; rather, such features may have originated under selection pressures for a locomotor versatility such as that displayed by the living chimpanzee. A second line of evidence may be drawn from resemblances between the wrists of living African and fossil Miocene apes. Casts of *Dryopithecus africanus* carpals show the following features: concavo-convexity on the proximal articular surface of the scaphoid; broad hamate with an oblique, spiral triquetral facet; centrale facet of the capitate extending onto the dorsal aspect of the capitate neck; and combined proximal articular surface of the scaphoid and lunate broader in a radioulnar than in a volar-dorsal plane. Each of these features is shared by modern African apes, as well as *Macaca,* and is substantially modified among gibbons and the orang. We conclude, therefore, that the structure and adaptations of the chimpanzee wrist may be close to the primitive condition for apes. On present evidence, there is little support for the theory that the wrist in African apes evolved through an evolutionary stage in which "suspension" and "brachiation" were used more extensively than in the living chimpanzee.

REFERENCES

LEWIS, O. J.

1972 Osteological features characterizing the wrists of monkeys and apes, with a reconstruction of this region in *Dryopithecus (Proconsul) africanus. American Journal of Physical Anthropology* 36:45–58.

TAYLOR, C. R., V. J. ROWNTREE

1973 Running on two or four legs: which consumes more energy? *Science* 179:186–187.

TUTTLE, R. H.

1967 Knuckle-walking and the evolution of hominoid hands. *American Journal of Physical Anthropology* 26:171–206.

1969 Quantitative functional studies on the hands of the *Anthropoidea*. I. The *Hominoidea*. *Journal of Morphology* 128:309–364.

1970 "Postural, propulsive and prehensile capabilities in the cheiridia of chimpanzees and other great apes," in *The chimpanzee: physiology, behavior, serology and diseases of chimpanzees*. Edited by G. H. Bourne, 167–253. Basel: S. Karger.

TUTTLE, R., J. V. BASMAJIAN, E. REGENOS, G. SHINE

1972 Electromyography of knuckle-walking: results of four experiments on the forearm of *Pan gorilla*. *American Journal of Physical Anthropology* 37:255–265.

TUTTLE, R., J. V. BASMAJIAN

1974 "Electromyography of forearm musculature in *Gorilla* and problems related to knuckle-walking," in *Primate locomotion*. Edited by F. A. Jenkins, Jr., 293–347. New York: Academic Press.

Discussion

KORTLANDT: Until 1960 taxonomists had good grounds to classify the Asian and African great apes together. In zoos they all three brachiated. Consequently, it was generally assumed that they all three occupied the same ecological niche in the canopy. This was a good premise to classify them in the same taxon. Since 1960, when field work started, the postulated facts employed by the taxonomists were proved untrue. Let me enumerate some of the new facts. First, chimpanzees are long distance ground walkers with a foraging range that varies from thirty to one hundred square kilometers, that is twelve to forty square miles, which is quite large. Second, we know that the population density of chimpanzees is highest in open types of semi-deciduous rain forest, broken forests, mosaic landscapes, woodland savannas, and so on. Third, they brachiate quite rarely and the adults mostly do so only in intimidation displays. The younger ones often brachiate but the adults rarely do so. They use their long arms primarily to reach around very tall tree trunks while walking bipedally up them in order to reach food in trees which cannot be climbed by monkeys or humans which do not have such long arms. Fourth, in the canopy, chimpanzees knuckle-walk on branches larger than three or four inches, whereas orangs hold branches with palmigrade grips even on very thick branches.

TUTTLE: Orangutans also fist-walk on large branches.

KORTLANDT: They fist-walk in the forest canopy in the wild?

TUTTLE: Yes, it was described by Alfred Russel Wallace in *The Malay Archipelago*. He said they were "knuckle-walking," but I assume that he meant fist-walking since scientists at that time did not clearly distinguish between the two hand postures.

KORTLANDT: What thickness of branches?

TUTTLE: Big branches.

KORTLANDT: Chimps have four or five different bipedal walking techniques on the ground in the wild, including both waddling and striding as described and defined by Napier, and three different jumping techniques. Therefore, to talk only about bipedal walking is just a simplification which confuses the facts. If we take all these different things together then the conclusion is that the ecological niches occupied by the Asian apes and the African ones are entirely different. Consequently, the argument used by the taxonomists in the old days is just not valid any more. They have not realized it. This is the point that should be made here.

TUTTLE: Modernization is going on in many areas of primatology not the least of which is the morphological part. Farish Jenkins, please tell us what cineradiography is and some of the problems that you have encountered while employing it?

JENKINS: Basically, cineradiography, or X-ray movies, involves two pieces of apparatus positioned on opposite sides of the animal. One is an X-ray source, a tube, and the other is an image intensifier which receives the X-ray beam and enhances the quality of the image. A movie camera takes a cinematic record of the X-ray image. Conceptually, it is a relatively simple system and has been used in diagnostic medicine for a number of years. Over the past several months I have been using biplanar cineradiography, that is to say two such apparatuses set in two planes, viz. the lateral plane and the dorsoventral plane. With this arrangement one can get a simultaneous three-dimensional record of the excursions, bony relationships, joint movement, and other anatomical details as the animal moves. We usually employ a treadmill. Most animals readily adapt to it. Hence they remain stationary with regard to the cineradiographic apparatus. I plan to attempt to use overhead treadmills, which might be called brachiation treadmills, to examine the functional anatomy of primates as they are arm-swinging or brachiating.

SIGMON: Is there any problem with radiation? What is the maximal build up of radiation?

JENKINS: Normally it is not necessary to run experimental animals very long under this condition. Once we train them to run on a treadmill, and they adapt very readily, the amount of actual radiation exposure is relatively small. We have never gotten into any difficulty using this technique. We freely use any mammal, with the exception of man, that will accommodate to our experimental situation. So there is essentially no problem here other than the fact that any radiation dosage involves some statistical chance of inducing neoplastic processes.

SIGMON: Is that the main reason for not using man?

JENKINS: We have not used man. Although we have contemplated it, and other laboratories have actually employed human subjects, there are difficulties for just that reason.

SECTION FIVE

Mechanisms and Evolution of Bipedalism in the Hominoidea

Functions and Evolution of Hominid Hip and Thigh Musculature

B. A. SIGMON

INTRODUCTION

Studies in primate anatomy have interested the academic community for a very long time, dating back to the first published primate dissection by Tyson in 1699. Throughout the eighteenth and early nineteenth centuries, occasional works appeared, but the first heavy wave of interest in primate anatomy occurred during the latter half of the nineteenth and the turn of the twentieth centuries. This is almost certainly correlated with the joint announcement by Darwin and Wallace in 1859 on the role of natural selection in species formation. Sonntag (1924) has an excellent review of the literature of this period. During the first half of this century, however, interest in anatomical studies of primates declined, as indicated by the decreased number of published reports. An interest in primate anatomy was not strongly revived until the middle of the century. During the last twenty to twenty-five years, a number of works have appeared dealing with the muscular anatomy of primates, and specifically and more recently concerning the hip and lower extremity (e.g. Blake 1967; Preuschoft 1961, 1970; Grand 1968; Uhlmann 1968; Sigmon 1969a, 1974; Stern 1971, 1972).

The renewal of interest in primate anatomical studies would appear to be related to two scientific events: the development of primate field studies, which got off the ground in the 1930's (e.g. Nissen 1931; Bingham 1932; Carpenter 1934), and then, during the late thirties, the acceptance by the scientific community of early hominid discoveries

I wish to acknowledge gratefully the assistance of Mrs. G. Anderson in the preparation of the diagrams.

being made in South Africa (Broom and Schepers 1946; Broom 1951). The recent generation of anatomists, utilizing the new sources of data provided by field studies and early hominid fossil discoveries, has been able to broaden its functional and evolutionary interpretations. This is particularly relevant in the field of comparative primate anatomy and in the study of the evolution of differing locomotor habits. The musculature itself, unlike the skeletal and dental systems, cannot be preserved by fossilization, although indications of muscles and their function are often revealed by muscle-attachment ridges, crests, and other bony projections, as well as by the relative proportions of various elements of the skeleton. A detailed study of skeletal remains using data from comparative anatomy of closely related animals makes it possible to draw some conclusions about locomotor patterns of extinct species.

I shall discuss differences in the hip and thigh musculature of the living hominoids and attempt to explain these differences in terms of their contributions toward the adaptation of the animal to its external environment. The hip and thigh are also of particular interest in considering the evolution of erect bipedalism in man. If one regards the ape grade of organization as representative of an early evolutionary stage through which man passed, as I shall do here, then a comparison between the two groups can point to evident differences in structure and function, and thus can reveal a stage, or stages, of change that might have occurred in the evolution of the hominid pattern of bipedal locomotion.

Robinson's recent monograph (1972) on early hominid posture and locomotion fills a major gap in our knowledge of the transition from pongid to early hominid grades of organization. I shall therefore not elaborate on this subject, which is best read in the original source, but shall instead concentrate on the hominoid patterns of musculature of the hip and thigh and their relationship to locomotion.

MUSCULAR PATTERNS IN THE HIP AND THIGH

The following data are based on dissections of twelve pongids and several humans as well as on observations of numerous human cadavers. The pongid sample includes two young male gorillas, two young and one adult male chimpanzee, one young male and two adult female orangutans, one young adult male and two young adult female gibbons, and one adult male siamang.

The muscles of the hip and thigh that were dissected and analyzed include iliacus, psoas major and minor, iliotrochantericus, tensor fasciae latae, gluteus maximus, gluteus medius, gluteus minimus, piriformis, gemellus superior and inferior, obturator internus and externus, quadratus femoris, sartorius, the quadriceps femoris muscles, semitendinosus, semimembranosus, biceps femoris, the adductor muscles, gracilis, and pectineus. A detailed description of each of these muscles can be found in Sigmon (1974). This article will include only a comparative summary emphasizing major differences in the anatomy of the hip and thigh among hominoids.

From both gross observation and more detailed muscular analyses of dissected specimens, it is readily apparent that the gluteal muscles (gluteus maximus, gluteus medius, and gluteus minimus) show significant differences among hominoids. This fact has been frequently noted by other authors (e.g. Washburn 1950; Napier 1967; Robinson 1968, 1972; Sigmon 1969a, 1974; Robinson, Freedman, and Sigmon 1972; Stern 1972). These three muscles vary in size, shape, areas of attachment, and innervation.

Other muscular variations that occur in hominoids are (1) the presence or absence of (a) tensor fasciae latae, (b) scansorius, (c) iliotrochantericus, and (d) adductor magnus long head, i.e. semimembranosus accessorius (Hartman and Straus 1933); and (2) the fusion or separation of (a) muscular parts of adductor magnus and (b) the two heads of biceps femoris.

Gluteal Muscular Patterns

Three definitive gluteal muscular patterns can be discerned for hominoids. The first pattern is characteristic of *Pan*, *Gorilla*, *Hylobates*, and *Symphalangus*; the second, of *Pongo*; and the third, of *Homo*.

In the first pattern (see Figures 1 and 4) gluteus maximus is an extensive muscle that covers a large portion of the hip and thigh. It extends from the gluteal aponeurosis, sacrum, and coccyx to the iliotibial tract laterally, the ischial tuberosity medially, and the femoral shaft distally from the gluteal tuberosity to the lateral epicondyle. In *Hylobates* the distal attachment extends only to midway along the femoral shaft, but in *Symphalangus* and the African apes it extends to the lateral epicondyle. The innervation for gluteus maximus is (1) from the inferior gluteal nerve, which supplies the cranial part, and (2) from the flexores femoris nerve, which supplies the distal portion of the muscle, the part distal to the ischial tuberosity. Functionally, the

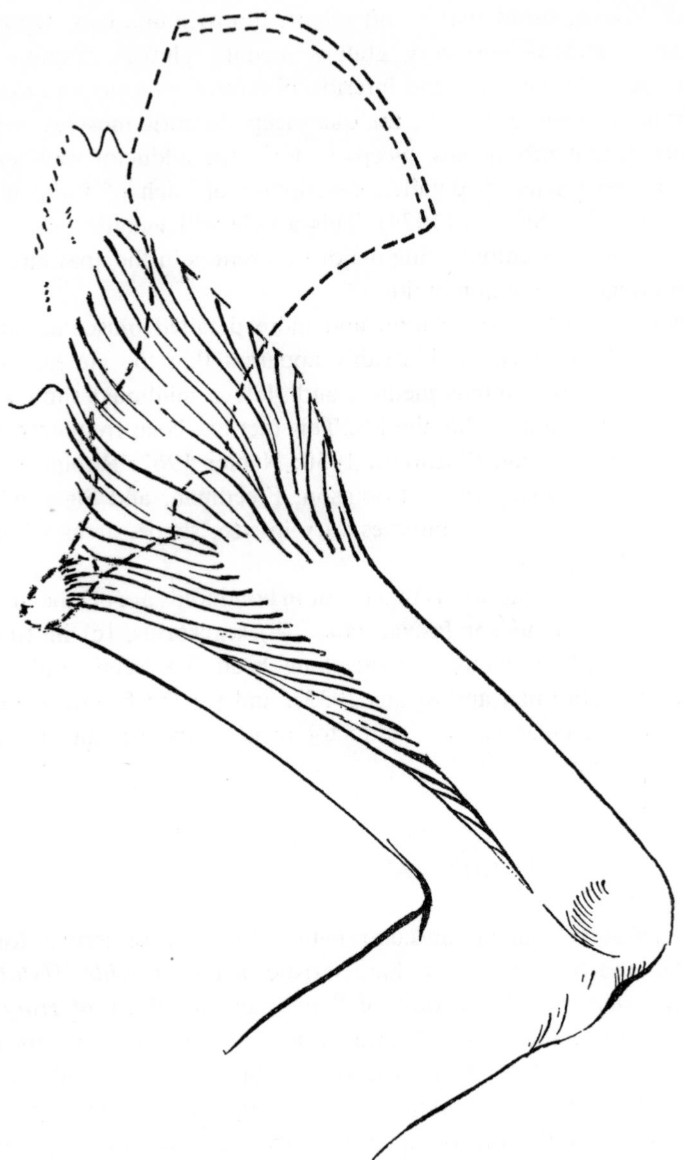

Figure 1. The pattern of gluteus maximus in the African apes and gibbons. (The drawing is of a chimpanzee)

thinner cranial part of gluteus maximus abducts and laterally rotates the thigh. Together with tensor fasciae latae (whose muscle fibers are joined to those of gluteus maximus), this cranial portion also acts to tense the iliotibial tract into which both muscles insert. The thicker,

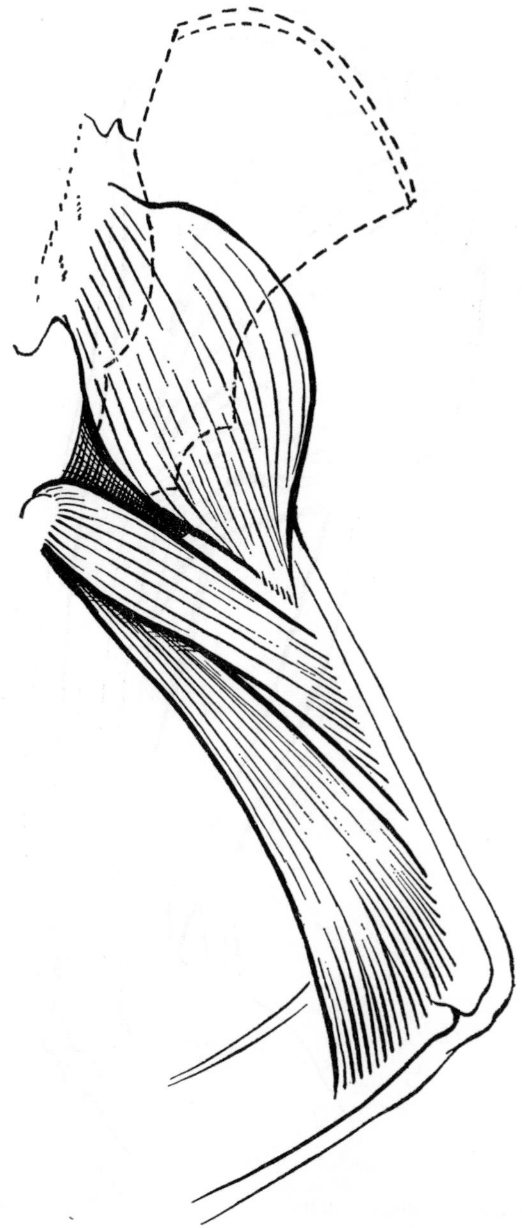

Figure 2. From the pelvis downward, the muscles are gluteus maximus proprius, ischiofemoralis, and biceps femoris long head in the orangutan

distal part of gluteus maximus adducts and laterally rotates the thigh at the hip and, most importantly, is a powerful thigh extensor.

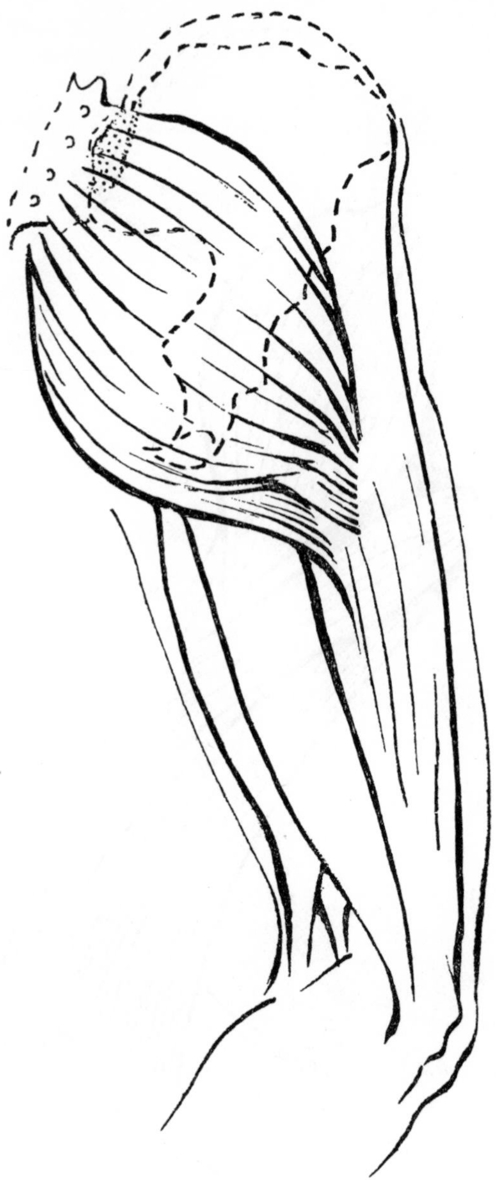

Figure 3. Gluteus maximus in man

Gluteus medius in pattern I is a very thick muscle that covers the whole of the dorsum of the ilium. In the African apes it is slightly larger in weight than gluteus maximus, whereas in the gibbons and in man, gluteus maximus is slightly larger in weight than gluteus medius

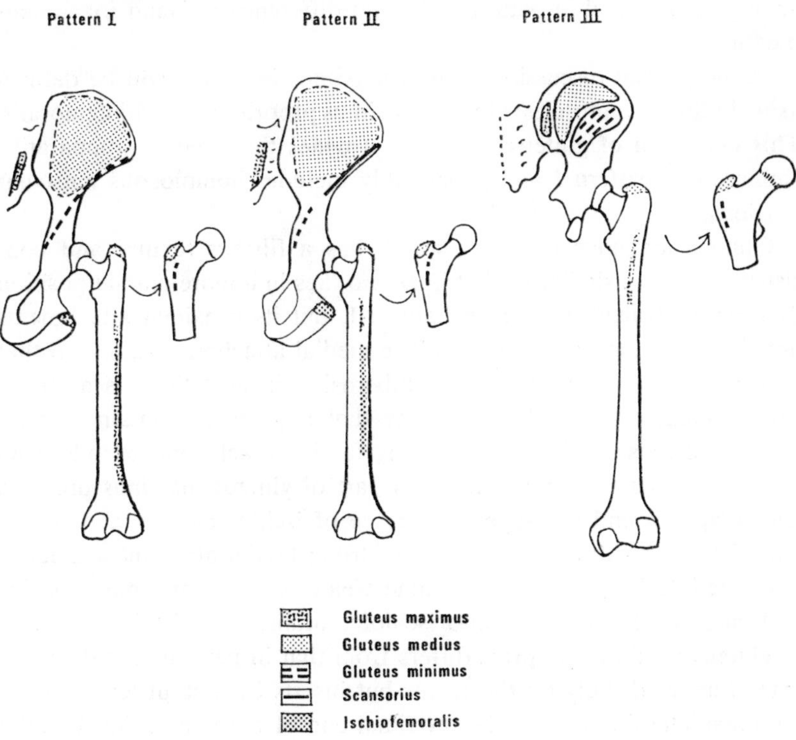

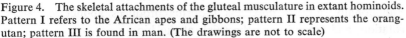

Figure 4. The skeletal attachments of the gluteal musculature in extant hominoids. Pattern I refers to the African apes and gibbons; pattern II represents the orang-utan; pattern III is found in man. (The drawings are not to scale)

(Haughton 1873; Preuschoft 1961; Blake 1967; Sigmon 1974). In pattern I the fibers of piriformis may join those of gluteus medius and insert together via a single stout tendon on the greater trochanter. Functionally, gluteus medius is a powerful thigh extensor; in addition, it acts in abduction and medial rotation of the thigh.

Gluteus minimus of pattern I is a wide, fan-shaped muscle covering, in the African apes, the dorsolateral border of the ilium and part of the ischium; in the gibbons the innominate attachment is less from the ilium and more onto the ischium. Its insertion is onto the anterior surface of the greater trochanter. Functionally, it can produce abduction, lateral rotation, and possibly some extension of the thigh; in the African apes it is in a position to produce flexion and medial rotation of the thigh as well.

Pongo is the only representative of pattern II (see Figures 2 and 4). Gluteus maximus and gluteus minimus differ considerably from the arrangement found in pattern I, but no difference is found for gluteus medius.

In the present discussion gluteus maximus in *Pongo* will be defined as including two muscles: gluteus maximus proprius and ischiofemoralis. This definition of gluteus maximus provides the greatest comparative similarity to pattern I and presumably includes homologous muscular portions.

Gluteus maximus proprius, which has a fibrous texture and consistent thickness similar to that in *Homo*, lies in a more cranial position than its equivalent portion in pattern I, but its proximal attachments are similar to those of pattern I. The medial attachment differs in that it does not pass over the ischial tuberosity; instead there is a strong fibrous connection to the tuberosity that appears to contain a small number of muscle fibers. This strong fascial attachment extends from the superior part of the mediodistal part of gluteus maximus proprius and wraps around the superior surface of ischiofemoralis and biceps femoris long head; a second equally strong fascial attachment extends from the inferior portion of the same area of gluteus maximus proprius and then attaches directly onto ischiofemoralis. The distal attachment of gluteus maximus proprius differs from that in pattern I. It does not extend as far distally on the femur but inserts by a stout tendon onto the dorsolateral border at the proximal end of the femur. An iliotibial tract is not present. Innervation is from the inferior gluteal nerve. Functionally, gluteus maximus proprius produces abduction, lateral rotation, and extension of the thigh at the hip.

The other portion of gluteus maximus, ischiofemoralis, which lies between the ischial tuberosity and the femoral shaft, is equivalent in location, innervation, and action to the distal portion of gluteus maximus in pattern I. Ischiofemoralis originates in common with the long head of biceps femoris from the ischial tuberosity. Its fibers separate from biceps femoris, and the muscle then inserts onto the posterolateral border of the femoral shaft just distal to the insertion of gluteus maximus proprius onto about the middle third or more of the shaft. The innervation is via a branch of the flexores femoris nerve. Functionally, the muscle is a thigh extensor, lateral rotator, and adductor.

Gluteus minimus in pattern II consists of two separate muscles that lie in approximately the same position as gluteus minimus does in pattern I. Together these two muscles form a thick, fan-shaped functional unit that has the same innervation, action, and general location as gluteus minimus in pattern I. The more laterally positioned muscle has been called *scansorius* (a word first used by Traill in 1818) and it extends a little more anteriorly and is a little thicker than the equivalent lateral part of gluteus minimus in pattern I. The medial part has been referred to as *gluteus minimus proprius* (Preuschoft 1961) and it acts in lateral rotation and possibly extension of the thigh. Innervation is via the superior gluteal nerve.

The third pattern of gluteal musculature is that seen in modern man (Figures 3 and 4). Each of the three gluteal muscles in pattern III shows important differences from both patterns I and II. First, gluteus maximus has no distal portion, that is, no muscular part extending between the ischial tuberosity and the femur. In man, gluteus maximus consists only of a cranial-positioned muscle whose shape is vaguely reminiscent of gluteus maximus proprius of *Pongo*. However, in man, gluteus maximus is unique in that it has a direct iliac attachment, no attachment to the ischial tuberosity, and is a much thicker, wider muscle than in any ape pattern. Gluteus maximus in pattern III inserts into the iliotibial tract and onto the gluteal tuberosity and lateral intermuscular septum. Innervation is solely from the inferior gluteal nerve. Functionally, its most important action is thigh extension and lateral rotation. The cranial fibers may act in abduction, and its lower fibers may produce some adduction. Its insertion into the iliotibial tract enables it to assist with bracing the knee during extension of the latter in erect posture and locomotion. Because of its skeletal position and attachments, gluteus maximus in pattern III is important in actions that require great effort and power.

Gluteus medius and gluteus minimus in man attach to the dorsum of the iliac blade and greater trochanter of the femur. Because of their location, they are in a prime position to provide the essential action of lateral balance control in upright walking. Functionally, they abduct the thigh and rotate it medially. During walking, when one foot is raised from the ground, the contractions of gluteus medius and minimus hold the innominate of the opposite side down close to the greater trochanter and thus prevent the slumping of the pelvis toward the unsupported side. Furthermore, by their rotary action, these two muscles assist in swinging the pelvis forward as a step is taken. Innervation is the same as in pongids, via the superior gluteal nerve.

In summary, patterns I and II show much greater resemblance to each other than either does to pattern III. In the pongids, gluteus maximus consists of a sacroiliac and an ischiofemoral portion, although in pattern I these two portions are joined to form a single muscle, whereas in pattern II the two portions are separate muscles. In hominids there is no ischiofemoral portion, as the attachment to the ischial tuberosity has been lost, and the femoral attachment has been reduced considerably, leaving an insertion only onto the proximal shaft of the femur and into the intermuscular septum. The sacroiliac portion in hominids has increased in width as well as in thickness and has developed a bony attachment to the iliac blade.

Second, gluteus medius in patterns I and II differs from that in pattern III. In hominids, gluteus medius is an abductor and medial rotator. In pongids, it performs these two actions, but in addition it acts in extending the thigh. The extensor function in gluteus medius has been lost in hominids.

Third, gluteus medius and gluteus minimus in hominids are in a position to function in lateral balance control, which is essential in upright bipedal walking. This adaptation is not developed in the quadrupedal pongids.

Other Muscular Variation

Tensor fasciae latae is absent in the orangutan but occurs in the other hominoids. In gibbons and African apes it is present as a thin muscle whose fibers are fused medially with those of gluteus maximus and laterally with gluteus medius and sometimes gluteus minimus. Through the latter two muscles its lateral attachment extends around to the iliac blade, where it attaches indirectly to the superior lateral border of the ilium. In man, tensor fasciae latae is comparatively thicker and is not joined to the gluteal muscles; it originates directly from the iliac blade in the area of the anterior superior spine and slightly above and below the spine. In the pongids (except *Pongo*) and in man, the insertion is into the iliotibial tract. The function of the muscle in both groups is also basically similar, being flexion, abduction, and medial rotation of the thigh, and aiding in tensing the iliotibial tract. In man, however, the latter function is of special importance because it helps to maintain the extended knee during erect posture. In comparison with tensor fasciae latae in the apes, that muscle in man has a more anterior location, is thicker, and has a direct attachment to the ilium. During contraction, its effect is to lock the knee into place during knee extension in erect posture and locomotion.

Scansorius (Sigmon 1969b) is a muscle occurring in *Pongo*. Although thicker and located somewhat more anteriorly, it is equivalent in location, function, and innervation to the lateral half of gluteus minimus in African apes.

Iliotrochantericus is a small slip of muscle that lies deep to the proximal head of rectus femoris. It has been found in all hominoids, including man, but its occurrence is inconsistent. Iliotrochantericus crosses the hip joint and has direct or indirect attachments to the ilium at the rim of the acetabulum and to the lesser trochanter of the femur. Its function in flexion of the thigh is of minor importance.

A muscle that occurs in some primates but not in man is adductor magnus long head, sometimes called semimembranosus accessorius (Hartman and Straus 1933). Functionally, this muscle acts as a member of both the adductor muscles and the hamstring group. In addition to being a powerful thigh adductor and extensor, it participates in lateral rotation of the thigh. Its nerve supply is from a branch of the flexores femoris nerve that also supplies the hamstring muscles. The long head of adductor magnus arises from the inferomedial border of the ischial tuberosity and inserts onto the medial epicondyle of the femur. It is a single, separate muscle in the African apes and in two of the gibbons. In the orangutans, siamang, and one gibbon, the proximal portions of the long and short heads of adductor magnus are joined but become separate distally, the long head inserting as in the other pongids onto the medial epicondyle and the short head inserting onto the middle to two-thirds of the dorsomedial border of the femur, similar to the insertion in man. Whether separate or partly fused to the short head of adductor magnus, the long head is always innervated by a branch of the flexores femoris nerve. In man, adductor magnus is innervated only by the obturator nerve.

The last point in muscular variation concerns the long and short heads of biceps femoris. In man, these two heads are joined, although each receives a different nerve supply. In pongids, there are two structural patterns: in the siamang, gibbons, and one chimpanzee, both heads are present and are joined; but in the gorillas, orangutans, and two other chimpanzees, the two heads are present but occur as separate rather than fused muscles. In both pongids and man, the origins and insertions are similar, varying only in extensiveness of attachment area. Innervation for the short head of biceps femoris in pongids and man is by the common peroneal nerve. However, the long head of biceps femoris in pongids is innervated by the flexores femoris nerve, not the tibial nerve as in man.

MOVEMENT AND MUSCULATURE

The Pongids

Thus far we have seen that there are detectable gross differences in the hip and thigh musculature of hominoids. The muscular patterns are expressions of the locomotor adaptations. Turning first to the locomotion of pongids, we can set up five locomotor categories, each of which characterizes one or more pongids. These groupings are a summary of observations by fieldworkers (Nissen 1931; Carpenter 1938, 1940; Kortlandt 1962; Schaller 1963, 1965; Goodall 1965; Reynolds 1965; Reynolds and Reynolds 1965; Horr 1972). The locomotor categories and respective pongids are seen in Table 1.

Table 1. Locomotor categories and respective pongids

	Gorilla	Chimpanzee	Orangutan	Gibbons
Terrestrial quadrupedalism	x	x		
Arboreal quadrupedalism	x	x	x	
Brachiation		x		x
Terrestrial bipedalism	x	x		
Arboreal bipedalism				x

This chart simply indicates patterns of locomotion, not frequency of occurrence. Because climbing and jumping are frequently seen in all the pongids, no separate category was established for these activities, but their occurrence should be duly noted. The chart shows that in almost all cases the African apes share the same patterns. In the one category, brachiation, in which they differ, it is interesting to note that observations of juvenile gorillas in zoos show that these apes may occasionally brachiate (Avis 1962). Gibbons differ in being highly skilled brachiators and in practicing arboreal bipedalism. The orangutan is almost exclusively arboreal.

A review of the anatomy and locomotion of pongids shows that (1) the anatomical pictures of the hips and thighs of the African apes are essentially identical and the locomotor patterns overlap considerably; (2) the anatomy of African apes is very similar to that of gibbons, but the locomotion is different; and (3) the orangutan has a different anatomical structure from the other three pongids (functionally, however, the musculature of *Pongo* is practically equivalent to that of the other pongids) and also a more limited locomotor repertoire. I have suggested elsewhere (1974) that the detailed differences between *Pongo* and the other pongids may be related to the former's highly specialized arboreality. The reason behind this suggestion is the trend in *Pongo* toward division of muscles into separate muscular portions. It is possible that these divisions may aid in providing greater independent action for the various separate parts of a given muscle and that this could affect the increased degree of mobility in a predominantly climbing form.

In summary, a comparison of pongid hip and thigh musculature shows a structural pattern for African apes and gibbons that differs from that of orangutans. Locomotor comparisons show three patterns: one for African apes, another for gibbons, and a third for orangutans. Several questions arise from these observations. First, are the muscular and locomotor differences due to geographical separation and adaptation to new and differing environments — and if so, why is gibbon anatomy similar to that of the African apes? Second, does the unique anatomical structure of the orangutan suggest that it is the most specialized — and if so, is it because of its more restricted habitat and locomotion? Third, is the anatomical pattern present in the two geographically separated taxa — African apes and gibbons — the more generalized pattern, possibly representative of the ancestral hominoid pattern? Of course these questions cannot be answered by looking only at one area of the body or only at pongids, but further investigation is certainly warranted.

Transition from a Pongid to a Hominid Grade of Organization

The erect, bipedal posture and locomotion of living hominids contrast sharply with the quadrupedal-climber habits of pongids. Although there are structural differences in the musculature of pongids, all pongids can be characterized functionally by a single basic pattern that contrasts with the pattern found in man. The muscular anatomy of the hip and thigh reflects these differences in the following ways. (1) There are more muscles in pongids than in man that contribute to the production of thigh extension. These include the distal part of gluteus maximus, gluteus medius, and the long head of adductor magnus, i.e. semimembranosus accessorius. (2) Gluteus medius and gluteus minimus in hominids have acquired a new and unique function, that of acting in lateral balance control during upright walking. This adaptation is accompanied by a loss of the ability of gluteus medius to produce thigh extension. (3) The thigh extensor mechanisms of pongids and man are differently adapted, as Robinson (1968, 1972) pointed out. The hamstring muscles (semitendinosus, semimembranosus, and the long head of biceps femoris) of the two taxa produce different results when they are acting to extend the thigh. The result in pongids is slow but powerful thigh extension, whereas extension in man is fast but relatively weaker, although the range of movement is greater. The reason for the difference in the effect of the extensor muscles lies in the relative lengths of the moment and lever arms. In both taxa, the muscle attachments are the same and the movements produced are also the same. The effective results of the hamstring actions, however, differ because in pongids the ischium (effective moment arm and area of proximal attachment) is longer than it is in man and the femur (distal attachment), as well as the total lower limb (effective lever length), is shorter. The actual lever length is decreased in pongids to an even greater degree because of their bent-knee gait.

These three areas of difference point to adaptations that each taxon has made in response to its locomotor requirements. An explanation for the added muscular elements for thigh extension in pongids plus the adaptation of these muscles for the provision of power in extension is that several pongid activities require this type of arrangement. For example, activities like climbing and jumping require that the body be pulled up against gravity. Shifting from a quadrupedal to a bipedal position is another movement in which the body must be pushed upward. In activities of this sort, which comprise a goodly proportion of pongid movement, power in thigh extension is of major importance in providing this upward thrust. Moreover, in all but the lightly built gibbons, it is a heavy body that is being moved against gravity.

Man, with his acquisition of upright bipedal posture and locomotion, has different problems of adjustment. First, walking on two rather than four limbs obviously requires a new system of balance control. Robinson (1972) has noted the importance of a shift downward in the center of gravity. This change, he suggests, would have preceded such skeletal modifications as the reduction of iliac height, widening of the ilium and sacrum, backward expansion of the ilium, development of lumbar curvature, repositioning of gluteus medius and gluteus minimus, and development of iliac buttressing in the area of the latter two muscles. Lateral balance control became possible as gluteus medius and minimus shifted laterally and became positioned in a more-or-less vertical orientation with their area of attachment onto the greater trochanter of the femur. Gluteus medius lost its capacity to produce thigh extension and increased its effectiveness as a thigh abductor. Thus, during walking, the contractions of gluteus medius and gluteus minimus act to prevent the pelvis on the supported side from slumping toward the unsupported side. Iliac buttressing in this area developed in response to stresses on the bone related to the function of these muscles in providing lateral stability.

Second, power in thigh extension is still necessary in man during movements that thrust the body upward against gravity, for example, rising from a stooped or seated position to a bipedal one, running or walking up a steep incline, or jumping across a stream. The major muscle of the thigh extensor group that acts in this capacity is gluteus maximus. Structurally, gluteus maximus in man differs considerably from that in pongids. It has lost its ischial attachment and most of its femoral one, has migrated more cranially, has formed a direct attachment onto the now broader ilium, and has developed into a much thicker muscle. Because its function as an extensor has not changed, the increased width and thickness were apparently a necessary adjustment to offset the loss of the powerful ischiofemoral portion that in pongids is the major part producing thigh extension.

Third, man is adapted for efficient bipedal striding, which is a relatively fast walking gait that necessitates taking long steps. The modification from power- to speed-oriented hamstring muscles (Robinson 1968, 1972) is an obvious adaptation to assist in meeting this need.

In considering how the hominid pattern of hip and thigh musculature evolved from a pongid grade of organization, we have seen that the major changes in musculature have been in the morphology and positions of the gluteal and hamstring muscles. We might expect that the fossil record would document a continuous gradation of change in the points just discussed, and to some extent a continuum of this sort does appear, as in the differences between *Paranthropus robustus* and *Homo africanus*. According to Robinson (1972), both early hominids possessed the balancing mechanisms of an upright biped, including both the downward shift in the center of gravity and the lateral balance control provided by gluteus medius and gluteus minimus. Both also had the human type of gluteus maximus. But the two taxa differ with regard to the hamstring thigh-extensor complex. *Paranthropus*, with its longer ischium and relatively shorter lower limbs, would have been adapted more toward the power-oriented thigh-extensor complex characteristic of pongids and very likely still practiced quadrupedal-climber habits in addition to erect bipedal locomotion. In contrast, *H. africanus*, with its humanlike short ischium and long lower limb, had developed the speed-oriented extensor complex characteristic of modern man. Efficient striding would thus have been possible only for *H. africanus*.

The fossil record is tantalizingly incomplete in providing evidence of the earliest transitional stages in the evolution of erect bipedalism in man. For example, we would like to know what the postcranial skeleton of *Ramapithecus* was like and to have additional information on the stages immediately preceding *Paranthropus*. As in many cases of transitional evolutionary periods, the one marking the junction between pongid and hominid grades of organization is poorly documented in the fossil record. It would seem reasonable to consider that this transitional period involved a fast or tachytelic rate of evolution, thus decreasing both the time factor and the number of individuals that lived during this period. The fossil record of this time, therefore, would be expected to be even more sparse than usual in preserving members of those populations who had begun the evolutionary trek into the unexplored areas of upright bipedal posture and locomotion.

REFERENCES

AVIS, V.
1962 Brachiation: the crucial issue for man's ancestry. *Southwestern Journal of Anthropology* 18:119–148.

BINGHAM, H. C.
1932 *Gorillas in a native habitat*. Carnegie Institution Washington Publication 426.

BLAKE, M. L.
1967 "The quantitative myology of the hind limb of primates with special reference to their locomotor adaptations." Unpublished doctoral dissertation, Magdalene College, University of Cambridge.

BROOM, R.
1951 *Finding the missing link*. London: Watts.

BROOM, R., G. W. H. SCHEPERS
1946 *The South African fossil ape-men: the* Australopithecinae. Transvaal Museum Memoir 2.

CARPENTER, C. R.
1934 *A field study of the behavior and social relations of howling monkeys (Alouatta palliata)*. Comparative Psychology Monograph 10:1–168.
1938 A survey of wild-life conditions in Atjeh, North Sumatra with special reference to the orang-utan. *Netherlands Committee for International Nature Protection, Communication* 12:1–34.
1940 *A field study in Siam of the behavior and social relations of the gibbon* (Hylobates lar). Comparative Psychology Monograph 16: 1–212.

GOODALL, J.
1965 "Chimpanzees of the Gombe Stream Reserve," in *Primate behavior*. Edited by I. DeVore, 425-473. New York: Holt, Rinehart and Winston.

GRAND, T. I.
1968 The functional anatomy of the lower limb of the howler monkey *(Alouatta caraya). American Journal of Physical Anthropology* 28:163-182.

HARTMAN, C. G., W. L. STRAUS, *editors*
1933 *The anatomy of the rhesus monkey*. Baltimore: Williams and Wilkins.

HAUGHTON, S.
1873 *Principles of animal mechanics*. London: Longman Green.

HORR, D. A.
1972 "The Borneo orang-utan: population structure and dynamics in relationship to ecology and reproductive strategy." Paper presented at the 41st Annual Meeting of the American Association of Physical Anthropologists, Lawrence, Kansas.

KORTLANDT, A.
1962 Chimpanzees in the wild. *Scientific American* 206:128–138.

NAPIER, J. R.
1967 The antiquity of human walking. *Scientific American* 216:56–66.

NISSEN, H. W.
1931 *A field study of chimpanzee*. Psychological Monographs 8:1–122.

PREUSCHOFT, H.
1961 Muskeln und Gelenke der Hinterextremität des Gorillas. *Morphologisches Jahrbuch* 101:432–540.
1970 "Functional anatomy of the lower extremity," in *The Chimpanzee*, volume three. Edited by G. H. Bourne, 221–294. Basel: S. Karger.

REYNOLDS, V.
1965 *Budongo: an African forest and its chimpanzees*. Garden City, New York: Natural History Press.

REYNOLDS, V., F. REYNOLDS
1965 "Chimpanzees of the Budongo Forest," in *Primate behavior*. Edited by I. DeVore, 368–424. New York: Holt, Rinehart and Winston.

ROBINSON, J. T.
1968 "The origin and adaptive radiation of the australopithecines," in *Evolution und Hominisation*. Edited by G. Kurth, 150–175. Stuttgart: Gustav Fischer Verlag.
1972 *Early hominid posture and locomotion*. Chicago: University of Chicago Press.

ROBINSON, J. T., L. FREEDMAN, B. A. SIGMON
1972 Some aspects of pongid and hominid bipedality. *Journal of Human Evolution* 1(4):361–369.

SCHALLER, G. B.
1963 *The mountain gorilla*. Chicago: University of Chicago Press.
1965 "Behavioral comparisons of the apes," in *Primate behavior*. Edited by I. DeVore, 474–481. New York: Holt, Rinehart and Winston.

SIGMON, B. A.
1969a "Anatomical structure and locomotor habit in Anthropoidea with special reference tot the evolution of erect bipedality in man." Unpublished doctoral dissertation, University of Wisconsin, Madison, Wisconsin.
1969b The scansorius muscle in pongids. *Primates* 10:246–261.
1974 A functional analysis of pongid hip and thigh musculature. *Jour-*

nal of *Human Evolution* 3:161–185.

SONNTAG, C. F.
1924 *The morphology and evolution of the apes and man.* London: J. Bale, Sons and Danielsson.

STERN, J. T.
1971 *Functional myology of the hip and thigh of cebid monkeys and its implications for the evolution of erect posture.* Basel: S. Karger.
1972 Anatomical and functional specializations of the human gluteus maximus. *American Journal of Physical Anthropology* 36:315–340.

TRAILL, T.
1818 Observations on the anatomy of an orang outang. *Memoirs of the Wernerian Natural History Society of Edinburgh* 3:1–49.

TYSON, E.
1699 *Orang-outang.* London: Thomas Bennet.

UHLMANN, K.
1968 Huft- und Oberschenkelmuskulatur: systematische und vergleichende Anatomie *Primatologia* 4(10).

WASHBURN, S. L.
1950 The analysis of primate evolution with particular reference to the origin of man. *Cold Spring Harbor Symposia on Quantitative Biology, Proceedings* 15:67–78.

Electromyography of the Gluteus Maximus Muscle in Gorilla and the Evolution of Hominid Bipedalism

RUSSELL H. TUTTLE, JOHN V. BASMAJIAN, and HIDEMI ISHIDA

Habitual bipedal posture and locomotion are major hallmarks of hominid status. Their imprint on the postcranial skeleton, especially the lower limb, is clear-cut. Thus, much of the evolutionary history of bipedalism could be traced assuredly in an appropriate series of fossils. Unfortunately, the fossil record of early Hominidae is now far more provocative than comprehensive. This promises to remain the case, particularly for pre-Pleistocene Hominidae, despite renewed efforts to exploit available Neogene deposits and to locate new ones in Eurasia and Africa. Accordingly, speculations and surmises on the phylogeny of hominid bipedalism will continue to draw heavily upon information from comparative studies of extant forms. Further, even if a relatively complete collection of fossils were available, their biomechanical and functional interpretation most surely would be premised on comprehensive comparative studies of living primates. Thus, even though indirect, kinesiological, electromyographic, cineradiographic, and other studies that require elaborate technology are required for the resolution of many problems pertaining to the mechanisms of postural and locomotive evolution in the Hominidae. Full-fledged modernization of the comparative method in evolutionary an-

This investigation was supported mainly by National Science Foundation Grant Number GS-3209 and by Public Health Service Research Career Development Award Number 1-K04-GM16347-01 from the National Institutes of Health. Supplementary support was provided by National Institutes of Health Grant Number RR-00165 to the Yerkes Regional Primate Research Center. We are especially thankful for the assistance of E. Regenos, J. Malone, J. Perry, Mrs. H. Ishida, R. Pollard, E. van Ormer, J. Roberts, Dr. Michale Keeling, J. Hudson, K. Barnes, J. Ford, and Gen. G. Duncan. We are grateful to Dr. Geoffrey H. Bourne, director of Yerkes Regional Primate Research Center, for accommodating our studies.

For Plates, see p. xxi, between pp. 560–561

thropology, with special emphasis on experimentation, has just begun, though the special importance of this effort was recommended in earlier decades. Washburn (1950) and Barnicot (1958) suggested that electromyography might be profitably employed to elucidate certain questions on hominid evolution.

During the period between September, 1970, and August, 1974, we developed and employed electromyographic (EMG) techniques that are especially suited to great apes. Our previous studies concentrated on the roles of certain forelimb muscles in posture and locomotion of gorilla (Tuttle et al. 1972; Tuttle and Basmajian 1974a, b, c; Basmajian and Tuttle 1973). Now we report results of the first EMG study on the gluteus maximus muscle in a gorilla as it engaged in bipedal behavior. Probably no other muscle has commanded the attention (both scientific and extracurricular) of anthropologists and human anatomists that the gluteus maximus has. We will not review previous studies comprehensively. Instead we will discuss the extent to which our EMG results confirm or deny inferences by several recent authors on the probable functions of the gluteus maximus muscle in African apes based on gross morphological studies of cadavers and observations of bipedal posture and locomotion in living subjects. We will conclude by speculating briefly on aspects of the evolution of hominid bipedalism to an extent that indeed surpasses the limits of our EMG results. But we hope that discussion may be further provoked herewith.

METHOD

Parts of the right and left gluteus maximus muscles were recorded during six recording sessions with one captive-born female lowland gorilla (*Pan gorilla gorilla*). The subject was between four years and ten months and five years and six months old and weighed 35.3 to 38.7 kilograms during the eight-month period in which this study was conducted. She was injected in the arm or shoulder with 15.0 milligrams/kilogram body weight of Ketelar (ketamine hydrochloride) and 0.5 milligrams of atropine. In each experiment five Karma fine-wire bipolar indwelling electrodes were implanted in selected muscles with 23- or 26-gauge hypodermic needles. Before withdrawing the needles, we manipulated the hip joint to verify positions of the electrodes.

After the needles were removed, the free (proximal) ends of the electrodes were attached to contact plates of differential preamplifiers by a conducting metallic suspension in quick-drying glue. The preamplifiers were attached with skin contact cement to the shaved surface of the hip or thigh. Lead wires from the differential preamplifiers were taped loosely to the thigh, hip, or back in a manner that would not impair free movement of the hip joint. The system was grounded by a metal plate cemented and taped to the thigh or gluteal region. To prevent displacement of electrodes, the thigh or pelvis or both were wrapped with an elastic surgical bandage and the subject was attired in custom-tailored denim trousers (Plate 1). The lead and ground wires and the component of a connector to which they attached were put through an opening into a pocket on the back of the trousers.

The subject was transported from the operating room to the testing area where she was connected via a ribbon cable to equipment in a separate recording booth (Tuttle et al. 1972: 256).

Five channels of electromyogram, one channel of reference pulse (i.e. discrete signals to mark time and routine behaviors such as "swing" and "strike" of the foot), and one channel of narration were calibrated and recorded on an Ampex SP 300 eight-channel tape recorder. Concurrently, the five EMG channels were displayed on a Model 564B Tectronix oscilloscope. A Panasonic split-screen television outfit was used to videotape behavior of the subject, the EMG display on the oscilloscope, and narration. The EMG display was recorded on the upper right-hand quadrant of video frames, and the activities of the subject occupied the remainder of the frames. Behavior and EMG displays are precisely synchronous on the videotapes.

Subsequent to the recording sessions, visicorder or pen-writer recordings of EMG activity were made from the FM tapes. Narration, time, and other referents were written along the bottom of the records. After identifying prominent activities of each muscle on the record of an experiment, the relative magnitudes of all other EMG action potentials were graded as marked, moderate, slight, negligible, or nil. Our method of scoring EMG potentials is based on that of Basmajian (1967: 46–47).

Behaviors that were accompanied by EMG potentials free of artifact on one or more channels were described on the basis of repeated examinations of the video tapes at normal and slow speeds with a Panasonic Tape-a-Vision Model NV-3020. Special attenion was given to position and movements of the hip joints and the relative amount of body weight borne by the hindlimbs.

The subject had the opportunity to walk freely on the floor and on a ramp, to climb onto a stage, and to hang from a trapeze. Candies and slices of fruits and vegetables were attached to the walls, hung above the trapeze, and held over her head in order to induce bipedal, climbing, suspensory, and manipulatory behavior.

The quality of our best EMG recordings was comparable to that in refined human EMG studies. An average experiment produced good to excellent results on at least one channel for 107 minutes. The longest recording session lasted 130 minutes. No session was less than 60 minutes.

RESULTS

We will report here the electromyographic activity of the gluteus maximus muscle only during bipedal behavior, except in a few instances in which other behavior elicited marked potentials and was especially indicative of a principal action of one of its parts. First, however, we will describe the behavior of the subject and the morphological terms employed in subsequent sections.

Bipedal Behavior

Once the chief effects of anesthesia had waned, the subject stood and walked bipedally at various rates either spontaneously or, more often, to reach for food and other incentives. Bipedal running was quite rare, occurring only when she threatened the investigators (a behavior that we discouraged). This was sometimes accompanied by chest beating. Typically during bipedal stance and locomotion, her knee and hip joints were flexed, her thighs were abducted, and her feet were plantigrade.

The locomotion of our gorilla subject basically resembles the bipedalism of chimpanzees (Elftman 1944; Tuttle 1970; Jenkins 1972). There was no evidence of a pelvic tilt mechanism like that of *Homo sapiens.* In fact, as in bipedal chimpanzees (Jenkins 1972), the hip bone on the side of the swing phase was characteristically elevated. The upper trunk shifted from side to side with each step, producing a waddling gait. During bipedal locomotion, the hip and knee joints never extended to the degree exhibited in certain bipedal reaching postures. Instead they remained partially flexed throughout each step or stride. Thus the knee joint did not pass directly beneath or behind the hip joint during the supportive and propulsive phases of the locomotive cycle, though it did closely approach the former relationship at the end of the propulsive phase in a few relatively long strides.

Hindlimb postures during bipedal stance were quite variable. The subject sometimes raised the heel of one foot off the substrate and even positioned the foot so that only the pulps of the five pedal digits were in contact with the substrate. We term the later foot posture "on points." It generally occurred as she was reaching overhead. In order to reach especially high incentives, she would stand with both feet on points and with her hip and knee joints remarkably extended so that the thigh and leg of each limb were aligned.

The subject also executed vertical jumps in order to reach objects overhead. She would crouch low before propelling herself upward by retraction of the thighs and extension of the knee joints. She engaged in a variety of other squatting and crouching postures as she rested, fed, and manipulated play objects. In full squats her ischial tuberosities might touch the support or only her feet might be in contact with the substrate. In less relaxed crouching postures, she in fact stood bipedally in quasi-upright postures, occasionally with her rump touching a wall or another vertical surface.

Bipedal behavior was momentarily employed as the subject descended feet-first from suspensory postures on the trapeze. Often one of her feet touched and began to bear weight before the other one did. She very rarely remained bipedal after alighting from the trapeze. Instead she characteristically proceeded to a knuckle-walking posture.

The subject frequently climbed onto a platform by propulsive effort of one hindlimb. Prior to elevation, the knee joint and hip joint of the other (i.e. major supportive) hindlimb were usually remarkably extended. Her forelimbs rested atop the stage. As she placed the foot of the propulsive limb atop the stage, the hip joint of her major supportive limb was often markedly abducted. Immediately prior to and during elevation, she leaned forward.

Notes on Morphology and Terminology

Morphological aspects of the gluteus maximus muscle in *Pan gorilla* have been described by numerous authors (Macalister 1874; Bischoff 1880; Symington 1889; Sommer 1907; Sonntag 1924; Gregory 1950; Preuschoft 1961, 1963; Uhlmann 1968; Stern 1971, 1972; Sigmon 1974, this volume). It is not fasciculated into distinct entities, but its extensiveness, attachments, and several directions of fibers indicate that different segments are capable of discrete action. We therefore placed electrodes centrally in each of three portions of the gluteus maximus muscle according to the following scheme.

UPPER PART This constitutes the superior part of the gluteus maximus proprius which originates from the gluteal fascia and inserts into the iliotibial tract (Sigmon, this volume). When the thigh is extended, it is oriented nearly vertically (Gregory 1950: 57, 157).

MIDDLE PART This is the inferior portion of the gluteus maximus proprius. It originates medially from the neural spines of the sacrum (Gregory 1950) or multifidus fascia (Stern 1972), sacrum, coccyx, and the sacrotuberous and sacroiliac ligaments. It inserts into the iliotibial tract (Sigmon, this volume). Its fibers are directed obliquely inferolaterally and laterally when the thigh is extended.

LOWER PART This is the "ischiofemoral portion" (Preuschoft 1961; Robinson, Freedman, and Sigmon 1972) of the gluteus maximus muscle. It originates from the ischial tuberosity and tendon of the long head of the biceps femoris muscle. It inserts to the femoral shaft between the gluteal tuberosity and the lateral epicondyle (Sigmon, this volume). When the thigh is extended, its fibers are directed obliquely inferolaterally.

Electromyography

UPPER PART The upper part of the gluteus maximus muscle was recorded on the right side in four experiments and on the left side in two experiments. It acted as an abductor and lateral rotator of the thigh and probably also as a stabilizer of the extended hip joint. Good or excellent results were obtained during all sessions. The most prominent EMG activity occurred as the subject (a) stood on one extended hindlimb and markedly abducted the ipsilateral hip in order to climb onto the stage; (b) stood on points at the top of the ramp and reached for objects overhead; and (c) while lying prone with thighs widespread, abducted and flexed the hip in order to protract the thigh against the frictional resistance of the substrate.

Bipedal walking occurred frequently in two sessions and occasionally in two other sessions. Bipedal running was rarely exhibited. The most comprehensive recordings are from the right side. Most EMG activity was uniphasic, occurring during the stance phase of the hindlimb. But occasionally short bursts of negligible activity were also exhibited during swing phase. Nearly all bipedal steps recruited some EMG activity in the upper part of the gluteus maximus muscle. Bipedal steps, including walking uphill on the ramp, usually recruited EMG potentials between negligible and slight-to-moderate. Higher potentials were infrequent. In one session, two of eighty-four bipedal steps were accompanied respectively by marked and moderate-to-marked EMG activity. The subject was walking beneath and reaching for the trapeze. If a hindlimb was otherwise especially heavily loaded, moderate potentials were recruited.

Most episodes of bipedal stance were accompanied by EMG potentials between negligible and slight-to-moderate, though erratic or consistent silence (nil potentials) was not unusual. Marked potentials were never recruited, and moderate or higher potentials were infrequent in the upper part of the gluteus maximus muscle during bipedal stance.

Rises from quadrupedal or sitting postures to bipedalism usually recruited slight or lower potentials in the upper part of the gluteus maximus muscle. It often (e.g. twenty-two of thirty-one rises in one session) remained silent as the subject stood up bipedally. In three sessions, no potentials greater than slight ones were recorded. In the fourth session, ten of twenty-five rises recruited potentials greater than slight ones. These (seven moderate and three slight-to-moderate) were exhibited as the subject rose at the top of the ramp and on the stage generally with the right hindlimb prominently loaded.

When the subject stood with hindlimbs fully extended and reached for objects overhead, marked, moderate-to-marked, and moderate potentials were exhibited in the upper part of the gluteus maximus muscle. But as weight shifted off the supportive limb (sometimes quite subtly) and as the subject stood quiescently on the fully extended limb, the muscle evidenced slight or lower potentials or fell silent.

Vertical jumps generally (ten of sixteen) recruited moderate or higher potentials in the upper part of the gluteus maximus muscle. But slight-to-moderate (two), slight (one), negligible-to-slight (one), and nil (two) potentials were also exhibited during jumps.

Squatting generally evidenced negligible or nil potentials in the upper part of the gluteus maximus muscle. However, one rapid crouch preparatory to a vertical jump recruited slight activity, and several episodes in which the subject crouched as she vigorously manipulated a towel were accompanied by slight and moderate potentials.

Descents from bimanual suspension onto the feet recruited slight, negligible, and nil potentials when the load was borne more or less equally by the right and left hindlimbs. In one session, five descents in which the right hindlimb was predominantly load-bearing recruited moderate (four) and moderate-to-marked (one) potentials in the upper part of the right gluteus maximus muscle.

The upper part of the gluteus maximus muscle typically (eight of twelve occasions) exhibited nil or negligible potentials as the ipsilateral hindlimb was extended to lift the subject onto the stage. However, on two occasions moderate potentials were recruited, and once each moderate-to-marked and slight potentials were recruited. Immediately prior to lifting by one hindlimb, the upper part of the gluteus maximus muscle of the contralateral (i.e. supportive) limb usually exhibited marked, moderate, or intermediate potentials as the hip was abducted. Lower potentials occurred before and after culminant effort to position the foot of the opposite limb atop the stage.

MIDDLE PART Good results were obtained from the middle part of the right gluteus maximus muscle in three experiments. This part acted as an abductor and lateral rotator of the thigh and as a stabilizer of the hip joint during a variety of flexed and extended positions of the thigh.

The circumstances in which most prominent EMG activity occurred in the middle part of the gluteus maximus muscle varied remarkably among the three sessions. In one, while hanging bimanually from the trapeze, the subject spread her thighs, an action that included abduction, lateral rotation, and slight flexion of the hip joint, in order to touch the edge of the ramp wih her toes. Her hindlimb was in free flight during marked bursts of EMG. In the second session, the most prominent EMG potentials were recruited as she stood on points at the top of the ramp and reached for objects overhead. Her knee joints were virtually fully extended and her hip joints were markedly extended and rotated laterally. In the third session, prominent EMG activity occurred as the groggy, quasi-reclining subject attempted to rise to a sitting position. Her weight rested mostly on the right hip. Her right hindlimb was flexed and seemed to be resting passively on the floor (though it was partly out of view) as she pushed herself up by extension of both forelimbs and the left hindlimb.

Bipedal walking occurred frequently and running rarely in one session. Bipedal walking occurred occasionally in a second session and never in a third. During the latter two experiments, the subject was unusually groggy and incoordinated through most of the recording period. EMG activity was uniphasic, occurring during the stance phase of the right hindlimb. No marked potentials were recorded in the middle part of the gluteus maximus muscle during bipedal locomotion. In the session wherein the subject was fully alert, negligible and negligible-to-slight potentials accompanied 54 percent (forty-six of eighty-four) of bipedal steps. Slight and slight-to-moderate potentials were recruited during 36 percent of steps, while moderate and negligible potentials accompanied 5 percent and 4 percent, respectively, of bipedal steps. In the second session, 65 percent (thirteen of twenty) of steps recruited slight and slight-to-moderate potentials. One step was accompanied by moderate-to-marked potentials, four by moderate potentials, and two by negligible potentials. In both sessions, the higher potentials usually occurred when the subject stumbled or otherwise shifted relatively more weight over the right hindlimb.

EMG activity was exhibited in the middle part of the right gluteus maximus muscle during all bipedal stances except when most of the load was over the left hindlimb. Relatively quiescent stance was typically accompanied by negligible or slightly higher potentials. No EMG potentials greater than moderate were exhibited. Moderate potentials were confined to one experiment in which the subject was groggy. In the other two sessions, the highest potentials were slight ones.

Rises from quadrupedal or sitting postures to bipedalism generally recruited slight or lower EMG potentials. But during the session wherein the subject was unusually groggy, two (of thirty-one) rises were accompanied by moderate potentials and one by moderate-to-marked potentials. The subject was at the top of the ramp with her right hindlimb downhill as she rose.

On two occasions the subject fully extended her hips and knees in order to reach objects on the wall above the ramp. Both episodes were accompanied by high EMG potentials in the middle part of the gluteus maximus muscle as she strained upward and by lower potentials as her efforts diminished.

In two sessions, eight of fifteen vertical jumps recruited moderate activity in the middle part of the gluteus maximus muscle. Slight potentials were exhibited during five jumps and negligible-to-slight and negligible potentials each during one jump. The lower potentials were associated with the less vigorous jumps.

Squatting was typically accompanied by negligible or nil EMG potentials in the middle part of the gluteus maximus muscle. One rapid crouch preparatory to a vertical jump recruited slight activity. Slight and slight-to-moderate potentials also occurred as the crouching subject kneaded and pulled on a towel.

Descents from suspension on the trapeze onto the hindlimbs recruited slight, negligible, or nil EMG potentials according to the extent of loading on the right hindlimb.

Climbing from the floor onto the stage by propulsive effort of the right hindlimb recruited nil (two instances) or negligible (one instance) EMG potentials in the middle part of the gluteus maximus muscle. By contrast, when the right foot was on the floor and the left foot was on the stage preparatory to lifting, moderate (seven instances), slight-to-moderate (two instances), or slight (six instances) potentials were recruited. The right hip was abducted then.

LOWER PART The lower part of the right gluteus maximus muscle was recorded in four experiments. It acted primarily as an extensor of the hip joint. Excellent or good results were obtained consistently in two sessions and erratically in one session. Poor results were obtained in one session. During the two best recording sessions, the most prominent activity occurred occasionally when the subject (a) walked bipedally; (b) pivoted over the right hindlimb while bipedal; and (c) stood bipedally at the edge of the stage with right foot foremost and stretched forward to grasp food incentives on a sill some distance from the stage. In the third session, the most prominent activity in the lower part of the gluteus maximus muscle occurred during the propulsive phase of a vertical jump which the subject executed from the top of the ramp in order to reach a slice of cucumber affixed to the wall. In the fourth session, the subject was partly out of view when the most prominent EMG activity occurred.

During bipedal walking (whether assisted or unassisted) and running, EMG activity was uniphasic, generally beginning at foot contact and lasting through most of the stance phase of the right hindlimb. In some episodes of rapid bipedalism, EMG began just prior to contact of the right foot with the floor. In some steps, particularly when the stride was relatively long, EMG ceased in the lower portion of the gluteus maximus muscle before the extensional movement of the hip joint (cf. retraction of the thigh) was complete.

Although marked EMG activity accompanied some bipedal steps in the two most successful experiments, this high level was not typical, accounting for only 10 percent (eleven of 105) and 6 percent (five of eighty-five) of bipedal steps in respective sessions. Other bipedal steps during the two sessions severally recruited lower levels of EMG potentials in the following percentages: moderate, 37 and 33 percent; slight or slight-to-moderate, 45 and 36 percent; negligible or negligible-to-slight, 8 and 25 percent. In a third session, only seven bipedal steps were accompanied by artifact-free EMG. Moderate-to-marked potentials were recruited during one step, moderate potentials during three steps, slight-to-moderate and slight potentials each during one step, and negligible-to-slight potentials during two steps. During the three sessions, no bipedal step was accompanied by complete silence in the lower portion of the gluteus maximus muscle.

EMG activity was evidenced during all episodes of bipedal stance in which the right hindlimb was supportive. The lower portion of the gluteus maximus muscle went silent only when the subject clearly shifted her weight predominantly onto the left hindlimb. No instances of marked EMG activity occurred, though on rare occasions (three times in one session and once in a second session) moderate-to-marked potentials were recruited. Moderate potentials were more common than higher ones (thirteen of sixty-one, four of forty-one, and two of six bursts) in the three sessions. But generally, slight or negligible potentials accompanied bipedal stance, particularly when the two limbs appeared to be equally loaded.

As the subject rose from quadrupedal to bipedal posture, moderate, slight-to-moderate, or slight potentials were typically exhibited by the lower portion of the gluteus maximus muscle. Occasionally, negligible potentials were evinced, but only in circumstances wherein the left hindlimb bore most of the load during hip extension.

When the subject fully extended her hindlimb in order to reach objects overhead, activity in the lower portion of the gluteus maximus muscle diminished (sometimes from relatively high levels) to silence as she achieved full extension of the hip joint.

The subject executed two vertical jumps which were accompanied respectively by marked and moderate-to-marked EMG potentials during retraction of the thigh.

Sustained squatting generally recruited slight and negligible potentials. But during instances in which the squatting subject shifted backward and forward over the right foot, as when she vigorously kneaded and shook a bath towel, moderate and moderate-to-marked potentials were interspersed with lower ones. Further, the subject was quite vigilant during episodes of towel manipulation, while in most other squatting bouts she seemed to be calm.

As the subject descended directly from the trapeze to the floor, negligible or slight potentials were exhibited in the lower portion of the gluteus maximus muscle. Negligible potentials were characteristic of episodes in which the left foot was first to contact the floor. Slight potentials occurred when the right hindlimb was prominently load bearing.

Climbing from the floor onto the stage by propulsive effort of the right hindlimb generally recruited negligible potentials, though slight EMG activity occurred during two ascents and the muscle was silent during two other ascents.

Simultaneity and Discreteness

The upper and middle parts of the right gluteus maximus muscle were recorded concurrently in two experiments, the upper and lower parts in two experiments, and the middle and lower parts in two experiments. During eleven minutes of one session, all three parts were recorded concurrently as the subject engaged in bipedal behavior. The upper parts of the right and left gluteus maximus muscles were recorded concurrently in two sessions.

The three parts of the gluteus maximus muscle are clearly capable of discrete activity. But often during bipedal behavior much of their activity occurred simultaneously, though at varying levels.

EMG activities in the upper and middle parts of the gluteus maximus muscle were sometimes reciprocal as the bipedal subject shifted about or swayed over the right hindlimb, jumped vertically, and climbed onto the stage. That is to say, while EMG activity occurred in the upper part of the muscle, the middle part might be silent or active at a lower level; but, in the next instance, the upper part might act at a lower level than the middle part or be inactive while the middle part was quite active. In one experiment the upper part seemed to act more prominently as an abductor than the middle part did, especially when the foot was in free flight during abduction of the thigh. During bipedal progression, the two parts were generally active simultaneously, though often at relatively different levels. In one session, the upper part acted at relatively higher levels than the middle part more frequently than vice versa. However, in another session, the middle part was often relatively more active than the upper part during rises to bipedalism and other bipedal behaviors.

The lower part of the right gluteus maximus muscle acted discretely from the upper and middle parts in a more clear-cut fashion than the latter two parts did from each other. The lower part was especially prominently active by comparison with the upper and middle parts as the subject crouched bipedally, stood bipedally with hip and knee joints partially flexed, and rose to bipedal postures, as well as sometimes during bipedal progression. It was silent in many instances of thigh abduction wherein the foot was in free flight and prominent activity was exhibited by the upper or middle or both other parts of the gluteus maximus muscle. Conversely, the latter two parts of the muscle were silent or active at low levels while the lower part was prominently active during some extensional movements of the hip joint in circumstances wherein resistance to thigh flexion was requisite to maintain bipedal posturing.

The upper parts of the right and left gluteus maximus muscles frequently acted simultaneously and at relatively equivalent levels during bipedal behaviors in which the hindlimbs were more or less equally supportive. Otherwise they acted discretely and often at remarkably different levels.

DISCUSSION

Washburn (1950) inferred and Breitinger (1959) concurred that in apes the gluteus maximus muscle is an abductor of the thigh because the relatively long ilium of their hip bones positions the muscle lateral to the greater trochanter of the femur. From this Washburn (1950) concluded that human evolution was initiated by the backward bending of the ilium so that the gluteus maximus muscle became an extensor of the hip joint while the gluteus medius muscle became an abductor, thereby taking over the prehominid function of the gluteus maximus.

Prior to 1964, Robinson (1962, 1963, 1964) accepted and reiterated Washburn's hypothesis. But subsequently, he and Sigmon disputed it on the basis of their dissections on specimens of all forms of extant apes (Sigmon and Robinson 1967; Sigmon 1971; Robinson 1968: 172–173, 1972: 79–82). They inferred that there is no major difference between apes and man in function of the gluteus maximus muscle (Sigmon and Robinson 1967). Instead they proposed that because of the different proportions and anatomical relationships of bony parts, it is only the effects of basically similar actions of the gluteus maximus muscle that differ between apes and man (Sigmon 1971; Robinson 1968: 173, 1972: 80). Accordingly, upstanding apes possess a relatively long moment arm (the ischium) and short lever arm (distance from the center of the acetabulum to the substrate), whereas bipedal man has a relatively long lever arm and a short moment arm. Although the gluteus maximus acts principally as an extensor of the hip joint in both man and apes, it chiefly provides speed of action in the former and power of action in the latter (Sigmon 1971, 1974; Robinson, Freedman, and Sigmon 1972).

Although available EMG data on gorilla do not take us to the bottom of the gluteus maximus problem, they at least provide a direct base for functional interpretation and establish a foundation for future refined biomechanical and kinesiological studies of apes and man. However, we would stress that the activities and functions of the gluteus maximus muscle are extremely complex, so oversimplification should be avoided in theoretical evolutionary schemes.

Our studies confirm that the gluteus maximus proprius, which we termed the "upper and middle parts" in previous sections, may act prominently as an abductor and lateral rotator of the thigh at the hip joint in gorilla. The lower or ischiofemoral part of the gluteus maximus muscle in gorilla acts primarily as an extensor of the hip joint. We cannot determine from available EMG data whether the gluteus maximus proprius also acts as an extensor of the hip joint or the extent to which the lower part of the gluteus maximus muscle might also act as an abductor or lateral rotator or both. For instance, when the subject stood on points and strained upward to reach objects overhead, the gluteus maximus proprius exhibited high potentials, the hip joint was dramatically extended, and the lower part of the gluteus maximus muscle was silent. This could be interpreted to mean that the gluteus maximus proprius in bipedal gorilla, as in man, is an extensor of the hip joint, especially during the final segment of extensional excursion. Per contra, the gluteus maximus proprius might instead be considered as a stabilizer of the fully extended hip joint, in which case it would not be an extensor per se in gorilla. Similarly, in many instances in which the lower part of gluteus maximus was active as an extensor of the hip joint, viz., during bipedal stance and locomotion, the hip joint was in abducted-laterally rotated positions.

Despite ambiguities that remain in regard to precise functions of the different parts of the gluteus maximus muscle in gorilla (and indeed also in man!), we conclude that there is no major factual impediment to theorizing the evolution of the human condition of the gluteus maximus muscle from one like that of the gorilla or its close counterpart the chimpanzee if such an African pongid were subjected to a selective complex favoring bipedalism of the human sort. The gluteus maximus proprius in the African ape clearly has the potential to act prominently when the hip joint is extended maximally. Further, it seems reasonable to propose that retrogression of the ischiofemoral portion of the gluteus maximus muscle from a prehominid African pongidlike condition would occur as full alignment of the hindlimb segments became increasingly habitual. Recall that in gorilla, the lower part of the gluteus maximus muscle fell silent as the animal achieved full extension of the hindlimb.

REFERENCES

BARNICOT, N. A.

1958 "The experimental approach to physical anthropology," in *The scope of physical anthropology and its place in academic studies.* Edited by D. F. Roberts and J. S. Weiner, 33–41. Cowley, Oxford, England: Church Army Press.

BASMAJIAN, J. V.

1967 *Muscles alive: their functions revealed by electromyography* (second edition). Baltimore: Williams and Wilkins.

BASMAJIAN, J. V., R. TUTTLE

1973 "EMG of locomotion in gorilla and man," in *Control of posture and locomotion.* Edited by R. B. Stein, K. B. Pearson, R. S. Smith, J. B. Redford, 599–609. London: Plenum Press.

BISCHOFF, T. L. W.

1880 Beiträge zur Anatomie des Gorillas. *Abhandlungen der königlich-bayerischen Akademie der Wissenschaften, München, Mathematisch-Physikalischen Classe* 13:1–48.

BREITINGER, E.

1959 "Zur frühesten Phase der Hominiden-Evolution," in *Beiträge Österreichs zur Erforschung der Vergangenheit und Kulturgeschichte der Menschheit.* Edited by E. Breitinger, J. Haeckel and R. Pittioni, 205–235. New York: Wenner-Gren Foundation for Anthropological Research.

ELFTMAN, H.

1944 The bipedal walking of the chimpanzee. *Journal of Mammalogy* 25:67–71.

GREGORY, W. K.

1950 *The anatomy of the gorilla.* New York: Columbia University Press.

JENKINS, F. A., JR.

1972 Chimpanzee bipedalism: cineradiographic analysis and implications for the evolution of gait. *Science* 178:877–879.

MAC ALISTER, A.

1874 The muscular anatomy of the gorilla. *Proceedings of the Royal Irish Academy* 1:501–506.

PREUSCHOFT, H.

1961 Muskeln und Gelenke der Hinterextremität des Gorillas. *Morphologisches Jahrbuch* 101:432–540.

1963 Muskelgewichte bei Gorilla, Orang-utan, und Mensch. *Anthropologischer Anzeiger* 26:308–317.

ROBINSON, J. T.

1962 "The origin and adaptive radiation of the australopithecines," in *Evolution und Hominisation.* Edited by G. Kurth, 120–140. Stuttgart: Gustav Fischer Verlag.

1963 "Adaptive radiation in the australopithecines and the origin of man," in *African ecology and human evolution.* Edited by F. C. Howell and F. Bourlière, 385–416. Chicago: Aldine.

1964 Some critical phases in the evolution of man. *South African Archaeological Bulletin* 19:3–12.

1968 "The origin and adaptive radiation of the australopithecines," in *Evolution und Hominisation*, (second edition). Edited by G. Kurth, 150–175. Stuttgart: Gustav Fischer Verlag.

1972 *Early hominid posture and locomotion*. Chicago: University of Chicago Press.

ROBINSON, J. T., L. FREEDMAN, B. A. SIGMON

1972 Some aspects of pongid and hominid bipedality. *Journal of Human Evolution* 1:361–369.

SIGMON, B. A.

1971 Bipedal behavior and the emergence of erect posture in man. *American Journal of Physical Anthropology* 34:55–60.

1974 A functional analysis of pongid hip and thigh musculature. *Journal of Human Evolution* 3:161–185.

SIGMON, B. A., J. T. ROBINSON

1967 On the function of m. gluteus maximus in apes and in man. *American Journal of Physical Anthropology* 27:245–246.

SOMMER, A.

1907 Das Muskelsystem des Gorillas. *Jenaische Zeitschrift für Naturwissenschaft* 42:181–308.

SONNTAG, C. F.

1924 *The morphology and evolution of the apes and man*. London: John Bale, Sons, and Danielsson.

STERN, J. T., JR.

1971 Functional myology of the hip and thigh of cebid monkeys and its implications for the evolution of erect posture. *Bibliotheca Primatologica* 14:1–318. Basel: S. Karger.

1972 Anatomical and functional specializations of the human gluteus maximus. *American Journal of Physical Anthropology* 36:315–340.

SYMINGTON, J.

1889 Observations on the myology of the gorilla and chimpanzee. *Report of the British Association for the Advancement of Science* 1889–1890: 629–630.

TUTTLE, R. H.

1970 "Postural, propulsive, and prehensile capabilities in the cheiridia of chimpanzees and other great apes," in *The chimpanzee*, volume two. Edited by G. Bourne, 167–253. Basel, New York: S. Karger.

TUTTLE, R. H., J. V. BASMAJIAN

1974a "Electromyography of forearm musculature in gorilla and problems related to knuckle-walking," in *Primate locomotion*. Edited by F. A. Jenkins, Jr., 293–347. New York: Academic Press.

1974b Electromyography of brachial muscles in *Pan gorilla* and hominoid evolution. *American Journal of Physical Anthropology* 41:71–90.

1974c "Electromyography of the manual long digital flexor muscles in gorilla," *Proceedings of the Sixth Congreso International de Medicina Fisica*, volume two. Edited by F. Barnoseu, 311–315. Madrid: Ministerio de Trabajo Instituto Nacional de Prevision.

TUTTLE, R. H., J. V. BASMAJIAN, E. REGENOS, G. SHINE
1972 Electromyography of knuckle-walking: results of four experiments on the forearm of *Pan gorilla*. *American Journal of Physical Anthropology* 37:255–266.

UHLMANN, K.
1968 Hüft- und Oberschenkelmuskulatur. Systematische und vergleichende Anatomie. *Primatologia* 4:1–442.

WASHBURN, S. L.
1950 The analysis of primate evolution with particular reference to the origin of man. *Cold Spring Harbor Symposia on Quantitative Biology*, Proceedings 15:67–78.

Function of the Gluteals in Man

ROBERT K. GREENLAW and JOHN V. BASMAJIAN

There seems to be some form of transition in the shape, size, and attachment of the gluteals from primitive forms to present-day man. Because presumably man has changed his form of ambulation from a type of quadrupedal to a bipedal gait pattern, it would be of interest to note the precise function of the gluteals in man and to compare these functions with those alterations of bone structure that have taken place in the various forms of primitive and present-day man.

MATERIAL AND METHODS

The precise activity of muscles acting about the hip during the performance of controlled test movements was studied in twenty-five normal, healthy, volunteer subjects in both the erect and recumbent positions, as well as during normal gait. The subjects averaged 21.6 years of age. A preliminary study using ten subjects and a definite study using fifteen subjects were carried out.

Fine wire electrodes were inserted into the belly of each muscle to be studied and the activity of from eight to ten muscles was recorded simultaneously on linograph ultraviolet-sensitive bromide paper. In addition, vertical deflections indicating signals from contact switches on different areas of the sole of the foot, as well as a time-marker showing one-tenth of a second intervals, were recorded on other channels. A classification of muscle activity was used in interpreting the electromyographic data and grades from zero (no activity) to four plus (very marked activity) were assigned.

Motion pictures of the subject were made simultaneously with the electromyographic recording procedure to assist in correlating motions of the pelvis and limb segments with the electromyographic activity recorded.

Detailed charts were made indicating the activity of each muscle during each tenth of a complete walking cycle for the various motions performed by the fifteen subjects.

In this article the function of the gluteal muscles will be considered for only the controlled test movements. A later work will deal with the function of these muscles during normal gait.

ABDUCTORS

Findings

In the relaxed, erect posture, minimal to no activity was noted in each of the muscles examined.

TENSOR FASCIAE LATAE Moderate activity was found on medial rotation of the fully extended limb, while no activity was found on lateral rotation. Moderate to marked activity was found on abducting the limb, but no activity was present on adduction. On straight leg raising, moderate to marked activity was found, and on flexing the hip with the knee flexed, moderate muscle activity was recorded. No activity was noted on extension of the thigh from the neutral position. Hypertension of the knee produced no activity.

GLUTEUS MEDIUS ANTERIOR Marked activity was noted on medially rotating the limb, while no activity was recorded on lateral rotation. Abduction to about thirty degrees produced marked activity throughout the full range of motion, while adduction revealed no activity. This portion of the gluteus medius showed slight to moderate activity on straight leg raising. Minimal activity was noted toward the extreme of extension of the thigh.

GLUTEUS MEDIUS POSTERIOR On medially rotating the right lower extremity, moderate activity was recorded in this part of the gluteus medius muscle, whereas on lateral rotation of the limb, no activity was noted. Abduction of the extremity produced moderate to marked activity, and adduction revealed no activity. This part of the gluteus medius was minimally active on straight leg raising. There was a slight degree of activity in the muscle on maximal extension of the thigh.

GLUTEUS MINIMUS A moderate degree of activity was noted on medial rotation of the thigh, as well as on abducting to forty-five degrees. There was no activity present on adduction of the limb and the muscle was electrically silent on lateral rotation. Straight leg raising elicited a slight response in the gluteus minimus muscle.

Discussion of Abductors

The minimal to zero activity noted in each of the muscles examined in the relaxed, erect posture coincides with the findings of Weddell, Feinstein, and Pattle (1944), Akerblom (1948), Arienti (1948), Wheatley and Jahnke (1951), Joseph and Nightingale (1954), Joseph and Williams (1957), Portnoy and Morin (1956), Joseph (1960), Jonsson and Steen (1966), and Basmajian (1974).

This negligible degree of activity is understandable as long as the line of gravity of the body, passing just anterior to the second sacral vertebra, passes through or slightly behind the transverse hip joint axes and through or slightly in front of the knee joint axes (Morton and Fuller 1952; Steindler 1955; Joseph 1960; Evans 1961; Williams and Lissner 1962; Basmajian 1974). A similar degree of electrical silence was observed in the relaxed recumbent position.

These muscles are classically known as abductors of the thigh and play an important role as stabilizers of the pelvis. They accomplish this by preventing rotation of the pelvis away from the weight-bearing limb during single-leg stance. This function has been emphasized by Inman (1947), Denham (1959), Elftman (1954), Paul (1965), Merchant (1965), McLeish and Charnley (1970), and others in functional and biomechanical considerations of the hip, mainly with respect to the frontal plane. As Inman (1947) pointed out, during single-leg stance, the abductor muscles in normals are capable of developing a force of 1.4 to 1.9 times the body weight in order to hold the pelvis in equilibrium.

Controversy exists with regard to the abductor function of the tensor fasciae latae. Kaplan (1958), using electrical stimulation techniques, did not consider the tensor as an abductor, while many other investigators thought that it possessed an important abductor function. From the present study, it is clear that the tensor fasciae latae is an abductor with the thigh extended or partly flexed. As Close suggested in a discussion of an article by Merchant (1965), this muscle may act as a guide rope in controlling medial and lateral rotation of the femur during abduction by its insertion into the iliotibial band. The upper part of the gluteus maximus, by its insertion into the iliotibial band, may exert a similar effect on the femur. The two muscles acting together may therefore control rotation of the femur during abduction. The tensor fasciae latae is also a medial rotator of the thigh in the standing and recumbent postures with the thigh in neutral extension and neutral abduction, and with the thigh in forty-five-degree flexion and neutral abduction. As stated above, the muscle has no significant activity as a lateral rotator of the thigh unless the thigh is in the abducted position. The rotatory effect (if any) of the tensor on the tibia was not studied. The tensor does not exert any extensor effect on the knee, as was suggested by Wheatley and Jahnke (1951) and Davies and Davies (1962).

The gluteus medius (anterior part) is a strong medial rotator of the hip with the thigh in either the neutral extended position or with the thigh flexed forty-five degrees. The gluteus minimus is also a medial rotator. Neither have any function as an active lateral rotator. Both muscles are also active abductors and flexors of the hip. The anterior part of the gluteus medius, the gluteus minimus, and the tensor fasciae latae act as flexors through the first twenty to twenty-five degrees of flexion to initiate the movement, after which the long flexors such as the iliopsoas take over.

There is still considerable uncertainty in the literature with regard to the possible functions of the posterior part of the gluteus medius. Duchenne (1867) considered the posterior fibers of the gluteus medius to be lateral rotators and extensors of the thigh. Steindler (1955) believed that portion of the gluteus medius to be an extensor of the thigh. Lockhart (1964) believed the posterior part to be a lateral rotator of the thigh. This study indicates that the posterior part of the gluteus medius is a medial and not a lateral rotator in both the standing and recumbent positions and with the thigh in various positions of flexion and abduction. While its extensor function is weak, there is even less activity as a flexor. The posterior part of the gluteus medius is a strong abductor of the thigh with the thigh in the position of neutral extension or flexed forty-five degrees.

Steindler (1955) believed in "the inversion of function" or "changes in the secondary muscle functions which occur as the position of the hip changes." He believed that the gluteus minimus changed from an abductor in the neutral position to an adductor in the flexed position. The findings of this study do not support such a statement.

The abductors pass from their site of origin on the lateral aspect of the ilium to their insertion in the superolateral aspect of the greater trochanter. The tensor fasciae latae passes in a similar direction but inserts into the iliotibial band. These muscles pass in a plane lateral to the mechanical axis of the femur, which is represented by an imaginary line passing from the center of the head of the femur to approximately the center of the distal femoral condyle. Such a relationship explains their function as abductors of the hip. Those abductors that have their line of action anterior to the line representing the mechanical axis of the femur would correctly be interpreted as flexors and medial rotators. From this consideration, one would expect the posterior part of the gluteus medius to be a lateral rotator and an extensor of the thigh. As was shown in this study, that part of the gluteus medius acts during medial rather than lateral rotation and does have a weak extensor function. The explanation of the medial rather than lateral rotatory function of the posterior part of the gluteus medius must be due to the relationship of the site of insertion of the muscle into the oblique ridge on the anterolateral surface of the greater trochanter and therefore the line of action passing slightly anterior to the mechanical axis of the femur, specifically at and near the site of insertion of the muscle.

GLUTEUS MAXIMUS

Findings

GLUTEUS MAXIMUS (UPPER THIRD) This portion of the gluteus maximus showed no activity when supporting the body weight on the right lower extremity, medially rotating the limb, abducting the thigh from the neutral position, straight leg raising, flexing the hip and knee simultaneously, increasing the arch of the back, or hanging on the right hip. Minimal activity was noted on lateral rotation of the extremity and slight to moderate activity on abducting the limb approximately forty-five degrees. It displayed moderate to marked activity on extending the hip actively from the neutral position. The activity as recorded for each of these movements was nearly maximal from the beginning and persisted to that degree throughout the full range of the movement.

GLUTEUS MAXIMUS (MIDDLE THIRD) In the erect position no activity was found when standing on the right leg. Nor was any activity noted on medially rotating the limb, straight leg raising, flexing the hip and knee simultaneously, adducting the extremity from the neutral position, increasing the arch of the back, or hanging on the right hip. Minimal activity was present on lateral rotation and this increased to slight activity on abduction. Extending the hip actively from the neutral position evoked moderate to marked activity in this portion of the muscle.

GLUTEUS MAXIMUS (LOWER THIRD) This portion of the gluteus maximus showed no activity on standing on the right lower extremity, medially rotating the limb, abduction or adduction from the neutral position, straight leg raising, flexion of the hip and knee simultaneously, increasing the arch of the back, or hanging on the right hip. Slight activity was recorded during lateral rotation of the limb and moderate activity on extending the thigh from the neutral position.

All portions of the gluteus maximus, as well as other gluteals, showed marked to very marked activity during maximum isometric contraction at the commencement and termination of the study.

Discussion of Gluteus Maximus

The function of the gluteus maximus as an extensor of the thigh is well known. Steindler (1955), however, considered the upper portion of the gluteus maximus to be a flexor of the thigh. Most workers understand the gluteus maximus to be a lateral rotator as well as an extensor of the thigh. The main controversy concerns the function of the upper and lower parts as abductors or adductors of the thigh respectively. The findings of this study show all three parts to be weak lateral rotators of the thigh; the upper and middle thirds are abductors and the lower third is inactive as an abductor or an adductor in the standing position. Only the upper part is an abductor in the recumbent position with the thigh either extended to neutral or flexed forty-five degrees. The lower third of the gluteus maximus shows weak activity as an adductor only with the thigh at forty-five degrees of flexion in the recumbent posture. As previously mentioned, the upper part of the gluteus maximus may act to tense the iliotibial tract, thereby assisting in the control of rotation of the femur during abduction of the thigh. The gluteus maximus does not assist in maintaining the equilibrium of the pelvis in the frontal plane during single-leg stance.

CONCLUSIONS

The following conclusions may be made from the foregoing study of function of the gluteal muscles during the performance of controlled test movements.

1. In the relaxed, erect posture, minimal to no activity was present in all the gluteal muscles.
2. With fine adjustments in posture, various individual muscles or groups of muscles revealed short periods of slight to moderate activity.
3. A considerable range of activity was noted for each muscle for most of the controlled test movements.
4. The posterior part of the gluteus medius was found to be a medial and not a lateral rotator of the thigh.
5. The tensor fasciae latae was clearly shown to be an abductor of the thigh, to clarify this controversial function. It did not exert any extensor effect on the knee.
6. There was no evidence to support the "inversion of function" hypothesis, advanced by Strasser and perpetuated by Steindler, for a change in function of the gluteus minimus from an abductor to an adductor with the thigh in a flexed position.
7. The abductor muscles stabilize the pelvis on the femur in the frontal plane during single-leg stance because of their abductor function. They are medial rotators and abductors of the thigh and strong flexors during the first twenty to twenty-five degrees of flexion.
8. The upper part of the gluteus maximus was shown to be an abductor and an extensor of the thigh. It was a weak lateral rotator with the thigh in neutral abduction but more active with the thigh in thirty degrees of abduction.
9. The middle third of the gluteus maximus was a strong extensor, a weak lateral rotator, and an abductor. It was more active as a lateral rotator with the thigh abducted thirty degrees. It was shown not to be an adductor or a medial rotator.
10. The lower third of the gluteus maximus was an extensor and was slightly active as a lateral rotator and as an adductor with the thigh flexed forty-five degrees. It was not active in adduction or abduction with the thigh in the neutral position.
11. The gluteus maximus does not assist in maintaining stability of the pelvis on the femur in the frontal plane, when standing erect, but does in the sagittal plane.

REFERENCES

AKERBLOM, B.
1948 *Standing and sitting posture.* Stockholm: A.-B. Nordiska Bokhandeln. (Translated by Ann Synge.)

ARIENTI, A.
1948 Analyse oscillographique de la marche de l'homme. *Acta Physiotherapy Rheumat. Belg.* 3:190–192.

BASMAJIAN, J. V.
1974 *Musces alive: their functions revealed by electromyography* (third edition). Baltimore: Williams and Wilkins.

DAVIES, D. V., F. DAVIES
1962 *Gray's Anatomy, descriptive and applied* (thirty-third edition). London: Longman's, Green.

DENHAM, R. A.
1959 Hip mechanics. *Journal of Bone and Joint Surgery* 41(B):550–557.

DUCHENNE, G. B. A.
1867 *Physiologie des mouvements.* Philadelphia, London: W. B. Saunders. (Translated by E. B. Kaplan [1949]; reissued in 1959.)

ELFTMAN, H.
1954 "The functional structure of the lower limb," in *Human limbs and their substitutes.* Edited by P. E. Klopsteg and P. D. Wilson. New York: McGraw-Hill.

EVANS, F. G.
1961 *Biomechanical studies of the musculo-skeletal system.* Springfield, Illinois: Charles C. Thomas.

GREENLAW, ROBERT K.
1973 "Function of muscles about the hip during normal level walking: an electromyographic and biomechanical study." Unpublished doctoral dissertation, Queen's University, Kingston, Ontario.

INMAN, V. T.
1947 Functional aspects of the abductor muscles of the hip. *Journal of Bone and Joint Surgery* 29:607–619.

JONSSON, B., B. STEEN
1966 Function of the gracilis muscle: an electromyographic study. *Acta Morphol. Neer-Scandinav.* 6:325–341.

JOSEPH, J.
1960 *Man's posture: electromyographic studies.* Springfield, Illinois: Charles C. Thomas.

JOSEPH, J., A. NIGHTINGALE
1954 Electromyography of muscles of posture: thigh muscles in males. *Journal of Physiology* 126:81–85.

JOSEPH, J., P. L. WILLIAMS
1957 Electromyography of certain hip muscles. *Journal of Anatomy* 91:286–294.

KAPLAN, E. B.
1958 The iliotibial tract. *Journal of Bone and Joint Surgery* 40(A):817–832.

LOCKHART, R. D.
1964 "Myology," in *Cunningham's Textbook of anatomy* (tenth edition). London: Oxford University Press.

MC LEISH, R. D., J. CHARNLEY
1970 Abduction forces in the one-legged stance. *Journal of Biomechanics* 3:191–209.

MERCHANT, A. C.
1965 Hip abductor muscle force: an experimental study of the influence of hip position with particular reference to rotation. *Journal of Bone and Joint Surgery* 47(A):462–476.

MORTON, D. J., D. D. FULLER
1952 *Human locomotion and body form: a study of gravity and man.* Baltimore: Williams and Wilkins.

PORTNOY, H., F. MORIN
1956 Electromyographic study of postural muscles in various positions and movements. *American Journal of Physiology* 186:122–126.

PAUL, J. P.
1965 "Bio-engineering studies of the forces transmitted by joints, engineering analysis," in *Bio-mechanics and related bio-engineering topics*. London: Pergamon Press.

STEINDLER, A.
1955 *Kinesiology of the human body under normal and pathological conditions.* Springfield, Illinois: Charles C. Thomas.

WEDDELL, G., B. FEINSTEIN, R. E. PATTLE
1944 The electrical activity of voluntary muscles in man under normal and pathological conditions. *Brain* 67:178–257.

WHEATLEY, M. D., W. D. JAHNKE
1951 Electromyographic study of the superficial thigh and hip muscles in normal individuals. *Arch. Phys. Med.* 32:508–515.

WILLIAMS, M., H. R. LISSNER
1962 *Biomechanics of human motion.* Philadelphia: W. B. Saunders.

Functional Adaptation to Posture in the Pelvis of Man and Other Primates

BENNO K. F. KUMMER

In tetrapods, the pelvis provides a stable connection between the free posterior extremities and the vertebral column. Since the pelvic girdle develops somewhat anterior to the cloacal region and later in time than the digestive tube, it forms a more or less elliptical or circular ring. For the purpose of mechanical analysis in a sagittal plane, however, it may be regarded as a two-armed lever. The hypomochlion of this lever is the hip joint (C in Figure 1a), one arm is loaded through the sacroiliac joint (O in Figure 1a) by a part of the body weight, the second arm acts as a lever for some muscles and the ischio-sacral ligaments.

The stress of the pelvic lever is determined by the two opposite rotational moments of the partial body weight and the resultant of all muscular forces due to the equilibrium conditions on the hip and sacroiliac joints. In the sacroiliac joint, the sacrum tends to rotate forward. This rotation is prevented by the ischio-sacral ligaments or the ischio-caudal muscles respectively (L in Figure 1b).

Even when the sacrum is fixed against the innominate bone, the whole complex tends to rotate forward in the hip joint. This results from a lordotic bending of the vertebral column, especially of the lumbar spine. The whole construction of the trunk is stabilized against ventral bending by a tensile string consisting of the ventral muscles, especially the rectus abdominis (Mr in Figure 1c). Theoretically, the abdominal muscles together with the erector spinae are sufficient to stiffen the entire trunk construction.

In reality there is an additional need for the fixation of the femur respective to the innominate bone, for in quadrupeds the hip and knee

For Plates, see p. xxii, between pp. 560–561

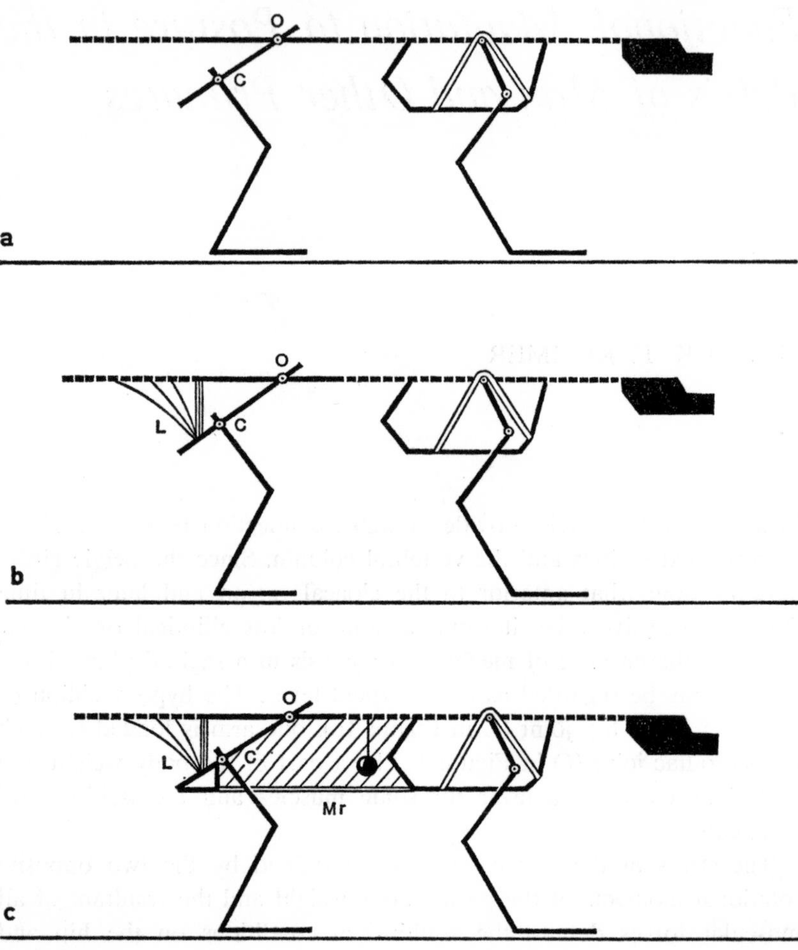

Figure 1 (a, b, c). The innominate bone of quadruped mammals as a two-armed lever
(a) without fixation
(b) fixation by ischio-sacral ligaments and ischio-caudal muscles
(c) additional fixation by the abdominal muscles

joints are in semiflexion and the support reaction on the ground causes further flexion of both joints. The flexion of the knee joint is prevented by the quadriceps femoris (M_q in Figure 2), but the hip joint can be stabilized by the extensors of the hip. In quadrupedal primates there are two main groups of hip extensors: the gluteal muscles (M_g in Figure 2) and the ischio-crural muscles (M_i in Figure 2). Both groups can also prevent the forward rotation of the pelvis in the hip joint and therefore discharge partially the ventral musculature.

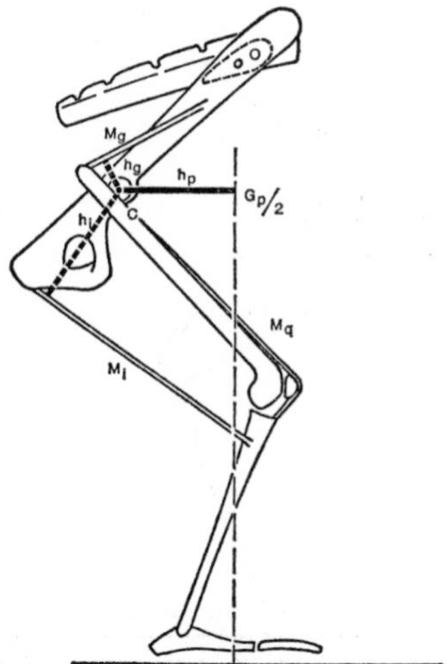

Figure 2. Balance of load and muscular moments at an innominate bone of a quadruped monkey

The innominate bone has to be adapted to the stress originating from the two opposite rotational moments as well as to the demands of the hip extensors. For the determination of the muscular forces and moments, the moment of the load must be known. This load moment depends on the weight to be borne by each hind leg ($\frac{G_p}{2}$ in Figure 2) and its lever arm h_p. The counteracting muscular moment is at least composed of the moment of the ischiofemoral muscles $M_i \cdot h_i$ and the moment of the gluteal muscles $M_g \cdot h_g$. Consequently the equilibrium conditions are:

$$\frac{G_p}{2} \cdot h_p = M_i \cdot h_i + M_g \cdot h_g.$$

This function is not absolutely determined, because the muscular moment could as well be provided by the ischiofemoral as by the gluteal muscles alone. In each case, the minimum muscular force is needed and the maximal functional adaptation is reached, when the lever arms of both muscle groups are greatest.

At a given length of the skeletal lever of a muscle (distance between bony insertion and center of rotation) the physical lever arm is greatest when the action line of the muscle extends rectangularly to the axis of the skeletal element, where the muscle is inserted. In this case the bony lever is identical to the imaginary lever arm (see Figure 3).

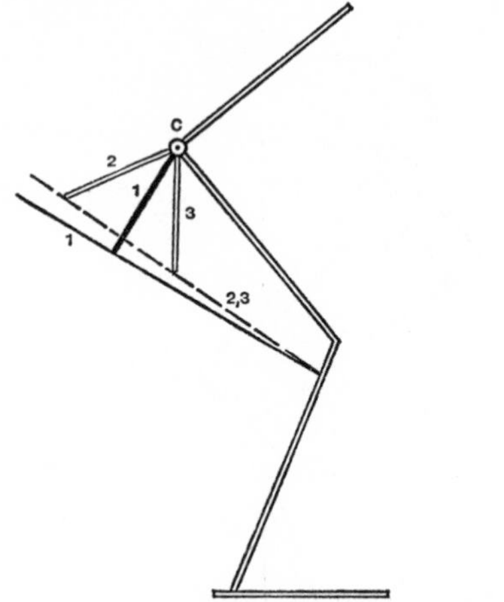

Figure 3. Change in length of the physical lever arm in different positions of the bony lever
C — Center of the hip joint
1, 2, 3 — Different positions of the ischium and the hamstring muscles respectively

In the quadrupedal monkeys the ischium seems to perform such an optimal lever for the ischiofemoral muscles (see Figure 4). The lever for the gluteal muscles is represented by the greater trochanter, belonging to the femur. In the most frequently adopted position of the femur, the gluteus medius muscle inserts on the trochanter at an almost right angle, when its origin is relatively far away. That accounts for a fairly long iliac bone.

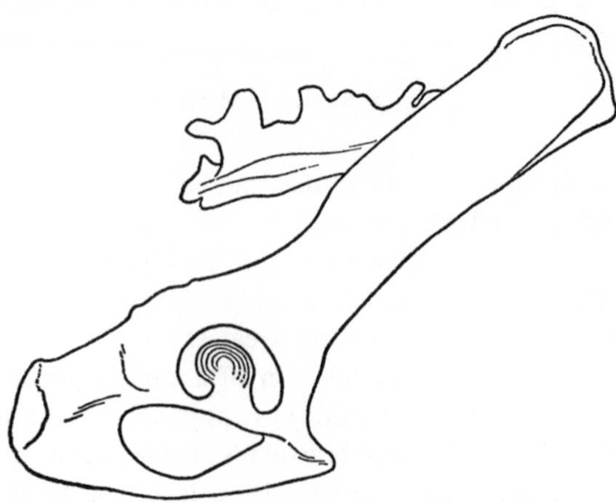

Figure 4. Right innominate bone and sacrum of *Cercopithecus aethiops*

Since the ilium has to serve at the same time as a force-transmitting construction between the leg skeleton and the spine, a strong bony beam has been developed from the sacroiliac to the hip joint. The part serving only as a surface of origin for the gluteal muscles may be represented by a considerably thinner osseous plate, reinforced however by a thickened border.

The same principle of a rigid-frame construction shows up still more elaborated in the ischio-pubic complex. There the central area is reduced to an aponeurotic membrane, fulfilling as well the function of a surface of origin for the inner and outer obturator muscles.

Elevation to bipedal standing requires a strong hip-extension mechanism. Not only the gluteal muscles but also the hamstrings have to be well developed. Therefore, in the temporarily erect apes, the surface of the ilium is considerably broadened. But this shape of the innominate bone and the sacroiliac junction are not yet adapted to a long-enduring stance or bipedal walking.

These relations may be analyzed in a bipedal standing chimpanzee (Figure 5). The gravity-center S of the entire body has to be held perpendicular above the area of support. This requires erection of the spine and extension of the hind legs. The extension in the hip joints, however is limited by the rotational moments of the muscles, necessary for the balance of the body weight. As was mentioned above, the moments of the hip extensors are greatest when their respective lever arms are longest, i.e. when the physical lever arms and skeletal levers

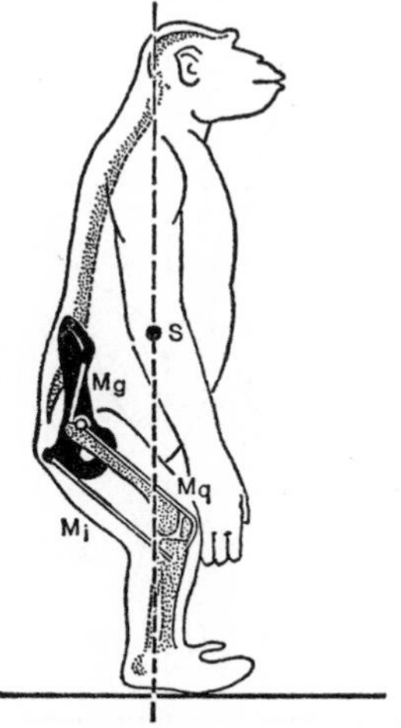

Figure 5. Bipedal standing chimpanzee (from live photograph) with the main muscle groups for the fixation of knee and pelvis

protrude. Under these circumstances the muscle inserts rectangularly on the bone. The skeletal lever for the gluteal muscles is the greater trochanter; the lever for the hamstrings is the ischium (see Figure 5). Both muscle groups insert almost rectangularly at their levers, when the femur is flexed to about ninety degrees in respect to the innominate bone. Further extension in the hip joint would shorten appreciably both lever arms and therefore diminish the extension moment, or for keeping the required moment, the muscles should develop a much greater force.

A more stable erect posture can be reached only by reduction of the load moment, while the muscular moment remains at least the same. Since the body weight can hardly be reduced without a reduction of the muscle masses and consequent weakening of their force, the moment of the mass to be borne in the hip joints must be diminished by shortening its lever arm. That means that the vertical from the gravity center of this mass has to be brought closer to the hip joint.

This adjustment can be provided by a lordotic curvation of the lumbar spine. But if it is reached only by erection of the vertebral column, the rotational moment of the same mass respective to knee joint increases (see the hypothetic posture of the chimpanzoid in Figure 6). The theoretical consequence is that the flexion moment must be reduced by extension of the knee joint, but the knee extension is impossible without accompanying hip extension, and this latter would reduce the moment of the extensor muscles.

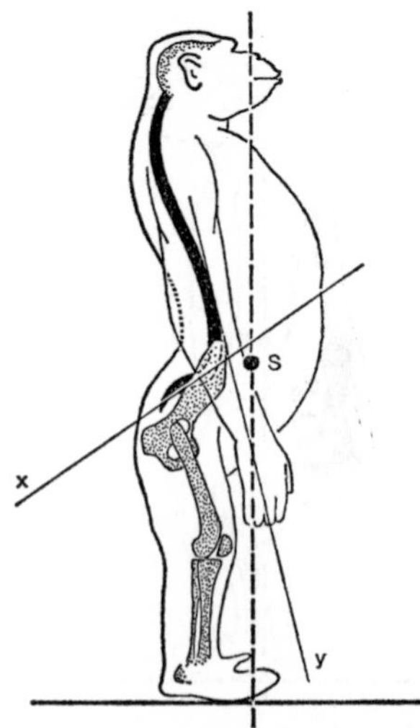

Figure 6. Hypothetical perfect erect posture of a bipedal standing chimpanzee. Axes x and y show main directions of sacrum and lumbar spine respectively

There seems to exist only one solution of this biomechanical problem: the innominate bone itself has to be curved in a lordotic sense so that the sacrum and the spine can be brought into a more upright position, while the ischium remains more or less angled with respect to the femur and therefore provides a sufficient lever arm for the hamstring muscles (see Figure 7). Only this shape of the innominate bone allows the fully erect posture, characteristic for man.

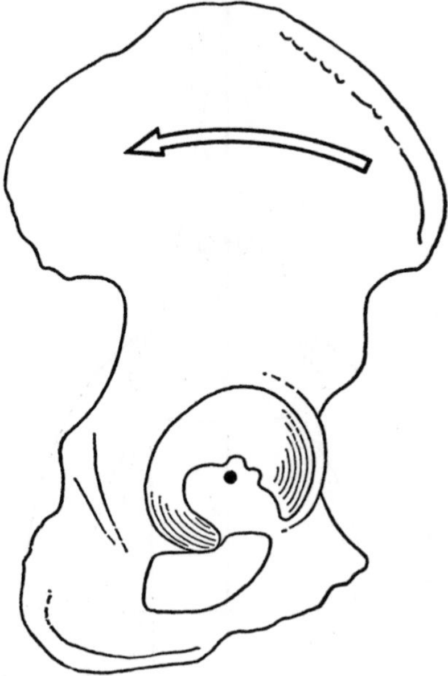

Figure 7. Right human innominate bone showing backward rotation of the ilium (arrow)

The angulation of the ilium against the ischium represents an adaptation to upright standing, but the bipedal gait requires further constructive changes. In human walking, the body is supported alternatively by only one leg. During the stance phase of the supporting leg, the pelvis tends to tilt to the opposite side, which is similar to adduction in the weight-bearing hip joint. In this situation a powerful abductor muscle group is required.

In typical quadrupedal locomotion there is practically no need for strong abduction in the hip, and consequently there is no pure abductor muscle. Such a functional group is developed by a change of the direction of the gluteus medius and minimus muscles. The ilium, already enlarged in Pongidae, turns from an almost frontal to a more sagittal plane, looking in a slightly caudal direction. By this transformation of the innominate bone, the small glutei come into a new position with respect to the hip joint and function as abductor muscles. Nevertheless, the gluteus maximus and a part of the medius do not lose their extensor function. Together with the hamstring muscles and the adductors, originating near the ischial tuberosity, they balance the body mass, whose ventrally tilting moment has been reduced by shortening of its lever arm.

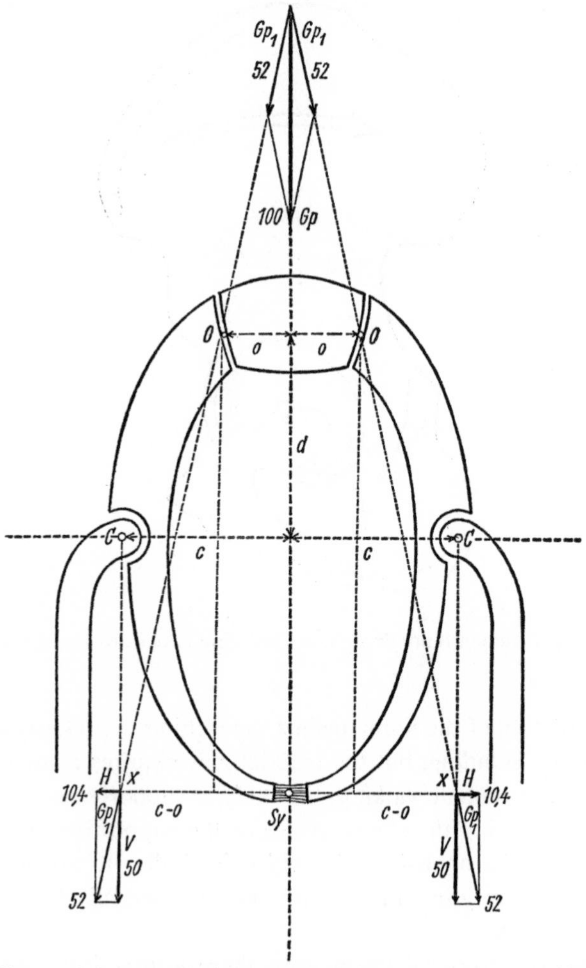

Figure 8. Stress of the os pubis and symphysis in a frontal plane in bipedal standing (Kummer 1959)
Important elements are: Gp — load of both posterior extremities in bipedal standing and body weight minus weight of legs; Gp_1 — load of one sacroiliac joint; O — sacroiliac joints; C — center of hip joint; Sy — symphysis pubis; H — horizontal component of Gp_1; V — vertical component of Gp_1

Finally, the stress of the pelvic girdle in the frontal plane should be discussed briefly. Following Pauwels (1948), in the standing man the force is transmitted from the sacroiliac joint to the hip joints in such a way that the pubic symphysis is stressed by tension (see Figure 8). This is true for quadruped mammals as well (see Kummer 1959).

It seems obvious that this kind of stress should also find its expression in an adapted structure of the innominate bone. In reality there can be seen reinforced beams running from the sacroiliac joint through the acetabular region to the tuber ischiadicum and to the symphysis respectively (see Figure 9). The ischium forms together with the ilium an angulated lever, reflecting the adaptation to the upright posture. On the other hand the same iliac beam is part of the pelvic ring, completed by the pubis.

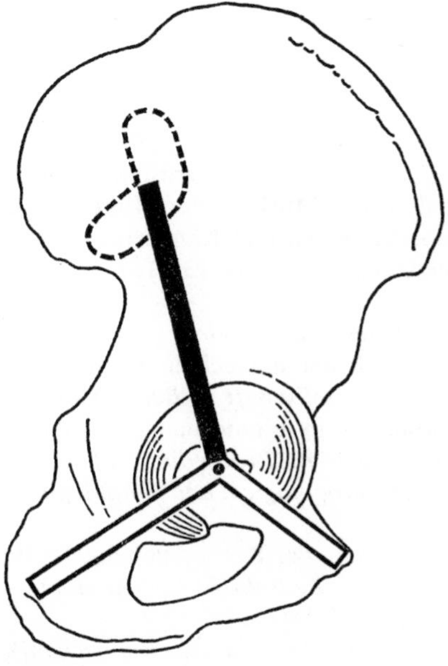

Figure 9. Right human innominate bone with indicated bony levers
Black — lever of the load
White — levers of the muscles and the symphysis respectively

The spongy architecture underlines the theoretically derived stress of the ischium and pubis. The ischium, as a bony lever for the hamstring muscles, inserted at almost a right angle, is stressed by bending approximately in a sagittal plane and consequently shows a cancellous structure in this plane, similar to a trajectoral pattern in a bent beam (compare Plate 1a and b). The pubis is bent in a frontal plane when standing on one leg or during walking while unilaterally supported (see Pauwels 1948). This is doubtless the situation of maximal stress to which the bone should be adapted. The expected bending pattern of the spongy structure can be seen clearly in the X-ray photograph (Plate 1c).

These observations demonstrate that the innominate bone shows in principle similar functional adaptations of shape and structure as in the long bones. Concerning the gross form in primates three functional types can be distinguished: the simple, straight two-armed lever of the quadruped monkeys; the straight two-armed lever within a frontal-plane enlarged ilium of the facultative bipedal apes, and the angulated two-armed lever with the more sagittally directed ilium of the fully bipedal man.

REFERENCES

BAUSCHULTE, C.

1972 Morphologische und biomechanische Grundlagen einer funktionellen Analyse der Muskeln der Hinterextremität (Untersuchung an quadrupeden Affen und Känguruhs). *Zeitschrift für Anatomie und Entwicklungsgeschichte* 138:167–214.

KUMMER, B.

1959 *Bauprinzipien des Säugerskelettes*. Stuttgart: Thieme.

1965 Die Biomechanik der aufrechten Haltung. *Mitteilungen der Naturforschenden Gesellschaft in Bern, Neue Folge* 22:239–259.

1968 General problems in biomechanics of the upright posture and gait: an introduction. *Proceedings of the Eighth International Congress of Anthropological and Ethnological Sciences* 1:316–322.

PAUWELS, F.

1948 Beitrag zur Klärung der Beanspruchung des Beckens, insbesondere der Beckenfugen. *Zeitschrift für Anatomie und Entwicklungsgeschichte* 114:167–180.

1965 *Gesammelte Abhandlungen zur Biomechanik des Bewegungsapparats*. Heidelberg, Berlin, New York: Springer.

Biomechanical Perspectives on the Lower Limb of Early Hominids

C. OWEN LOVEJOY

The characteristic locomotor pattern of *Homo sapiens* is made possible by a series of morphological features of his lower limb. These may be said to constitute its total morphological pattern (LeGros Clakr 1964). The individual features of this pattern are well known and include a number of distinctive characteristics of the ilium and femur. While significant alterations of the tibia, fibula, tarsus, ischium, and pubis are apparent, these are generally more conservative and thus retain more similarity with those of other higher primates.

In the interpretation of fossil limb samples (as with those of *Australopithecus*) an adherence to a strict morphological interpretation of individual features is usually unsatisfactory if the object of study is a reconstruction of locomotor pattern. A morphological alteration is not of itself an adaptation. Rather, it is the mechanical EFFECT of the anatomical change that constitutes the actual adaptation. Morphological changes can thus be direct or indirect; i.e. they may themselves cause a mechanical effect or they may be an alteration produced BY a mechanical alteration.

Each of the adaptations to bipedalism characteristic of the human

I wish to thank Dr. Kingsbury G. Heiple and Dr. Albert Burstein for their valuable discussions and criticisms; Dr. Michael Day for a cast of OH-20; and Dr. Alan Walker for a cast of his reconstruction of the australopithecine femur based on KNM-ER-993 and OH-20. I wish also to thank Dr. Milford Wolpoff for measurements of australopithecine specimens and discussions of their morphology and condition, and Mr. Brad Thorton and Mr. Terry Calhoun for measurements of Amerindian pelves. The photographs are by Mr. Larry Rubin.

For Plates, see pp. xxiii–xxv, between pp. 560–561

lower limb has been the result either of natural selection or of the well-documented phenomenon of mammalian musculoskeletal plasticity. What must then be regarded as significant in the reconstruction of gait patterns is not fossil morphology but its resultant — something that we may call the total biomechanical pattern. That is, study of morphological change in limb segments must have as its objective the understanding of the effects of alterations of form upon the mechanics of function. The biomechanical pattern that emerges should be our primary objective.

Isolated morphological features vary significantly more than do the mechanical attributes that are their result. To state this in other terms, the total morphological pattern and its individual elements are distinctly more variable than the total biomechanical pattern. For example, occasionally a first metatarsal can be found that has no facet for articulation with the second metatarsal. The hallux of such an individual, however, is fully adducted, and his gait pattern is completely normal. The morphological feature (the articular facet) serves as an indication of the position of the hallux. It is the latter that is important to the gait pattern not the former. Both nonmetric and metric variations of the hominid postcranial skeleton are extensive and must be given full consideration in the reconstruction of locomotor patterns of extinct related species.

The first task in the reconstruction of locomotor patterns from fossil samples lies, then, in the assessment of the biomechanical significance of each of its morphological features — that is to say, in determining whether or not the feature IS of mechanical significance.

We shall review the morphological features of each of the limb segments of the australopithecine lower limb. We shall attempt to isolate those features that are of mechanical significance and, once these have been established, we shall compare them to their counterparts in *Homo sapiens*. Those differences that are revealed by using this approach can then serve as an indication of the mechanical differences in the limb skeletons of *Australopithecus* and *H. sapiens*. This will then allow an interpretation of the australopithecine locomotor pattern.

Most previous accounts of australopithecine postcranial material have been based primarily upon material from South Africa, as the East African material has only recently become available for analysis. Casts of some of these newer specimens have been made generally available through an ambitious casting program of the Kenya National Museum. Therefore, in this paper both South and East African material will be discussed. In general, specimens from both regions show marked similarity in both anatomical and biomechanical features. This will be given further discussion below.[1]

ILIUM

The general morphological pattern of the australopithecine ilium is clearly hominid, and the available specimens are strikingly similar to the modern human ilium. This includes a large and distinct posterior portion. This indicates that the origin of the gluteus maximus was equally favorable to its position in modern man for femoral extension. The clearly formed sciatic notch in STS–14, STS–65, TM–1517, and SK–50 is ample evidence of this point. The retroauricular part is also substantial, indicating a well-developed sacroiliac articular complex (Dart 1957), although the robusticity of the ilium in this region can only be observed in STS–14 and the two adolescent ilia from Makapan (MLD–7 and MLD–25). These specimens demonstrate only limited robusticity in this region, and Robinson believes the auricular surface of STS–14 to be small compared to *H. sapiens*. However, both of these factors are most likely due to the relatively small body size of these specimens. When dealing with the surface areas of joints, linear normalization for body size is not justified, as body weight is of prime consideration. Robinson (1972) bases his opinion upon the breadth of the auricular surface of STS–14 (29.5 millimeters). The same measurement on a small sample of *H. sapiens* gave a mean value of 62 millimeters (Schultz 1930). Robinson's estimate for body size in females such as STS–14 is 40–60 pounds. Thus the static pressure on the auricular joint surface would be the same in STS–14 and *H. sapiens* if the specimens measured by Schultz had body weights of about 80–120 pounds. It seems as if a more detailed study might reveal that STS–14 had a BROADER auricular surface relative to the modern average. In general, with the exceptions of some of those particular features to be noted below, the consensus of most authors is that the ilium of *Australopithecus* is very similar to that of modern man (Dart 1949, 1957, 1958; LeGros Clark 1967; Lovejoy, Heiple, and Burstein 1973; Lovejoy 1973; Robinson 1972).

[1] All measurements reported in this paper were made on original specimens or taken from the literature

Anterior Inferior Iliac Spine

A large anterior inferior iliac spine is clearly present in all adult australopithecine ilia (Lovejoy, Heiple, and Burstein 1973; Lovejoy 1973; Robinson 1972). Robinson points out that impressions for the iliofemoral ligament and the reflected head of the rectus femoris are both distinctly present.

Lateral Iliac Flare

A more pronounced lateral iliac flare among australopithecine specimens has been pointed out by a number of authors (LeGros Clark 1967; Lovejoy, Heiple, and Burstein 1973; Lovejoy 1973; Robinson 1972; Zihlman 1969). The immediate mechanical import of this feature is an increased distance (along a horizontal through both acetabulae in an articulated pelvis) from the acetabulum to the lateralmost extent of the iliac crest. It is thus a feature fully commensurate with a long femoral neck, and its mechanical effects are the same as those mentioned below.

Anterior Superior Iliac Spine

An additional feature also noted by most authors is the distinctive anterior prolongation of the anterior superior iliac spine in australopithecine ilia. As Robinson (1972) points out, this prolongation is associated with a greater robusticity of the ilium in this region. Various interpretations have been suggested for this feature. It seems most likely that it is simply a secondary result of the greater iliac flare. Such flare places the anterior part of the ilium in a more posterior position than in *H. sapiens* (Lovejoy, Heiple, and Burstein 1973). The prolongation of the spine in *Australopithecus* compensates for this and results in a similar position (relative to the hip joint) of the inguinal ligament and sartorius (Lovejoy, Heiple, and Burstein 1973; Lovejoy 1973). Furthermore, as slight variations in the degree of lateral iliac flare would have substantial effects upon the position of these structures, greater variation in the projection of the anterior superior spine should be expected. That is, while the depth of the notch separating anterior superior and inferior spines is variable in *H. sapiens*, it must be expected to vary to a greater degree in australopithecines as a result of the greater lateral iliac flare in the latter (Figure 1).

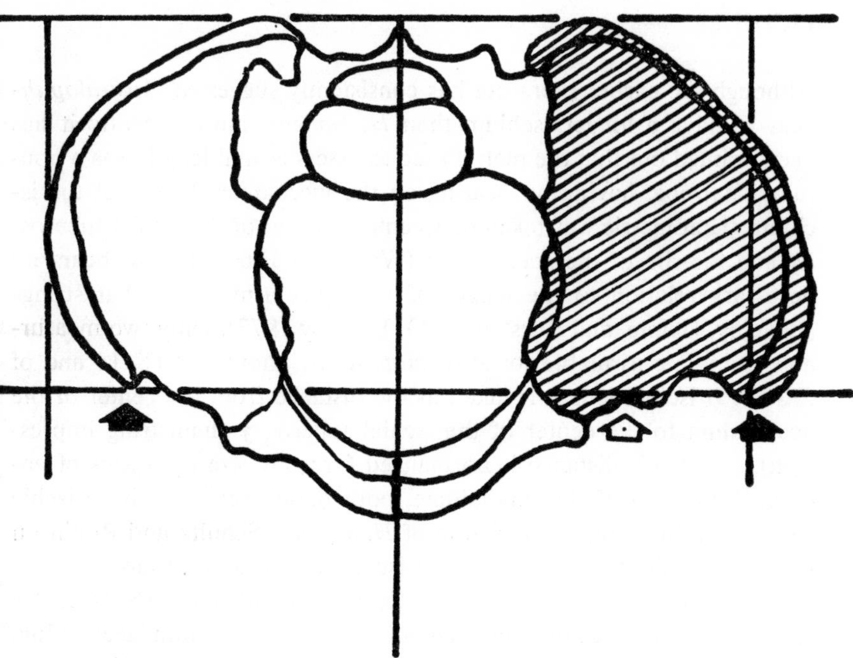

Figure 1. Superior view of MLD-7 articulated with a Bushman pelvis of equivalent osteological age. Symmetrical coordinate lines have been included to demonstrate the relative spatial positions of various bony features. Note the more pronounced lateral flare in MLD-7, resulting in a more lateral position of the abductors relative to the hip joint. Note that the positions of the anterior superior iliac spines are equivalent in both ilia (solid arrows) despite the much deeper notch separating it from the anterior inferior spine in MLD-7. The well-developed iliopsoas groove in the australopithecine specimen is indicated with an open arrow. (Drawn from a photograph in Dart 1949)

Iliac Pillar

Most authors now agree that a distinct iliac pillar is present in australopithecine ilia (Dart 1957; Day 1959; Lovejoy, Heiple, and Burstein 1973; Lovejoy 1973; Robinson 1972; Zihlman 1969). However, Robinson and Lovejoy, Heiple, and Burstein point out that it differs somewhat from that of sapiens, in that its position is more anterior than is usually the case in modern man. This feature can again be related to the greater lateral flare of autralopithecine ilia as discussed above (Lovejoy, Heiple, and Burstein 1973; Lovejoy 1973; Robinson 1972) (Figure 1).

ISCHIUM

Although the earlier literature has consistently suggested *Australopithecus* to have a longer ischium than *H. sapiens,* more recently it has been pointed out that the metric used to assess ischial length was a nonfunctional one, having no bearing on the mechanical length of the ischium. That metric was taken between the border of the ischial tuberosity and the rim of the acetabulum (Washburn 1963). It thus bears no necessary relation to the length of the lever arm of the hamstrings (Lovejoy, Heiple, and Burstein 1973; Lovejoy 1973). Only two measurable ischia are available for *Australopithecus,* those of STS–14 and of SK–50. If ischial length is taken as the distance from the center of the acetabulum to the center of the ischial tuberosity (hamstring impression), and if this distance is normalized for body size by means of another dimension of the innominate, both these specimens have ischia well within the range of variation of *H. sapiens*. Schultz and Robinson utilize the ratio between functional ischial length and acetabulum diameter as an index of ischial length. Schultz found that STS–14 had a relatively SHORT ischium and that SK–50 had an ischium/acetabulum ratio almost identical to modern man (Table 1). Lovejoy, Heiple, and

Table 1. Relative ischial length in *Australopithecus* and *Homo sapiens*

Observer Metric		STS-14	SK-50	Number	Modern man mean	Standard Deviation
Schultz (1969)						
$\frac{\text{Acetabulum diameter}}{\text{Functional ischial length}}$	$\times 10^2$	80	67	24	67.6	—
Robinson (1972)						
$\frac{\text{Acetabulum diameter}}{\text{Functional ischial length}}$	$\times 10^2$	87	62	40	68.4	4.3
Lovejoy et al. (1973)						
$\frac{\text{Iliac height}}{\text{Functional ischial length}}$	$\times 10^2$	47	—	25	48	3.4

Burstein reached a similar conclusion for STS–14 by comparing ischium length to ilium height. The ratio between these metrics in STS–14 was almost identical to the human mean, but the ilium height of SK–50 could not be measured. Robinson concluded that the ischial length of modern man was significantly shorter than that of SK–50. However, the data that he used do not justify his interpretation. He found that the mean value of the ischium/acetabulum ratio (multiplied by 100) was 68 in modern man (N=40) with a standard population range of 56–81. His ratios for STS–14 and SK–50 were 87 and 62 respectively.[2] Thus, one can only conclude that the data of Robinson and Schultz show both australopithecine specimens to have ischia of similar length to those of modern man (although the ischium of STS–14 appears to be quite short).

Lovejoy, Heiple, and Burstein (1973)have suggested that the form of the ischial tuberosity of STS–14 differed from that of modern man. This statement can now be shown to be in error as a result of the recent description of the specimen by Robinson (1972). He points out that the actual surface of the ischial tuberosity was not fully preserved and thus no statements can be made of its form. The only specimen that can thus afford knowledge of the tuberosity is MLD–8. This specimen has an ischial tuberosity whose form is essentially identical to that of modern man (Lovejoy, Heiple, and Burstein 1973).

PUBIS

Although a portion of the pubic ramus was preserved in STS–65, only in STS–14 was the symphysis also preserved. Robinson notes no particular difference in this specimen and the pubis of modern man,

[2] Robinson states (1972: 93) that the acetabulum diameter of SK-50 is 62 percent of its ischium length. I was unable to locate anywhere in his text (1972) the actual estimates for acetabulum diameter or functional ischium length. Robinson does give the distance from the acetabular rim to the nearest edge of the tuberosity (27 millimeters), but this is not an estimate of functional ischial length, as Robinson points out. Lovejoy, Heiple, and Burstein (1973) estimated the functional ischial length in SK-50 as 60 millimeters, and this has subsequently been confirmed on the original specimen by Dr. Milford Wolpoff. Broom, Robinson, and Schepers (1950) and Schultz (1969) use 50 millimeters as an estimate for acetabular diameter in SK-50. THIS GIVES A FUNCTIONAL ISCHIAL LENGTH RATIO OF 83 PERCENT, ALMOST IDENTICAL TO THAT OF STS-14, IN WHICH IT IS 87 PERCENT! In order to obtain the 62 percent suggested by Robinson for SK-50 (using the Lovejoy, Heiple, and Burstein estimate of functional ischial length), an acetabulum diameter of 37 millimeters is required. This is clearly too small because the diameter of the femoral head of SK-97 (which Robinson has suggested to be a good fit for SK-50) is also 37 millimeters. Allowing a conservative 4-millimeter increase over femoral head size to acetabulum size for SK-50, functional ischial length would become 68 percent — IDENTICAL TO THE MEAN OF ROBINSON'S MODERN HUMAN SAMPLE! If the opinion stated in this paper is correct — that the femoral head (and acetabulum) diameters of australopithecines were probably somewhat smaller than those of modern man — this would imply that the functional ischial length of SK-50 is actually SHORTER than that of modern man.

save a relatively marked length (although the specimen is clearly within the range of variation of modern man).[3] While the length of the pubis is not critical to an interpretation of australopithecine locomotion, it is of some interest with respect to the dimensions of the birth canal in these early hominids and will be discussed further below.

FEMUR

Lesser Trochanter[4]

The form and position of the lesser trochanter are well within the range of variation of their position in *H. sapiens*. Some authors have stated that its position on the femoral shaft is more lateral than in modern man (Broom, Robinson, and Schepers 1950; Day 1969; LeGros Clark 1967; Napier 1964). However, a metric assessment of the position of the lesser trochanter with respect to the femoral shaft was made using a moderate sample of Amerindian femora. Both SK–82 and SK–97 were within one standard deviation of the mean of this modern sample (Lovejoy and Heiple 1972). Robinson (1972) states that the lesser trochanter of STS–14, while not fully preserved, can be located because the bone surface forming its base was preserved. He concludes that its position in this specimen is "slightly unusual" because it probably did not protrude beyond the medial border of the shaft, while in *Homo sapiens* "the lesser trochanter is so situated that when the femur is viewed directly from the back, the trochanter protrudes past the medial border of the shaft" (Robinson 1972: 130). This is only true in selected specimens. In the Amerindian population studied by Lovejoy and Heiple (1972), the modal position of this apophysis was one in which it failed to protrude by a significant distance. Variability is great, however, as can be seen by reference to Figure 2. Furthermore, the functional position of this feature varies with anteversion of the femoral neck (Lovejoy and Heiple 1972; Walker 1973). The newer East African material (cf. Figure 2) confirms that *Australopithecus* was equally as variable

[3] I have recently had the opportunity to study a complete cast of the STS-14 pelvis. In my opinion, the pubic bones have been reconstructed with too great a ventral deviation; that is, the pubic symphysis would appear to have been in a more dorsal position than is indicated by the reconstruction. This alteration would considerably shorten the pubic bones.

[4] The present discussion does not include the new femoral material recently recovered at East Rudolph. Comment on these specimens will be deferred until more detailed information is available.

as modern man in this feature, and that australopithecine and modern femora do not differ significantly in this regard.

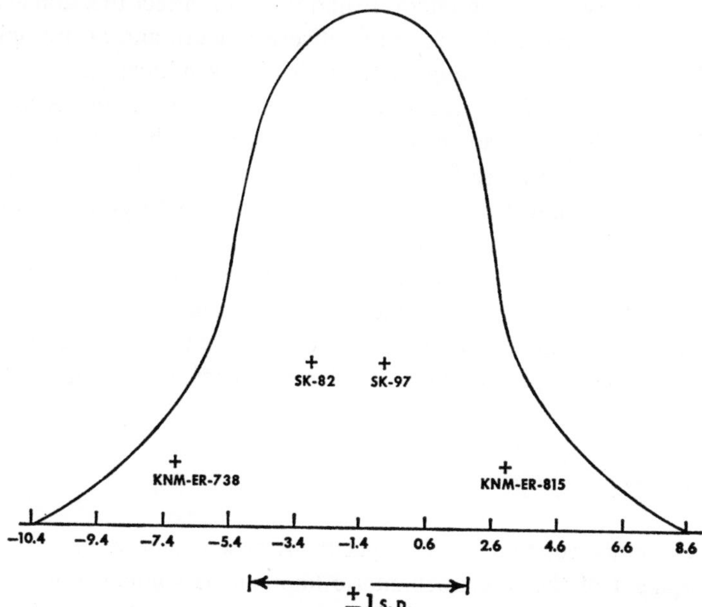

Figure 2. Normal curve fitted to sample of ninety-six human femora (ninety-six individuals) measured for the position of the lesser trochanter relative to the femoral shaft (all measurements in millimeters). Identical measurements made on australopithecine specimens are 0 (SK-97); −3 (SK-82); −7 (KNM-ER-738); +3 (KNM-ER-815). The mean of the Amerindian sample was −1.4 millimeters; S.D. = 3.6; range = +8 to −8.5; X^2 for fit data to normal distribution was P = .26

Greater Trochanter

The position of the greater trochanter in australopithecine femora appears to have been slightly different from its position in modern man, although an overlapping range of variation in the two species is clearly indicated. In *Australopithecus* the lateral flare of this apophysis from the shaft of the bone is somewhat less pronounced than in *H. sapiens.* We have elsewhere (Lovejoy and Heiple 1972) suggested that this is perhaps due to a more laterally situated femoral shaft than in sapiens. Walker (1973) has suggested that the condition might be related to the somewhat higher bicondylar angle of australopithecine femora. In Robinson's opinion (1972), the difference is due to a less prominent distal part and slightly more anterior position of the gluteus minimus attachment. But again, this is a highly variable feature in modern femora. In any case, the position of the greater trochanter with respect to the center of the hip joint is the critical dimension, because this directly determines the mechanical advantage of the anterior gluteals. Where the trochanter lies with respect to the femoral shaft does not affect this dimension. Thus this morphological difference between modern and australopithecine femora is not one of immediate mechanical significance.

Although the STS–14 femur is damaged in this region, Robinson (1972) suggests that a somewhat greater flare may have been present in this specimen. In those East African femora in which the position of the greater trochanter can be observed, it appears to conform to the pattern described above (Walker 1973).

Additional minor morphological differences between the proximal surface anatomy of australopithecine and sapiens femora have been described, including the rather deep trochanteric fossa. None of these, however, would appear to have any significant effect upon gait pattern.

Intertrochanteric Line

Walker points out that of five specimens now available in which the development of the intertrochanteric line can be studied, none shows this feature to be well developed. Day has suggested that the development of the intertrochanteric line is related to its tension during life. This would appear not to be the case on the following grounds:

1. It is absent or only slightly developed in a significant proportion of modern femora (over 50 percent of a large Amerindian sample and over 25 percent of a Zulu sample (Lovejoy and Heiple 1972).
2. Specimens can be found in which the heaviest development of cortical bone is in that region of the ligament's insertion where it is most slackened (the medial synovial reflection).
3. Other, almost equally large ligamentous structures fail to produce rugosities similar to the intertrochanteric line.
4. The development of the intertrochanteric line is clearly age-related and is almost always absent in Amerindian femora prior to fusion of the femoral epiphyses.

The lack of an intertrochanteric rugosity in australopithecine femora is thus problematical, although no mechanical significance is apparently involved. The massive anterior inferior iliac spine is a clear indication that a well-developed Bigelow's ligament was present in *Australopithecus* (Lovejoy, Heiple, and Burstein 1973; Robinson 1972). We would venture to say that its clear association with age and its limited expression in five australopithecine specimens simply reflects a younger age of death in these specimens than in those usually found in dissection rooms. In any case, there appears to be no mechanical significance attributable to this feature.

Obturator Externus Groove

A distinct obturator externus groove is identifiable in at least several australopithecine specimens, including OH–20 (Day 1969) and SK–82 and SK–97 (Robinson 1972). It is variably developed in *H. sapiens* and again is a morphological feature of no immediate mechanical significance. However, its presence serves as an indication that the obturator externus tendon was closely applied to the posterior surface of the femoral neck, a situation only explicable by consistent full extension of the hip.

Collo-Diaphyseal Angle

The neck-shaft angles of several australopithecine specimens are given in Table 2. All are well within the range of variation of *H. sapiens*, although their mean value lies well below that of most sapiens populations. While Robinson attributes no significance to these lower values, Walker

Table 2. Metric parameters of australopithecine and modern human femora

	SK-97	SK-82	KNM-ER-815	KNM-ER-738	STS-14	OH-20
Neck-shaft angle	118	120	115	115	118	115
Maximum femoral length	—	—	—	—	—	—
Maximum diameter femoral head	37	34	—	34	31	—
Biomechanical neck length	67	64	—	54	53	78
$\frac{\text{Biomechanical neck length}}{\text{Maximum femoral length}} \times 10^3$	—	—	—	—	—	—
$\frac{\text{Maximum diameter femoral head}}{\text{Maximum femoral length}} \times 10^3$	—	—	—	—	—	—
$\frac{(\text{Maximum diameter femoral head})^2}{(\text{Maximum femoral length})^3} \times 10^6$	—	—	—	—	—	—

Table 2. (Continued)

STS-14 Reconstruction Lovejoy and Heiple	Robinson	KNM-ER-993/OH-20 Reconstruction Walker	Amerindian Mean	Standard deviation
118	118	116	128	3.6
280	310	360	450	29
31	31	34	45	3.4
53	53	72	68	5.3
189	171	200	151	7
111	100	94	100	4.4
44	32	25	22	2.4

(1973) believes the low neck-shaft angle to be a populational characteristic of *Australopithecus*. From the number of specimens now available, it would appear that the population means of the two taxa do differ. On the other hand, the great range of variation in *H. sapiens* indicates that the angle is not critical to locomotor pattern. The net biomechanical effect of a lower collo-diaphyseal angle is an increase in the distance between the greater trochanter and femoral head, i.e. a greater effective neck length. This appears to have been the primary import of this feature in *Australopithecus* (see below).

Femoral Neck Length

Most students of australopithecine postcranial morphology have commented upon the unusually long neck of the femur (Campbell 1966; Day 1969; LeGros Clark 1967; Napier 1964; Zihlman 1969). In Robinson's opinion, the necks of STS–14, SK–82, and SK–97 are relatively long, but as he points out, "such a statement is not easy to document even though it is an obvious impression from visual observation" (1972: 128). He further notes that a problem of definition is immediately apparent when australopithecine neck length is considered:

> The point I wish to make is that there appear at first glance to be two differences between the *Paranthropus* and *H. sapiens* femora — smaller head and more tapering, longer neck in the former — but these are really two aspects of one difference. Both types of femur have much the same functional distance between the acetabulum and the shaft axis; since the head in *Paranthropus* occupies a smaller part of that functional distance, the neck occupies more (1972: 145).

A variety of metrics have been suggested for use in estimating the relative length of the femoral neck (see, for example, Napier 1964). However, most of these are unsatisfactory because they are dependent upon other morphological landmarks, which in turn vary independently of neck length (as Robinson points out). Using various metrics, Walker was able to demonstrate a statistically significant, longer neck length in his reconstruction (based primarily on specimens KNM–ER–993 and OH–20). Thus, MORPHOLOGICALLY, the neck length of the australopithecine femur can be considered greater that that of *H. sapiens*. This kind of measurement, however, fails to clarify the important question that Robinson posed.

Because our concern here is the reconstruction of gait pattern, our primary interest should lie in the mechanical significance of femoral neck length. While an increase in neck length results in a greater distance from origin to insertion of many of the muscles about the hip, it

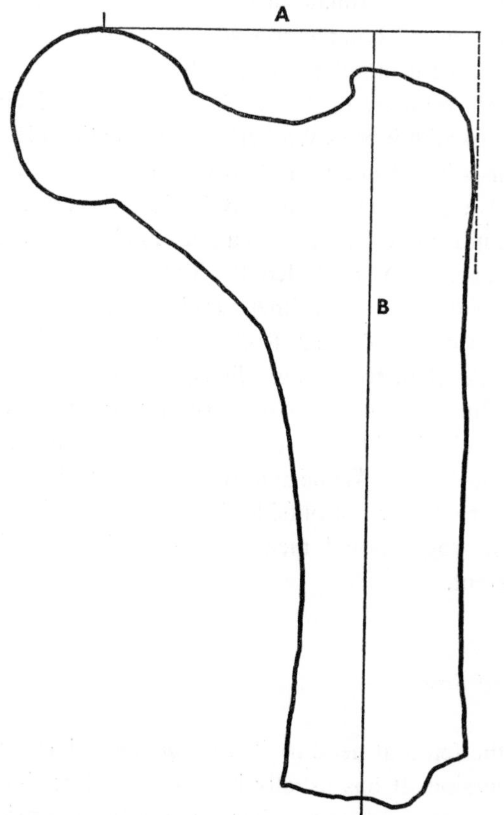

Figure 3. Biomechanical length of the femoral neck (A). This metric may be defined as the length of a line from the most lateral point on the greater trochanter to its tangential point of intersection with the most cephalad point on the femoral head. It is taken perpendicular to the centroidal axis of the shaft (B). (See Lovejoy, Heiple ,and Burstein 1973)

has relatively little effect upon their mechanical function, with two exceptions — gluteus medius and gluteus minimus. Their lever arm in effecting abduction is the normal from their line of action to the center of the hip joint. An increase in the length of the femoral neck increases this lever arm. We have elsewhere suggested the use of a metric that directly approximates this distance (from the femur alone) and is at the same time unaffected by morphological variations not immediately involved. This metric (biomechanical length of the femoral neck) is defined and illustrated in Figure 3. When this metric is normalized (for body mass and stature) by femoral length, it provides a direct measure of the relative length of the abductor lever arm. Unfortunately, most of the femoral specimens of *Australopithecus* are not sufficiently preserved for accurate estimate of their overall length, and this is a necessity for meaningful comparison with *H. sapiens* and other primate species. A sufficient amount of the STS–14 femur was preserved for a reasonable estimate of its length (Lovejoy and Heiple 1970; Robinson 1972). In addition, as Walker's reconstruction (1973) of the East African femur is based upon an almost complete femoral shaft (KNM–ER–993) and a proximal portion (OH–20) of very similar size, robusticity, and morphology, it is also a reasonable one for use in estimating relative mechanical neck length. Values for normalized femoral neck length for these two specimens and a moderate sample of Amerindians are provided in Table 2. Both specimens have significantly longer femoral necks than the Amerindians, and it should be remembered that these values are INDEPENDENT OF FEMORAL HEAD SIZE. Thus, the impression obtained by most observers is confirmed, despite the reservations of Robinson. While relative femoral neck length in *Australopithecus* was probably not outside the range of modern sapiens, it appears that the populational means for this biomechanical characteristic are different.

Femoral Head Size

The size of the femoral head in *Australopithecus* has also been a topic of some discussion. It has usually been regarded as significantly smaller than that of *H. sapiens* and has thereby been considered evidence for incomplete bipedal adaptation in these early hominids. Normalization by femoral length, however, is even more necessary for femoral head diameter than for neck length, because the former is a metric whose value is directly proportional to a joint surface. It therefore requires consideration of the square-cube law; i.e. if an object is increased in size, its surface area increases in proportion to the square of a characteristic dimension, while its mass increases in proportion to the cube of that characteristic dimension. Thus, if the mass of an animal increases, its joint surface areas must increase at a much greater rate if articular cartilage is to be sufficient for the increased loads. Therefore, in order to determine whether or not the femoral head of australopithecine specimens is small, we must also know femoral length so that some relationship with body mass and stature can be included. This, again, is only possible for two specimens — STS–14 and the Walker reconstruction. When the head diameters of these specimens are normalized either partially (head diameter/femoral length) or completely (head diameter^2/femoral length^3), both fall well within the range of variation of modern femora (Table 2).

There remain, however, several additional australopithecine specimens for which head diameter is known but for which no reliable estimate of femoral length is possible. Robinson has normalized the South African specimens (STS–14, SK–82, and SK–97) by means of shaft diameters below the lesser trochanter. While the resulting ratios for STS–14 are similar to those for his sapiens sample, they are somewhat lower for SK–82 and SK–97, implying either a more robust shaft relative to femoral head diameter or a relatively small head. In Walker's opinion (1973) the former of these two possible interpretations is correct: "The femoral heads in *Australopithecus* do not seem, therefore, as writers have suggested, to be small for the femur length, although since the femur is very robust the heads may be small relative to the shaft dimensions."

Walker's choice of these two interpretations appears to be quite reasonable and soundly based. The femoral shaft of KNM–ER–993 was complete from distal end to lesser trochanter. Thus, despite the fact that his femoral length is dependent upon reconstruction, any error will be minimal. When shaft diameters of the specimen are normalized by its length, the results are ratios that indicate a shaft robusticity somewhat greater than that of sapiens. Therefore, Robinson's use of shaft robusticity as a normalization factor for head diameter would appear to be the poorer choice. Such is not completely the case, however. Why there should be greater shaft robusticity in *Australopithecus* becomes a legitimate question. Possibly it was the result of somewhat greater muscularity in australopithecines and perhaps greater body weight relative to sapiens. This would then beg the question of femoral head size once more.

From the evidence presented thus far, it is our opinion that the populational means of femoral head diameter were possibly slightly lower than those of sapiens, although certainly not outside the modern range of variation. This is made clear not only by the above metrics but also by the acetabular study of Schultz. He concluded:

> From these observations it is evident that the acetabulum of *Australopithecus africanus* does not significantly differ from that of recent man, particularly, that its large proportionate size indicates the acquisition of the erect posture .... It seems most likely that *Australopithecus robustus* also has a relative acetabular diameter equalling that of recent man and surpassing the corresponding values of other recent primates (1969: 197).

Finally, we have elsewhere pointed out (Lovejoy, Heiple, and Burstein 1973; Lovejoy 1973) that the dimension that is critical to the interpretation of gait pattern is not femoral head size per se but the resultant pressure imposed upon the articular cartilage of the femoral head. This will be discussed further below.

Femoral Head Coverage

Recently, Jenkins (1972) made observations on the form of the femoral head in *Australopithecus*. He suggested that a prolongation of the articular surface of the femoral head onto the neck of the femur occurs anteriorly in modern man and posteriorly in the chimpanzee, and that the former is "related to a relatively deep and ventrally facing acetabulum" in man and a shallower and more laterad acetabulum in the chimpanzee. He then concludes that:

> The intermediate configuration of the femoral head margin in *A. robustus* ... together with the relatively shallow acetabulum ... is evidence that femoral excursion was of an intermediate pattern .... If the *A. robustus* femur were adducted as much as in man, a disproportionate area of articular surface would lie outside the bony acetabulum (1972: 879).

These conclusions are based upon conjectures that are not permissible and they are contrary to the evidence. The following points may be raised:

1. Jenkins's observations require a detailed knowledge of acetabular form. The specimen he used was SK–50, the acetabulum of which required extensive reconstruction. In his description of the original specimen Robinson points out that a 9-millimeter crack passing through the upper portion of the acetabulum has caused it to lie:

in a quite unnatural position in relation to the other portion. The remainder of the acetabulum has been warped so that the pubic margin lies closer to the ischial margin than was originally the case and thereby the acetabular notch is reduced to approximately half of its original width (1972: 88).

2. Femoral head coverage depends upon the orientation of the innominate in space. The posterior part of the ilium of SK—50 is poorly preserved and there is no auricular surface. Nor is there a sacrum for this specimen.
3. The proximal femoral specimen used was that of SK–82, which is not the same individual represented by SK–50. Robinson's observations on the relation between SK–50 and the Swartkrans proximal femoral samples are particularly interesting with regard to Jenkins's reconstruction: "It is clear, however, that the head of SK–97 would fit this acetabulum [SK–50] more successfully than would SK–82 — in fact, the former appears to be of exactly the right size for the acetabulum" (1972: 142). In any, case, slight differences in femoral head coverage cannot be demonstrated using specimens from different individuals.
4. The extension of the articular surface that occurs in the SK–82 specimen is not similar to that of the chimpanzee. It is a distinct localized projection onto the femoral neck which may be matched with some frequency in Amerindian femora. Its form shows it to be clearly unrelated to femoral head coverage. On the other hand, SK–97 shows a form of its articular surface which matches Jenkins's description of modern man perfectly (see Robinson 1972: Figure 82).
5. Orientation of the femoral fragment requires both a knowledge of anteversion and of the bicondylar angle (shaft obliquity). Both of these were unknown for SK–82.
6. The acetabula of modern man and chimpanzee are not different with regard to depth (as Jenkins suggested). Schultz, in his study of the STS–14 acetabulum (he rightly concluded that the SK–50 specimen was too distorted for study), found that its relative acetabular depth stood "well within the range of the same relation [depth/diameter] among recent genera, whose averages have been found to differ remarkably little" (1969: 194).

Linea Aspera

Robinson has recently concluded that the linea aspera of STS–14, while small in development relative to its usual condition in modern man, "is of the *H. sapiens* type in principle and is well defined" (1972: 131). He points out that the Swartkrans specimens are too poorly preserved to make observations. Leakey, Mungai, and Walker (1972) report the presence of a linea aspera in the newer East African specimens, including KNM–ER–736 and KNM–ER–361.

Intercondylar Notch

We have elsewhere pointed out that the intercondylar notch of *Australopithecus* is similar to that of *H. sapiens* (Heiple and Lovejoy 1971). There appears to be no disagreement with this assessment in the recent literature (see Robinson 1972; Walker 1973). The greater depth of the intercondylar notch in hominids can be related to the more elliptical form of the femoral condyles (Heiple and Lovejoy 1971). The attachments for the anterior and posterior cruciate ligaments are like those in *H. sapiens* (Robinson 1972).

Lateral Condylar Projection

We have elsewhere pointed out that the form of the femoral condyles in STS–34 and TM–1513 is like that of *H. sapiens* and unlike that of quadrupedal primates. In hominids, both condyles show a distinct elliptical shape (Figure 4), indicating a specialization for maximum cartilage contact in the knee joint only during full extension of the lower limb. In quadrupeds, on the other hand, the condyles show no such specialization to one position, being essentially circular in cross-sectional outline. Walker (1973) reports a similar condition in KNM—ER–993.

Bicondylar Angle

The bicondylar angles of STS–34 and TM–1513 have been the topic of some discussion. LeGros Clark (1947) originally reported TM–1513 to have an angle of AT LEAST 7°, and Kern and Straus (1949) incorrectly assumed this to mean exactly 7°. We have elsewhere pointed out that the methods usually employed in obtaining the obliquity of the shaft have been inadequate, because they employed specific morphological landmarks of no mechanical significance. We have used as a definition the angle between the condylar plane and the centroidal axis of the shaft. We found that using sharp shadow tracings, the bicondylar

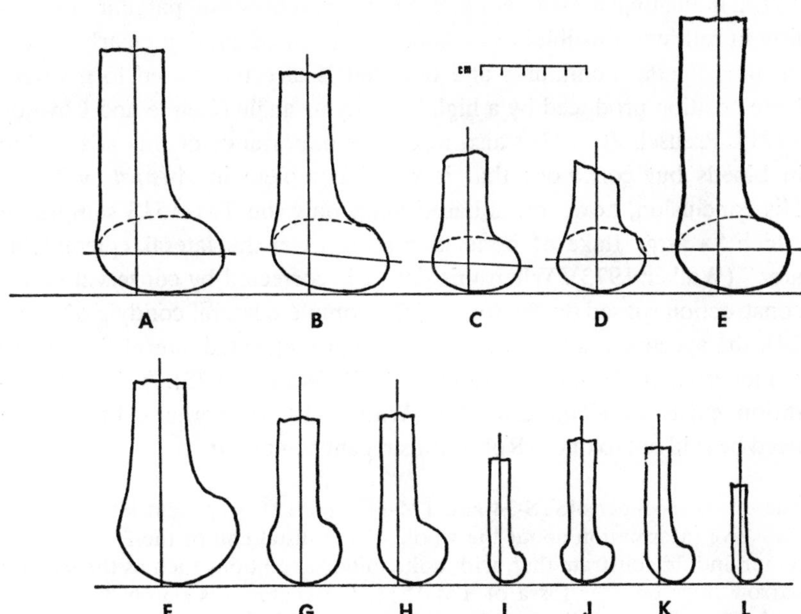

Figure 4. Lateral condylar projections of a number of primates. Each is a tracing of a photograph of the lateral articular surface taken perpendicular to the bicondylar plane. Top row: A and B. *Homo sapiens* (Amerindian); C. TM-1513; D. STS-34 (reversed); E. KNM-ER-993-Walker reconstruction (reversed). Note that the long axis of the ellipse in B and C can be made parallel to the bicondylar plane by slight anterior bowing of the femur or by slight hyperextension of the knee. Bottom row: F. *Pan gorilla* (CMNH-B1431); G. *Pan troglodytes* (CMNH-B1769); H. *Pongo* (CMNH-B1055); I. *Hylobates* (CMNH-B161); J. *Papio* (CMNH-B1043); K. *Pygathrix* (CMNH-B1511); L. *Macaca* (KSU-12). (CMNH: Cleveland Museum of Natural History; KSU: Kent State University)

angle (so defined) could be obtained from only the distal portion of a femur (equal to the amount preserved in STS–34 and TM–1513) within ± 1° of the actual value assessed from the complete femur (Lovejoy and Heiple 1971). Values obtained for STS–34 and TM–1513 were 14° and 15° respectively. Robinson gives values of 8° and 9° for these specimens but does not specify his methods. An additional specimen in which almost all of the shaft is preserved, KNM–ER–993, is now available. Walker reports the shaft obliquity as 15°.

Patellar Groove

We have elsewhere pointed out that a deep patellar groove and high lateral lip are present on the distal femur specimens STS–34 and TM–

1513, indicating a clear adaptation to prevention of patellar dislocation in full femoral-tibial extension. This is an adaptation clearly absent in quadrupedal hominoids and one that is directly related to a valgus knee position produced by a high bicondylar angle (Heiple and Lovejoy 1971). Preuschoft (1971) also notes the importance of this adaptation in bipeds but concludes that it was incomplete in *Australopithecus*. His conclusion, however, is based upon only the TM–1513 sample, in which "a large flake of bone is missing from the lateral epicondylar area" (Walker 1973). When this defect is corrected by conservative reconstruction (based on the form of the complete lateral condyle of STS–34), the specimen is found to have a clearly elevated lateral lip similar to modern man (Heiple and Lovejoy 1971; Walker 1973). A similar condition exists in KNM–ER–993 (Walker 1973). Perhaps little more need be said but to quote Robinson's recent summary:

> These two specimens [STS-34 and TM-1513] are of very great interest since they give information about the whole of the distal end of the *H. africanus* femur and demonstrate that, with quite minor exceptions such as the slightly narrow intercondylar fossa of TM-1513, the anatomy is simply that of *H. sapiens* to an extraordinarily detailed extent (1972: 137).

TIBIA

The australopithecine tibia is now known to a limited extent from two specimens that have received preliminary description: OH–6 (Davis 1964) and KNM–ER–741 (Leakey, Mungai, and Walker 1972). The distal joint surface is known only from OH—6. As far as could be detected from this specimen, no significant differences exist with respect to *H. sapiens* (Davis 1964).

With respect to the proximal part of the bone, Davis has suggested three distinct differences from the typical human condition. These are a greater extent of the tibialis posterior relative to that of the flexor digitorum longus, a somewhat smaller soleus, and a large popliteus in which "the direction of muscle pull was nearly vertical" (Davis 1964: 968). Several comments seem necessary concerning this interpretation. First, the proximal end of the bone was not fully preserved. The extent of the areas of origin and insertion of the proximal musculature in the fossil therefore depend to some extent upon its reconstructed length (this is especially true of the popliteus). The estimate made by Davis was 277 ± 10 millimeters. It was "deduced from comparisons of the relative length of the shaft below the nutrient foramen in the fossil and in other higher primates" (Davis 1964: 947). The position of the nutrient foramen is highly variable in the human tibia and should not, therefore, be used as a basis for metrical analysis (Hrdlicka 1898; Lovejoy 1970). We mention this point because, in our opinion, the actual length of the fossil tibia was less than 277 millimeters. A visual impression of this may be obtained by reference to Plate 1.

The lowermost portion of the area of origin of the tibialis posterior is clearly defined on the posterolateral aspect of OH–6, the typical V-form of its most distal extent being clearly marked and similar to its sapiens position. The majority of its origin, however, is somewhat disturbed by damage to the shaft's posterolateral aspect (near the postmortem break with the missing proximal portion (Plate 2). While the large, posterior, vertical ridge is accentuated by this defect, it is nonetheless clearly a true morphological feature of the bone and thus very probably the soleal line. Here we are in disagreement with Davis, who notes the presence of this bony ridge but does not identify it. He suggests that below the area of the popliteus, there is "a strongly marked crest which continues into a short weakly marked soleal line which does not gain the lateral border of the bone" (1964: 968).

The interpretation of these two crests is clearly required for a complete understanding of the morphology of OH–6. The "strongly marked crest" of which Davis speaks is homologous to a well-developed UPPER part of the soleal line seen in some sapiens specimens in which this rugosity is divided into two distinct portions or in which its course is nearly vertical prior to its juncture with the area of origin of the flexor digitorum longus. This may be seen in OH–6 and in an Amerindian specimen shown in Plate 2. In both specimens the soleal line descends almost vertically along the proximal part of the shaft and then makes a well-defined medialward shift as it reaches the area of origin of the flexor digitorum longus. At the juncture of the shaft, a ridge continues as well on the posterolateral aspect of the bone, defining the medialmost extent of the tibialis posterior. The area enclosed by these two divisions is occupied by the flexor digitorum longus. As OH–6 is distinctly similar to this type of sapiens morphology, there is little reason to suggest that the relative development of the flexor digitorum longus and tibialis posterior were significantly different in OH–6. In fact, the relationships of these three muscles is so highly variable in both extent of origin and location that Davis's conjecture is not permissible. Vallois describes specimens in which

> . . . la ligne oblique fait defaut ou est à peine indiquée; dans d'autres, elle ne s'unit pas au bord interne de l'os et se continue directement avec la crête

longitudinale qui, sur la face postérieure, sépare le jambier postérieur du fléchisseur commun des orteils (1938: 98).

Furthermore, if the present interpretation is correct, rather than displaying a weakly developed soleal line, OH–6 displays a soleal rugosity comparable to those most robustly developed in the Amerindian population used for comparison in this analysis. The most important aspect of the posterior morphology of OH–6 is thus the presence of the large soleal line on both tibia and fibula, because in the gorilla the origin of the soleus is usually restricted to the fibula, save a "rudimentary" origin from the popliteal line (Gregory 1950).

Finally, some comment seems in order concerning Davis' conclusions regarding the popliteus. He has remarked that the texture of the bone in the region of its origin "suggests that the direction of muscle pull was nearly vertical" (1964: 968). This seems highly improbable. First, the top one-half of the area of popliteal origin is missing in the fossil (if the length estimate of Davis is accepted, almost all of it is missing). Second, a vertically oriented tendon for the popliteus would be contrary to its condition in all other higher primates, where it is angled laterally about 45°.

Evidence is now available concerning the above points from the newer specimen KNM–ER–741, in which most of the proximal joint surface is well preserved. This specimen is very similar to many Amerindian tibiae; in fact, the detailed description provided by Leakey, Mungai, and Walker (1972) serves as an accurate description of many Amerindian tibiae because of their great similarity to the fossil. Unfortunately, despite its greater size relative to OH–6, it is a quite gracile specimen and its regions of muscular origin are therefore only lightly marked. The following points can be made, however.

On the posterior-medial aspect of the shaft, a concave impression for the origin of the flexor digitorum longus is clearly present and identical to its condition in many modern tibiae. Although the area for origin of the tibialis posterior is not clearly marked, its anterior limit (i.e. the anterolateral limit of the posterior compartment) can be palpated. There is no evidence that the relative areas of origin of these two muscles are not similar to their condition in modern man. The soleal line is not prominent, but its course is similar to its path in numerous modern specimens. Although the lateral condyle is damaged, Leakey, Mungai, and Walker point out that a popliteus groove is detectable and in a position similar to modern tibiae.

In summary, combining the evidence from OH–6 and KNM–ER–741, one may conclude that both the proximal and distal joint surfaces and the shaft of the bone indicate that the australopithecine tibia approximates the modern human pattern with such fidelity that no locomotor or mechanical differences are implied by the morphology of these bones.

FIBULA

Davis (1964) concluded that the shaft of the OH–6 fibula "in many ways resembles that of *H. sapiens*; indeed, there are fibulae from modern human beings which resemble it almost perfectly" (1964: 968). His conclusions concerning the lateral malleolus were that it was essentially similar to the *H. sapiens* condition.

TARSUS

The foot of *Australopithecus* is partially known from two specimens, an incomplete talus from Kromdraai (TM–1517) and an almost entire foot from Olduvai (OH–8). The striking similarity of these specimens to those of modern man has been generally recognized. However, minor morphological variations of these specimens have been used to suggest that they are not indicative of a fully bipedal gait. As pointed out earlier, minor morphological variations are in themselves of such small significance as to make them dubious in reconstructing gait pattern.

Both the Olduvai and Kromdraai specimens display features clearly indicative of complete upright bipedalism. In fact, as far as we can detect, they do not differ from modern specimens in any detail, when the range of variation of modern man is given proper consideration. While our study of these specimens is based upon available casts and published measurements (the cast available for OH–8 is an articulated specimen so that joint surfaces cannot be completely studied), those differences that have been asserted to exist with modern specimens are primarily features of the talus, and an individual cast is available for this bone.

Of primary significance to most workers appears to be the "horizontal axis of the talar neck," the magnitude of which is said to lie outside the range of modern human variation (Day and Napier 1964; Day and Wood 1968; Robinson 1972). This angle is given by Day and Wood as 28° in OH–8 and 32° in TM–1517. Their sample of 128 human tali yielded a mean value of 19° with a standard deviation of 3.4°. Thus the Olduvai specimen would appear to lie just inside and the Kromdraai specimen just outside three standard deviations from the human mean. A primary problem, of course, lies with the adequacy of the modern sample. The average Amerindian talus appears to display considerably greater divergence of the talar neck than was the case in the sample used by Day and Wood. This could be related to footwear, substrate, posture, locomotor habits, etc. In any case, the divergence of the talar neck is as great in numerous Amerindian specimens as it is in the two australopithecine tali. The divergence of the neck is difficult to measure reliably (Barnett 1955). For this reason, we have not attempted to assess this feature quantitatively for the Amerindian population used in this study, but two samples from this population are included in Plate 3 for comparison with the australopithecine specimens.

Many workers have assumed that a high angle of divergence of the talar neck is related to divergence of the hallux. This would appear doubtful for several reasons. First, three joint surfaces separate the talar neck from the hallux. Slight alterations in the form of these would have far greater effect uppon hallucal divergence than would the deviation of the talar neck from the central axis of the trochlear surface. Second, Barnett measured this angle in a number of primates and found it to be about equal to the human value in a number of forms (rhesus, baboon, orangutan), all with fully divergent halluces (Barnett 1955). From his own study he concluded:

> Medial deviation of the neck within the foot is found in species with a wide foot, for example, those with a plantigrade gait or a fossorial habit, and in arboreal species in which the body weight is deviated within the foot towards the medial side (1955: 229).

Finally, it should also be pointed out that the angle of divergence of the talar neck in the adult foot is the result of a REDUCTION of its original angle of divergence in the infant, where it averages about 35° (Trotter 1966). The talar neck angle is thus probably higher in Amerindians (and australopithecines) than in some other modern human populations because of factors such as those mentioned above, and the high angles of divergence in TM–1517 and OH–8 do not indicate any differences in the gait patterns of australopithecines and modern man.

A second feature that has been suggested to differ in the modern and australopithecine foot is the metatarsal robusticity index. When the middle circumference of the bone is divided by its length, some indication of the "robusticity" of the metatarsal is obtained (roentgenographic determination would of course be more accurate). When the five metatarsals from a single individual are compared, the relative robusticity of the metatarsals shows distinctive patterns in hominids and pongids, although both show great variation. Archibald, Lovejoy, and Heiple (1972) studied the distribution of the metatarsal robusticity pattern in a modern sample of Amerindian feet. They found that the pattern that characterizes the OH–8 metatarsus was the second most frequently occurring pattern in the Amerindian population and that it differed substantially from the pongid pattern.

THE TOTAL BIOMECHANICAL PATTERN OF THE LOWER LIMB SKELETON OF *AUSTRALOPITHECUS*

For the most part it is apparent that most of the morphological features of the australopithecine lower limb are within the range of variation of *H. sapiens.* For some of these features there appears to be little or no difference between sapiens and australopithecine populations. For others, however, there is an apparent overlap between the two populations, but the average expressions or populational means appear to differ. A summary of morphological differences between *Australopithecus* and *H. sapiens* is presented in Table 3. The most immediate implications of this summary are that the total morphological patterns of *Australopithecus* and *H. sapiens* differ only slightly, and that a great wealth of features indicating a completely bipedal gait are present, although there are some consistent differences, especially with regard to the hip joint. In order to interpret the latter, it is first necessary to compare australopithecines and modern man with respect to those morphological features that have mechanical importance. Table 4, therefore, lists the mechanical differences that are important to gait pattern and that result from the morphological differences listed in Table 3.

Only one significant difference between *H. sapiens* and *Australopithecus* emerges from Table 4. This can be shown to be a difference in femoral head pressure (Lovejoy, Heiple, and Burstein 1973). That is, whereas the femoral head of *Australopithecus* is slightly smaller than that of *H. sapiens,* the lever arm of the abductors is at the same time greater than in *H. sapiens.* Lovejoy, Heiple, and Burstein (1973) calculated the resultant femoral head pressure in STS—14 (which includes a whole pelvis and much of a femur from the same individual) and a series of Amerindians. The effects of the greater length of the abductor lever arm were found to be quite substantial. Despite a slightly smaller femoral head in STS–14, the static pressure on the articular cartilage of the hip joint was found to be only HALF that of the Amerin-

Table 3. Morphological differences in the lower limb skeleton of *Australopithecus* and *Homo sapiens*

BONE Morphological feature	Difference between *H. sapiens* and *Australopithecus*
Femur	
Neck-shaft angle	Somewhat lower populational mean (116°) in *Australopithecus*
Femoral neck length	Somewhat greater in *Australopithecus* when normalized by femoral length
Bicondylar angle	Slightly higher in *Australopithecus*
Flare of greater trochanter	Somewhat less in *Australopithecus*
Intertrochanteric line	Average expression slightly less in *Australopithecus*?
Position of lesser trochanter	None
Intercondylar notch	None
Femoral head coverage	None on basis of present evidence
Linea aspera	None on basis of present evidence
Lateral condylar projection	None
Patellar groove	None
Ilium	
Size of auricular surface	None when normalized for body weight
Anterior inferior iliac spine	None
Lateral iliac flare	Greater in *Australopithecus* but populational overlap with *H. sapiens*
Iliac pillar	Position more anterior in *Australopithecus*
Anterior superior iliac spine	More protuberant in *Australopithecus*
Ischium	
Functional length	None
Morphology of ischial tuberosity	None on basis of present evidence
Pubis	
Length	Slightly lower in *Australopithecus* than in *H. sapiens* (but well within range of variation) on basis of one specimen
Tibia	
Proximal region and joint surface	None
Shaft	None
Distal region and joint surface	None
Fibula	
General morphology	None
Tarsus	
Horizontal angle of talar neck	Slightly greater in *Australopithecus* but well within range of variation of *H. sapiens*
Robusticity pattern of metatarsals	None

Table 4. Biomechanical differences in the lower limb skeleton of *Australopithecus* and *Homo sapiens*

BONE Biomechanical feature	Difference between *H. sapiens* and *Australopithecus*
Femur	
Mechanical length of femoral neck	Greater in *Australopithecus* as a result of both a lower neck-shaft angle and a greater morphological neck length
Femoral head size	Slightly greater in *H. sapiens* relative to body weight
Position of knee joint in locomotion	None
Ilium	
Position of abductors	More lateral in *Australopithecus*. Commensurate with longer femoral neck length. Causes protuberance of anterior superior spine and more anterior position of iliac pillar
Ischium	
No differences	
Pubis	
No differences	
Tibia	
No differences	
Fibula	
No differences	
Tarsus	
Angle of talar neck	Greater frequency of flatfoot in *Australopithecus*?

dian average. They concluded that the morphology of the australopithecine hip complex was equally or more favorably adapted to bipedal locomotion than that of *H. sapiens*. Those morphological changes that separate *Australopithecus* and *H. sapiens* were judged to result from an enlarged birth canal in the latter and not from any difference in gait pattern. This is illustrated in Figure 5. As the dimensions of the fetal cranium increased during the Pleistocene, changes were required in the dimensions of the hip complex. The posterior extension of the ilium and of the caudal portion of the sacrum were already present in *Australopithecus* (Robinson 1972). The increase in the size of the birth canal between *Australopithecus* and *H. sapiens* therefore took the form of an increase in interacetabular distance. This increase in the coronal diameter of the birth canal in turn caused a reduction in lateral iliac flare and a commensurate decrease in the lever arm of the abductors. Such a decrease would have resulted in femoral head pressures beyond physiological limits were the relative size of the femoral head not correspondingly increased as well.

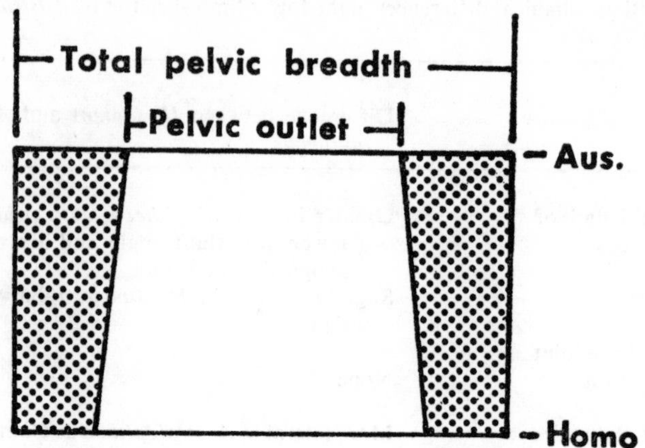

Figure 5. Schematic representation of pelvic evolution during the Pleistocene. While total pelvic breadth (relative to stature) remains substantially unchanged, the coronal diameter of the birth canal (pelvic outlet) increases in response to greater term fetal cranial capacity. This increases the torque developed about the hip joint during the stance phase of gait, and at the same time reduces the lever arm of the abductors. These changes required greater iliac robusticity and relative femoral head size in later Pleistocene hominids. The reduction of lateral iliac flare resulted in a less protuberant anterior superior spine, a more posterior position of the iliac pillar, a reduction in femoral neck length, etc. see Lovejoy, Heiple, and Burstein 1973; Lovejoy 1973)

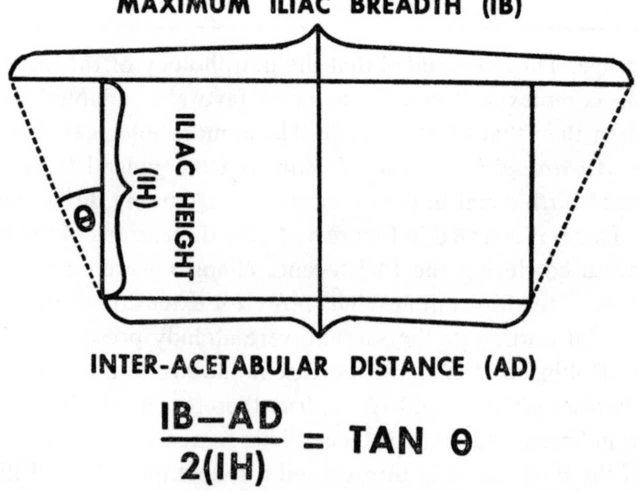

$$\frac{IB-AD}{2(IH)} = \tan\theta$$

Figure 6. Metrics used to determine the degree of iliac flare in an articulated pelvis. When the interacetabular distance (distance between the centers of the acetabula) (AD) is subtracted from maximum iliac breadth (IB) and divided by two times the iliac height, the result is the tangent of angle theta. Angle theta is defined for this study as the amount of lateral iliac flare

As a wide birth canal is essentially required only in females, it might be expected that modern males would have a greater tendency to retain those abductor advantages seen in *Australopithecus,* i.e. they should demonstrate a greater lateral flare than females. A series of metrics were therefore taken from a sample of articulated Amerindian pelves, the purpose of which was to quantify the amount of lateral flaring of the iliac blades. These metrics are explained in Figure 6 and the results of the survey are given in Figure 7. As can be seen by reference to the latter figure, a bimodal distribution of lateral iliac flare resulted from this survey, with males having a greater average degree of flare. The distributions were significantly different (P<.001). It was also suggested above that greater lateral flare should result in greater relief of the anterior superior iliac spine. This feature was also assessed in the Amerindian

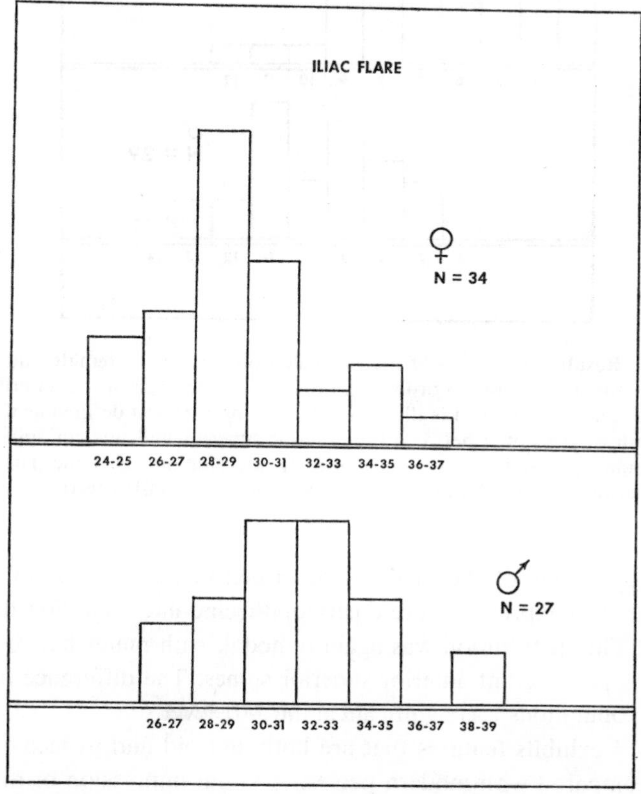

Figure 7. Results of the metrics taken on 34 female and 27 male articulated Amerindian pelves (as described in Figure 6), in order to measure differences in lateral flare. The male mean was about 31° and that of the females 28°. The populations are distinctly bimodal and differ significantly (P = .001; t test)

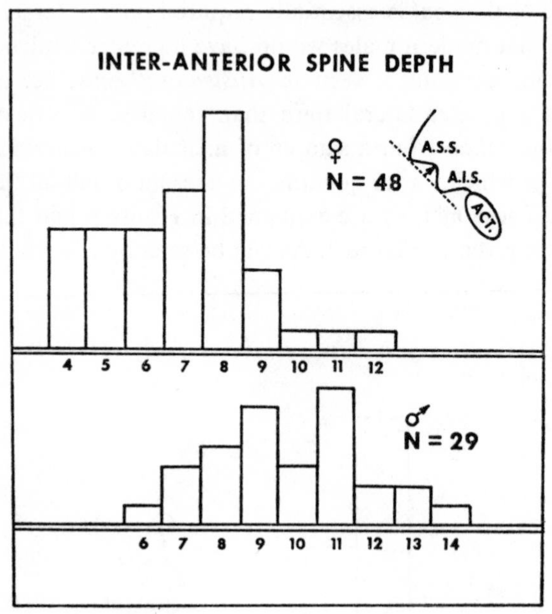

Figure 8. Results of a series of metrics taken on forty-eight female and twenty-nine male Amerindian ilia in order to compare protuberance of the anterior superior spine. The metric taken is illustrated by the inset. It was defined as the maximum depth of the notch between the anterior superior and inferior spines taken perpendicular to a tangent to the most anterior extension of each spine. The populations are distinctly bimodal and differ significantly (P = .001; t test)

sample by means of the methods described in Figure 8. Again males were found to express a more australopithecine-like condition than did females. The distribution was again bimodal, with males having generally more protuberant anterior superior spines. The difference between the two populations was significant at the .001 level.

STS–14 exhibits features that are both android and gynecoid in nature if compared with modern pelves. A visual impression of this relationship can be obtained by comparing STS–14 with modern pelves of fairly marked sexual dimorphism (Figure 9). The marked similarity of the australopithecine specimen with that of the male can be readily seen with respect to lateral flaring, while on the other hand, the subpubic angle of the former is obtuse, resembling that of the modern female. This is most likely a product of the relatively high interacetabular diameter of STS–14, which is in turn probably due to both the small stature of this particular specimen and to the fact that is almost certainly a female. Male australopithecine specimens (e.g. SK–50?) are likely to exhibit

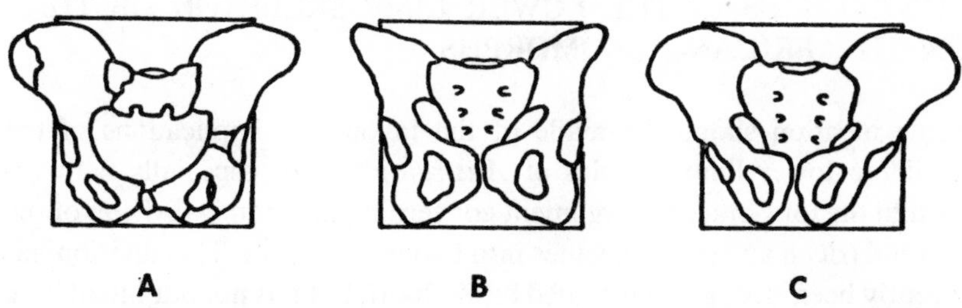

Figure 9. Photographic tracings of three pelves in anterior view. Coordinate lines have been inserted over each to clarify its width in relation to its height. Specimen A (STS-14: Robinson reconstruction) is 47 percent broader than it is high. Specimen B (KSU-99902) (female) is 29 percent broader than it is high, while specimen C (KSU-02055B) (male) is 58 percent wider than it is high. Note the pronounced lateral flaring in specimen C compared to that of B, but the similarity in subpubic angle in B and A. Both Amerindian specimens are from the same skeletal population. For further discussion see text

smaller interacetabular distances and therefore more lateral flaring and greater relief of the anterior superior iliac spine.

In summary, it must be pointed out that pelvic form is a highly variable and complex trait and that those factors enumerated above, while contributing significantly to the form of the adult pelvis, are most certainly not the only factors involved. This, in conjunction with the very limited sample available from which to reconstruct the australopithecine pelvis, means that a quantitative test of the hypothesis being presented here is not possible; yet when the factors of hip joint pressure and parturition are combined in the analysis of bipedal hominids, it would appear that what evidence is available at this point strongly favors the present explanation of pelvic differences in australopithecines and modern man.

If the iliac position and form in the modern male is more conservative than that of the modern female, it might also be expected that males would tend to be more conservative with regard to proximal femoral morphology as well. Although biomechanical neck length of the femur is not generally available in the literature, the angle between the shaft and neck is a frequently recorded metric for most skeletal populations. Interestingly, Walker points out that the neck-shaft angle does "demonstrate sexual dimorphism in man with females having higher angles than males by sometimes as much as 3° between the means of the sexes" (1973).

DIFFERENCES IN THE LOWER LIMB SKELETON OF THE SOUTH AFRICAN ALLOMORPHS

Some mention should be made of the taxonomic implications of the available lower limb samples of *Australopithecus,* especially with regard to the long-standing argument concerning taxonomic division of the South African australopithecines into two distinct taxa. This division has recently been strongly questioned by Wolpoff, but it is not our intent here to attempt any resolution of this argument. Rather, we wish only to discuss the lower limb in particular. The question may also arise as to differences between South and East African samples. These will also be discussed.

When the total evidence is considered, it would appear unlikely that any differences can be shown to exist between samples of the two alleged allomorphs of South Africa with regard to their lower limb skeletons. Rather, there appears to be a wealth of indications that no significant mechanical differences exist between these supposed taxa. Walker (1973) and Zihlman (1969) have reached similar conclusions.

This conclusion can be most easily demonstrated by briefly repeating what we have done through this paper, i.e. by comparing the mechanical features of the specimens of *Australopithecus* with those of *H. sapiens*. Taking, for example, proximal femoral anatomy, we find that STS–14 (attributed to the gracile form) and SK–97 and SK–82 (attributed to the robust form) share the same features that distinguish them from modern man. All three specimens have a somewhat lower neck-shaft angle, a longer femoral neck, a similar position of the lesser trochanter, etc. Turning to the pelvis, we find the same conditions to hold true. Both SK–50 (robust) and STS–14 (gracile) have protuberant anterior superior spines, greater lateral flare, well-developed inferior spines, an anterior pillar position, etc. Robinson bases his distinction of the gracile and robust forms primarily upon ischial length, which he believes to be significantly greater in the robust than in the gracile form. As pointed out above, however, both of these ischia have functional lengths well within the range of variation of modern man; they therefore cannot be used for taxonomic distinctions.

A similar situation would appear to hold true for specimens from East and South Africa, although to date only comparisons between femora can be made. Again, the East African specimens demonstrate the same kinds of differences from the modern condition as do those from South Africa: slightly smaller head, longer neck, lower neck-shaft angle, less greater trochanteric flare, and a distal femur similarly adapted as in

H. sapiens (essentially indistinguishable save for the higher bicondylar angle).

SUMMARY

When the lower limb samples of *Australopithecus* (including both South and East African samples described to date) are analyzed with regard to morphological features of biomechanical significance, it is found that only minor differences exist with respect to the lower limb skeleton of modern man and that these differences indicate no difference in gait pattern but only one of response to encephalization.

For a number of years and throughout much of the literature there has been an a priori assumption that australopithecine locomotion and postcranial morphology were "intermediate" between quadrupedalism and the bipedalism of modern man. There is no basis for this assumption either in terms of Neo-Darwinian theory or, as pointed out above, in terms of the lower limb skeleton of *Australopithecus*. It is often claimed, principally on the basis of this a priori assumption, that morphological features shared by both modern man and *Australopithecus* do not necessarily indicate similar gait patterns (see, for example, Jenkins 1972). Although this might be true in terms of a single feature, it is demonstrably not true when the total mechanical pattern is considered. As we have seen, the only significant difference between the total biomechanical patterns of *Australopithecus* and *H. sapiens* is one that indicates that *Australopithecus* was at an advantage compared with modern man (femoral head pressure). This brings us to a second point.

There also appears in the literature a tendency to regard human bipedalism as a kind of locomotor pinnacle. Such is not the case. Human bipedalism is merely the combination of three simple elements (trunk progression, limb progression, control of pelvic tilt) (see Lovejoy 1973). Only the last of these is not part of the locomotor adaptation of any terrestrial mammal. No mysterious requirements need be satisfied for man to walk erect. He must simply obtain (by natural selection or by musculoskeletal plasticity) those basic adaptations of his joints and orientations of his muscles that are necessary to effect the above three requirements. All of these adaptations (a valgus knee position, a mechanism to prevent lateral patellar dislocation, an increased cartilage contact in the knee joint, a well-developed iliofemoral ligament, a long abductor lever, a posterior position of the gluteus maximus, etc.) are demonstrably present in *Australopithecus*.

In summary, the lower limb skeleton of *Australopithecus* points to a long history of bipedalism among hominids. If bipedalism was fully evolved during the basal Pleistocene, then the transition from quadrupedalism to bipedalism must lie in earlier strata. Just how old bipedalism is and under what conditions selection favored its adoption are important questions that can only be answered by further excavations of fossil strata that predate Pleistocene man.

REFERENCES

ARCHIBALD, J. DAVID, C. OWEN LOVEJOY, KINGSBURY G. HEIPLE
1972 Implications of relative robusticity in the Olduvai metatarsus. *American Journal of Physical Anthropology* 37:93–96.

BARNETT, C. H.
1955 Some factors influencing angulation of the neck of the mammalian talus. *Journal of Anatomy, London* 89:225–230.

BROOM, ROBERT, JOHN T. ROBINSON, G. W. H. SCHEPERS
1950 *Sterkfontein ape-man* Plesianthropus. Transvaal Museum Memoir 4. Pretoria: Transvaal Museum.

CAMPBELL, BERNARD G.
1966 *Human evolution*. Chicago: Aldine.

DART, RAYMOND
1949 Innominate fragments of *Australopithecus prometheus. American Journal of Physical Anthropology* 7:301–334.
1957 The second adolescent (female) ilium of *Australopithecus prometheus. Journal of the Palaeontology Society of India* 2:73–82.
1958 A further adolescent ilium from Makapansgat. *American Journal of Physical Anthropology* 16:473–479.

DAVIS, P. R.
1964 Hominid fossils from Bed I, Olduvai Gorge, Tanganyika: a tibia and fibula. *Nature* 201:967–970.

DAY, MICHAEL H.
1959 *Guide to fossil man*. London: Camelot Press.
1969 Femoral fragment of a robust australopithecine from Olduvai Gorge, Tanzania. *Nature* 221:230–233.

DAY, MICHAEL H., J. R. NAPIER
1964 Hominid fossils from Bed I, Olduvai Gorge, Tanganyika: fossil foot bones. *Nature* 201:967–970.

DAY, MICHAEL H., BERNARD A. WOOD
1968 Functional affinities of the Olduvai Hominid 8 talus. *Man* 3:440–455.

GREGORY, WILLIAM K., *editor*
1950 *The anatomy of the gorilla*. New York: Columbia University Press.

HEIPLE, KINGSBURY G., C. OWEN LOVEJOY
1971 The distal femoral anatomy of *Australopithecus. American Journal of Physical Anthropology* 35:75–84.

HRDLICKA, ALES
1898 Study of the normal tibia. *American Anthropologist* 11(old series): 307–312.

JENKINS, FARISH A., JR.
1972 Chimpanzee bipedalism: cineradiographic analysis and implications for the evolution of gait. *Science* 178:877–879.

KERN, H. M., WILLIAM L. STRAUS
1949 The femur of *Plesianthropus transvaalensis*. *American Journal of Physical Anthropology* 7:53–77.

LEAKEY, RICHARD E. F., J. M. MUNGAI, ALAN C. WALKER
1972 New australopithecines from East Rudolf, Kenya (II). *American Journal of Physical Anthropology* 36:235–251.

LE GROS CLARK, WILFRID E.
1947 Observations on the anatomy of the fossil Australopithecinae. *Journal of Anatomy, London* 81:300–313.
1964 *The fossil evidence for human evolution* (second edition). Chicago: University of Chicago Press.
1967 *Man-apes or ape-men? The story of discoveries in Africa*. New York: Holt, Rinehart and Winston.

LOVEJOY, C. OWEN
1970 "Biomechanical methods for the analysis of skeletal variation with an application by comparison of the theoretical diaphyseal strength of platycnemic and euricnemic tibias." Unpublished doctoral dissertation, University of Massachusetts, Amherst, Massachusetts.
1973 The biomechanics of stride and their bearing on the gait of *Australopithecus*. *Yearbook of Physical Anthropology* 17:147–161.

LOVEJOY, C. OWEN, KINGSBURY G. HEIPLE
1970 A reconstruction of the femur of *Australopithecus africanus*. *American Journal of Physical Anthropology* 32:33–40.
1971 Femoral anatomy of *Australopithecus africanus* and *robustus* (abstract). *American Journal of Physical Anthropology* 35:286.
1972 Proximal femoral anatomy of *Australopithecus*. *Nature* 235:175–176.

LOVEJOY, C. OWEN, KINGSBURY G. HEIPLE, ALBERT H. BURSTEIN
1973 The gait of *Australopithecus*. *American Journal of Physical Anthropology* 38:757–779.

NAPIER, J. R.
1964 The evolution of bipedal walking in the hominids. *Archives de Biologie* (Liège) 75:673–708.

PREUSCHOFT, H.
1971 Body posture and mode of locomotion in early Pleistocene hominids. *Folia Primatologica* 14:209–240.

ROBINSON, JOHN T.
1972 *Early hominid posture and locomotion*. Chicago: University of Chicago Press.

SCHULTZ, ADOLPH H.
1930 The skeleton of the trunk and limbs of higher primates. *Human Biology* 2:303–438.

1969 Observations on the acetabulum of Primates. *Folia Primatologica* 11:181–199.

TROTTER, MILDRED

1966 "Osteology," in *Morris' Human anatomy*. Edited by Barry J. Anson, 133–315. New York: McGraw-Hill.

VALLOIS, H. V.

1938 Les méthodes de mensuration de la platycnémie: étude critique. *Bulletin et Mémoires de la Société d'Anthropologie, Paris, Série 8* 9:97–108.

WALKER, ALAN C.

1973 New *Australopithecus* femora from East Rudolf, Kenya. *Journal of Human Evolution* 2:545–555.

WASHBURN, SHERWOOD L.

1963 "Behavior and human evolution," in *Classification and human evolution*. Edited by Sherwood L. Washburn, 190–203. Chicago: Aldine.

ZIHLMAN, ADRIENNE L.

1969 "Human locomotion: a reappraisal of the functional and anatomical evidence." Unpublished doctoral dissertation, University of California, Berkeley, California.

1971 The question of locomotor differences in *Australopithecus*. *Proceedings of the 3rd international congress of primatology*. Basel: S. Karger.

Comparative Osteometry of the Foot of Man and Facultatively Bipedal Primates

J. LESSERTISSEUR, and F. K. JOUFFROY

The uniqueness of the bony foot of man, with respect to his particular aptitude for erect posture and bipedal locomotion, is denoted by well-known anatomical arrangements: metatarsal arch, shape and disposition of the big toe and of the tarsal region, etc. We will show that it is evidenced in the simplest metric characters, that is, by the longitudinal proportions of the foot considered as an ensemble with respect to the length of the hind limb, or by examination in detail of the relationships existing between the principal elements themselves.

There exist throughout the order, forms capable of practicing bipedal locomotion in natural conditions, but more or less occasionally. The best known examples are *Indri* among the prosimians and the gibbon and the gorilla among the anthropoids. In fact, nearly all primates are capable of standing erect and many can walk or run on their hind limbs. This aptitude, like that of sitting, is certainly not alien to arboreality which demands a certain extensibility of the trunk and limb articulations.

We are concerned here only with the simian primates which practice terrestrial bipedal locomotion most readily (the bounding bipedalism of the Indriidae and several other prosimians is in fact very different from human walking). These are *Ateles* and *Lagothrix* among the platyrrhines and all of the apes among the catarrhines. The proportions of their feet will be compared, first, with those of man, then, with those of some related genera that are normally quadrupedal and less familiar with bipedal locomotion (*Cebus, Macaca*). We will inquire, thereby, if it is possible to pick out of this ensemble certain comparable metric tendencies which could indicate to some degree bipedal adaptation.

THE HUMAN FOOT

Man is the only accomplished bipedal primate and this singularity leads one to consider his foot (Figure 1) as the best reference for the study of anatomical specializations linked to this type of locomotion.

A comparison between human and simian feet has been the object of many studies often with ambiguous conclusions: Volkov 1903–1904; Mollison 1910; Weidenreich 1921; and among more recent authors, those of Schultz 1963; Napier 1964; Oxnard 1972; Lessertisseur and Jouffroy 1973. We will be occupied here only with proportions not the form. In this perspective the best work remains that of Schultz. We have no other ambition than to complete it by some supplementary indications (in particular by axony — the consideration of the placement of the morphological axis of the foot) and to add several reflections.

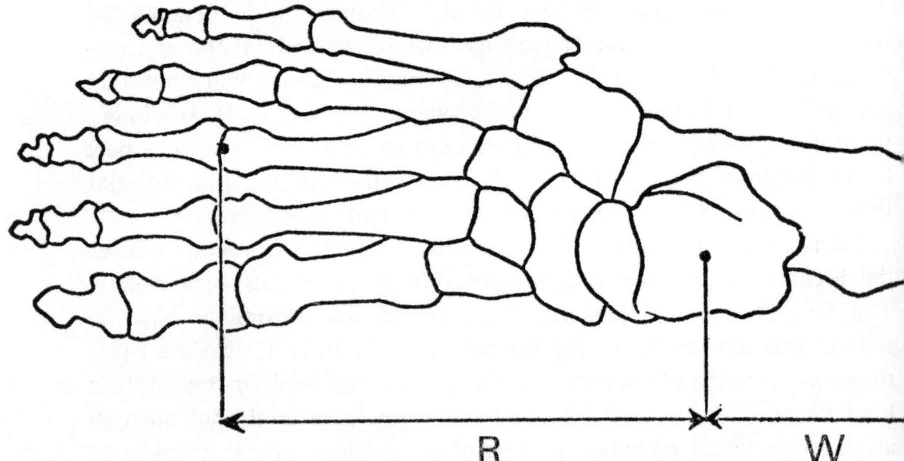

Figure 1. Dorsal view of the skeleton of the human foot. W: arm of force, R: arm of resistance, of the foot lever.

In the four aspects that interest us — total length, relative length of the different segments, length of the hallux and axony — the proportions of the human foot are, even for a primate, quite unusual.

1. With respect to the total length of the hind leg (Figure 2) it is by far the shortest of all (22–23 percent as against 28–25 percent for all simians; 32 percent in the macaque). With respect to the length of the trunk — Schultz' mode of evaluation — the difference is not significant (man 44 percent; macaque 43 percent). It is the rest of the limb, and especially the thigh, which elongates: the femur of man is very

long (43 percent of the hind limb, 64 percent of the trunk). Generally, the length of the foot and the length of the femur vary inversely, as we have established in previous studies (Lessertisseur 1970; Lessertisseur and Jouffroy 1973).

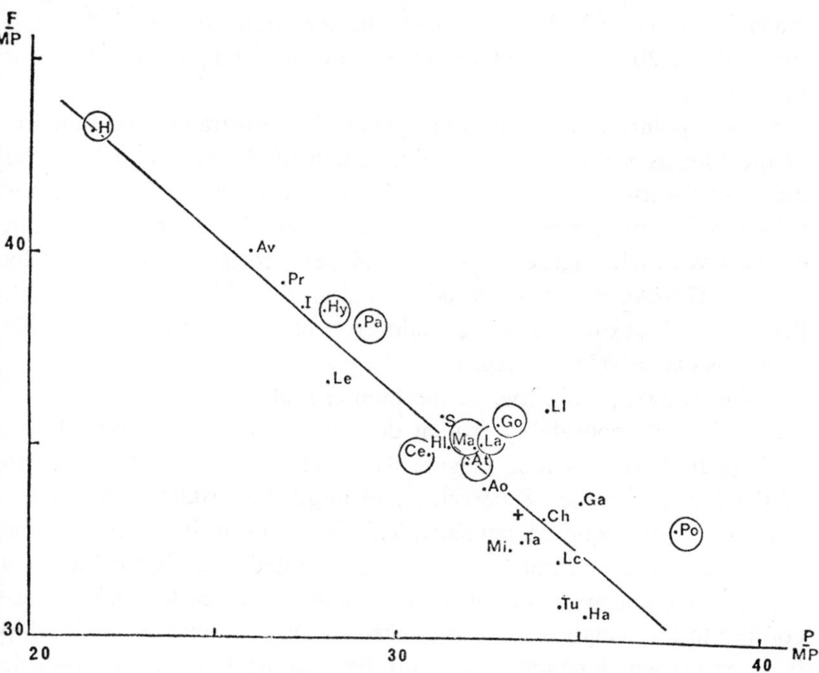

Figure 2. Comparison between the relative length of the femur and that of the foot. Abscissa: the length P of the foot with respect to that of the hindlimb, MP. Ordinate: the same measurement F for the femur. The relationships are expressed in percentages.

Ao *Aotus*
At *Ateles*
Av *Avahi*
Ce *Cebus*
Ch *Cheirogaleus*
Ga *Galago*
Go *Gorilla*
H *Homo*
Ha *Hapale*
Hl *Hapalemur*
Hy *Hylobates*
I *Indri*
La *Lagothrix*
Lc *Leontocebus*
Le *Lemur*
Ll *Lepilemur*
Ma *Macaca*
Mi *Microcebus*
Pa *Pan*
Po *Pongo*
Pr *Propithecus*
S *Semnopithecus*
Ta *Tarsius*
Tu *Tupaia*

2. The intrinsic proportions — those of the tarsus, the metatarsus, and the phalanges — are no less original. The tarsus is very long: more than 50 percent of the length of the foot (macaque 33 percent),

a figure which is only attained or exceeded among primates by the most specialized prosimian leapers *Tarsius* and *Galago*, with a completely different morphology. The metatarsus remains of average proportions (man 30 percent; macaque 32 percent), contrary to the general rule in primates in which the tarsus and metatarsus are generally inversely variable. It is, then, the toes that are especially short (man about 20 percent; macaque 36 percent), a figure much lower than in any other primate.

Schultz points to an interesting proportion illustrating the function of the foot as a lever: the posterior length of the tarsus (behind the center of the astragalar articulation, i.e. the power arm of the lever) is related to its anterior length plus the metatarsus (i.e. the resistance arm of the lever). The figure for man, 39.4 percent, is only exceeded by that for *Gorilla*, which suggests a relationship with corporal weight. (The feeble index of the orang could be explained by the fact that the animal is exclusively arboreal.)

3. The hallux, or big toe, of the human foot ($m_1 + o_1$), beyond the fact of its nonopposability (which does not enter in its proportions), is singular. It is very long (Figure 3), about 50 percent of the length of the foot (macaque 38 percent) and more than 100 percent of the middle toe (macaque 55 percent). This is obviously in relation to the shortness of the external toes. As Morton noted, the big toe supports alone, in the course of walking, nearly half the forces transmitted, according to the length of the foot. One can also establish a relationship between the length of the hallux and the placement of the morphologic axis of the foot (axony).

4. The morphologic axis of the foot, defined in the skeleton by the longest radius (Figures 3 and 4), passes, in principal, in simians by the third radius (mesaxony); this is what is considered as the "primitive" disposition of the mammalian autopod. Most often, however, a strong tendency toward equalization of the third and fourth radii (paraxony) is observed in cynomorphs and platyrrhines, whereas in prosimians the rule is ectaxony, or passage of the axis through the fourth radius. Man is the only primate in which the internal radii, I and II, essentially equal, are the longest. Muscular morphology confirms this originality. The interossei dorsales are symmetrically disposed with respect to the second radius. The human foot is therefore entaxonic, a rare occurrence in mammals. This singularity is obviously in relation to the particular mode of human plantigrady, and the latter in correlation with bipedalism. One can translate this by the relationships m_2+o_2/m_3+o_3 and m_4+o_4/m_3+o_3, or, respectively 107 and 92.3 percent in man, as

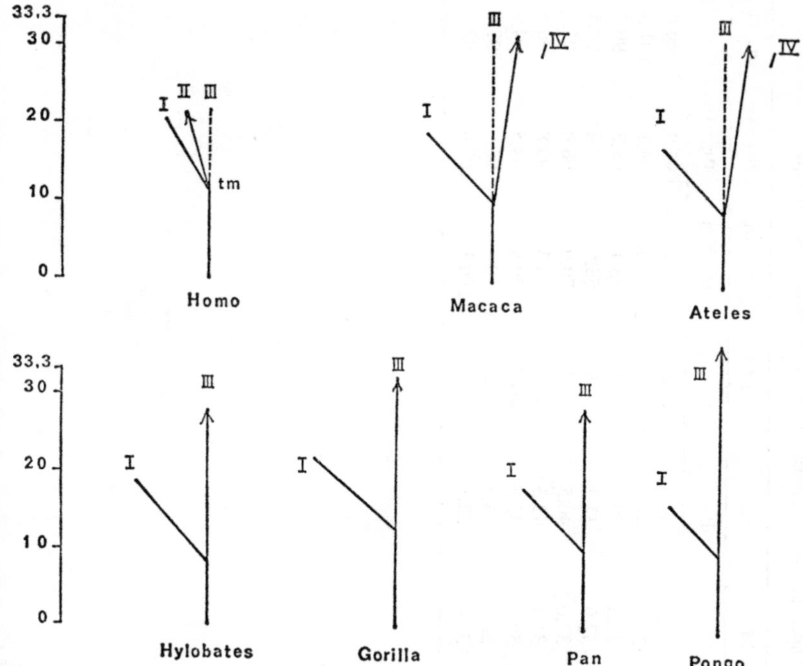

Figure 3. Schematic representation of the principal characteristics of the foot of man and certain apes and monkeys. The vertical segment in general represents the length of the foot as a percentage of that of the hindlimb. Each segment represents the relative length of the corresponding part of the foot. *tm*: the level of the tarso-metatarsal articulation. The arrow indicates the position of the morphologic axis

against 88 and 99 percent in the macaque.

In summary, from the four features chosen here, the proportions of the foot of man indicate a very clear specialization, which permits the definition of a foot adapted to orthogrady as follows: (1) it is very short with respect to the hind limb, in particular to the femur; (2) it presents a very long tarsus and very short external toes; (3) it has a very long hallux; and (4) its morphologic axis is displaced towards the interior, in an entaxonic position.

We have now to examine to what degree facultatively bipedal primates would present comparable tendencies in foot proportions.

THE FOOT OF FACULTATIVELY BIPEDAL PRIMATES

We have assembled in two tables (Tables 1 and 3) the mean values of the following indices, obtained (excepting those taken from Schultz

Table 1. Mean values of indices obtained from measuring the bony foot of specime ns of genera having a tendency toward bipedal locomotion

Genus	$P/_{tr}$	$F/_{MP}$	$P/_{MP}$	$t/_{P}$	$W/_{R}$	$\frac{M_m}{P}$	$\frac{o_m}{P}$	$\frac{m_1+o_1}{P}$	$\frac{m_1+o_1}{m_3+o_3}$	$\frac{m_2+o_2}{m_3+o_3}$	$\frac{m_4+o_4}{m_3+o_3}$
Cebus	46.2	34.9	30.9	31.3	22.8	31.6	37.2	45.0	65.4	95.9	99.9
Lagothrix	44.8	35.2	32.3	30.1	19.9	27.7	41.9	41.5	59.4	99.1	101.5
Ateles	58.0	34.7	31.9	30.2	18.0	31.3	40.0	36.6	53.1	96.2	99.7
Macaca	43.1	35.1	32.1	33.3	22.3	32.0	37.2	37.9	55.5	87.6	99.4
Hylobates	51.6	38.6	28.0	29.1	18.2	32.0	40.5	50.1	70.9	96.0	97.6
Pongo	59.3	33.0	37.6	27.9	19.6	31.1	42.5	24.4	33.3	93.8	96.8
Pan	47.0	38.3	28.9	34.9	28.2	32.5	35.5	46.5	70.9	94.5	94.9
Gorilla	46.1	35.7	32.7	39.2	46.1	28.9	34.4	43.1	70.6	96.0	97.6
Homo	43.8	43.2	21.6	53.3	39.4	30.6	22.1	48.9	100.1	107.6	92.4

Table 2. Conventions used for compilation of Table 3 (numbers are percentages)

		– – Very short	– Short	0 Medium	+ Long	++ Very long
Foot	P/MP	25	25–30	30–32.5	32.5–35	35
Tarsus	t/P	28	28–33	33–38	38 –45	45
Metatarsus	M_m/P	25	25–30	30–32.5	32.5–35	35
Toes	o_m/P	30	30–35	35–38	38 –40	40
Hallux	m_1+o_1/P	35	35–40	40–45	45 –50	50
	m_1+o_1/m_3+o_3	45	45–55	55–70	70 –90	90
Axony*		Entaxony	Parentaxony	Mesaxony	Paraxony	Ectaxony (1)

* Ectaxony (predominance of the fourth radius), normal in prosimians, is rare in simians (*Aotus*); paraxony (III = IV) is considered as existing in forms where the value IV/III lies between 99 and 103; "parentaxony" would be a disposition where II = III; it is not found in any living primate, but must have existed in the ancestors of man, the only entaxonic primate (predominance of the second radius).

Table 3. Interpretation of principal results shown in Table 1 based on conventions shown in Table 2

Genus	P/MP	t/P	M_m/p	o_m/P	$\frac{m_1+o_1}{P}$	$\frac{m_1+o_1}{m_3+o_3}$	Axony
Homo	– –	++	0	– –	+	++	– –
Gorilla	+	+	–	–	0	+	0
Pan	–	0	0	0	+	+	0
Pongo	++	– –	0	++	– –	– –	0
Hylobates	–	–	0	++	++	+	0
Macaca	0	0	0	0	–	0	+
Ateles	0	–	0	++	–	–	+
Lagothrix	0	–	–	++	0	–	+
Cebus	0	–	0	0	0	0	+

1963) by measuring the bony foot of sixty specimens in the collections of the Laboratoire d'Anatomie comparée du Muséum national d'Histoire naturelle, and belonging to genera considered above as presenting some natural tendency toward bipedal locomotion; to these, for comparison, we have added *Cebus* and *Macaca*.

P/Tr: length of the foot divided by that of the trunk (from Schultz 1963)

P/MP: length of the foot divided by that of the free hind limb

t/P: length of the tarsus divided by that of the foot

W/R: length of the arm of force of the foot lever divided by that of the arm of resistance (Figure 1) (from Schultz 1963)

M_m/P: length of the longest metatarsal (M_3 in the lower primates, M_2 in anthropoids and man) divided by that of the foot

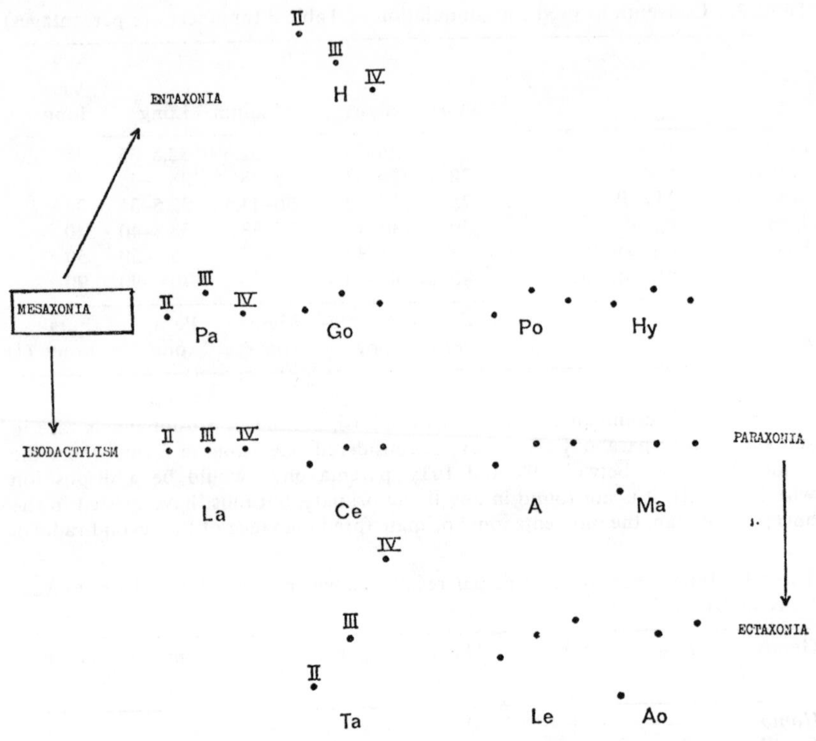

Figure 4. Schematic representation of the length of the second, third and fourth toes (m+o) in different primates. The foot axis passes through the longest toe: II: entaxony, III: mesaxony, III=IV: paraxony, IV: entaxony. (Isodactylism refers to the exceptional case of *Lagothrix*, where II=III=IV.) Same symbols as in Figure 2

o_m/P: length of the longest free toe (o_2 in man, o_3 in all other genera) divided by that of the foot

$M_1 + o_1/P$: total length of the hallucal radius divided by that of the foot

$\frac{m_1+o_1}{m_3+o_3}$: total length of the hallucal radius divided by that of the third radius (considered as typically axial in primates)

$\frac{m_2+o_2}{m_3+o_3}$ and $\frac{m_4+o_4}{m_3+o_3}$: total length of the second and fourth radii divided by that of the third.

Table 3 interprets the principal results shown in Table 1 in relation to the four following considerations, which seemed to us the most important: relative length of the foot, relative length of each of the three segments of the foot, tarsus, metatarsus, and the longest free toe; relative length of the hallucal radius; axony (defined by the longest radius). This interpretation, intended to render the resemblances and the differences more rapidly legible is an indication of the numerical results based on the conventions shown in Table 2.

DISCUSSION

If we consider the principal metrical characters of the human foot (its shortness, the length of the tarsus, the large development of the first radius, the relative shortening of the other free toes, and finally, the entaxony) as linked to bipedalism, we note that all of these traits are not combined in any other primate. However, certain partial or imperfect resemblances appear in other simian forms that we studied as follows:

1. A certain shortness of the foot, relative to the hind limb, is found, though to a lesser degree than in man, in *Gorilla* (28 percent as against 21.6 percent);
2. A tarsus as long as that of man (more than 50 percent of the length of the foot) is only found in the most specialized leaping prosimians. Nevertheless, with 40 percent the tarsus of *Gorilla* approaches *Homo*. It should be noted that in the "lever index" of Schultz (motor arm/resistance arm) the tarsus of *Gorilla* also approaches that of man (46 and 40 percent respectively);
3. In the same fashion the length of the human hallux (nearly 50 percent of MP, more than 100 percent of R_3) is closer to that of the prosimians than to that of apes and monkeys; however, the gibbon also has a very long hallux (50 percent of MP, 70 percent of R_3), but, obviously, in a different total morphological context;
4. The chimpanzee and the gorilla have free toes that are notably shorter than in most other primates (30 – 35 percent of the length of the foot), but they are still far from the 20 percent of man;
5. Finally, entaxony is a human characteristic. A human disposition of the pedal interossei dorsales has been cited in some gorillas. This hardly influences the metric proportions of the toes, *Gorilla* remains clearly mesaxonic, like the other anthropoid apes.

This comparison can be better brought out in a "genus by genus" study.

Ateles and *Lagothrix,* the best bipeds among the platyrrhines, have hardly any points of pedal morphology in common with man. The morphology of their feet resembles more that of their relative, *Cebus,* although the phalanges are distinctly longer and the big toe shorter.

It is among the anthropoid apes that one finds the closest similarities. But the diversity of the measurements renders impossible the definition of an "average anthropoid ape foot." One must distinguish at least three distinctly different modalities.

The foot of the gibbons (*Hylobates* and *Symphalangus*) approaches that of man, and differs from that of the macaque in its relative shortness (28 percent of MP) and hallux length (50 percent of MP). It differs by the shortness of the tarsus (28 percent of P) the lever index of Schultz (about 20 percent), the extreme length of the phalanges (more than 40 percent of P), and its mesaxony.

The orangutan foot is for all the characters studied extremely distant from that of man: total length (37 percent of MP), shortness of the tarsus (27 percent of P), and of the hallux (25 percent), feeble lever index (20 percent) – despite the weight of the animal – extremely long phalanges (43 percent of P), and mesaxony.

The chimpanzee and, still more, the gorilla, shows certain "humanoid" tendencies, in particular the length of the tarsus (40 percent in *Gorilla*), lever index (46 percent) and the relative shortness of the free toes (33 percent). But these figures (except the second) are still very far from human proportions. Finally, mesaxony is virtually retained.

These comparisons also bring out:

1. The relative originality of the human foot, which, by its proportions in general, and in particular by its entaxony, represents a distinctly aberrant form among the primates;
2. The fact that the few resemblances noted present rather a "mosaic" distribution; each genus, and man in particular, approaches more or less (according to the character considered) either one or another genus. However, the human foot seems the least divergent from that of the most usually bipedal anthropoid apes, the gibbon and the gorilla.

It remains, then, to try to interpret these similarities.

It is obviously hardly possible, in view of so few characters, so capriciously distributed, to distinguish between those which point to the possibility of a more or less distant common origin both of man and anthropoid apes and those which imply morphological convergences. Because it is an organ essentially marked by the function it assumes, we will adopt the traditional functional point of view and will try to relate the morphologic resemblances and differences to resemblances and differences in the mode of locomotion of the forms considered.

In this respect, a first remark is necessary: all the primate genera designated above as practicing to some degree terrestrial bipedal locomotion are, in current ecoethologic classifications put in the categories "brachiators" or "semi-brachiators," which is metrically denoted thus: in these animals the forelimb is equal to or longer than the hindlimb. If this relationship is not due to chance (the genera studied are sufficiently numerous for this to be unlikely), it is necessary first to seek a relationship between suspended brachial locomotion and bipedalism.

This relationship has been emphasized for many years by the partisans of the ancient thesis maintaining the brachiating origin of man. Keith (1923) first (who was to abandon this theory later), then and especially Gregory (1928) and Morton and Fuller (1952). These authors emphasize that the "orthostatic" attitude — all the body articulations being placed in complete extension (with, precisely, the exception of the hands of the brachiators and the feet of the bipedal walkers!) — is common to the suspended position and to erect posture. In order to illustrate this theory, one could have said that it sufficed to unhook a suspended gibbon from its branch and to place it on the ground for it to assume vertical bipedalism. (In the same way, man, by his erect posture, is capable of brachiation, as in exercises on a trapeze.) Note, however, that the forces exerted in the two positions are inverse, traction on the hands and forelimbs in one case and pressure on the hindlimbs and feet in the other. Brachiators would therefore be in some way preadapted to the bipedal position and reciprocally, the quadrupedal climbers would remain naturally quadrupedal on the ground. This is an interesting observation, but one which denotes probably only a convergence since, due to this inversion of the forces working in the two cases, the proportions and muscular requirements of the two limbs are strictly opposite.[1] It is no less thinkable that the few resemblances observed in the foot of the gibbon and that of man are in accordance with this reciprocal preadaptation.

The resemblances between the feet of man and gorilla can be the result of another analogy. Both are large forms in which the foot must submit to morphological modifications in accordance with the particular exigencies of supporting a heavy animal. The short proportions ("breviligne") of the foot (in opposition to the long foot — "longiligne" — of light brachiators), the relative elongation and reinforcement of the tarsal region, the correlative shortening of the toes, even, if it is real in the *Gorilla,* the entaxonic tendency, and lastly the high figure of the

1 The great length of the forelimb (not found in man) tends to place the trunk in an inclined position when the animal is on all fours, and even quasi-vertical in the gibbon. It is also a facilitation. Moreover, *Ateles* and the gibbon are not only brachiators but also excellent arboreal leapers whose hindlimbs are very long. There exist convergences in proportions between the hindlimb of man and that of the best leaping primates (in particular the Indriidae).

"lever index" of Schultz, must result from this common exigency. The adult *Gorilla,* by its excessive weight, is moreover much less arboreal than the young, and it is claimed that the Kivu form (*G. beringei*), which can attain the largest size, is more voluntarily bipedal than its relative of the plains (*G. gorilla*). The orangutan cannot be considered here: with a form equally heavy, but exclusively arboreal, it presents no convergence in proportions of the foot either with man or with the gorilla.

It seems to us that these two simple notations — the orthostatic position preadapting the genera with suspended locomotion to that of bipedalism, and the heavy weight of some of them — suffice for explaining the few points of resemblance without having recourse to a near-common origin, as advocated by the "brachiating ancestor" theory.

The foot of man owes its originality to a long independent adaptation to terrestrial life, probably, as Osborn thought as early as 1927, a life on the steppes. The discovery by Leakey of a nearly complete skeleton of the foot of an *Australopithecus ("Homo habilis"),* already very comparable to a human foot although nearly two million years old, pleads to a certain extent in favor of this high antiquity for human bipedalism. The conditions under which this human bipedalism were acquired would be without relation with those of the facultative or secondary bipeds that constitute divers brachiating primates. The few resemblances observed are limited to functional convergences that are but little marked.

REFERENCES

ASHTON, E. H., C. E. OXNARD

1964 Locomotor patterns in primates. *Proceedings of the Zoological Society of London* 142:1–28.

GREGORY, W. K.

1928 Were the ancestors of man primitive brachiators? *Proceedings of the American Philosophical Society* 67:129–150.

1930 The origin of man from a brachiating anthropoid stock. *Science* 71:645–650.

JENKINS, F. A., JR.

1972 Chimpanzee bipedalism, cineradiographic analysis and implications for the evolution of gait. *Science* 178:877–879.

KEITH, A.
1923 Man's posture, its evolution and disorders. VI. Evolution of the human foot. *The British Medical Journal* 1:687–689.

LESSERTISSEUR, J.
1968 Du bipède animal au bipède humain. *Bulletin de la Société zoologique de France* 93:505–534.
1970 Les proportions du membre postérieur de l'Homme comparées à celles des autres Primates. Leur signification dans l'adaptation à la bipèdie érigée. *Bulletin et mémoires de la Société anthropologique de Paris* 6(12):227–241.

LESSERTISSEUR, J., F. K. JOUFFROY
1973 Tendances locomotrices des primates traduites par les proportions du pied. *Folia Primatologica* 20:125–160.

MIVART, ST. G.
1869 On the appendicular skeleton of the primates. *Philosophical Transactions of the Royal Society of London* 157:299–429.

MOLLISON, T.
1910 Die Körperproportionen der Primaten. *Morphologisches Jahrbuch* 42:79–304.

MORTON, D. J., D. D. FULLER
1952 *Human locomotion and body form.* Baltimore: Williams and Wilkins.

NAPIER, J. R.
1964 Evolution of bipedal walking in the hominids. *Archives of biology* 75:673–708.

NAPIER, J. R., PH. NAPIER
1967 *A handbook of living primates.* London: Academic Press.

OSBORN, H. F.
1927 Recent discoveries relating to the origin and antiquity of man. *Science* 65:481–488.

OXNARD, C.
1972 Some African fossil foot bones. *American Journal of Physical Anthropology* 37:3–12.

PREUSCHOFT, H.
1963 Beitrag zur Funktion des Pongidenfusses. *Zeitschrift für Morphologie und Anthropologie* 53:19–28.
1969–1970 Statische Untersuchungen am Fuss der Primaten. I. (1969) Statik der Zehen und Mittelfusses. II. (1970) Statik des ganzen Fusses. *Zeitschift für Anatomie und Entwicklungs-Geschichte* 131:156–192.

SCHULTZ, A. H.
1963 "The relative length of the foot skeleton and its main parts in primates," in *The primates.* Edited by J. Napier, 199–206. Symposium of the Zoological Society of London 10.
1963 Relations between the lengths of the main parts of the foot skeleton in primates. *Folia Primatologica* 1:150–171.

TUTTLE, R. H.
1970 Postural, propulsive and prehensile capabilities in the cheiridia of chimpanzees and other great apes. *Chimpanzee* 2:167–253.

VOLKOV, T.

1903–1904 Les variations squelettiques du pied chez les primates et dans les races humaines. *Bulletin et mémoires de la Société anthropologique de Paris*, séries 5, 4:632–708; 5:1–50 and 201–331.

WEIDENREICH, F.

1921 Der Menschenfuss. 2. *Morphologie und Anthropologie* 22:51–282.

1931 Der primäre Greifcharacter der menschlichen Hände und Füsse und Seine Bedeutung für das Abstammungsproblem. *Verhandlungen Gesellschaft für Physiologie und Anthropologie* 5:97–110.

Discussion

BASMAJIAN: (While showing slides to illustrate EMG techniques). In human bipedalism there are specific phases. The kinesiologist is interested in not just how the subject achieves the erect posture but also what the specific elements of bipedalism are and where the various muscle actions and various swings and shifts take place. Thus kinesiologists interested in human posture and locomotion, have conceptualized the entire cycle of walking into various parts. It is almost magical the way it divides into approximately 60 percent right stance phase, 40 percent right swing phase, and vice versa with approximately 10 percent overlap. Each situation is complex. For instance, in the gluteal muscles there is a complex change in the various 10 percent elements of the entire cycle. The gluteus maximus muscle is silent during parts of the walking phase when we might expect it to be active. This warns us to be chary of implications from the anatomical locations of muscles as to the role that they might play in locomotion.

LOVEJOY: I have some new data that might be of interest. Dr. Milford Wolpoff has had the opportunity to study the new femurs that were recovered with skull KNM-ER 1470 from East Rudolf. It has been stated that they are modern looking, and in some respects they are, including a flare of the greater trochanter which in some specimens, like SK 82, is not present. However, one interesting metrical aspect of these femurs is that the biomechanical neck length in KNM-ER-1481 is clearly in the range of *Australopithecus* and is over four standard deviations from the human mean. It is one of the few complete australopithecine femurs that are available.

KUMMER: May I ask you what you are calling biomechanical neck length? Because it is often thought that one morphological parameter alone has little or no biomechanical significance. Generally groups of morphological parameters are linked together by mechanical or genetic rules. Only this linkage or interaction of biomechanical significance is significant for the whole situation. In this way, biomechanical requirements can be fulfilled by different morphological solutions. Under these circumstances, what will you call biomechanical neck length?

LOVEJOY: The problem here is that we are dealing with a series of fossil specimens where we usually do not have the links available. We usually find isolated femurs. The only exception in *Australopithecus* is STS 14, which I will return to in a second. What we are defining as biomechanical neck length is the distance from the abductor insertion, as judged to be mostly the exterior of the greater trochanter, to the center of the femoral head which we are assuming to be fairly near the center of the hip joint. While it may not be the actual axis of rotation, and in fact sometimes is not, it is the best we can do on an isolated specimen. Previous estimates of neck length were of a different type and I think were less correlated with what the actual link system would show to be a biomechanically meaningful neck length. In STS 14 we have a proximal femoral fragment and a pelvis. Thus our analysis included both elements and did attempt to reconstruct the link system of the abductors. This showed that STS 14, because of greater lateral flare in the ilium and longer biomechanical neck length of the femur, had a joint reaction force which was somewhat lower than in modern man.

KUMMER: In other words, it is the lever arm of the abductors that you determine?

LOVEJOY: Yes, that is what we are attempting to approximate.

LASKER: In considering such a matter, one should bear in mind the relationship to additional factors which you cannot measure from the parts that are present. That is, the length of the link or the fraction of the link from the axis of rotation of the hip to the insertion of the abductors is only meaningful if we know also the distance from the abductor insertion to the effective points that we are moving, be it the foot or the knee. In the upright position, of course, it is the foot. Identical or similar shapes but at different scale permit an evaluation of the mechanics involving parts that are not present in these fossil specimens. That is why we have to have a model based on contemporary species in order to work with these dimensions.

GOODMAN: If we compare types of walking behavior in the Hominoidea would we say that the chimp and gorilla are closer to the orangutan than to man? And is there any evidence from this behavior in contemporary forms and from the fossils to give us a clue, strictly from this perspective as to when the line originated which led to the human species? Does the data on walking allow any phylogenetic inference or not?

TUTTLE: I think we might pose this a bit differently: Given available information on bipedalism in *Australopithecus* how many millions of years might we project further in time for the origin of bipedalism? This requires speculation. But I would be most interested in what my colleagues who have worked on the australopith materials might conjecture about this?

LOVEJOY: From my viewpoint all of the fossil evidence from the basal Pleistocene indicates a full and complete adaptation both to erect posture and bipedal walking. In regard to the phase of transition from quadrupedalism to bipedalism or whatever the previous mode of locomotion was, there is no evidence in the fossil record indicating its time of occurrence. We would have to reconstruct it from other forms of posture and locomotion in the hominoids and I do not believe that at this point the evidence is good enough to attempt an accurate estimate of that sort.

TUTTLE: As mentioned in the paper by Basmajian, Ishida, and me, in terms of at least one muscle, the gluteus maximus viewed morphologically and now electromyographically, I do not see any major difficulties in a rather rapid transition, from a condition like gorilla and presumably also like chimpanzee, to that of man.

SIGMON: The work that Tuttle and Basmajian are doing is excellent. It is something that a number of us have been wanting to do for several years but we thought it was not feasible. They draw and interesting conclusion that I would like to hear more about. There are several parts to the gluteus maximus in the African apes. They discuss the EMG results of three different parts. They conclude that in a completely extended position which seems to me to be hyperextension as when the animal is standing upright and reaching for something, action recorded was predominantly from the upper part of gluteus maximus rather than from the lower portion even though the lower portion appears to be the heavier extensor section of the muscle. The authors suggest that since action is recorded mostly in the upper part of the muscle, during hyperextension or complete extension, this might say something about why the gluteus maximus in man is migrated cranially and the ischiofemoral portion has been more or less lost. I would ask the authors to comment on this particular point in terms of the comparability of hyperextension in gorilla and man. What are the EMG results in man during hyperextension? In this position the moment arm of the lower part of the muscle would predictably not be very effective. Also I would like for them to comment on possible side effects of action like lateral rotation and abduction that may be recorded in this hyperextended position.

TUTTLE: John, if you will provide information on man, I will speak about the situation in gorilla.

BASMAJIAN: It should be pointed out that in man's erect posture there is virtually no activity in the gluteus maximus. This approximates the extended position of the gorilla reaching position and it also emphasizes another point, i.e. in man the muscles that might be used in the dynamic phase of achieving a posture, in a nonevolutionary sense, may become completely silent upon that achievement. And the reason for this seems to be that once the posture is reached there is no particular reason for muscle activity because the subject hangs from ligaments or uses various columns of bones, etc. So it is a fallacy to believe that you require muscles to maintain a particular posture if you are a human. Now in contrast to this, the gorilla is becoming bipedal, i.e. at the experimental stages, employing something that is not what we might call common to his everyday behavior. So having reached an awkward posture for him, he is continuing the muscle activity very often in a fashion that man does not need. The point is that in man there is no need for gluteus maximus activity in that so-called hyperextended or extended position.

TOBIAS: John, when you say it is silent during that particular phase of the walking cycle, are you referring to both the contralateral and the ipsilateral muscles?

BASMAJIAN: Generally, yes. In normal human locomotion, muscles are hardly needed at all. I might emphasize that in normal human locomotion at a moderate pace the amount of energy consumed is only slightly greater than that used sitting in a chair. During the entire cycle of normal locomotion, the gluteus maximus muscle is virtually inactive, rising to SLIGHTLY ACTIVE during the swing phase of that side.

TUTTLE: At the point behaviorally upon which our rather brief discussion of gorilla gluteus maximus EMG activity is based, the subject stands with her knee and hip joints fully extended. This truly is hyperextension of the hip joints. Even more remarkably, the animal is in a position which we term "on points," viz. on the tips of all toes with the ankles markedly extended. This is not an habitual posture of gorillas or of any other primate. It is most interesting that as final hyperextension of the hip is achieved, i.e. when she is really straining upward to get the food incentive, we record high bursts of EMG potentials in the upper part of the gluteus maximus muscle. Although there are differences in details of the attachments of this muscle in gorilla and man it is a good counterpart of the gluteus maximus muscle in man. Presumably the attachments could change rather rapidly if selection pressures were rigorous enough. And I assume that they were rigorous during the transition from a quadrupedal or bimanual suspensory form to a bipedal form. Thus we might expect that the upper portion of the gluteus maximus muscle would increase its attachments to the sacrum and ilium as the hominid condition was achieved. And if the lower or ischiofemoral portion were no longer of use, for instance in climbing, which is what we assume the big ischiofemoral portion is most used for in gorilla, then it would diminish. Whether or not it "migrated" as Becky said, I would not speculate. But it is quite reasonable to expect it to diminish if it were no longer being used for climbing in the manner that it is used for climbing in gorilla and chimpanzee. I think that the behavior that makes it so important in gorilla and chimpanzee is climbing vertical tree trunks as opposed to almost any other mode of climbing, e.g. climbing out in terminal branches like the orangutan which concomitantly has a somewhat different gluteal arrangement (see Sigmon, this volume). When our gorilla climbs onto a platform she simply leans over the top of the platform and elevates herself by extension of hip and knee. This is accompanied by little EMG activity in the ischiofemoral portion of the gluteus maximus muscle. It is while climbing vertically and therefore when gravity is acting mostly against the animal that this muscle would be prominently active. And, of course, this is precisely what chimpanzees and gorillas do in the wild that might require it.

GOODMAN: Your comments show very nicely where one can bring in selective factors to interpret the changes that take place. But I submit that you have not the least idea as to how extensive the actual genetic changes are. I suspect that they are rather trivial seeing how close chimpanzee and gorilla are to man with respect to their DNA and their proteins. *Per contra* our molecular data, which deal with a different area of the problem, do lend themselves to very precise quantification.

SIGMON: I would like to pursue one aspect of my initial question about the implications of the main results of Tuttle, Basmajian, and Ishida's paper. They seem to suggest that because the ape was in the hyperextended position, presumably as it began bipedal walking, that the strong EMG activity of the gluteus maximus proprius muscle could perhaps be comparable to the strong EMG activity of the gluteus maximus in man, which has only the upper or cranial portion. But is it practicable at this moment to draw evolutionary conclusions regarding the two portions of gluteus maximus and are the two postures really comparable?

TUTTLE: We did not mean to imply that the upper portion is in any way functioning similarly in the two forms. We were only commenting that it is available, should selection act to develop in the direction of the human muscle for whatever reason it would be required in the human mode of bipedalism. My suspicion is that in the hyperextended position the muscle is acting more as a stabilizer of the hip (and this is implied in the paper) rather than as an extensor of the hip. When the gorilla is standing on the points of its toes, with the hip hyperextended, the hip is probably also laterally rotated. The animal is bandaged and wearing pants. Thus we would need cineradiography to clarify the exact positioning of the joints. But we suspect that both lateral rotation and hyperextension are occurring to stabilize the joint (or, to maintain it in hyperextension) and to give maximum reach, however that is achieved biomechanically. One other point, the animal never walks in this position. It walks with a bent hip, bent knee gait. This is what is customarily observed in chimpanzees and gorillas and is the basis for the commonly stated generalization that great apes cannot approximate the fully extended human posture of hip joint and knee joint such that the long bones of the hindlimb are aligned. This is sheer nonsense. An orangutan upon which we are conducting EMG studies and our gorilla demonstrate that this is feasible at least until seven to eight years of age in orangutan and gorilla.

KUMMER: There is a very simple mechanical explanation for the different behavior of gluteus maximus in man and gorilla. In upstanding man, the gravitational vertical oscillates only very little about the hip joint. In gorilla, it is always considerably forwards (ventral) to it. So giving a tilting moment for the whole body the extensors of the hip must be in action to prevent this tilting. Also in bipedal standing pongids, for reasons of equilibrium, the gravitational vertical must be ventral to the hip joint so the extensors of the hip joint have to be active.

JENKINS: We studied several chimpanzees by cineradiography using a treadmill device to which they adapted very readily. We found that in the bipedal mode of locomotion, the postures and the excursions of the lower extremities were essentially similar to those used in a quadrupedal support pattern. In other words, in order to achieve the bipedal position, the chimpanzee would rotate its pelvis, but the femoral positions and excursions remained very similar to those observed in quadrupedal walking.

TOBIAS: I would like to comment on Morris's specific question about phylogenetic and possibly even chronological inferences on hominid bipedalism. The question assumes that we can answer another point. Is there a precise osteological correlate of upright stance and bipedal striding gait? Can we pinpoint the bony features which connote that particular functional complex? There is more than one opinion on the subject now. On the one hand, we have the opinions of Robinson, Walker, and others, that the pattern of anatomy of the limb bones and girdle bones shown by australopithecine and other fossil remains from Africa is not the same morphological complex that we normally associate with upright stance and bipedal striding gait. On the other hand, Lovejoy and his colleagues have made a very telling case for this functional complex being compatible with the kind of anatomy we find in the early hominids from Africa. So at the outset this basic point has not been resolved. Obviously we cannot precisely interpret the fossils until we resolve the differences between these two viewpoints. I am sympathetic with the viewpoint that Lovejoy and his colleagues have been developing lately that the head size of the newborn baby is more important in molding the anatomy of the pelvis and associated upper end of the femur, than are the relatively minor adjustments in walking to which Tuttle has just referred and which may have required only a relatively small number of genic changes to have been effected. A further difficulty then is the incompleteness of the fossil record. We have no relevant fossils from which we could draw any inferences earlier than approximately three million years. The only good pelvic remains earlier than this that might be relevant to the discussion are those of *Oreopithecus* whose whole status is terribly uncertain. The oldest femora which we have, and to which Lovejoy referred, are the two that were found approximately in the same level as the KNM-ER 1470 man at East Rudolf. These were dated originally as older than 2.6 million years because they came from below a tuff which has been dated by K/Ar as 2.6 million years B.P. On the basis of paleomagnetic determinations, they have been redated to approximately 2.9 million years. Earlier than that we simply have nothing at all. And we do not have any pelves as early as 2.9 million years. So we cannot give a specific answer. Any further comment would be complete speculation. It may be reasonable to make informed speculations on this subject. But we lack consensus on the osteological correlates of the functional complex and, secondly, we do not have the fossils to answer the question.

TUTTLE: Some authors now write about *Paranthropus*, the robust form of australopith as a knuckle-walker, whereas the more gracile form of australopith, *Homo africanus*, was a biped. Certainly if the hindlimb evidence shows that both forms were bipeds it is hard to make *Paranthropus* a knuckle-walker as well.

TOBIAS: It has very long arms.

JENKINS: I have presented an alternative viewpoint to Lovejoy's interpretation of the proximal femoral anatomy in australopithecines. Drawing on analogous data from humans and chimpanzees, I do not find that the femoral head coverage in australopithecines was quite the same as in modern man. Although there may be good reasons to criticize any interpretation based principally on the fossils at hand, because of their incompleteness and poor preservation, perhaps Lovejoy would comment further on this matter.

LOVEJOY: Our difference of opinion rests mainly on which pelvic specimen to use. Dr. Jenkins used SK 50 in his reconstruction. The acetabulum of SK 50 was crushed rather extensively whereas that of STS 14 is better preserved. While there is a difference of opinion about the taxonomic status of these two specimens I treat them as being within the range of variation of one species at least postcranially. STS 14 has a hip joint coverage that is fully comparable to modern man. The condition in the SK 50 specimen depends on how one reconstructs it. That is where our difference of opinion seems to lie.

JENKINS: In chimpanzee and gorilla there is an extension of the articular area along the posterolateral aspect of the femoral head onto the neck. In man the extension of the articular area occurs on the anterolateral aspect of the head. I have seen neither extension on casts and photographs of australopithecine material. Here you have a clear distinction between the australopithecine femoral heads and those of modern man. I would interpret this in terms of femoral head coverage which relates to SLIGHT differences in the normal posture, i.e. the way the australopithecines held the femur in normal stance and gait.

LASKER: The scale by which we can measure what is a very slight difference is the scale of intraspecific variation. In looking at these studies I think that the intraspecific variation, for instance, in Basmajian's studies on man, provides an excellent scale. It is my impression that the range of physiological variation tends to be slightly larger than we anatomists would consider it to be in morphological terms. Is this correct?

BASMAJIAN: Yes, that is quite correct.

LASKER: Perhaps Dr. Basmajian would say a little bit about pathological variation too. Because this gives us a better way to approach Professor Goodman's molecular questions about how to view the variation within the species.

BASMAJIAN: People with extensive pathology can still maintain essentially a normal gait. Clothed patients with absolute, bilateral gluteus maximus paralysis can walk on a flat surface with no evidence of their serious disability. But when they reach any elevation that requires climbing they exhibit their deficiency. So in everyday imitations of normality there can be considerable ranges of human disability morphologically that can be accommodated by using that better brain that we talk about.

LASKER: Perhaps we have studied the variation a little less among nonhuman primates. I recall from some ancient conversations with Sherwood

Washburn that during his first trip to Siam he encountered a free-ranging gibbon with one arm. He never saw its gait because the animal was shot and brought to camp, but the animal must have managed to get about until it was shot.

KUMMER: Cartilage cover of the femoral head is very much related to the range of movement we find in the hip joint. We see it in man. And I have seen several cases where the femoral head on the medial side was not covered by cartilage. Several months ago we found exactly the same pattern in a gorilla, dissected in our institute. In all other respects this gorilla was absolutely normal, it was not a pathological case. It was not osteoarthritis. It had normal cartilage on the head, except on the medial (inner) side of the head and neck.

TUTTLE: Was it a zoo gorilla that might have been bipedal?

KUMMER: It was a zoo gorilla. But man also is bipedal and man has this side of his femoral head covered with cartilage. We find it in man only if there is diminished range of movement in the hip joint.

SECTION SIX

Brain Evolution in the Hominoidea and the Evolution of Human Language

Brain Evolution in the Hominoidea

PHILLIP V. TOBIAS

INTRODUCTION

Ten years ago, I published an estimate of the endocranial capacity of Olduvai hominid 5, then known as *Zinjanthropus boisei* (Tobias 1963) and subsequently renamed *Australopithecus boisei* (Tobias 1967). The opportunity was taken then to compile all available data on the cranial capacities of early hominids. Including *Homo erectus,* the total amounted to fifteen determinations or estimates. In the space of a decade that number has doubled: we have today some thirty capacities of early hominids. These include some new determinations on old discoveries, especially by Holloway (1970a, 1970b, 1972a, 1972b, 1973a, 1973b), and as a result we can be much more confident about the raw data for this study than we could a decade ago. Nevertheless, it remains a poor sample when one recalls that it is all we know of the size and shape of the braincases of hominids of various individual ages, presumably of both sexes, of several different species and even more than one genus, derived from two widely separated continental areas, and spanning perhaps two and a half million years in time. These five possible sources of variance compel us to divide the fairly respectable total of thirty values into a number of subsets. The sample size for each subset

My grateful thanks are extended to the South African Medical Research Council and the S. L. Sive Memorial Travelling Fellowship Committee, the Wenner-Gren Foundation, the L. S. B. Leakey Foundation, the University of the Witwatersrand and its Bernard Price Institute for Palaeontological Research; and to Mr. B. Brink, Mr. R. J. Clarke, Mrs. K. Copley, Mr. P. Faugust, Mr. R. E. F. Leakey, Miss C. J. Orkin, and Miss J. Walker.

is thus reduced to exiguous proportions, enough to daunt the most ardent believer in the validity of small sample statistics.

In this review, I shall endeavor to appraise the most recent determination or estimate of the cranial capacity of each of the thirty specimens. I shall then consider these capacities in systematic categories and attempt to assess 95 percent population limits. The data will next be viewed in relation to the newest estimates of the geological age of the specimens. Finally, I shall explore what evidence there is upon which to base an approach to the question of sexual dimorphism of cranial capacity among the early hominids.

THE ENDOCRANIAL CAPACITIES OF EARLY HOMINIDS

Taung

The child skull of Taung has an endocast which has been the subject of numerous volumetric estimates. These have been reviewed in detail by Tobias (1971a) and, as it now seems that the former estimates were too high, the earlier work will not be summarized or appraised here. In a meticulous restudy, Holloway (1970a) made three new reconstructions of the incomplete endocast: the volume of the most reliable of his reconstructions was 404 cubic centimeters — as compared with earlier estimates ranging from 450 to 520 cubic centimeters. With hindsight, it is now possible to see that Keith's estimates of "less than 450" cubic centimeters (1925:234) and "a minimum size" of 450 cubic centimeters (1931:61–65) were closest to the mark. Extrapolation from the cranial capacity of the Taung child, with its newly erupted first permanent molars, to the probable capacity of the adult could be based on the fact that by the dental age of the Taung child, the capacities of various hominoids have reached 90 to 94 percent of the adult mean values (gorilla 90, orangutan 91 to 92, chimpanzee 94, man 94). The unweighted mean percentage for the four kinds of hominoid is 92.5 percent (Tobias 1967:79, 1971a:15). On this percentage, the Taung "adult value" might be expected to have been 438 cubic centimeters. Holloway (1972a) chose to use 92 percent, giving an "adult value" of 440 cubic centimeters, a figure which, for practical purposes, we may adopt here. A reasonable range of adult estimates, based on 90 to 94 percent, is 430 to 449 cubic centimeters.

Sterkfontein

STS 60. The value obtained by Schepers (Broom and Schepers 1946) was 435 cubic centimeters and by Broom and Robinson (1948) about 450 cubic centimeters. Schepers' estimate has been confirmed by Holloway (1970b) with a value of 428 cubic centimeters which is adopted here.

STS 71. The earlier estimate of 480 to 520 cubic centimeters (Broom, Robinson, and Schepers 1950) seems to have been too high: Holloway's new determination yields 428 cubic centimeters.

STS 19/58. Broom and Robinson's (1948) reconstruction of this endocast from the base (Sts 19) and the calotte (Sts 58) gave a value of 530 cubic centimeters. Schepers subsequently gave values of 550 to 570 cubic centimeters. Holloway (1970b) based his reconstruction on the basis cranii (Sts 19) alone and obtained a value of only 436 cubic centimeters.

STS 5. Broom and Robinson (Broom, Robinson, and Schepers 1950) estimated the capacity of this beautifully preserved cranium as 482 cubic centimeters. Schepers (Broom, Robinson, and Schepers 1950) and Robinson (1954) accepted the figure of 480 cubic centimeters, as I do in the present study. Holloway's (1970b) study confirmed this result with a value of 485 cubic centimeters.

Thus, of the four Sterkfontein crania which have yielded capacity estimates, two capacities have been confirmed by Holloway's restudy and two have been downgraded considerably — by 18 to 22 percent for Sts 19 and by 11 to 18 percent for Sts 71. The sample mean for the four Sterkfontein crania has therefore dropped from about 486 to about 444 cubic centimeters.

Makapansgat Limeworks

MLD 37/38. Dart (1962) had estimated that the capacity of this specimen was about the same as that of Sts 5, namely, 480 cubic centimeters, and I accepted that capacity in my former computations (Tobias 1963, 1971a). However, Holloway (1972b) has recalculated the capacity of this specimen and obtains a lower value (435 cubic centimeters). He used the MLD 1 parieto-occipital fragment to compute the bone thickness of MLD 37/38 in three regions. This may introduce a source of error into his recomputation, as MLD 1, with its converging temporal crests leading, in all probability, to an anteriorly placed sagittal crest, may well have belonged to a young adult MALE, whereas MLD 37/38, with no comparable development of muscular markings, could have belonged to a young adult FEMALE. Nevertheless, despite this possible source of error, Holloway's revised estimate of 435 cubic centimeters has been accepted here as being probably more reliable than the previous estimate.

MLD 1. This parieto-occipital portion of a calvaria is a most interesting specimen. Although its median sagittal contour is similar to that of Sterkfontein 5 (Robinson 1954), the occipital sagittal dimensions exceed those of Sts 5 and of all other measurable australopithecine occipitals. Thus, its occipital sagittal chord (lambda-opisthion) is 68.0 millimeters, in contrast with about 58.5 millimeters in Sts 5, 59.0 millimeters in MLD 37/38, and 57.8 millimeters in Olduvai hominid 5 *(A. boisei)*. This value of 68.0 millimeters even exceeds the 64.6 millimeters of Olduvai hominid 13 (which is one of the paratypes of *H. habilis* and is even regarded by some as belonging to *H. erectus*), but it falls short of the 71.0 millimeters for the occipital sagittal chord of Olduvai hominid 24, which, too, is regarded as a member of *H. habilis* (Leakey, Clarke, and Leakey 1971; Tobias 1972a). It would seem that MLD 1 possessed a more capacious occipital squama than any other australopithecine from South Africa; presumably, too, the endocranial capacity of this part of the braincase was somewhat more voluminous than that of any of the other australopithecines. Furthermore, the biasterionic arc breadth of the MLD 1 occipital (115.0 millimeters) exceeds that of MLD 37/38 (90.0 millimeters), Sts 5 (about 90.0 millimeters), Olduvai hominid 5 (112.0 millimeters), and Olduvai hominid 24 (about 104.0 millimeters), though it is exceeded by that of the very robust KNM-ER-406 (about 120.0 millimeters). This massive occipital arc breadth of MLD 1 is occasioned at least in part by its marked torus as well as by its strong transverse curvature.

All of this evidence suggests that the capacity of MLD 1 was probably greater than that of Sterkfontein 5 (with 480 or 485 cubic centimeters), and certainly greater than that of MLD 37/38 (with 435 cubic centimeters). Holloway (1973b) has made an estimate of 500 cubic centimeters for MLD 1, and it seems to me that this estimate may even err a little on the low side, in light of the excessively large occipital measurements of MLD 1. However, using the partial endocast method on MLD 1, Holloway found that two trials gave fairly different results. For the present, I have not included this estimate of the capacity of MLD 1 in my calculations.

Incidentally, this relatively large cranial capacity may well prove another feature relating MLD 1 to *A. robustus/A. boisei.* The latter hominids from Swartkrans, Olduvai, and East Rudolf have values of 530, 530, 510 and 506 cubic centimeters. In contrast, the bigger-brained early hominids of Olduvai *(H. habilis)* have cranial capacities ranging from about 600 cubic centimeters to 684 cubic centimeters and, further, this larger cranial capacity is accompanied by temporal lines placed much more widely apart on the calvaria. Both in its probable capacity and in its virtually certain possession of a sagittal crest, MLD 1 agrees with the *A. robustus* superspecies rather than with *A. africanus* on the one hand or with *H. habilis* on the other.

In passing, it might be noted that the features of MLD 1 are not the only ones which tend to relate some of the Makapansgat specimens to the robust australopithecine. Although the Makapansgat hominids are usually classified in *A. africanus,* in 1967 I drew attention to some "robust" features in some of the crania, jaws, and teeth from that site (Tobias 1967:244):

> In these respects, the Makapansgat specimens seem to show a somewhat nearer approach to *A. robustus* than do the Sterkfontein specimens. This reduces the distinctness of the lineages and renders it less likely that they represented two clades, the members of which should be regarded as generically distinct from each other.

Since then, Aguirre (1970) has studied the early hominid mandibles from South Africa. He has identified a constellation of morphological features characterizing the mandibles of *A. robustus* from Swartkrans. These features, he believes, are clearly shown by the jaw MLD 2 of Makapansgat, which he states should be regarded unequivocally as a "young male *A. robustus*." To Aguirre, it appears indubitable that there is more than one species of hominid at Makapansgat, a thought I had raised previously as a tentative suggestion (Tobias 1968a, 1969).

Perhaps another way of looking at the somewhat intermediate features shown by the Makapansgat hominids is to suggest that they resemble a population closer to the point of speciation between *A. africanus* and *A. robustus*. In such a population, anatomical polymorphisms could have coexisted, foreshadowing the later speciation of the *A robustus/A. boisei* lineage from the basic *A. africanus*, which it seems reasonable to suppose was the ancestor.

Swartkrans

SK 1585. Thus far, only one of the South African frankly robust specimens has yielded an endocast so well preserved as to permit an estimate of its volume. This specimen, SK 1585, proved to have a capacity of 530 cubic centimeters (Holloway 1972a), exactly the same value as had earlier been obtained for the very robust Olduvai hominid 5 (Tobias 1963).

Olduvai

OH 5. This specimen, the type of *A. boisei,* has a capacity of 530 cubic centimeters (Tobias 1963) and this value has not been changed by the more recent studies of Holloway (1972b). It was the first positive indication that the robust group of australopithecines might have possessed a somewhat larger capacity than *A. africanus.*

OH 7. The type specimen of *H. habilis* (Leakey, Tobias, and Napier 1964) was estimated to possess a capacity of 363.4 cubic centimeters for the biparietal partial endocast and, by computation, 657 cubic centimeters for the total endocast (Tobias 1971a). If it is assumed that the mandible included as part of the holotype of *H. habilis* belongs to the same individual as do the parietals, then this set of bones represents an individual who, by modern dental standards, was about twelve years of age. It has been estimated from comparative hominoid data that the cranial capacity at this age would represent about 96 percent of the capacity in adulthood. Accordingly, a value of 684 cubic centimeters has been estimated for the "adult value" of OH 7. This value, or at least a somewhat earlier estimate of 687 cubic centimeters (Tobias 1968b), has been accepted most recently by Holloway (1937a).

OH 13. Using the part-endocast method, I was able to obtain values for the partial endocast of about 392 cubic centimeters, for the entire endocast of 639 cubic centimeters, and for the "adult value" of 652 cubic centimeters. Holloway's (1973a) most recent study has confirmed this value — his figure is 650 cubic centimeters.

OH 16. This specimen, which has been provisionally referred to *H. habilis*, is a much-fractured calvaria. It is sufficiently preserved to make clear that the specimen was a complete skull, including all thirty-two of the permanent teeth, at the time when it "had been washed out by heavy rainfall at Site F.L.K. II, Maiko Gully; it had, moreover, been afterwards trampled on and very badly broken up by herds of Masai cattle before it was discovered by one of our senior African staff" (Leakey and Leakey 1964:6). A reasonable inference, confirmed by the later discovery of some parts of the same specimen *in situ,* was that it derived from deposits three to four feet above the Marker Tuff If at the base of Bed II. That is, it derived from the lower part of Bed II BEFORE the faunal break.

As there has been some discussion on the validity as well as the taxonomic affinities of the reconstructed specimen, the following account is given of the reconstruction:

The calvaria has been reconstructed from no fewer than 107 fragments. The first reconstruction by M. D. Leakey and a modified version of it made on casts of the fragments by L. Distiller and myself both erred in placing an elongate compound fragment of bone in the left temporal fossa. As this fragment was orientated with its long axis (52.5 millimeters in length) anteroposterior, it had the effect of greatly elongating the reconstructed cranium, which, at this stage, had an estimated maximum glabello-occipital length of 159 to 160 millimeters. Furthermore, the long ovoid appearance of norma verticalis was strongly reminiscent of some of the Asian specimens of *Homo erectus.*

In January, 1965, when I had the opportunity to re-examine the original fragments in Nairobi, I noticed a clear beveled sutural edge on the elongate fragment, which betrayed its true identity, namely, part of the right temporal bone. The removal of the offending fragment permitted a better alignment to be effected between the left frontal and left parietal parts: this converted the whole vault into a short ovoid, or even spheroid, vault as seen in norma verticalis, and resulted in a maximum glabello-occipital length of only 144 millimeters, i.e. 15 to 16 millimeters shorter than the earlier reconstructions. The general "pithecanthropine" resemblance, suggested by the first reconstructions, likewise largely disappeared.

The final reconstruction incorporates twenty-nine fragments of the frontal, twenty-five of the left parietal, forty-two of the right parietal, and eleven of the occipital.

In order to make a partial endocranial cast, the reconstructed vault was smoothed off inferiorly with plasticine, along a curved line corresponding closely to the lower margins of the parietals and passing through the cerebellar fossae at about the level of the posterior intraoccipital synchondrosis. The transverse limb of the cruciate eminence was partly intact and could be reconstructed in the missing part. Thus the lower margin of the cerebral fossae of the occipital is clear. Anteriorly, the endocranial aspect of the frontal squama is present as far as the front edge of the floor of the anterior cranial fossa.

An endocranial cast was then made by Mr. R. J. Clarke and the base of this was smoothed and hollowed to coincide on each side with the notched lower margin of the parietal bones. The resulting cast comprises the part of the braincase occupied by the major part of the cerebrum, down to the line of recurvation of the frontal lobes anteriorly and the lower margin of the occipital pole posteriorly. The parts missing from the cast comprise the rostrum, the temporal lobes, the cerebellum, and the area occupied by brainstem from about the level of hypothalamus to medulla oblongata, parts which collectively seem to occupy about one-third of the total endocranial volume.

The part-cast was varnished with a coating of shellac, and the author, assisted by Mr. Clarke, determined its volume by volumetric displacement of water. Eight determinations were made and their values were as follows: 408, 409, 410, 410, 411, 411, 412, and 414. The mean of these eight readings is 410.6 cubic centimeters. The problem now was to determine the probable ratio of the capacity of the part-cast to the total endocranial capacity. To compute this ratio, recourse was had to two australopithecine endocranial casts, namely, those of the two very complete specimens Sts 5 *(A. africanus)* and OH 5 *(A. boisei),* for both of which the total endocranial volume is known (480 and 530 cubic centimeters respectively). From total plaster endocasts of these two crania, part-casts were prepared by Mr. Clarke under the author's direction, the basal parts being removed along a curved line corresponding to the lower margin of the frontal lobe impression in front and that of the occipital lobe impression behind. The volumes of the resulting two part-casts were determined by eight volumetric displacements of water and the values were as follows:

Sts 5 Part-cast: 317, 317, 317, 318, 319, 320, 321, and 321.

Mean: 318.75

OH 5 Part-cast: 345, 349, 350, 351, 352, 352, 353, and 353.

Mean: 350.625

Next, the ratios between the part-cast volume and the known total volume for each of these two specimens were calculated. The results were remarkably similar:

Sts 5: 66.4063 percent
OH 5: 66.1556 percent
Mid value: 66.28095 percent

Using the mid value, we obtained a total for OH 16 of 619.97 or 620 cubic centimeters. With the Sts 5 ratio (66.4063) the figure came to 618.4; with the OH 5 ratio (66.1556), the value was 620.7 cubic centimeters. In other words, the method yielded a range of estimates of 618.4 to 620.7 cubic centimeters. For practical purposes, a central value of 620 cubic centimeters may be accepted.

The state of the teeth of OH 16 indicates that the individual was of about the same age as OH 13 and that it probably possessed some 98 percent of its adult capacity. The "adult value" computed on this basis is 633 cubic centimeters and this value has been used in my studies. It should be mentioned here that Holloway (1973a) has not reconstructed an endocast of OH 16, as the cranial reconstruction is not good enough, in his judgment, to give an accurate internal surface replica (1973a:98). He adds, however, "Although the value of 650 cm³ for OH 16 may be doubtful in view of the fragmentary nature of the skull, it is unlikely that it is grossly inaccurate if the large size of the frontal portions and the associated dentition are considered" (1973a:98), and indeed, he has included the figure of 650 cubic centimeters for OH 16 in his "habiline sample."

OH 24. This much-crushed cranium has been developed and reconstructed in masterly fashion by Mr. Clarke. As in all the other Olduvai hominids thus far found, no natural endocast was contained within the remains of the calvaria of OH 24. However, following his reconstruction of the cranium, Mr. Clarke was able to make a plaster and a plastic cast of the interior of the braincase. As the braincase, as such, had not been restored by the correction of the fracture-depression of the calotte, nor of that of the base, the resulting endocast was likewise unrestored. Thus it was flattened from above and somewhat stove inward from the base.

Mrs. Margaret Leakey and Dr. Alan Walker then determined the volume of the endocast by displacement of water. In six determinations, they obtained these readings: 556, 582, 575, 562, 555, and 574 cubic centimeters.

The mean of these six readings amounts to 567.3 cubic centimeters. They then checked their technique against mine, by making four displacement readings on the endocast of OH 5, obtaining readings of 538, 536, 528, and 539 cubic centimeters, with a mean of 535 cubic centimeters. This compares with my own determination of 530 cubic centimeters (Tobias 1963), later confirmed by Holloway (1970a). Their readings for OH 5 being thus slightly on the high side, Mrs. Leakey and Dr. Walker, in an unpublished report, suggested that "perhaps, then, around 565 cubic centimeters would be right for OH 24."

In their preliminary announcement of the discovery of OH 24 and brief description of it, M. D. Leakey, Clarke, and L. S. B. Leakey stated that the preliminary determinations gave a figure "of the order of 560 cm³." At the same time they made it clear that "the cranium is still warped slightly" and "the crushing of the whole cranium has also to be taken into account when considering the cranial capacity, which must inevitably have been greater than the absolute capacity as measured now."

These caveats were unfortunately disregarded in an unsigned editorial comment, headed "Confusion over fossil man," in *Nature* (Anonymous 1971), which suggested that OH 24 is disqualified from membership in the genus *Homo* because it "does not fulfil all the generic criteria outlined in the 1964 revision [of Leakey, Tobias, and Napier 1964]." In particular, the editorial stated that "the revision calls for a minimum cranial capacity of 'about 600 cm³'. Although some gorillas have more than 600 cm³, OLDUVAI HOMINID 24 HAS ONLY 560 CM³" (emphasis mine).

Although the comment in *Nature* went on to say, "This is admittedly a preliminary estimate," and "if cranial capacity cannot be accurately determined . . .," it is clear that the writer of the unsigned comment considered that the capacity disqualified the specimen from falling into a group for which "about 600 cm³" has been diagnosed as a minimum capacity.

Tobias (1972a), in commenting on the unsigned editorial, stated:

> Now, it is an arguable point and might be deemed by some to be a quibble, whether a capacity "in the order of 560 cm³" qualifies to be included under the formula "about 600 cm³". When one considers that the mean cranial capacity of *Australopithecus africanus* is of the order of 450 cm³ and the sample range 428 to 485 cm³, (Tobias 1971a), it might well be considered that 560 cm³ is "about 600 cm³". Even the robust australopithecines have cranial capacities of 500-530 cm³ (n = 3); thus every proven *Australopithecus* capacity is exceeded by the value 560 cm³.

I went on to point out, "Much more important, though, is the fact that 560 cm³ is the capacity of the calvaria in its present rather crushed state — it might be said to be the 'taphotype', but not the phenotype of OH 24."

How much should one allow for the crushing of the cranium? From the region of the lambda behind to that of the metopion in front, the calotte or roof of the calvaria shows a fracture-depression downward and into the upper part of the braincase. Furthermore, a large part of the cranial base is stove inward, particularly the posterior cranial fossa. Thus, on both the roof and the floor of the endocranial cavity, damage to the lining bones tends to reduce the measurable capacity. The value of 567 cubic centimeters is uncorrected for the cranial distortion, as mentioned above: a restoration on paper of the calvaria to its probable contours before crushing has added up to 5.0 millimeters in vertical height to the calotte and several millimeters to the base, as a minimum correction. A careful computation, based on such a restoration, indicates that approximately 24 cubic centimeters should be added to the top of the endocranial cavity and 6 cubic centimeters to the base. This gives a total value of approximately 597.0 cubic centimeters.

Working independently, Holloway has made a plastic restoration of the uncrushed endocast, based on the endocast taken from Clarke's reconstruction. Correcting for the distortion, Holloway (1973a) has obtained a figure of 590 cubic centimeters, compared with mine of 597 cubic centimeters. An average value between Holloway's and my estimates would place the restored cranial capacity at some 593 to 594 cubic centimeters. For practical purposes, we may accept the value of 593 cubic centimeters as a not unreasonable estimate of the original cranial capacity of OH 24, before its cranium was crushed.

A careful study of the teeth of OH 24 shows that in dental eruption age, OH 24 would have been older than OH 13 and slightly older than OH 5, in both of whom the upper third molars were in the process of erupting. It is concluded that OH 24 was dentally on the brink of adulthood. No correction of the estimated cranial capacity need therefore be made, and the value of 593 cubic centimeters is accepted for practical purposes as the adult value for this specimen of *H. habilis* (Tobias 1972a).

OH 9. The large cranium, assigned to *H. erectus*, early yielded an estimate of 1,000 cubic centimeters (Tobias 1965). Since then, the base of the interior has been skillfully cleaned of matrix by Dr. Alan Walker, permitting a new estimate of 1,067 cubic centimeters to be made by Holloway (1973a). This value is accepted here.

OH 12. This thick-skulled, fragmentary cranium has been reconstructed by Holloway (1973a) and has yielded a possible estimate of 727 cubic centimeters. It should be noted that Holloway warns that the reconstruction of OH 12 could show considerable error (1973a:98). The figure has been used in certain of my computations here.

East Rudolf

KNM-ER-406. This large, crested skull from East Rudolf has been assumed to be a male of *A. boisei.* Holloway (1973a) has used measurements and a formula to arrive at an estimate of 510 cubic centimeters for the capacity of this member of the robust superspecies.

KNM-ER-732. This East Rudolf cranium is considered on morphological grounds to be a female of *A. boisei.* Holloway's latex mold of the endocranium of the original, further modeled with plasticine, gave a value of 506 cubic centimeters (Holloway 1973a).

Homo erectus from Asia

The seven Indonesian specimens from Trinil and Sangiran which have yielded cranial capacity determinations are listed here, as they appear in the earlier literature and as listed by me in 1971. Trinil 2 of 1891 (see new scheme of numbering in Jacob 1973) was formerly estimated to have a capacity of 900 cubic centimeters (Dubois 1898, 1921). A new study enabled me to arrive at the reduced value of 850 cubic centimeters for this specimen. Holloway has been making new studies on the other Indonesian specimens (personal communication), but his new estimates and determinations of cranial capacity are not yet available. Hence the data as listed in 1971 are used here. Similarly, the published data for the six Chinese *H. erectus* (five from Choukoutien and one from Lantian) are employed here.

MEANS AND LIMITS OF CRANIAL CAPACITY IN EARLY HOMINID TAXA

The data for the thirty crania are summarized in Tables 1 to 7, in which the available samples are sorted into the probable systematic categories. For this purpose, Taung is kept in *A. africanus,* although I have elsewhere questioned whether this is indeed correct (Tobias 1973). Similarly, MLD 37/38 is placed in *A. africanus,* while MLD 1 is omitted. Olduvai hominids 7, 13, 16, and 24 are placed in *H. habilis.* The four robust specimens — SK 1585, OH 5, KNM-ER-406, and KNM-ER-732 — are included in the *A. robustus/A. boisei* superspecies.

For each taxon, the sample range, mean, and standard deviation are

Table 1. Cranial capacities of *A. africanus* (cubic centimeters)

Specimen	Cranial capacity
Taung	440
Sterkfontein	
Sts 60	428
Sts 71	428
Sts 19	436
Sts 5	480
Makapansgat	
MLD 37/38	435
Sample range	428–480
Sample mean	*441.2*
95 percent confidence limits of mean	430.3–452.0
Standard deviation (s)	*19.6002*
95 percent confidence limits of s	14.3496–30.9080
Degrees of freedom	5
t_5 (95 percent confidence limits)	2.571
$t_5 \times s$	50.39
95 percent confidence limits of population	*390.8–491.6*

Table 2. Cranial capacities of *A. robustus/A. boisei* superspecies (cubic centimeters)

Specimen	Cranial capacity
Swartkrans	
SK 1585	530
Olduvai	
OH 5	530
East Rudolf	
KNM-ER-406	510
KNM-ER-732	506
Sample range	506–530
Sample mean	*519.0*
95 percent confidence limits of mean	511.9–526.1
Standard deviation (s)	*12.8062*
95 percent confidence limits of s	9.3757–20.1945
Degrees of freedom	3
t_3 (95 percent confidence limits)	3.182
$t_3 \times s$	40.76
95 percent confidence limits of population	*478.2–559.8*

Table 3. Cranial capacities of *H. habilis* (cubic centimeters)

Specimen	Cranial capacity
Olduvai	
OH 7	684
OH 13	652
OH 16	633
OH 24	593

Table 3. (Continued)

Sample range	593–684
Sample mean	*640.5*
95 percent confidence limits of mean	619.4–661.6
Standard deviation (s)	*38.0219*
95 percent confidence limits of s	27.8364–59.9577
Degrees of freedom	3
t_3 (95 percent confidence limits)	3.182
$t_3 \times s$	121.01
95 percent confidence limits of population	*519.5–761.5*

Table 4. Cranial capacity of *H. erectus erectus* of Indonesia (cubic centimeters)

Date of discovery	New designation of specimen (Jacob 1973)	Old designation	Cranial capacity
1891	Trinil 2	*Pithecanthropus I*	850
1937	Sangiran2	*Pithecanthropus II*	775
1938	Sangiran 3	*Pithecanthropus III*	890
1938–1939	Sangiran 4	*Pithecanthropus IV*	750
1963	Sangiran 10	*Pithecanthropus V* (1964) *Pithecanthropus VI* (1968)	975
1965	Sangiran 12	*Pithecanthropus VII*	915
1969	Sangiran 17	*Pithecanthropus VIII*	1,029 approx.

Sample range	750–approximately 1,029
Sample mean	*883.4*
95 percent confidence limits of mean	827.5–939.4
Standard deviation (s)	*101.0723*
95 percent confidence limits of s	73.9966–159.3833
Degrees of freedom	6
t_6 (95 percent confidence limits)	2.447
$t_6 \times s$	247.39
95 percent confidence limits of population	*636.0–1130.8*

Table 5. Cranial capacity of *H. erectus pekinensis* of Choukoutien (cubic centimeters)

Specimen	Cranial capacity
Choukoutien	
II	1,030
III	915
X	1,225
XI	1,015
XXI	1,030

Table 5. (Continued)

Sample range	915–1,225
Sample mean	*1043.0*
95 percent confidence limits of mean	980.7–1105.3
Standard deviation (s)	*112.5056*
95 percent confidence limits of s	82.3671–177.4127
Degrees of freedom	4
t_4 (95 percent confidence limits)	2.776
$t_4 \times s$	312.30
95 percent confidence limits of population	*730.7–1355.3*

Table 6. Cranial capacity of *H. erectus* of Asia (cubic centimeters)

Specimen		Cranial capacity
Lantian 1		780
Trinil 2		850
Sangiran 2		775
Sangiran 3		890
Sangiran 4		750
Sangiran 10		975
Sangiran 12		915
Sangiran 17	approximately	1,029
Choukoutien II		1,030
Choukoutien III		915
Choukoutien X		1,225
Choukoutien XI		1,015
Choukoutien XXI		1,030
Sample range		750–1,225
Sample mean		*936.85*
95 percent confidence limits of mean		863.1–1010.6
Standard deviation (s)		*133.1795*
95 percent confidence limits of s		97.5027–210.0139
Degrees of freedom		12
t_{12} (95 percent confidence limits)		2.179
$t_{12} \times s$		290.24
95 percent confidence limits of population		*646.6–12271*

Table 7. Cranial capacity of *H. erectus* of Asia and Africa (cubic centimeters)

Specimen		Cranial capacity
Lantian 1		780
Trinil 2		850
Sangiran 2		775
Sangiran 3		890
Sangiran 4		750
Sangiran 10		975
Sangiran 12		915
Sangiran 17	approximately	1,029
Choukoutien II		1,030
Choukoutien III		915

Table 7. (Continued)

Choukoutien X	1,225
Choukoutien XI	1,015
Choukoutien XXI	1,030
OH 9	1,067
OH 12 approximately	727
Sample range	727–1,225
Sample mean	*931.5*
95 percent confidence limits of mean	854.1–1008.9
Standard deviation (s)	*139.7430*
95 percent confidence limits of s	102.3080–220.3640
Degrees of freedom	14
t_{14} (95 percent confidence limits)	2.145
$t_{14} \times s$	299.66
95 percent confidence limits of population	*631.9–1231.2*

given, as well as the estimated 95 percent limits for the population mean and the population standard deviation. To compute the 95 percent confidence limits of the sample, I have assumed that cranial capacity is a normally distributed variate. Instead of using limits which are 2, 2.5, or 3 standard deviations away from the sample mean, I have used 't' standard deviations on either side of the mean, the formula being $\bar{x} \pm ts$. The value of 't' is obtained from tables of Student's 't' values for small samples and varies with the degree of freedom and with the probability. In the computation of population sample limits here, I have used $p=.95$. I am most grateful to Dr. David Pilbeam for helpful discussions and advice on the statistical handling of these small samples.

The 95 percent sample confidence limits are given in Table 8 and depicted in Figure 1. The population ranges for the two australopithecine species overlap to a small extent, though the sample means are significantly different ($t=2.46$, $p<0.02$, <0.05 [Holloway 1973a]). It is of interest that there is no overlap between the ranges for *A. africanus* (391 to 492 cubic centimeters) and for *H. habilis* (520 to 762 cubic centimeters): the means are very significantly different ($t=5.76$, $p<0.001$). On the other hand, the upper half of the *H. habilis* range overlaps the *H. erectus* range. These results confirm the claims made that *H. habilis* has a significantly greater mean capacity than either australopithecine group (Pilbeam 1969; Campbell 1972; Holloway 1973a).

Before attempting to analyze the pattern of change of cranial capacity among the various taxa, it is important to recall that both sexes

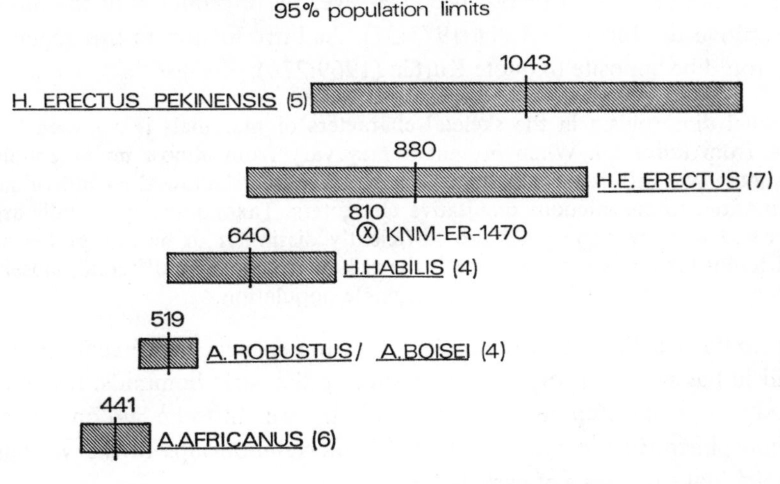

Figure 1. Cranial capacities of various early hominids. For each taxon, the mean and 95 percent population limits are shown, as described in the text. The numbers in parentheses after each taxonomic nomen are the respective sample sizes

Table 8. Population limits (95 percent) for Early Hominid Taxa (cubic centimeters)

Taxon	n	95 percent population limits
A. africanus	6	390.8–491.6
A. robustus/A. boisei	4	478.2–559.8
H. habilis	4	519.5–761.5
H. erectus erectus	7	636.0–1,130.8
H. erectus pekinensis	5	730.7–1,355.3
H. erectus of Asia	13	646.6–1,227.1
H. erectus (total)	15	631.9–1,231.2

are represented in our total sample of thirty specimens and, probably, in most of the subsets.

SEXUAL DIMORPHISM OF CRANIAL CAPACITY

Brace (1973) and Wolpoff (1973) have rendered a valuable service to paleoanthropologists by directing their attention powerfully to the need to take into account sexual dimorphism in our fossil samples and, especially, Bonnet's "largely forgotten assertion that sexual dimorphism in the hominid fossil record becomes 'ever more pronounced the more primitive the form' " (Brace 1973:31). As introduction to this section, it would be apposite to quote Kurtén (1969:226):

> Sexual dimorphism in the skeletal characters of mammals is common but far from universal. When present it may vary from almost imperceptible average size differences, which are completely overshadowed by individual variation, to conspicuous qualitative characters. Taxonomically, pitfalls are created whenever the sexes are sufficiently dissimilar to be interpreted as different taxa. Conversely, there is the risk of treating two different, closely related taxa as sexual dimorphs of a single population.

It would, I believe, be true to claim that the existence of sexual dimorphism has not been forgotten in studies on the early hominids: the only real source of difference of opinion is in the weight to be laid on sexual dimorphism, in the assessment of the interrelationships of the various individual specimens of early hominids.

Holloway (1973a) draws attention to the features of KNM-ER-732 that mark it as most probably a female robust australopithecine skull. He adds, "The value of 506 cm^3 for ER 732 represents 95 percent of the 530 cm^3 values for OH 5 and for SK 1585, a value also consistent with sexual dimorphism as an explanation of the difference" (1973a:98). This reasoning is perfectly acceptable when there is other collateral evidence for the sex of the specimen. However, it leaves unanswered the question of the low capacity — 510 cubic centimeters — in the obviously male cranium of KNM-ER-406, for this capacity is only 96 percent of the value in the two robust crania with 530 cubic centimeters (as against 95.5 percent for the female cranium, KNM-ER-732). This example raises the question: when should one invoke the factor of sexual dimorphism when dealing with an array of cranial capacities?

A similar problem is raised by the sample of four *H. habilis* crania from Olduvai. Leakey, Clarke, and Leakey (1971) suggested the wholly reasonable proposition that, on dental and cranial morphology, OH 7 and OH 16 should be regarded as males and OH 13 and OH 24 as females. The cranial capacities sort themselves rather awkwardly: the two supposed males, OH 7 and OH 16, have 684 and 633 cubic centimeters, while the two supposed females, OH 13 and OH 24, have 652 and 593 cubic centimeters. The two extreme values sort well, whereas the two intermediate ones do not. Here again, the problem arises: when would it be valid to invoke a sexual explanation and when not? The array of capacities might seem to fall into Kurtén's category of "almost imperceptible average size differences, which are completely overshadowed by individual variation." To obtain a body of firm data with which to approach this problem, I have surveyed virtually all that is known or available at present about sexual dimorphism in cranial capacity in living hominoids, including modern man.

Sexual Dimorphism of Cranial Capacity in Living Hominoids

The mean cranial capacity of adult females may be as low as 81.3 percent and as high as 97.6 percent of the mean capacity of males in different populations of hominoids. There are differences among various series drawn from the same species and there are interspecific differences. The following are among the various modes of expressing sexual dimorphism:

$$♂\bar{x}/♀\bar{x}\,\%,\ ♀\bar{x}/♂\bar{x}\,\%,\ \frac{♂\bar{x} - ♀\bar{x}}{♂\bar{x}}\,\%.$$

In this analysis I shall use the third form, i.e. the actual difference of the means will be expressed as a percentage of the male mean.

In a detailed study of all available data for hominoids (Tobias 1971a, 1971b), the following values were found for hylobatines:

Siamang *(Symphalangus syndactylus)*	2.4 percent
Gibbon *(Hylobates lar)*	3.0 percent

The data on which the siamang index is based are pooled from earlier studies, while those for *H. lar* are based on a single good series of males and of females, measurements for which were kindly placed at my disposal by Dr. A. Schultz. These low values bespeak the smallest degree of sexual dimorphism in all hominoid series available to me.

Table 9 gives the values for numerically adequate individual series as well as for pooled means in all pongid series available.

For chimpanzees, the index of sexual dimorphism ranges from 6.9 to 8.4 in various series. The index based on the largest pooled samples of males and of females is 6.9 percent.

The index for five series of orangutan ranges from 9.5 to 18.7 percent, the index for the largest pooled samples being 13.8 percent.

Four lowland gorilla series have indices between 11.8 and 17.2, with an index of 14.8 percent based on the largest pooled series.

Hence, although Table 10 gives a summary of the indices based largely on pooled samples, individual — and substantial — samples within each species may vary widely in the degree of sexual dimorphism

Table 9. Sexual dimorphism of pongid cranial capacities

Species	Male mean	Female mean	Male mean–female mean as percent of Male mean	Reference
Chimpanzee (*Pan troglodytes*)	398.5	371.1	*6.9*	Tobias 1971a, 1971b (pooled data)
	420.0	390.0	7.1	Selenka 1899
	410.0	380.0	7.3	Ashton and Spence 1958
	381.0	350.0	8.2	Schultz 1965
	399.5	365.8	8.4	Zuckerman 1928
Orangutan (*Pongo pygmaeus*)	395.0	357.6	9.5	Oppenheim 1911–1912
	434.1	389.8	10.2	Gaul 1933
	415.0	370.0	10.8	Ashton and Spence 1958
	434.4	374.5	*13.8*	Tobias 1971a, 1971b (pooled data)
	455.0	390.0	14.3	Selenka 1898, 1899
	416.0	338.0	18.7	Schultz 1965
Gorilla (*Gorilla gorilla gorilla*)	510.0	450.0	11.8	Selenka 1899
	534.6	455.6	*14.8*	Tobias 1971a, 1971b (pooled data)
	543.0	461.0	15.1	Randall 1943–1944
	550.0	460.0	16.4	Ashton and Spence 1958
	535.0	443.0	17.2	Schultz 1962, 1965

Table 10. Tabular summary of indices of sexual dimorphism of cranial capacity among living nonhuman hominoids (percent)

Siamang	2.4
Gibbon (*H. lar*)	3.0
Chimpanzee	6.9
Orangutan	13.8
Gorilla	14.8

Table 11. Sexual dimorphism of cranial capacity in modern man, distribution of percentage indices

Percent index	5–6	6–7	7–8	8–9	9–10	10–11	11–12	12–13	13–14	14–15	15–16	16–17	17–1
Number of series	1	4	4	6	12	14	11	7	2	3	0	1	1

of cranial capacity. The indices for individual samples and for pooled series are represented diagrammatically in Figures 2 and 3.

For modern man, data have been assembled for sixty-seven human populations. While not laying claim to being an exhaustive compilation, the list embraces a fair world-wide coverage. If the sixty-seven popula-

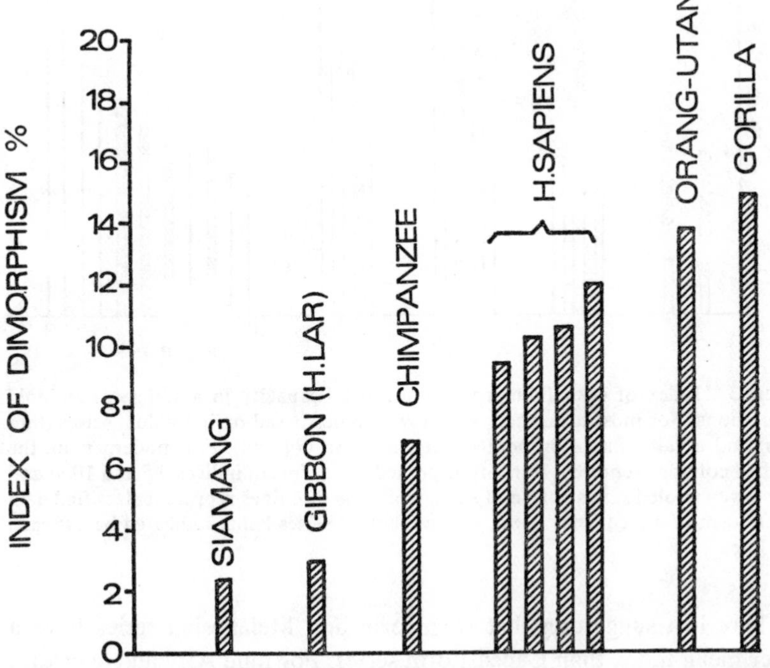

Figure 2. Index of sexual dimorphism of cranial capacity in modern Hominoidea. The values for siamang, chimpanzee, orangutan, and gorilla are based on pooled male and pooled female samples; that for gibbon is based upon a single population of male and of female *Hylobates lar.*

The values for *Homo sapiens* are based upon mean weighted indices for thirty-four male and female series (9.5 and 10.3 percent) and for sixty-seven pooled unweighted series (10.6 and 12.0 percent).

The range of human indices shown therefore represents several estimates of an overall species mean for *H. sapiens*

tions are grouped into categories roughly in accordance with Garn's (1965) classification of living peoples, there are 5 Australian, 33 Caucasiform, 9 Melanesian, 9 Negriform, 3 Polynesian, 3 Indian, 4 Mongoliform, 1 Amerind, and 1 Tahitian hybrid series. The values of the index of sexual dimorphism for individual series vary even more markedly than in the pongids. Thus, the index ranges from 5.2 percent in a Chinese series to 18.4 percent in a Singhalese sample. Table 11 summarizes the distribution of indices. The modal class is 10 to 11 percent and the mean of the sixty-seven indices is 10.57 percent (Figure 4).

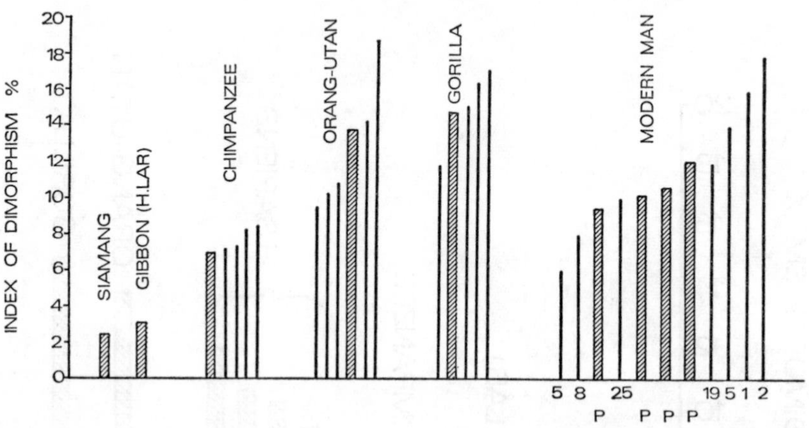

Figure 3. Index of sexual dimorphism of cranial capacity in a series of hominoid populations. For most taxa, there are shown values based on individual series (thin lines) and a value based on pooled data (hatched column). For modern man, the hatched columns represent thirty-four pooled series (mean indices 9.5 and 10.3) and sixty-seven pooled series (10.6 and 12.0), while the thin lines represent classified data in the form of a frequency chart, the number of series being indicated below each thin line

There is a suggestion that Negriform and Melanesian series have a lower mean index than Caucasiform series. For nine African Negriform series, the average index is 8.64 percent; for nine Melanesian series, 9.99 percent; and for thirty-three Caucasiform series, 10.82 percent. Other ethnic subsets comprise too few samples (from one to five series per subset) for separate analysis.

The low mean value for African series as compared with the European mean is interesting in light of some work on sexual dimorphism of stature. It has been shown by Hiernaux (1968) and by Tobias (1962, 1970a, 1972b) that sexual dimorphism of stature seems to be a sensitive indicator of environmental adequacy. Under conditions of malnutrition or other forms of environmental inadequacy, males are more adversely affected than are females — and sexual dimorphism of stature is lower. Under conditions of environmental amelioration, the degree of sexual dimorphism of stature may be expected to increase. In view of the prevalence of poor nutritional and other living circumstances in Africa, it is not surprising that the mean index of sexual dimorphism of stature among forty-nine African populations (6.212 percent) is lower than the

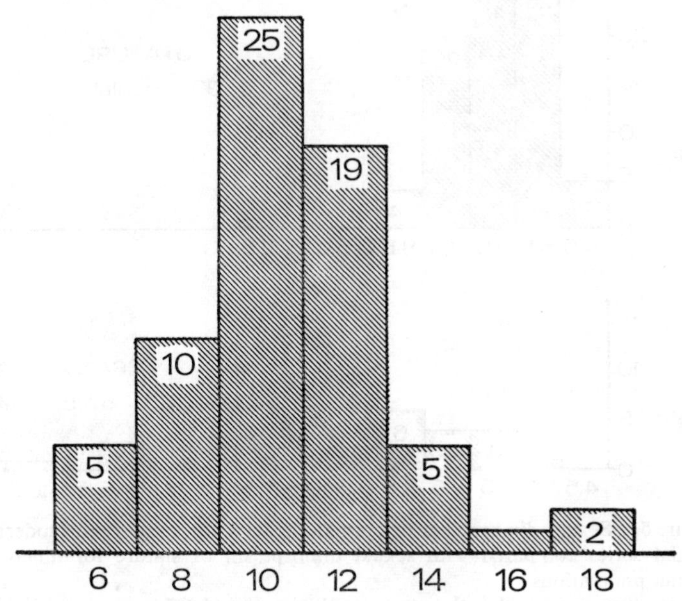

Figure 4. Percentage index of sexual dimorphism of cranial capacity in sixty-seven modern human cranial series. The mean indices have been grouped in classes with 2 percent intervals: thus, the label "6" stands for "the class 5.0 to 6.9 percent." The modal class is the 10 percent class, with the means of twenty-five series falling within it. The 12 percent class is almost as common, with the means of nineteen series in it

mean index among forty-one European populations (6.784 percent).

It has been shown that brain size is positively correlated with bodily stature (Pakkenberg and Voigt 1964; Spann and Dustmann 1965; Tobias 1970b). It is possible, therefore, that the low index of sexual dimorphism of cranial capacity among African series is simply a reflection of the low dimorphism index of stature among African populations.

In general, the index of dimorphism of cranial capacity is higher than that of stature (Figure 5). Partly, this may be due to the fact that, relative to each unit of stature, females have a smaller weight of brain. Spann and Dustmann (1965) showed that adult men have on the average 8.3 grams of brain for every centimeter of body stature, whereas adult women have on the average only 8.0 grams of brain for every centimeter of stature. Thus, women have smaller brains than men, not

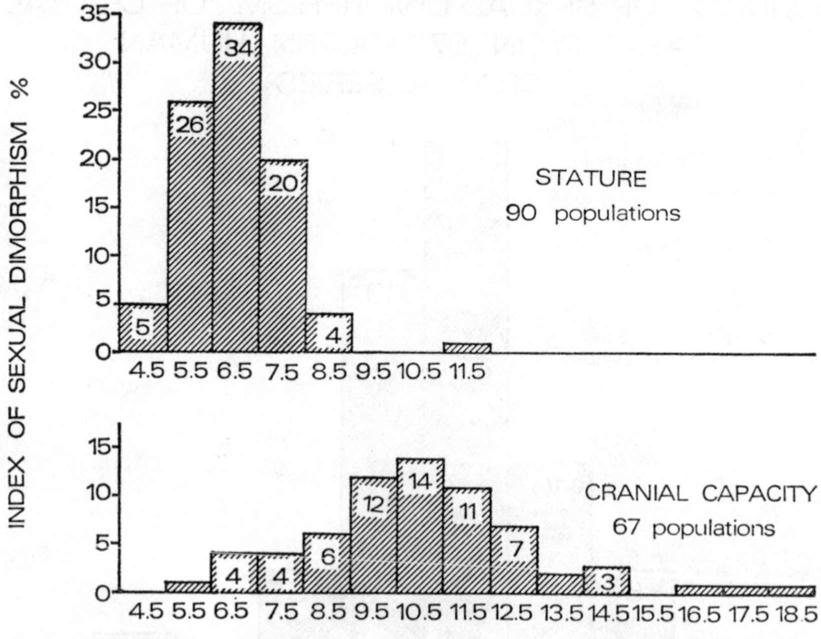

Figure 5. Sexual dimorphism of cranial capacity for sixty-seven modern human cranial series compared with sexual dimorphism of stature for ninety modern human populations.

Note that compared with stature, with a mode of 6.5 percent, cranial capacity shows a decided shift to the right, with a mode of 10.5 percent

only because they are shorter, but because they have less brain tissue per unit of stature. This factor might be sufficient to account in large measure for the index of dimorphism of cranial capacity being greater than that of stature. Partly, too, the fact that cranial capacity is a cubical measure and stature a linear measure might be expected to contribute to a larger male-female discrepancy of cranial capacity.

It is clear, from what has been demonstrated, that sexual dimorphism of cranial capacity is a most variable character in living hominoids: some human populations have over three times as much dimorphism of this trait as others! Similarly, some pongid series have about three times as much sexual dimorphism of cranial capacity as others. Thus, populations with high dimorphism would have rather more extreme upper and lower values where males and females would be clearly recognizable by cranial capacity alone. On the other hand, populations with low dimorphism would have relatively few capacities at the male upper and female lower extremes and so would provide no assistance in the sexing of specimens. In either category, whether sexual dimorphism is 6 percent or 18 percent, the majority of capacities would be expected to lie in the area of overlap of the two distribution curves.

Sexual Dimorphism of Cranial Capacity in Fossil Hominids

In the case of fossil groups, it would be extremely hazardous to use the unsupported evidence of cranial capacity alone to allocate a particular specimen to one or the other sex. Such a procedure would be especially questionable when (a) sample size is very small; and (b) there is insufficient evidence on which to decide whether a particular fossil sample represented a high-dimorphism or low-dimorphism taxon.

In light of this comment, it would, for instance, be foolhardy to attribute Sterkfontein 5 (known for decades as "Mrs. Ples") to the MALE sex simply because that cranium has the largest internal capacity of the four Sterkfontein crania of *A. africanus* — unless other evidence, such as robusticity, muscle markings, and tooth root size indicated the need for such a reattribution.

Similarly, it would be unjustified to assign KNM-ER-406 to the female sex simply because it has the second smallest capacity (510 cubic centimeters) of the four values of the specimens in the *A. robustus/A. boisei* superspecies, in the face of overwhelming morphological evidence, based on muscle markings and crests, that ER 406 represents a male!

I conclude that sexual dimorphism of cranial capacity can be used on fossil hominids only with utmost caution and circumspection. At this stage of our knowledge, we should consider this population parameter as being simply of exploratory interest and heuristic value. It should be our aim to determine how capacity varies with sex when sex can be determined on other criteria, rather than to use cranial capacity to help to determine sex.

NEW THOUGHTS ON THE PATTERN OF HOMINID PHYLOGENY

We may now return to the cranial capacities which, irrespective of sex, we had classified into various taxa. The problem now is to determine whether any phylogenetic trends in the development of the brain can be detected. To approach this question, we need to know something of the trait under investigation (e.g. cranial capacity), but we also need to know the position of each taxon in time and phylogeny. We shall therefore turn aside from the brain briefly and attempt to synthesize the newer facts bearing on hominid phylogeny in general.

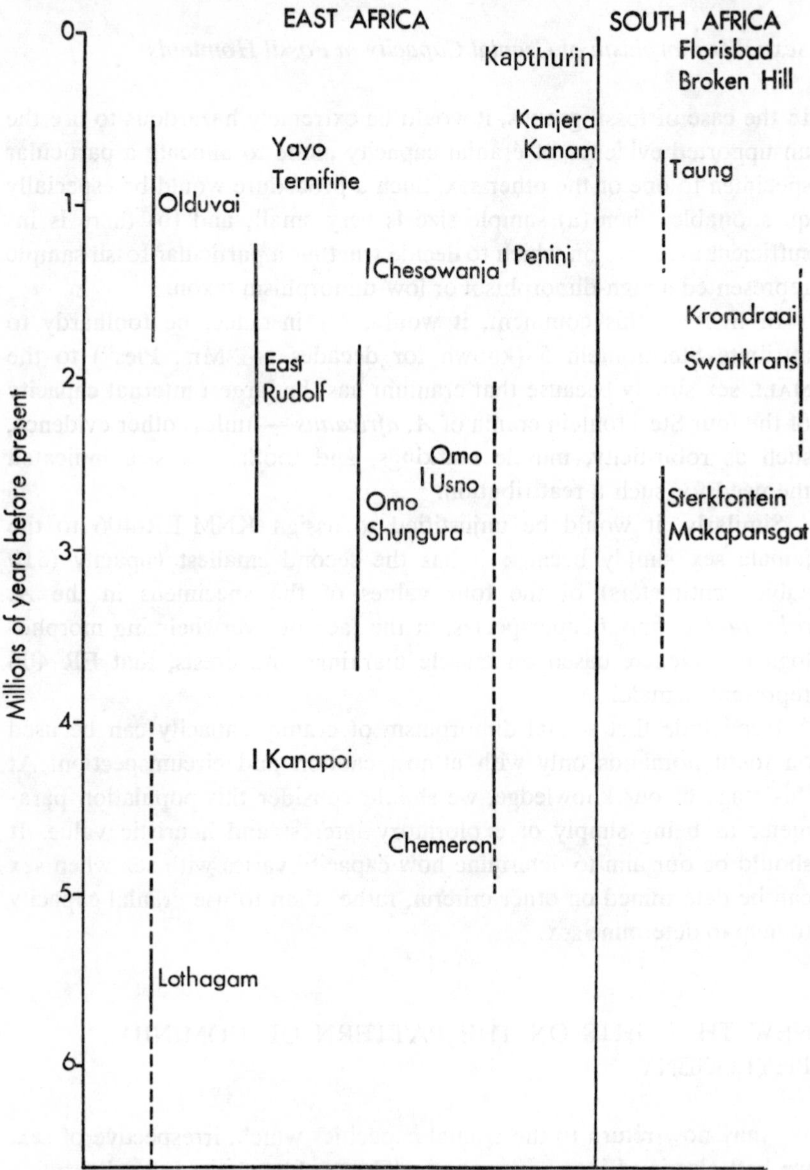

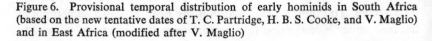

Figure 6. Provisional temporal distribution of early hominids in South Africa (based on the new tentative dates of T. C. Partridge, H. B. S. Cooke, and V. Maglio) and in East Africa (modified after V. Maglio)

The time scale of hominid evolution in East Africa is becoming progressively clearer, with new age determinations based upon the potassium-argon method, paleo-magnetism reversals, fission tracking, and faunal correlations. It is now clear that the well-attested East African hominids span nearly 5.0 million years, from about 5.5 million years B.P. to >1.0 million years B.P. Various parts of this time range are occupied by at least four hominid taxa: *Australopithecus c.f. africanus, A. boisei, Homo habilis,* and *H. erectus.* At each well-sampled time level in the 5.0-million-year span, at least two different sympatric species of hominid coexisted. This fact refutes the so-called principle of competitive exclusion, according to which, on a priori grounds, only one hominid species could exist at any one time (Figure 6).

At last, the long-uncertain dating of the South African australopithecine cave deposits is yielding to analysis by geomorphological methods and by faunal correlations both *inter se* and with the well-calibrated East African faunas. The work of T. C. Partridge suggests that the Makapansgat cave deposit is the oldest of the five South African australopithecine sites, the cave having opened probably about 3.7 million years B.P. and the dated fauna therein being at least 2.5 to 3.0 million years old (Cooke 1970; Maglio 1973). Sterkfontein cave, it is inferred, opened about 3.3 million years B.P. and its dated fauna is about 2.5 to 3.0 million years old. Swartkrans cave seems to have opened about 2.6 million years B.P. and its dated fauna is at least as old as the Upper Member of Olduvai Bed 1 (about 1.7 to 1.8 million years B.P.). Most surprisingly, the Taung deposit — long regarded as the oldest of the five South African australopithecine deposits — turns out to be far and away the youngest. According to Wells' faunal analyses (1969) and Butzer's geomorphological studies (1974), Taung is at the oldest as young as the Swartkrans-Kromdraai Faunal Span, but Partridge's work seems to indicate that the Taung cave did not open until <0.9 million years B.P. The Taung hominid itself may be as young as 0.8 or even 0.7 million years B.P.! (Figure 7).

The South African deposits thus appear to span nearly 3 million years — from about 3.5 million years B.P. to perhaps 0.7 million years B.P. Within this span, at least three different hominid taxa are represented: *A. africanus, A. robustus,* and *Homo* sp. (exemplified by "Telanthropus" from Swartkrans, which is regarded by some as *H. erectus* but by the author as *H. habilis*).

When the total assemblages of South and East African early hominids are plotted against time, a clear-cut cladistic pattern of hominid evolution emerges (Figure 8). The morphological, chronological, and geo-

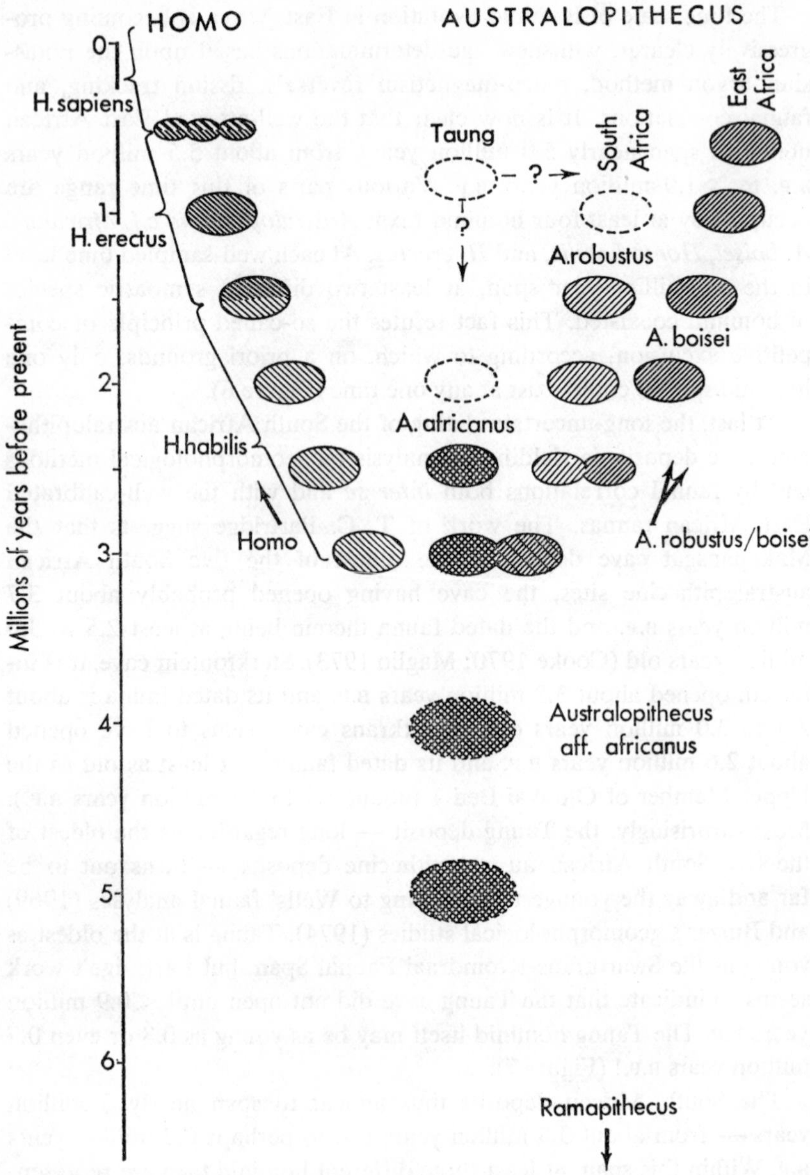

Figure 7. Populations of early hominids identified systematically and arranged chronologically. The horizontal distance between any pair of population ovals is approximately proportional to the morphological and taxonomic distance between the taxa represented by those ovals

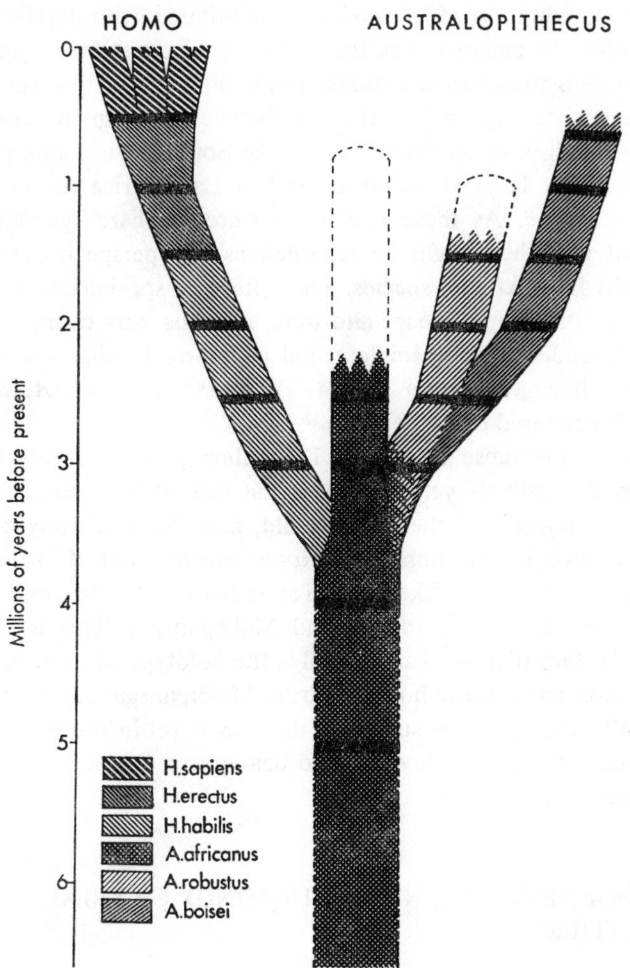

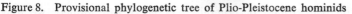

Figure 8. Provisional phylogenetic tree of Plio-Pleistocene hominids

graphical evidence is consistent with the following interpretation. The ancestral Pliocene population of hominids was *A. africanus.* This relatively unspecialized hominid is best represented at present in the samples from Makapansgat and Sterkfontein. About 3.0 million years B.P. (or even earlier), a branch of *A. africanus* underwent strong selection for cerebral enlargement, out of proportion to bodily size: this branch is the *Homo* lineage, perhaps the earliest known member of which is Richard Leakey's new large-brained hominid cranium, KNM-ER-1470, found some distance below the KBS Tuff (2.6 million years B.P.) at East Rudolf. This *Homo* lineage was characterized from an early period by strong dependence upon tool making and tool using.

Some populations of *A. africanus* continued with relatively little change after the emergence of the *Homo* lineage. Yet others underwent a series of dental specializations, developing an increasingly robust body, under dietary or behavioral influences, thus giving rise to the robuster lineages of *Australopithecus*. In South Africa, this produced the moderately large *A. robustus,* and in East Africa the excessively robust *A. boisei*. As these two forms were nowhere sympatric, it is suggested that they might be regarded as a superspecies comprising South and East African species. These lines of specialization diverged away from the *Homo* lineage and were, it seems, NOT characterized by strong dependence upon implemental activities. Having spawned two derivative lineages, *Homo* and *A. robustus/A. boisei, A. africanus* largely disappeared from the scene.

The apparent lapse of at least 1.0 million years and very likely as much as 2.0 million years between the last of the well-attested *A. africanus* samples and the Taung child, and the synchrony of Taung with only two known hominids, *Homo erectus* and *A. robustus/A. boisei,* makes it most unlikely that Taung belongs to the same taxon as the hominids from Sterkfontein and Makapansgat. This is suggested despite the fact that the Taung skull is the holotype of *A. africanus,* to which taxon most of the hominids from Makapansgat and Sterkfontein are usually assigned. It is suggested that the as yet incompletely studied child skull from Taung may prove to belong to a late surviving population of the robust lineage!

PHYLOGENETIC TRENDS IN HOMINID CRANIAL CAPACITIES

Against the background of hominid phylogeny just limned, we may now attempt to reconstruct what has been happening to cranial capacity.

The pattern is not a simple anagenetic one, as Holloway (1973a) has stressed. Cladogenetic elements are present as well: this is suggested by the appearance, AT LEAST TWICE, of a trend toward increase of cranial capacity. In my latest reconstruction of hominid phylogeny, I suggest that from the basic *A. africanus* or *A. c.f. africanus* stock, one of two different lines of development gave rise to early *Homo*, with its precocious and disharmonic emphasis on brain enlargement; while the other gave rise, perhaps somewhat later, to a progressively more robust and big-toothed lineage, that of *A. robustus/A. boisei*. The latter lineage, too, shows signs of brain enlargement. However, it could pertinently be asked whether the increase in brain size in *A. robustus/A. boisei* may have been related, in part at least, to the general increase in body bulk that seems to have accompanied the evolution of the robust lineage. *A. robustus/A. boisei* has been shown to comprise essentially short individuals, not differing in stature from *A. africanus* (Burns 1971; McHenry 1972, 1974). On the other hand, the robust form of South African australopithecine does appear to have been "a good deal heavier," to judge by the size of the teeth and skulls (McHenry 1974). Is brain size related to body weight or to body stature or to both?

It was Cuvier who first introduced the concept of relative brain weight, that is, the weight of the brain expressed as a fraction of the weight of the body. It followed, perhaps expectedly, that early workers such as Matiegka (1902) and Pearl (1905) should claim that, in modern man, brain weight varies with body weight and with body height. That is, they claimed to find that taller people and heavier people have larger brains. However, more recent workers have questioned the correlation claimed to exist between brain weight and body weight WITHIN the human species. Pakkenberg and Voigt (1964), in a more refined analysis on the brains of European subjects, showed that the increasing brain weight with increasing body weight found by earlier workers is really attributable to the fact that people with higher body weight are usually taller than average. The earlier workers had failed to correct for body height when evaluating the relationship between brain weight and body weight. When this correction was made, it was found that brain weight depends significantly on body height but NOT ON BODY WEIGHT (Tobias 1970b). Their results were confirmed by Spann and Dustmann (1965), while Schreider (1966) reanalyzing some old brain and body measurements made by Paul Broca in Paris in 1865–1870, found that between brain weight and body height there was a positive correlation coefficient of 0.26 for males and 0.31 for females.

Thus, WITHIN the modern human species, brain size does NOT vary with body weight. Is it possible, however, that there could be a correlation when different species are compared?

An extensive literature has grown up, since the pioneering work of Snell (1892) and Dubois (1897), culminating in the studies on insectivores and primates by Bauchot and Stephan (1964–1969), and Thenius (1969). Their results may be summarized thus: "The relation of brain weight to body weight is found to be linear on a double logarithmic scale, IF CLOSELY RELATED SPECIES ARE COMPARED." (Stephan 1972:157). I do not propose here to evaluate this approach and the results (cf. Thenius 1969; Stephan 1972; Holloway 1973b). Notwithstanding, the position seems sufficiently clear to conclude that, in two closely related species, the one with a heavier mean body weight might be expected to have a larger brain than the one with a lighter body weight. This seems to match the relationship between *A. africanus* and *A. robustus/A. boisei*: although they do not seem to have been of different stature, the evidence for the heavier body weight of the latter superspecies might lead one to expect a bigger brain — WITHOUT ANY INDICATION OF ADDITIONAL PROGRESSIVE ENCEPHALIZATION. In contradistinction, the brain enlargement in the *Homo* lineage would seem to be accompanied by much evidence of progressive encephalization, culminating in the position where Stephan (1972:173–174) can write:

> The size of the brain, considered in conjunction with the differences in body weight by aid of the allometry formula (= encephalization), is not more pronounced in Primates than in other orders. A Prosimian stage is reached by many mammals and a Simian or even Pongid stage is matched by several semi-aquatic and/or aquatic groups. Only man has encephalization which exceeds that of all animals. He is the only Primate with an outstanding brain size.

Total brain size is of course a relatively crude measure of encephalic advancement, and Stephan's work has indeed led him fruitfully to apply his approach to various parts of the brain individually. Nevertheless, the relevance in the present context is that we are confronted with a situation where a small-brained ancestral *A. africanus* seems to have undergone cladistic evolution. Cladogenesis seems to have occurred, giving rise to at least two different lines, each characterized by brain enlargement, while a third line may represent the fairly short-lived persistence of populations of little-changed *A. africanus*. In the one instance — that of the robust lineage — it seems that brain enlargement accompanied an increase in body bulk, but it is questionable whether this enlargement represented progressive encephalization. In the other instance, the lineage of early *Homo* leading to *H. habilis*, brain enlargement seems to have been selected in its own right, without evidence for concomitant increase in body size. In this lineage, therefore, one is able to see early steps in the marked and progressive encephalization that is the hallmark of the genus *Homo* and ultimately, in its extreme manifestation, of the species *H. sapiens*.

If this interpretation is correct, one should perhaps be able to detect differences between the brain morphology of the progressive *Homo* line, on the one hand, and that of the ancestral *A. africanus* and of the nonencephalizing derivative, *A. robustus/A. boisei*, on the other hand. Such differences might be sought at the level of the surface morphology of the endocasts, as indicators of changes in the underlying structure and organization, as was stressed earlier by Dart (1956) and repeatedly in recent years by Holloway.

INDICATIONS OF ENCEPHALIC REORGANIZATION IN THE EARLY HOMINIDS

Much has been written on the morphological features that serve to distinguish the australopithecine from the pongid brain (Broom and Schepers 1946; Broom, Robinson, and Schepers 1950; LeGros Clark 1947; Dart 1956; von Bonin 1963; Tobias 1967; Holloway 1972a). These features include marked prominence of the inferior frontal convolution, forward placement of the brainstem, enlargement and medial encroachment of the cerebellar hemispheres, a tendency toward parietal expansion, and the underslung cerebellum bearing a humanlike relationship to the overlying cerebral hemisphere (Tobias 1967).

We may next enquire whether any features distinguish the endocasts of early *Homo* from those of *Australopithecus.* The part-endocast of OH 13 shows a clear vertical expansion of the cerebrum beyond the dimensions in some australopithecine casts; thus the maximum height in the plane of the coronal suture (54 millimeters) is greater than in Sts 5 (39 millimeters) and even than in the high-brained *A. boisei,* OH 5 (48 millimeters). If the maximum height is measured above the plane of the notch in the squamosal margin of the parietal bone (which at this point marks the lower margin of the part-endocast), the value in OH 13 (62 millimeters) far exceeds those of two high-brained australopithecine part-endocasts which had been especially cut down for comparison (Sts 5: 48.5 millimeters; OH 5: 51 millimeters).

The following first detailed description of the original endocast of OH 24 brings out further points of encephalic reorganization and advancement, as compared with the brains of australopithecines.

The gyral and other impressions on the endocranial surface of the vault bones have permitted the identification of several encephaloscopic features. The impression of the rostrum shows that it was not as exaggeratedly developed as in several of the australopithecine endocasts (e.g. Sts 5 and Taung). The impressions of the superior frontal gyrus can be identified on both sides, as well, probably, as that of the middle frontal gyrus on the left. Other impressions underlying the parietal bone probably represent three parts of the parietal lobe, namely, the superior and inferior parietal lobules and the arcus parieto-occipitalis, possibly the parieto-occipital sulcus, and the intraparietal sulcus.

Nothing corresponding to the lunate sulcus can be identified on the endocast — which recalls LeGros Clark's (1964:135) emphatic statement that it is really not possible to identify the lunate sulcus with certainty from the impressions on the australopithecine endocasts. Weidenreich (1936) said the same about the endocasts of *H. erectus pekinensis* and von Bonin (1963) about that of *H. erectus erectus* I.

Another well-marked impression may represent — on both sides — the posterior end of the middle frontal gyrus, or a lateral part of the precentral gyrus. The impression of the temporal lobe suggests that it is smaller and more attenuated than in OH 5, Sts 5, or SK 1585.

In keeping with the very anterior position of the foramen magnum, the impression of the brainstem is placed further forward and looks more vertically downward, than in australopithecine endocasts.

As in other early hominids, the impression of the cerebellum does not form the most posterior part of the endocast: the impression of the occipital pole of the cerebrum marks the posterior limit and that of the cerebellum is well tucked under anteriorly. In fact, it is further forward from the occipital pole impression than in any of the australopithecine endocasts, e.g. Sts 5, Taung, SK 1585, or OH 5. As seen in side view, there appears to have been a more substantial posterior pole of the cerebrum behind the plane of the cerebellum, not only in antero-posterior extent, but, too, in vertical height. This feature would probably have been even more striking if the fracture-depression in the upper part of the hind end of the calvaria had not influenced the shape of the posterior part of the endocast.

As seen in basal view, the endocast shows an important difference from those of the australopithecines. In all of the latter, the cleft between the cerebellar impression and the temporal lobe impression, normally occupied by the petrous pyramid, extends posterolaterally to the very edge of the endocast. In OH 24, the cleft stops short of the edge; beyond it a well-expanded cerebrum can be seen anterolateral and posterolateral to the cleft. Another way of expressing this relationship is to state that in the endocasts of OH 5, SK 1585, and Sts 5, the maximum width across the impressions of the two cerebellar hemispheres is approximately equal to the maximum breadth across the cerebrum just above the impressions of the most lateral poles of the cerebellar hemispheres; whereas in OH 24, the cerebral impressions appear to balloon outward above the cerebellar impressions, so that much more cerebral cast can be seen in norma ventralis (basalis) lateral to, as well as behind, the cerebellar impressions.

In keeping with the expanded breadth of the cranium, to which reference has already been made, and with due allowance for some broadening by distortion, the whole endocast of OH 24 shows a great lateral expansion. While this is most strikingly apparent in the posterior two-thirds of the endocast, it is also impressive in the region of the frontal lobes of the endocast.

The moderately expanded height of the endocasts of OH 5, SK 1585, and Sterkfontein "type II," as well as the marked expansion of the vertical diameter of that of Sts 5, are lacking in the unrestored endocast of OH 24: as seen in side view, it looks flattish compared with these others. Restoration on the upper and lower surfaces, however, imparts a less flat and more rounded contour in norma lateralis.

It seems that the endocasts of *H. habilis* do show some signs of further reorganization and advancement which are not present in the robust australopithecines — nor yet in *A. africanus.* Although the evidence is still relatively sparse, it would seem that we are justified in recognizing two patterns of brain enlargement among the early hominids. In one line, that of *A. robustus/A. boisei,* we have a combination of (1) bigger teeth, robuster bones, and heavier muscles; (2) a concomitantly enlarged brain; and (3) absence of indications of progressive brain reorganization. In the other line, that of early *Homo,* we have the complex (1) smaller teeth, and probably gracile bones and lighter muscles; (2) disproportionally enlarged brain; and (3) suggestions of progressive brain reorganization beyond the australopithecine grade. To these morphological complexes we might add behavioral traits, the most obvious overt manifestation of which is culture-dependence in the *Homo* lineage but not in the *A. robustus/A. boisei* superspecies.

At this level of hominid phylogeny, it seems that the changes marking the inception of the early *Homo* line are predominantly cerebral and cultural-behavioral and only minimally dental and gnathic. On the other hand, the changes marking the initial kick on the robust line seem to be predominantly dental and gnathic, probably under dietary and behavioral control, but, apart from overall increase in body bulk (including brain bulk), only minimally cerebral and cultural-behavioral. Thus, the divergence of *Australopithecus* into two different lineages is effected by markedly disparate kinds of mosaic development. In one, the evolution of the brain is not blatantly involved; in the other, it plays an all-important and pivotal role.

REFERENCES

AGUIRRE, E.

1970 Identificación de "Paranthropus" en Makapansgat. *Crónica del XI Congreso Nacional de Arqueología, Mérida,* 1969, 98–124.

ANONYMOUS

1971 Confusion over fossil man. *Nature* 232:294–295.

ASHTON, E. H., T. F. SPENCE

1958 Age changes in the cranial capacity and foramen magnum of hominoids. *Proceedings of the Zoological Society of London* 130: 169–181.

BAUCHOT, R., H. STEPHAN

1964 Le poids encéphalique chez les Insectivores Malgaches. *Acta Zoologica* 45:63–75.

1965 Hirn-Körpergewichtsbeziehungen bei den Halbaffen (Prosimii). *Acta Zoologica* 46:209–231.

1966 Données nouvelles sur l'encéphalisation des Insectivores et des Prosimiens. *Mammalia* 30:160–196.

1967 Encéphales et moulages endocraniens de quelques insectivores et primates actuels. Problèmes actuels de paléontologie. *Colloques Internationaux du Centre National de la Recherche Scientifique* 163:575–586.

1968 Etude des modifications encéphaliques observées chez les Insectivores adaptés à la recherche de nourriture en milieu aquatique. *Mammalia* 32:228–275.

1969 Encéphalisation et niveau évolutif chez les simiens. *Mammalia* 33:225–275.

BRACE, C. L.

1973 Sexual dimorphism in human evolution. *Yearbook of Physical Anthropology 1972* 16:31–49.

BROOM, R., J. T. ROBINSON

1948 Size of the brain in the ape-man, *Plesianthropus. Nature* 161 (4090):438.

BROOM, R., J. T. ROBINSON, G. W. H. SCHEPERS

1950 *Sterkfontein ape-man, Plesianthropus.* Transvaal Museum Memoir 4.

BROOM, R., G. W. H. SCHEPERS

1946 *The South African fossil ape-men, the* Australopithecinae. Transvaal Museum Memoir 2.

BURNS, P. E.

1971 New determination of australopithecine height. *Nature* 232:350.

BUTZER, K. W.

1974 Paleo-ecology of South African australopithecines: Taung revisited *Current Anthropology* 15:367–382, 398–426.

CAMPBELL, B. G.

1972 Conceptual progress in physical anthropology: fossil man. *Annual Review of Anthropology* 1:27–54.

COOKE, H. B. S.

1970 Notes from members. Canada: Dalhousie University, Halifax.

Society of Vertebrate Paleontology Bulletin 90:2.

DART, R. A.

1956 Relationships of brain size and brain pattern to human status. *South African Journal of Medical Science* 21:23–45.

1962 The Makapansgat pink breccia australopithecine skull. *American Journal of Physical Anthropology*, n.s. 20:110–126.

DUBOIS, E.

1897 Über die abhängigkeit des *Hirngewichts* von der Körpergrösse bei den Säugetieren. *Archiv für Anthropologie* 25:1–28.

1898 Remarks upon the brain-cast of *Pithecanthropus erectus. Proceedings of the Fourth International Congress of Zoology, Cambridge*, 85–86.

1921 On the significance of the large cranial capacity of *Homo Neandertalensis. Proceedings Koninklijke Nederlandse Akademie van Wetenschappen* 23(8):1271–1288.

GARN, S. M.

1965 *Human races* (second edition). Springfield, Illinois: Thomas.

GAUL, G.

1933 Über die Wachstumsveränderungen am Gehirnschädel des Orangutans. *Zeitschrift für Morphologie und Anthropologie* 33:362–394.

HIERNAUX, J.

1968 Variabilité du dimorphisme sexuel de la stature en Afrique Subsaharienne et en Europe," in *Anthropologie und Humangenetik: Festschrift zum Karl Saller*, 42–50. Stuttgart: Gustav Fischer Verlag.

HOLLOWAY, R. L.

1970a Australopithecine endocast (Taung specimen, 1924): a new volume determination. *Science* 168:966–968.

1970b New endocranial volumes for the australopithecines. *Nature* 227: 199–200.

1972a New australopithecine endocast, SK 1585, from Swartkrans, South Africa. *American Journal of Physical Anthropology* 37:173–186.

1972b "Australopithecine endocasts, brain evolution in the Hominoidea, and a model of hominid evolution," in *The functional and evolutionary biology of primates*. Edited by R. Tuttle, 185–204, Chicago: Aldine.

1973a New endocranial values for the East African early hominids. *Nature* 243:97–99.

1973b Endocranial volumes of early African hominids, and the role of the brain in human mosaic evolution. *Journal of Human Evolution* 2:449–459.

JACOB, T.

1973 Palaeo-anthropological discoveries in Indonesia with special reference to the finds of the last two decades. *Journal of Human Evolution* 2:473–485.

KEITH, A.

1925 The fossil anthropoid ape from Taung. *Nature* 115(2885):234–235.

1931 *New discoveries relating to the antiquity of man*. London: Williams and Norgate.

KURTÉN, B.

1969 "Sexual dimorphism in fossil mammals," in *Sexual dimorphism in fossil metazoa and taxonomic implications*. Edited by G. E. G. Westermann, 226–233. International Union of Geological Sciences, Series A, (1). Stuttgart: E. Schweizerbartische Verlag.

LEAKEY, L. S. B., M. D. LEAKEY

1964 Recent discoveries of fossil hominids in Tanganyika: at Olduvai and near Lake Natron. *Nature* 202:5–7.

LEAKEY, L. S. B., P. V. TOBIAS, J. R. NAPIER

1964 A new species of the genus *Homo* from the Olduvai Gorge. *Nature* 202:7–9.

LEAKEY, M. D., R. J. CLARKE, L. S. B. LEAKEY

1971 New hominid skull from Bed I, Olduvai Gorge, Tanzania. *Nature* 232(5309):308–312.

LE GROS CLARK, W. E.

1947 Observations on the anatomy of the fossil *Australopithecinae*. *Journal of Anatomy* 81:300–333.

1964 *The fossil evidence for human evolution* (second edition). Chicago: University of Chicago Press.

MAGLIO, V. J.

1973 Origin and evolution of the Elephantidae. *Transactions of the American Philosophical Society*, n.s. 63(3):1–149.

MATIEGKA, H.

1902 Über das Hirngewicht, die Schädelkapazität und die Kopfform, sowie deren Beziehungen zur psychischen Tätigkeit des Menschen. *S. B. kgl. böhmische Gesellschaft der Wissenschaften*, Prague *Math-nat. Cl.* 20:1–75.

MCHENRY, H. M.

1972 "Postcranial skeleton of early Pleistocene hominids." Unpublished doctoral dissertation, Harvard University, Cambridge, Massachusetts.

1974 How large were the australopithecines? *American Journal of Physical Anthropology* 40:329–340.

OPPENHEIM, S.

1911–1912 Zur Typologie des Primatencraniums. *Zeitschrift für Morphologie und Anthropologie* 14:1–204.

PAKKENBERG, H., J. VOIGT

1964 Brain weight of the Danes. *Acta Anatomica* 56:297–307.

PARTRIDGE, T. C.

1973 Geomorphological dating of cave opening at Makapansgat, Sterkfontein, Swartkrans and Taung. *Nature* 246(5428):75–79.

PEARL, R.

1905 Biometrical studies in man. I. Variation and correlation in brain weight. *Biometrika* 4:13–104.

PEARSON, E. S., J. WISHART, *editors*

1947 *Student's collected papers* (second edition). London: Biometrika Office.

PILBEAM, D. R.

1969 Early Hominidae and cranial capacity. *Nature* 224:386.

RANDALL, F. E.
1943–1944 The skeletal and dental development and variability of the gorilla. *Human Biology* 15:236–254, 307–337; 16:23–76.

ROBINSON, J. T.
1954 The genera and species of the Australopithecinae. *American Journal of Physical Anthropology* 12(2):181–200.

SCHREIDER, E.
1966 Brain weight correlations calculated from original results of Paul Broca. *American Journal of Physical Anthropology* 25:153–158.

SCHULTZ, A. H.
1962 Die Schädelkapazität männlicher Gorillas und ihr Höchstwert. *Anthropologischer Anzeiger* 25(2-3):197–203.
1965 The cranial capacity and the orbital volume of hominoids according to age and sex. *Homenaje a Juan Comas en su 65 anniversario*, volume two, 337–357. Editorial Libros de Mexico.

SELENKA, E.
1898 *Menschenaffen (Anthropomorphae). Studien über Entwicklung und Schädelbau*, volume one: *Rassen, Schädel und Bezahnung des Orangutans*, 1–91. Studien über Entwicklungsgeschichte der Tiere, Heft 6. Wiesbaden: C. W. Kreidel.
1899 *Menschenaffen (Anthropomorphae). Studien über Entwicklung und Schädelbau*, volume two: *Schädel des Gorillas und Schimpanses*, 95–160. Studien über Entwicklungsgeschichte der Tiere, Heft 7. Wiesbaden: C. W. Kreidel.

SNELL, O.
1892 Die Abhängigkeit des Hirngewichts von dem Körpergewicht und den geistigen Fähigkeiten. *Archiv für Psychiatrie und Nervenkrankheiten* 23:436–446.

SPANN, W., H. O. DUSTMANN
1965 Das menschliche Hirngewicht und seine Abhängigkeit von Lebensalter, Körperlänge, Todesursache und Beruf. *Deutsche Zeitschrift für gerichtliche Medizin* 56:299–317.

STEPHAN, H.
1972 "Evolution of primate brains: a comparative anatomical investigation," in *The functional and evolutionary biology of primates.* Edited by R. Tuttle, 155–174. Chicago: Aldine.

THENIUS, E.
1969 Stammesgeschichte der Säugetiere (einschliesslich der Hominiden). *Handbuch der Zoologie*, Band 8: *Mammalia*, Teil 2; Lieferung 47, 1–368. Berlin: W. de Gruyter.

TOBIAS, P. V.
1962 On the increasing stature of the Bushmen. *Anthropos* 57:801–810.
1963 Cranial capacity of *Zinjanthropus* and other australopithecines. *Nature* 197 (4869):743–746.
1965 New discoveries in Tanganyika: their bearing on hominid evolution. *Current Anthropology* 6(4):391–399, 406–411.
1967 *The cranium and maxillary dentition of* Australopithecus (Zinjanthropus) boisei. Cambridge: Cambridge University Press.

1968a "New African evidence on human evolution." Wenner-Gren Foundation Supper Conference, New York City, April, 1968.
1968b Cranial capacity in anthropoid apes, *Australopithecus* and *Homo habilis* with comments on skewed samples. *South African Journal of Science* 64(2):81–91.
1969 Commentary on new discoveries and interpretations of early African fossil hominids. *Yearbook of Physical Anthropology 1967*. Edited by S. Genoves, 24–30.
1970a Puberty, growth, malnutrition and the weaker sex — and two new measures of environmental betterment. *The Leech* XL(4): 101–107.
1970b Brain size, grey matter and race — fact or fiction? *American Journal of Physical Anthropology* 32(1):3–26.
1971a *The brain in hominid evolution*. New York/London: Columbia University Press.
1971b The distribution of cranial capacity values among living hominoids. *Proceedings of the Third International Congress of Primatology* 1:18–35. Basel: Karger.
1972a "Dished faces", brain size and early hominids. *Nature* 239 (5373): 468–469.
1972b "Growth and stature in southern African populations," in *Human biology of environmental change*. Edited by D. J. M. Vorster, 96–104. Adaptability Section, IBP, held in Blantyre, Malawi, April 1971.
1973 Implications of the new age estimates of the early South African hominids. *Nature* 246(5428):79–83.

VON BONIN, G.
1963 *The evolution of the human brain*. Chicago: University of Chicago Press.

WEIDENREICH, F.
1936 *Observations on the form and proportions of the endocranial casts of* Sinanthropus pekinensis, *other hominids and the great apes: a comparative study of brain size*. Paleontologia Sinica, series D, 7, 50 pages.
1943 *The skull of* Sinanthropus pekinensis. Paleontologia Sinica, 127, 486 pages.

WELLS, L. H.
1969 Faunal subdivision of the Quaternary in southern Africa. *South African Archaeological Bulletin* 24:93–95.

WOLPOFF, M. H.
1973 "Sexual dimorphism in the australopithecines," in *Paleoanthropology*. Edited by Russell H. Tuttle. World Anthropology. The Hague: Mouton.

ZUCKERMAN, S.
1928 Age-changes in the chimpanzee, with special reference to growth of brain, eruption of teeth, and estimation of age; with a note on the Taung ape. *Proceedings of the Zoological Society of London* 1:1–42.

Early Hominid Endocasts: Volumes, Morphology, and Significance for Hominid Evolution

R. L. HOLLOWAY

INTRODUCTION

The only direct evidence we have of the evolution of the hominid brain during the past three or four million years is paleoneurological, i.e. based on the observations and measurements of the endocranial casts of the fossil hominid specimens. To be sure, there are other lines of evidence, but those are indirect. For example: (1) the remaining hominid bony fragments that indicate different behavioral adaptations based on musculoskeletal patterns requiring reorganized neural contents (Holloway 1970c, 1973); (2) associated faunal and archaeological contexts such as stone tools made to standardized patterns, their spatial in situ distributions suggesting living, butchering, and/or camping sites, and the incorporation of larger protein-yielding mammals, which is a form of indirect evidence for increasing sophistication of hunting behavior, and its social nexus; all of these suggest changing adaptive behavioral patterns, both at the individual and social group levels, mediated by specific organizations of different neural centers and pathways of the brain; and finally, of course, is (3) our knowledge of present-day

Most of the data reported in this article were collected with the aid of National Science Foundation Grants 2300 and 92231 X, for which I am grateful. I wish to express my sincerest thanks to Professor Tobias and his staff at the University of Witwatersrand, South Africa, for encouragement, cooperation, and facilities; to the late Dr. L. S. B. Leakey, his wife Mary, and Richard E. Leakey for their cooperation and help in working on the East African hominids and to their staff; to Dr. A. Walker, University of Nairobi for his advice, encouragement, and friendship. Finally, I wish to thank Roberta Britt for her editorial assistance and typing of this manuscript.

Homo sapiens' behaviors and neurological organization, which uniquely show, when compared to any other living primates, symbolization and language, creativity, high degrees of foresight, memory, egocentrism, hedonism, self-perception, and identity, a very large mass of neural tissue (both absolutely and relatively), and expansion of a number of neural subsystems (e.g. Broca's and Wernicke's areas, the septum, amygdala, cerebellum, cells of Betz, etc.). We must assume these reorganizational changes were gained through natural selection for adaptive behavioral patterns from some apelike pongid of the late Miocene or early Pliocene. Indeed, it is the contention of this author that many of these changes were already present some two to three million years ago (Holloway 1966, 1967, 1970c, 1972a, 1973).

This paper will concentrate on the results of the last three or four years of research on the endocast remains (i.e. the direct evidence) of the fossil hominids discovered in both South and East Africa. In addition, a few preliminary results will be presented for hominids from Indonesia. Cranial capacity, or endocranial volumes, is seen as an important parameter for both taxonomic and functional (behavioral) considerations, but in a restricted way.

CRANIAL CAPACITY: SOME METHODOLOGICAL THOUGHTS

Cranial capacity is only an approximation of the size of the brain because, in operational terms, it measures only the volume of space inside the internal table of bone of a skull that can be filled with air or some other substance, such as water, seed, shot, etc., and includes non-neural tissues such as the meninges (including tentoria), blood vessels, cerebrospinal fluid, ventricles, and various cisternae, which may reach one-third of the volume. Yet, as with any morphological feature, or complex, it is measurable, and thus a true parameter possessing not only a potential for characterizing biological populations, but also relationships, both functional (i.e. "behavior," brain-body allometric relations), and evolutionary, i.e., rates of changes through time. Admittedly, it is a very gross parameter considered in any meaningful (substantive) functional sense, but its change through time should enable us to speculate, if nothing else, about probable selection pressures in the evolutionary past. As I have discussed elsewhere (Holloway 1972a), cranial capacities should be treated as an important population parameter; thus it is essential that the measurement of this variable be as accurate as possible, particularly in view of the returning interest in the problem of allometric growth and brain-body relationships (e.g., Count 1947; Sholl 1948; Jerison 1970; Kinsey 1972; Holloway 1972a, 1973; Stephan 1972; Leutenegger 1973, Gould 1966, 1971). In addition, of course, despite the usual and frustrating paucity of faithful imprints of the actual underlying cerebral morphological patterning of gyri and sulci, SOME patterning of a gross kind is discernable; this provides clues about reorganizational changes in cortical structure (e.g., lunate sulcus and association cortex) and thus, by linkage with comparative material on extant primate brains, on subcortical organization.

It is therefore surprising, at least to this author, that relatively little research effort has been directed toward a fuller understanding of this parameter and its accurate determination. As I have shown elsewhere (Holloway 1970a, 1970b, 1972a, 1973), many of the values previously published for the early hominids, particularly those of South Africa, were grossly in error. More recent work still in progress indicates that a number of the East Asian *Homo erectus* fossils are also incorrectly reported (e.g. Tobias 1971).

There is yet another reason for renewed efforts to study this parameter. Fossil hominids are usually quite "inconsiderate" to their discoverers because the fossil specimens are seldom complete or undistorted. It is difficult to write about methods of reconstruction and volume determination because each specimen often requires its own methodology, and few, if any, studies have carefully tested methods for accuracy and replicability, a sine qua non for scientific analysis. For example, Tobias (1971) has provided a number of calculations for cranial capacities of hominids from South and East Africa as well as from Indonesia, based on a "partial endocast" method, relying on extremely small samples and only a very few replications. I hasten to add, of course, that the same criticism can be applied to my own methods as described elsewhere (Holloway 1970a, 1970b, 1972a, 1973). Moving from value determinations for a moment, there have as yet been few if any studies on the mensuration of endocasts in terms of bivariate plots, allometric relationships, or multivariate analysis. In the latter case, I am aware of only one study: Sacher's (1970) factor analysis of quantitative primate neuroanatomical data. Unfortunately, this study, introduced as a critique of my own efforts to understand quantitative reorganizational changes (Holloway 1964, 1968), had indeed not "thrown out the baby with the bath," but simply drowned the beast in a plethora of well-known previously established generalities with no specific behavioral or functional relationships. It is a classic example of using techniques simply because they exist, without first asking the prior questions concerning what the mathematical manipulations can generate in terms of new hypotheses to be tested.

Since 1969, I have been fortunate to have the original fossils available for study, and a number of new volumetric determinations have been made. Wherever possible, I have attempted to make full endocast reconstructions, as these, if carefully done, are probably the most accurate way of obtaining the closest approximation to real values. A number of additional studies are under way at present, which are attempting to: (1) gain a large sample of accurate latex casts of extant primates; (2) compare these actual values with X-ray measurements of the same skulls; (3) study the interrelationships of a large number of endocast measures both in bivariate and multivariate ways; (4) study the question of laterality and cerebral dominance; (5) provide as accurate a basis as possible for extension of values to studies of brain-body relationships; (6) provide a minimal but accurate basis for reconstructing volumes from fragmented specimens; and (7) find measures and reorganizational endocast features suitable for correlation with functional ("behavioral") attributes. Perhaps a caveat is in order here: these studies in no way represent a total approach, and this paper should not be construed as a statement that paleoneurology is the only approach to the study of the evolution of the brain.

SOME RESULTS: ENDOCAST VOLUME DETERMINATION

Table 1 presents some endocast volume determinations resulting from studies since 1969, involving both South and East African early hominids. A few comments on several of these specimens are necessary. The value for the Taung specimen, 404 milliliters, is that for the actual child specimen; the adult value of 440 milliliters is suggested on the basis of a 92 percent completion of the growth figure on the basis of the dentition (Holloway 1970a, for references). Tobias' (1971) insistence on values of 500 milliliters (for the infant) and 540 milliliters (for the adult) are not based, as far as I am aware, on any actual determination on his part. Indeed, in 1969, both he and Alan Hughes corroborated my midline placement (Holloway 1970a). The MLD 37/38 specimen, which I list as 435 milliliters, is considered by Tobias (1971) as 480 milliliters on the basis of Dart's (1962) earlier analysis of external measurements of height and width. As Tobias (1971: 17) points out, the MLD 37/38 specimen is both wider and shorter than

Table 1. Some endocranial capacities for early hominids

Specimen	Region	Taxon	Capacity (cubic centimeters)	Method
Taung	South Africa	*A. africanus*	440 *	A — 1
STS60	South Africa	*A. africanus*	428	A — 1
STS71	South Africa	*A. africanus*	428	C — 2, 3
STS19/58	South Africa	*A. africanus*	436	B 2
STS5	South Africa	*A. africanus*	485	A 1
MLD37/38	South Africa	*A. africanus*	435	D 2
MLD1	South Africa	?	500 ± 20	B 3
SK1585	South Africa	*A. robustus*	530	A 1
OH5	East Africa	*A. robustus*	530	A 1
OH7	East Africa	*Homo habilis*	687	— 2
OH13	East Africa	*Homo habilis*	650	C 2
OH24	East Africa	*Homo habilis*	590	A 2
OH9	East Africa	*Homo erectus*	1067	A 1
OH12	East Africa	?	727	A 3
ER406	East Africa	*A. robustus*	510 ± 10	D 2
ER736	East Africa	*A. robustus*	504	A 1

* Refers to adult value. A refers to direct H_2O displacement of full or hemi-endocast with minimal plasticine reconstruction; B refers to partial endocast method; C refers to extensive plasticine reconstruction up to one-half of the endocast; D refers to use of MacKinnon et al. (1956) formula. Scale of 1–4 refers to confidence in reconstruction, with 1 highest.

STS 5, but the width is very little more, and the height is quite a bit lower. Using hemiskull sections from the right and left halves respectively of MLD 37/38 and STS 5 and opposing them so that the foramen magnum and occipital base line up, it is evident that the MLD 37/38 specimen is smaller, and thus I believe the 435 milliliter determination to be more accurate than Dart's (1962) and Tobias' (1971) 480 milliliter figure. MLD 1, consisting of an occipital fragment, was based on the partial endocast method (Tobias 1967, 1971), but only two determinations were attempted, giving a value of 500 ± 20 milliliters, but a low evaluation (three out of a scale of one to four); thus as Tobias (1971) suggests, further work is required on this specimen, which suggests a form perhaps intermediate between *A. africanus* and *A. robustus* taxa. Deleting it from the total gracile sample, the mean is 442 milliliters (adult) and not 494 milliliters, as Tobias (1971) claims. It is curious that Tobias disregards the STS 19 specimen's determination of 436 milliliters as "less reliable" (1971: 20), even though based on Tobias' own partial endocast methods, and his substitution of 530 cubic centimeters is based on no published methodology that I am aware of. Similarly, Tobias (1971) uses a value of 500 cubic centimeters for the SK1585 specimen discovered at Swartkrans by Brain (1970), based on a compromise of 475 milliliters by Brain and my determination of 530 milliliters, based on a hemiendocast reconstruction (Holloway 1972b). As I have shown in that publication, the similarity between SK1585 and Olduvai Hominid 5 is almost one of identity. Tobias' figure of 500 milliliters is not based on any actual determination as far as I can tell. Incidentally, it should be pointed out that Tobias' (1967) reconstruction of the O.H. 5 as 530 millimeters is in error, because he has reconstructed the anterior poles of the temporal lobes too far anteriorally (Holloway 1972b: Figure 8), although the actual volume difference would only change slightly, i.e. 522 milliliters. There simply are no hominids with temporal poles extending to the orbital nasal rostrum!

Table 2 presents my own results (these should be regarded as preliminary) for the Indonesian *Homo erectus* specimens, based on actual endocast reconstruction rather than partial endocast or partial H_2O displacements, which have inherent methodological difficulties. In the case of *Homo erectus* II, the value of 815 milliliters is based on a reconstruction made on a totally accurate, cured latex mold taken from the original specimen in G. H. R. von Koenigswald's laboratory in Frankfort; the full description is currently under preparation. The value given for *Homo erectus* I (943 milliliters) is based on a plaster cast made by the late Professor McGregor, checked against original

Table 2. Some tentative *Homo erectus* volumes

Specimen	Locality	Previous estimate	Current estimate	Method
Homo erectus I	Trinil	850 Tobias 1971*	943	A — 1
Homo erectus II	Sangiran	775 Tobias	815	A — 1
Homo erectus III	Sangiran	890 Tobias	Too Frag.	—
Homo erectus IV	Djetis, Sangiran	750 Tobias	900	B — 2
Homo erectus VI	Sangiran	975 Tobias	900+	A — 1
Homo erectus VII	Sangiran	915 Tobias	None	—
Homo erectus VIII	Sangiran	1029 Tobias	None	—

* All estimates taken from Tobias (1971), which should be consulted for details and past values published.

dimensions, and not based on the as yet unproven method of Tobias (1971). I believe McGregor's reconstruction is faultless, with a particularly excellent basal reconstruction. The value of 890 milliliters for *Homo erectus* III given by Tobias (1971) is interesting, but it only rests on the single parietal; it would be wise to refrain from accepting this value as final.

Homo erectus IV is another matter. The 750 milliliter value, reported by Tobias (1971) and originally published by von Koenigswald (1967), is based on a reconstruction that does not account for errors of misarticulation of the parietal upon the temporals and the consequent flattening of the vault. My own reconstruction of *H. erectus* IV, based on a very accurate latex mold of the original specimen and subsequent reconstruction, is 900 milliliters, a very considerable difference indeed. *Homo erectus* VI, discovered in the Sangiran dome in 1963 (Jacob 1964, 1966), is given as 975 milliliters in Tobias (1971) on the basis of Jacob (1966) and von Koenigswald (1967). Through the courtesy and cooperation of Dr. Jacob, I was able to make my own endocast of rubber latex in 1971, the reconstruction of which yields 900+. However, as some shrinkage occurred in the mold, the figure of 925 should only be regarded as a closer approximation until a new endocast is made and reconstructed. The remaining *Homo erectus* VII and VIII specimens require new molds before accepting the figures of 915 and 1029 milliliters respectively (Tobias 1971).

However, Tobias and I seem to be in very close agreement regarding the endrocranial volumes of the East African hominids, i.e. O.H. numbers 7, 13, 24, and the *H. erectus* O.H. number 9 from the LLK site, Bed II. Description of the methods used for these hominids, as well as those from East Lake Rudolf, have been published elsewhere (Holloway 1973), but a few comments are necessary. Unlike the South African forms, the East African materials do not include any natural endocasts, and reconstruction methods differ in that these are based on addition of plasticine to missing areas, with the exception of O.H. number 9 and E.R. 406. The parietals of O.H. number 7 fit most closely the 650 milliliter reconstruction of O.H. number 13 and the 727 milliliter reconstruction of O.H. number 12, from V.E.K. IV, which is perhaps the most dubious of all the reconstructions. The left parietal of O.H. number 7 extends over three-fourths of the O.H. number 5 whole endocast, and when approximated to the 590 milliliter O.H. number 24, extends beyond the midsagittal plane. The values of 510 ± 10 milliliters for the ROBUST E.R. 406 are based on the MacKinnon, et al. (1956) formula: $V = f\,[1/2\,(LWB) + 1/2\,(LWH)]$, where $f = 0.4518$ from the O.H. number 5 endocast, and L, W, B, H measurements are taken from the external bony points on E.R. 406, and bone thicknesses based on O.H. 5 are deducted from the external measurements. Incidentally, the above formula, applied to a growing sample of actual latex endocasts from gorilla and chimpanzee skulls, indicates a small range of *f*, which when averaged, allows specific prediction of volumes usually within 2 percent of the actual value. Furthermore, the coefficient *f* seems to be specific for each taxon (i.e. robust australopithecines, *Homo habilis*, and *Homo erectus*), and preliminary studies suggest it will be useful for estimating full volume where fragments are available. Indeed, the formula and the *f* coefficient are sensitive enough to differentiate *Pan paniscus* from *Pan troglodytes* endocasts, but this is so far based only on a sample of N = 6 for the *paniscus* group.

SOME STATISTICAL RESULTS

Table 3 presents a statistical analysis on the endocast volumes presented in Table 1. Needless to say, these results should not be accepted without a great deal of caution, considering the very small sample sizes and the inherent difficulties of reconstruction of volumes. The results clearly support the view of four distinct taxa when the Indonesian *Homo erectus* fossils are included.

Table 3. Some statistical results for the early hominids

Comparsion	T	P	
A. africanus versus *A. robustus*	2.69	< 0.05	$> .02$
A. africanus versus *H. habilis*	5.76	$< .001$	
A. robustus versus *H. habilis*	2.91*	$< .02$	$> .05$
A. taxa versus *H. habilis*	5.38	$< .001$	
A. africanus (N = 7) average = 442 milliliters			
A. robustus (N = 4) average = 517 milliliters			
H. habilis (N = 4), including OH #16, = 637 milliliters			

S. D's from assuming coefficient of variation at 10 percent, where $C.V. = \frac{S.D \times 100}{Mean}$

All P values from two-sided tables.

$$T = x - y \quad \sqrt{\frac{N_1 N_2}{N_1 N_2}}$$

$$\sqrt{\frac{(N_1 - 1)\, S.D._x^2 + (N_2 - 1)\, S. + Dy^2}{N_1 + N_2 - 2}}$$

S.D., *africanus* = 44 milliliters; *robustus* = 52 milliliters; *habilis* = 64 milliliters

* N.B., with N = 6 for both groups, T = 3.56, P < .01 > .001 (see Holloway 1973 for further explanation).

Of more interest, however, are the results shown in Table 4 on a few of the indices calculated from measurements taken directly on the endocasts rather than line-drawing projections. These figures illustrate that the morphological pattern of large cranial height, relative to the

Table 4. Some indices for endocranial casts

Specimens	Volume in milliliters	D arc / L arc	D arc / Length	L / H	H^3 / V
Taung	404	1.13	1.48	1.41	1.41
STS60	428	1.00	1.35	1.40	1.29
STS3	485	1.08	1.39	1.42	1.27
OH5	530	1.47	1.37	1.45	1.20
SK1585	530	1.73	1.42	1.43	1.37
ER732	506	1.06	1.42	1.48	1.13
OH24	590	1.01	1.29	1.40	1.32
OH13	650	1.17	1.49	1.48	1.16
OH9	1067	1.05	1.31	1.55	1.18
OH12	727	1.11	1.41	1.60	0.97
HEI	943	1.07	1.35	1.63	0.94
HEII	815	1.06	1.35	1.53	1.08
HEVI	900	1.00	1.26	1.60	1.01
Pan paniscus Av.:	328	.98	1.32	1.44	1.05
(N = 7) + range:	266–376	.96–1.01	1.28–1.37	1.34–1.53	.87–1.23
Pan trog. Av.:	406	.94	1.26	1.46	1.09
(N = 16) + range:	355–484	.87–1.01	1.20–1.36	1.39–1.56	.88–1.22
Gorilla gor. Av.:	516	.95	1.22	1.52	1.06
(N = 15) + range:	390–578	.90–1.01	1.19–1.28	1.47–1.60	.95–1.21

D and L arcs are tape measured on endocasts from frontal to occipital poles. L and H are length and height, being chord measurements from above landmarks. Height is from vertex to lowest portion of temporal lobe.

volume, is shared by the *A. africanus* and *H. habilis* taxa, and indeed, is a distinct pattern in comparison to either pongids (except *P. paniscus*) or *H. erectus* samples. It is interesting too that the *A. robustus* sample also shows a fairly high height index. These results give support, I believe, to the taxonomic relationships given by Eldredge and Tattersall (forthcoming) based on the doming versus platycephaly configuration found in these hominids. At the time of writing this report, I have only seen casts of Richard Leakey's new 2.6×10^6 year-old E.R. 1470 skull, but my impression is that it too will show a relatively high index when endocast.

Multivariate analysis, particularly by discriminant functions and canonical analysis is now underway, and results will be published at some later time. Naturally, results differ depending on the number and kind of variables used, but it is clear so far that at least six or seven variables

Table 5. Some speculative results on brain-body allometric relationships

Specimen	Capacity (milliliters)	Probable body weight (pounds)	"Progression index"
Taung	440	45	19.8
STS60	428	43.5	19.6
STS71	428	43.5	19.6
STS19/58	436	44	19.8
STS5	485	49	20.6
MLD37/38	435	44	19.8
MLD1	500	50.9	20.8
SK1585	530	54	21.2
OH5	530	54	21.2
OH7	687	69.9	23.4
OH13	650	66.1	22.9
OH24	590	60	22.1
OH9	1067	108	27.6
OH12	727	74	23.9
ER406	510	52	20.9
ER732	506	50.9	20.8

are necessary before unambiguous clusters, without overlapping, occur between the fossil hominids and small samples of gorilla and chimpanzee (*paniscus* and *troglodytes*) endocasts. Much more experimentation with sample sizes and variables is necessary before the significance of the results can be understood.

ALLOMETRY: BRAIN-BODY WEIGHT RESULTS

One of the most important uses of accurate endocranial volumes relates to the question of allometric change during the evolution of the hominid brain. Obviously, until we have better methods of ascertaining body size parameters, any discussion of these relationships is highly speculative. At the expense of being premature, at least on the basis of sample sizes and current understanding of body weights for the fossil hominids, Table 5 presents some hypothetical body weights and "progression indices" (see Stephan 1972) for the hominids. These results are based on the following:

$X = cY^b$, where X = brain weight in grams and Y = body weight, also in grams. Then, $\text{Log}_e X = \log_e c + b\log_e Y$.

These formulas rest upon the work of Snell (1892), Dubois (1897), and von Bonin (1937), and were throughly discussed by Count (1947) and Sholl (1948; see also Gould 1966, 1971 for further discussion of the problems associated with using these relationships).

During the Burg-Wartenstein Conference in 1970 (Holloway 1972a), I used Lovejoy and Heiple's (1970) estimate of gracile australopithecine body weight at forty-five pounds and my derived mean of 442 milliliters for brain volume. This suggested a brain-body ratio of 1 : 46, as in present *Homo sapiens*. Using this ratio and assuming it was the same in all gracile australopithecines, it was possible to calculate probable body weights and then solve simultaneously for c and b in the above equation. This led to an exponent b = 1 and c = 0.02165, giving an equation:

$$\mathrm{Log}_e X = -3.83244 + \log_e Y.$$

The equation above was then checked using Tobias' (1971) figures for modern man.

Thus, these preliminary results are in agreement with Kinsey's (1972) speculation that selection pressures for increased body size during hominid evolution might account for the large amount of increase in brain weight. Of course, two equations are probably necessary: one for log-log regressions within taxa and another one for regressions between taxa. The above equation has been treated as if it were for both within and between taxa, which is surely erroneous. But our data are nowhere complete or reliable enough to entertain any confidence in these relationships at present. Equally speculative are the "progression indices" given in Table 5 based on the use of this equation and Stephan's (1972) basal line of:

$$\mathrm{Log}_{10} H = 1.632 + 0.63 \log_{10} b.$$

The results do place the hominids, even the robust and gracile australopithecines, within the range of values for modern man. I would like to make it clear that I do not place any great confidence in these preliminary results thus far and look forward to seeing critiques and further work on this problem and its interpretation by my colleagues (see Holloway 1973 for further skepticism).

SOME MORPHOLOGICAL CONSIDERATIONS

Degrees of Cerebral Folding

Unfortunately, the faithfulness with which cerebral sulci and gyri leave their imprints through the cerebrospinal fluid and meninges to the internal bony table of the skull leaves much to be desired. In the australopithecines, only Taung, STS60, Type 3, and SK1585 show any definable sulcal morphology. O.H. number 5 and the *Homo habilis* specimens show none, nor do any of the erectus types, except I and II from Java; neither do adult chimpanzee and gorilla endocasts. Nevertheless, when one compares the Taung, STS60, and Type 3 endocasts with present chimpanzee or gorilla endocasts or with photographs of the actual brain, there is clearly increased fissuration observable in the frontal lobe, i.e. anterior to the central sulcus. This is extremely difficult to quantify, but perhaps a metric analysis of distances between apexes of gyri might indicate this. Part of this problem, of course, relates to the age of the individual specimen; the sulci and gyri being more apparent in younger individuals, as is the case for the increased "progression indices," the high relative brain size, and the expansion of height variables, more cortical folding, particularly, would be a logical outcome.

Position of the Lunate Sulcus

Elsewhere (Holloway 1970a, 1972a), I have suggested that the disposition of this landmark is indeed in a posterior position compared to any of the pongid brains, at least in the Taung and SK1585 endocasts. Unfortunately, none of the other hominid specimens show this landmark, and even endocasts of adult pongids are very difficult for any precise location of the sulcus, the major evidence coming from the original brains and/or their photographs (e.g. Connolly 1950; Retzius 1906). Surely, Dart (1925, 1956) was correct in his posterior placement of the sulcus, as was Schepers (1946). The significance of this has been pointed out many times (e.g. Dart 1925, 1956; Schepers 1946; Holloway 1964, 1966, 1968, 1970c, 1972a). It is perhaps the most conclusive proof for reorganization of the brain from a pongid to human pattern, as it correlates with increased expansion of height and posterior parietal "association" cortex.

Temporal and Cerebellar Lobes

Overall, there is a distinct difference between the temporal-cerebellar cleft formed by the petrous portion of the temporal bone between pongids and the early hominids. The angle is indeed more acute, suggesting an expansion of the latero-basal and posterior portions of the temporal lobe because there do not appear to be any significant differences in the shape of the anterior cerebellar lobes between pongids (chimpanzee and gorilla) and hominids. In addition, the anterior tip of the temporal lobe is significantly enlarged and pointed in hominids when compared to pongids. Part of this difference rests with the different growth and shape of the wings of the sphenoid, which sharply delineate temporal from frontal cortex in the hominid, but not the pongid, endocasts.

Cerebellar morphology on endocasts has not been thoroughly studied using large samples of pongid endocasts; this study is currently in progress in my laboratory. Judging from what I have examined thus far, there is a considerable range of shape in pongids, and I do not feel that hominid endocasts are going to show any strikingly different patterns. The cerebellar lobes of SK1585, O.H. numbers 5, 13, 24, 9, and *Homo erectus* II and VI seem advanced in comparison to those of Taung, STS60, and STS19/58. STS5 defies description, but might be related to distortion in this region of the skull and to preparation.

Frontal Lobe and Rostrum

In all the hominid specimens, in which this region is available for examination, clear differences exist when compared to any of the pongids. The frontal lobes are more rounded and broader in their anterior portion, and all show a more pronounced inferior third frontal gyrus that is deeper and usually cleanly separated from the supra-anterior aspect of the temporal lobe. To be sure, a large series of pongid endocasts shows considerable variation in morphological shape; but in addition to the differences noted above, one usually finds a more defined concavity in the orbital portion of the hominid frontal, and the rostrum resting on the cribriform plate is usually further back and not as punctate as in pongids.

I have tried a small pilot study of surface areas for the endocasts, which so far indicates no significant differences in frontal lobe size between hominids and pongids (for a review on actual brains, see Holloway 1968), but this depends on where one places the central sulcus.

In sum then, the whole brain of hominids, based on the endocast studies conducted so far, shows a number of reorganized features, mainly based on expansion of posterior and upper parietal cortex, expansion of inferior and anterior temporal cortex, more gyral and sulcal folding, and more modern disposition of the so-called "Broca's area" of the frontal lobe.

LATERALITY AND CEREBRAL DOMINANCE

A number of interesting new observations have appeared recently on the questions of laterality and cerebral dominance. LeMay and Culebras (1972) have found that both coronal sections of brains and carotid arteriograms are able to demonstrate more highly developed parietal operculi in thirty-eight of forty-four right-handed people (see also Geschwind and Levitsky 1968). They also examined the La Chapelle-aux-Saints skull and suggested that the sylvian point was higher on the right. Having examined this endocast myself, I am not certain that the sylvian fissures can be so readily distinguished. In any event, none of the australopithecine or *Homo erectus* endocasts permit extension of these methods. McAdam and Whitaker (1971) found slow negative potentials a maximum over Broca's area of the left hemisphere during subject pronunciation and bilaterally symmetrical potentials for non-speech control gestures. These constitute the first physiological evidence of a direct nature for localization of language production in normal humans. Morrell and Salamy (1971) also showed consistently high amplitudes of cortical evoked responses from the left hemispheres. Kinsbourne (1972) has shown that right- and left-handed people differ in the direction they look when thinking about either verbal or numerical and spatial problems. When solving verbal problems, right-handers look right, but they look left when doing numerical and spatial problems. This fits perfectly with conceptions of lateralization of language functions to the left cerebral hemisphere and spatial and temporal processes to the right.

Most recently, Kimura (1973) has summarized the results of her research at Montreal Neurological Institute. Hemispheric specializations were found for both right and left sides: dichotomic listening tasks gave higher scores in the right ear, and thus the left cerebral hemisphere; melodies were better scored by the left ear (thus, the right hemisphere) as were other vocal nonspeech sounds, e.g. laughing, crying, and coughing, but consonant-vowel sounds were better heard through the right ear, suggesting a specialized function of the left hemisphere. Using a tachiscope, Kimura found better recognition of words and letters by the right visual field than the left, whereas location of dots in a spatial field was better performed by the left visual field. Depth-perception test scores were higher when information was presented to the right cerebral hemisphere. These data lend considerable support to the data assembled from other tests and ablation studies regarding dominance of left cerebral hemisphere for language tasks, and the right for spatial temporal appreciation.

Two questions might be discussed with regard to these findings: (1) what do the endocast studies show in terms of lateralization, and (2) what do these studies suggest in the way of a clearer basis for speculation regarding language origins and functions?

First, the endocasts existing so far for the South and East African australopithecines, including fossils designated *Homo habilis*, are not adequate for measuring lateralization. Only O.H. number 5 is complete on both sides, but the presence of excrescences from fissures make exact measurements impossible. The *Homo erectus* materials from Indonesia offer a better chance, and these (I, II, and VI) are currently under investigation. The main problem is to place a midsagittal plane [MSP] and accurately measure lateral deviations from this plane, sampling numerous points with calipers coordinated equally with the MSP. The major areas for measuring a large cluster of points would be Broca's area, the supratemporal regions, Wernicke's area, and the level of the sylvian fissure apex. Needless to say, there are a number of inherent difficulties with this approach.

With regard to language, the most extensively cited frameworks are those of Geschwind (1965) and Lancaster (1968), which consider early language development (sensu phylogenetics) as mainly devoted to the evolution of "object naming," which assumes that human communication is more of a cerebral operation than in other primates, among whom communication is mostly emotional. That is, humans are capable of nonlimbic to nonlimbic associations, whereas other primates are programmed for cortical-limbic operations. These views are based on a large amount of clinical data (viz. Geschwind 1965) and on a not very clear appreciation of cortical-to-cortical and cortical-subcortical pathway differences in the neural organization of different primates. In recent years, one important basis for the above viewpoint has undergone some crucial revamping: the problem of cross-modal perception. Recent studies have shown human infants without language abilities capable of cross-modal transfers between touch and vision, and more importantly, Davenport and Rogers (1970) have shown chimpanzees and orangutans capable of some cross-modal matching (see also Drewe et al. 1970, for a critical appraisal of cross-modal matching).

The question is, does the neuroanatomical and neurophysiological evidence jibe with the above hypotheses? That other primates are incapable of cortico-cortical connections is not based on any real evidence. As far as the comparative evidence is concerned, the higher primates, at least, share the major structures (i.e. posterior parietal association cortex, two-way connections between areas 37 and the pulvinar of the thalumus, and cortico-cortical fibers, both U-shaped, and the longitudinal fasçiculi). In addition, children show an extremely early capacity for generation of language skills long before the cortical areas supposedly responsible for these abilities have matured (e.g. see Conel 1963). Another criticism is that as Bronowski and Bellugi (1970) and also Lenneberg (1967) have shown, human language involves far more than simply "object naming" even in its earliest ontogenetic manifestation (see also Church 1971, McNeill 1970). Finally, but perhaps even more importantly, is the question of learning and memory (coding, storage, retrieval, recomposition, etc., i.e. John 1971), and how we view the operation of neural subsystems, i.e. in strict localizationist, equipotential, or some combination of viewpoints. In other words, the systems of fibers and tissues that mediate human language (involving reception, articulation, and composition of symbolic streams of communication) may indeed be quantitatively greater in human than in nonhuman brains, but one is still left with the question of ability to encode symbols at the microanatomical and thus neurochemical levels. I do not think that either the neurophysiological or neuroanatomical evidence can support a view so dichotomous in nature about the separation of emotional (i.e. "limbic") and purely cognitive (i.e. "cerebral") operations in communicative behavior. Memories do not become established without the operation of both cortical and subcortical components, and communication per se is always a stream of ongoing accommodations among social actors invoking emotional involvement at some level. Indeed, even self-communication, i.e. thought, planning, "rehearsing," etc., are usually imbued with some degree of emotion. Finally, as the evidence of Stephan (1972) and Stephan and Andy (1969) indicates, the human brain has not just invoked evolutionary enlargement of the cortical structures above. Consequently, while the frameworks of Geschwind (1965) and Lancaster (1968) have correctly emphasized the importance of cortical evolutionary changes and human language, they have done so at the expense of oversimplifying the nature of the evidence and the need for looking at language phenomena at a more molecular level. These viewpoints and popularizations of them greatly confuse, I believe, the probable evolutionary significance of language, its role in past human adaptations, and the interplay among the evolution of language, motor skills, tool-making, hunting abilities, social behavior, and lateralization of function. Obviously, "object-naming," i.e. the assignation of standardized codes for referents would have had great selective advantage, but this aspect is but one part of a more complex whole that needs to receive more thought than it has before.

SOME SPECULATION

The endocasts studied thus far of the East and South African early hominids show evidence for an earlier antecedent stage of reorganization along human lines prior to significant enlargement (see Holloway 1966, 1968, 1972a, b, 1973, for discussion and relevance to our understanding of human mosaic evolution). This fact has a significance because it is in direct contrast to the point made recently by Washburn and Strum (1972) that tool elaboration starts late in the hominid record. The probable brain-body ratios and the eruption sequence of the dentition all suggest that an important component of early hominid adaptation was an increased duration of growth and probably an increased post-natal dependency time. As I have suggested elsewhere (Holloway 1968, 1969), I believe that SOCIAL CONTROL was one of the most important aspects of early human evolution and that language was a critical component of engendering social control. Language in its broadest sense and tool-making are examples of social control and reflect a very substantial similarity of cognitive structuring, as I have suggested elsewhere (Holloway 1969). At the same time, adaptation to a savanna econiche accompanied by an increasing emphasis on the procurement of resources that are rich in protein by small groups, in which adults are responsible for infant care for longer durations, would have placed strong selection pressures for cooperative behavior, developed through social control and nourishment, as well as finely coordinated motor skills, involving increasing utilization of the environment for tools and weapons and appreciation of complex spatiotemporal relationships. Not only are the hand-eye and left-right hand coordination mechanisms, as used in making a hand-axe for example, involved here, but also the ability to compute trajectories for throwing objects at moving animals (predators and prey) and for traversing the savanna econiche to find water sources, feeding areas, home bases, shelters, and spoors. Both humans and apes may indeed be capable of showing underarm and overhead throwing motions, but only the human animal is capable of delivering great power, accuracy, and distance with overhead throwing and thrusting, a point that Washburn and Strum (1972) fail to emphasize. The archeological record, at least for the early hominids, shows a large number of spheroidal stone objects (e.g. Leakey 1971) that were most likely used as projectiles. Indeed, throwing objects with considerable force and accuracy over a significant distance must have been an important component of early hominid scavenging, hunting, and predator protection from the beginning. The ability of chimpanzees to engage in this activity has been well documented (e.g. Goodall 1971). As far as I am aware, only the human brain is capable of complex computations and coordinations involving accurate and forceful throwing of objects at both moving and stationary targets. Indeed, is there any culture existing in which object-throwing is not a considerable component of both child and adult play, in which symbols, fantasies, and social control are not operative? Most of human existence, except for the last eight to ten thousand years, has not been sedentary, and one should expect that evolution would work for a neural system of components that would best integrate both hand-eye and language coordination. These skills were surely extremely important in human evolution, but they did not develop in the abstract, i.e. outside the contexts of social existence; consequently, one must wonder at the significance of, and problems associated with, the continued evolutionary elaboration of the human brain, musculoskeletal system, prolonged duration of growth, and social control.

As Washburn and Strum (1972) have noted, the corpus callosum is certainly the largest in man and must have extremely important functions; this is confirmed by the split-brain experiment of Gazzaniga (1970) and Sperry (1968). Indeed, its significance lies in coordinating and exchanging information between hemispheres and cortical-subcortical subsystems, between cognition shaped through symbol systems and coordinated action in spatiotemporal, and, one should add, social environments. Also, the current data (e.g. Kimura 1973) on sex differences in human abilities relating to higher scores for females in verbal tests and higher scores on spatiotemporal tasks for males, based on both psychological and neurological data, raise some interesting implications regarding our present speculative frameworks about sexual division of labor in early human evolution, as do Kimura's observations of the free use of the right hand in communicative actions. Are there sex-related genetic differences existing for the differential development of these skills in the sexes? Or are these the result of developmental differences, i.e. the timing of maturation of particular cortical-subcortical regions in male and female? My own belief is that natural selection did favor a kind of sexual specialization and division of labor of skills that were complementary to a full social adaptive existence early in hominid evolution (e.g. Holloway 1966, 1967, 1972) that related to developmental rather than genetic differences between males and females. That is, females have always matured earlier than males, linguistic specialization or competence comes earlier in females than in males, and the dominant hemisphere's neural development (nerve cells and mylinogenesis) develops earlier on the left than on the right side. The right hemisphere, however, develops later in both males and females, but in males it develops in a milieu of economic and play behaviors reflecting an early division of roles and tasks between the sexes. Obviously, this is a system with considerable plasticity in it, with genetic components shared both by male and female chromosomes, but in which other genetic differences related to maturation schedules and endocrine target tissue relationships differ between the sexes.

The large-scale later evolution of the brain, i.e. following the early hominid australopithecine phases when the brain more than doubled itself in size (e.g. from about 450 milliliters to 1,400 milliliters), is not, I believe, tied in directly with the elaboration of stone tools. I believe the significance of stone tools as direct read-outs, as it were, of hominid neurological organization and motor skill has been greatly overemphasized. The stone tools, associated faunal remains, and traces of shelters and camping sites are but clues to a more important matrix of social behavioral adaptations that involved cooperation, symbolic cognitive structuring, sexual division of labor, and prolonged dependency, maturation, and training of offspring. The radical innovation that melded these components together was an evergrowing sophistication of symbolically mediated systems of social controls and a positive interrelationship between prolonged growth, social nurturing, and cultural and neural complexity (Holloway 1967). The study of endocasts shows, I suggest, that this process began quite early in hominid evolution.

REFERENCES

BRAIN, C. K.

1970 New finds at the Swartkrans Australopithecine site. *Nature* 225: 1112–1118.

BRONOWSKI, J., U. BELLUGI

1970 Language, name, and concept. *Science* 168:669.

CHURCH, J.

1971 "The ontogeny of language," in *The ontogeny of vertebrate behavior*. Edited by H. Moltz, 451–479. New York: Academic Press.

CONEL, J. L.
1963 *The postnatal development of the human cerebral cortex*, volumes one through seven. Cambridge, Massachusetts: Harvard University Press.

CONNOLLY, C. J.
1950 *External morphology of the primate brain*. Springfield, Illinois: C. C. Thomas.

COUNT, E. W.
1947 Brain and body weight in man: their antecedents in growth and evolution. *Annals, New York Academy of Science* 46:993–1122.

DART, R. A.
1925 *Australopithecus Africanus*: the man-ape of South Africa. *Nature* 115:195–199.
1956 The relationship of brain size and brain pattern to human status. *South African Journal of Medical Science* 21:23–45.
1962 The Makapansgat pink breccia Australopithecine skull. *American Journal of Physical Anthropology* 20:119–126.

DAVENPORT, R. K., C. M. ROGERS
1970 Intermodal equivalence of stimuli in apes. *Science* 168:279.

DREWE, E. A., G. ETTLINGER, A. D. MILNER, R. E. PASSINGHAM
1970 A comparative review of the results of neuropsychological research on man and monkey. *Cortex* 6:129–163.

DUBOIS, E.
1897 Über die Abhängigkeit des Hirngewichts von der Körpergrösse bei den Säugetieren. *Archiv für Anthropologie* 25:1–28.

GAZZANIGA, M. S.
1970 *The bisected brain*. New York: Appleton-Century-Crofts.

GESCHWIND, N.
1965 Disconnexion syndromes in animals and man. *Brain* 88:237–294, 585–644.

GESCHWIND, N., W. LEVITSKY
1968 Human brain: left-right asymmetries in temporal speech region. *Science* 161:186–187.

GOODALL, J.
1971 *In the shadow of man*. London: Collins.

GOULD, S. J.
1966 Allometry and size in ontogeny and phylogeny. *Biological Review* 41:587–640.
1971 Geometric similarity in allometric growth: a contribution to the problem of scaling in the evolution of size. *American Naturalist* 105:113–136.

HOLLOWAY, R. L.
1964 "Some quantitative relations of the primate brain." Unpublished doctoral dissertation, University of California at Berkeley.
1966 Cranial capacity, neural reorganization and hominid evolution: a search for more suitable parameters. *American Anthropologist* 68:103–121.
1967 The evolution of the human brain: some notes toward a synthesis

between neural structure and the evolution of complex behavior. *General Systems* 12:3–19.

1968 The evolution of the primate brain: some aspects of quantitative relationships. *Brain Research* 7:121–172.

1969 Culture: a *human* domain. *Current Anthropology* 10:395–412.

1970a Australopithecine endocast (Taung specimen, 1924): a new volume determination. *Science* 168:966–968.

1970b New endocranial values for the Australopithecines. *Nature* 277: 199–200.

1970c "Neural parameters, hunting, and the evolution of the human brain," in *The primate brain.* Edited by C. R. Noback and W. Montagna, 299–310. New York: Appleton-Century-Crofts.

1972a "Australopithecine endocasts, brain evolution in the Hominoidea, and a model of hominid evolution," in *The functional and evolutionary biology of the primates.* Edited by R. Tuttle 185–204. Chicago: Aldine.

1972b New Australopithecine endocast, SK 1585, from Swartkrans, South Africa. *American Journal of Physical Anthropology* 37: 173–186.

1973 Endocranial capacities of the early African hominids and the role of the brain in human mosaic evolution. *Journal of Human Evolution* 2:449–459.

JACOB, T.

1964 A new hominid skull cap from Pleistocene Sangiran. *Anthropologica* 6:97–104.

1966 The sixth skull cap of *Pithecanthropus erectus. American Journal of Physical Anthropology* 25:243–260.

JERISON, H. J.

1970 "Gross brain indices and the analysis of fossil endocasts," in *The primate brain.* Edited by C. R. Noback and W. Montagna, 225–244. New York: Appleton-Century-Crofts.

JOHN, E. ROY

1971 "Brain mechanisms of memory," in *Psychobiology*. Edited by J. L. McGaugh, 200–284. New York: Academic Press.

KIMURA, D.

1973 The asymmetry of the human brain. *Scientific American* 228(3): 70–78.

KINSBOURNE, M.

1972 Eye and head turning indicates cerebral lateralization. *Science* 176:539–541.

KINSEY, W. G.

1972 Allometric transposition of brain/body size relationships in hominid evolution. *American Journal of Physical Anthropology* 37:442.

LANCASTER, J. B.

1968 "Primate communication systems and the emergence of human language," in *Primates.* Edited by P. C. Jay, 439. New York: Holt, Rinehart, and Winston.

LEAKEY, M. D.
1971 *Olduvai Gorge*, volume three. Cambridge: Cambridge University Press.

LE MAY, M., A. CULEBRAS
1972 Human brain — morphological differences in the hemispheres demonstrable by carotid arteriography. *The New England Journal of Medicine* 287:168–170.

LENNEBERG, E. H.
1967 *The biological foundation of language*. New York: Wiley.
1969 On explaining language. *Science*, 164:635–642.

LEUTENEGGER, W. A.
1973 Encephalization in Australopithecines: a new estimate. *Folia Primatologica* 19:9–17.

LEVY, J.
1969 Possible basis for the evolution of lateral specialization of the human brain. *Nature* 224:614–615.

LOVEJOY, C. O., K. G. HEIPLE
1970 A reconstruction of the femur of *Australopithecus Africanus. American Journal of Physical Anthropology* 32:33–40.

MAC KINNON, I. L., J. A. KENNEDY, T. V. DAVIES
1956 The estimates of skull capacity from Roentgenologic measurements. *American Journal of Roentgenography, Radiation Therapy, and Nuclear Medicine* 76:303–310.

MC ADAM, D. W., H. A. WHITAKER
1971 Language production: electroencephalographic localization in the normal human brain. *Science* 172:499-502.

MC NEILL, D.
1970 "The development of language," in *Carmichael's manual of child psychology*, volume one. Edited by P. H. Mussen, 1061–1162. New York: Wiley.

MORRELL, L. K., J. G. SALAMY
1971 Hemispheric asymmetry of electrocortical responses to speech stimuli. *Science* 174:164–166.

RETZIUS, G.
1906 *Das Affenhirn*. Jena: G. Fischer.

SACHER, G. A.
1970 "Allometric and factorial analysis of brain structure in insectivores and primates," in *The primate brain*. Edited by C. R. Noback and W. Montagna, 245–288. New York: Appleton-Century-Crofts.

SCHEPERS, G. W. H.
1946 "The endocranial casts of the South African ape-men," in *The South African fossil ape-men, the Australopithecinae*. Edited by R. Broom and G. W. H. Schepers, 167–272. Transvaal Museum Memoir 2.

SHOLL, D. A.
1948 The quantitative investgation of the vertebrate brain and the applicability of allometric formulae to its study. *Proceedings of the Royal Society (Biology)* 135:243–258.

SNELL, O.

1892 Die Abhängigkeit des Hirngewichts von dem Körpergewicht und geistigen Fähigkeiten. *Archive für Psychiatrie und Nervenkrankheiten* 23:436–446.

SPERRY, R. W.

1968 *Mental unity following surgical disconnection of the cerebral hemispheres.* The Harvey Lectures 62:293–323.

STEPHAN, H.

1972 "Evolution of primate brains: a comparative anatomical investigation," in *The functional and evolutionary biology of primates.* Edited by R. Tuttle, 155–174. Chicago: Aldine.

STEPHAN, H., O. J. ANDY

1969 Quantitative comparative neuroanatomy of primates: an attempt at phylogenetic interpretation. *Annals, New York Academy of Science* 167:370–387.

TOBIAS, P. V.

1967 *Olduvai Gorge,* volume two. Cambridge: Cambridge University Press.

1971 *The brain in hominid evolution.* New York: Columbia University Press.

VON BONIN, G.

1937 Brain weight and body weight in mammals. *Journal of Genetic Psychology* 16:379–389.

VON KOENIGSWALD, G. H. R.

1967 Neue Dokumente zur menschlichen Stammesgeschichte. *Ecologae Geologicae Helvetiae* 60:641–655.

WASHBURN, S. L., S. C. STRUM

1972 "Concluding comments," in *Perspectives in human evolution,* volume two. Edited by S. L. Washburn and P. C. Dolhinow, 469–491. New York: Holt, Rinehart, and Winston.

Maturation and Longevity in Relation to Cranial Capacity in Hominid Evolution

GEORGE A. SACHER

INTRODUCTION

A characterizing feature in the evolution of genus *Homo* was the increase in brain size. The fossil evidence indicates that this increase was extraordinary in both magnitude and rate. It was accompanied by the development of speech and symbolic behavior, which unfortunately left no artifacts prior to the cave art of the Upper Paleolithic, and by the development of toolmaking behavior, for which there is voluminous evidence. The successful accomplishment of this remarkable transition required that a number of other anatomical and physiological adaptations accompany the modifications of brain and behavior. Some of these leave traces in the fossil record, but the majority do not.

One characteristic that has had great significance for the course of human evolution is length of life. Man is, by a wide margin, the longest-lived primate and also, by a smaller margin, the longest-lived mammal. This longevous trait was acquired during the course of human evolution, and it is distinctive and important enough to merit being listed, along with symbolic and toolmaking behavior, as a distinguishing feature of the human species.

I shall look at the human lifespan in three contexts that are necessary, though not by themselves sufficient, for an understanding of how human longevity evolved in the past and for an apprecation of some

Work supported by the United States Atomic Energy Commission. I wish to make special acknowledgment of the contribution of Mr. M. L. Jones, who has given me free access to the extensive and thoroughly documented unpublished data gathered in his research project on the survival and reproduction of mammals in captivity.

of the ways in which it may evolve in the future. One context is concerned with the constitutional factors, including cranial capacity, that are associated with length of life in recent and fossil mammals, including hominids. Another examines the selective forces that operated in the evolution of mammalian and primate longevity, both at the population level and at higher levels of phylogenetic branching. The third outlook is that of the gerobiologist, examining the problem of the finitude of life from the standpoint of the evolved molecular-genetic mechanisms that combat aging processes and extend life.

It will be seen that some determiners of man's longevity lie far back in his mammalian heritage, while others derive from his primate, hominid, or human nature. The data about the more specific adaptations at the genus or species levels are limited, and my competence in that domain is limited also, but I hope I shall be able to raise some questions that others will find it worthwhile to answer.

MEASURES OF LENGTH OF LIFE

There are several ways of estimating the longevity parameter for a sample. Among the most widely used is the life expectation, which is the average survival time of a sample, measured from some specified age. However, the life expectation cannot be used for the analysis of species differences in longevity, because the principal sources of longevity data for the analysis are published zoo reports, and these almost always consist of tabulations of the longer survival times, and frequently of only the maximum survival, for each species. This means that we must abandon the use of mean or median value statistics and resort instead to the use of extreme value statistics. This is now a highly developed branch of statistics (Gumbel 1958). The measure I shall use to represent the species longevity parameter is the maximum longevity reported for the species in properly documented tabulations of survival data. This is, fortunately, a usable measure in the situation where we have only approximate estimates of the sizes of the samples on which the maximum values are based, because of the mathematical properties of the Gompertz mortality function that characterizes the mortality processes of all mammalian species. The defining property of the Gompertz equation is that the age-specific death rate for a population increases exponentially with age.

$$\rho = -\frac{1}{N}\frac{dn}{dt} = \rho_0 e^{\alpha t}. \tag{1}$$

The number, N, living at age t is then

$$N = N_0 \exp\left[-\frac{\rho_0}{\alpha}\left(e^{\alpha t} - 1\right)\right] \tag{2}$$

For large values of t this reduces to

$$\frac{N}{N_o} = \exp\left[-\frac{\rho_0}{\alpha} e^{\alpha t}\right] \tag{3}$$

The expected time, t_{max}, at which one out of an initial sample of N_o will be found alive is, therefore,

$$t_{max} = \frac{1}{\alpha}\left(\log \log N_o - \log \frac{\rho_0}{\alpha}\right) \tag{4}$$

In consequence, the maximum expected survival increases very slowly with N_o. What this means in practice, as I have by now confirmed for a large number of species, is that as the number of maximum survival times from different zoos increases, the maximum of this set of values increases very slowly and becomes virtually stationary for practical purposes.

In summary, the maximum longevity statistic is a theoretically appropriate estimate of the species longevity parameter. More sophisticated extreme value statistics are available if needed (Gumbel 1958), but the results I have obtained would not be materially altered thereby.

THE ROLE OF BRAIN AND BODY WEIGHT IN MAMMALIAN LONGEVITY

Rubner, one of the first students of mammalian energy metabolism, showed in 1908 that the metabolic rate per gram of tissue is an inverse function of body size and that the lifetime energy expenditure, estimated as (metabolic rate) × (lifespan), for several species of domestic animals (ranging in body size from cat to cow) is approximately constant, with an average value of roughly 200 kilocalories per gram (Rubner 1908). This was widely accepted for many years as evidence for a "wear-and-tear" theory of aging, which posited that each species has a lifespan determined by the rate at which it exhausts a fixed number of calories' worth of metabolic capacity. However, Rubner also reported that the lifetime energy expenditure for man is more like 800 kilocalories per gram. This discordant finding, together with data for a few other species that differ markedly in lifespan although they are roughly equal in body weight, led a contemporary anatomist, Friedenthal, to modify Rubner's rule by adding the further hypothesis that big-brained animals live longer than small-brained animals of equal body size (Friedenthal 1910). However, Friedenthal's conclusion did not find general acceptance, for it was only rarely cited in following years, and I was unaware of it in 1955 when I rediscovered the same relationship (Sacher 1959). Since that time I have analyzed data on several hundred species, thereby giving quantitative expression to the generalizations of Rubner and Friedenthal and, moreover, providing evidence for other constitutional factors that are functionally related to lifespan in mammals.

Mammalian lifespans have a nominal fiftyfold range of variation; body weights vary by a factor of 4×10^7 and brain weights by a factor of 8×10^4. Theory and observation agree that the relations of body dimensions over such wide magnitudes of variation are best represented by the use of the logarithmically transformed variables, which typically yield linear allometric relations of the form

$$\log y = a \log x + k. \tag{5}$$

Here the slope, a, is the allometry coefficient, so called because when a is not equal to unity, the relation of the two variables is not one of simple proportionality, or isometry. The constant k is the scaling term that adjusts y to x for some fixed value, x_o,

$$k = \log y_0 - a \log x_0 \tag{6}$$

The allometric relation of brain weight to body weight (Figure 1) has been extensively studied and written about for more than a century, but unfortunately this was largely a meaningless activity because it was based on the premise that the constant k in Equation 5, the so-called index of cephalization, or some closely related parameter is a measure of the "intelligence" or "psychic perfection" of the species (Dubois 1928). In default of any objective comparative data on intelligence, a lack that is still with us today, the chief support for these theories was that the index of cephalization for man is greater than that for any other species (Figure 1), and that the great apes lie below man but above the higher monkeys, which are in turn superior to most nonprimates. This rather anthropocentric view was seriously shaken when it became evident that some dolphins and small odontocete whales have cephalization indices higher than the pongids and quite close to man (Gihr and Pilleri 1969).

In 1955, intrigued by the indications of a relationship between brain size and longevity, I undertook a statistical analysis of the relation of lifespan (L) to brain weight (E) and body weight (S) in the placental

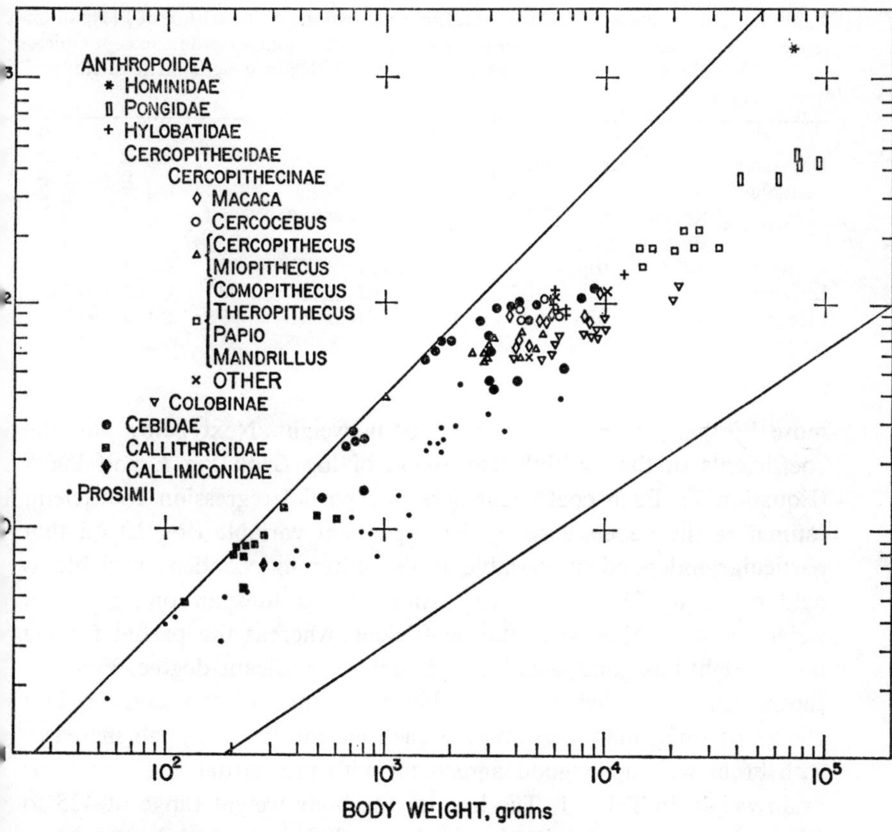

Figure 1. Relation of adult brain and body weights for primates. Data from numerous sources, including von Bonin (1937) and Count (1947). Data plotted on double logarithmic scales. The upper line, with slope +1, and the lower line, with slope +2/3, are upper and lower bounds for the distribution of mammalian brain and body weights. The upper line, which is equal to a brain weight : body weight ratio of 4 percent, is seen to be a sharp limit for the brain weights of primates weighing les than 2 kilograms.

mammals. The logarithmic allometry relation was used, but in a multidimensional form:

$$\log L = a_e \log E + a_s \log S + k. \qquad (7)$$

The first report (Sacher 1959) was based on sixty-three species, but I shall here report the data for a subsequent analysis based on 239 species of mammals, from twelve orders (Sacher 1966). Table 1 gives the results of that analysis. The first two lines give the coefficients of univariate regression of log lifespan on log brain weight and log body weight. Both regressions are positive, but brain weight accounts for

Table 1. Least squares simple and multiple regressions of logarithm of lifespan on logarithms of brain and body weight for all major mammalian orders except Chiroptera. Also given is the regression of logarithm of brain weight on logarithm of body weight

Dependent variable	Independent variables: Regression coefficients, Brain weight	Body weight	Intercept	d.f.	Error of estimate	Squared correlation
Lifespan	0.282 ± .012	--------	0.704 ± .021	237	0.152	0.711
Lifespan	--------	0.172 ± .010	0.502 ± .040	237	0.190	0.546
Lifespan	0.519 ± .036	−0.173 ± .025	0.9818 ± .044	236	0.139	0.760
Brain weight	--------	0.665 ± .013	−0.923 ± .053	237	0.251	0.914

more lifespan variance than does body weight. Next below are the coefficients of the multiple regression of log L on log E and log S (Equation 7). Each coefficient here is a partial regression coefficient, estimating the dependence of the dependent variable (log L) on that particular independent variable if the other independent variable is held constant. The partial regression of log lifespan on log brain weight is larger than the total coefficient, whereas the partial for log body weight has gone negative to a highly significant degree. Figure 2 shows graphically what these relations mean for two body weight classes of small mammals. Within each weight class lifespan increases with brain weight, in good agreement with the partial coefficient for brain weight in Table 1. The line for the body weight range of 425 to 1000 grams lies BELOW that for the 100 to 300 gram animals, consistent with the negative partial coefficient for lifespan on body weight at constant brain weight.

The allometry of lifespan was also evaluated for a half-dozen individual orders and suborders and yielded consistent estimates of a_e and a_s. The statistics for the suborder Anthropoidea are given in Table 2. There are forty-three species, and it can be seen that the relations are much the same as those found for all mammals in Table 1, except that the total and partial coefficients for lifespan on brain weight are somewhat larger. The differences between the coefficients for the Anthropoidea and all mammals are not significant.

In a later study the influence of metabolic rate and body temperature on lifespan was investigated. It was found that there is a highly significant negative partial coefficient for log lifespan on log metabolic rate, independent of body weight, and a significant tendency for lifespan to INCREASE with increasing body temperature, an unexpected but very important finding (Sacher, unpublished data).

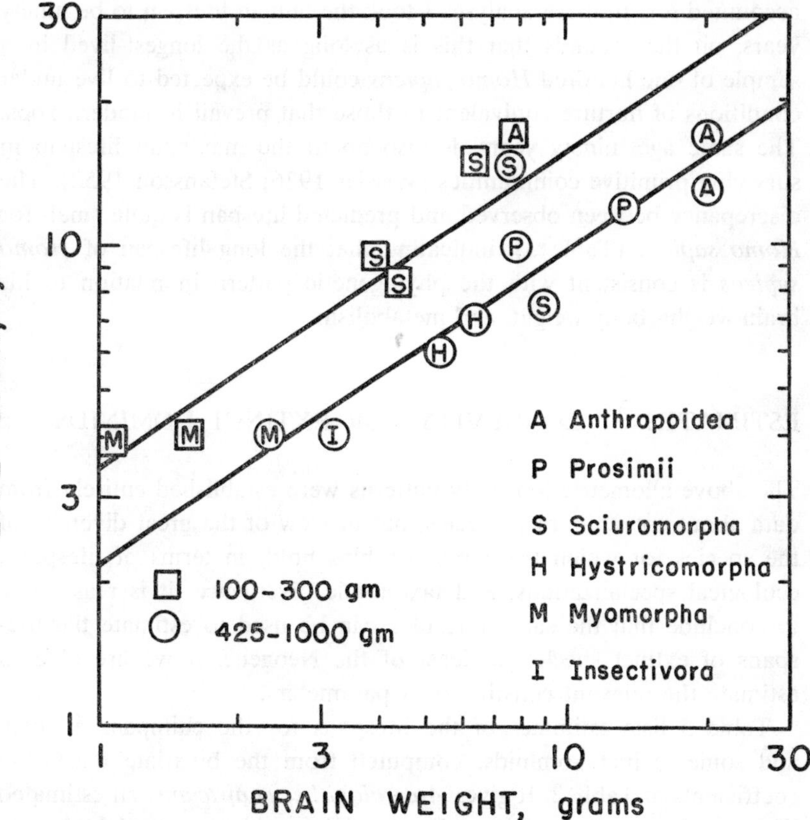

Figure 2. Relation of lifespan to brain weight for two body weight classes of small mammals. Lifespan and brain weight on double logarithmic grid

Table 2. Least squares simple and multiple regressions of logarithm of lifespan on logarithms of brain and body weight of the suborder Anthropoidea. Also given is the regression of logarithm of brain weight on logarithm of body weight.

Dependent variable	Independent variables: Regression coefficients, Brain weight	Body weight	Intercept	d.f.	Error of estimate	Squared correlation
Lifespan	0.379 ± .039	– – – – – – –	0.640 ± .074	41	0.118	0.698
Lifespan	– – – – – – –	0.232 ± .034	0.501 ± .127	41	0.148	0.524
Lifespan	0.648 ± .112	–0.202 ± .079	0.871 ± .114	40	0.111	0.740
Brain weight	– – – – – – – –	0.669 ± .036	–0.570 ± .132	41	0.154	0.895

The predictive power of these relationships is quite high. The squared multiple correlations for the several analyses range from 0.74 to 0.85, indicating that 80 percent or more of the lifespan variance is accounted for. In these analyses I took the human lifespan to be ninety years, on the grounds that this is as long as the longest-lived in a sample of one hundred *Homo sapiens* could be expected to live under conditions of nurture equivalent to those that prevail in modern zoos. The same age, ninety years, is also about the maximum lifespan in surviving primitive communities (Wissler 1936; Stefansson 1958). The discrepancy between observed and predicted lifespan is quite small for *Homo sapiens* (Table 3), indicating that the long lifespan of *Homo sapiens* is consistent with the phylogenetic pattern in relation to his brain weight, body weight, and metabolism.

ESTIMATES OF LONGEVITY FOR EXTINCT HOMINIDS

The above allometric longevity patterns were established entirely from data about contemporary species, but in view of the great diversity of the species for which these relationships hold, in terms of lifespans, ecological specializations, and taxonomic divergence, it is reasonable to conclude that the same formulas can be used to estimate the lifespans of extinct species, at least of the Neogene, if we are able to estimate the relevant constitutional parameters.

Table 3 lists estimates of the lifespans for the chimpanzee, man, and some extinct hominids, computed from the bivariate regression coefficients in Table 2. It gives *Australopithecus africanus* an estimated lifespan about equal to those for the living pongids, as might be expected from its chimpanzee-sized brain and body. Potential lifespans for *Australopithecus habilis*, *Homo erectus*, and *Homo neanderthalensis* are also recorded. If we take these estimates at face value, an approximately twofold increase in lifespan occurred during hominid evolution.

The right-hand column of Table 3 gives the maximum age estimates for some of these populations based on various criteria of skeletal aging. It is more than likely that the use of alternative criteria would lead to somewhat different age estimates from the same material. For example, in one extensive appraisal of the South African australopithecine material (Mann 1968), evidence that the sequence of molar eruption is the same for *Australopithecus* as for modern man is made the basis for the implicit assumption that the absolute rates of dental maturation are the same for the two species; this assumption is carried over to the time scales for skeletal maturation and aging. An alternative view of maturation rates in *Australopithecus* and *Homo sapiens* is given below.

Table 3. Cranial capacity, body weight, and lifespan for some living and extinct hominoids

	Cranial capacity milliliters	Body weight [d] grams	Lifespan Predicted[e] years	Lifespan Observed years
Pan troglodytes	394[a]	45,000	43	49[f]
Australopithecus africanus	442[b]	40,000	47	35–40[g]
Australopithecus sp. (Olduvai Hominid 7)	657[a]	50,000	58	—
Homo erectus	974[a]	60,000	72	40–60[h]
Homo neanderthalensis	1,425[c]	70,000	89	40–60[h]
Homo sapiens	1,400[c]	70,000	89	90[i]

a Tobias (1963)
b Holloway (1970)
c Weidenreich (1936)
d based on Schaeffer (1962)
e predictions based on the bivariate regression of log lifespan on log brain weight and log body weight from Table 2
f Anonymous (1972), captivity record
g Mann (1968)
h Vallois (1960)
i based on survival in primitive societies, e.g. Wissler (1936) and Stefansson (1958)

Another difficulty with the maximum lifespan estimates from fossil materials is the possibly great differences in the quality of life in the different evolutionary stages and their effect on mortality rates. I suggest that this was not a major factor, insofar as the life table was concerned, except in transient phases of adaptation to new environments or development of new food supplies. In all likelihood, even periods of great technological and social invention, such as the early Neolithic, did not extend the lifespan nearly as much as they increased the carrying capacity of the land.

Taking these considerations into account, the skeletal data are not inconsistent with the estimates from brain size, and the indications agree, therefore, that potential lifespan increased considerably during the evolution from *Australopithecus* to *Homo sapiens*, *pari passu* with the threefold increase in brain size. If we accept the evidence of brain size, the modern potential lifespan was fully attained in the Upper Paleolithic, for the Neanderthals achieved brain weights fully equal to the modern values, and possibly greater on the average.

FACTORS INFLUENCING THE INCREASE IN CRANIAL CAPACITY AND LONGEVITY

The facts presented thus far indicate that there is a close functional relationship between longevity and brain size for mammals that holds equally for the subhuman primates and man. The existence of such a functional relationship does not by itself imply anything about the causal processes responsible for the relation. These must be established by experimental intervention and by examining the relationships with additional variables.

There are three basic kinds of explanation for the relation of longevity to brain size. One (which I shall call H1) is that the brain itself participates in the stabilization of the life processes of the organism in such a way that the invariance of the internal milieu, and longevity in consequence, increases as an allometric function of brain size. In other words, the brain is postulated to be an ORGAN OF LONGEVITY as well as an organ for interaction with the external environment. The second hypothesis (H2) is that the evolution of a larger brain imposes on the species an added metabolic and developmental burden, and a consequent decreased reproductive rate that can only be compensated by means of an extension of the reproductive span, and hence of the lifespan.

The third logical possibility (H3) is that an evolutionary increase of longevity is invariably followed by an increase of brain size, for no other reason than that it is possible. In my opinion, although H3 is logically possible, it is scientifically meaningless because it is not a falsifiable hypothesis in the sense of Popper. Therefore, I shall not consider it further.

H1 and H2 are independent, so that either H1 can hold, H2 can hold, or both can hold. If H3 is excluded, then one of these three cases must obtain. I shall offer evidence for H2, the hypothesis that the reproductive cost of a larger brain makes a longer lifespan necessary. It is considerably more difficult to establish or reject H1, the hypothesis that the brain is an organ of longevity, but some indicative facts will be discussed in the next section.

The hypothesis that brain size imposes a reproductive cost is confirmed if it can be shown that development time, maturation time, and litter size are more strongly dependent on the size of the developing brain than on any other factor. This question was examined by gathering data on the gestation times, litter sizes, and neonatal and adult brain and body weights for ninety-one species, including nineteen primate species. The data for the insectivores and primates are given in Table 4. Multiple regressions of log gestation time on the other five variables were computed. Of the five variables, gestation time had significant partial regressions on three: neonatal brain weight (E_n), brain weight advancement (A_e),[1] and litter size (N). The multiple regression equation is

$$\begin{aligned} \log \text{gestation time} = {} & (0.274 \pm 0.015) \times \log \mathrm{E_n} \\ & + (0.144 \pm 0.058) \times \log \mathrm{A_e} \\ & - (0.173 \pm 0.065) \times \log \mathrm{N} \\ & + 1.853 \pm 0.039. \end{aligned} \tag{8}$$

The squared multiple correlation, which measures the fraction of gestation time variance accounted for, is 0.926, indicating a high degree of relationship. Neonatal brain weight and brain size advancement between them account for most of the gestation time variance. Body weight and body size advancement had no significant partial coefficients with gestation time.

Large neonatal brain weight, or high brain weight : body weight ratio at birth, has a depressing effect on litter size, which reinforces the negative influence of neonatal brain weight on reproductive rate. These data support H2, the hypothesis that a large brain imposes a reproductive cost.

The main conclusion of my study of the relation of gestation time to brain size was that all mammalian brains conform to a common law of growth: the cube root of brain weight increases as a linear function of gestation time, and the characteristic mammalian rate of brain growth is the rate-limiting process for all other aspects of somatic growth (Sacher and Staffeldt 1974). This law holds both within species, for the ontogeny of the fetal brain, and between species, for the phylogenetic relation of gestation time to neonatal brain weight. An important implication is that the time needed for a brain to reach a given stage of growth or to attain full growth can be estimated from a knowledge of its size alone.

This provides an objective basis for the estimation of relative maturation times of related species that differ in brain size. The rule is that the ratio of brain maturation times varies as the ratio of the cube roots of the brain weights. Let us compare the maturation of the chimpanzee and man in terms of this relationship. The age at sexual maturity is about nine years for the female chimpanzee (Napier and Napier 1967) and fourteen for the human female, so the ratio is 14:9, or 1.55. Their

1 Brain weight advancement at birth is the ratio of neonatal to adult brain weight.

Table 4. Gestation times, litter sizes, neonatal and adult brain and body weights, and advancement factors for brain and body growth at birth for insectivores and primates. From Sacher and Staffeldt (1974), whereliterature citations are given

Species	Gestation time	Litter size	Neonatal Brain weight	Neonatal Body weight	Adult Brain weight	Adult Body weight	Advancement Brain weight	Advancement Body weight
		Insectivora						
Erinaceus europaeus	34.	4.6	0.313	13.9	3.50	928.	0.089	0.015
Tupaia glis	46.	3.0	0.530	9.2	3.15	150.	0.168	0.061
Elephantulus intufi	51.	1.5	0.673	10.5	1.14	49.	0.590	0.214
Elephantulus myurus	46.	1.5	0.580	9.0	1.37	64.	0.423	0.140
		Primates — Prosimii						
Lemur catta	135.	1.0	8.78	78.0	22.0	2,100.	0.399	0.037
Nycticebus coucang	90.	1.2	4.00	30.5	12.8	1,230.	0.312	0.024
Galago crassicaudatus	135.	1.0	4.00	40.0	9.9	700.	0.404	0.057
		Primates — Anthropoidea						
Alouatta paliatta	139.	1.0	30.8	440.0	54.0	7,670.	0.570	0.057
Cebus capucinus	180.	1.0	29.0	250.0	73.0	3,700.	0.397	0.067
Saimiri sciurea	150.	1.0	14.0	100.0	25.0	779.	0.560	0.128
Ateles dariensis	140.	1.0	58.0	407.0	114.0	9,100.	0.508	0.044
Ateles geoffroyi	140.	1.0	64.0	512.0	109.0	7,640.	0.587	0.067
Hapale leucocephala	145.	2.0	3.7	35.3	7.8	220.	0.474	0.160
Macaca mulatta	175.	1.0	58.0	540.0	84.6	5,980.	0.685	0.090
Macaca mulatta	165.	1.0	51.5	394.0	107.0	8,700.	0.481	0.045
Macaca maurus		1.0	32.0	390.0	72.0	7,400.	0.444	0.052
Papio hamadryas	180.	1.0	75.0	443.0	183.0	20,700.	0.409	0.021
Papio papio	180.	1.0	53.0	335.0	179.0	32,000.	0.296	0.010
Cercopithecus pygerythrus	195.	1.0	33.5	227.0	67.0	4,600.	0.500	0.049
Presbytis obscurus	168.	1.0	43.0	514.0	65.5	5,800.	0.656	0.088
Colobus polykomos		1.0	38.0	340.0	96.0	6,800.	0.395	0.050
Hylobates lar	210.	1.0	65.0	400.0	102.0	5,500.	0.637	0.072
Pongo pygmaeus	270.	1.0	129.0	1,500.0	343.0	36,900.	0.376	0.040
Pan troglodytes	230.	1.0	128.0	1,560.0	360.0	45,000.	0.355	0.034
Gorilla gorilla	265.	1.0	227.0	1,750.0	406.0	140,000	0.559	0.012

respective brain sizes are about 350 and 1,400 grams, for a ratio of 4:1. The cube root of 4 is 1.59, so the agreement is good. Although there is no known relationship between brain maturation and sexual maturation, as a general rule they are closely related in mammalian development, a point that has not yet been examined closely.

If we apply this relationship to the fossil hominids, we estimate their maturation times to be, relative to 14.5 years (average of male and female) for man:

Australopithecus africanus 10 years
Australopithecus sp. (Olduvai Hominid 7) 11 years
Homo erectus 13 years
Homo neanderthalensis 14.5 years

This relationship needs to be confirmed by a more extensive study of the relation between brain size and maturation time in the higher primates, but pending the outcome of such a study, I believe that this rule provides a better basis for the discussion of maturation times in fossil hominids than does, for example, the assumption that the maturation times of hominids get longer because they have more to learn (Dobzhansky 1962, cited by Mann 1968), because the latter assumption is not falsifiable. Hominids do indeed have more to learn, but the essence of hominization is that they are able to learn more rapidly. A more reasonable assumption, supported by comparisons of learning rates between *Pan* and *Homo*, is that the learning process speeds up to fit into the maturation period defined by an optimum program of mammalian brain growth (Sacher and Staffeldt 1974).

The increase of brain size during hominid evolution was presumably accompanied by a decrease of neonatal brain growth advancement. The living pongids and the terrestrial monkeys have advancement factors of 0.35–0.40 (Table 4). This would correspond to newborn human brain weights of 400 to 550 grams, obviously much too large for successful parturition. At what stage of human evolution this decrease occurred is a matter for conjecture, but one can conclude that the shift to the lower advancement stage was accompanied by commensurate evolution of the social behavior and shelter technology needed for the protection and nurture of an infant born at that earlier stage of neurobehavioral development (Hockett and Ascher 1964).

Leutenegger (1970) showed that sexual dimorphism in pelvic dimensions of both Old World and New World simians increases as the relative head breadth (ratio of head breadth to transverse diameter of pelvis) of the newborn increases. The measure of sexual dimorphism used by Leutenegger — the ratio of the ischio-pubal index in the two sexes — is near unity for the gorilla and chimpanzee, species in which the newborn is relatively small, but near the upper limit for primates in *Homo sapiens*. This extreme dimorphism of the human pelvis suggests that the rate of evolution of hominid brain size may have been limited, not only by the selection toward earlier birth, but also by the increase in breadth of the female pelvic girdle and by the problems arising from a high degree of sexual dimorphism in pelvic dimensions.

BRAIN STRUCTURE AND LONGEVITY

The strong relation of longevity to brain weight leads one to ask whether any specific brain structure is associated with longevity in mammals. In 1970 I began the investigation of that question (Sacher 1970) by carrying out a multiple factor analysis of a set of measurements made by Stephan, Bauchot, and Andy (1970) on the volumes of twelve brain regions in sixty-three species of insectivores and primates. The twelve structural variables, together with brain weight, body weight, and seventeen derived variables computed as ratios of some of the original fourteen variables, constituted a 31 × 31 correlation matrix. The matrix was factored by the principal components method and rotated to simple structure by the varimax method. Four factors for brain structure were found, as summarized in Table 5.

The largest factor is factor I, NEOCORTICALIZATION, which is so named because its largest loadings are for the neocortex volume: telencephalon volume ratio (variable 28) and the absolute neocortex volume (variable 12). Absolute olfactory bulb volume (variable 6) and paleocortex volume (variable 7) have the smallest loadings on factor I. The negative loadings of variables 17–20 and 22–27 arise from the linear dependence among the volume ratio measures, so this group of variables need not be considered in the interpretation of Factor I.

The leading variables that identify the ALLOCORTEX factor, factor II, are the volumes of olfactory bulb, paleocortex, septum, schizocortex, and hippocampus. These constitute a broad group of paleocortical and archicortical brain structures, and the fact that they have remained in close structural association throughout insectivore and primate phylogeny reinforces the growing body of evidence for close functional interrelations among these areas with respect to learning, motivation, and affective behavior (Adey and Tokizane 1967).

All the absolute brain volume measures (variables 1–12) have 90

Table 5. Factor loadings for the four rotated factors for brain structure obtained from the 31 × 31 correlation matrix formed as described in the text. Variables 1–14 and 16 are original measurements, while variables 17–28 are ratios of the first 15. Variables 15 and 29–31 are omitted because they are irrelevant to the present discussion. The bottom line, variance, is the sum of squares of the factor loadings and is an estimate of the importance of the factor. From Sacher (1970)

Variable number	Name	Factors Neocortex	 Allocortex	 Cerebellum	 Subcortical
		I	II	IV	V
1	Medulla	0.73	0.58	+0.02	+0.30
2	Cerebellum	0.79	0.52	−0.00	+0.32
3	Mesencephalon	0.77	0.56	+0.06	+0.24
4	Diencephalon	0.82	0.51	+0.07	+0.24
5	Telencephalon	0.80	0.48	+0.10	+0.06
6	Olfactory bulb	− .04	0.85	−0.24	−0.06
7	Paleocortex	0.57	0.74	+0.10	+0.35
8	Septum	0.72	0.61	+0.03	+0.31
9	Striatum	0.82	0.49	+0.07	+0.28
10	Schizocortex	0.74	0.62	−0.02	+0.22
11	Hippocampus	0.74	0.60	−0.01	+0.25
12	Neocortex	0.86	0.41	+0.09	+0.27
13	Brain weight	0.80	0.50	+0.08	+0.33
14	Body weight	0.69	0.58	+0.03	+0.33
16	Total brain volume	0.80	0.50	+0.08	+0.33
17	1/16	−0.82	−0.27	−0.18	−0.37
18	2/16	−0.13	0.20	−0.90	−0.20
19	3/16	−0.74	−0.26	−0.13	−0.50
20	4/16	−0.29	−0.18	−0.12	−0.94
21	5/16	0.75	−0.16	+0.40	+0.33
22	6/5	−0.88	−0.05	−0.22	−0.39
23	7/5	−0.94	−0.12	−0.10	−0.27
24	8/5	−0.86	−0.20	−0.23	−0.35
25	9/5	−0.43	−0.21	−0.31	−0.60
26	10/5	−0.75	−0.09	−0.35	−0.49
27	11/5	−0.79	−0.21	−0.28	−0.44
28	12/5	0.96	0.11	+0.02	−0.03
	Variance	14.75	5.46	1.56	3.57

percent or more of their variance accounted for by these two variables. Factor IV is more specific, having to do with the ratio of cerebellum to telencephalon volume. Factor V is defined by the volume ratios of diencephalon, mesencephalon, striatum, and schizocortex, and it is evidently concerned with the relations between cortex and lower brain regions. There was also a fifth factor, defined by the brain weight: body weight ratio, but no brain regions had significant loadings on it.

Figure 3 shows how the three most important factors, for neocortical, allocortical, and subcortical structures, are related. The absolute volume

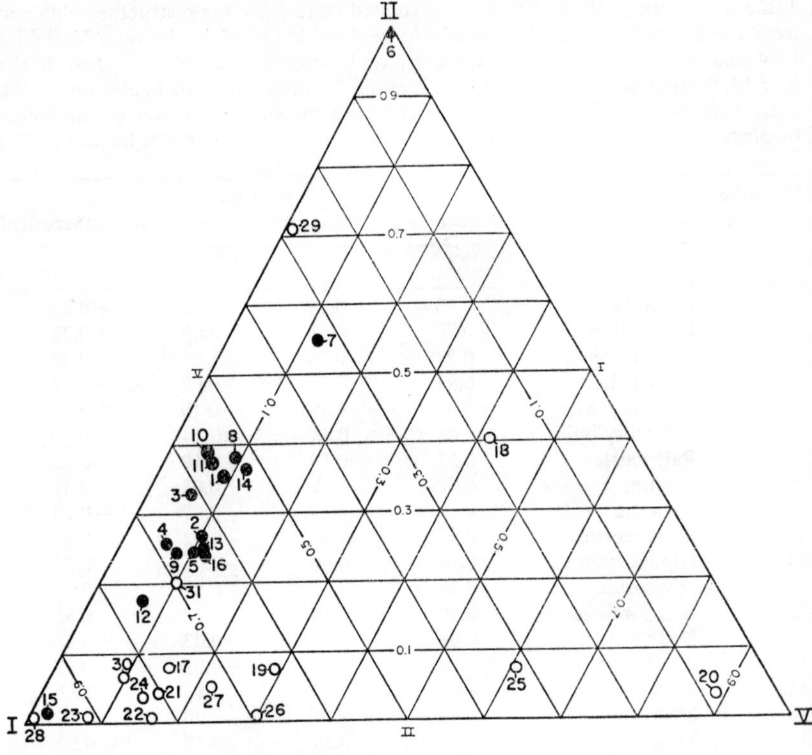

Figure 3. Plot of factor loadings for three factors of brain structure, the neocortical (I), allocortical (II), and subcortical (V). The points are the squares of the loadings on factors I, II, and V from Table 5, normalized to unity. The filled circles are the fourteen original variables, and the open circles are the ratio variables, as defined in Table 5.
From Sacher (1970), reprinted with permission of Appleton-Century-Crofts

variables, 1 through 12, are governed by the relations between neocortex (factor I) and allocortex (factor II), for each one has its projection almost entirely in the I-II plane. The ratio variables, on the other hand, are dominated by the relations of the neocortex to the subcortical centers, for all of them lie in the I-V plane, which is defined by the axis from neocortex to striatum, diencephalon, and mesencephalon. The cerebellum volume ratio (variable 18) is the only brain measure that does not have most of its variance projected into these three dimensions.

When the factor analysis was carried out (Sacher 1970), there were not enough primate lifespan data to permit an investigation of the relation of lifespan to the brain structure factors, but more data have since become available (Jones, unpublished data) and I was able to tabulate lifespans for forty-three of the sixty-three insectivore and primate species. The statistical analysis of the relation of lifespan to the four factors is given in Table 6.

Table 6. Relation of lifespan to the four factors of brain structure in forty-three species of insectivores and primates

I. Simple correlations and regression of logarithm of lifespan with logarithms of variables listed

	neocortex volume ratio I	olfactory bulb volume II	diencephalon volume ratio V	cerebellum volume ratio IV	total brain volume –
regression coefficient	0.435*	0.049	0.923*	0.216	0.164*
correlation coefficient	0.711*	0.144	0.687*	0.113	0.919*
squared correlation	0.505	0.021	0.472	0.013	0.845

* Significant at 1 percent level

II. Coefficients of multiple regression of log lifespan on the logs of the three brain variables that have significant influence on lifespan

$$\begin{aligned} \text{log lifespan} = & (0.377 \pm 0.044) \times \text{log neocortex ratio} \\ & + (0.080 \pm 0.024) \times \text{log olfactory bulb volume} \\ & + (0.680 \pm 0.096) \times \text{log diencephalon ratio} \\ & - 0.837 \pm 0.273 \end{aligned}$$

squared multiple correlation, $R^2 = 0.805$

In this analysis, the dependence of lifespan on five brain structure variables is examined. Four of them, i.e. neocortex volume ratio, olfactory bulb volume, diencephalon volume ratio, and cerebellum volume ratio, are leading variables on the four brain structure factors. The fifth, total brain volume, is the sum of all the regional volumes. The correlation coefficients in part I of Table 6 indicate that lifespan has close relations to the neocortex volume ratio (factor I) and the diencephalon volume ratio (factor V), but its closest relation is to total brain volume, which is equivalent to a general factor.

The coefficients of multiple regression in part II of Table 6 are based on only three of the brain variables. The fourth, cerebellum volume ratio, was excluded because it did not have a significant partial regression coefficient with lifespan. All three partial regression coefficients are positive and highly significant, even that for olfactory bulb volume, which does not have a significant simple regression coefficient with lifespan (part I). Of the three variables, neocortex volume ratio is the most influential, diencephalon volume ratio is somewhat less so, and olfactory bulb volume has a relatively minor effect. The squared multiple correlation, which measures the fraction of log lifespan variance accounted for by the three variables, is 0.805. It is interesting to note that the squared correlation for total brain volume by itself (part I of Table 6) is 0.845, significantly greater than the squared multiple correlation of 0.805 for the three variables.

These findings taken together suggest that there are several independent structural entities in the central nervous system that are related to the stabilizing and life-prolonging functions of the organism. It is not suggested that the three systems identified in this study form the complete set. The encouraging thing is that even at the coarse level of analysis attained by dividing the whole brain into twelve major regions, it is possible to discover major independent structural unities within the brain and to relate them to a significant integrated performance of organisms.

The point of view of this presentation is that length of life is the expression of the total capability of a set of physiological, biochemical, and behavioral performances that are all directed toward stabilizing the organism and thereby maintaining life. In this sense, longevity is analogous to another global performance of the brain — cognitive intelligence — except that in the case of longevity there is no validity problem: it is an unambiguous performance in a way that intelligence can never be. This analogy is further substantiated in the analysis of the relation of longevity to brain structure, where the total brain volume is seen to be a better predictor of longevity than is the sum of the three factors so far identified (Table 6). Total brain volume is, therefore, a composite measure, or score, of the total longevity capability, in much the same sense as the intelligence quotient (IQ) is a weighted sum of part scores for various specific mental abilities.

Insofar as the relation of the brain volume to longevity is shown to consist of a sum of contributions of distinct brain structures, there is reinforced confidence in H1, the hypothesis that the brain makes an active contribution to assuring the length of life of the organism of which it is a part.

GENETIC FACTORS IN THE EVOLUTION OF BRAIN AND LONGEVITY

The time course of expansion of hominid cranial capacity has been analyzed by Kurtén (1971), on the basis of recent advances in absolute dating. He concludes that the rate was very low for *Australopithecus*, increased to an average value of about 4.6 percent per 100,000 years for *Homo erectus*, and increased again to perhaps 7.5 percent per 100,000 years for the *Homo neanderthalensis* group. The Neanderthal brain attained the size of the modern *Homo sapiens* brain at least 100,000 years ago, and since that time there has been no further increase in brain size, although there is evidence from endocranial casts that there has been change in the relative sizes of the major cortical regions.

If this chronology is accepted, then most of the increase of brain size, from australopithecine to modern dimensions, took place in a period that began about 2,000,000 years ago and ended about 100,000 years ago. The forty-year increase of maximum lifespan indicated in Table 3 must then have taken place over the same time span. The average absolute rates of the two processes, about 0.35×10^{-6} per year, or 350 milliDarwins,[2] for increase in brain size, and about 250 milliDarwins for increase in lifespan, are extremely rapid — tachytelic — in comparison to typical rates of evolutionary change, which are in the range of tens of milliDarwins (Haldane 1949). The genetic basis of such rapid rates of evolution is not yet clear, but they alert us to the possibility that those very considerable increases in brain size and longevity were accomplished by allelic substitution at a comparatively small number of loci (Kimura 1960). This conclusion is encouraging in relation to the possibility that the human life history can be modified in beneficial ways by means of euphenic procedures (Lederberg 1963) for introducing appropriate sets of genes into the genomes of the somatic cells of the organism. If on the order of a few hundred loci were involved in the transition from *Australopithecus* to *Homo sapiens*, then a considerably smaller number of genes might be able to effect notable improvements in general vigor or intelligence in an evolutionarily natural way. The feasibility of this program depends on two key steps. One is the development of the very advanced technology needed for the parasexual transfer of genetic information. I believe we can consider this development to be a certainty within this century. The other, and more difficult, problem is to identify the relevant genes or linkage systems in experimental animals and to effect their isolation in a fashion suitable for transfer to human cells. Success in this step depends critically on the validation of certain hypotheses about the nature of the genetic systems that govern longevity in mammals and about certain

[2] The Darwin is a unit of rate of evolutionary change and is equal to the change of a dimension by a factor of $e = 2.718\ldots$ per 1,000,000 years (Haldane 1949).

aspects of the genetics of size and conformation of the body and organs.

THE POTENTIALITY FOR FURTHER EVOLUTION OF MAN'S BRAIN STRUCTURE, LONGEVITY, AND PSYCHOLOGICAL NATURE

Human brain weight is about 2 percent of body weight (Table 4) and has remained at that level for about 100,000 years, but insofar as dimensional and metabolic factors are concerned, there is no impediment to renewed expansion of the brain. In Figure 1, the upper side of the distribution of brain weight : body weight values for primates is bounded by a line of unit slope; this line truncates the distribution, for a number of points approach or touch the line on the lower side, but none cross it. This line, which represents a brain weight : body weight ratio of 4 percent, is the upper limit for adult brain weight : body weight ratios in all orders of mammals and probably indicates an upper limit of brain metabolism that mammals can support. Other groups besides primates that have species with brain weight : body weight ratios approaching the 4 percent value are: the didelphid and dasyurid marsupials; the vespertilionid bats; the squirrel family, rodents of the families Muridae and Cricetidae; and the weasels. The New World monkeys of the family Cebidae are the largest monkeys, and the largest mammals, to reach the 4 percent limit (Figure 1). A similar limit was long ago described for birds (Lapicque and Dastre 1908), but the mammalian limit has not been reported previously.

It is not out of the question for a future human subspecies or species to attain the 4 percent limit. This would be equivalent to an adult having the brain weight : body weight ratio of a nine year old (Blinkov and Glezer 1968). Such a transition could come about by comparatively minor degrees of paedogenetic natural selection or possibly by the parasexual euphenic procedures referred to above.

If the linkage between brain size and longevity were maintained through this transition, the new men, with their 2.5- to 3-kilogram brains, might have maximum lifespans of 140 years. There are also plausible genetic mechanisms for life prolongation that would not involve an increase of brain size. Because of limits on brain size at birth, a hominid with a 3-kilogram brain could have a neonatal brain weight of no more than 300-400 grams, and hence a gestation period of no more than nine months, so that the newborn brain could have an advancement of at most 10-12 percent, about equivalent in neurobehavioral development to a six-month human fetus. This would be a viable schedule only under the conditions of civilized life.

My purpose in giving these examples is to underline the fact that the extremely rapid evolution of brain and longevity within the past million years presages the possibility of far more rapid evolution in the future, either by eugenic or euphenic means.

The major remaining question is whether such a transformation would be beneficial to the species, to society, or to the person. This is related to the question of why increase of brain size ceased so abruptly a hundred millennia ago. Let us examine that question briefly.

As we noted earlier, man is not unique in the possession of a large brain. The elephants and numerous whale species have much larger brains, and several species of dolphins have brain : body ratios considerably higher than the pongids and not much below the human. I suggest that until about 100,000 years ago the hominids were in a neuropsychological situation very like those other species, in that comparatively complex traditions of hunting, migration, social organization, toolmaking, and environment control were being implemented by comparatively inefficient nonsymbolic neural processes for learning, memory storage, and innovation, presumably based on highly evolved capacities for mental imagery, imitation, and dreaming. The advantages of their niche, coupled with the inefficient use of neural capacity by the supporting neural processes, led to strong selection for increased brain size in hominids. At some point, a long series of pre- and protolinguistic preadaptations coincided with the evolution of the brain to a critical size and resulted in the sudden — in evolutionary terms almost instantaneous — invention of language. The resulting enormous increase in information-processing capacity of the brain meant that as of that moment the amount of cortex was no longer the limiting factor in man's cognitive apprehension of his environment, so that, also as of that moment, selection for increased brain size ceased. There may, indeed, have been a transient tendency toward decreased overall brain size while selection was effecting the initial neural reorganization for speech and symbolic behavior in general. The rapidity of this reorganization suggests, however, on the same grounds of genetic load adduced earlier in connection with the overall evolution of hominid brain size, that the brain reorganization was of a minor and superficial nature and was accomplished by changes at a relatively small number of gene loci. In short, the transformation from protoman to true man must have been accomplished primarily by a "software" revolution, rather than by any far-reaching rewiring of the neural circuitry. This schema differs in major respects from the consensus among anthropologists, as presented by Hockett and Ascher (1964).

On the basis of this conjecture, man's biological evolution toward greater brain size and longevity stopped because there was no longer selective advantage in the continuation of that trend. The paradoxical implication is that resumption of the trend must depend on renewed selection for nonsymbolic modes of cognition, for increase in nonlinguistic mental activities and behaviors, and for more adequate and functional use of reverie, dream, and other intuitive behaviors. The persistence of those traits in the human personality implies that selection in favor of them has never ceased, so that the human psyche represents a stable or fluctuating balance between man's prelinguistic heritage and the new symbolic thought processes. The way that balance shifts in the future, whether by natural selection, random drift, or human agency, will be perhaps the most significant current in man's future history.

The conjecture that extensive reorganization of the hominid brain occurred (Holloway 1966, 1967) still awaits substantive experimental support. If we consider the observable data of hominid brain evolution, then the salient feature of that evolution has been an increase in brain size, accompanied by changes in the sizes of brain regions and in the numbers and densities of cellular components that are, on the whole, in keeping with the allometry of primate and mammalian brain structure. The various aspects of that increase that are unique to the Hominidae — e.g. differentiation of the motor speech area — still need to be sought and validated, but this does not mean that the extensive data on observed quantitative relations should be disparaged because of the asserted greater importance of conjectural qualitative changes still unseen. The hypothesis of important qualitative reorganization also faces the difficulty that the expansion of the hominid brain occurred with extreme rapidity, and it is difficult to understand what kind of major reorganization of neural structure could have occurred in the short time available. It will also be difficult to dissociate the changes arising from the putative reorganization from those due to the remarkable lability of neural tissue, as manifested in its response to changes in experiential environments (Diamond et al. 1972), hormone levels (Clendinnen and Eayrs 1961), and other nongenetic factors.

To recapitulate, increase in overall size of the neopallium is the major, though not the sole, evolutionary change in the hominid nervous system. The best basis for inference about the change in overall intelligence is that it underwent a monotonic allometric increase with brain size in regard to any common set of abilities and performances. However, the invention of symbolic recoding of experience increased the informational capabilities of the hominid brain to an incalculable degree and led to an abrupt change in the direction of brain evolution and in the evolution of the human species.

REFERENCES

ADEY, W. R., T. TOKIZANE, *editors*
1967 *Structure and function of the limbic system.* Amsterdam: Elsevier.

ANONYMOUS
1972 Wendy remembered. *Yerkes Newsletter* 9:16–17.

BLINKOV, S. M., I. I. GLEZER
1968 *The human brain in figures and tables.* New York: Basic Books.

CLENDINNEN, B., J. EAYRS
1961 The anatomical and physiological effects of prenatally administered somatotrophin on cerebral development in rats. *Journal of Endocrinology* 22:183–193.

COUNT, E. W.
1947 Brain and body weight in man: their antecedents in growth and evolution. *Annals of the New York Academy of Sciences* 46:993–1122.

DIAMOND, M. C., M. R. ROSENZWEIG, E. L. BENNETT, B. LINDNER, L. LYON
1972 Effects of environmental enrichment and impoverishment on rat cerebral cortex. *Journal of Neurobiology* 3:47–64.

DOBZHANSKY, T.
1962 *Mankind evolving.* New Haven: Yale University Press.

DUBOIS, E.
1928 The law of necessary phylogenetic perfection of the psychencephalon. *Proceedings of the Royal Academy of Sciences Amsterdam* 31:304–314.

FRIEDENTHAL, H.
1910 Über die Giltigkeit der Massenwirkung für den Energieumsatz der lebendigen Substanz. *Zentralblatt für Physiologie* 24:321–327.

GIHR, M., G. PILLERI
1969 "Hirn-Körpergewichts-Beziehungen bei Cetaceen," in *Investigations on Cetacea.* Edited by G. Pilleri, volume one, 109–126. Berne: University of Berne.

GUMBEL, E. J.
1958 *Statistics of extremes.* New York: Columbia University Press.

HALDANE, J. B. S.
1949 Suggestions as to quantitative measurement of rates of evolution. *Evolution* 3:51–56.

HOCKETT, C. F., R. ASCHER
1964 The human revolution. *Current Anthropology* 5:135–168.

HOLLOWAY, R. L.
1966 Cranial capacity, neural reorganization, and hominid evolution: a search for more suitable parameters. *American Anthropologist* 68:103–121.
1967 The evolution of the human brain: some notes toward a synthesis between neural structure and the evolution of complex behavior. *General Systems* 12:3–19.
1970 New endocranial values for australopithecines. *Nature* 227:119–200.

KIMURA, M.
1960 Optimum mutation rate and degree of dominance as determined by the principle of minimum genetic load. *Journal of Genetics* 57:21–34.

KURTÉN, B.
1971 Time and hominid brain size. *Commentationes Biologicae Societis Scientiarum Fennicae* 32(36).

LAPICQUE, L., M. DASTRE
1908 Limite supérieure de la proportion d'encéphale par rapport au poids du cops chez les oiseaux. *Compes Rendus de l'Académie des Sciences Paris* 147:1421–1423.

LEDERBERG, J.
1963 Molecular biology, eugenics and euphenics. *Nature* 198:428–429.

LEUTENEGGER, W.
1970 Beziehungen zwischen der Neugeborenengrösse und dem Sexualdimorphismus am Becken bei simischen Primaten. *Folia Primatologica* 12:224–235.

MANN, A. E.
1968 "The paleodemography of *Australopithecus*." Unpublished doctoral dissertation, University of California, Berkeley. Ann. Arbor: University Microfilms.

NAPIER, J. R., P. H. NAPIER
1967 *A handbook of living primates*. New York: Academic Press.

RUBNER, M.
1908 *Das Problem der Lebensdauer und seine Beziehungen zum Wachstum und Ernährung*. Munich: Oldenbourg.

SACHER, G. A.
1959 "Relation of lifespan to brain weight and body weight in mammals," in *Ciba Foundation Colloquia on Ageing*. Volume five: *The lifespan of animals*. Edited by G. E. W. Wolstenholme and M. O'Connor, 115–133. London: Churchill.
1966 Dimensional analysis of factors governing longevity in mammals (abstract). *Proceedings of the Eighth International Congress of Gerontology*, Vienna.
1970 "Allometric and factorial analysis of brain structure in insectivores and primates," in *Advances in primatology*. Edited by C. R. Noback and W. Montagna, 245–287. New York: Appleton-Century-Crofts.

SACHER, G. A., E. F. STAFFELDT
1974 Relation of gestation time to brain weight for placental mammals: implications for the theory of vertebrate growth. *American Naturalist* 108:593–615.

SCHAEFFER, U.
1962 Gehirnschädelkapazität und Körpergrösse bei Vormenschenfunden in allometrischer Darstellung. *Zoologischer Anzeiger* 168: 149–164.

STEFANSSON, V.
1958 Eskimo longevity in northern Alaska. *Science* 127:16–19.

STEPHAN, H., R. BAUCHOT, O. J. ANDY
1970 "Data on size of the brain and of various brain parts in insectivores and primates," in *The primate brain.* Edited by C. R. Noback and W. Montagna, 289–297. New York: Appleton-Century-Crofts.

TOBIAS, P. V.
1963 Cranial capacity of *Zinjanthropus* and other australopithecines. *Nature* 197:743–746.

VALLOIS, H. V.
1960 "Vital statistics in prehistoric populations as determined from archaeological data," in *The application of quantitative methods in archaeology*. Edited by R. F. Heizer and S. F. Cook, 186–222. Chicago: Quadrangle Books.

VON BONIN, G.
1937 Brain-weight and body-weight of animals. *Journal of Genetic Psychology* 16:379–389.

WEIDENREICH, F.
1936 *Observations on the form and proportion of the endocranial casts of* Sinanthropus pekinensis, *other hominids and the great apes: a comparative study of brain size*. Paleontologia Sinica, series D, 7, fascicle 4, 50 pages.

WISSLER, C.
1936 Distribution of deaths among American Indians. *Human Biology* 8:223–231.

Estimation of the Cranial Capacity of Fossil Hominids

G. OLIVIER, and J. M. DRICOT

The cranial capacity of fossil hominids has a taxonomic value that is at least as great as that of morphology. Professor P. Tobias wrote a book on the subject (1971). But it is often impossible to measure this capacity. Indirect estimates are to be cautioned against since the equations used to make them differ from one form to another.

In the following article we propose a new approach to the problem, along with solutions which can be used when only one skull fragment is being examined.

CRITICISM OF USUAL TYPES OF ESTIMATION PROCEDURES

Capacity is a function of the dimensions of the cranium. It always provides correlations with the different measurements of the vault, and the "most probable value" of the capacity is furnished by the regression of this capacity in relation to one dimension. Since precision depends upon the closeness of the correlation, we can sometimes associate several dimensions together in a "module" (for example, the product of the diameters) when one of the correlation coefficients is neither high nor significant enough and when it is desirable to do without equations of multiple regressions. But this method is only valuable for subjects from the reference population or neighbors of these subjects. It is not useful in dealing with fossil men, especially the oldest of these.

With the aid of skulls from our osteology laboratory (Olivier and Tissier 1970), we drew a graph of capacity in relation to an arbitrary dimension, for example the occipital one (lambda-opisthion). We calculated the regression line of the capacity in relation to this chord,

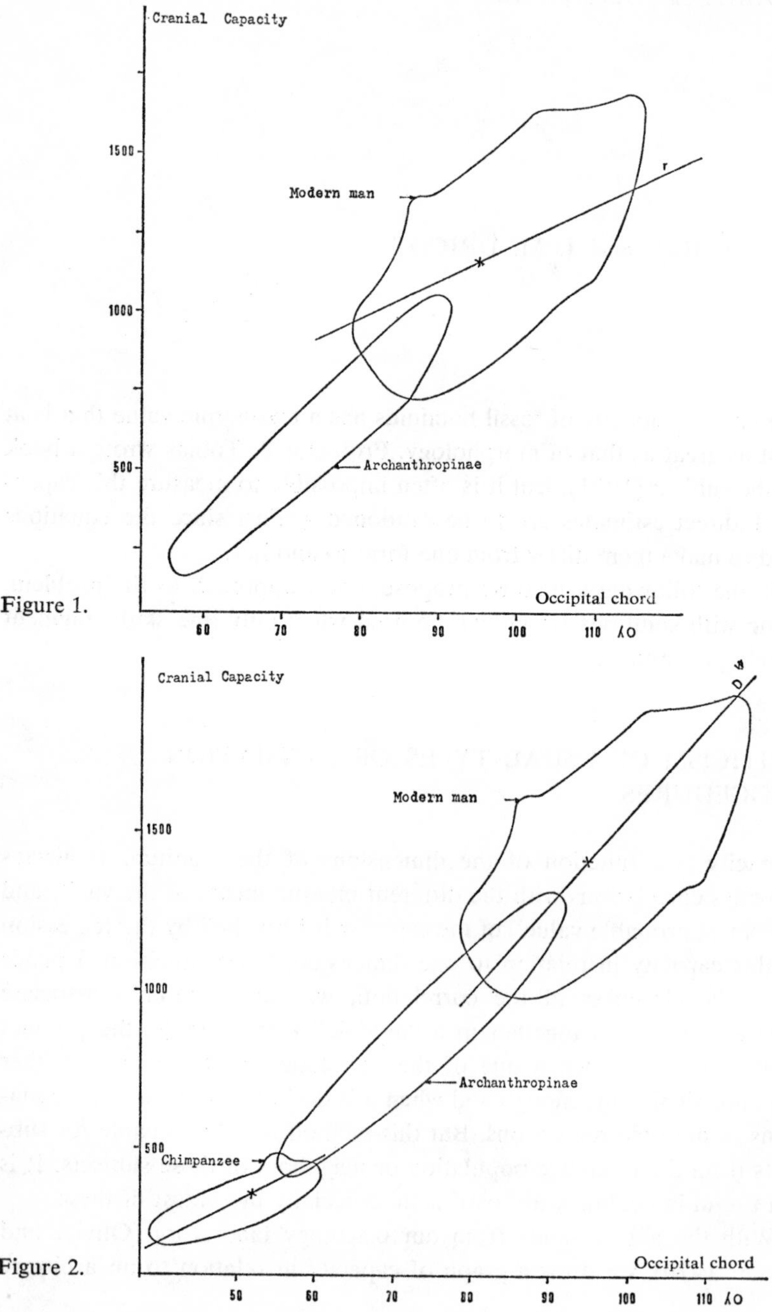

Figure 1.

Figure 2.

and then put the values for Archanthropinae on the graph. Certain systematic discrepancies appeared (see Figure 1): the observed values are always less than those predicted by the regression line that was calculated. This is not the case if known values are compared with those found from the correlation axis. For simplicity, we have used here the D line of Teissier (1948).

The explanation of this is quite simple: regression presupposes a cause and effect relationship between the two variables. Let us return to this notion at its most basic level using Galton's old example: the size of the sons will depend upon that of the fathers. There is "filial regression" and not vice versa. In our case per contra the RELATIONSHIP IS REVERSIBLE. Capacity conditions the dimensions of the skull and, conversely, these dimensions determine capacity. Regression loses its significance here. A similar observation was made by Masset (1971) regarding the correlation between age and the degree of cranial synostosis.

The use of the D line or of the correlation axis nevertheless presents two drawbacks:

1. It necessitates a higher correlation value (Salmon et al. 1970).
2. There will be some degree of doubt for the oldest hominids because their capacity values are quite low, which places them far apart on the axis. A very minor error made in the slope or the angle of the axis used could introduce huge variations and a large factor of uncertainty. Thus, the angle will vary from sample to sample.

All this suggested that we might seek out possible common relationships between the Pongidae and the Hominidae.

ESTIMATES COMMON TO MAN AND CHIMPANZEE

We selected the chimpanzee in order to alleviate the problem of cranial "superstructure" and because we have sufficient data. We recorded the dimensions that seemed most likely to resolve our problem. R. Deblock furnished a good deal of his own data for which we are greatly indebted to him.

Consider again the example of the occipital chord. The correlation is higher in the chimpanzee for two reasons. One is of a theoretical and taxonomic nature and is developed further by Olivier and Tissier in this volume. The other is of a practical nature. The association of the two species of chimpanzee (*Pan troglodytes* and *Pan paniscus*) "extends" the correlation and raises the coefficient.

But one essential difference between the slopes of the clusters of correlations is remarkable. The angle is more significant in man. The grouping together of the chimpanzee and human correlations is only possible if it is assumed that the line is curvilinear and has an "empty center" which would correspond to fossil forms between man and chimpanzee (Figure 2).

It is known that some curvilinear correlations can be made linear by means of logarithmic coordinates. In our example, the transformation of the data into logarithmic values leads to the placement of the two sets of points in such a way that their axes are aligned. Around this common axis fossil men will then be quite naturally grouped: Paleoanthropinae, Archanthropinae, and australopithecines (Figure 3). Logarithmic transformation of data is a well-known procedure for making linear correlations from curvilinear ones. The technique is described in various works, particularly one dealing with quantitative anthropology (Anonymous 1972).

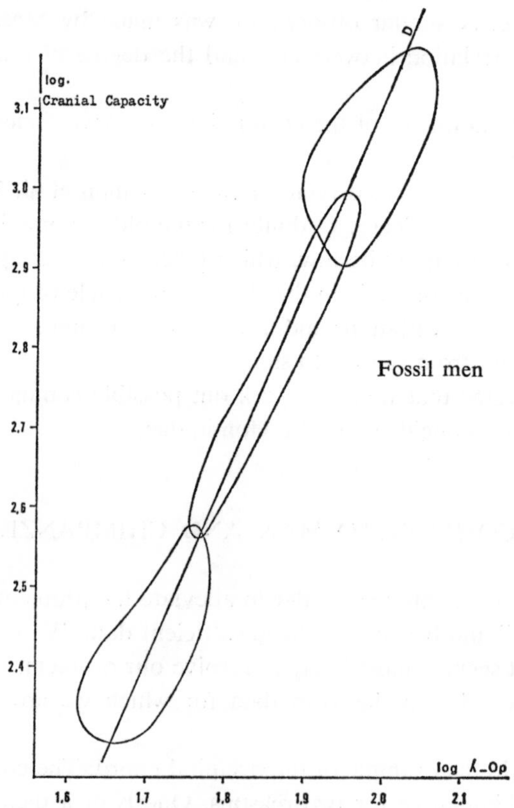

Figure 3.

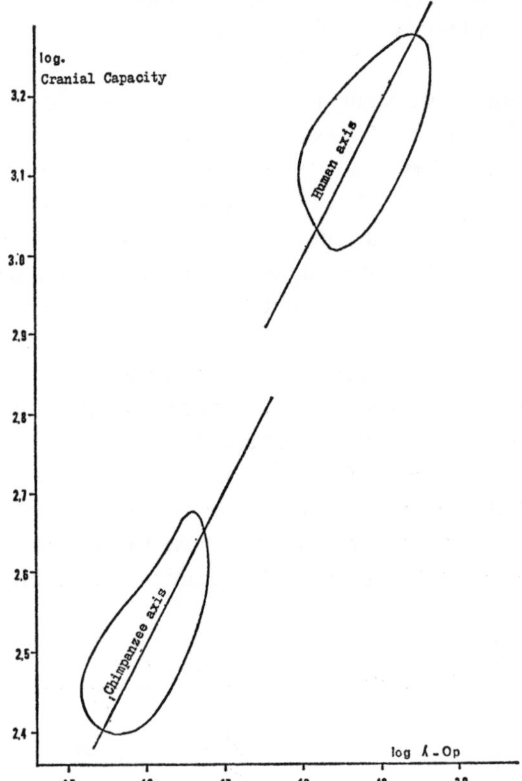

Figure 4.

CRANIAL ALLOMETRY

Hemmer demonstrated that certain phylogenetic lags exist between the principal relationships of cranial allometry, depending on the groups being compared. It might appear that we are contradicting this fact with our single correlation, but this is not so. If the axes of each correlation are calculated separately (logarithmically), it will be clear that they do not coincide: they are parallel and quite close to one another (Figure 4). The axis for man falls above that of the chimpanzee. Hemmer is therefore correct. It is only for practical purposes of simplification that we have joined them on a single major axis in this case. In other cases, the question will arise as to the point at which the two axes should be distinguished from one another. In fact, it is the placement of known fossils that guides us in this matter and directs us to use either an intermediary axis or even the chimpanzee axis.

CRITICISM OF ESTIMATES USING LOGARITHMIC TRANSFORMATIONS

First and foremost, we shall use, at least for reference purposes, the cranial capacity values of fossil men. They must be employed with some caution, for very few of them result from regular measuring procedures. But it appeared to us that capacities determined by careful experimenters were quite useful data and had as much value as capacities measured by different techniques. In some cases, we shall note certain anomalies, which will doubtlessly lead to some revision of the measurements.

The objection might be raised that our human sample is not representative of all humanity since it is composed entirely of Frenchmen. It was not possible for us to collect all of the necessary measurements from a correct assortment of all the world's various races. But, for the major cranial diameters on which there is a good deal of data, we verified that our sample is really quite close to the general mean, for its correlations at least (Figure 5). The cranium of the Frenchmen is a

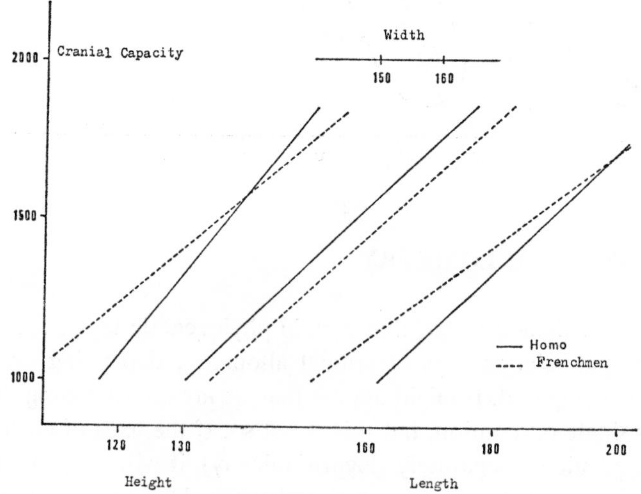

Figure 5.

bit larger (it is especially wider) than the average for the world's populations that was used by Olivier and Tissier (1970). Luck is with us for the slopes of the correlation axes are close to those of all humans. It might be thought that our sample's approximate representation of all humans will not be limited to the major diameters, but will extend to the other measurements of the skull as well. When it was necessary (in making logarithmic transformations), we corrected the angle of the axis by finding the mean value between that of the Frenchmen and that of the chimpanzee.

Sexual differences were not taken into account in these estimations. Ordinarily, it is assumed that the female has a skull that is less thick than that of the male. The female's cranial dimensions would supposedly lead to greater cranial capacity values. In our data, this is not the case. The axes for each sex are parallel and quite often are the same. For certain dimensions, the male's axis corresponds to a cranial capacity that is a bit greater than that of the female's axis. This is the case in man and the chimpanzee. In the procedure proposed here, the estimation of the capacity will be the same regardless of sex. Sexual differences are not very well known for fossil men.

Another criticism stems from the different sizes of the two samples. There are fifty-six chimpanzees (males, females, and young) and 117 humans (of both sexes). If the two groups are made equal (by lowering the number of humans used), the general mean will be lower, but the slope of the axis will remain at log. 2.24 and its ordinate will only vary from log. –0.1285 to log. –0.129, which is so small that it is insignificant.

We have also used the absolute value of the cranial capacity instead of the cube root as Hemmer (1967) did. Teissier (1948) demonstrated that in allometry the square root value provides the best adjustment of the points for the weight/stature relationship. This is also the case for the capacity/dimension relationship of the cranium. In research which seeks to make proper estimations of cranial capacity, we found that the results will be the same whether we used cube roots, square roots, or normal values for cranial capacity.

Indeed, a very real objection to our procedure might be the following: we do not use the biological interpretation of allometry. Instead we use a logarithmic transformation to obtain linear correlations. But the results of these correlations vary from one dimension to another: solutions to our problem other than that associated with occipital line values exist. It will be seen later that, for some cranial dimensions, the values for australopithecines and Archanthropinae are near the cluster of values for the chimpanzee, while Neanderthal's values are in an intermediate position between the two. For other dimensions, the estimates for ancient fossils are on an axis intermediary between those of man and chimpanzee. In brief, there is no single rule, for the thickness of the fossil skull does not always manifest itself in the same way and the evolution of different parts of the skull has certainly not been synchronous. A grave defect in our procedure resulted from this. Sometimes one must know in advance which type of human one is looking at in order to know what sort of relationship to apply. Capacity can no longer be invoked as a taxonomic criterion since the latter must be known in advance. But this case is rare. On the other hand, for skulls with known capacity but uncertain morphology, the relationships between dimensions and capacity can be used as arguments in favor of a particular taxonomic classification.

ACCURACY OF ESTIMATES AND PERMISSIBLE DEVIATION

A line of regression can be surrounded by two others, corresponding to ± 1 associated variation types, i.e. to 5 percent accuracy. The major axis, or reversible angle, can also be surrounded by two segments of curves whose formula can be found in Salmon et al. (1970); but because we are working with logarithms, this procedure is difficult to apply.

We have handled this difficulty in the following manner. First, when one is using two separate and quite distant samples, the correlation is high and the regression line is so close to the major axis that the standard deviation of the regression line can be used.

Second, our samples were of different sizes, as we mentioned earlier. During our efforts to correct for this in order to align our correlations and to maintain the same type of variability throughout, we noticed that the correlation coefficient was hardly at all modified because it was already quite high. As a result, we continued to use the group coefficient (Man + Chimpanzee) without making any corrections, but using logarithmic coordinates.

The last difficulty we shall mention stems from the very use of logarithms whose correlations will not necessarily have the same meaning as when normal coordinates are used. When we return to these normal coordinates, we find that we have a curved line which is no longer framed by two parallels, but rather by two divergent curves: it is natural that the margin of error should not be the same for the lower values as it is for the higher ones, which makes this different from a normal correlation. And even more important, these two curves are at different distances from the principal curve. As a result of the properties of logarithms, the addition of the antilog of the standard deviation gives a higher value than does the subtraction of the same value. This is purely illogical, and it would perhaps be better to use an average value to surround the curve made by the most probable values. Nevertheless, we cannot prove that the margin of error is not asymmetrical. Finally, we have retained the values we found in their original form, leaving to the reader the calculation of a deviation range (variable for each estimate).

RESULTS

We shall present the results in three classes according to whether the estimate is intermediary between man and chimpanzee, or is the same for both species (according to the example given), or is analogous to that of the chimpanzee.

Estimates Intermediate between Man and Chimpanzee

Five dimensions fit into this category, but two of these are doubtful.

FRONTAL LINE The frontal chord (nasion-bregma) gives the best results (Figure 6). While the Neanderthalers can be placed within the

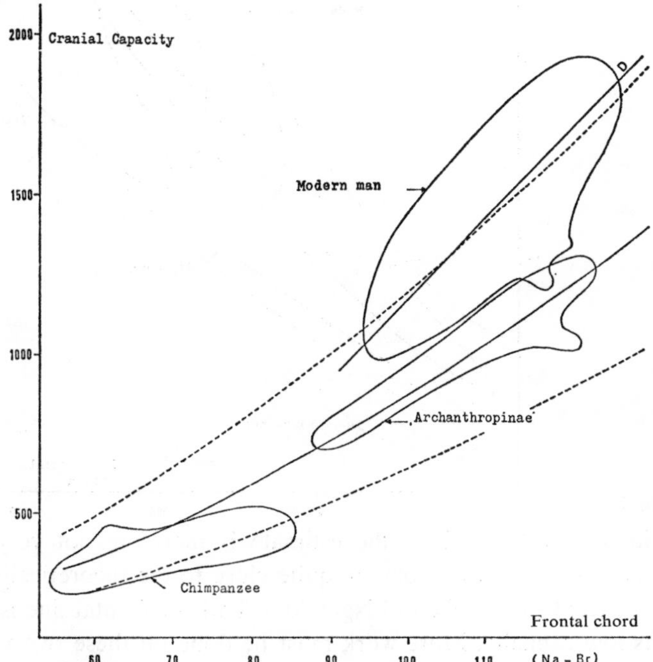

Figure 6.

region of present-day men (where they are indicated by small circles), and while we haven't data on the australopithecines, the Archanthropinae fit into a cluster which is intermediate between man and chimpanzee. As a precaution, we shall assign them a slope that is also intermediate between these two groups, and their capacity can be calculated by the following relationship (where X represents the dimension under consideration, as it will throughout this article):

Cranial capacity $= 0.2963\ X^{1.734}$

or,

log. Cranial capacity $= 1.73435$ log. X – log. 0.5283 ± 0.232 k log. 0.30.

Figure 6 represents the curve of the most probable values by a continuous line. It is surrounded by the discontinuous lines of divergent curves which correspond to the antilogs of the intervals of possible deviation. For capacities between 800 and 1200 cc., a "mean" standard variation would be on the order of ±330 cc., with an error of 5 percent, but varying quite a bit with the measurement concerned: ± 260 cc. for 800 cc., ± 400 for 1200 cc. For this dimension, as for many others

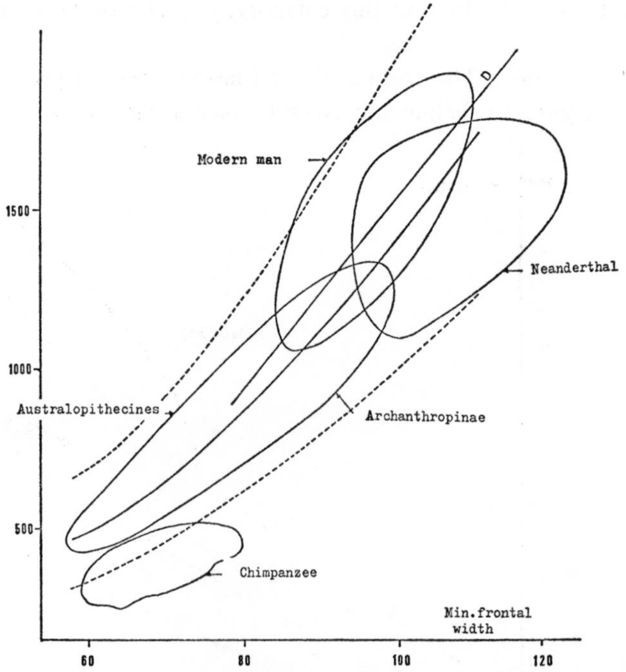

Figure 7.

considered by themselves, the estimate is therefore not very precise. However, the data available are quite close to the theoretically defined curve, except for the skull of Ngandong 1 whose frontal line is too long for its low capacity. More work must be done on these two values.

For the Neanderthalers, the major axis of the correlation from our sample of present-day men could be used; we would thus have for them:

Cranial capacity = 25.28 X – 1316 cc.

Eventually a slope between those of man and chimpanzee could also be assigned to them.

MINIMUM FRONTAL WIDTH The minimum frontal width gives less significant results, although two values of the australopithecines are aligned with those of the Archanthropinae. The permissible deviation is a bit greater than for the frontal line; but the fossils that are known are widely dispersed between the two statistical boundaries. At any rate, the following relationships are found:

Cranial capacity = $0.060\ X^{2.19}$

or,

log. Cranial capacity = 2.1867 log. X – log. 1.2226 ± 0.254 k log. 0.30.

It is interesting that the Neanderthals have a frontal width that is greater than that of present-day man, but their capacity is on the same order as that of modern man. The result of this is that they are situated around the curve of the formula given above. This curve can therefore be used for estimates of all ancient fossils, no matter what their taxonomic position may be (Figure 7).

OCCIPITAL WIDTH The occipital width (biasteric) gives even worse results because it developed quite early in the course of our phylogenesis and still presents a great deal of variability both in the chimpanzee and in present-day and fossil man. For the australopithecines and the Archanthropinae, we find:

Cranial capacity = $0.05\ X^{2.09}$

or,

log. Cranial capacity = 2.08895 log. X – log. 1.3026 ± 0.26 k log. 0.30.

The Neanderthals are placed between the Archanthropinae and present-day man. Perhaps the estimation of their cranial capacity can be made by drawing a major axis, similar to that of present-day man, through the averages of the values we have. We would then have:

Cranial capacity = 26.07 X – 1684 cc.

ANTERIOR RIDGE OF THE PARIETAL The anterior ridge of the parietal (bregma-propterion chord) can perhaps permit us to estimate the cranial capacity of ancient hominids by the relationships:

Cranial capacity = $0.089\ X^{2.09}$

or,

log. Cranial capacity = 2.09095 log. X − log. 1.0517 ± 0.201 k log. 0.301.

But we have only five control data; three are on the australopithecines and two on the Archanthropinae. They provide us with absolutely no certainty as to the intermediate nature of the estimate. Because we have insufficient data, we do not know where to place the Neanderthals or whether the relationships above are applicable to them.

INFERIOR RIDGE OF THE PARIETAL The inferior ridge of the parietal (propterion-asterion chord) is even more subject to uncertainty; the same subjects that we used above lead to the possibility of two different relations, one for the australopithecines and one for the Archanthropinae. Neanderthals, moreover, are lacking. Provisional (and perhaps valid?) relationships are:

Cranial capacity = $0.156\ X^{1.88}$

or,

log. Cranial capacity = 1.8796 log. X − log. 0.8074 ± 0.3575 k log. 0.301.

Estimates Common to Both Man and Chimpanzee

From a very practical point of view, we do not have to know whether we are dealing with phylogenetic properties or with variations in the thickness of certain parts of the skull. Let us simply state that five dimensions reveal major axes of correlation that are somewhat similar in man and in the chimpanzee (both in logarithmic coordinates).

OCCIPITAL CHORD The occipital chord, as was seen above, permits us to estimate the capacity by the formulae:

Cranial capacity = $0.044\ X^{2.28}$

or,

log. Cranial capacity = 2.2773 log. X − log. 1.357 ± 0.188 k log. 0.30.

As far as we currently know, these relationships are equally valid for the Neanderthals; but Figure 8 shows that the occipital line of Jebel Ighoud I is far too great, or the capacity is far too small. Between 800 and 1200 cc., the capacity is estimated at ± 140 cc., with 5 percent error.

BASIO-BREGMATIC HEIGHT Basio-bregmatic height can be estimated as follows:

Cranial capacity = $0.00015\ X^{3.3}$

or,

log. Cranial capacity = 3.3 log. X – log. 3.825 ± 0.1725 k log. 0.299.

It is quite probable that the Neanderthals are worthy of a special relationship which is difficult to establish inasmuch as Boskop man (here classed as a Neanderthaler) has values that are obviously too low. For these Paleoanthropinae, we can use either the formula above or the major axis of present-day man's correlations, drawing the line through their mean points, or:

Cranial capacity = 25.67 X – 1735 cc.

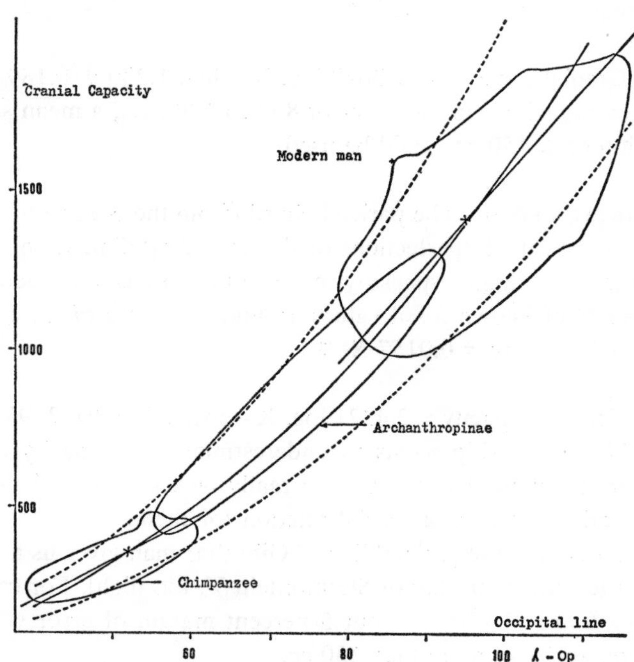

Figure 8.

AURICULAR HEIGHT Auricular height from the porion to the vertex, should be in more common use than the preceding measurement. Its relationships with capacity are:

Cranial capacity = 0.00756 $X^{2.56}$

or,

log. Cranial capacity = 2.5635 log. X – log. 2.1215 ± 0.156 k log 0.30.

Here again, the Neanderthals might merit a special formula because the values found with our relationships above are about 200 cc. too low (this is the same for basio-bregmatic height). Therefore, it might be possible to use for them the major axis of correlation for present-day man and the mean points of the Neanderthals. For more ancient hominids, a mean deviation type, valid for these two heights, would be on the order of 145 cc. for capacities between 800 and 1200 cc.

POSTERIOR RIDGE OF THE PARIETAL The posterior ridge of the parietal (mean of the linear distance from lambda to the asterion on each side) has a minimal correlation with cranial capacity, both in man and in the chimpanzee. Moreover, we have only found five pieces of data on ancient hominids (and none on Neanderthalers). But these five values fit so neatly within our calculated line that we must recommend the following formulae for them:

Cranial capacity $= 0.0577\ X^{2.26}$

or,

log. Cranial capacity $= 2.2628$ log. X – log. 1.239 ± 0.189 k log. 0.30.

For capacities on the order of 800 to 1200 cc., a mean standard deviation of ± 150 cc. could be used.

PARIETAL CHORD The parietal chord (from the bregma to the lambda) exaggerates the imperfections of the preceding dimension: the correlation is not as high, especially in the chimpanzees, and there is a wider dispersal of known fossil values around the curve of the formulae:

Cranial capacity $= 0.0157\ X^{2.42}$

or,

log. Cranial capacity $= 2.4221$ log. X – log. 1.803 ± 0.2395 k log. 0.30.

This relationship seems to underestimate the capacity of Neanderthalers by about 100 cc., but we really lack sufficient data to confirm this and to establish a special relation for them.

At any rate, the parietal line of Gibraltar man gives us a value which is far too low (and that of Sterkfontein V, too high). For capacities between 800 and 1200 cc., our 5 percent margin of error would lead to discrepancies of more than 150 cc.

Estimations Analogous to Those of the Chimpanzee

The phylogenetic distance between present-day man and certain ancient fossils is such that the latter can be placed practically on the extension of the line for the chimpanzee. From the point of view of biometrics, Neanderthalers will thus be clearly distinguishable from Archanthropinae, which will be confused with australopithecines until our knowledge of these fossils improves enough to permit us to more easily separate them from one another.

MAXIMUM LENGTH OF THE SKULL The maximum length of the skull is always increased by supraorbital "superstructures." It can therefore be expected that all ancient fossils will have a relationship that is different from that of present-day man without any torus. But this is not the case: australopithecines and Archanthropinae alone correspond to an extension of the relationship for the chimpanzees, the Neanderthalers being in a sort of intermediate position between these two. For the australopithecines, then, we have:

Cranial capacity $= 0.0057\ X^{2.28}$ (Figure 9)

or,

log. Cranial capacity $= 2.2859$ log. X – log. 2.2406 ± 0.27 k. log. 0.154.

The length (width as well) of the skull of *Zinjanthropus* is too great, and we propose to reduce it to 160 millimeters (and to 110 millimeters for the width).

The cranial capacity of the Neanderthalers can be estimated by the axis for our sample of present-day men, by passing through the mean points for these fossils; we then have:

Cranial capacity $= 20.42\ X - 2581$ cc.

MAXIMUM WIDTH OF THE SKULL Measurements of the maximum width of the skull of australopithecines present widely divergent results. However, with the exception of *Pithecanthropus* IV which is definitely aberrant, the relationship for the Archanthropinae is an extension of that of the chimpanzees:

Cranial capacity $= 0.0011\ X^{2.17}$

or,

log. Cranial capacity $= 2.7754$ log. X – log. 2.9525 ± 0.254 k log. 0.1446.

Contrary to what was the case with the length of the skull, the Neanderthalers are here situated within the region of present-day men (Figure 10) and their values can be estimated by the axis of this correlation:

Cranial capacity $= 23.18\ X - 1945$ cc.

MODULE The module (length × width) is a product which is quite tempting to use, although we are a bit suspicious of the use of modules in general. Besides, we can obtain results with sums that are just as good as those obtainable from products, as Welcker (1885) has shown (his tables give quite good results for present-day man, without needing to distinguish index classes). The module set-up with the product above gives the following estimate (Figure 11):

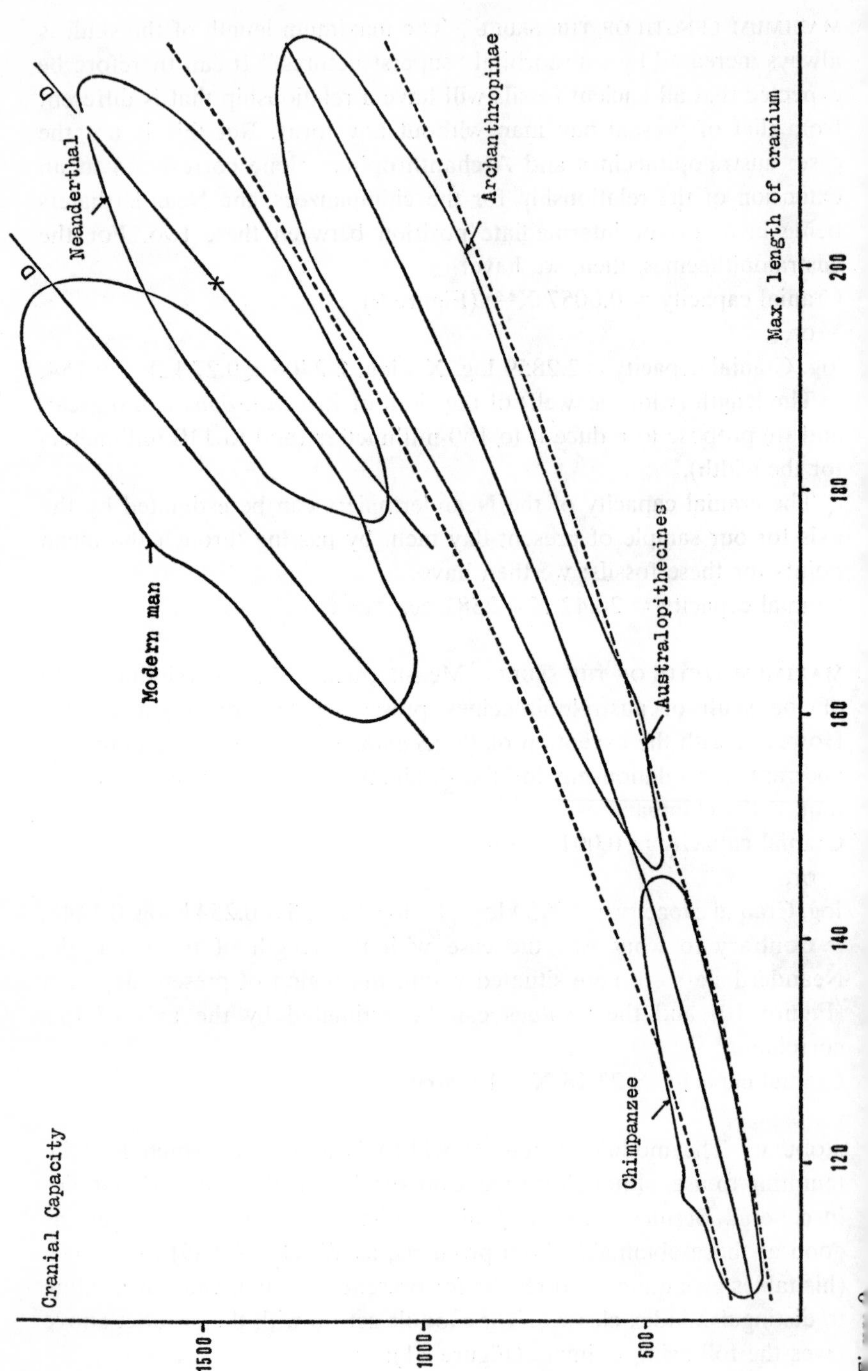
Cranial Capacity
1500
1000
500
Max. length of cranium
120
140
160
180
200
Modern man
Neanderthal
Archanthropinae
Australopithecines
Chimpanzee
D
D

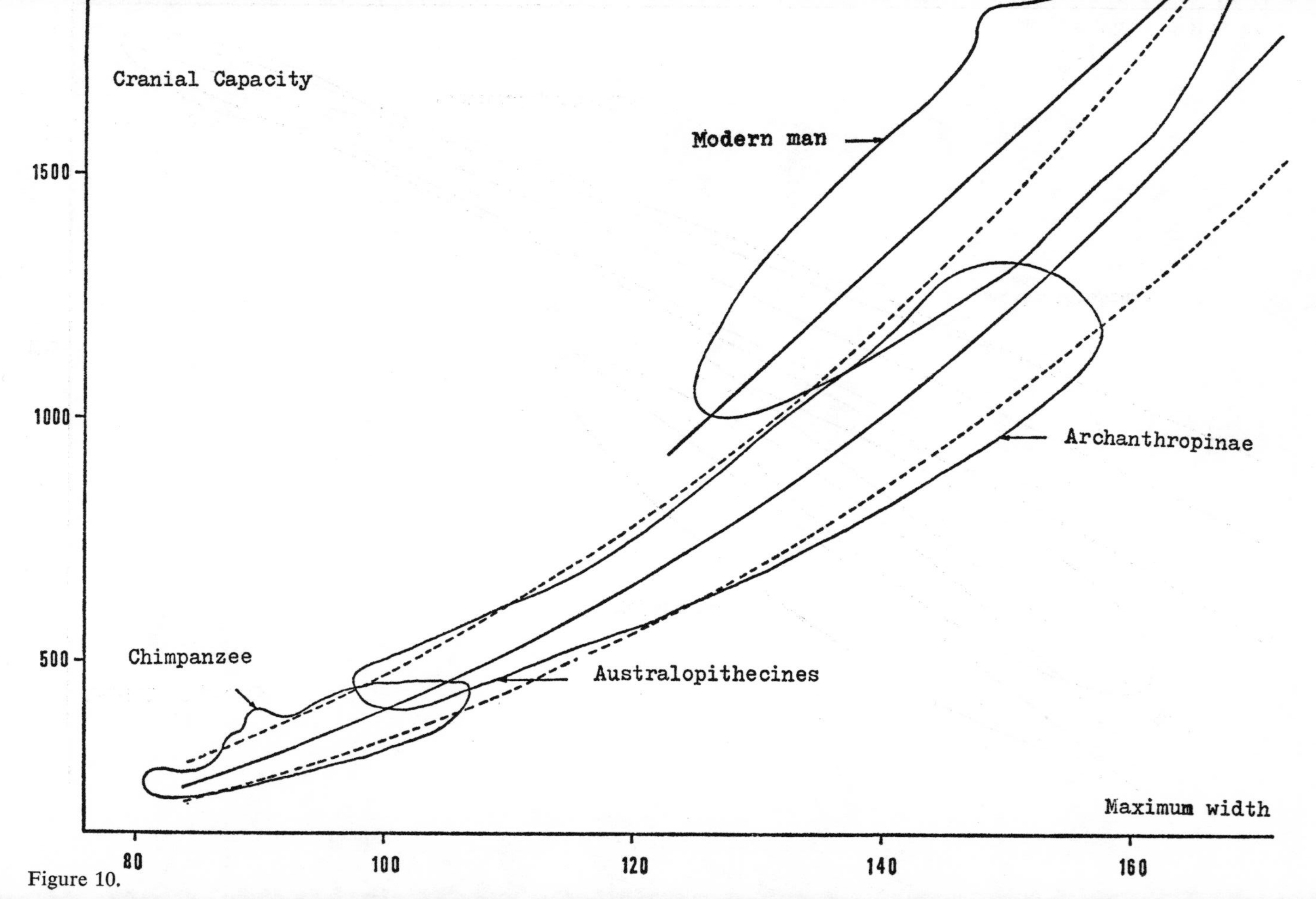

Cranial Capacity
1500
1000
500
Modern man
Archanthropinae
Chimpanzee
Australopithecines
Maximum width
80
100
120
140
160

Figure 10.

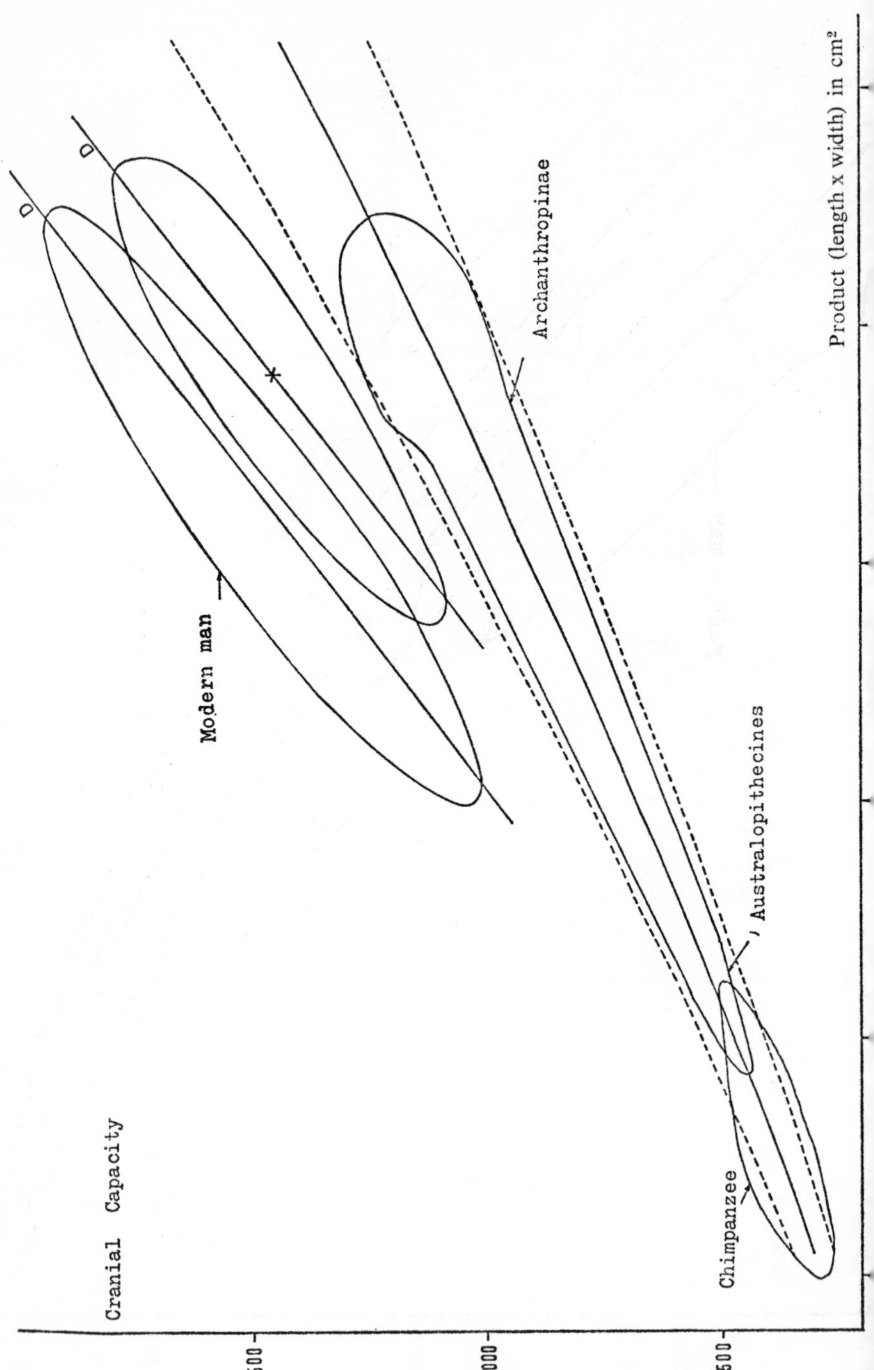
Cranial Capacity
1500
1000
500
Product (length x width) in cm²
Modern man
Archanthropinae
Australopithecines
Chimpanzee
D
D

Cranial capacity = $0.0023\ X^{1.27}$.

or,

log. Cranial capacity = 1.2694 log. X – log. 2.628 ± 0.211 k log. 0.149.

The Neanderthalers can be estimated by the axis of the correlation of present-day men, scaled so as to pass through their mean points, thus:

Cranial capacity = 8.0 X – 869 cc.

CONCLUSIONS

Estimation of cranial capacity ought not to be done by use of regression lines and "most probable values." Biological reasons point instead toward the use of the axis of the correlations between dimensions and capacity to obtain estimates that are correct and that are without any prejudgment about possible causality between sets of data. For the most ancient hominids, relationships common to man and chimpanzee must be sought. They can be derived by means of logarithmic co-ordinates.

Between the axes of correlation for present-day man and for the chimpanzee, there may be "phylogenetic lag." When this is minimum, an approximated common axis connects the two cranial capacity correlations with the dimensions concerned and permits a simple estimate of the values for fossil men.

When the lag is clearer, the ancient hominids will fit either on the extended axis for the chimpanzee, or in a position that is intermediate between that extended axis and the axis of present-day man; by using the values that are known for these hominids, the axis which corresponds to the best estimates can be determined.

The Neanderthalers are placed in the intermediate position when the Archanthropinae fit on the extended line for the chimpanzee; in this case, a special relation can be established for them. In other cases, the cranial capacity of the Neanderthalers can be estimated either by the general formula we have given or by the axis of the correlation of present-day man, but never by regression.

A series of formulae has been given in order to permit correct estimation of the cranial capacity of a fossil by means of one dimension of the skull vault, often from the measurement of a single bone of the skull. It will rarely be necessary to know in advance what was the taxonomic position of the fossil.

The same method can be extended to present-day man.

APPENDIX

Table 1. Data utilized

	117 Frenchmen			56 Chimpanzees		
	Mean	Deviation	Correlation with (1)	Mean	Deviation	Correlation with (1)
1. Cranial Capacity	1411.4	157.4	1.0	363.4	44.7	1.0
2. Maximum length of skull	178.4	7.71	0.719	126.2	8.38	0.785
3. Maximum width of skull	143.3	6.79	0.788	96.66	4.74	0.769
4. Basio-bregmatic height	129.6	6.13	0.657	86.29	4.14	0.672
5. Porion-vertex height	113.5	5.92	0.737	67.07	3.68	0.595
6. Minimum frontal width	96.1	5.22	0.611	67.25	4.13	0.543
7. Frontal chord (Na-Br)	109.8	6.23	0.580	68.51	5.84	0.645
8. Parietal chord (Br-L)	110.25	7.58	0.592	63.40	4.37	0.159
9. Bregma-propterion chord	94.9	4.63	0.790	64.48	4.39	0.720
10. Lambda-asterion chord	86.75	4.99	0.479	47.56	3.05	0.532
11. Propterion-asterion chord	96.65	5.34	0.679	75.00	5.51	0.713
12. Occipital chord (L-Op)	95.0	5.80	0.451	52.46	3.51	0.577
13. Occipital width (Bi-ast.)	111.85	6.04	0.592	76.93	4.54	0.402
14. Module (length × width)	255.6	19.68	0.905	122.5	12.96	0.841

Table 2. Equations of the axis of correlations

In the 117 French subjects *(Standard deviation of the regressions)*

Cranial capacity = 20.42 (Length of skull) — 2.232 cc ± 214.5
" " = 23.18 (Width of skull) — 1911 cc ± 189.9
" " = 25.67 (Basio-bregmatic height) — 1.916 cc ± 232.7
" " = 26.58 (Porion-vertex height) — 1.605 cc ± 208.6
" " = 30.15 (Minimum frontal width) — 1.485 cc ± 244.3
" " = 25.28 (Frontal chord) — 1.364 cc ± 251.5
" " = 20.76 (Parietal chord) — 877 cc ± 248.7
" " = 34.02 (Bregma-propterion chord) — 1.818 cc ± 189.2
" " = 31.53 (Lambda-asterion chord) — 1.324 cc ±270.9
" " = 29.48 (Propterion-asterion chord) — 1.438 cc ± 226.6
" " = 27.13 (Occipital chord) — 1167 cc ± 275.3
" " = 26.07 (Occipital width) — 1.505 cc ± 248.7
" " = 8.0 (Length × width module) — 634 cc ± 131.5

Table 2. (Continued)

In 1656 Homo sapiens	
Cranial capacity = 19.0	(Length of skull) — 2.063 cc ± 261.6
„ „ = 18.8	(Width of skull) — 1.194 cc ± 208.1
„ „ = 24.7	(Basio-Bregmatic height) — 1871 cc ± 258.2

REFERENCES

ANONYMOUS

1972 "Anthropologie quantitative." Cours polycopié, Association cooporative des Etudiants en Sciences. Paris.

HEMMER, H.

1967 Allometrie — Untersuchungen zur Evolution des menschlichen Schädels und seiner Rassentypen. *Fortschritte der Evolutionsforschung* 3. Stuttgart: Fischer.

1969 A new view of the evolution of man. *Current Anthropology* 10: 179–180.

MASSET, C.

1971 Erreurs systématiques dans la détermination de l'âge par les sutures crâniennes. *Bulletins et Mémoires de la Société d'Anthropologie de Paris* 7:85–105.

OLIVIER, G., H. TISSIER

1970 Données sur le crâne des Français. *Bulletins et Mémoires de la Société d'Anthropologie de Paris* 6:307–310.

1972 Les corrélations structurales entre grands diamètres crâniens. *Bulletins de l'Association des Anatomistes* 154:1109–1116.

PEARSON, K.

1926 On the reconstruction of cranial capacity from external measurements. *Man* 26:46–50.

RIGAUD, A., P. BONJEAN, R. RIQUET, J. LAULAN, R. STEFANIAK

1967 Etude comparative de deux procédés de mesure indirecte d'évaluation de la capacité crânienne. *Bulletins de l'Association des Anatomistes* 136:891–905.

SALMON, D., *et al.*

1970 The reversible line: a statistical comparison of two methods of measurements. *Revue européenne d'études cliniques et biologiques* 15:1132–1140.

TEISSIER, G.

1948 La relation d'allométrie, sa signification statistique et biologique. *Biometrics* 4:14–53.

TOBIAS, P. V.

1971 *The brain in hominid evolution.* New York and London: Columbia University Press.

WEIDENREICH, F.

1943 *The skull of* Sinanthropus pekinensis. Palaeontologia Sinica, 127, 486 pages.

WELCKER, H.

1885 Die Kapazität und die drei Hauptdurchmesser der Schädelkapsel bei den verschiedenen Nationen. *Archiv für Anthropologie* 16:1–159.

Correlations Between Major Cranial Diameters of Man and Pongidae

G. OLIVIER and H. TISSIER

INTRODUCTION

The notion of the correlation coefficient was first conceived to express the degree of relationship among species; but it has many other uses as well. It has been employed commonly by biologists. The goal of our scientific study is to explain nature and to find some order where there seems to be only anarchy. A natural step in this direction is to seek out the links, however weak or statistical, between phenomena. In the best cases, there will be a cause-effect relationship; but more often, we will be led to the research of yet a third factor which is responsible for connecting the two phenomena under study.

It will be seen that this is the case with correlations between cephalic diameters. Several authors — Dahlberg (1941), Khérumian and Boulanger (1949), Olivier and Nistri (1957) — have noted the high-valued coefficients occurring in isolated populations and have interpreted them as indicative of the homogeneity of genetic heritage. This was an error, for they neglected the fact that the variability in these cephalic dimensions was the same everywhere and that there could therefore not possibly have been any accumulation of "homozygotic polygenies." If that had been true, it would have been so in all populations of this type, which was not the case. Moreover, the correlation coefficient has a fluctuating nature and often provides one with unpredictable variations; often, only the highest coefficients can be retained, i.e. those whose square (r^2) is great enough to have some biological significance. In regard to correlations between the major cranial diameters of man, all sorts of values can be found, both null and significant. On the other hand, the correlations seem to be more stable and certain for the

Pongidae. The cause of the insufficiency of the correlation coefficient in man is doubtlessly related to the presence of a GENERAL SIZE FACTOR; this is manifested by a correlation between stature and head dimensions which is on the order of about 0.20 in the living subject (it is more significant for the length than for the width of the skull). In skeletons, the size of the entire body can be determined from cranial capacity, whose correlation with the major diameters is on the order of 0.65 (it is more significant for the width than for the length or height of the skull). This last correlation is present in man as well as in the Pongidae.

Thus we decided to study the partial correlations of the diameters with one another using, as a factor of equal size, constant cranial capacity. It will be found that the disappointing results of the simple correlations will thus be avoided and results will be clearer.

MATERIAL AND METHODS

The data were obtained from measurements of 1,656 human skulls and one hundred chimpanzee skulls. The former were taken from scientific literature and the groups were chosen so as to represent all the races and areas of the globe. For one particular demonstration, we added a homogeneous lot of 1,000 skulls whose sex was rigorously determined. In all cases, we made certain that the cranial capacity had been correctly measured and that it corresponded closely to the results obtained by using the Welcker procedure (which is the best for estimating such values).

The measurements of the chimpanzee skulls were furnished by R. Deblock. There were forty-one *Pan troglodytes* and fifty-nine *Pan paniscus* skulls in the group. All were adults.

From these data, we calculated in a circular permutation the correlation coefficients between length, width, and basio-bregmatic height of the skulls (we made certain that the height of the brainpan would have given us the same results). With the aid of these preliminary correlation coefficients, we were then able to calculate partial correlations using standard cranial capacity values and partial correlations of two dimensions, assuming the third remained constant. The formulae for these coefficients are programmed in any laboratory and only the interpretations are interesting to report here.

RESULTS

As is always the case in the study of correlations, the results are presented here in the form of numerical tables with commentary. Before arriving at the partial correlations which are the principal object of this study, we must report the values of the simple correlations.

Simple Correlations

In both groups in Table 1, width is closely related to cranial capacity; the other values are all higher for the chimpanzee. We might note the importance of the test *t* results between the correlation coefficients for width/length of the skull, although the values are significant in both cases. But it is certain that these values will be affected by variable factors acting in a quite random manner because the sexes, the many races of man, and the two species of chimpanzee were all mixed together.

Table 1. Natural correlations

	1,656 Men	100 Chimpanzees	Test *t*
Width/length	+0.101***	+0.701***	10.6***
Height/length	+0.334***	+0.628***	4.5**
Width/height	+0.147***	+0.576***	6.0**
Length/cranial capacity	+0.536***	+0.702***	3.1**
Width/cranial capacity	+0.741***	+0.794***	1.4
Height/cranial capacity	+0.553***	+0.672***	2.1*

Let us examine the influence of sex alone upon the data; here we shall use two large groups of Portuguese skulls. The cranial capacity was not measured in the same way that it was in the other samples, but the sex is clearly established (by the birth certificates of the subjects):

Table 2. Sexual differences of correlations

	Portuguese			Chimpanzee		
	494 Men	506 Women	Total	50 Males	50 Females	Total
Width/length	+0.225	+0.270	+0.411	+0.692	+0.679	+0.701
Height/length	+0.317	+0.339	+0.537	+0.619	+0.499	+0.628
Width/height	+0.210	+0.255	+0.395	+0.580	+0.611	+0.576
Length/cranial capacity	+0.606	+0.623	+0.736	+0.712	+0.680	+0.702
Width/cranial capacity	+0.646	+0.657	+0.717	+0.855	+0.739	+0.794
Height/cranial capacity	+0.521	+0.492	+0.664	+0.642	+0.641	+0.672

No difference between the two sexes is very large. For the chimpanzee, the values are no different from those of the total group of one hundred; but this might be due to the fact that, within each sex category, there are pygmy chimps *(paniscus)* and ordinary ones *(troglodytes)*. Grouping them together may have increased the correlation. The values of Table 3, compared with those of Table 1, show that this is partly true anyway, particularly for the height/length correlation in the chimpanzee skulls. The values found for each sex in the human group are always significantly less than those of the two sexes combined.

It also can be noted that the values given for the Portuguese group are, on the whole, higher than those given earlier in Table 1 for man in general. This is due to the fact that there are great differences between samples; details on this fact will be found in another table. For the moment, here are the relationships between the lowest and highest values observed in our thirteen groups of human populations (in parentheses, the sample size):

Table 3. "Racial" differences of correlations

	Minimum	Maximum	Test *t*	Group (1,656)
Width/length	−0.116 (61)	+0.607 (79)	4.9**	+0.101
Height/length	+0.073 (56)	+0.553 (129)	3.2**	+0.334
Width/height	+0.170 (193)	+0.551 (45)	3.0**	+0.147
Length/cranial capacity	+0.487 (56)	+0.884 (79)	3.8**	+0.536
Width/cranial capacity	+0.534 (193)	+0.856 (129)	5.7**	+0.741
Height/cranial capacity	+0.540 (85)	+0.828 (45)	3.2**	+0.553

In man, all the minimum values of the correlation coefficients differ significantly from the maximum values, but this difference will diminish somewhat in the partial correlations. These gross fluctuations reveal not only the differences in genetic heritage among the populations but also the heterogeneity of the sample groups (some included equal numbers of subjects of both sexes, and others did not). Finally, we must take into account the inaccuracy of the correlation coefficient.

In the chimpanzee, comparison of the coefficients found for each species points out no differences; but this might be due to the reduced size of the samples and to the fact that the values are already increased because males and females are treated together:

Table 4. Specific differences of correlations

	41 *Pan troglodytes*	59 *Pan paniscus*	Test *t*	Group (100)
Width/length	+0.739	+0.518	1.8	+0.701
Height/length	+0.483	+0.379	0.6	+0.628
Width/height	+0.595	+0.503	0.6	+0.576
Length/cranial capacity	+0.627	+0.441	1.3	+0.702
Width/cranial capacity	+0.817	+0.713	1.2	+0.794
Height/cranial capacity	+0.627	+0.480	1.0	+0.672

The coefficients found for *P. troglodytes* are all higher than those of *P. paniscus,* but they are neither significant nor conclusive (this might be due to a single subject with extreme traits). However, two correlations of *P. paniscus* differ significantly from those of the rest of the chimpanzees: these are the ones relating height and length of the skull, and length and cranial capacity.

Partial Correlations

Here, we obtain a clearer perspective on the situation. Let us begin with constant cranial capacity and with group values:

Table 5. Generic differences of partial correlations

	1,656 Men	100 Chimpanzees	Test *t*
Width/length	−0.517***	+0.325***	9.2***
Height/length	+0.053	+0.235*	1.9*
Width/height	−0.476***	+0.159	6.4**

We compare these results with the simple correlations of Table 1: the order of the differences is the same; all of the correlations decrease; when they are slightly low, they become insignificant (height/length in man, width/height in the chimp). The reason is that secondary correlations of skull volume came into play here; when the simple correlations were almost null, they reversed themselves and became negative and clearly significant. The difference between man and chimpanzee rests in these last correlations which are a property of man. The chimpanzee will never provide us with negative partial correlations, if the cranial capacity is kept constant, because the dimensions concerned will always reveal enough relationships for the SHAPE of the skull to be maintained. In man, on the other hand, the correlations are smaller in general; those of width are greatly influenced by volume. Abstracting from this, we observe good INVERSE correlations, the meaning of which is quite clear. There is a retention of the FORMAT (size) at the expense of the FORM (shape). Cerebral volume is so essential to man that the format of the skull takes priority over the form. This is the "compensation" process of diameters described by J. Leschi and found here in another fashion. In the Pongidae, the form is almost always translatable as taxonomic reality. Man is a singular being by virtue of the priority given to brain volume.

Of course, these partial correlations, with volume kept constant, will vary just as the preceding values did according to sex, race, and species:

Table 6. Sexual differences of partial correlations

	Portuguese			Chimpanzees		
	494 Men	506 Women	Total	50 Males	50 Females	Total
Width/length	−0.274***	−0.236***	−0.247***	0.228	0.357***	0.325***
Height/length	0.002	0.047	0.095**	0.301*	0.112	0.235*
Width/height	−0.194**	−0.104*	−0.156***	0.078	0.265	0.159

There is no sexual difference in the partial correlations, with capacity kept constant, in man or in the chimpanzee. In this case the values for each sex are no greater than for the group composed of both sexes.

There also do not appear to be any differences between the species of chimpanzee, but perhaps this is due to the causes given after the Table 3 data above:

Table 7. Specific differences of partial correlations

	41 *Pan troglodytes*	59 *Pan paniscus*	Test *t*	Group total (100)
Width/length	+0.505***	+0.323*	1.1	+0.325***
Height/length	+0.148	+0.212	0.3	+0.235*
Width/height	+0.184	+0.261*	0.5	+0.159

On the other hand, differences between human samples are discernible. It does not seem that these differences are linked to the shape of the skull as it is determined by the horizontal or height cranial indices. We must therefore be dealing with different genetic material in each population, or with interaction among the subjects which is different from the rest of the genus. The size of the groups is found between parentheses:

Table 8. "Racial" differences of partial correlations

	Minimum	Maximum	Test *t*	Group total (1,656)
Width/length	+0.022 (184)	−0.568*** (138)	5.1	**−0.517*** **
Height/length	+0.161* (184)	−0.509*** (328)	8.1	+0.053
Width/height	−0.003 (140)	−0.611*** (129)	6.0	−0.476***

We wondered why the different diameters revealed different correlations in man and in the chimpanzee, particularly for the partial correlations of skull height with both width and length. We tried to find the correlation values between the two diameters with the third dimension held constant. We were not able to derive much information from this. There is some lowering of the simple correlations of Table 1, with differences that are less than those observed when the cranial capacity was constant:

Table 9. Partial correlations with third dimension constant

	1,656 Men	100 Chimpanzees	Test *t*
Width/length	+0.056*	+0.528***	6.2**
Height/length	+0.324***	+0.306**	0.2
Width/height	+0.121***	+0.329***	2.2*

Everything occurs just as if the third dimension did not have the kind of importance held by capacity in the correlation between the two others and this is easily understood.

As in the preceding case, there is no sexual difference; the differences between human samples remain, but are less significant. Finally, a specific difference between the two species of chimpanzee appears: it seems that in *P.troglodytes* there is a strong partial correlation between width and length, and in *P. paniscus* there is a strong partial correlation between height and length. In both cases the third dimension is held constant. Numerical proof of this follows:

Table 10. Sexual differences of multiple partial correlations

	Portuguese			Chimpanzees		
	494 Men	506 Women	1000 Total	50 Males	50 Females	100 Total
Width/length	+0.171**	+0.202***	+0.257***	+0.520***	+0.545***	+0.528
Height/length	+0.283***	+0.290***	+0.227***	+0.370**	+0.145	+0.306**
Width/height	+0.150**	+0.181***	+0.447***	+0.267	+0.428**	+0.329***

Table 11. "Racial" differences of multiple partial correlations

	Minimum	Maximum	Test t	Group total (1,656)
Width/length	—0.240 (61)	+0.537*** (79)	2.03*	+0.056*
Height/length	+0.064 (56)	+0.469*** (138)	2.7**	+0.324***
Width/height	+0.119 (193)	+0.413*** (138)	2.9**	+0.121***

CONCLUSIONS

The study of PARTIAL CORRELATIONS between major CRANIAL DIAMETERS, with the cranial capacity kept constant, sheds new light on the uncertain results previously obtained by means of simple correlations. Instead of finding genetic homogeneity in isolated populations, we were able to establish the following facts:

1. In the chimpanzee there is some persistence of the proportions and of the FORM (shape), regardless of skull size;
2. In man we observed some persistence of the FORMAT (size) by a sort of compensation between major diameters; a general rule gives a MAJOR TAXONOMIC character to the form; but in man the cerebral volume, manifested in the skull format, is preponderant and becomes the generic classification criterion.

Carried out on more than 1,000 human skulls and on one hundred skulls of two different species of chimpanzees, this study has enabled us to discover certain fluctuations within each group and between human races and species of chimpanzee. Further research will perhaps lead to an explanation of these variations.

Appendix 1.

		Length		Width		Height		Cranial Cap.		Sources
CHIMPANZEE POPULATIONS		m	σ	m	σ	m	σ	m	σ	
Pan troglodytes	22 males	138.1	5.23	101.6	3.20	92.2	4.03	420.5	34.1	Documents Deblock
	19 females	131.5	4.67	97.6	3.77	88.8	3.16	376.9	36.9	Documents Deblock
	41 total	135.0	6.15	99.8	3.67	90.6	3.94	400.3	40.8	Documents Deblock
Pan paniscus	28 males	123.8	3.14	95.3	4.33	87.1	3.20	363.8	32.0	Documents Deblock
	31 females	124.8	5.39	96.0	3.59	86.2	3.20	340.1	34.7	Documents Deblock
	59 total	124.3	4.43	95.7	3.78	86.6	3.40	351.3	34.9	Documents Deblock
All chimpanzees	50 males	130.3	8.22	98.0	4.92	89.3	4.32	388.8	42.8	Documents Deblock
	50 females	127.4	5.98	96.6	3.60	87.2	3.36	354.1	39.2	Documents Deblock
	100 total	128.8	7.33	97.3	4.38	88.3	4.02	371.4	44.5	Documents Deblock
HUMAN POPULATIONS										
Ameridians	62 M	181.7	5.39	140.6	4.50	130.7	3.67	1,396.9	91.5	Hrdlicka 1924
(Santa Cruz)	67 F	172.7	4.19	135.0	3.72	125.1	3.75	1,222.8	71.4	Hrdlicka 1924
	129 M+F	177.0	6.55	137.7	4.98	127.8	4.63	1,306.5	119.3	Hrdlicka 1924

Appendix 1. (Continued)

HUMAN POPULATIONS		Length		Width		Height		Cranial Cap.		Sources
		m	σ	m	σ	m	σ	m	σ	
Southern Australians	185 M	190.9	5.61	133.1	4.46	130.8	5.24	1,395.4	99.9	Hrdlicka 1924
	143 F	181.1	5.11	128.3	4.59	124.9	4.80	1,211.1	88.7	Hrdlicka 1924
	328 M+F	186.8	7.19	131.0	5.10	128.2	5.83	1,315.0	131.9	Hrdlicka 1924
Auvergne residents (France)	85M+F	174.6	6.75	146.8	6.17	129.3	6.05	1,524.5	138.0	Documents Broca
South Chinese	56 M+F	179.5	6.00	138.7	5.16	136.9	4.55	1,421.6	63.4	Olivier 1966
Corsicans (France)	79 M+F	180.5	8.52	135.1	5.40	128.1	6.03	1,299.2	146.9	Documents Broca
Eskimos	78 M	187.3	5.82	138.0	4.59	138.9	4.67	1,528.0	104.8	Hrdlicka 1924
	62 F	179.7	4.67	132.4	5.07	132.0	5.07	1,360.6	91.1	Hrdlicka 1924
	140 M+F	183.9	6.53	135.5	5.56	135.9	5.65	1,453.9	129.5	Hrdlicka 1924
French	63 M	181.8	6.46	145.1	6.58	132.0	5.83	1,486.7	134.9	Olivier 1970
	56 F	174.8	7.84	140.7	6.50	126.6	5.52	1,326.6	136.1	Olivier 1970
	119 M+F	178.4	7.82	143.5	6.79	129.6	6.14	1,411.4	157.4	Olivier 1970
Mongols	113 M	184.2	6.00	150.1	5.59	131.1	4.71	1,575.7	110.9	Hrdlicka 1924
	71 F	173.6	6.00	143.0	5.19	125.3	4.00	1,406.6	128.0	Hrdlicka 1924
	184 M+F	180.1	7.90	147.4	6.45	128.8	5.27	1,510.5	143.7	Hrdlicka 1924
Negrillos	45 M+F	174.4	6.34	132.3	5.46	128.7	5.60	1,238.1	126.7	Documents Marquer

Appendix 1. (Continued)

HUMAN POPULATIONS		Length		Width		Height		Cranial Cap.		Sources
		m	σ	m	σ	m	σ	m	σ	
New Caledonians	86 M	184.1	6.85	132.3	4.86	139.5	3.91	1,423.1	99.4	Sarasin 1916–1922
	52 F	178.3	5.93	127.5	5.32	133.6	3.47	1,284.5	92.4	Sarasin 1916–1922
	138 M+F	181.9	7.10	130.5	5.57	137.4	4.72	1,370.9	117.8	Sarasin 1916–1922
New Guineans	124 M	177.6	6.88	131.4	5.09	131.6	4.06	1,279.6	99.9	Hambly 1940
	69 F	170.4	5.22	126.4	4.54	128.6	4.71	1,153.6	76.0	Hambly 1940
	193 M+F	175.0	7.22	129.6	5.46	130.5	4.53	1,234.6	110.1	Hambly 1940
Senegalese	99 M+F	177.8	6.87	129.8	4.16	130.2	5.42	1,245.6	114.1	Documents Laffont
Vietnamese	61 M+F	175.4	6.54	139.0	5.44	137.0	4.60	1,413.9	61.2	Olivier 1966
TOTAL	1,656 M+F	180.2	8.32	135.9	8.41	130.8	6.40	1,361.0	158.1	
Portuguese	494 M	185.0	6.37	137.8	5.55	134.1	5.20	1,517.9	126.5	Documents De Macédo
	506 F	176.5	5.88	133.3	4.94	127.5	4.78	1,341.1	113.0	Documents De Macédo

Appendix 2. "Racial" correlation variations

SIMPLE CORRELATIONS

Width / Length		Height / Length		Width / Height	
79 Corsicans	.607***	Amerindians	.553***	Negrillos	.551***
129 Amerindians	.550***	Negrillos	.548***	Amerindians	.480***
328 Australians	.514***	Mongols	.525***	French	.419***
184 Mongols	.512***	French	.518***	Eskimos	.415***
85 Auvergne residents	.496***	Senegalese	.518***	Mongols	.413***
99 Senegalese	.444***	Eskimos	.517***	Australians	.393***
119 French	.380***	Corsicans	.513***	Senegalese	.356***
45 Negrillos	.350*	Australians	.488***	New Caledonians	.354***
140 Eskimos	.285***	New Caledonians	.421***	Corsicans	.338**
193 New Guineans	.153*	New Guineans	.412***	Vietnamese	.256*
56 Chinese	.044	Vietnamese	.384**	Auvergne residents	.248*
138 Caledonians	.049	Auvergne residents	.294**	Chinese	.235
61 Vietnamese	–.116	Chinese	.073	New Guineans	.170*

Appendix 2. (Continued)

PARTIAL CORRELATION (with cranial capacity kept constant)	Width / Length		Height / Length		Width / Height
Negrillos	–.598***	Australians	–.509***	Corsicans	–.613***
New Caledonians	–.568***	Senegalese	–.489***	Amerindians	–.611***
Vietnamese	–.562***	Corsicans	–.456***	Australians	–.383***
Amerindians	–.485***	Chinese	–.375***	Senegalese	–.360***
French	–.426***	Negrillos	–.337*	Vietnamese	
Chinese	–.387***	Amerindians	–.024	Negrillos	–.341*
New Guineans	–.367***	Auvergne residents	–.046	Chinese	–.306*
Senegalese	–.346***	Eskimos	–.051	New Guineans	–.247***
Eskimos	–.340***	New Guineans	–.096	French	–.207*
Australians	–.335***	Vietnamese	–.244**	Auvergne residents	–.190
Corsicans	–.330**	New Caledonians	+.049	Mongols	–.082
Auvergne residents	–.033	French	+.093	New Caledonians	–.057
Mongols	+.022	Mongols	+.161*	Eskimos	–.603

Appendix 2. (Continued)

MULTIPLE PARTIAL CORRELATIONS	Width/Length		Height/Length		Width/Height
Corsicans	.537***	New Caledonians	.469***	Negrillos	.447***
Auvergne residents	.404***	Eskimos	.454***	New Caledonians	.413***
Australians	.401***	Vietnamese	.431***	Eskimos	.321***
Amerindians	.389***	Senegalese	.430***	French	.281**
Mongols	.369***	French	.427***	Vietnamese	.253**
Senegalese	.325***	Corsicans	.412***	Amerindians	.253**
New Caledonians	.233**	Mongols	.406***	Chinese	.233*
French	.210*	New Guineans	.396***	Auvergne residents	.212*
Negrillos	.114	Amerindians	.395***	Mongols	.195**
Eskimos	.103	Negrillos	.390***	Australians	.190**
New Guineans	.092	Australians	.369***	Senegalese	.164
Chinese	.028	Auvergne residents	.158	New Guineans	.119
Vietnamese	–.240	Chinese	.064		

REFERENCES

CHABEUF, M.
1969 Les caractères physiques de sept populations malgaches. *Bulletins et Mémoires de la Société d'Anthropologie de Paris* 4:181–207.

DAHLBERG, G.
1941 *The race biology of the Swedish Lapps.* Uppsala.

KHÉRUMIAN R., J. BOULANGER
1949 Contribution à l'étude biométrique des principaux diamètres et indices cranio-faciaux. *Bulletins et Mémoires de la Société d'Anthropologie de Paris* 10:70–88.

LESCHI, J.
1954 Forme du crâne et capacité crânienne. Variations compensatrices des trois diamètres crâniens. *L'Anthropologie* 58:29–61.

OLIVIER G., R. NISTRI
1957 Les corrélations céphalo-faciales dans les races humaines. *Bulletins et Mémoires de la Société d'Anthropologie de Paris* 8:31–46.

OLIVIER G., H. TISSIER
1970 Données sur le crâne des Français. *Bulletins et Mémoires de la Société d'Anthropologie de Paris* 6:307–310.

VASSAL P., H. PINEAU
1955 Etude corrélative de quelques mesures de la tête. *Comptes-rendus de l'Association des Anatomistes* 6:1350–1359.

A Comparison of the Neurocranium and the Splanchnocranium in Recent and Fossil Primates

FRANCISZEK M. ROSIŃSKI and ANNA SZWEDZIŃSKA

A significant factor in the process of hominization was the accelerated growth rate of the neurocranium, which was accompanied by a reduction of the proportion of the facial area in the skull during the hominid phase. Different methods have been proposed for a quantitative assessment of the relationship between these two segments of the skull (see Stratz 1904; Oppenheim 1911; Sergi 1940; and Hemmer 1967).

Herein we will devote particular attention to Stratz's method. It is principally based on natural skull proportions. From outline sketches of skulls on millimeter graph paper in norma lateralis the surface areas of the neurocranium and the splanchnocranium are calculated by simple addition of the squares. The face-brain index ("Stratzindex") is calculated thus:

$$\frac{\textit{Surface area of the splanchnocranium} \times 100}{\textit{Surface area of the neurocranium}}$$

Stratz's method is very time-consuming, therefore we employed a planimeter, which is a mechanical integrator for areal measurements of plane figures. This simplified measuring considerably. We used median sagittal outline sketches and photographs of skulls in norma lateralis. These were taken in part from the works of Stratz (1904), with information on fifteen skulls, as well as from Oppenheim (1911), Schreiner (1927), Weidenreich (1943), Broom and Schepers (1946), Snow (1948), Broom and Robinson (1950, 1952), Hill (1953–1970), Milicerowa (1955), Wokroj (1955), Hofer et al. (1956), Górny (1957), Martin and Saller (1957), Piveteau (1957), Gieseler (1959), Belniak et al. (1961), Genet-Varcin (1963), Davis and Napier (1963), Strauss (1964), Tobias (1967), and Müller (1970).

The amount of material that was available to us and the demarcation line between the face and brain skull areas advocated by Stratz did not guarantee a completely satisfactory calculation of the Stratz index in every case. In the reconstruction of different fossil hominid skulls, the values are only approximate. Nevertheless, the information presented here might give some new insights into the interrelationships between the two parts of the skull in different primate forms. We followed the systematics of Genet-Varcin (1963) and Stęślicka-Mydlarska (1967). The face-brain index values for the 363 primate skulls may be found in the following tables:

	Total	Table
Prosimiae, recent	33	1
Prosimiae, fossil	17	1
Simiae, recent	73	2
Simiae, fossil	7	2
Hominidae, fossil	28	3
Homo sapiens, recent	190	4
Neonate, infant and juvenile	15	5

Examination and overview of the final results reveals a very diversified picture. In comparison with other groups, the Lemuriformes (see Table 1) have relatively high index values premised on the considerable development of the facial area of the skull and low volume of the neurocranium. Among the Prosimiae a number of Lorisiformes and Tarsiiformes exhibit relatively low values as a result of significant reduction in the splanchnocranium and the rounder brain cavity. However, this is not associated with phylogenetic increase in brain size. For instance, the brain of *Loris tardigradus* is barely six grams (Brauer and Schober 1970).

The platyrrhine monkeys have brains that are qualitatively and quantitatively better developed than prosimian brains. For example, the brain weight of *Lagothrix humboldti* is 112 grams (Spitzka 1903) while that of *Lemur mongoz* is just eighteen grams (Brauer and Schober 1970). The Stratz index also demonstrates a more strongly pronounced tendency towards rounding of the general skull profile in extant Platyrrhini (see Table 2). The arithmetic mean value of twenty-one recent Platyrrhini is 105.8. It is 153.6 for twenty recent lemuriforme skulls.

In the Cercopithecoidea, the relationship between the neurocranium and the splanchnocranium is quite variable. Although many of them have a relatively large brain volume (e.g. *Papio hamadryas* is 186.4 grams [Brauer and Schober 1970]), their index value is very high as a

Table 1. The face-brain skull index in recent and fossil Prosimiae

Infra-order	Family	Genus	N	Index value
	Tupaiidae	*Tupaia*	2	134.2; 170.9
		+*Anagale*	1	c. 228.0
	Apatemyidae	+*Sinclairella*	1	c. 173.0
		+*Stehlinella*	1	c. 164.0
Lemuriformes	Lemuridae	*Lepilemur*	1	163.3
		Hapalemur	1	154.7
		Lemur	7	118.6–187.9
		Cheirogaleus	1	183.1
		Microcebus	1	134.3
		Phaner	1	118.1
		+*Megaladapis*	2	307.1; 324.4
		+*Archaeolemur*	1	191.1
		+*Hadropithecus*	1	180.6
	Indriidae	*Indri*	1	201.9
		Avahi	1	200.0
		Propithecus	2	170.6; 179.5
		+*Palaeopropithecus*	2	268.9
		+*Archaeoindris*	1	196.3
		+*Mesopropithecus*	2	140.9; 143.2
	+Notharctidae	+*Notharctus*	2	181.6; 212.5
	+Plesiadapidae	+*Plesiadapis*	1	191.7
	+Adapidae	+*Adapis*	2	172.6; 177.3
	Daubentoniidae	*Daubentonia*	2	107.7; 123.1
Lorisiformes	Lorisidae	*Perodicticus*	1	228.0
		Nycticebus	1	161.4
		Loris	2	77.5; 140.1
		Arctocebus	1	121.9
	Galagidae	*Galago*	2	173.9; 125.6
		Euoticus	1	111.7
		Galagoides	1	94.6
Tarsiiformes	Tarsiidae	*Tarsius*	4	79.3–111.9
	Anaptomorphidae	+*Tetonius*	1	145.9

result of the highly developed muzzle region. The opposite is true of *Cercopithecus talapoin*, Schreber, which has a brain weight of barely 38.5 grams (Brauer and Schober 1970). But with regard to the Stratz index it falls next to that of modern *Homo sapiens*. To a greater extent than in any other nonhuman primate, the talapoin monkey exhibits a significant reduction in jaw prognathism with simultaneous rounding of the neurocranium. The skull profile of fully adult specimens is in

Table 2. The face-brain skull index in recent and fossil Simiae

Infra-order	Family	Genus	N	Index value
Platyrrhini	Cebidae	*Alouatta*	1	190.4
		Pithecia	1	138.3
		Cacajao	1	133.7
		Brachyteles	1	127.5
		Chiropotes	1	122.2
		Aotes	1	111.8
		Cacajao	1	110.7
		Lagothrix	1	103.7
		Callicebus	1	98.2
		Callimico	1	75.7
		Cebus	3	81.5–101.5
		Ateles	3	67.6– 88.3
		+*Cebupithecia*	1	117.7
	Callitrichidae	*Cebuella*	1	87.1
		Hapale	2	77.3; 87.0
		Tamarin	2	102.7; 103.8
Catarrhini	Cercopithecidae	*Theropithecus*	1	238.0
		Papio	4	154.4–228.4
		Mandrillus	1	210.4
		Cynocephalus	1	203.1
		Macaca	3	98.6–199.5
		Comopithecus	1	189.3
		+*Gorgopithecus*	1	179.6
		Semnopithecus	4	75.4–154.2
		Cercocebus	1	144.9
		Cynomolgus	1	139.3
		Simias	1	136.7
		Allenopithecus	1	120.3
		Cercopithecus	2	102.5; 124.5
		Cercopithecus talapoin	2	50.6; 60.6
		Erythrocebus	2	75.4; 99.6
		Colobus	1	79.2
		+*Mesopithecus*	1	166.2
		+*Parapapio*	1	125.3
		+*Dolichopithecus*	1	106.6
	Hylobatidae	*Hylobates*	6	67.1– 88.6
	Pongidae	*Pongo*	6	102.0–173.2
		Gorilla	5	140.0–167.4
		Pan	8	81.0–128.0
		+*Proconsul* (2 reconstructions)	1	90.7; 239.8
		+*Oreopithecus*	1	76.2

many ways reminiscent of early ontogenetic stages in other species of *Cercopithecus*.

Among the anthropoid apes, the lowest index values (67.1–88.6) occur in the relatively primitive *Hylobates,* although according to Tobias (1963) the average brain capacity is only 89.3 cubic centimeters. The difference between the great apes and *Homo* is more telling, with the fossil hominids occupying an intermediary position (see Table 3). The median value for eight variably reconstructed australopithecine skulls

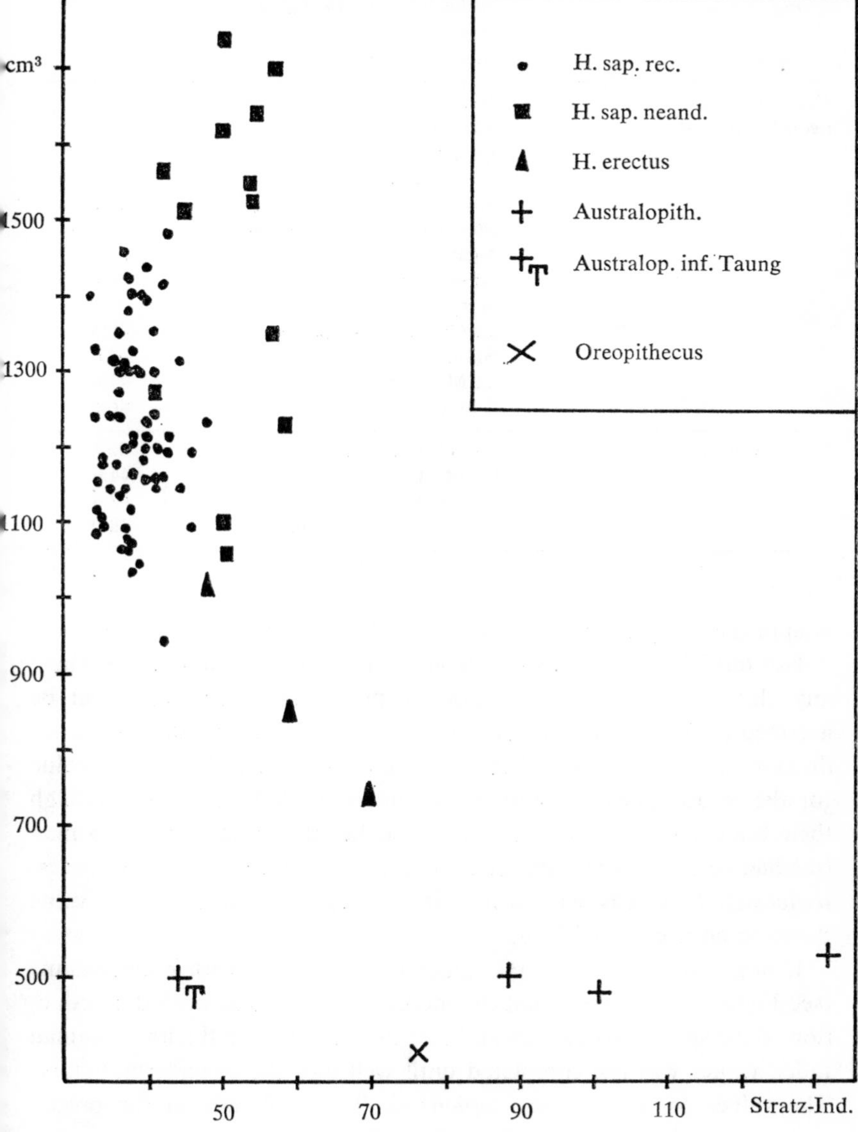

Figure 1. The face-brain skull index in proportion to brain volume

Table 3. The face-brain skull index in fossil hominids (mostly reconstructed)

Systematic division	Common name	Index value
Australopithecinae	*Zinjanthropus*	131.8
	Plesianthropus 5	100.7
	Plesianthropus 7	88.2
	5 other Australopithecines (largely reconstructed)	84.9–103.4
Homo erectus	*Pithecanthropus robustus*	69.5
	Homo erectus I Trinil	59.0
	Sinanthropus XI	47.9
Homo sapiens neanderthalensis	Neanderthal	58.4
	Shanidar	57.0
	La Quina	56.8
	La Ferrasie	54.3
	Spy I	53.9
	Monte Circeo	53.4
	Ngandong	50.3
	Amud I	50.0
	Africanthropus	50.0
	La Chapelle-aux Saints	49.5
	Skhūl V	44.8
	Le Moustier	41.6
	Tabun	40.0
Homo sapiens	Cro-Magnon male	45.1
	Combe Capelle	44.0
	Predmosti (male)	43.4
	Afalou-bou-Rhummel	38.0

is approximately 99, thereby falling squarely in the pongid range.

Not until *Homo erectus* and *Homo sapiens neanderthalensis* is there any clear trend toward reduction of the index values. This can be ascribed to the increase in brain volume and also to the significant reduction of the facial part of the skull. But even then, the median value for the Stratz index for thirteen Neanderthal skulls is 50.8, although their brain volume is on average no smaller than that of modern man (median value is 1,451 cubic centimeters for the *Homo sapiens neanderthalensis*). It is only with recent *Homo sapiens* that the index value drops to an average of 37.8.

If hominid face-brain skull values are contrasted with brain volume (see Figure 1), it is clear that the increase in brain size preceded reduction of the splanchnocranium and that the transition to the lower human index values was not completed until well into the Neanderthal stage. The values for four *Homo sapiens* skulls are already in the border region of modern man (see Table 3).

There are no major differences in the Stratz index for geographically dispersed human races, as Stratz himself pointed out. However, the index values for male skulls are on average higher than for female skulls (see Table 4).

In early development stages, the index value is much lower than in adult individuals. For example, in *Cercopithecus* the index value of infants is 29.1, of juveniles is 34.9 and 102.5 and 124.5 for two fully grown individuals. The relatively small difference in index values for immature individuals of different primate species, in contrast to much larger differences among mature specimens, is in keeping with the fact that the skull shapes of different species are more similar during the early developmental stages.

Table 4. The face-brain skull index in different series of *Homo sapiens*

Series	♂ Male		♀ Female		Male and Female		
	N	x	N	x	N	x	Minimum–maximum
Central European (Wokroj 1955)	47	36.4			47	36.4	31.3–41.2
North European (Schreiner 1927)	17	38.3	5	35.9	22	37.7	32.4–43.0
African (Górny 1957)	25	38.9	20	36.5	45	37.8	31.6–48.4
Red Indian (Snow 1948)	6	38.3	7	37.4	13	37.8	32.8–43.6
Australian (Milicerowa 1955)	27	40.1	17	36.6	44	38.8	32.9–48.5
Various others	16	39.8	3		19	39.5	30.1–44.6
Total:	138	38.3	52	36.4	190	37.8	30.1–48.5

Table 5. The face-brain skull index in a number of newborn, infant, and young anthropoid skulls

Monkeys and Apes	Index value	Hominids	Index value
Cercopithecus sabaeus (neonate)	29.1	*Australopithecus* (Taung infant)	44.4
Cercopithecus hamlyni (juvenile)	34.9	*Paranthropus crassidens* (infant)	48.0
Hylobates (newborn)	20.4	Teshik-Tash (Neanderthal, infant)	30.5
Pongo (juvenile)	49.1	Grimaldi (juvenile)	27.0
Gorilla (juvenile, male)	95.7	*Homo sapiens* (newborn)	17.5
Gorilla (juvenile, female)	70.9	*Homo sapiens* (new born)	17.6
Pan (juvenile)	55.3	*Homo sapiens* (new born)	17.8
		Homo sapiens (infant I)	20.9

Table 6. The proportion of the length of the face to the length of the neurocranium (index median values)

Primates	basion–prosthion × 100 / greatest length	basion–nasion × 100 / greatest length	basion–prosthion × 100 / basion–nasion
Lemur	150.8	107.8	140.4
Hapale	86.6	83.6	103.7
Mycetes	160.5	108.2	148.4
Cebus	86.5	77.3	112.1
Cynocephalus	120.2	80.6	146.0
Theropithecus	123.2	86.2	143.3
Macaca cynomolgus	120.0	89.2	130.2
Macaca nemestrina	131.2	90.6	141.8
Macaca sinica	123.9	84.2	142.4
Cercocebus collaris	126.1	70.7	162.1
Semnopithecus	95.1	83.5	115.1
Hylobates syndactylus (male)	114.4	89.4	128.0
Hylobates syndactylus (female)	109.3	86.3	126.7
Hylobates lar	93.6	80.1	119.9
Hylobates entelloides	98.3	84.6	116.1
Pongo (male)	134.8	84.1	160.2
Pongo (female)	113.2	80.4	141.6
Pongo (juvenile)	95.1	71.8	133.9
Gorilla (male)	141.8	104.3	136.0
Gorilla (female)	118.6	94.3	126.1
Gorilla (juvenile)	109.8	84.6	130.4
Pan (male)	108.8	81.2	134.0
Pan (female)	105.9	82.0	130.0
Pan (juvenile)	78.8	70.7	112.7
Pongo	115.5	75.4	153.3
Gorilla	103.5	73.2	141.3
Pan	99.0	73.4	134.9
Sterkfontein 5	83.1	66.4	125.1
Zinjanthropus	79.2	65.0	121.8
Homo erectus	58.9	56.9	108.1
Homo sapiens neanderthalensis	57.3	56.6	102.1
Homo sapiens	54.2	55.7	98.2

Although recent man diverges much from the nonhuman primates in regard to the face-brain skull index, we cannot agree with Stratz (1904: 93) "... that Man as an entity differs sharply from all animal groups in his face-brain skull index." The index value is low in certain nonhuman species like the talapoin monkey, which approaches values of the *Homo sapiens neanderthalensis*. In a sufficiently large selection of skulls of talapoin monkeys, and possibly in other species of animals particularly domesticated ones, index values less than 50.6 may be found. Since in the phylogenetically primitive primates, the index values only exhibit a partially increasing tendency, it is not advisable to attribute any major importance to this factor in modeling the evolutionary changes in skulls. On the other hand, the face-brain skull index may well be more suitable for the quantitative characterization of ontogenetic skull development or for quantitative expressions of sexual dimorphism.

Oppenheim (1911) demonstrated the interrelationship between the neurocranium and the splanchnocranium by means of 3 indices. These are reproduced in the first part of Table 6. But instead of the indices: $\frac{\textit{maximum length} \times 100}{\textit{basion-prosthion length}}$ and $\frac{\textit{basion-nasion length} \times 100}{\textit{basion-prosthion length}}$ we considered reverse relationships. The data were correspondingly converted as follows, $\frac{(\quad 10{,}000 \quad)}{\textit{index value}}$. Unfortunately, it was not possible to establish which measuring points Oppenheim used to obtain "maximum lengths." In the second part of the table, which contains data on anthropoid apes, fossil hominids, and modern man, glabella-opisthocranion lengths are shown. Table 7 gives further information on these indices.

As can be seen from the data given for the first and second indices it is not only *Homo sapiens* but also the fossil hominids that differ from the nonhuman primates. In the third index, modern man differs from the anthropoid apes, but not from all nonhuman primates, e.g. *Hapale* (see Table 6).

We also used traditional and some new cranio-facial indices in which modern man differed from the Pongidae, to establish further interrelationships between the splanchnocranium and the neurocranium. In this analysis the anthropoid apes were not considered to be phylogenetically basic forms. Instead they were considered systematically, more primitive comparative forms and at best working models of the more distant hominid predecessors. For the elaboration of these indices we partly used the graphic representations of individual skull dimensions of anthropoid apes in the work of Heintz (1966).

The data quoted with regard to pongid skulls in Tables 5 and 6 are based on measurements made on specimens in the Institut de Paléontologie Humaine, the Muséum National d'Histoire Naturelle in Paris and the Muzeum Antropologiczne in Wrocław. The other skull

Table 7. Cranio-facial index values in hominids and pongids[1]

Index	*Homo sapiens* (recent)			*Homo sapiens neanderthalensis*			*Homo e*		
	N	M	Minimum Maximum	N	M	Minimum Maximum	N	M	Min Max
1. Stratzindex	190	37.7	30.1– 48.5	13	50.8	40.6– 58.4	3	63.4	47.
2. ba–n × 100 / g–op	782	55.7	47.1– 64.0	7	56.6	51.0– 60.1	3	56.9	54.
3. ba–pr × 100 / po–b	279	87.9	73.9–108.0	5	104.6	98.3–112.4	1		121.
4. ba–pr × 100 / g–op	637	54.2	45.7– 66.0	5	57.3	54.8– 60.0	1		58.
5. ba–pr × 100 / eu–eu	695	72.7	58.7– 99.2	5	77.0	72.3– 80.4	1		84.
6. ba–pr × 100 / ba–b	640	71.9	62.4– 96.4	5	89.9	87.1– 95.3	1		99.
7. n–pr × 100 / eu–eu	788	50.5	38.3– 66.2	5	56.1	51.0– 65.8	1		55.
8. l–o × 100 / ba–pr	341	96.5	70.1–120.0	5	79.8	72.9– 88.2	1		75.
9. n–pr × 100 / ba–b	730	50.6	38.3– 64.6	5	65.6	56.6– 73.8	1		66.
10. n–pr × 100 / g–op	796	37.8	28.2– 45.6	5	41.8	38.0– 45.3	1		40.
11. n–pr × 100 / ft–ft	794	73.0	55.6– 90.3	5	81.6	73.7– 97.6	1		91.
12. n–ns × 100 / ba–b	760	36.7	27.5– 44.8	5	46.2	41.1– 50.4	1		45.
13. n–ns × 100 / ft–ft	827	53.1	40.4– 65.8	5	57.3	53.5– 60.5	1		62
14. zy–zy × 100 / ba–b	638	97.7	85.0–111.3	5	112.8	108.1–116.8	1		128
15. ba–pr × 100 / n–ba	702	98.2	79.1–117.3	5	102.1	94.4–117.3	1		108.
16. zy–zy × 100 / eu–eu	762	97.9	78.4–112.7	5	96.7	90.0–101.7	1		109.
17. ol–sta × 100 / g–op	382	25.7	20.9– 32.0	3	29.5	27.5– 31.3	1		27

[1] ba = basion; n = nasion; g = glabella; op = opisthocranion; po = porion; eu = euryon; b = bregma; o = opisthion; ns = nasospinale; ol = orale; sta = staphylion; ft = frontotemporale; zy = zygion; pr = prosthion; l = lambda

Table 1. (Continued)

Sterkfontein 5	*Pan*			*Gorilla*			*Pongo*		
	N	M	Minimum-Maximum	N	M	Minimum-Maximum	N	M	Minimum-Maximum
100.7	8	101.7	81.0–128.0	5	150.6	139.9–167.4	6	132.5	102.0–173.2
66.4	15	73.4	70.8– 79.4	17	73.2	66.2– 84.7	10	75.4	71.9– 83.6
158.4	17	193.3	168.3–216.2	18	230.9	188.5–304.6	9	195.2	162.0–227.6
83.1	15	99.0	91.9–107.9	17	103.5	93.0–140.3	10	115.5	100.0–129.1
123.2	15	129.4	117.6–146.0	17	149.3	136.2–168.9	10	139.5	120.8–155.9
122.0	15	152.4	138.0–169.0	17	169.2	148.4–192.2	10	152.0	134.1–177.4
75.8	18	80.1	67.3– 95.0	19	91.7	82.2–100.9	11	88.1	74.2–113.5
47.9	17	39.1	32.6– 47.2	18	39.1	30.9– 47.6	9	40.2	35.2– 47.7
75.0	15	94.0	82.0–109.2	17	104.6	89.8–121.1	10	93.3	83.0–106.5
51.1	15	61.0	54.1– 65.2	17	63.7	52.6– 78.2	10	71.0	59.0– 86.8
129.3	18	116.7	95.7–150.8	19	147.4	129.4–171.6	11	143.4	116.1–193.8
46.0	17	63.7	55.4– 82.2	18	86.9	73.5–100.0	10	69.7	53.8– 86.0
79.3	18	79.8	67.6–109.5	19	122.9	105.9–144.6	11	107.6	79.0–147.7
127.0	14	143.4	130.0–154.0	17	158.3	133.3–182.1	10	144.7	126.0–173.5
125.1	15	134.9	127.5–150.5	17	141.3	124.0–165.7	10	153.3	138.6–165.2
128.3	14	122.1	115.3–130.0	18	139.2	126.9–159.2	11	134.9	115.0–165.0
50.1*	18	50.2	41.1– 59.1	18	55.1	48.6– 69.4	10	57.9	50.8– 64.9

* from prosthion

dimensions are taken largely from the works mentioned above (with the Stratz index).

A comparison of the results in Table 7 shows that the fossil hominids belong between the Pongidae and *Homo sapiens* as far as the individual indices are concerned, yet the degree of similarity to *Homo sapiens* varies quite considerably from case to case. For example the similarity of the gracile *Australopithecus africanus* specimen "Sterkfontein 5," to *Homo sapiens* is much greater than that of the robust *Australopithecus, "Zinjanthropus boisei."*

In order to arrive at a better quantitative intermediary definition of the forms mentioned, we established a "bipolar similarity index." We calculated the difference between the median values for *Homo sapiens* and the average mean value of the three pongid genera (for which we correspondingly took the polar value of 100 percent and 0 percent of the *sapiens* similarity). Then we calculated the difference between the index value of Sterkfontein 5 and *Zinjanthropus,* on the one hand, and the mean pongid value. From this data, we constructed the index, which has a certain similarity with the dimorphism index proposed by Stęślicka (1958). If a hominid index value lay below the average median value of the pongids, it was counted as a negative or "dissimilarity value."

Figure 2 contains the graphic representation of the bipolar *sapiens* similarity index values for *Zinjanthropus,* Sterkfontein 5 and the reconstructed *Sinanthropus* skull.

The considerable scatter of the individual index values seems to point to a perceptible disproportion in the morphological structure and a different level of hominization dynamics in the individual skull elements in the australopithecines. *Homo erectus pekinensis* is considerably more balanced as far as the morphodynamics are concerned. A summary *sapiens* similarity value was calculated experimentally on the basis of the individual *sapiens* similarity index values. This was 5.0 for *Zinjanthropus,* 35.8 for Sterkfontein 5, and 77.4 for *Homo erectus pekinensis* in terms of the indices mentioned above.

Although the skull is remarkably resistant to evolutionary change (Washburn 1951), a partial analysis of this part of the skeleton reveals a very differentiated picture of different morphodynamic tendencies, both phylogenetically progressive and regressive in nature, which is manifested very clearly in a comparison between the neuro- and the splanchnocranium. At the same time, the relatively large amount of variation in anthropoid apes points to a wide range of trait variability in fossil hominids, whose morphological variability was certainly no less than in *Homo sapiens* populations, or in a large group of chimpanzees.

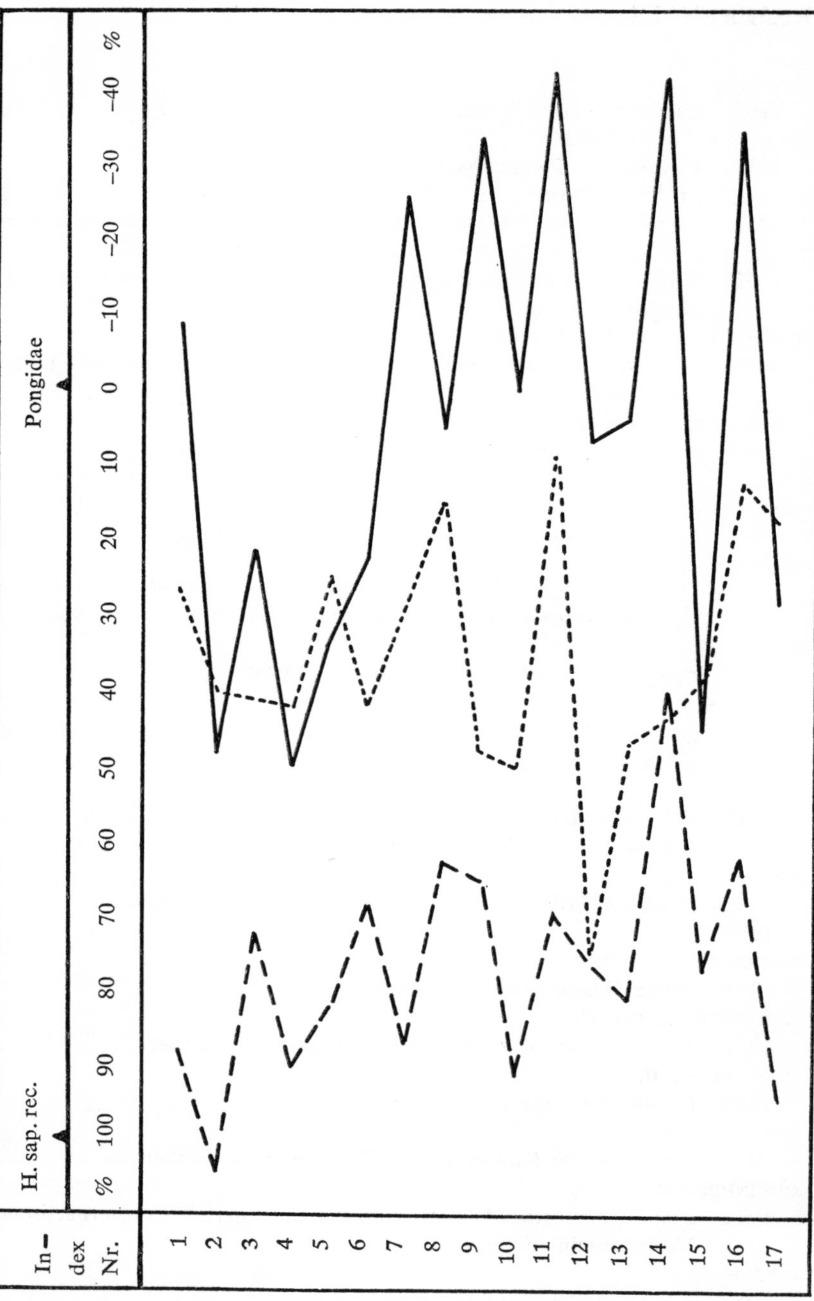

Figure 2. Bipolar sapiens similarity with regard to the cranio-facial indices in *Homo erectus pekinensis* (– –), Sterkfontein 5 (- - -), and *Zinjanthropus* (—)

REFERENCES

BELNIAK, T., *et al.*
1961 *Cmentarzysko w Gródku nad Bugiem*. Wrocław: PWN.

BRAUER, K., W. SCHOBER
1970 *Katalog der Säugetiergehirne*. Jena: G. Fischer.

BROOM, R., J. T. ROBINSON
1950 *Further evidence of the structure of the Sterkfontein Ape-Man* Plesianthropus. Transvaal Museum Memoir 4. Pretoria.
1952 *Swartkrans Ape-Man* Paranthropus crassidens. Transvaal Museum Memoir 6. Pretoria.

BROOM, R., G. W. H. SCHEPERS
1946 *The South African fossil Ape-Men, the Australopithecinae*. Transvaal Museum Memoir 2. Pretoria.

DAVIS, P. R., J. NAPIER
1963 A reconstruction of the skull of *Proconsul africanus* (R.S. 51). *Folia Primatologica* 1(1):20–28.

GENET-VARCIN, E.
1963 *Les singes actuels et fossiles*. Paris: N. Boubée.

GIESELER, W.
1959 "Die Fossilgeschichte des Menschen," in *Evolution der Organismen*. Edited by G. Heberer, 951–1109. Stuttgart: G. Fischer.

GÓRNY, S.
1957 *Crania Africana Uganda*. Wrocław: PWN.

HEINTZ, N.
1966 Le crâne des anthropomorphes. *Koninklijk Museum voor Midden Afrika* 4. Tervuren, Belgium.

HEMMER, H.
1967 *Allometrie-Untersuchungen zur Evolution des menschlichen Schädels und seiner Rassentypen*. Stuttgart: G. Fischer.

HILL, O. W. C.
1953–1970 *Primates*. Edinburgh: University of Edinburgh Press.

HOFER, H., *et al.*
1956 *Primatologia*. Basel: S. Karger.

MARTIN, R., K. SALLER
1957 *Lehrbuch der Anthropologie*. Stuttgart: G. Fischer.

MILICEROWA, H.
1955 *Crania Australica*. Wrocław: PWN.

MÜLLER, A. H.
1970 *Lehrbuch der Paläozoologie III/3*. Jena: G. Fischer.

OPPENHEIM, S.
1911 *Zur Typologie des Primatencraniums*. Stuttgart: Schweizerbartische Verlagsbuchhandlung.

PIVETEAU, J.
1957 *Traité de Paléontologie*. Paris: Masson.

SCHREINER, K. E.
1927 *Menneskeknoklene fra Osebergskibet og andre Norske Jernalderfund*. Oslo: Univ. Anat. Instit. den Antr. Avdel.

SERGI, S.
1940 Der Neandertalschädel vom Monte Circeo. *Anthropologischer Anzeiger* 16:203–217.

SNOW, C.
1948 *Indian Knoll skeletons.* Lexington: University of Kentucky.

SPITZKA, E. A.
1903 Brainweights of animals with special reference of the weight of the brain in the macaque monkey. *The Journal of Comparative Neurology* 13:9–17.

STĘŚLICKA, W.
1958 Wskaźniki dymorfizmu. *Materiały i Prace Antropol.* 45:5–44.

STĘŚLICKA-MYDLARSKA, W.
1967 "Rząd: naczelne – Primates," in *Zoologia.* Edited by Z. Grodziński 419–430. Warszawa: PWN.

STRATZ, C. H.
1904 Das Verhältnis zwischen Gesichts- und Gehirnschädel beim Menschen und Affen. *Archiv für Anthropologie* 3:85–93.

STRAUS, W. L.
1964 "The classification of *Oreopithecus,*" in *Classification and human evolution.* Edited by S. L. Washburn, 146–177. London: Methuen.

TOBIAS, P.
1963 Cranial capacity of *Zinjanthropus* and other australopithecines. *Nature* 197:743–746.
1967 "The cranium and maxillary dentition of *Australopithecus (Zinjanthropus) boisei,*" in *Olduvai Gorge.* Edited by L. S. B. Leakey. Cambridge: Cambridge University Press.

WASHBURN, S. L.
1951 The new physical anthropology. *Transactions of the New York Academy of Sciences II* 13(7):298–304.

WEIDENREICH, F.
1943 *The skull of* Sinanthropus pekinensis. Palaeontologia Sinica, 127, 486 pages.

WOKROJ, F.
1955 Fotografie 50 czaszek z Ostrowa Lednickiego omawianych na konferencji metodologicznej i typologicznej. *Przegląd Antropologiczny* 21:3.

The Brain of Primitive Man

HANNIBAL HAMLIN

Knowledge about human brain evolution, if collated with modern neurological discipline, might reasonably reach retrograde beyond the extant geographic representatives of *Homo sapiens*, probably as far back as Neanderthal. In this context, what is actually known anatomically about the brain of primitive man should be derived partly from contemporary surviving groups of primitive people.

A few autopsy specimens from one such rare source have been given competent, although selective and sketchy, neurohistologic appraisal. These were contributed by a Stone Age mountain enclave of south-central New Guinea, having been collected by Carleton Gajdusek of the National Institutes of Health; they have been studied under light microscopy by Professor Elizabeth Beck, neuropathologist at Maudsley Hospital, London. Remarkable features were (1) unusually large midline septal nuclei and massa intermedia, the transverse connection between right and left thalami (head ganglia of sensorimotor integration) and (2) what appeared to be accessory hypothalamic nuclei and smaller inferior frontal lobes. Poorly staining white matter was noted in certain areas and suggested inadequate myelination due to deficient protein intake during maturation. Physical habitus and metabolic pattern of the Fore people have been described in studies by Gajdusek and co-workers and can be briefed as follows: delayed growth and maturation with short stature and low weight, and amazingly high toleration for pain; low water intake and urinary output; low protein/fat ratio with high carbohydrate diet and low nitrogen and amino acid excretion; also reversal of urinary sodium/potassium ratio, low serum cholesterol, and low BP — but a high level of physical fitness.

An empirical generalization about the functional brain of early mankind during its distant past is linked with the evolution of ability to communicate linguistic speech (verbalization) and its subsequent correlation with handedness. Archaeologic evidence would suggest a wide temporal gap between ethologically conditioned talk and the choice between right-left preferential lateralization of spearhead action to one side of the midline plane of somatic symmetry. The latter would seem to have developed during the late Paleolithic — dextro in about three-fourths of us, levo in about one-fourth — the unique feature of human telokinesis, apparently associated with optional dominance of the leading hand in concordance with proplasia of certain parts of the corresponding cerebral hemisphere contralateral to that hand, notably the *planum temporale* on the left side, which can often be seen in horizontal section through the level of auditory cortex.

No right-left neuroblastic predominance was observed in tissue blocs taken from either side of the cortical matrix in sixteen- to twenty-six-week-old fetal brains. Physiologic investigation disclosed unilateral cortical electroencephalograph activity in response to bilateral visual photic stimuli among neonates which might appear to presage cerebral dominance. Psychological data described directional gaze in right-handed adults when cogitating, supposedly pointing to lateralization of language in the left hemisphere and stereognosis in the right. No indication has been found of disparate memory storage vis-à-vis right or left hemisphere.

Intriguing evidence confronts us in the right-sided preponderance that extends from the primary Betz cortical cells caudally into the motor tracts from internal capsule down through brainstem and into the crossed-over final common pathway in the spinal cord where pyramidal right-of-way is greater on the right side than the left at and below the medullary decussation, continuing into the anterior horn cells and internuncial neurones which direct all efferent systems. This most epochal discovery since the early descriptions of the human pyramidal tract was recently formulated from studies of precursory neuronal migrations in the premyelinated central nervous systems of young embryos.

Millennia of humanoid central nervous system evolution preceded the relatively recent and comparatively secondary influence of the making and manipulating of tools and weapons on brain morphology. For instance, findings of as many right-handed as left-handed flint artifacts and correlative postural representations depicting right-left actions in mesolithic cave art lend support to such a concept. During the major part of their neuro-evolution, our hominid ancestors were more likely to have been browsers than hunters.

The evolutionary importance to modern man of fossil craniometry, brain size, and brain configuration with relevance to longevity and other factors has been well formulated by competent scholars. But I must submit that the notion of "paleoneurology" which would include neuroanatomy and physiology, and even ethology, indulges not speculation but fantasy. Consider the fantastic individual variation of the human brain, wherein every neuron (nonregenerative) carries its special DNA genome. Except for the close simulation between identical twins, none of our brains are alike. The brain — not the heart — is indeed the chalice of individual personality.

Speculation about the brain of primitive man would be more realistic if it pertained to the ancient living races — the geographic representatives of the human species. Comparative information from surviving groups similar to the Fore people of New Guinea (i.e. Australian aborigines, African or South American isolates) is nonexistent. Furthermore, it is likely that systematic studies of brain samples from such diminishing geographic varieties of mankind — while still available — would provide additional insight toward appreciation of the brain with particular relevance (in consideration of other standard criteria) to its unique taxonomic priority as the progenitor of anthropology.

On the Evolution of Language: A Unified View

PHILIP LIEBERMAN

A unified theory for the evolution of human language centrally involves the comparative, ontogenetic, and evolutionary studies of speech production with which I and my colleagues are closely identified. It also crucially involves the consideration of other recent, and not so recent, studies of cognitive ability in nonhuman primates: hunting, bipedal posture, the neural correlates of auditory perception, visual perception in adult and infant humans, speech perception in humans, play activity, gesture, etc. I shall attempt here to synthesize a great deal of data into what I hope is a coherent theory. I somewhat redundantly stress that this may result in a theory that is testable. Like all theories, it cannot account for everything. This theory does, however, appear to "explain" and relate a number of phenomena that otherwise appear to be quite unrelated. Moreover, it appears to point to a coherent evolutionary process that relates the communications systems of other animals to human language. Most importantly, it points out a number of questions that can be resolved through controlled experiments and careful observations.

I have drawn on a number of seemingly disparate ethological, anatomical, psychological, and anthropological sources because I think that it is obvious that there is no single factor that is, in itself, responsible for the evolution of human language. Evolution is a complex process that inherently involves all aspects of the life cycle and environment of a species and its relationships to other species. Although particular factors like, for example, gestural communication (Hewes 1971) undoubtedly had an important role in the evolution of human language, no single factor can, in itself, provide, as it were, the "central key" to the

For Plates, see pp. xxvi–xviii, between pp. 560–561

puzzle. Everything depends on everything else and the interaction is the "crucial" factor if anything is. Gestural communication, for example, depends on the prior existence of visual pattern recognition, analysis, cognitive ability, and bipedal posture. Visual pattern identification probably depends, in turn, on natural selection for visual ability in an arboreal environment. Bipedal posture, in turn, probably again depends on prior selection for brachiation in an arboreal environment (Campbell 1966).

Note that I am not saying that we cannot analyze the factors that underlie the evolution of human language. I am proposing that the process involved many factors. One of these factors appears to be the process of "preadaptation"; that is, natural selection channeled development in particular directions because of previous modifications selected for some other role. Darwin's (1859) comments concerning the evolution of the lung from the swim bladder perhaps constitute one of the first and most convincing examples of preadaptation.

Let me begin by listing the evolutionary factors that I will discuss here. There probably are more, but I suggest that these are the central factors in the evolution of human language. I shall order the factors in terms of their probable role in differentiating the language of modern man from that of progressively earlier hominids and other animals. In other words, I shall first list the factors that I think were most important in the late stages of human evolution and proceed to factors that probably were more imporant in earlier stages. It is important to note that I am not categorically differentiating human language (i.e. the language of present-day *Homo sapiens*) from other languages (e.g. the possible language of present-day chimpanzees).

Linguists have been somewhat anthropocentric in defining language to be necessarily human language. I will define a language to be a communications system that is capable of transmitting new information. In other words, I am defining language operationally as a communications system that places no inherent restriction on the nature or quality of the information transferred. It is obvious that this definition does not require that all languages have all of the properties of human language.

FACTOR 1: SPECIALIZED SPEECH ENCODING AND DECODING

Modern man's communications achieve a high rate of transmission speed by means of a process of speech encoding and decoding. The rate at which meaningful sound distinctions are transmitted in human speech is about twenty to thirty segments per second. That is, phonetic distinctions that differentiate meaningful words, e.g. the sounds symbolized by the symbols [b], [æ], and [t] in the word "bat," are transmitted, identified, and sorted at a rate of twenty to thirty segments per second. It is obvious that human listeners CANNOT simply transmit and identify these sound distinctions as separate entities. The fastest rate at which sounds can be identified is about seven to nine segments per second. Sounds transmitted at a rate of twenty per second indeed merge into an undifferentiable "tone." The linguist's traditional conception of phonetic elements comprising a set of "beads on a string" clearly is not correct at the acoustic level. How. then, is speech transmitted and perceived?

The results of the past twenty years of research on the perception of speech by humans demonstrated that the individual sounds like [b], [æ], and [t] are encoded, that is, "squashed together," into the syllable-sized unit [b æ t] (Liberman et al. 1967). A human speaker in producing this syllable starts with his supralaryngeal vocal tract – i.e. his tongue, lips, velum, etc. – in the positions characteristic of [b]. He, however, does not maintain this articulatory configuration but instead moves his articulators towards the positions that would be attained if he were instructed to maintain an isolated, steady [æ]. He never reaches these positions, however, because he starts towards the articulatory configuration characteristic of [t] before he ever reaches the "steady state" (isolated and sustained) vowel [æ]. The articulatory gestures that would be characteristic of each isolated "sound" are never attained. Instead, the articulatory gestures are melded together into a composite, characteristic of the syllable.

The sound pattern that results from this encoding process is itself an indivisible composite. Just as there is no way of separating with absolute certainty the [b] articulatory gestures from the [æ] gestures (you can't tell exactly when the [b] ends and the [æ] begins), there is no way of separating the acoustic cues that are generated by these articulatory maneuvers. The isolated sounds have a psychological status as motor control or "programming" instructions for the speech production apparatus. The sound pattern that results is a composite and the acoustic cues for the initial and final consonants are largely transmitted as modulations imposed on the vowel. The process is, in effect, a time-compressing system. The acoustic cues that characterize the initial and final consonants are transmitted in the time slot that would have been necessary to transmit a single isolated [æ] vowel.

The human brain decodes, that is, "unscrambles," the acoustic signal in terms of the articulatory maneuvers that were put together to generate the syllable. The individual consonants [b] and [t], although they have no independent acoustic status, are perceived as discrete entities. The process of human speech perception inherently requires "knowledge" of the acoustic consequences of the possible range of human supralaryngeal vocal tract speech articulation (Liberman et al. 1967; Lieberman 1970, 1972). The special speech processing involved appears to involve crucially the dominant hemisphere of the human brain (Kimura 1964; Shankweiler and Studdert-Kennedy 1967; Liberman et al. 1967). We will discuss the process of human speech perception in more detail with respect to its interrelation with the anatomy of the human vocal tract. For the moment, we will note that the special neural devices necessary for the "decoding" of human speech may be comparatively recent evolutionary acquisitions.

FACTOR 2: SPECIAL SUPRALARYNGEAL VOCAL TRACT ANATOMY

Modern man's speech-producing apparatus is quite different from the comparable systems of living nonhuman primates (Lieberman 1968; Lieberman et al. 1969; Lieberman, Crelin, and Klatt 1972). Nonhuman primates have supralaryngeal vocal tracts in which the larynx exits directly into the oral cavity (Negus 1949). In the adult human the larynx exits into the pharynx. The only function for which the adult human supralaryngeal vocal tract appears to be better adapted is speech production.

Understanding the anatomical basis of human speech requires that we briefly review the source-filter theory of speech production (Chiba and Kajiyama 1958; Fant 1960). Human speech is the result of a source, or sources, of acoustic energy being filtered by the supralaryngeal vocal tract. For voiced sounds, that is, sounds like the English vowels, the source of energy is the periodic sequence of puffs of air that pass through the larynx as the vocal cords (folds) rapidly open and shut. The rate at which the vocal cords open and close determines the fundamental frequency of phonation. Acoustic energy is present at the fundamental frequency and at higher harmonics. The fundamental frequency of phonation can vary from about 80 hertz (Hz) for adult males to about 500 Hz for children and some adult females. Significant acoustic energy is present in the harmonics of fundamental frequency to at least 3000 Hz. The fundamental frequency of phonation is, within wide limits, under the control of the speaker who can produce controlled variations by varying either pulmonary air pressure or the tension of the laryngeal muscles (Lieberman 1967). Linguistically significant information can be transmitted by means of these variations in fundamental frequency as, for example, in Chinese where these variations are used to differentiate different words.

The main source of phonetic differentiation in human languages, however, arises from the dynamic properties of the supralaryngeal vocal tract acting as an acoustic filter. The length and shape of the supralaryngeal vocal tract determines the frequencies at which maximum energy will be transmitted from the laryngeal source to the air adjacent to the speaker's lips. These frequencies, at which maximum acoustic energy will be transmitted, are known as formant frequencies. A speaker can vary the formant frequencies by changing the length and shape of his supralaryngeal vocal tract. He can, for example, drastically alter the shape of the airway formed by the posterior margin of his tongue body in his pharynx. He can raise or lower the upper boundary of his tongue in his oral cavity. He can raise or lower his larynx and retract or extend his lips. He can open or close his nasal cavity to the rest of the supralaryngeal vocal tract by lowering or raising his velum. The speaker can, in short, continually vary the formant frequencies generated by his supralaryngeal vocal tract.

The acoustic properties that, for example, differentiate the vowels [a] and [i] are determined solely by the shape and length differences that the speaker's supralaryngeal vocal tract assumes in articulating these vowels. The situation is analagous to the musical properties of a pipe organ where the length and type (open or closed end) of pipe determines the musical quality of each note. The damped resonances of the human supralaryngeal vocal tract are, in effect, the formant frequencies. The length and shape (more precisely, the cross-sectional area as a function of distance from the laryngeal source) determine the formant frequencies.

The situation is similar for unvoiced sounds, for which the vocal cords do not open and close at a rapid rate releasing quasi-periodic puffs of air. The source of acoustic energy in these instances is the turbulence generated by air rushing through a constriction in the vocal tract. The vocal tract still acts as an acoustic filter but the acoustic source may not be at the level of the larynx as, for example, in the sound [s], for which the source is the turbulence generated near the speaker's teeth.

The anatomy of the adult human supralaryngeal vocal tract permits modern man to generate supralaryngeal vocal tract configurations that involve abrupt discontinuities at its midpoint. These particular vocal tract shapes produce vowels like [a], [i], and [u], which have unique acoustic properties, as well as consonants like [g] and [k]. The acoustic properties of these particular sounds will be discussed in detail, but for the moment I will simply note that they are sounds that minimize the problems of precise articulatory control. A speaker can produce about the same formant frequencies for an [i], for example, while he varies the position of the midpoint area function discontinuity by one or two centimeters (Stevens 1972). They are also sounds that are maximally distinct acoustically. They, moreover, are sounds that a human listener can efficiently use to establish the size of the supralaryngeal vocal tract that he is listening to. This last property relates to Factor 1, the specialized speech encoding and decoding that characterizes human language. The reconstructions of the supralaryngeal vocal tracts of various fossil hominids that my colleague, Edmund S. Crelin, has made indicate that some extinct hominids lacked the anatomical basis for producing these sounds while other hominids appear to have the requisite anatomical specializations for human speech. I will, of course, return to this topic.

FACTOR 3: COGNITIVE ABILITY AND AUTOMATIZATION

There are two interrelated aspects to the cognitive abilities that underlie language. One is the process that I will term automatization. Human language involves rapidly executing complex sequences of articulatory maneuvers or making equally complex perceptual decisions regarding the identity of particular sound segments. At a higher level, complex phonological and morphophonemic relationships must be determined. None of the processes is, however, what the speaker or listener is directly concerned with. The semantic content of the message is the primary concern of the speaker or listener. The sending and receiving processes are essentially automatic. No conscious thought is expended in the process of speech production, speech perception, or any of the syntactic or morphophonemic stages that may intervene between the semantic content of the message and the acoustic signal. It is clear that "automatized" skills are not unique to human language. Other aspects of human activity – dance, for example – involve similar phenomena. The novice dancer must learn the particular steps and movements that characterize a particular dance form. Once the steps have been learned, they must become automatized. The dance itself involves the complex sequences. Playing the piano or violin, skiing, or driving a car all involve automatized behavior.

The bases for the automatized behavior that is a necessary condition for human language may reside in cross-modal transfers from other systems of hominid and hominoid activity. Tool use, for example, requires a high degree of automatization if it is to be effective. You cannot stop to think how to use a hammer every time you drive a nail in. Hunting is perhaps a still stronger case. A successful hunter must be able to thrust his spear accurately without pausing to think about the mechanics of spear thrusting. Natural selection would quickly favor the retention of superior automatization. Automatized behavior pervades all aspects of culture. Indeed a cultural response is, to a degree, a special case of automatized behavior. In simpler animals cultural responses are perhaps less subject to environmental pressures. In humans they may be more subject to external forces than to innate mechanisms, but they are no less automatized once learned.

A special factor that may be germane to automatized behavior is that a "plastic" period appears to be involved. It is comparatively easy to shape behavior during the "plastic" period. Afterwards it is either impossible or relatively difficult to modify automatized behavior. Puppies thus can be trained more readily than adult dogs. All humans can readily learn different languages in their youth. Most humans can learn a foreign – thus unfamiliar – language only with great difficulty (or not at all) during adult life. The same comments probably apply to learning to play the violin, tightrope walking, etc., although no definitive studies have yet been made.

Cognitive Ability

Cognitive ability is a necessary factor in human language. Linguists often tend to assume that cognitive ability IS linguistic ability. Indeed, since the time of Descartes the absence of human language in other animals has been cited as a "proof" of man's special status and the lack of cognitive ability in all other species. Human language has been assumed to be a necessary condition for human thought. The absence of human language has been, conversely, assumed to be evidence of the lack of all cognitive ability.

It is clear that cognitive (i.e. logical) abilities can be demonstrated or observed in many animals. Behavioral conditioning, for example, which can be applied with great success to pigeons and rats, itself can be viewed as a demonstration of logical ability on the part of the "conditioned" animal. Pavlov's dogs had to make a logical association between the bell and food. Calling the animal's response a "conditioned reflex" obscures the fact that the animal had to be able to connect LOGICALLY the sound of the bell with food. The same "conditioned" response often can be observed when a human gourmet regards the menu. In both cases cognitive ability must interpose between the token of the food that is anticipated and the observed physiological response. The human gourmet is presumably more flexible, adaptive, and discriminating than Pavlov's dogs; however, the basic process is similar. In *Homo sapiens* the cognitive abilities that underlie this particular aspect of behavior are simply more complex than is the case for *Canis familiaris*. The difference is, however, quantitative rather than qualitative.

The particular cognitive abilities associated with presumably "unique" human behavioral patterns like tool use have been observed in chimpanzees (Goodall 1971) and sea otters (Kenyon 1969). Some of the cognitive abilities that have been traditionally associated with human language have likewise been demonstrated by Gardner and Gardner (1969) and by Premack (1972). Premack's experiments, in particular, clearly demonstrate that cognitive ability and human language CANNOT be regarded as the same biologic ability.

Chimpanzees do not possess the phonetic apparatus of human language. They have available a subset of the phonetic distinctions that are available to modern man. Chimpanzees COULD, using the phonetic distinctions that are available to them, establish a language. This language's phonetic system might not be as efficient as modern man's, but it could form the basis of a language, where we have operationally defined a language to be a communications system capable of transmitting unanticipated, new knowledge.The difference, at the phonetic level, between human language and this hypothetical chimpanzee language would be quantitative rather than qualitative. Premack's experiments demonstrate that the cognitive abilities of chimpanzees are, at worst, restricted to some subset of the cognitive abilities available to humans. The difference at the cognitive level is thus also probably quantitative rather than qualitative.

It is important to note here that quantitative functional abilities can be the base of behavioral patterns that are qualitatively different. I think that this fact is sometimes not appreciated in discussions of gradual versus abrupt change. A modern electronic desk calculator and a large general-purpose digital computer, for example, may be constructed using similar electronic logical devices and similar magnetic memories. The large general-purpose machine will, however, have 1,000 to 10,000,000 times as many logical and memory devices. The structural differences between the desk calculator and the general-purpose machine may thus simply be quantitative rather than qualitative. The "behavioral" consequence of this quantitative difference can, however, be qualitative. The types of problems that one can solve on the general-purpose machine will differ in kind, as well as in size, from those suited to the desk calculator. The inherent cognitive abilities of humans and chimpanzees thus could be quantitative and still have qualitative behavioral consequences.

The cognitive abilities that are typically associated with human language may have their immediate origins in the complex patterns of hominid behavior associated with tool use, toolmaking, and hunting. Hewes (1971) makes a convincing case for the role of gestural communication in the earliest forms of hominid language and associates language with the transference of cognitive ability from these complex behavioral patterns. I would agree with Hewes, but I would not limit the earliest hominid languages to gestures, nor would I restrict the cognitive abilities that underlie language to hominids. Tool use and hunting certainly are not exclusively hominid patterns of behavior.

We can get some insights on the neural abilities that nonhuman primates possess by taking note of the phylogenetic evolution of the peripheral systems involved in information gathering and communication. The acute color vision of primates, for example, would have had no selective advantage if it were not coupled with matching cognitive processes. Gestural communication is consistent with the evolution and retention of increasingly complex facial musculature in the phylogenetic order of primates. It is likewise unlikely that gestural communication was at any stage of hominid evolution the SOLE "phonetic" medium. Negus (1949), by the methods of comparative anatomy, demonstrates that the larynges of nonhuman primates are adapted for phonation at the expense of respiratory efficiency. The far simpler larynx of the lung fish is better adapted for respiration and protecting the lungs. Clearly, mutations that decreased respiratory efficiency would not have been retained over a phylogenetic order unless they had some selectional advantage.

The cognitive skills that underlie linguistic ability in hominids thus probably evolved from cognitive facilities that have a functional role in the social behavior and communications of other animals. Like automatization, these skills would appear to be part of the biologic endowment of many species and their continued development in "higher" species is concomitant with behavioral complexity. The transference of these cognitive skills to human language thus could be viewed as yet another instance of "preadaptation," the use of cognitive processes for language that originally evolved because of the selective advantages conferred on activities like hunting, evading natural enemies, food-gathering, etc.

THE SPEECH ABILITIES OF NEANDERTHAL AND OTHER FOSSIL HOMINIDS

As I noted above, it is apparent that no single factor can be in any reasonable way identified as the "key" to language. The two factors that appear to be most recent in shaping the particular form of HUMAN language are, however, speech-encoding and speech-producing anatomy. Certain neural mechanisms must be present for the perception of speech (Lenneberg 1967). It is difficult to make any substantive inferences about the presence or absence of particular neural mechanisms in the brains of extinct fossil hominids because we can deduce only the external size and shape of the brain from a fossil skull. Also, we lack a detailed knowledge of how the human brain functions. We could not really assess the linguistic abilities of a modern man simply by examining his brain. Fortunately, we can derive some insights on the nature of speech perception in various fossil hominids by studying their speech-producing anatomy. The relationship between speech anatomy and speech perception is very much like that which obtains between bipedalism and the detailed anatomy of the pelvic region. The anatomy is a necessary condition, although neural ability is also necessary.

The methodology that has enabled us, and I must emphasize that this research has been a joint enterprise, to reconstruct the speech-producing anatomy of extinct hominids is that proposed by Darwin. Darwin, in chapters ten and thirteen of *On the origin of species* (1859), discussed both the "affinities of extinct Species to each other, and to living forms," and "Embryology." We have applied the methods of comparative and functional anatomy to the speech-producing anatomy of present-day apes and monkeys and to the normal human newborn. We first assessed the speech-producing abilities of these living animals in terms of their speech-producing anatomy. We found that their supralaryngeal vocal tracts inherently restricted their speech-producing abilities. We then noted that certain functional aspects of the morphology of the skulls of these living animals resembled similar features of extinct fossil hominids.

The reconstructions of the supralaryngeal vocal tracts of the La Chapelle-aux-Saints, Es-Skhūl V, Broken Hill, Steinheim, and Sterkfontein 5 fossils were made by Crelin, by means of the homologues that exist between these skulls and living forms, the marks of the muscles on the fossil skulls, and the general methods of comparative anatomy. Crelin's (1969) previous experience with the anatomy of the newborn was especially relevant in that we can see in the human newborn many of the relevant skeletal features associated with the soft tissue structures that must have occurred in certain of these now-extinct hominid forms. In most cases we made use of casts of the fossil material made available by the Wenner-Gren foundation. For the La Chapelle-aux-Saints and Steinheim fossils, casts made available by the University Museum, Philadelphia, Pennsylvania were employed. The original La Chapelle-aux-Saints fossil as well as the La Ferrasie and La Quina child's fossil were also examined with the cooperation of the Musée de l'Homme in Paris and the Musée des Antiquités Nationales in St. Germain-en-Laye. We attempted to examine the original Steinheim fossil but were not successful.

The details of the reconstructions are discussed in our published and forthcoming papers (Lieberman and Crelin 1971; Lieberman, Crelin, and Klatt 1972; Crelin et al. f.c.). I will, however, note some of the salient points in the discussion of particular fossils. I will first discuss the computer-modeling technique that we employed to arrive at a functional assessment of these supralaryngeal vocal tracts. I think that it makes sense to approach the discussion of the reconstructions by first discussing the modeling technique because one of the points that I hope will emerge from the discussion of the modeling technique is the question of how much of the detail of the supralaryngeal vocal tract's morphology we need to know in order to make meaningful statements about speech ability. The answer to this question is that we really need to know only a few, fairly gross aspects of the morphology of the supralaryngeal vocal tract. The reason that this is so is itself one of the functional characteristics of human speech.

I shall begin the discussion of the modeling technique by returning to our studies of the speech capabilities of living nonhuman primates. This is a useful way to start because we can compare the results of our

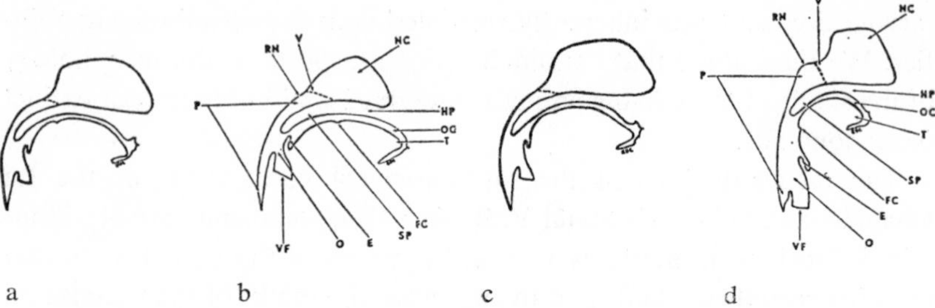

Figure 1. Diagrams of the air passages of (a) newborn human, (b) adult chimpanzee, (c) Neanderthal man, and (d) adult human. The anatomical details that are keyed on the chimpanzee and adult man are as follows: P = Pharynx, RN = Roof of Nasopharynx, V = Vomer Bone, NC = Nasal Cavity, HP = Hard Palate, OC = Oral Cavity, T = Tongue, FC = Foramen Cecum, SP = Soft Palate, E = Epiglottis, O = Opening of Larynx into Pharynx, VF = Level of Vocal Folds (after Lieberman et al. 1972)

modeling with the actual phenomena. Plate 1 shows the left half of the head and neck of a young adult male chimpanzee sectioned in the midsagittal plane. Silicone rubber casts were made of the air passages, including the nasal cavity, by filling each side of the split air passages separately in the sectioned head and neck to insure perfect filling of the cavities. The casts from each side of a head and neck were then fused together to make a complete cast of the air passages. In Plate 2 the cast of the chimpanzee airways is shown together with casts made, following the same procedures, for a newborn human and an adult human. A cast of the reconstructed supralaryngeal airways of the La Chapelle-aux-Saints fossil also appears in Plate 2. In Figure 1 equal-sized outlines of the air passages for these four vocal tracts are sketched.

Note the high position of the larynx in the newborn human and adult chimpanzee vocal tracts where the soft palate and epiglottis can be approximated. In the adult human vocal tract the soft palate and epiglottis are widely separated and cannot be approximated. The tongue is likewise at rest in the newborn human and chimpanzee completely within the oral cavity, whereas in the adult man the posterior third of the tongue is in a vertical position forming the anterior wall of the supralaryngeal pharyngeal cavity. Note, in particular, that there is practically no supralaryngeal portion of the pharynx present in the direct airway out from the larynx when the soft palate shuts off the nasal cavity in the newborn human and in the chimpanzee. In the adult man half of the supralaryngeal vocal tract is formed by the pharyngeal cavity.

This difference between the chimpanzee and newborn supralaryngeal vocal tracts and that of adult *Homo sapiens* is a consequence of the opening of the larynx into the pharynx directly behind the oral cavity. In other words, the larynx opens almost directly into the oral cavity. This is the case for all living animals (Negus 1949) with the exception of adult *Homo sapiens*. We really should use the term "adultlike" rather than adult because these differences appear to be fully developed by two years of age and are probably largely differentiated by six months of age (Lieberman, Harris, et al. 1972).

The functional distinctions that these anatomical differences confer on adult humans have been determined for respiration, swallowing, and the sense of smell. Kirchner (1970) notes that the respiratory efficiency of the adult human supralaryngeal airways is about half that of the newborn. The right-angle bend in the adult human supralaryngeal airway increases the flow resistance. The nonhuman supralaryngeal anatomy allows the oral cavity to be sealed from the rest of the airway during inspiration. This aids the sense of smell (Negus 1949) and also allows an animal to breathe while its mouth contains a liquid (e.g. when a dog laps water). The adult human supralaryngeal airways also increase the possibility of asphyxiation. Food lodged in the pharynx can block the entrance to the larynx. This is not possible in nonhumans, because the supralaryngeal pharynx serves as a pathway for both food and liquids and as an airway only in adult *Homo sapiens*.[1]

The functional distinctions that the differences in the anatomy of the supralaryngeal airways confer on speech production can be determined by modeling techniques. The source-filter theory of speech production, as I have noted before, states that speech is the result of the filtering action of the supralaryngeal vocal tract on the acoustic sources that excite it. Because the properties of the filter are uniquely determined by the shape and length (the cross-sectional area function) of the supralaryngeal vocal tract, it is possible to assess the properties of a particular vocal tract once we know the range of shapes that it can assume.

Note that this type of analysis will not tell us anything about the total range of phonetic variation. We would have to know the properties of the laryngeal source as well as the degree of motor control that

[1] The human vocal tract is also inferior to the vocal tracts of hominids like La Chapelle-aux-Saints with respect to chewing. The reduction in the body of the mandible in modern *Homo sapiens* has reduced the tooth area. Dental studies have determined (Manly and Braley 1950; Manly and Shiere 1950; Manly and Vinton 1951) that chewing efficiency in primates is solely a function of swept tooth area. Hominid forms that have smaller tooth areas have less efficient chewing. The reduction of the mandible in modern man therefore cannot be ascribed to enhancing chewing efficiency.

a particular organism possessed. We can however, assess the restraints that the supralaryngeal vocal tract itself imposes on the possible phonetic repertoire. The situation is similar to that which would occur if we found an ancient woodwind instrument made of brass. We would probably not be able to say very much about the reed, which would have decayed, but we would be able to determine some of the constraints that the instrument imposed on a performance. These constraints obviously would inherently structure the musical forms of the period. We would not know all of the constraints, we could not say very much about the manual dexterity of the players or the general musical theory, but we would know more than would be the case if we had not found the ancient instrument.

We are in a somewhat better position when we study the reconstructed supralaryngeal vocal apparatus of an extinct hominid. We can tell something about the constraints on the phonetic repertoire. The interconnections that exist between the vocal apparatus and the perception of speech in *Homo sapiens,* however, allow us to make some more general inferences than would otherwise be the case.

The technique that we have employed to assess the constraints imposed by the supralaryngeal vocal apparatus of an animal makes use of a computer model of the vocal tract. We really do not have to make use of this model. It would be possible, although somewhat tedious, to make actual models of possible supralaryngeal vocal tract configurations. If these models, made of plastic or metal, were excited by means of a rapid quasi-periodic series of puffs of air (i.e. an artificial larynx), we would be able to hear the actual vowellike sounds that a particular vocal tract configuration produced. If we systematically made models that covered the range of possible vocal tract configurations, we could determine the constraints that the supralaryngeal vocal tract morphology imposed, independent of the possible constraints determined by limitations on motor control, etc. We would, of course, be restricted to steady-state vowels in that we could not rapidly change the shape of the vocal tract, but we could generalize our results to consonants because we could model the articulatory configurations that occur at the start and end of typical consonant-vowel sequences.

Note that these modeling techniques allow us to assess the limits on the phonetic repertoire that follow from the anatomy of the supralaryngeal vocal tract, independent of muscular or neural control and independent of the dialect, habits, etc. of the animal whose vocal tract we would be modeling. The technology for making these mechanical models existed at the end of the eighteenth century. Von Kempelen's

(1791) famous talking machine modeled the human vocal tract by mechanical means. The method that we have employed simply makes use of the technology of the third quarter of the twentieth century.

CHIMPANZEE AND NEWBORN AND ADULT *HOMO SAPIENS*.

In Figure 2 three area functions are shown for the chimpanzee vocal tract derived from the sectioned head and neck shown in Plate 1. The silicone rubber casting and schematic drawing of this vocal tract are shown in Plate 2 and Figure 1 respectively. The area functions shown in Figure 2 represent the best approximations that we could get to the human vowels [a], [i], and [u]. With a light pen we systematically drew area functions on an oscilloscope input to a PDP 9 computer. The computer had been programmed to calculate the formant frequencies that corresponded to these area functions. The details of the computer program are discussed by Henke (1966). The computer allowed us to make hundreds of possible supralaryngeal vocal tract models conveniently and rapidly. We thus could explore the acoustic consequences of all possible chimpanzee supralaryngeal vocal tract configurations without waiting for a chimpanzee actually to produce these shapes. We used the same procedure to explore the possible range of supralaryngeal vocal tract shapes for the newborn human supralaryngeal vocal tract shown in Plate 2 and Figure 1. We were guided in these simulations by the morphology of the head and neck, i.e. the relative thickness and position of the tongue, the lips, and the velum, and the position of the pharynx relative to the larynx and oral cavity.

We were also able to make use of cineradiographic pictures of newborn infants during cry and swallowing (Truby et al. 1965). The results of these simulations are shown in Figure 3. In Figure 3 the formant frequencies of the three area functions of Figure 2 are plotted, together with an additional data point (X) for the human newborn. The loops labeled with phonetic symbols represent the data points for a sample of real utterances derived from seventy-six adult men, women, and adolescent children producing American English vowels (Peterson and Barney 1952). In Figure 4 we have reproduced the actual data points for this sample of real human vowels. Note that the chimpanzee and newborn human utterances cover only a small portion of the adult human "vowel space." In other words, the chimpanzee and newborn vocal tracts, according to this modeling technique, inherently do not appear to be able to produce vowels like [a], [i], and [u].

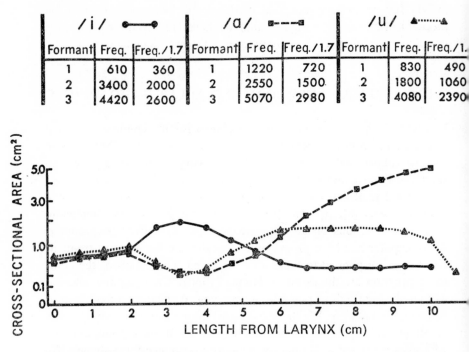

/i/ ●—●			/a/ ■---■			/u/ ▲·····▲		
Formant	Freq.	Freq./1.7	Formant	Freq.	Freq./1.7	Formant	Freq.	Freq./1.
1	610	360	1	1220	720	1	830	490
2	3400	2000	2	2550	1500	2	1800	1060
3	4420	2600	3	5070	2980	3	4080	2390

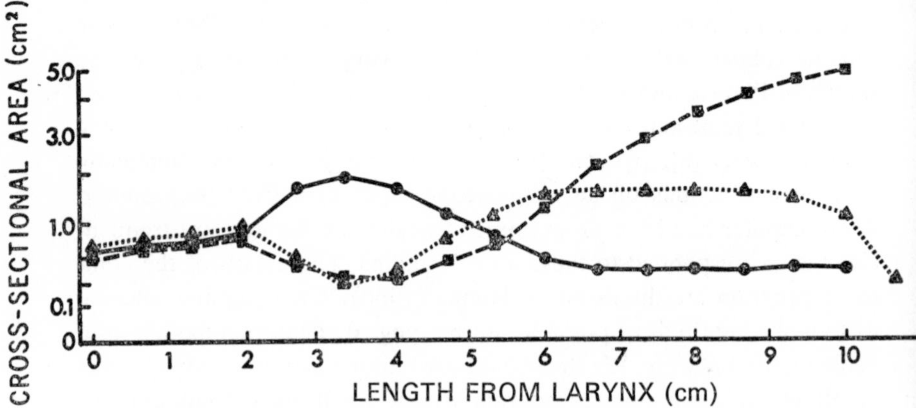

Figure 2. Chimpanzee supralaryngeal vocal tract area functions modeled on a computer. These functions were the "best" approximations that could be produced, given the anatomic limitations of the chimpanzee, to the human vowels [i], [a], and [u]. The formant frequencies calculated by the computer program for each vowel are tabulated and scaled to the average dimensions of the adult human vocal tract (after Lieberman et al. 1972)

All normal human speakers can inherently produce these vowels. Any human, if he is raised in an American English environment, will be able to produce these vowels. The modeling of the chimpanzee and newborn vocal tracts indicates that they could not, even if they had the requisite motor and neural abilities. The question that we are addressing is, thus, not whether chimpanzees and newborns can speak American English, but whether they have the anatomical apparatus that would allow them to speak.

The results of the modeling technique can, of course, be checked against the actual utterances of chimpanzees and newborn *Homo sapiens*. When this is done it is evident that the actual vowels of newborn *Homo sapiens* agree with the computer simulation (Irwin 1948; Lynip 1951; Lieberman, Harris, et al. 1972). The chimpanzee simulation appears to encompass a greater range than has been observed so far in the acoustic analysis of chimpanzee vocalizations (Lieberman

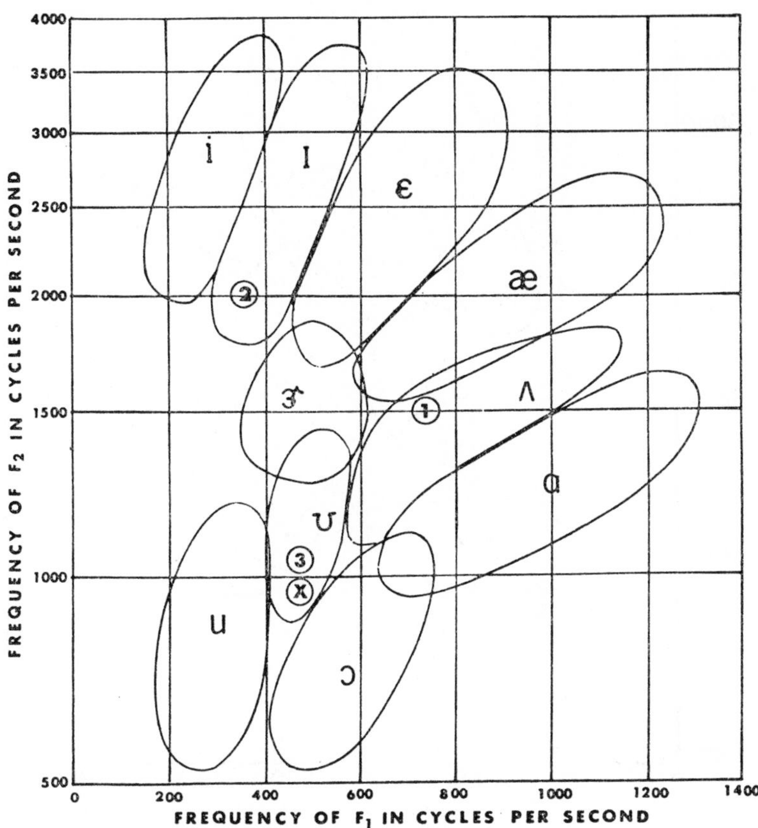

Figure 3. Plot of formant frequencies for chimpanzee vowels of Figure 2, data points (1), (2), and (3), scaled to correspond to the size of the adult human vocal tract. Data point (X) represents an additional point for the human newborn. The closed loops enclose ninety percent of the data points derived from a sample of seventy-six adult men, women, and children producing American English vowels (Peterson and Barney 1952). Note that the chimpanzee and newborn vocal tracts cannot produce the vowels [i], [u], and [a] (after Lieberman et al. 1972)

1968). This may merely indicate that the acoustic analyses so far derived from chimpanzees do not represent the total chimpanzee repertoire. It is, however, apparent that the computer simulation does not appear to be showing a SMALLER vowel space than is actually the case. The computer simulation for adult *Homo sapiens* corresponds with that observed (Chiba and Kajiyama 1958; Fant 1960; Peterson and Barney 1952) and is not plotted here.

The vowel diagrams in Figures 3 and 4 are really an indirect way of showing that the chimpanzee and newborn cannot generate supralaryn-

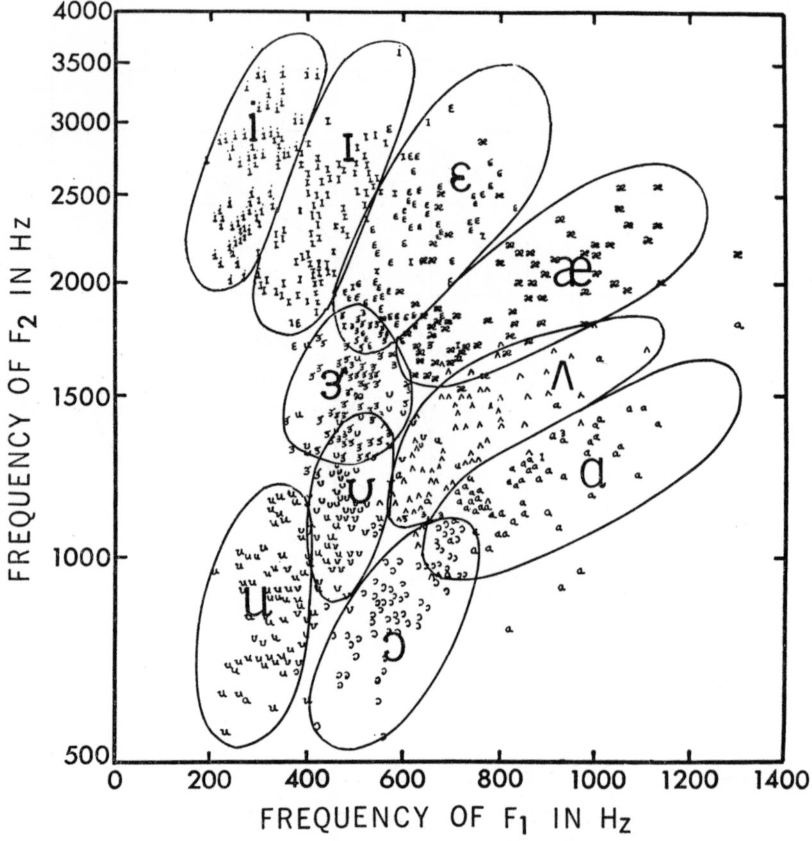

Figure 4. Formant frequencies of American English vowels for a sample of seventy-six adult men, adult women, and children. The closed loops enclose ninety percent of the data points in each vowel category (after Peterson and Barney 1952)

geal vocal tract area functions like those shown in Figure 5. These three configurations are the limiting articulations of a vowel triangle that is language-universal (Troubetzkoy 1939). It is not a question of the chimpanzee and newborn not being able to produce American English vowels. They could not produce the vowel range that is necessary for any other language of *Homo sapiens*. Particular modern languages may lack one of these articulations, but they always include at least one of these vowels and/or the glides [y] and [w], which are functionally equivalent to [i] and [u].

It is important to remember that we are discussing the PHONETIC level rather than the PHONEMIC. Claims that a particular language,

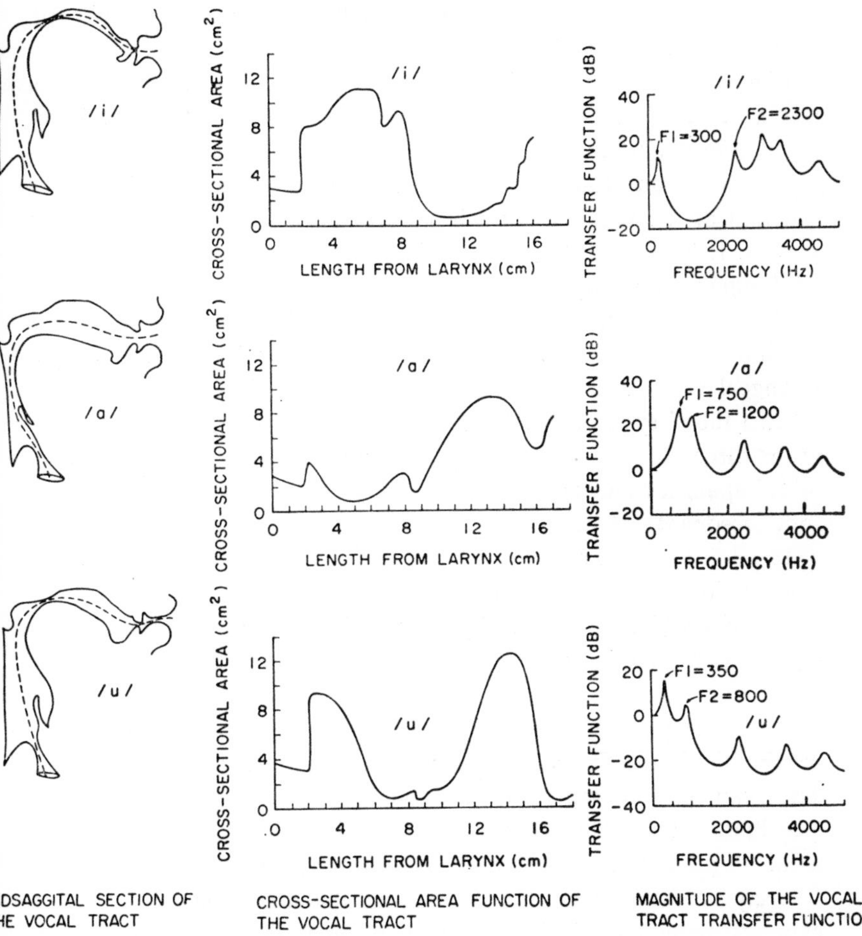

Figure 5. Illustrations of approximate (a) midsagittal sections, (b) cross-sectional area functions, and (c) acoustic transfer functions of the vocal tract for the vowels [i], [a], and [u] (after Lieberman et al. 1972)

e.g. Kabardian (Kuipers 1960), has only "one" centralized vowel generally concern the phonemic level, i.e. the claim is that a particular language does not differentiate words at the phonemic level through vowel contrasts. At the phonetic level these languages make use of vowels like [i], [u], and [a], although these vowels' occurrences are conditioned by other segments. It is also important to note that a vocal tract that cannot produce the area functions necessary for [i], [a], and [u] also cannot produce velar consonants like [g] and [k]. These consonants also involve discontinuities at the midpoint of the supralaryngeal vocal tract. Dental and bilabial consonants like [d], [t], [b], and [p] are, however, possible.

Figure 5 shows a midsagittal outline of the vocal tract for the vowels [i], [a], and [u], as well as the cross-sectional areas of the vocal tract (Fant 1960) and the frequency domain transfer functions for these vowels (Gold and Rabiner 1968). Ten-to-one discontinuities in the area function at the vocal tract's midpoint are necessary to produce these vowels. It is possible to generate these discontinuities with the "bent" adult human supralaryngeal vocal tract because the cross-sectional areas of the oral and pharyngeal cavities can be independently manipulated in adult humans while a midpoint constriction is maintained. The supralaryngeal vocal tract in adult humans thus can, in effect, function as a "two tube" system. The lack of a supralaryngeal pharyngeal cavity in the direct airway from the larynx, at a right angle to the oral cavity, in chimpanzees and newborn humans restricts these forms to "single tube" resonant systems.

In adult humans, muscles like the genioglossus can pull the pharyngeal portion of the tongue in an anterior direction, enlarging the pharyngeal cavity while the oral cavity is constricted, as in the production of [i]. In the production of [a], in adult humans, the pharyngeal constrictors reduce its cross-sectional area while the oral cavity is opened by lowering the mandible. It is impossible to articulate these extreme discontinuities in the chimpanzee and newborn supralaryngeal vocal tracts. They can only attempt to distort the tongue body in the oral cavity (see Plate 2 and Figures 1 and 2) to obtain changes in cross-sectional area. The intrinsic musculature and elastic properties of the tongue severely limit the range of deformations that the tongue body can be expected to employ. This is evident in cineradiographic observations of newborn cry and swallowing (Truby et al. 1965), baboon cries (Zhinkin 1963), and the deformations of the oral and pharyngeal portions of the tongue in adult humans (Perkell 1969).

Note that Figure 5 shows that the discontinuities in the [a], [i], and [u] area functions occur at or near the midpoint of the supralaryngeal vocal tract. Stevens (1972) has shown that the midpoint area discontinuity has an important functional value. It allows human speakers to produce signals that are acoustically distinct with relatively sloppy articulatory maneuvers. The first and second formant frequencies are maximally separated for [i], maximally centered for [a], and maximally lowered for [u]. When a human speaker wants to produce one of these vowels it is not necessary for him (or her) to be very precise about the position of the tongue. All that is necessary is an area function discontinuity within one centimeter or so from the midpoint. The formant frequencies will not perceptibly vary[2] (Flanagan 1955) when the discontinuity shifts plus or minus one centimeter from the midpoint. This would not be the case for similar articulations if they were generated at any point other than the midpoint of the vocal tract.

The vowels [a], [i], and [u] are thus optimal acoustic signals for communication. The speaker can produce maximally differentiated sounds without having to be terribly precise. All other vowels are both less distinct and less "stabile." The speaker must be more precise to produce acoustic signals that are not as distinct and separable. This factor is germane to one of the points that I raised earlier: how precise does the reconstruction of the supralaryngeal vocal tract of an extinct hominid have to be to yield meaningful data? The answer is that we can derive useful information without having to reconstruct fine detail because the crucial factor is essentially the ability to generate area discontinuities at or near the midpoint.

La Chapelle-aux-Saints

In Plate 2 and Figure 1 a silicone rubber model and a sketch of the supralaryngeal vocal tract of the La Chapelle-aux-Saints Neanderthal fossil are shown. It obviously was not possible to obtain this information directly from the soft tissue of this fossil hominid. The reconstruction of the supralaryngeal airways was effected by Edmund S. Crelin using the similarities that exist between this fossil and a newborn human as a guide (Lieberman and Crelin 1971; Lieberman, Crelin, and Klatt 1972). The possible arthritic condition (Straus and Cave 1957) of the La Chapelle-aux-Saints fossil has been raised in some criticisms of Crelin's reconstruction. Arthritic changes could no more have affected his supralaryngeal vocal tract than is the case in modern man.

Figure 6 shows a lateral view of the skull, vertebral column, and larynx of newborn and adult *Homo sapiens* and the reconstructed La Chapelle-aux-Saints fossil. Note that the geniohyoid muscle in adult *Homo sapiens* runs down and back from the symphysis of the mandible. This is necessarily the case because the hyoid bone is positioned below the mandible in adult *Homo sapiens*. The two anterior portions of the

[2] Flanagan (1955) shows that human listeners are not able to discriminate stimuli that differ solely with respect to a single formant frequency unless the difference exceeds sixty Hz.

digastric muscles, which are not shown in Figure 6, also run down and back from the mandible for the same reason. When the facets into which these muscles are inserted at the symphysis of the mandible are examined, it is evident that the facets are likewise inclined to minimize the sheer forces for these muscles. The human chin appears to be a consequence of the inclination of these facets. The outwards inclination of the chin reflects the inclination of the inferior plane of the mandible at the symphysis.

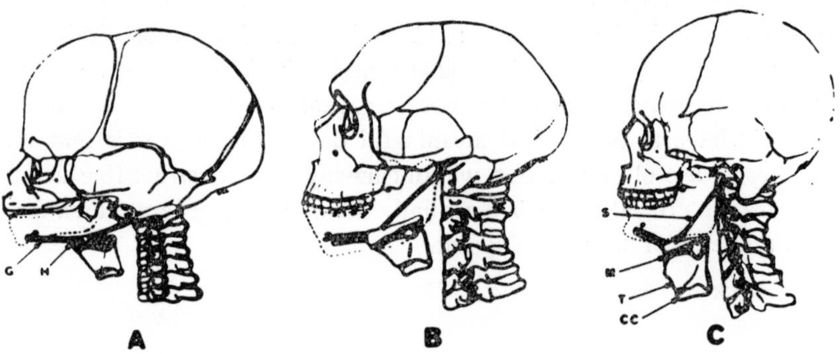

Figure 6. Skull, vertebral column, and larynx of newborn (A), and adult Man (C), and reconstruction of Neanderthal (B). G = Geniohyoid Muscle, H = Hyoid Bone, S = Stylohyoid Ligament, M = Thyrohyoid Membrane, T = Thyroid Cartilage, CC = Cricoid Cartilage. Note that the inclination of the styloid process away from the vertical plane in newborn and Neanderthal results in a corresponding inclination in the stylohyoid ligament. The intersection of the stylohyoid ligament and geniohyoid muscle with the hyoid bone of the larynx occurs at a higher position in newborn and Neanderthal. The high position of the larynx in the Neanderthal reconstruction follows, in part, from this intersection (after Lieberman and Crelin 1971)

Muscles are essentially "glued" in place to their facets. Tubercles and fossae in this light may be simply regarded as adaptations that increase the strength of the muscle-to-bone bond by increasing the "glued" surface area. The inclination of the digastric and geniohyoid facets likewise serves to increase the functional strength of the muscle-to-bone bond by minimizing sheer forces. As Campbell (1966: 2) succinctly notes, "Muscles leave marks where they are attached to bones, and from such marks we assess the form and size of the muscles." This is no less true for living than for extinct forms. When the corresponding features are examined in newborn *Homo sapiens* (Figure 6) it is evident that the nearly horizontal inclination of the facets of the geniohyoid and digastric muscles is a concomitant feature of the high position of the hyoid bone (Crelin 1969: 107–110). These muscles are nearly horizontal

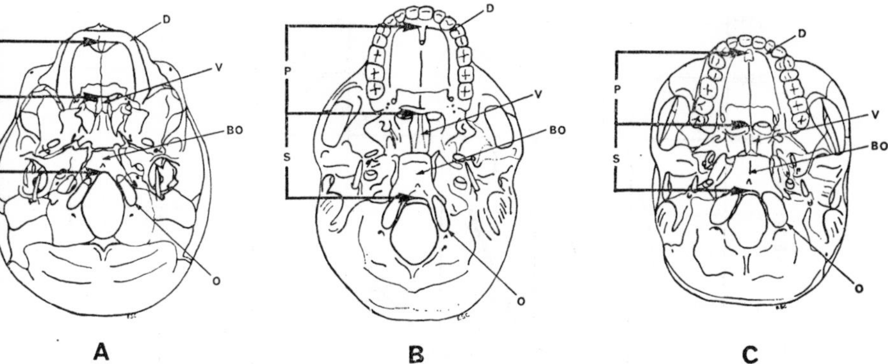

Figure 7. Inferior views of base of skull of Newborn (A), Neanderthal (B), and adult Man (C). D = Dental Arch, P = Palate, S = Distance Between Palate and Foramen Magnum, V = Vomer Bone, BO = Basilar Part of Occipital, O = Occipital Condyle (after Lieberman and Crelin 1971)

with respect to the symphysis of the mandible in newborn *Homo sapiens*. The facets therefore are nearly horizontal to minimize sheer forces. Newborn *Homo sapiens* thus lacks a chin.[3]

When the mandible of the La Chapelle-aux-Saints fossil is examined, it is evident that the facets of these muscles resemble those of newborn *Homo sapiens*. The inclination of the styloid process away from the vertical plane is also similar in newborn *Homo sapiens* and the La Chapelle-aux-Saints fossil. When the base of the skull is examined (Figure 7) for newborn and adult *Homo sapiens* and the La Chapelle-aux-Saints fossil, it is again apparent that the newborn *Homo sapiens* and fossil forms have many common features that differ from adult *Homo sapiens*. The sphenoid bone is, for example, exposed in newborn *Homo sapiens* and the La Chapelle-aux-Saints fossil between the vomer and the basilar part of the occipital. This is a skeletal feature that provides room for the larynx, which is positioned high with respect to the mandible. There has to be room for the larynx behind the palate in newborn *Homo sapiens* and in the La Chapelle-aux-Saints fossil. The qualitative difference in the morphology of the base of the skull, i.e. the exposure of the sphenoid, is a skeletal consequence of this anatomical necessity.

We do not claim that all the features of the La Chapelle-aux-Saints fossil are found in newborn *Homo sapiens*. This is definitely NOT the

[3] The human chin is sometimes stated to be a reinforcement for the mandible. This is probably not the case. It more likely is a stress concentration point. It would be rather simple to resolve this point using the methods of stress analysis common in mechanical and civil engineering.

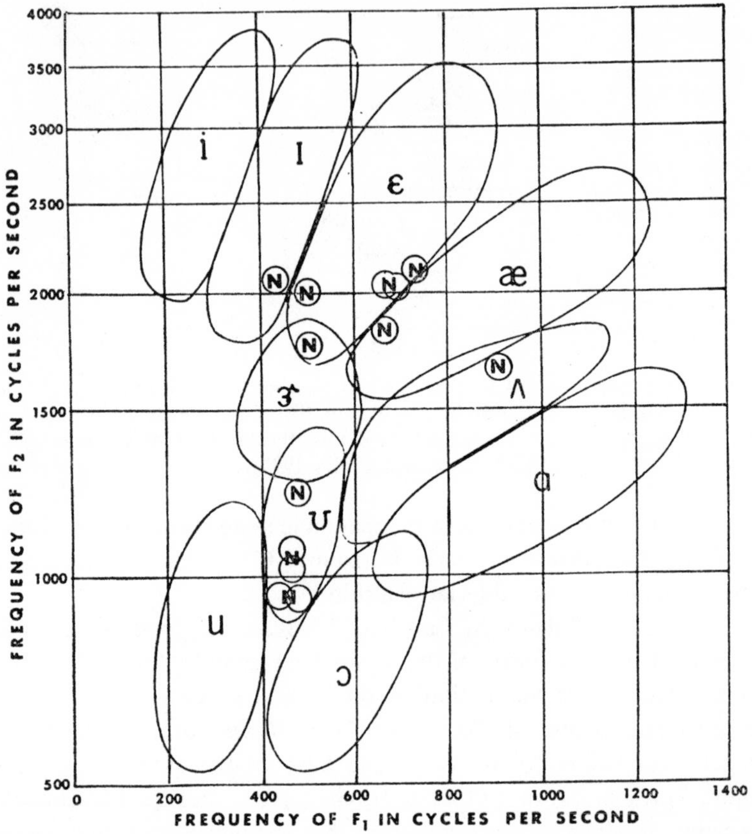

Figure 8. Plot of formant frequencies for reconstructed La Chapelle-aux-Saints supralaryngeal vocal tract in attempts to produce the vowels [i], [u], and [a]. Note that none of the data points (N) fall into the vowel loops that specify these vowels (after Lieberman and Crelin 1971)

case. We are claiming that certain features, particularly those relating to the base of the skull and mandible, are similar. These similarities make possible a reasonably accurate reconstruction of the supralaryngeal vocal tract of the La Chapelle-aux-Saints fossil. Our observations are in accord with the results of Vlček's (1970) independent "onto-phylogenetic" study of the development of a number of fossil skulls of Neanderthal infants. Vlček notes the presence of skeletal characteristics that are typical of both infant and adult Neanderthal fossils that are manifested during particular phases of the ontogenetic development of contemporary man. Other features that characterize adult Neanderthal man never appear in the ontogenetic development of contemporary man, while still other features that characterize contemporary man never are manifested in the fossil skulls. I will return to these data when I discuss the status of classic Neanderthal man. For the moment, it is relevant as an independent replication of the similarities between newborn *Homo sapiens* and the La Chapelle-aux-Saints fossil. Crelin's reconstruction of the supralaryngeal vocal tract of this fossil is also in accord with earlier attempts like that of Keith, which is discussed by Negus (1949) as well as the inferences of Coon (1966).

In Figure 8 the vowel space of the reconstructed La Chapelle-aux-Saints supralaryngeal vocal tract is presented. Each of the data points (N) represents attempts to produce vowels like [a], [i], or [u]. The labeled loops again refer to the Peterson-Barney (1952) data for actual human vowels. Note that the vowel space of the fossil is a subset of the human vowel space and that it is impossible to produce the "extreme" vowels [a], [i], and [u]. It is likewise impossible to produce the glides [y] or [w] or velar consonants like [g] and [k]. The Neanderthal supralaryngeal vocal tract also probably is not capable of making nasal versus nonnasal contrasts. Everything will tend to be nasalized. The modeled Neanderthal vowel space is probably too large in that we allowed articulatory maneuvers that would have been rather acrobatic in modern man (Lieberman and Crelin 1971). We tried to err on the side of making this fossil's phonetic ability more humanlike whenever we were in doubt.

Sterkfontein 5

In Plate 3 a silicone rubber model of the airways of the reconstructed supralaryngeal vocal tract of the Sterkfontein 5 cranium (Mrs. Ples) is shown together with the chimpanzee airways that appeared in Plate 2. Note the similarities. Crelin's reconstruction follows from the similarities that exist between this fossil and the present-day orangutan and, to a lesser degree, the chimpanzee. The reconstructed vocal tract has the same phonetic limitations as present-day apes. (The details of this reconstruction and the others that follow are discussed in detail elsewhere [Crelin et al. f.c.]).

Es-Skhūl V and Steinheim

In Plate 4 silicone rubber models of the reconstructed airways of the

Es-Skhūl V and Steinheim fossils are shown together with the supralaryngeal airways of adult *Homo sapiens*. Note that the reconstructed supralaryngeal airways both have right-angle bends, that the pharyngeal cavity is part of the direct airway out of the larynx, and that both resemble the supralaryngeal airways of adult modern man. The reconstructed Es-Skhūl V airway is completely modern. It would place no limits on its owner's phonetic repertoire if he attempted to produce the full range of human speech. The Steinheim supralaryngeal airway, although it has some pongid features, is also functionally equivalent to a modern supralaryngeal vocal tract. It would have placed no restrictions on its owners's phonetic repertoire if he attempted to produce the full range of human speech.

Broken Hill (Rhodesian Man)

In Plate 5 a silicone rubber model of the reconstructed supralaryngeal airways of Rhodesian man is shown together with a casting of the supralaryngeal airways of adult *Homo sapiens*. Note that despite the large oral cavity which follows from the large palate of this fossil, there is a right-angle bend in the supralaryngeal airway. This vocal tract appears to be an intermediate form. When it is modeled it can produce acoustic signals appropriate to the human vowels [a], [i], and [u], although supralaryngeal vocal tract configurations that are needed are not as stabile, i.e. resistant to articulatory sloppiness, as equivalent human vocal tract configurations. Note that the large palate in this fossil form occurs with a bent supralaryngeal vocal tract. The reduction of the palate in forms like Steinheim, Es-Skhūl V, and modern *Homo sapiens* therefore cannot be the factor that caused the larynx to descend.

SIGNIFICANCE OF RESULTS

In Table 1 the results of the reconstructions and computer modeling so far discussed are presented together with the results that would be obtained for various fossils that are similar to the ones that we have examined. I have not attempted to list all the similar forms. Note that we have divided the table into two categories: fossil hominids who had the anatomical specializations that are necessary for human speech and fossils who lacked these specializations.

Table 1. Results of reconstructions and computer modeling

	— Human supralaryngeal vocal tract	+ Human supralaryngeal vocal tract
	Australopithecines: africanus	
	robustus	
	boisei	
	Saccopastore I	Steinheim
Classic Neanderthal	Monte Circeo	
	Teshik-Tash (infant)	
	La Ferrassie I	
	La Chapelle-aux-Saints	
	La Quina (infant)	Broken Hill
	Pech-de-l'Azé	
		Es-Skhūl V
		Djebel Kafzeh
	Solo 11	
	Shanidar I	Cro-Magnon
		modern *Homo sapiens*

Neoteny

The first point that I want to make is that the anatomy necessary for producing the full range of sounds necessary for human speech represents a particular specialization that, at the present time, occurs only in normal adult *Homo sapiens*. It is clear that adult *Homo sapiens* does not particularly resemble newborn *Homo sapiens*.[4] This is, in general, true of all primates (Schultz 1968). The infantile forms of primates often do not resemble their adult forms. Schultz (1944, 1955), moreover, shows that the infantile forms of various nonhuman primates resemble newborn *Homo sapiens* whereas the adult forms of these nonhuman primates diverge markedly from adult *Homo sapiens*. This, however, does not mean that adult *Homo sapiens* has evolved by preserving neonatal features (Montagu 1962), because it is apparent that modern man has his own unique specializations. The unique specializations of modern man include the anatomy necessary for the production of human speech. Table 1 shows that these specializations have evolved over at least the past 300,000 years and that until comparatively recent times, various types of hominids existed, some of whom

4. Benda (1969) shows that Down's Syndrome (Mongolism) involves the retention of infantile morphology. Victims of this pathology, in some instances, retain the general proportions of the newborn skull. Their supralaryngeal vocal tracts retain the morphology of the newborn and they are unable to speak. They strikingly demonstrate that *Homo sapiens* has not evolved by retaining infantile characteristics.

lacked the anatomical mechanisms necessary for articulate human speech.

The "Neanderthal Problem"

Note that Table 1 places a number of fossil forms that lacked speech into a category labeled "classic Neanderthal." A view that has enjoyed some popularity in recent years is that Neanderthal fossils do not differ substantially from modern *Homo sapiens*, that they simply form a subset of hominids who have characteristics that grade imperceptibly with those typical of the modern population of *Homo sapiens*. An extreme formulation of this view is, for example, that ". . . no single measurement or even set of measurements can set Neanderthals apart from modern man" (Nett 1973). In other words, Neanderthal man cannot be regarded as a separate species or even a separate variety distinct from *Homo sapiens*.

This claim can be substantiated only if one includes fossils like Steinheim and Es-Skhūl V in the same class as forms like La Chapelle-aux-Saints. Quantitative multivariate analysis like that of Howells (1968) demonstrates that fossils like La Chapelle and La Ferrasie form a class that is quite distinct from modern man. The measurements contained in Patte's (1955) comprehensive work as well as the observations of Vlček (1970) on the ontogenetic development of Neanderthal infants indicate that this class of fossils, classic Neanderthal man, represents a specialization that diverged from the line (or lines) that contains more direct ancestors of *Homo sapiens*. Fossils like Steinheim and Es-Skhūl V, which are sometimes categorized as "early" Neanderthal, are functionally distinct from classic Neanderthal. These fossils exhibit the anatomical specializations necessary for human speech.

A general overlap between modern man and Neanderthal man is possible only if forms like Steinheim and Es-Skhūl V are put into the same class as La Chapelle, La Ferrasie, Monte Circeo, etc. Hominids who could have produced human speech would have to be classified with hominids who could not have produced human speech. This would be equivalent to putting forms that had the anatomical prerequisites for bipedal posture into the same class as forms that lacked this ability.

A question immediately arises. Is this category, i.e. set of fossils labeled "classic Neanderthal," a separate species? It is useful to remember Darwin's definition of the term "species." Darwin (1859: 52) viewed the term ". . . as one arbitrarily given for the sake of convenience to a set of individuals closely resembling each other, and that it does not essentially differ from the term variety, which is given to less distinct and more fluctuating forms." Darwin later notes (1859: 485): "... the only distinction between species and well-marked varieties is that the latter are known, or believed, to be connected at the present day by intermediate gradations, whereas species were formerly thus connected."

It is evident that intermediate fossil forms like Broken Hill man bridge the gap between classic Neanderthal man and modern *Homo sapiens*. We do not know, and we probably never will be able to know, all the traits that may have differentiated various hominid populations that are now extinct. We do not, for example, know whether viable progeny would have resulted from the mating of forms like Cro-Magnon and La Quina. Even if we did know that viable progeny would result from the mating of classic Neanderthal and early *Homo sapiens* populations, we would not necessarily conclude that these forms were members of the same species.

"Species," as Darwin noted, is simply a labeling device. *Canis lupus* and *Canis familiaris* are considered to be separate species even though they may freely mate and have viable progeny. The behavioral attributes of wolves and dogs make it important for people, e.g. shepherds, to place these animals into different species, even though some dogs, e.g. chihuahuas and St. Bernards, are more distinct morphologically and behaviorally and cannot mate. The question of separate species labels for classic Neanderthal and other fossil hominid populations is thus probably an empty question. We simply can note that different types of hominids apparently coexisted until comparatively recent times and that some of these hominids do not appear to have contributed to the present human gene pool.

Table 1 does have some bearing on the apparent absence of the specializations typical of classic Neanderthal man (e.g. La Chapelle, La Ferrasie, etc.) in modern man. Animal studies (Capranica 1965) have established the role of vocalizations in courtship and mating. The presence, or absence, of humanlike speech probably would have served as a powerful factor in assortative mating. In the present population of modern man it is evident that linguistic differences and affinities play a powerful role in mate selection. We would expect this phenomenon to be accentuated when different hominid populations inherently were unable to produce the sounds of other groups. Sexual selection determined by speech patterns may thus have played a significant role in the divergence of groups like classic Neanderthal in Western Europe and the ancestral forms of modern *Homo sapiens*.

The Evolutionary Sequence

There is, unfortunately, a large gap in Table 1 in that we have not yet been able to examine specimens of *Homo erectus* with intact skull bases. It is, however, likely that the situation that typifies later hominid forms will also characterize *Homo erectus;* most probably *Homo erectus* specimens will not have the anatomy necessary for the production of the full range of human speech. Some forms, however, will undoubtedly be found that either had the necessary anatomy or that were intermediate forms. Evolution goes in small steps, and forms intermediate between Steinheim and the australopithecines must have existed. We still are, like Darwin, at the mercy of the "imperfection of the geological record."

We can, despite this gap, draw several inferences from Table 1. I would like to propose the following evolutionary sequence. The first phase of the evolution of human language must have relied on a system of gestures, facial expressions and vocal signals like those of present-day apes to communicate the semantic, i.e. cognitive, aspects of language. Although the cognitive abilities of early australopithecines were probably near the levels of present-day apes, late forms would have developed superior abilities as evolution continued step-by-step and mutations favoring larger relative brain sizes were retained. The retention of mutations leading to larger relative brain sizes is itself a sign that cognitive ability had a selective advantage. We can reasonably infer that activities like toolmaking and collective social enterprises like hunting were important attributes of australopithecine culture.

Although the vocal apparatus of forms like *Australopithecus africanus* does not appear to differ significantly from those of present-day apes, vocal communications undoubtedly played a part in their linguistic system. Our reconstructions can tell us nothing about the larynx; however, it is almost certain that the laryngeal mechanisms of these forms were at least as developed as those of present-day apes. As Negus (1949) observed, there is a continual elaboration of the larynx as we ascend the phylogenetic scale in terrestrial animals. The larynges of animals like wolves are capable of producing a number of distinct calls that serve as vehicles of vocal communication. The same is true for the larynges of chimpanzees and gorillas.

Studies like that of Kelemen (1948), which have attempted to show that chimpanzees cannot talk because of laryngeal deficiencies, are not correct. Kelemen shows that the chimpanzee's larynx is different from the larynx of a normal adult human male. The chimpanzee's larynx will not produce the range of fundamental frequencies typical of adult human males; however, it can produce a variety of sound contrasts. Many of these sound contrasts indeed occur in human languages. A present-day chimpanzee, if it made maximum use of its larynx and supralaryngeal vocal tract, could, for example, produce the following sound contrasts:

1. VOICED VERSUS UNVOICED, i.e. excitation of the vocal tract by the quasi-periodic output of the larynx versus turbulent noise excitation generated by opening the larynx slightly and expelling air at a high flow rate.
2. HIGH FUNDAMENTAL VERSUS NORMAL FUNDAMENTAL, i.e. adjusting the larynx so phonation occurs in the falsetto register rather than the modal chest register (van den Berg 1960). The larynx has several modes of phonation which result in acoustic signals that are quite distinct. In falsetto the fundamental frequency is high and the glottal source's energy spectrum has comparatively little energy at its higher harmonics.
3. LOW FUNDAMENTAL VERSUS NORMAL FUNDAMENTAL, i.e. adjusting the larynx to a lower register. This lower register, termed "fry," produces very low fundamental frequencies (Hollien et al. 1966) that are irregular (Lieberman 1963).
4. DYNAMIC FUNDAMENTAL FREQUENCY VARIATIONS, e.g. low to high, high to low. Variations like these occur in many human tone languages.
5. STRIDENT HIGH ENERGY LARYNGEAL EXCITATION, i.e. the high, fundamental frequency, breathy output that can be observed in some chimpanzee vocalizations (Lieberman 1968) as well as in the cries of human newborn (Lieberman, Harris, et al. 1972).
6. CONTINUENT VERSUS INTERRUPTED, i.e. the temporal pattern of laryngeal excitation can be varied. This can be observed in the calls of present-day monkeys and apes (Lieberman 1968).
7. ORAL VERSUS NONORAL, i.e. the animal can produce a call with his oral cavity sealed or with his oral cavity open. This can be observed in present-day gorillas, in which the low-energy, low fundamental frequency sounds that sometimes accompany feeding appear to be produced with the oral cavity sealed by the epiglottis (Lieberman 1968).
8. LIP-ROUNDING AND LARYNGEAL LOWERING. Chimpanzees have the anatomic ability of rounding their lips and/or lowering their larynges while they produce a call. Both of these articulatory gestures could produce a formant frequency pattern that had falling transitions.
9. FLARED LIPS AND LARYNGEAL RAISING. Chimpanzees could either

flare their lips and/or raise their larynges while they produced a call. This would generate a rising formant frequency pattern.

10. BILABIAL CLOSURES AND RELEASES. Sounds like [b] and [p] as well as prevoiced [b] (like that occurring in Spanish, for example [Lisker and Abramson 1964]), could be produced by controlling the timing between the opening and closing of the larynx and the lips.

11. DENTAL CLOSURES AND RELEASES. Sounds like [d] and [t] (Lisker and Abramson 1964) could be produced by varying the timing between a closure effected by the tongue blade against the alveolar ridge and the opening and closing of the larynx.

Australopithecines could have generated all of the above sound contrasts if they had the requisite motor control and the neural ability to perceive the differences in sound quality that are the consequences of these articulatory maneuvers. Most of these phonetic contrasts, i.e. "features" (Jakobson et al. 1952), have been observed in the vocal communications of present-day nonhuman primates. Present-day human languages make use of all of these sound contrasts. The combination of articulatory features like (j) and (k) and timing features like (f) could also generate sounds like [f], [v], [s], etc. It is quite probable that late australopithecines and various forms of *Homo erectus* made use of these sound contrasts to communicate. The transference of patterns of "automatized" behavior, discussed above, from activities like toolmaking and hunting would have facilitated the acquisition of the motor skills necessary to produce these sounds. The role of hunting would have placed a premium on communication out of the line of sight, communication that, furthermore, left the hunter's hands free.

The neural mechanisms necessary for the differentiation of these sounds appear to exist in present-day primates. Wollberg and Newman (1972), for example, have shown that squirrel monkeys (*Saimiri sciureus*) possess auditory receptors "tuned" to one of the vocal calls that these monkeys make use of in their communications. Similar results have been demonstrated for frogs (Capranica 1965). Although gestural communication (Hewes 1971) undoubtedly played a more important role in the communications of these early hominids than is the case for modern man, I think that it is most unlikely that vocal communications also did not play an important role.

The crucial stage in the evolution of HUMAN language would appear to be the development of the "bent" supralaryngeal vocal tract of modern man. Table 1 shows a divergence in the paths of evolution. Some hominids appear to have retained the communications system that was typical of the australopithecines, a mixed system that relied on both gestural and vocal components. Other hominids appear to have followed an evolutionary path that resulted in almost total dependence on the vocal component for language, relegating the gestural component to a secondary "paralinguistic" function. The process would have been gradual, following from the prior existence of vocal signals in linguistic communication.

As I have noted before, the bent supralaryngeal vocal tract that appears in forms like present-day *Homo sapiens*, and the Steinheim, Es-Skhūl V, and Broken Hill fossils, allows its possessors to generate acoustic signals that have very distinct acoustic properties and that are very easy to produce. These signals are, in a sense, optimal acoustic signals (Lieberman 1970). If vocal communications were already part of the linguistic system of early hominids, then mutations that extended the range and the efficiency of the signaling process would have been retained in forms like Steinheim. The "bent" supralaryngeal vocal tract is otherwise a burden for basic vegetative functions. It would not have been retained unless it had conferred an adaptive advantage. The initial adaptive value of the bent supralaryngeal vocal tract would have been its value in increasing the inventory of vocal signals and, moreover, in providing more efficient vocal signals.

The neural mechanisms necessary to perceive these new signals would, in all likelihood, have been available to hominids like Steinheim. Recent electrophysiological data (Miller et al. 1972) shows that animals like the rhesus monkey, *Macaca mulatta*, will develop neural detectors that identify signals important to the animal. Receptors in the auditory cortex responsive to a 200 Hz sinusoid were discovered after the animals were trained by the classic methods of conditioning to respond behaviorally to this acoustic signal. These neural detectors could not be found in the auditory cortex of untrained animals. The auditory system of these primates thus appears to be "plastic." Receptive neural devices can be formed to respond to acoustic signals that the animal finds useful.

These results are in accord with behavioral experiments involving human subjects where "categorical" responses to arbitrary auditory signals can be produced by means of operant conditioning techniques (Lane 1965). They are also in accord with the results of classic conditioning experiments like those reported by Pavlov. The dogs learned to identify and to respond decisively to the sound of a bell, an "unnatural" sound for a dog. The dog obviously had to "learn" to identify the bell. Hominids like Steinheim, who had the potential to make "new" acoustic signals, would also have had the ability to "learn" to respond to these sounds in an automatized way. The plasticity of the primate auditory system would have provided the initial mechanism for "learning" these new sounds.

Later stages in the evolution of human language probably involved the retention of mutations that had "innately" determined neural mechanisms that were "tuned" to these new sounds. By innately determined, I do NOT mean that the organism needs no interaction with the environment to "learn" to perceive these sounds. The evidence instead suggests that humans are innately predisposed to "learn" to respond to the sounds of speech. Experiments with six-week-old infants (Eimas et al. 1971; Morse 1971) show that they respond to the acoustic cues that differentiate sounds like [b] and [p] in the same manner as adults. These acoustic distinctions involve ten millisecond differences in the timing of the delay between the start of the acoustic signal that occurs when a human speaker opens his lips and the start of phonation. It is most improbable that six-week-old infants could "learn" to respond to these signals unless there was some innate predisposition for this sound contrast to be perceived. This surely is not surprising. Human infants really do not "learn" the complex physiological maneuvers associated with normal respiration. They have built-in "knowledge."

The case for the neural mechanisms that are involved in the perception of human speech is not as simple as that for respiration. Some contact with a speech environment is necessary. Deaf children, for example, although they at first produce the vocalizations of normal children, become quiet after six months of age (Lenneberg 1967). Nottebohm (1970) shows similar effects in birds. Some aspects of the bird's vocal behavior are manifested even when the bird is raised in isolation. Other, important aspects of the bird's vocal behavior develop only when the bird is exposed to a "normal" communicative environment.

At some late stage, that is, late with respect to the initial evolution of the "bent" supralaryngeal vocal tract, the neural mechanisms that are necessary for the process of speech encoding would have evolved. The humanlike supralaryngeal vocal tract would have been retained initially for the acoustically distinct and articulatory facile signals that it could generate. The acoustic properties of sounds like the vowels [a], [i], and [u] and the glides [y] and [w], which allow a listener to determine the size of the speaker's supralaryngeal vocal tract, would have preadapted the communications system for speech encoding.

When a human listener hears a sound like the word "bat" as it is produced by an intermediate-sized supralaryngeal vocal tract, it is indeterminate. Ladefoged and Broadbent (1957), for example, show that a listener will perceive this sound as the word "bit" if he is led to believe that it was produced by a long vocal tract. The same listener will perceive the same sound as "but" if he is led to believe that it was produced by a small, i.e. short vocal tract. The listener, in effect, "normalizes" the signal to take account of the acoustic properties of different-sized vocal tracts. The listener responds as though he is interpreting the acoustic signal in terms of the articulatory gestures that a speaker would employ to generate the word.

The perception of human speech is generally structured in terms of the articulatory gestures that underlie the acoustic signal (Liberman et al. 1967). This process, as I noted earlier, is the basis of the encoding which allows human speech to transmit information at the rate of twenty to thirty segments per second. Signals like the vowels [a], [u], and [i] and the glides [y] and [w] are determinate in the sense that a particular formant pattern could have been generated by means of only one vocal tract using a particular articulatory maneuver (Stevens and House 1955; Lindblom and Sundberg 1969). A listener can use these vowels to identify instantly the size of the supralaryngeal vocal tract that he (or she) is listening to (Darwin 1971; Rand 1971). These vowels can indeed serve the same function in the recognition of human speech by computer. Gerstman (1967), for example, derives the size of a particular speaker's vocal tract from these vowels to identify the speaker's other vowels. Without this information it is impossible to assign a particular acoustic signal into the correct vowel class. The computer, like a human, has to know the size of the speaker's supralaryngeal vocal tract.

The process of speech encoding need not have followed the exact path that I have proposed. Other sounds, like [s] can provide a listener (or a computer) with information about the size of the speaker's vocal tract. As I noted before, the australopithecines had the anatomical prerequisites for producing sounds like [s], so the process of speech encoding and the evolution of the human supralaryngeal vocal tract may have been coeval. It is clear, however, that evolution goes by small steps and what we have in present-day man is a fully encoded speech system with a speech-producing anatomy that is highly adapted to this function. Other, now extinct, hominids like classic Neanderthal man had speech-producing anatomy that clearly was not as well adapted for speech encoding. It is, therefore, reasonable to conclude that speech encoding was either more rudimentary or not present.

It is, however, important to conclude with the point that language does not necessarily have to involve the process of speech encoding and rapid information transfer. The remains of Neanderthal culture all point to the presence of linguistic ability. Conversely, birds may have the potential for rapid information transfer (Greenewalt 1967); however, birds lack the cognitive ability that is also a necessary factor in language. It is most unlikely that birds could develop a complex language unless they also had larger brains.

Human language is the result of the convergence of many factors: automatization, cognitive ability, and speech encoding. The particular form that human language has taken, however, appears to be the result of the evolution of the human supralaryngeal vocal apparatus. The supralaryngeal vocal apparatus that differentiates present-day *Homo sapiens* from all living animals thus is as important a factor in the late stage of hominid evolution as dentition and bipedal posture were in earlier stages.

REFERENCES

BENDA, C. E.
1969 *Down's syndrome, Mongolism and its management*. New York: Grune and Stratton.

CAMPBELL, B.
1966 *Human evolution, an introduction to man's adaptations*. Chicago: Aldine.

CAPRANICA, R. R.
1965 *The evoked vocal response of the bullfrog*. Cambridge, Massachusetts: M.I.T. Press.

CHIBA, T., M. KAJIYAMA
1958 *The vowel, its nature and structure*. Tokyo: Phonetic Society of Japan.

COON, C. S.
1966 *The origin of races*. New York: Knopf.

CRELIN, E. W.
1969 *Anatomy of the newborn: an atlas*. Philadelphia: Lea and Febiger.

CRELIN, E. W., P. LIEBERMAN, D. H. KLATT
f.c. "Anatomy and related phonetic ability of the Skhūl V, Steinheim, and Rhodesian fossils and the Plesianthropus reconstruction."

DARWIN, C.
1859 *On the origin of species* (Facsimile edition). New York: Atheneum.

DARWIN, C. J.
1971 Ear differences in the recall of fricatives and vowels. *Quarterly Journal of Experimental Psychology* 23:386–392.

EIMAS, P. D., E. R. SIQUELAND, P. JUSCZYK, J. VIGORITO
1971 Speech perception in infants. *Science* 171:303–306.

FANT, G.
1960 *Acoustic theory of speech production.* The Hague: Mouton.

FLANAGAN, J. L.
1955 A difference limen for vowel formant frequency. *Journal of the Acoustical Society of America* 27:613–617.

GARDNER, R. A., B. T. GARDNER
1969 Teaching sign language to a chimpanzee. *Science* 165:664–672.

GERSTMAN, L.
1967 "Classification of self-normalized vowels," in *Proceedings of IEEE Conference on Speed Communication and Processing,* 97–100.

GOLD, B., L. R. RABINER
1968 Analysis of digital and analog formant synthesizers. *IEEE-Trans. Audio Electroacoustics, AU-16,* 81–94.

GREENEWALT, C. A.
1967 *Bird song: acoustics and physiology.* Washington, D.C.: Smithsonian Institution.

HENKE, W. L.
1966 "Dynamic articulatory model of speech production using computer simulation." Unpublished doctoral dissertation (Appendix B), Massachusetts Institute of Technology, Cambridge, Mass.

HEWES, G. W.
1971 *Language origins: a bibliography.* Boulder, Colorado: University of Colorado, Department of Anthropology.

HOLLIEN, H., P. MOORE, R. W. WENDAHL, J. F. MICHEL
1966 On the nature of vocal fry, *Journal of Speech and Hearing Research* 9:245–247.

HOWELLS, W. W.
1968 Mount Carmel man: morphological relationships. *Proceedings of the Eighth International Congress of Anthropological and Ethnological Sciences,* volume one. Tokyo.

IRWIN, O. C.
1948 Infant speech: development of vowel sounds. *Journal of Speech and Hearing Disorders* 13:31–34.

JAKOBSON, R., G. FANT, M. HALLE
1952 *Preliminaries to speech analysis.* Cambridge, Massachusetts: M.I.T. Press.

KELEMEN, G.
1948 The anatomical basis of phonation in the chimpanzee. *Journal of Morphology* 82:229–256.

KENYON, K. W.
1969 *The sea otter in the eastern Pacific Ocean.* Washington: United States Government Printing Office.

KIMURA, D.
1964 Left-right differences: the perception of melodies. *Quarterly Journal of Experimental Psychology* 16:355–358.

KIRCHNER, J. A.
1970 *Pressman and Kelemen's physiology of the larynx* (revised edition). Rochester, Minnesota: American Academy of Ophthalmology and Otolaryngology.

KUIPERS, A. H.
1960 *Phoneme and morpheme in Kabardian*. The Hague: Mouton.

LADEFOGED, P., D. E. BROADBENT
1957 Information conveyed by vowels. *Journal of the Acoustical Society of America* 29:98–104.

LANE, H.
1965 Motor theory of speech perception: a critical review. *Psychological Review* 72:275–309.

LENNEBERG, E. H.
1967 *Biological foundations of language*. New York: Wiley.

LIBERMAN, A. M., F. S. COOPER, D. P. SHANKWEILER, M. STUDDERT-KENNEDY
1967 Perception of the speech code. *Psychological Review* 74:431–461.

LIEBERMAN, P.
1963 Some acoustic measures of the periodicity of normal and pathologic larynges. *Journal of the Acoustical Society of America* 35:344–353.
1967 *Intonation, perception, and language*. Cambridge, Massachusetts: M.I.T. Press.
1968 Primate vocalizations and human linguistic ability. *Journal of the Acoustical Society of America* 44:1574–1584.
1970 Towards a unified phonetic theory. *Linguistic Inquiry* 1:307–322.
1972 *The speech of primates*. The Hague: Mouton.

LIEBERMAN, P., E. S. CRELIN
1971 On the speech of Neanderthal man. *Linguistic Inquiry* 2:203–222.

LIEBERMAN, P., E. S. CRELIN, D. H. KLATT
1972 Phonetic ability and related anatomy of the newborn, adult human, Neanderthal man and the chimpanzee. *American Anthropologist* 74:287–307.

LIEBERMAN, P., K. S. HARRIS, P. WOLFF, L. H. RUSSELL
1972 Newborn infant cry and nonhuman primate vocalizations. *Journal of Hearing Research* 14:718–727.

LIEBERMAN, P., D. H. KLATT, W. A. WILSON
1969 Vocal tract limitations on the vowel repertoires of rhesus monkey and other nonhuman primates. *Science* 164:1185–1187.

LINDBLOM, B., J. SUNDBERG
1969 *A quantitative model of vowel production and the distinctive features of Swedish vowels*. Speech Transmission Laboratory Report 1. Stockholm, Sweden: Royal Institute of Technology.

LISKER, L., A. S. ABRAMSON
1964 A cross-language study of voicing in initial stops: acoustical measurements. *Word* 20:384–422.

LYNIP, A. W.
1951 The uses of magnetic devices in the collection and analysis of the preverbal utterances of an infant. *Genetic Psychology Monograph* 44:221–262.

MANLY, R. S., L. C. BRALEY
1950 Masticatory performance and efficiency. *Journal of Dental Research* 29:448–462.

MANLY, R. S., F. R. SHIERE

1950 The effect of dental deficiency on mastication and food preference. *Oral Surgery, Oral Medicine, and Oral Pathology*, 3:674–685.

MANLY, R. S., P. VINTON

1951 A survey of the chewing ability of denture wearers. *Journal of Dental Research* 30:314–321.

MILLER, J. M., D. SUTTON, B. PFINGST, A. RYAN, R. BEATON

1972 Single cell activity in the auditory cortex of rhesus monkeys: behavioral dependency. *Science* 177:449–451.

MONTAGU, M. F. A.

1962 "Time, morphology and neoteny in the evolution of man," in *Culture and the evolution of man*. Edited by M. F. A. Montagu, 324–342. New York: Oxford University Press.

MORSE, P.

1971 "Speech perception in six-week old infants." Unpublished doctoral dissertation, University of Connecticut, Storrs.

NEGUS, V. E.

1949 *The comparative anatomy and physiology of the larynx*. New York: Hafner.

NETT, E. G.

1973 A note on phonetic ability. *American Anthropologist* 75:1717–1719.

NOTTEBOHM, F.

1970 Ontogeny of bird song. *Science* 167:950–956.

PATTE, E.

1955 *Les Néanderthaliens, anatomie, physiologie, comparaisons*. Paris: Masson.

PERKELL, J. S.

1969 *Physiology of speech production: results and implications of a quantitative cineradiographic study*. Cambridge, Massachusetts: M.I.T. Press.

PETERSON, G. E., H. L. BARNEY

1952 Control methods used in a study of the vowels. *Journal of the Acoustical Society of America* 24:175–184.

PREMACK, D.

1972 Language in chimpanzee? *Science* 172:808–822.

RAND, T. C.

1971 Vocal tract size normalization in the perception of stop consonants. *Haskins Laboratories Status Report on Speech Research*, SR-26/26, 141–146.

SCHULTZ, A. H.

1944 Age changes and variability in gibbons. *American Journal of Physical Anthropology*, n.s. 2:1–129.

1955 The position of the occipital condyles and of the face relative to the skull base in primates. *American Journal of Physical Anthropology*, n.s. 13:97–120.

1968 "The recent hominoid primates," in *Perspectives on human evolution I*. Edited by S. L. Washburn and P. G. Jay, 122–195. New York: Holt, Rinehart and Winston.

SHANKWEILER, D., M. STUDDERT-KENNEDY
1967 Identification of consonants and vowels presented to left and right ears. *Quarterly Journal of Experimental Psychology* 19:59–63.

STEVENS, K. N.
1972 "Quantal nature of speech," in *Human communication, a unified view*. Edited by E. E. David and P. B. Denes. New York: McGraw Hill.

STEVENS, K. N., A. S. HOUSE
1955 Development of a quantitative description of vowel articulation. *Journal of the Acoustical Society of America* 27:484–493.

STRAUS, W. L., JR., A. J. E. CAVE
1957 Pathology and posture of Neanderthal man. *Quarterly Review of Biology* 32:348–363.

TROUBETZKOY, N. S.
1939 *Principes de phonologie*. Paris: Klincksieck. (1949, translated by J. Cantineau).

TRUBY, H. M., J. F. BOSMA, J. LIND
1965 *Newborn infant cry*. Uppsala: Almqvist and Wiksells.

VAN DEN BERG, J. W.
1960 Vocal ligaments versus registers. *Current Problems in Phoniatrics and Logopedics* 1:19–34.

VAN LAWICK-GOODALL, JANE
1971 *In the shadow of man*. New York: Dell.

VLČEK, E.
1970 "Étude comparative onto-phylogénétique de l'enfant du Pech-de-l'Azé par rapport à d'autres enfants néandertaliens," in *L'enfant du Pech-de-l'Azé*. Edited by D. Feremback et al., 149–186. Paris: Masson.

VON KEMPELEN, W. R.
1791 *Mechanismus der menschlichen Sprache nebst der Beschreibung seiner sprechenden Maschine*. Vienna: J. B. Degen.

WOLLBERG, Z., J. D. NEWMAN
1972 Auditory cortex of squirrel monkey: response patterns of single cells to species-specific vocalizations. *Science* 175:212–214.

ZHINKIN, N. I.
1963 "An application of the theory of algorithms to the study of animal speech — methods of vocal intercommunication between monkeys," in *Acoustic behavior of animals*. Edited by R. G. Busnel, 132–180. Amsterdam: Elsevier.

Discussion

WOLPOFF: In these papers we are presented with essentially two different models about why man's brain reached its present size. Both suggest that it is the result of selection, presumably for greater learning capacity and a greater storage capacity. But one model, based on the Neanderthals, suggests that although this selection occurred slowly and continuously, it left us about 100,000 years ago with a brain which though very large, was really not much different in organization from other primates. Then language originated, perhaps 100,000 years ago. According to this model the storage, information, and learning capacity resulting from neural changes due to structured human language allowed man's development to continue exponentially. The other model, which I think is Ralph Holloway's more than anybody else's, suggests that the hominid brain has been subject both to vast increase in size and neural reorganization. Holloway suggests that the major selective pressure for this neural reorganization is "social control." Perhaps a better term for it would be "encephalization of structure" because it seems clear that social behaviors like language are highly structured phenomena wherein the structure is largely within the brain itself, much in the same way that there is a structure within a computer. The computer programs will tell the computer what to do. This is analogous to what we learn. But the structure is already there, allowing us to write programs of certain sorts very easily just as it is possible to learn certain behaviors easily. Now it is difficult to choose hypotheses when we are speculating. This is essentially what we are doing here. Lieberman has suggested, in a very ingenious attempt to reconstruct the anatomy of the vocal tract of Neanderthals, that perhaps the former model rather than the latter is correct. He believes that there is corroborating evidence suggesting that until very recently hominids did not have the capability for fully articulate human language of a modern sort. While many of his analytical techniques are modern, the reconstruction itself is subject to very serious question. First, his case is weakened by use of Boule's reconstruction of La Chapelle and distorted specimens such as Steinheim. Second, it is very difficult, if not impossible, to reconstruct the gross anatomy of the vocal tract. Most of my criticism centers about his position of the larynx in Neanderthals. His positioning is based on the line between the position of the genial tubercles and the styloid process. I have observed many genial tubercles. They do not form lines. Instead they are little bumps. You could put this almost anywhere you want because the genial tubercles themselves do not indicate any muscle direction. Unfortunately he chose to put the intersection above the angle of the mandible which leads to an anatomical problem that I would like to have his comment on. It seems to me that Neanderthals could not swallow. If you look at Lieberman's diagram of the newborn infant and modern man, the anterior bellies of the digastric muscles will allow the hyoid to go anterior and SUPERIOR when the muscle is fired. However, the Neanderthal's larynx, indicated by the hyoid position, is located so high that it would have to go anterior and INFERIOR during swallowing. Thus I believe swallowing would not be possible because the respiratory tract would not be closed as it is in modern man.

LIEBERMAN: You have posed a number of questions. Let me take them in order. One, my paper indicated that the possession of a modern vocal tract anatomy is not all that recent, Steinheim and Skūhl V seem to have had it. These are fully developed ones. The model is in fact consistent with the notion of several species coexisting. It is rather reassuring that Phillip Tobias finds independent evidence for the existence of more than one hominid form at one period. Secondly, tubercles and fossae are essentially devices to increase surface area so that the glue joint is a little stronger. If you look at the plane of the digastric muscle of La Chapelle or La Ferrassie, and a whole range of fossils, you will note that the angulation of the system is designed to minimize shear forces that are going straight back from the mandible. Now if you consider a muscle system that is optimized to minimize a shear force, e.g. a newborn human or any living ape or monkey, you will find that the alignment of muscles like the digastric and the geniohyoid is such that they run straight back. The angulation furnished by the styloid (as inferred from the base of the styloid) is such that the whole larynx is positioned high. The total morphological system of classic Neanderthal, or for that matter *A. africanus*, is such that there is a high larynx. This total morphology is almost identical with that of living apes; I could further extend that to be practically identical to that of all living animals except man. Further, you would be incorrect to propose that the neural mechanisms that are specific to language can be entirely responsible for the organization of the brain. The neural mechanisms of language would appear to be operant in all sorts of other human activities that we also find in other primates and non-primate animals. Language need not be present in its fully developed form to get the human brain.

WOLPOFF: I would still like to know how Neanderthals could swallow with the anterior digastrics positioned as they are in your reconstruction?

LIEBERMAN: You are wrong in your notion that a low hyoid is essential for swallowing. Victims of Down's syndrome provide another interesting test case. They preserve the morphology of the infant. Normal infants swallow with a high position of the hyoid. The angulation of the mandible is similar to that in various fossils like La Chapelle. Further, the larynx is high. The sphenoid is exposed. The synchondrosis between the base of the occipital and the vomer bone is not present in any of these forms, i.e. newborns, classic Neanderthals, or *A. africanus*. Instead the sphenoid is exposed because the larynx has to be up there. It is up and back. In brief, classic Neanderthal could swallow with a hyoid positioned as per our model just as all living nonhuman primates with this morphology swallow.

TUTTLE: We might swallow that.

VOGEL: Dr. Tobias, upon what evidence is the new dating of the South African australopithecine sites based? Other than the new dating of the Taung site what evidence, especially dental traits, supports reassignment of the Taung child to the robust australopithecines?

TOBIAS: The new dates are based on geomorphological considerations applied by T. Partridge of Johannesburg and K. Butzer of Chicago. Partridge's approach is based on the rate of cutting back of the nickpoint of the river near four of the five South African sites. It is premised on geomorphological constants such as the rate of valley widening which was necessary for the subterraneously developed cave to open to the surface. Butzer's analysis is based on a different set of geomorphological yardsticks. It is based on correlation between the sequence inferred in the Harts River Valley in which Taung is situated and the Vaal River Valley, where there is a good implemental and faunal sequence. Further evidence is provided by Cooke's and Maglio's studies of the suid fauna from Sterkfontein and the suid and proboscidian fauna from Makapansgat and a comparison of these faunal elements with the well-dated, well-calibrated succession of Suidae and proboscidians in East Africa. These can be regarded as independent lines of evidence. There is a chronology of Suidae in East Africa. We know what pigs were living at two million, three million, and four million years B.P. There is a proboscidian chronology in East Africa and so we know what elephants were living at any half million year period. Comparing suids from Sterkfontein and Makapansgat with those of East Africa, and comparing the elephants from Makapansgat with the well-dated proboscidian sequence of East Africa, we find the equivalent forms dated to about two-and-a-half to three million years B.P. We should do this for a great number of other mammals, such as hippos, rhinos, cercopithecoids, antelopes, and other animals. Hopefully we shall ultimately be able to regard the hominids as an additional element for correlation. In response to the question, "Are there any morphological criteria associating Taung with *robustus?*" Although the Taung specimen was discovered forty-nine years ago it has not been fully described. Dart's 300 page monograph which he wrote in the 1920's was not published. There is no complete description of the Taung skull available. We now have a number of juvenile specimens from Swartkrans, including very recently discovered ones. The time is now ripe for a major Weidenreich-style definitive study on the Taung skull.

SZALAY: If Phillip Tobias' new taxonomic assessment of the Taung child as a robust australopith is validated, and I suspect that it will be, this should warn anthropologists in the future to abide by the rules of zoological nomenclature if we are to avoid complete chaos regarding hominid systematics. Further, this new assignment of the Taung child may mean that the nomen *Australopithecus* may have to be suppressed.

WOLPOFF: The demise of *Australopithecus* is perhaps a bit premature.

TOBIAS: I agree with Milford on this point. And I am delighted that Fred Szalay agrees with my suggestion about the Taung child which is very tentative at this stage. The taxonomic implications of removing the Taung child from *A. africanus* (of which it is the type specimen) have been investigated very carefully. The skull should never have been made the type skull of a new species because it is a juvenile with an inadequate number of clearly defined morphological features. There is a strong advisory ruling of the International Commission on Zoological Nomenclature that juveniles should not be made types of species in such circumstances. The next described specimen attributed to *A. africanus* would become the lectotype of *A. africanus*. And the nomen would persist. Conversely, placing the child from Taung into *A. robustus* will not make it the type specimen of *A. robustus*. The type specimen of *A. robustus* will remain the first discovered specimen, TM 1517 from Kromdraai, because, again as a child, Taung is not suitable to be the type for a species. I have two publications in press that detail the taxonomic systematic implications of taking Taung out of *A. africanus*.

TUTTLE: Perhaps there is a need here for children's liberation.

ECKHARDT: Your phylogenetic chart on the Hominidae (Figure 6) showed hominids in Africa extending back to 5.5 million years B.P., the earliest specimen being Lothagam and another one following that being the Baringo specimen.

TOBIAS: The latter is the Chemeron temporal bone recovered near Lake Baringo. The Kanapoi humeral fragment is also early.

ECKHARDT: You omitted the Baringo molar tooth which has been discussed as an early australopithecine. Would you agree with me that this specimen might not be a hominid?

TOBIAS: Are you referring to the Ngorora specimen?

ECKHARDT: Yes.

TOBIAS: It is too uncertain and too indefinite. I would accept it as HOMINOID. I would not accept that there is enough evidence to declare it unequivocally HOMINID.

ECKHARDT: I agree with that completely. And I would extend the uncertainty to Lothagam which now seems to be uniformly accepted as hominid. It can be matched, almost characteristic after characteristic, by modern chimpanzee and gorilla material. There is a strong indication that we should place a large question mark next to Lothagam which would affect dating the beginning of the hominid sequence. If that is the case it might also have ramifications for the rest of the branch points that you drew (Figure 6) because it is going to allow the possibility for interpreting the differences as intraspecies variation instead of interspecific differences. This would change the shape of your phylogenetic chart rather substantially. The other point that I should like to make pertains to sample sizes. You gave sample sizes and ranges based on those and 95 percent confidence limits. All of these sample sizes were quite small. It must be emphasized that you are dealing with "populations" inferred from specimens which may not by any means represent biological populations. These specimens might well be drawn from rather vastly different points in time. Since this is a period during which there is strong evidence that rapid evolution in brain size was occurring you must correct these population ranges for rates of change through time. It could be done rather readily. But this might extend the degree of overlap so enormously that, depending on one's point of view, we might find ourselves in the delightful or unhappy position that we cannot really solidly demonstrate that we are dealing with separate evolving lines or merely one evolving line.

TOBIAS: I fully accept everything you said on the latter part. Obviously this whole question is hedged in with a great number of cautionary messages and it really is very subjunctive if not highly subjective at this stage.

As regards the early Lothagam specimen, what you say is extremely interesting to me. W. W. Howells is here and has been working on that mandible. Bill would you like to comment on it before I do?

HOWELLS: It is not my bone. It is Bryan Patterson's and he is still working on it. I cannot tell you anything about it now.

TOBIAS: It is perfectly correct that the record at that lower part of my line (Figure 6) is extremely sparse. I did not start at six million years B.P. because there were no relevant fossils earlier than that. I was not intending a dogmatic statement. It was merely convenient for me to start the graph there. And if the bottom part of the graph looks straight, and somewhat phyletic, I am quite sure that it is merely owing to what Charles Darwin called the imperfection of the fossil record. Once again, when we have a large number of hominids from that late Pliocene period it is pretty clear that they will represent the same kind of cladistic or even reticulate pattern, perhaps with the coexistence of two or more species at several different times. Perhaps they will be semispecies as I have suggested *robustus* and *boisei* are. Ultimately perhaps the two semispecies will come to be recognized as two subspecies. But at the moment I think that we are in a state of flux because of the rapidity of new discoveries. I fully agree with Eckhardt that the story from three million years B.P. back in time is very uncertain. The Kanapoi distal humerus which is put at 4.5 million and the Chemeron temporal are hominid. The humerus was described as being very close to an *africanus* humerus but it is extremely imperfect material on which to base any inference about the hominids at that level. If *Ramapithecus* is not a hominid, then the options are open for verifying Sarich's suggestion that hominid emergence occurred five million years ago (or maybe, at the earliest to which he is prepared to push it back on his molecular clock, six to eight million years ago). This would not be at all at serious variance with the paleontological facts at present available.

TUTTLE: This is becoming literally a brainless discussion. Might we try to get back to the brain. Dr. Sacher would you please comment now?

SACHER: The focus of my own work has been not so much on the evolution of the hominid brain *per se* as on what it implies about the evolution of the human lifespan. The conclusion is that lifespan has evolved *pari passu* with brain size in hominids, as in all mammals, because of the overriding requirements of reproduction. If the length of time that it takes for an organism to develop to sexual maturity is a function primarily of the size of the brain that has to be developed, this will determine the reproductive rate, and hence his reproductive span and lifespan.

LIEBERMAN: One factor that seems to be emerging out of many studies is that there is extreme lateralization in the perception of human speech. What can be said definitively about evidence of lateralization in fossil hominids?

TOBIAS: The subject is dealt with pretty fully in Holloway's paper (see Holloway, this volume). There is increasing evidence that, while we have two brains, one is not just a carbon copy of the other. There is a bilateral localization of various kinds of skills. Speech is one, manual dexterity another. Not all of the skills have been assessed. But the psychomotor tests that have been performed show them not to be localized in the same hemisphere. Thus the view that has gone by the board is the idea of a dominant hemisphere. Each hemisphere is dominant for particular functions.

TUTTLE: Unfortunately, much of the endocast evidence is very one-sided. I might also add that despite all the pongid brains that have been examined, I am not aware of any study that has attempted specifically to document quantitative and morphological differences between the two sides.

LIEBERMAN: We reviewed that literature and found it is deficient in this regard.

WOLPOFF: I would like Tobias to comment on the following two matters regarding the evolution of early hominid brains. The first deals with the way the samples are treated. Holloway employed t-tests to show that *robustus* cannot be *africanus*, *africanus* cannot be *habilis*, and so forth. However, the use of the t-test in these sorts of studies can be very misleading. With them I could "prove" to a 5 percent significance level that *H. erectus* in Java cannot be *H. erectus* in China and yet we still do not consider them to be different taxa. With a single sample t-test you could "prove" that skull 10 from Choukoutien does not belong in that sample. But, of course there is a lot of good evidence that it does. Consequently, I question the use of statistical tests on samples of this size, given that we can use these same tests on other samples and get results that we clearly do not like. Secondly, we are in a terribly confusing position right now *vis-à-vis* what happened in regard to the brain size of early hominids. I do not think that it is a simple problem. In the lower Pleistocene of Africa we have small hominids with small teeth and small brains, such as *A. africanus;* we also have small hominids with small teeth and larger brains (if the capacities are correct), such as *H. habilis;* we have large hominids with larger teeth and slightly larger brains, *A. robustus;* and finally we have larger hominids with typically robust australopithecine type morphology of the face and dentition but with very large brains. There are at least two examples of this now, KNM-ER 1470 and KNM-ER 1590. It strikes me that we are faced with two alternatives: (1) that there were four or five different taxa of hominids in the lower Pleistocene. This is essentially what Phillip Tobias suggests; or (2) there was one taxon of hominids in the lower Pleistocene and there is virtually no relation whatsoever between body size, brain size and tooth size. Phillip, specifically what sort of evidence would help us to decide between these two hypotheses?

TOBIAS: Surely the critical point here is that we must consider the total morphological pattern of specimens in any study of this sort. The two most complete East Rudolf robust specimens show all the classical features which distinguish hominoid males from hominoid females. The total morphological pattern might indeed help us. A second important point to remember is the occurrence of mosaic evolution. It has been very obvious in the whole story of man. There is little doubt that brain change was much more relevant to diversification of hominids at some stages in that four million year period than at others. Further, there is little doubt that dental change, i.e. change in dental size, was more relevant in certain stages in hominization than in others and in certain parts of the matrix of hominization. Therefore, I am not at all put off by the fact that you could get a significant t-test result between *H. erectus erectus* and *H. erectus pekinensis*. At that stage brain size seems to be a much less significant parameter of change than at the level between *Australopithecus* and *H. habilis* where it is associated with evidence of behavioral change, e.g. the Oldowan culture. Such cultural evidence must be taken into consideration. So the fact that a t-test is accepted as indicative of different taxa at one level but not at another level must be seen in relation to the lineage, the total morphological and ethological pattern, and also the particular point in the mosaic of diversification which we recognize at that level. Brains are more important at some points and, similarly the attainment of erectness is obviously more important at some stages than at others. We have not uncovered the stage where the attainment of erectness really is critically important. This is still in a no-man's-land where we do not have the fossils.

GOODMAN: Dr. Sacher (see Sacher, this volume) brought out the very important point that increase in brain size is correlated with increasing generation length. In terms of his efforts to make correlations, it should be pointed out that there is reason to think that increasing generation times, particularly if they reduce the sidereal time of the cell divisions involved in the maturation of the sperm and the ovum or lengthen it within a particular generation, would have the effect of reducing the number of mutations due to mistakes of replication in the DNA on a sidereal or time basis. There are other arguments that can be offered in terms of selective processes. One would expect mutations to be much more detrimental during the embryonic and fetal stages of life than at late stages of life. Thus there is less chance of spreading mutations in a population. When we consider such factors it seems that molecular evolution has been slowing somewhat in the higher primates, particularly in the line going to man where generation length has been increasing quite a bit. This is a point that Lovejoy has drawn upon to try to substantiate a fifteen million year separation between us and the chimps instead of some time within the last few million years. The best molecular data which gives a full estimation of mutational divergence would, when subjected to the clock concept probably separate man and chimp only about one million years ago. On that basis I am quite willing to accept Sarich's thought that we probably did not separate any more than eight million years ago. But I see no *a priori* reasons to have a bias toward either view. We must wait until the fossil evidence helps us to decide the matter, though the clock model is a useful one in suggesting alternative times.

TUTTLE: So we have won you over to morphology? I hoped that if I had you sit here long enough this might happen.

TOBIAS: Morris, I am inclined to agree with you rather than with Vincent Sarich on this. The assumption of CONSTANCY in molecular change seems to fly in the face of everything. Would you accept that what I said about mosaic evolution at the morphological level is no less evident at the molecular level? Were there times when molecular changes in albumin occurred more rapidly than at other times? Were changes of particular molecules of different significance in various lineages? Might this also apply to the DNA analyses and the immunological assays?

GOODMAN: Sudden changes do occur in rates of evolution at the molecular level. Over long periods of time, rates seems more regular. But whether the pattern is linear or whether some other curve describes it remains to be seen. Over fifty million year periods, one can expect some rather striking differences in the rates of change. These might result from gene duplication.

TOBIAS: And by chromosome changes at the Chiarelli level.

SACHER: I come in carefully, as I am not a paleoanthropologist or a systematist, but I am interested in a group of questions that are impacted by these disciplines. These have to do with the evolution of the brain in its structural aspects — the question of how many independent factors or evolutionary properties we must postulate to account for the human brain in its divergence from the ancestral hominoid brain. The word empirical should be retained because it is possible to have an empirical science of form and particularly one in which qualitative shape and form properties can be dealt with quantitatively, not necessarily in absolute numerical terms, but quantitatively in terms of various concepts of scaling. There is especially a need to assemble an adequate data base, consisting of multivariate measurements of brain structures on the fossil endocasts, in ways that can be duplicated by measurements on recent brains. Then we can develop a basis for an analysis of brain evolution that will enable us to use all of the salvageable information about the endocasts.

TOBIAS: I appreciate what George said. Both Holloway (see Holloway, this volume) and I (see Tobias, this volume) dealt in some detail with parameters other than size. Sir Arthur Keith, von Bonin, Holloway, and others have stressed reorganization of the cerebrum and cerebellum. Features other than the neopallium also show quite marked changes. Hence, we must take as many different parameters into account as we can in our assessments. There are undoubtedly signs of reorganization in the brain of *Australopithecus* as compared with the pongid brain. In my paper (see Tobias, this volume) I tried to suggest some indications of reorganization in the *Homo habilis* brain which distinguish it from the *Australopithecus* brain, apart from the size parameter which is the grossest and most easily determined of all the criteria we can use. So I would assure George Sacher that this is being attended to, however inadequately, at the moment. We will not lose sight of it. Dr. Hamlin's (see Hamlin, this volume) point about variability in modern human brains deserving much more attention is also well taken. Not early enough work has been done on that.

SACHER: There has to be a methodology for deciding how many form factors there are.

TOBIAS: Yes.

SACHER: Before we can effectively investigate reorganization, we have to provide objective evidence that we can falsify the hypothesis that the evolution of the hominid brain is simply an increase in a general size factor. Most uses of multivariate analysis in this area are to serve the systematists' interests in classifying. I am talking about it more from the aspect of a factor analysis which permits us to look for the structural factors rather than the taxonomic groupings, although in actuality each implies the other.

SZALAY: You are talking about two distinctive types of procedures. Taxonomic procedures are primary. They are simply a means to determine the biological validity of the samples and are widely used to determine this key question, i.e. whether the samples were of the same species or not.

HOWELLS: In regard to multivariate analysis, it is important to understand that taxonomic results and intraspecies results should and can be compared and also interpreted. They make very good checks against one another, as I have been trying to do with hominid skulls, checking factor analysis and multiple discriminants within and between populations.

Biographical Notes

JOHN V. BASMAJIAN (1921–) is a Canadian anatomist and neurophysiologist now working at Atlanta's Emory University. A medical graduate of the University of Toronto, he has taught anatomy and conducted research at that university as well as at Queen's University in Canada and St. Thomas's Hospital Medical School in London. He is the author of two widely-used anatomy textbooks and several monographs on electromyography, electrodiagnosis, and muscle function.

SUSAN MARIE CACHEL (1949–) received a B.A. (1970) and an M.A. (1971) from the University of Chicago. She is currently a Ph.D. candidate in physical anthropology at the University of Chicago and is doing research on the origins of the anthropoid grade.

BRUNETTO CHIARELLI (1934–) was born in Florence, Italy. He holds a Ph.D. in Anthropology, Biology, and Zoology and is Professor of Primatology and Anthropology at the University of Turin. From 1969–1974 he was Visiting Professor at the University of Toronto, Department of Anthropology. His publications include works on comparative genetics, cytogenetics, taxonomy of primates, and the biology of living and protohistoric human populations. He is Director of the International School of Human Biology at the Center "E. Majorana" and Editor of the *Journal of Human Evolution*.

ERIC DELSON (1945–) was born in New York, received his B.A. from Harvard College and his Ph.D. (Geology) from Columbia University. After a year at the University of Pittsburgh, he returned home to teach in the City University of New York, where he has been Assistant Professor of Anthropology at Lehman College since 1973. His major interests span paleoanthropology and primatology, centering on the evolutionary development of catarrhine primates, especially the Cercopithecidae. Current research involves studies of European, Asian, and African fossil cercopithecines and the cranial and dental morphology of all Old World monkeys.

JEAN DRICOT (1946–) was born in Belgium, has a "doctorat de 3ème cycle" from the University of Paris-VI, and is now working in Peru.

JOHN G. FLEAGLE (1948–) graduated from Yale University (B.S. 1971) with Distinguished Honors in Geology and Geophysics. He continued his studies at Harvard University (M.S. 1973) where he is currently a candidate for the Ph.D. degree in Anthropology. He has had extensive field experience in collecting fossil primates, and has recently undertaken field research on the behavior and ecology of Malaysian forest primates. His publications deal with diverse paleoprimatological subjects as well as growth, nutrition, and locomotion of living primates.

MORRIS GOODMAN (1925–) was born in Milwaukee. He received his bachelor's degree, M.S., and Ph.D. from the University of Wisconsin with a dissertation on the precipitin behavior of avian antibodies. His research of the past sixteen years has dealt with the molecular evolution of *Homo sapiens* and other primates. He is Professor of Anatomy at Wayne State University, Detroit and Coeditor of the *Journal of Human Evolution.*

ROBERT K. GREENLAW (1930–), a native of New Brunswick, Canada, graduated in Medicine at Dalhousie University in Halifax. He received orthopedic surgical training at McGill University in Montreal and at the University of California in San Francisco. In 1973 he received his Ph.D. in Anatomy for work done with Professor J. V. Basmajian at Queen's University in Canada. He now practices surgery in Nova Scotia.

HANNIBAL HAMLIN (1904–) received his Ph.B. in Natural Science from Yale in 1927, an M.S. (Anatomy and Zoology), and an M.D.,

1933–36. He was Field Leader of the Whitney South Sea Expedition from 1927–1930 and a neurosurgeon in the United States Naval Reserves Medical Corps from 1941–1945 and at Massachusetts General Hospital of Harvard University. He is an Honorary Life Member of the American Museum of Natural History and a member of the American Association of Physical Anthropologists. His research interests center on Anthropo-geography and Neuro-evolution.

RALPH L. HOLLOWAY (1935–), Professor of Anthropology at Columbia University, received his B.S. in Geology from the University of New Mexico in 1959 and his Ph.D. from the University of California at Berkeley in 1964. He has taught at Columbia University since 1964. Currently the recipient of a Guggenheim Fellowship, he is studying and reconstructing the fossil hominid endocasts obtained during visits to Kenya, South Africa, and Indonesia. Professor Holloway's specialty is the evolution of the brain and behavior.

HIDEMI ISHIDA (1939–) was born in Mie, Japan. He studied at Kagoshima University (B.A. 1962) and Kyoto University (M.A. 1966). He received his Ph.D. in Anthropology from Kyoto University in 1971. He was a member of the Primate Research Institute of Kyoto University from 1967 to 1971, and is now at the Laboratory of Physical Anthropology, Kyoto University (Instructor in Physical Anthropology since 1971). His special interests include primatology, anthropology, and hominization.

FARISH A. JENKINS, JR. (1940–) studied at Princeton (B.A. 1961) and Yale (M.S. 1966, Ph.D. 1969), and taught anatomy at the College of Physicians and Surgeons of Columbia University from 1968 to 1971. Currently he is Professor of Biology at Harvard University and Curator of Vertebrate Paleontology at the Museum of Comparative Zoology. His research has focused on both paleontological and neontological problems, particularly the evolution of mammal-like reptiles, early mammals, and the biomechanics of the musculoskeletal system.

FRANÇOISE K. JOUFFROY is Chargée de Recherches at the Centre National de la Recherche Scientifique (France). She is doing her research in the Laboratoire d'Anatomie Comparée du Muséum National d'Histoire Naturelle de Paris. Her present research interest is in the evolutionary morphology and the functional anatomy of mammals, particularly primates.

Benno K. F. Kummer (1924–   ) was born near Frankfurt and studied medicine at the Universities of Königsberg, Jena, and Frankfurt, receiving his Dr. med. in 1950 (Frankfurt). He is Professor of Anatomy in Cologne (1962) and the Director of the Anatomisches Institut der Universität. His special field is the biomechanics of the loco-quarterly *Human Biology* and the author of *Physical anthropology* (1973).

Gabriel W. Lasker received his bachelor's degree from the University of Michigan and his M.A. and Ph.D. from Harvard. He is Professor of Anatomy at Wayne State University, Detroit, and has done fieldwork in Mexico, Peru, and the United States. He is Editor-in-Chief of the quarterly *Human Biology* and the author of *Physical anthropology* (1973).

Jacques Lessertisseur is Maître de Conférences, sous-directeur au Laboratoire d'Anatomie Comparée du Muséum National d'Histoire Naturelle de Paris (55, rue de Buffon, 75005 Paris). His interest is concerned with the comparative anatomy of the skeleton and musculature of mammals and more particularly of primates. Presently, his research interests include osteometric studies of the cranium and appendicular skeleton, with application of the factorial analysis method.

Philip Lieberman (1934–   ) was born in New York. He received a B.S. and M.S. in Electrical Engineering from the Massachusetts Institute of Technology in 1958 where he also received a Ph.D. in Linguistics in 1966 with a dissertation on the physiology, acoustics, and grammatical function of intonation in English. He was a member of the research staff at Air Force Cambridge Research Laboratories and Haskins Laboratories. From 1967 to 1974 he taught at the University of Connecticut and is now Professor of Linguistics at Brown University.

C. Owen Lovejoy (1943–   ) is Associate Professor of Anthropology at Kent State University and Assistant Clinical Professor of Orthopedic Surgery at Case Western Reserve University. He received his B.A. from Western Reserve University in 1965, an M.A. from the Case Institute of Technology in 1967, and a Ph.D. in Physical Anthropology from the University of Massachusetts in 1970. From 1970–1973 he undertook post-doctoral study in biomechanics at the Case Institute of Technology. His principal research interests include human osteology, biomechanics, human paleontology, primate taxonomy, and paleodemography. He is a member of the Board of Directors of the Human Biology Council.

PETER MURRAY (1942–) is a Research Associate in the Department of Anatomy, the University of Tasmania, Australia. He received his B.S. from Portland State University, Portland, Oregon, and in 1973 received a Ph.D. from the University of Chicago. His special interest is in the morphology and behavior of primates and marsupials, and he is currently studying the behavior of the brush-tail possum (*Trichosurus vulpecula*).

GEORGES OLIVIER (1912–) is Professor of Physical Anthropology at the University of Paris-VII. His main works are *Pratique anthropologique* (translated into English under the title *Practical anthropology*) and *Anatomie anthropologique*. He was Vice-President of the *International Union of Anthropological Sciences* (1964–1973) and founder of the *Journées anthropologiques de langue française*.

FRANCISZEK M. ROSIŃSKI (1932–) studied philosophy in Lublin and Warsaw, receiving his Ph.M. in 1966. He then studied Natural Sciences in Wrocław and received his Sc.D. in 1974. He taught cosmology and anthropology at the High Seminary in Kłodzko and at the Academy of the Theologie Catholic in Warsaw. He is continuing his anthropological research by order of the University of Wrocław and of the Polish Academy of Sciences. His publications include works on the prehistory of religion, anthropogenesis, clinical anthropology, and dermatoglyphics.

GEORGE A. SACHER (1917–) is Senior Biologist at Argonne National Laboratory and Lecturer in the Committee on Evolutionary Biology at the University of Chicago. He received his training in psychology and physiology at the University of Chicago and has been at Argonne Laboratory since 1942. His long involvement with the problem of evaluating the effects of ionizing radiations and other environmental pollutants on human mortality and longevity provided both the motivation and the orientation for his research on the biology of aging, which includes work on the stochastic theory of mortality and aging and current investigations on the evolutionary and genetic factors that determine the lifespans of vertebrate species. His laboratory research focuses on comparative and genetic studies of aging processes in several species of myomorphic rodents.

BECKY A. SIGMON (1941–) is Associate Professor of Anthropology and is also on the faculty of the Department of Anatomy at the University of Toronto where she has been since 1969. She received her B.A. in Anthropology from the University of North Carolina in 1963, and her M.S. and Ph.D. in Human Biology from the University of Wisconsin in 1966 and 1969 respectively. Her research interests lie in the early transitional stages of hominid evolution and hominid adaptability. A major focus of her research thus far has been on the evolution of human locomotion as reflected through studies in comparative primate anatomy and on the hominid fossil material from East and South Africa.

FREDERICK S. SZALAY (1938–) was born in Hungary. He studied biology at Mt. St. Mary's College (B.S. 1961), zoology at the University of Massachusetts (M.S. 1963), and received his Ph.D. in 1967 in Vertebrate Paleontology from Columbia University and the Museum of Natural History. He is presently a Professor of Anthropology at Hunter College, City University of New York, and Research Associate in Vertebrate Paleontology at the American Museum of Natural History. His research interests center on the interpretation of the primate fossil record as well as on methods of inference (phylogenetic and functional) needed to overcome problems in the study of fossil morphology.

ANNA S. SWEDZIŃSKA (1947–) studied physical anthropology of the University in Wrocław and received her Sc.M. in 1970. She taught biology at the Medical Academy and anthropology at the University in Wrocław. Since 1972 she has been a member of the Department of Anthropology at the University in Wrocław and of the Polish Academy of Sciences in Wrocław. Her interests include ontogeny, anthropometry, and the descent of man.

HENRI TISSIER (1919–) is a biometrician attached to the Laboratoire d'Anthropologie biologique, Université Paris-VII.

PHILLIP V. TOBIAS (1925–) was born in Durban, Natal. He received his education at the University of the Witwatersrand, Johannesburg, and at Cambridge University, England, and is a Doctor of Science and Doctor of Philosophy, as well as being medically qualified. His researches have been in the fields of cytogenetics and human biology, and he is author of *Chromosomes, sex cells and evolution* (1956); *Man's anatomy*, three volumes, with M. Arnold (first edition 1963–64, second edition 1967); *The cranium of* Australopithecus (Zinjanthropus) boisei (1967); *Man's past and future* (1969, 1971); *The brain in hominid evolution* (1971); *The meaning of race* (1961, 1972); numerous chapters in books; and articles in learned journals. In 1959, he succeeded R. A. Dart to the Chair of Anatomy at the University of the Witwatersrand. A founder-member of the special committee for Human Adaptability (I.B.P.), he founded and presided over the Institute for the Study of Man in Africa, the Anatomical Society of Southern Africa, the South African Society for Quaternary Research, and serves on international scientific bodies and editorial boards in a number of countries. He is a Fellow of the Linnean Society (of London) and a Fellow (and past President) of the Royal Society of South Africa. His main recent researches have dealt with the peoples of Sub-Saharan Africa (especially the Khoisan and Negro peoples) and with the early hominids of South and East Africa.

RUSSELL HOWARD TUTTLE (1939–) is Associate Professor in Anthropology and Evolutionary Biology at the University of Chicago and Visiting Research Scientist at Yerkes Regional Primate Research Center of Emory University. He received a B.S. degree (Anatomy, 1961) and an M.A. (Anthropology, 1962) from the Ohio State University and a Ph.D. (Anthropology, 1965) from the University of California at Berkeley. He has conducted field studies on non-human primates and associated fauna in Rhodesia, Ceylon, Kenya, and Tanzania. His principal research on the functional morphology and evolutionary biology of primates has been conducted at primate research centers, museums, and anthropological institutes in the United States, Japan, Switzerland, and Italy. He is the editor of *The functional and evoluionary biology of primates* (1972) and the author of more than thirty scientific papers.

PHILLIP L. WALKER (1947–) received his B.A. from Indiana University in 1970, an M.A. from the University of Chicago in 1971, and a Ph.D. in Anthropology from the University of Chicago in 1973. He is currently Assistant Professor in the Department of Anthropology at the University of California at Santa Barbara. His special interests include human evolution, functional anatomy, primate ecology, and primate behavior.

Plates

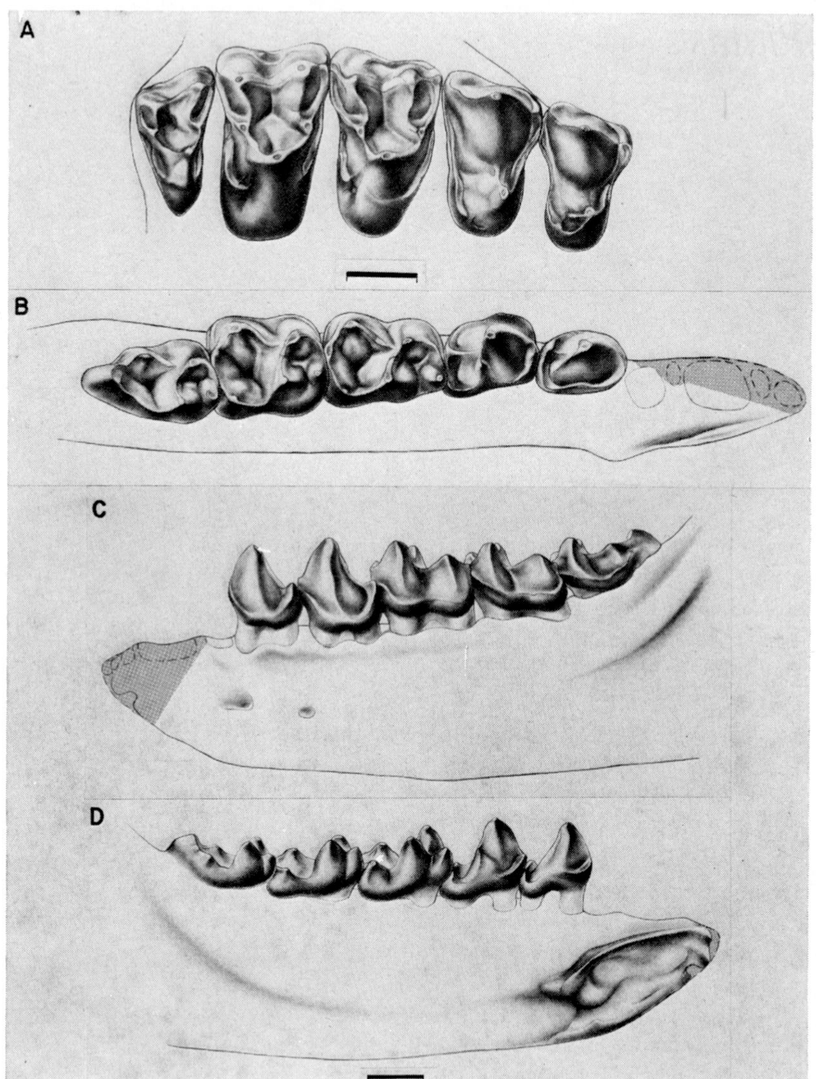

Plate 1. *Teilhardina belgica*, early Eocene of Belgium. A. Right P^3–M^3, occlusal view, above; B. left mandibular ramus with P_3–M_3, occlusal view; C. left mandibular ramus with P_3–M_3, lateral view; D. left mandibular ramus with P_3–M_3, medial view. Stippled areas are reconstructed. Scale represents 1 millimeter

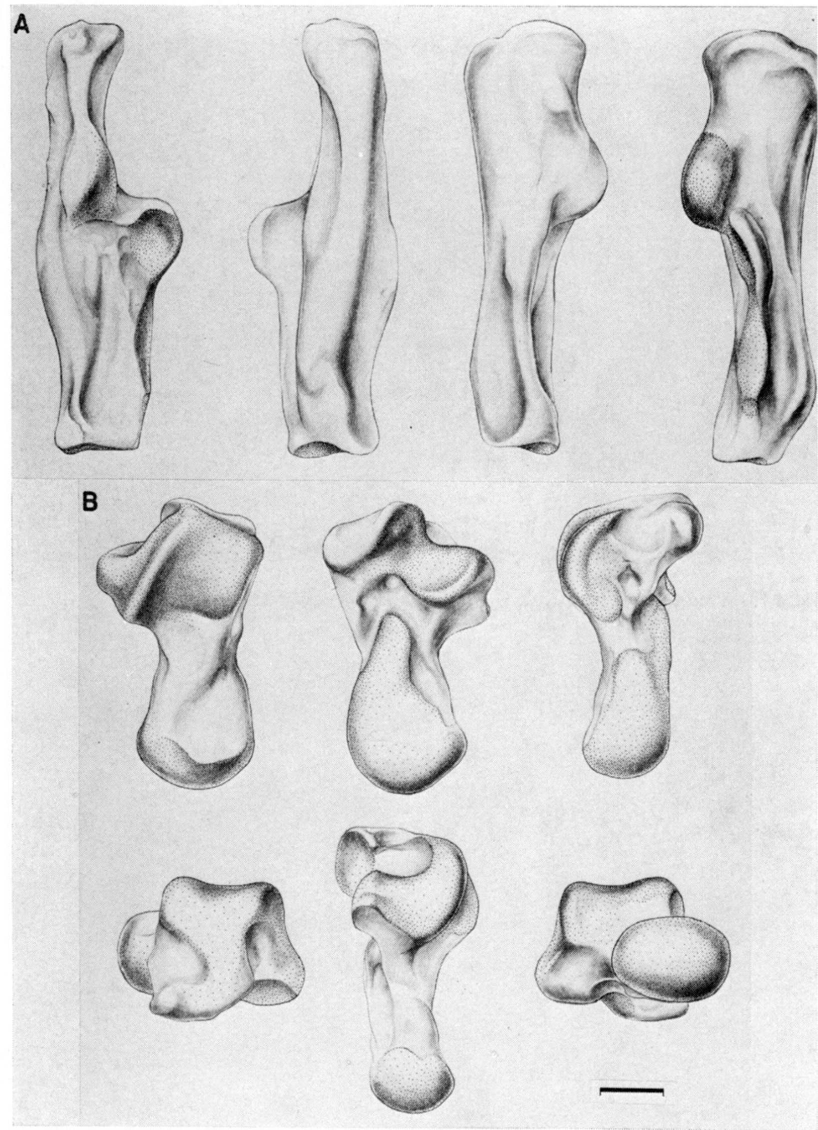

Plate 2. *Teilhardina belgica*, early Eocene of Belgium. A. Right calcaneum. From left to right: dorsal, plantar, lateral, and medial views. B. Right astragalus. From left to right: dorsal, plantar, medial, proximal, lateral, and distal views. Scale represents 1 millimeter

Plate 1. Tree shrew (*Tupaia glis*). Photograph by Edwardas Reklys

Plate 2. Elephant shrews (*Nasalio brachyrhyncus brachyrhyncus*) mother and two-week-old infant. Photograph by Edwardas Reklys

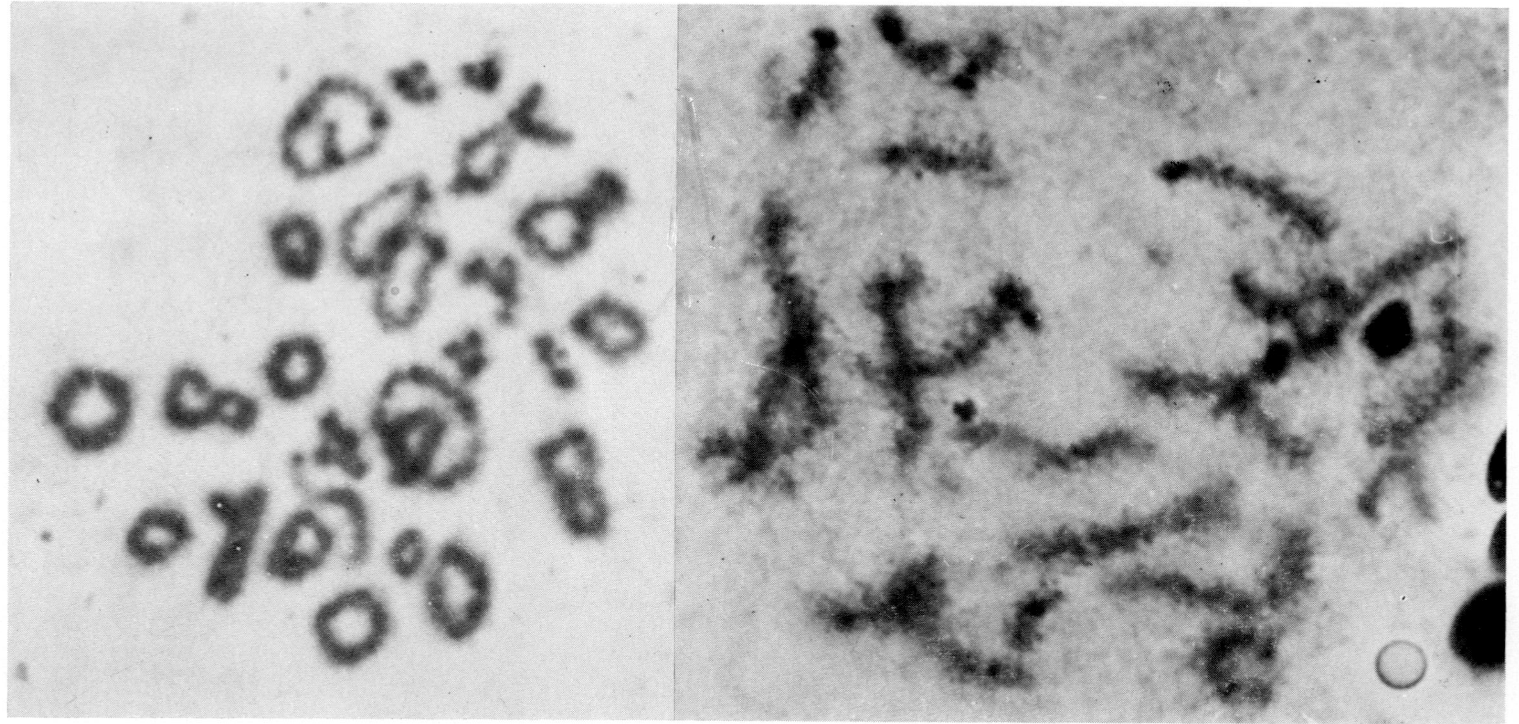

Plate 1. Meiotic chromosomes. Left: a diakinetic stage of *Papio* hamadryas
Right: a zygotic stage of *Macaca nemestrina*

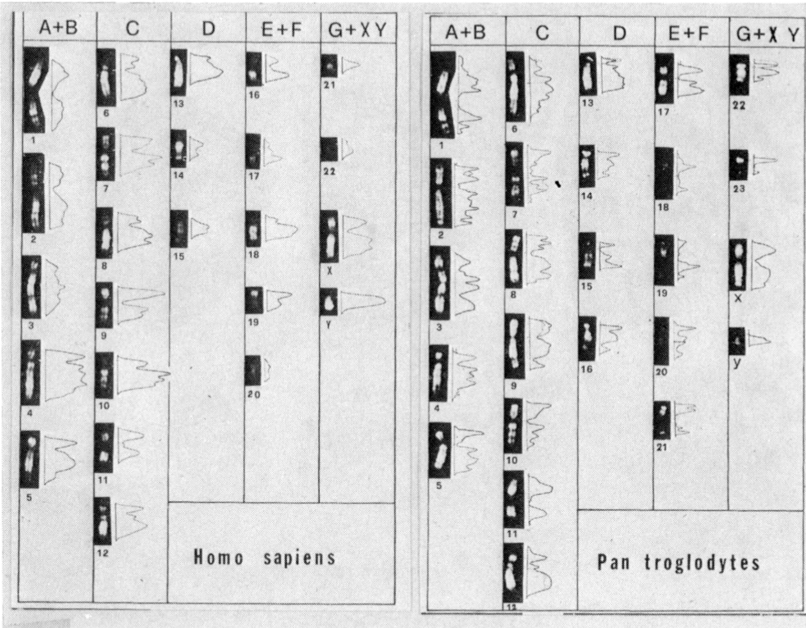

Plate 2. Chromosomes of man and chimpanzee stained with quinacrine fluorescent mustard and their absorption curves. They may allow a direct and quantitative comparison of the chromosome bands

Plate 1. Photograph of whole and partially chewed fruits and seeds from the stomach of a gibbon (*Hylobates lar*)

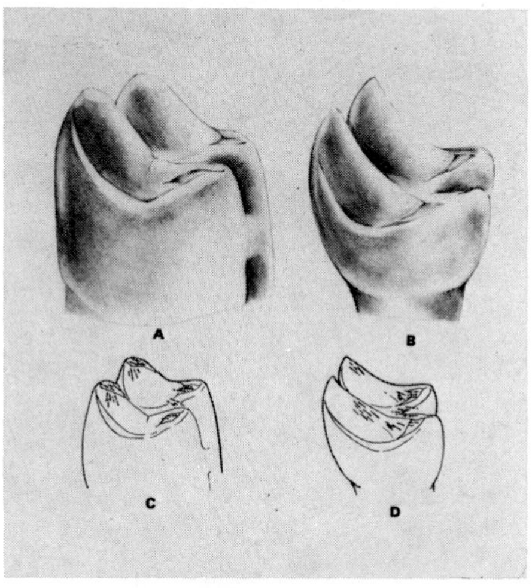

Plate 2. Mandibular second molar of *Presbytis rubidicundus* (B), and *Macaca fascicularis* (A). Schematic representations of the orientation and concentration of wear striations on the mandibular second molars of *Presbytis* (D), and *Macaca* (C)

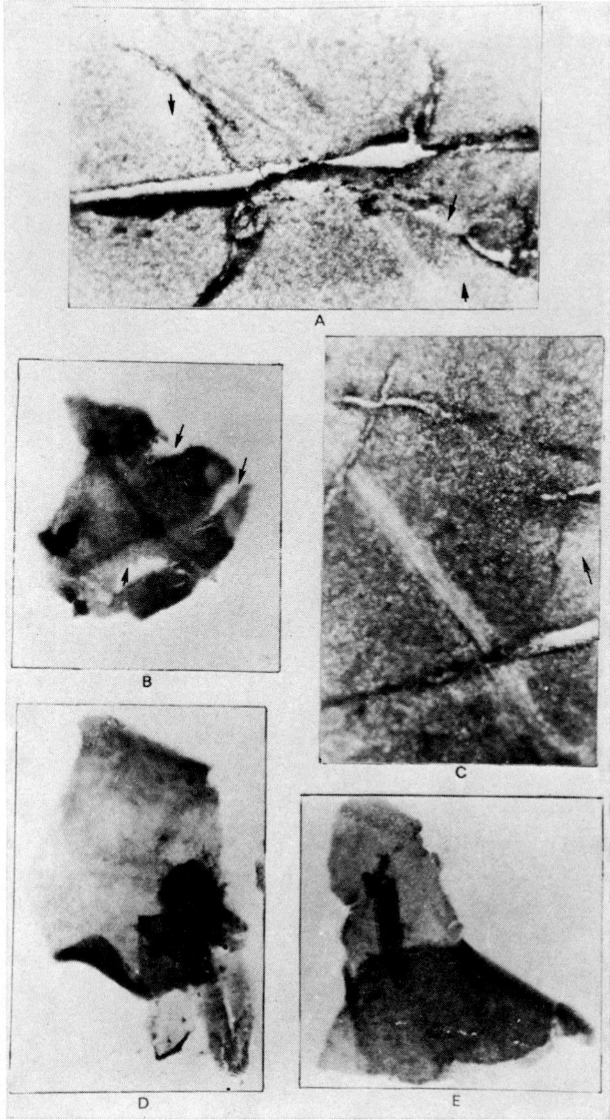

Plate 3. A and C photomicrographs of leaf fragments recovered from the stomach of *Macaca* showing crushing (arrows) and lop cuts produced by the detention. Whole mount, 40×. B, D and E photomicrographs of leaf fragments recovered from *Presbytis* stomachs showing typically small, clean cut pieces. Note puncture from cusp tip in B (arrow), and sharply demarcated borders suggesting efficient shearing action of the dentition in D. Whole mount, 40×

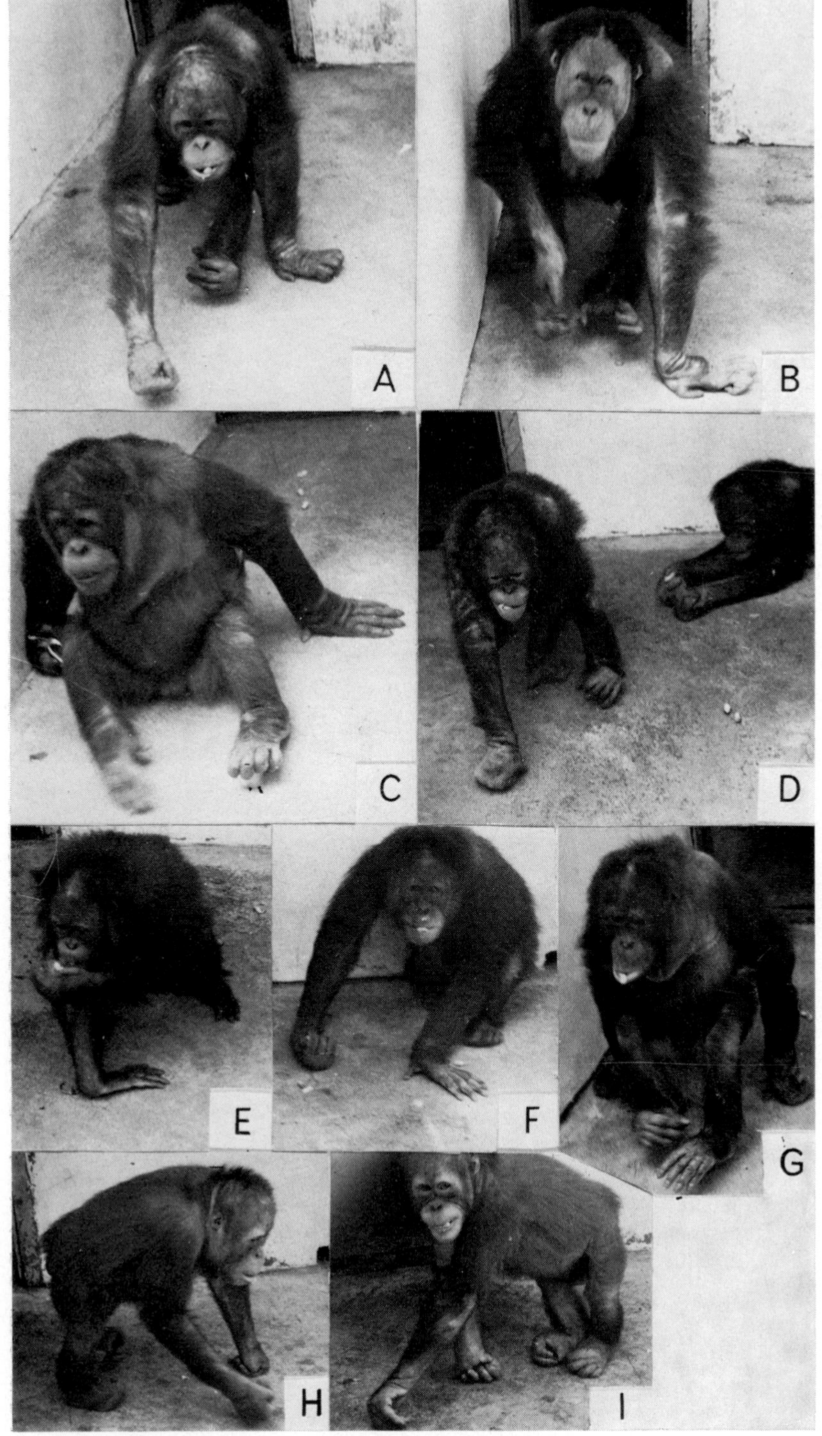
A
B
C
D
E
F
G
H
I

Plate 1. (A) Juvenile orangutan progressing with left hand in modified palmigrade posture and right hand in fist-walking posture; (B) Subadult orangutan progressing with left hand in modified palmigrade posture. The animal also ran quadrupedally with the fingers of both hands fully extended. (C) Juvenile orangutan with left hand palmigrade. (D) Juvenile orangutan progressing with both hands in modified fist-walking posture. Note contact of pollices with substrate. (E) Juvenile orangutan with right hand palmigrade. (F) Juvenile orangutan with left hand palmigrade and right hand resting on the dorsum of the metacarpal region. (G) Juvenile orangutan crutch-walking with hands in modified fist-walking postures. (H) Juvenile orangutan fist-walking. Note that left pollex is tucked under the lateral fingers. (I) Juvenile orangutan with right hand in fist-walking posture. (Photographs by Dr. I. S. Bernstein, Yerkes Regional Primate Research Center)

Plate 2. Felix, an adult male orangutan, sitting-feeding with left hand resting in knuckled posture. (Photograph by L. La France, Chicago Zoological Park)

Plate 3. Felix knuckle-walking on a wet substrate. (Photograph by L. La France, Chicago Zoological Park)

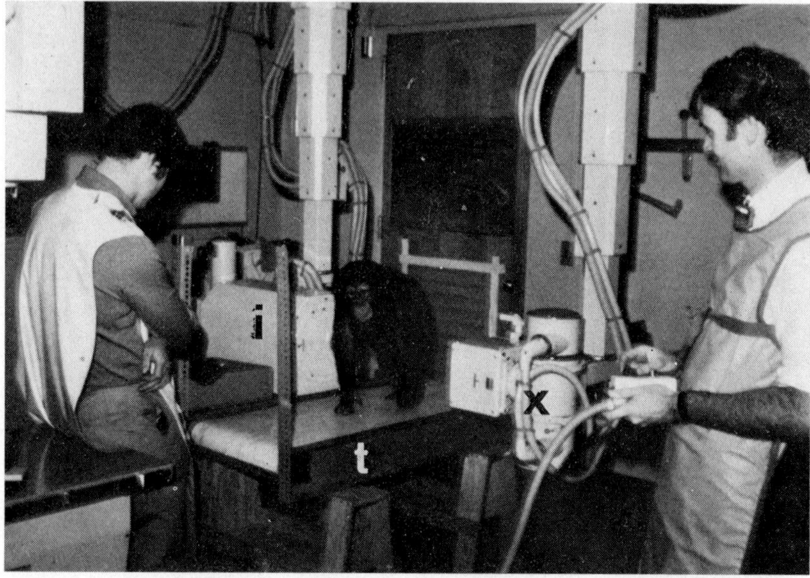

Plate 1. Cineradiography of a knuckle-walking chimpanzee. The chimpanzee is moving on a variable speed treadmill (t) controlled by an investigator (right). The radiographic apparatus consists of an x-ray source (x) and an image intensifier and camera system (i)

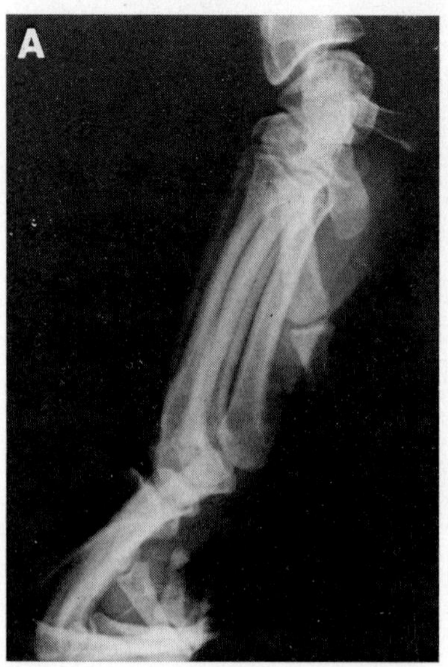

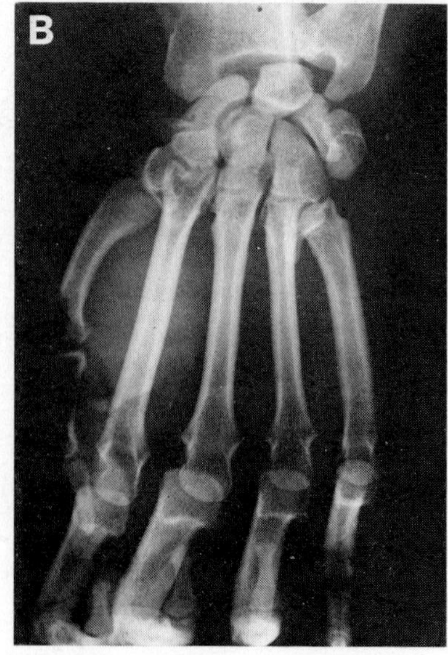

Plate 2. Lateral (A) and anteroposterior (B) radiographic projections of a chimpanzee right hand (LEMSIP number 250) in a simulated knuckle-walking posture

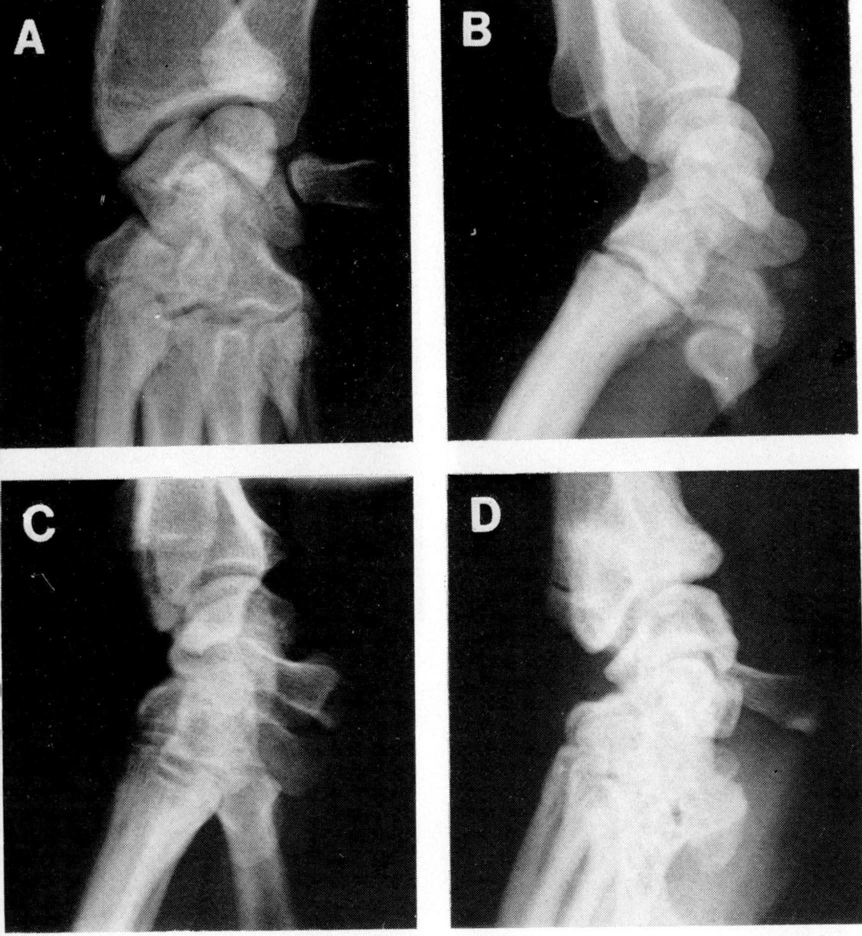

Plate 3. Oblique (A) and lateral (B–D) radiographic projections of the right wrists of four different chimpanzees

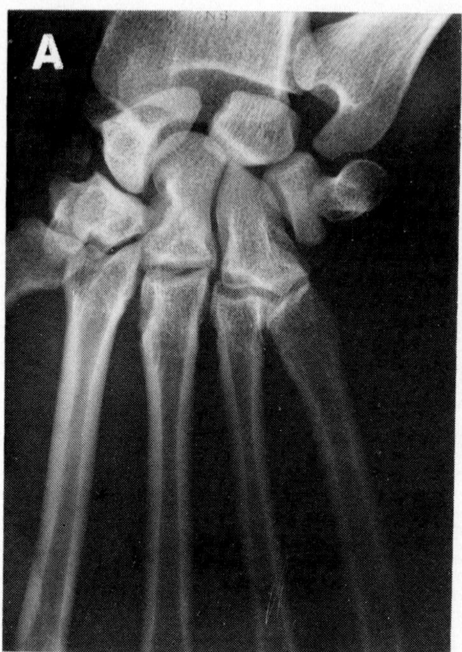

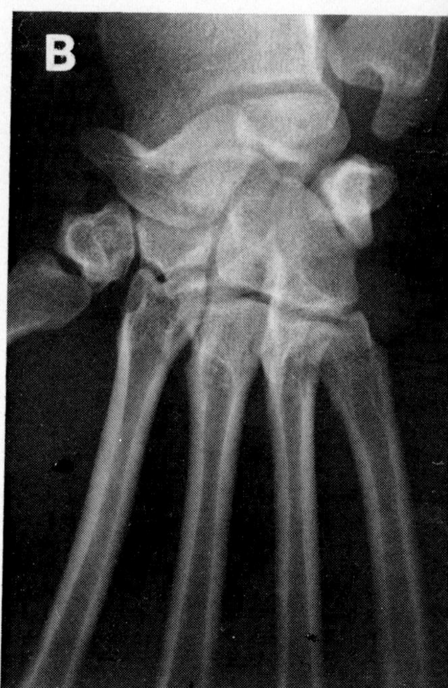

Plate 4. Anteroposterior radiographic projections of chimpanzee wrists. The projection in (A) is directly anteroposterior; the projection in (B) is slightly oblique

Plate 5. Radiographs of a passively manipulated chimpanzee right wrist (LEMSIP number 250). Anteroposterior projection of maximum ulnar deviation (A) and maximum radial deviation (B). Lateral projection of maximum flexion (C) and maximum extension (D) ▶

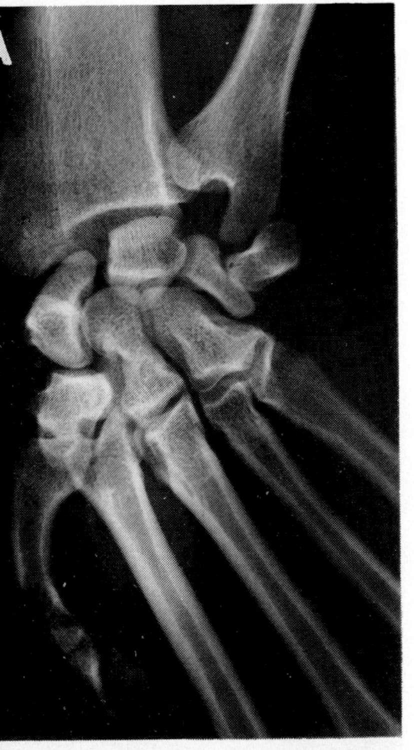
A

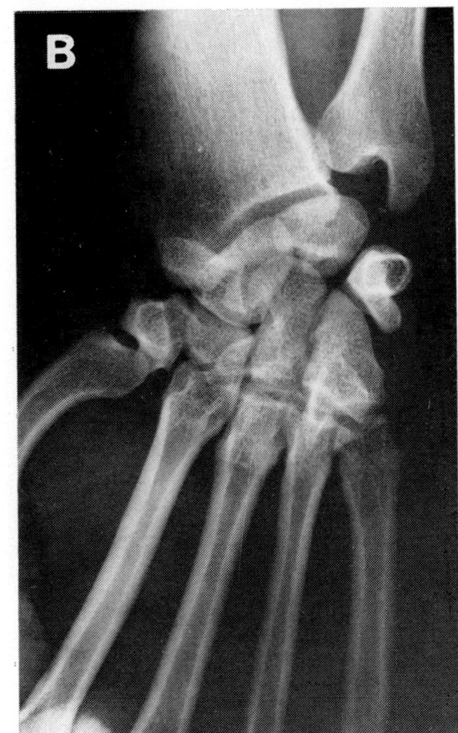
B

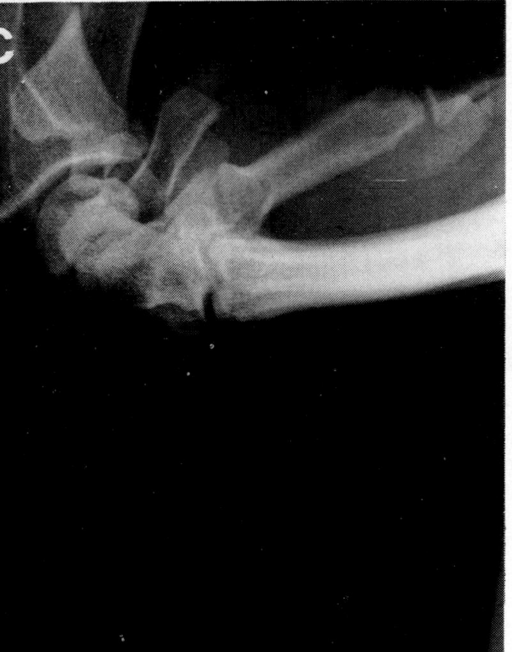
C

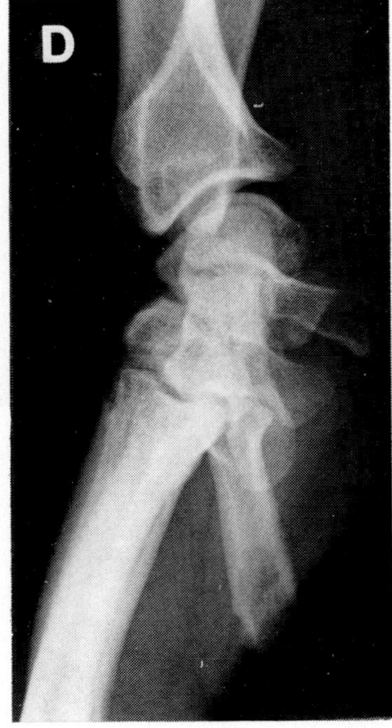
D

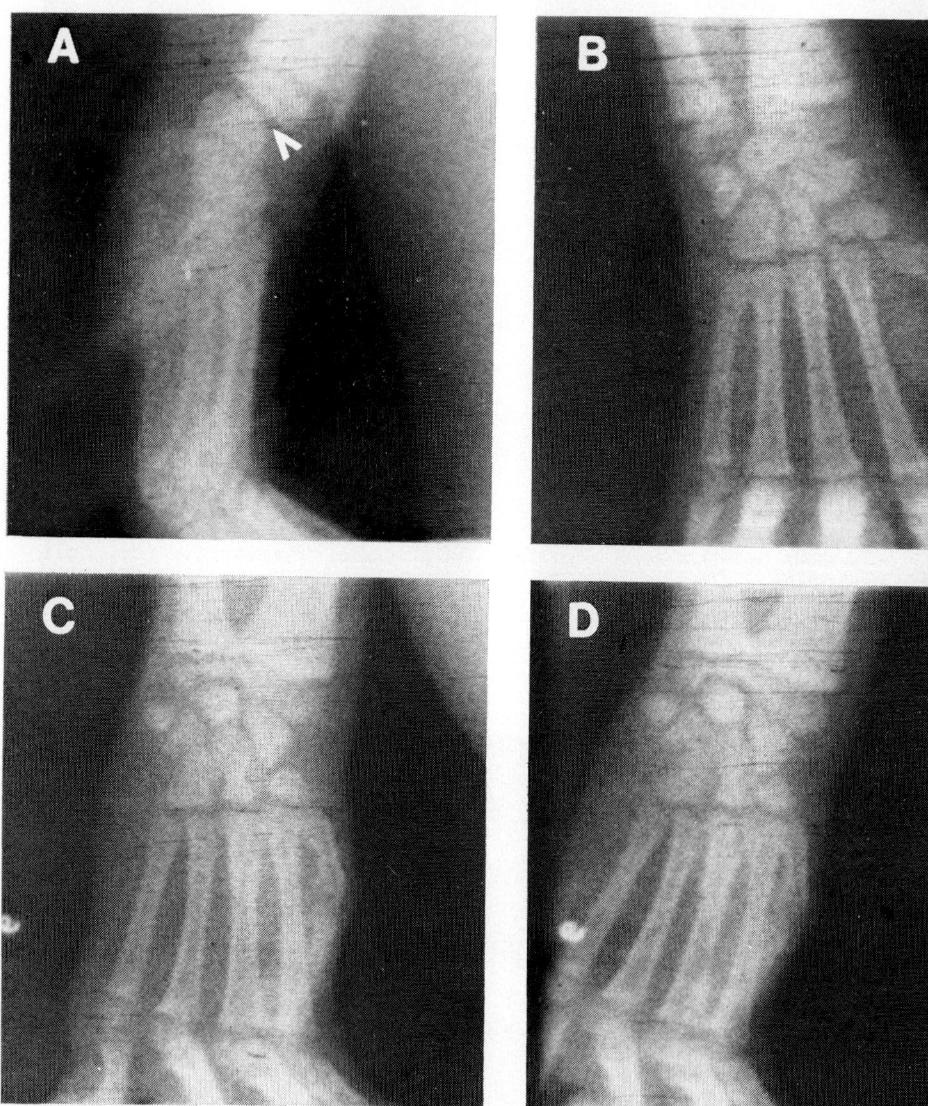

Plate 6. The wrist in a knuckle-walking chimpanzee as recorded cineradiographically on 16-millimeter film. (A) Lateral projection of the wrist during the second half of the propulsive movement; note the degree of extension at the proximal carpal joint (arrow). (B) Anteroposterior projection of the wrist during the first half of a propulsive movement. (C–D) Slightly oblique anteroposterior projections taken from a different sequence than B

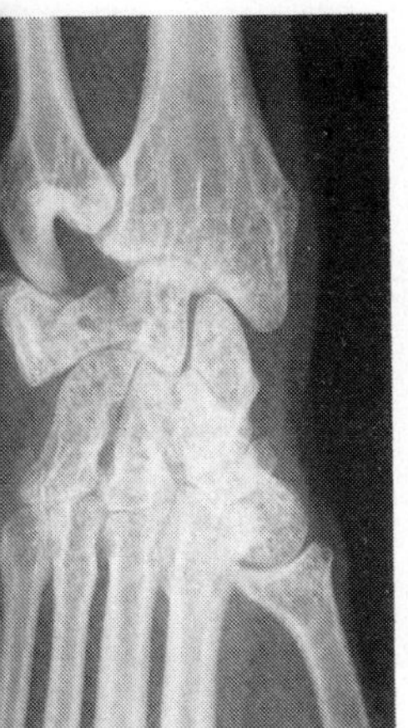

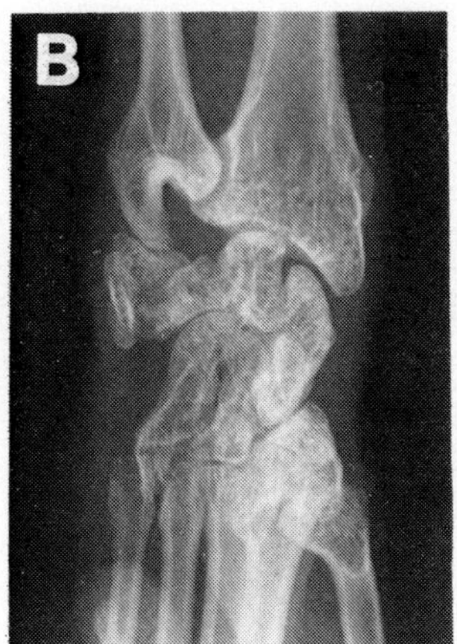

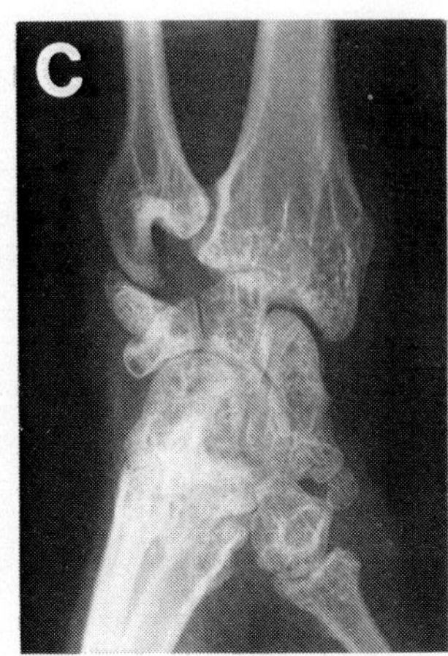

Plate 7. Radiographs of a passively manipulated gibbon wrist (*Hylobates lar*, LEMSIP number 1). (A) Anteroposterior projection of the wrist in neutral position. With the forearm held stationary, the manus was manipulated toward a pronated (B) and supinated (C) position. These maneuvers are accomplished with all intercarpal joint surfaces remaining in articular contact. Similar maneuvers performed on macaque wrists result in disarticulation or noncongruent relationships between joint surfaces

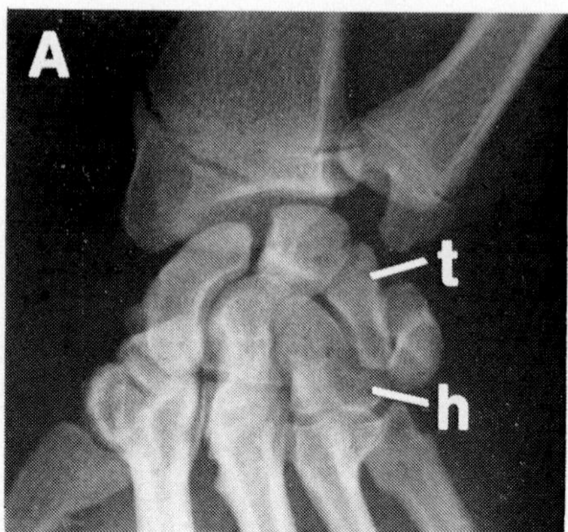

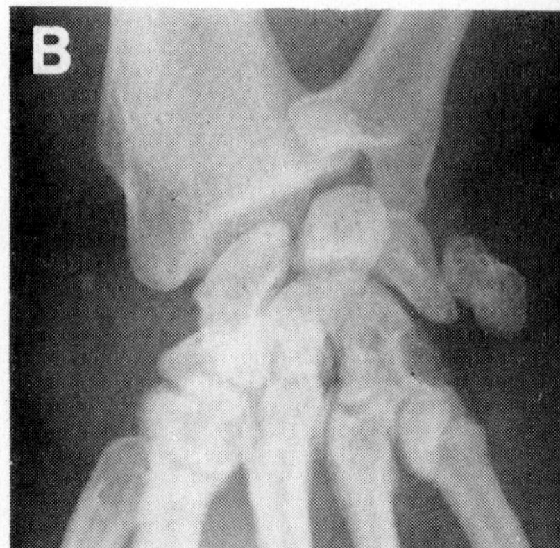

Plate 8. Radiographs of passively manipulated chimpanzee wrists (A, C, LEMSIP number 16; B, number 1) in anteroposterior projection. (A) Wrist maximally extended, showing triquetral (t) positioned toward the ulnar side on the hamate (h). (B) Wrist maximally extended in a supinated position, showing the triquetral placed relatively more centrally on the hamate than in (A); it has been suggested that this triquetral-hamate relationship correlates with wrist extension. However, the same relationship occurs in the supinated wrist in the neutral position (C) and does not invariably occur in an extended wrist (A)

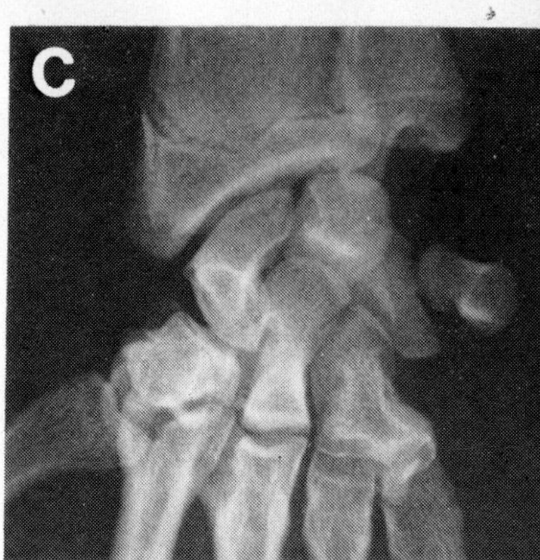

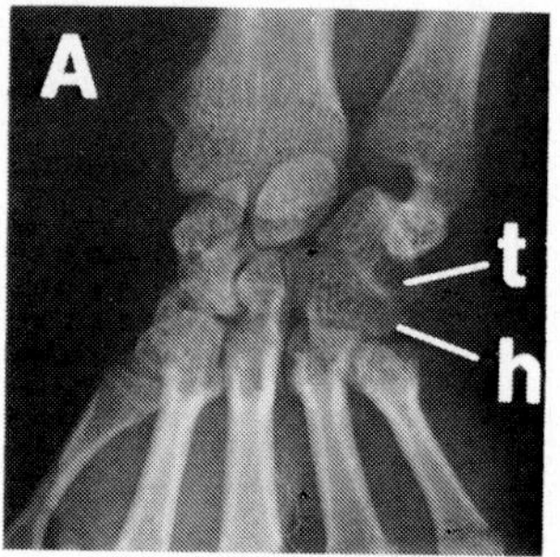

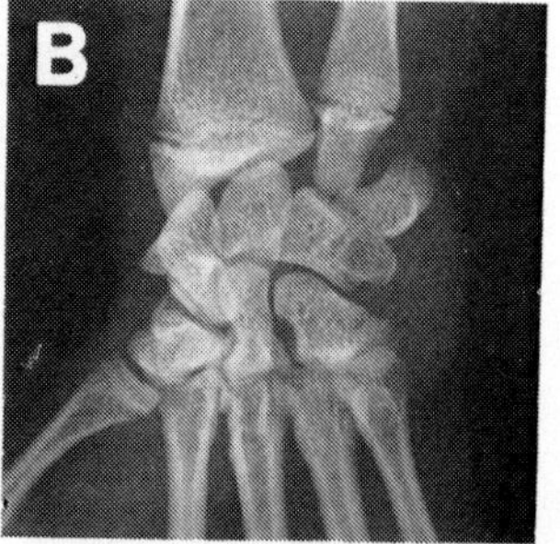

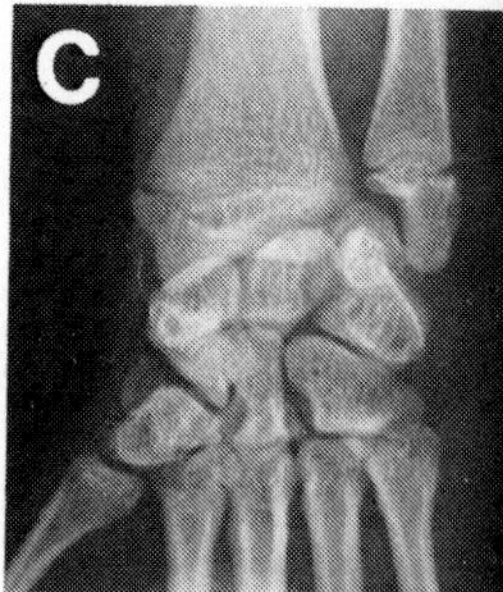

Plate 9. Radiographs of a passively manipulated rhesus macaque wrist (LEMSIP number 564) to show triquetral-hamate relationships. In extension(A), the triquetral (t) moves toward the ulnar side on the hamate (h). In supination (B), the triquetral is in its most central position with respect to the hamate, whereas in pronation (C), the positioning is intermediate

Plate 1. Inaki (four years and ten months old) walking bipedally up a ramp. Note flexed and abducted hip/flexed knee posture and plantigrade feet

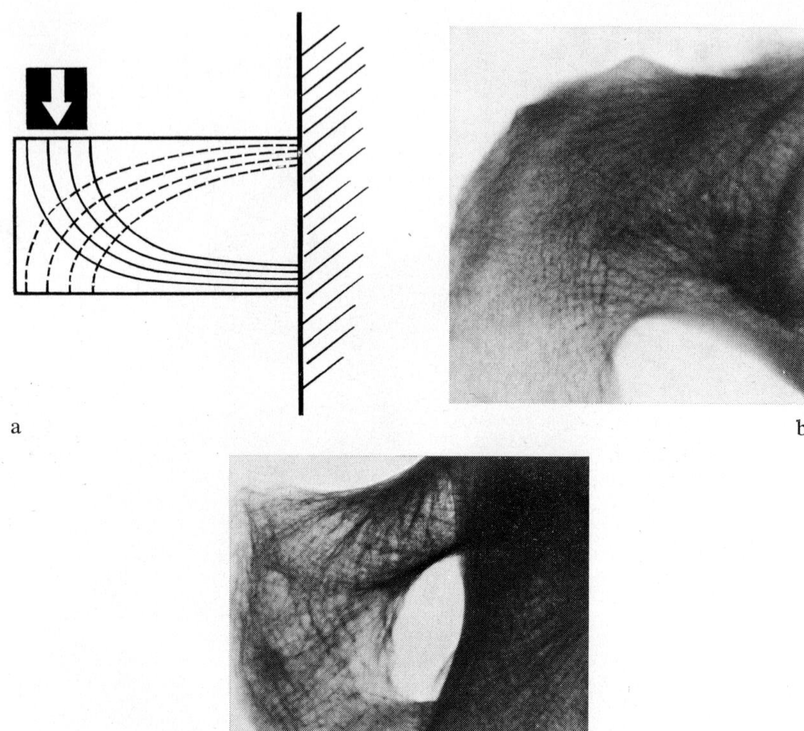

Plate 1. Bending structures in the pelvic levers
(a) Stress trajectories in a horizontal beam, bent by a load
(b) Trajectoral structure of the os ischii in an almost sagittal plane (X-ray photograph)
(c) Trajectoral structure of the os pubis in an almost frontal plane (X-ray photograph)

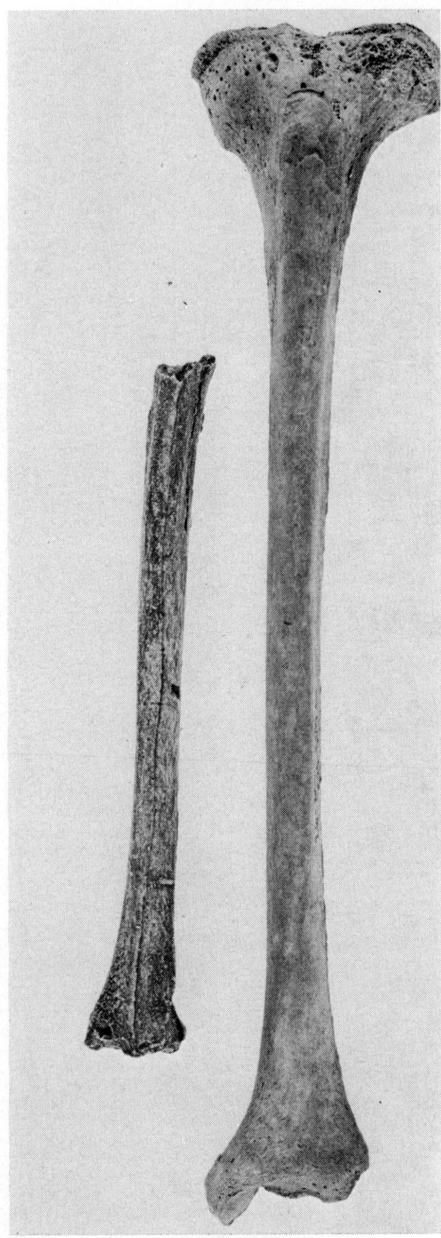

Plate 1. Cast of OH-6 and an Amerindian tibia (KSU-26503). The midpoint (of physiological length) of the australopithecine specimen (based upon the Davis length estimate) has been aligned with that of the Amerindian tibia. It can be seen that when this is done, the missing proximal portion of OH-6 would require disproportionate length if the Amerindian specimen were to be longer than the complete australopithecine specimen by equal increments at both proximal and distal ends. This can be visually corrected by lowering the estimated midpoint of OH-6, i.e. lowering the length estimate of the bone

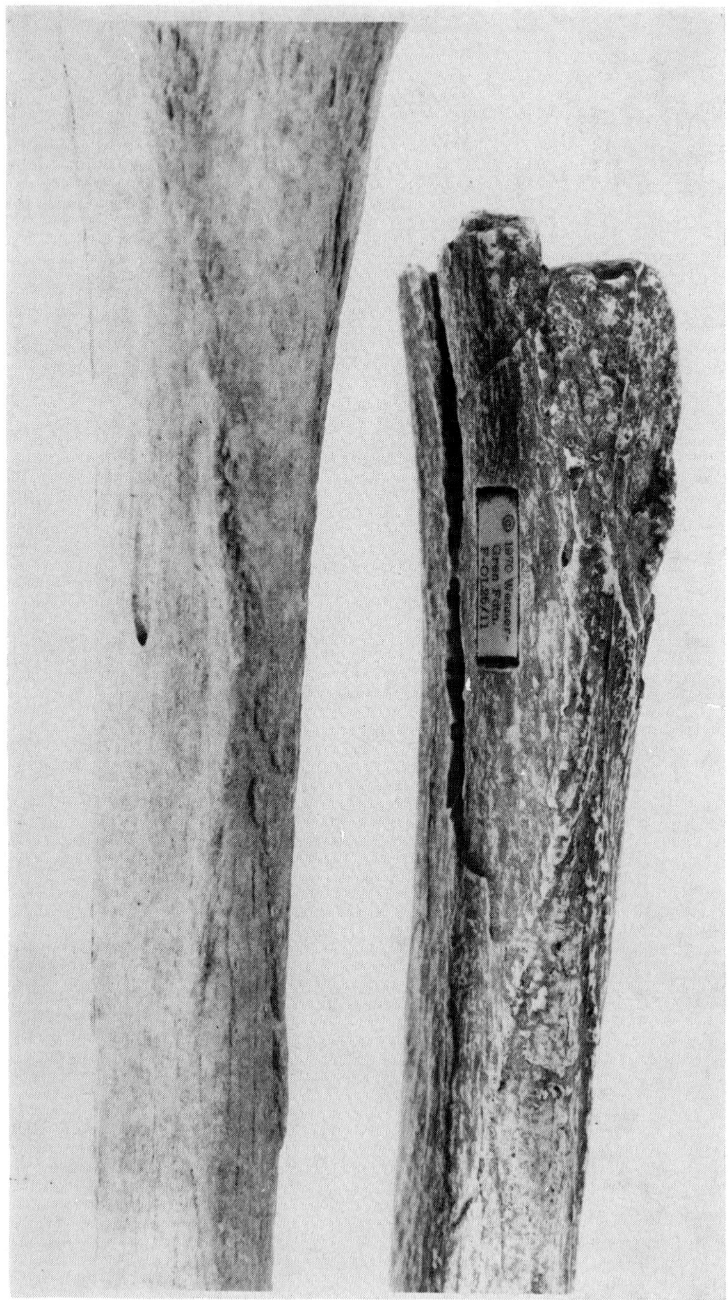

Plate 2. Cast of OH-6 compared with an Amerindian tibia (KSU-02254A). Crushing of the posterolateral aspect of the shaft of OH-6 is evident, accentuating the vertical bony ridge. Note, however, that the ridge is homologous to the soleal line in the Amerindian specimen, and that upon reaching the most proximal extent of the origin of the flexor digitorum longus, it divides in both specimens, circumscribing the area of origin of this muscle. This morphology is typical of numerous Amerindian specimens, although this region of the tibia is highly variable

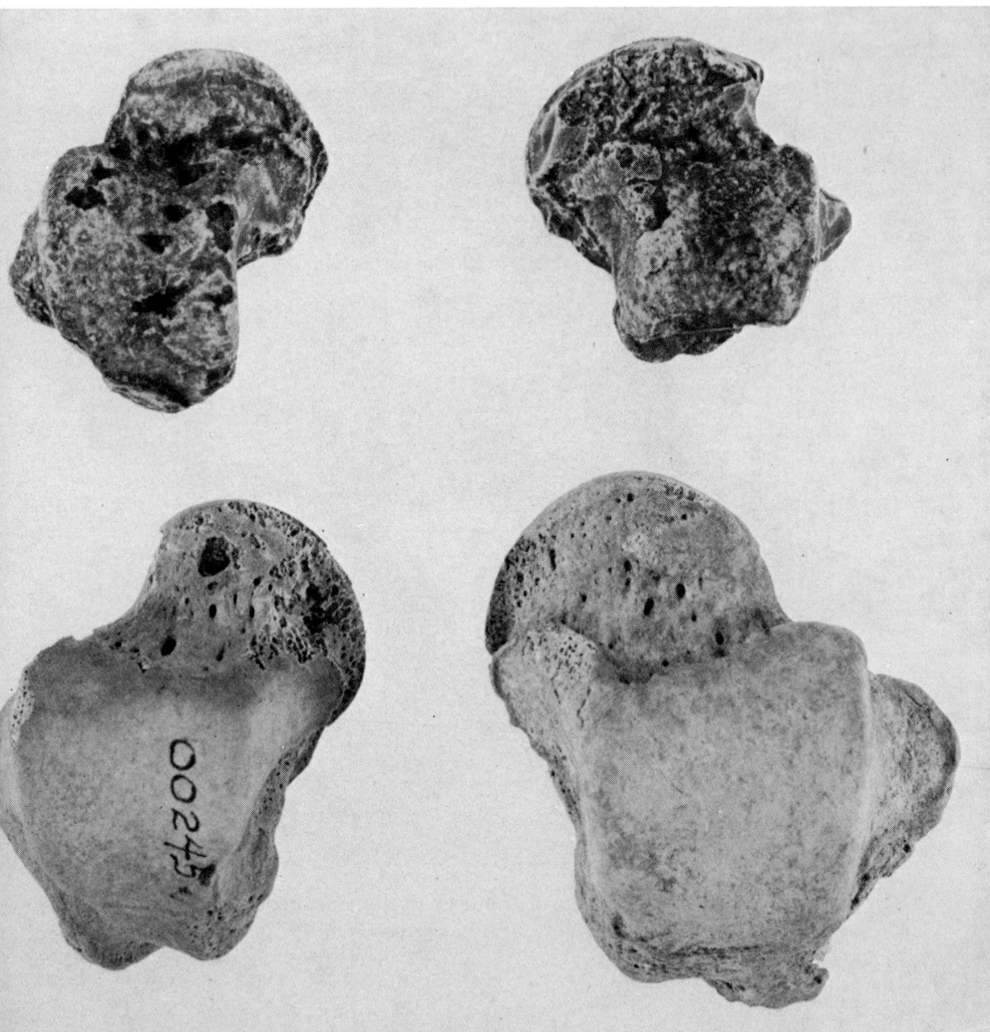

Plate 3. Casts of TM-1517 (top, right) and OH-8 (top, left) compared with two Amerindian tali, KSU-00245 (bottom, left) and KSU-26403 (bottom, right). The trochlear surfaces have been aligned. The equivalence of the talar neck angles in these specimens is clear, especially when the resultant direction of the navicular joint surface is visually considered (in the latter case, KSU-00245 has the most medially directed joint surface). Note also that the marked excavation of the articular facet for the medial malleolus is also present in the Amerindian specimens

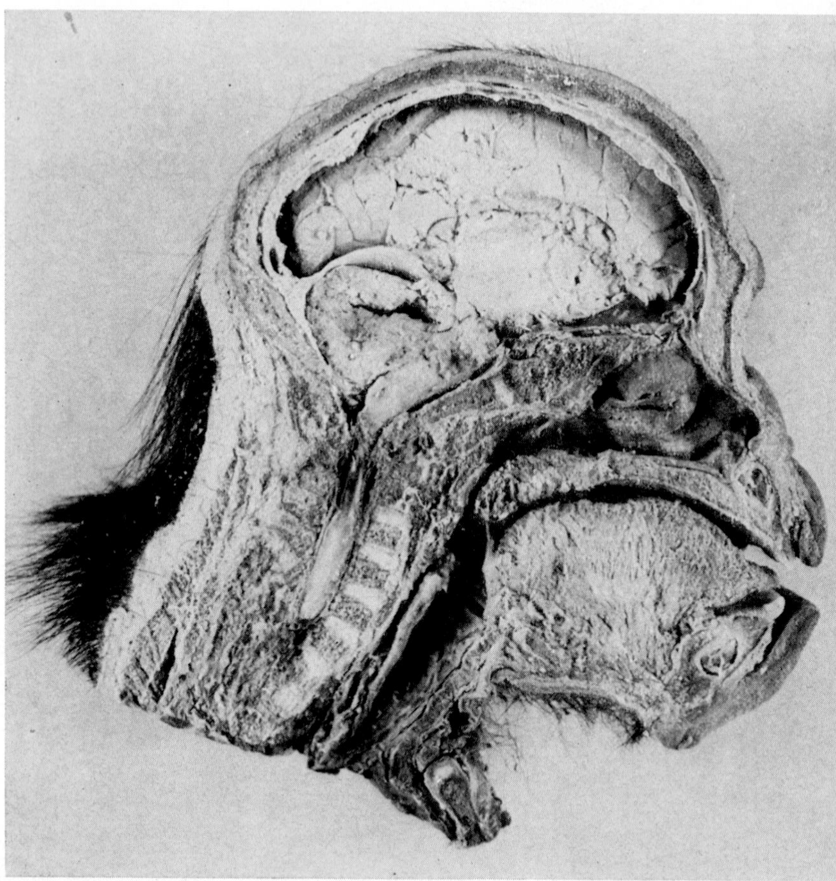

Plate 1. Left half of the head and neck of a young adult male chimpanzee sectioned in the midsagittal plane (after Lieberman et al. 1972)

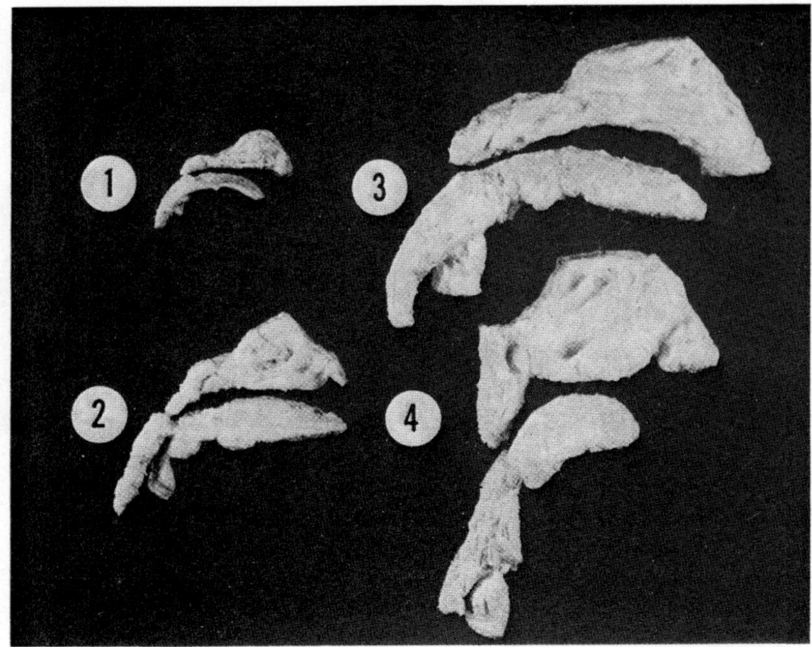

Plate 2. Casts of the nasal, oral, pharyngeal, and laryngeal cavities of (1) newborn *Homo sapiens,* (2) adult chimpanzee, (3) La Chapelle-aux-Saints reconstruction, and (4) adult *Homo sapiens* (after Lieberman et al. 1972)

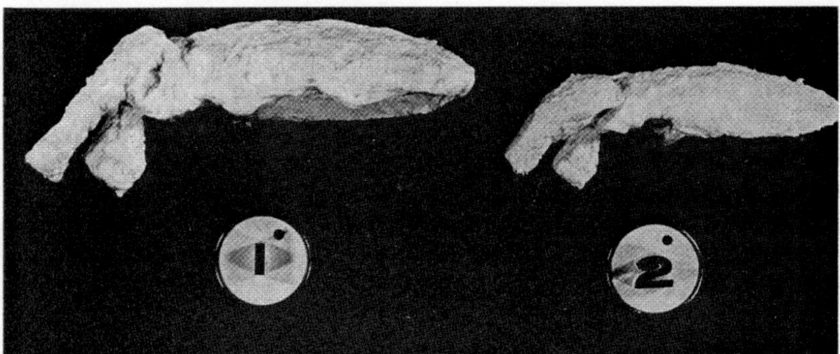

Plate 3. Casts of the oral, pharyngeal, and laryngeal cavities of the (1) Sterkfontein 5 reconstruction and (2) chimpanzee. Note that the supralaryngeal airways of the Australopithecine fossil and chimpanzee are almost identical except for their size. The nasal cavities have been omitted to make the similarities in these "one tube" supralaryngeal vocal tracts more apparent

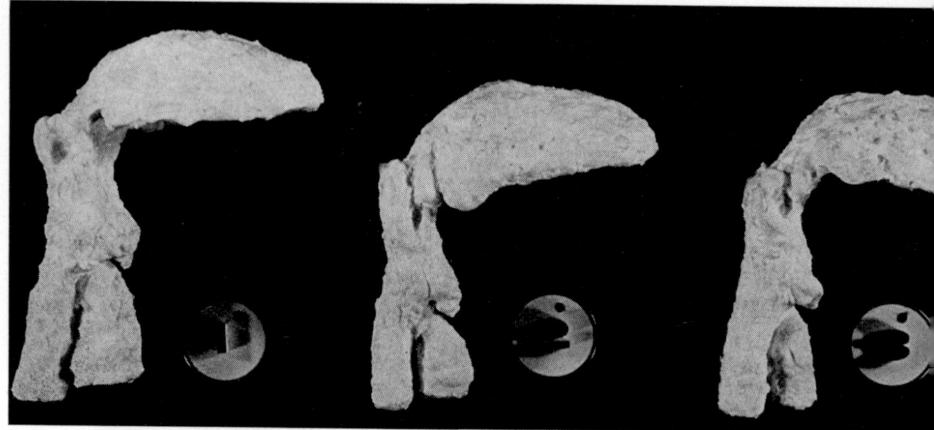

Plate 4. Casts of the oral, pharyngeal, and laryngeal cavities of (1) Es-Skhūl V reconstruction, (2) Steinheim reconstruction, and (3) adult *Homo sapiens* (refer back to the key on Figure 1 for anatomical details). Note that the two fossil reconstructions' supralaryngeal airways both have a right-angle bend and a pharyngeal cavity similar to that of modern *Homo sapiens*

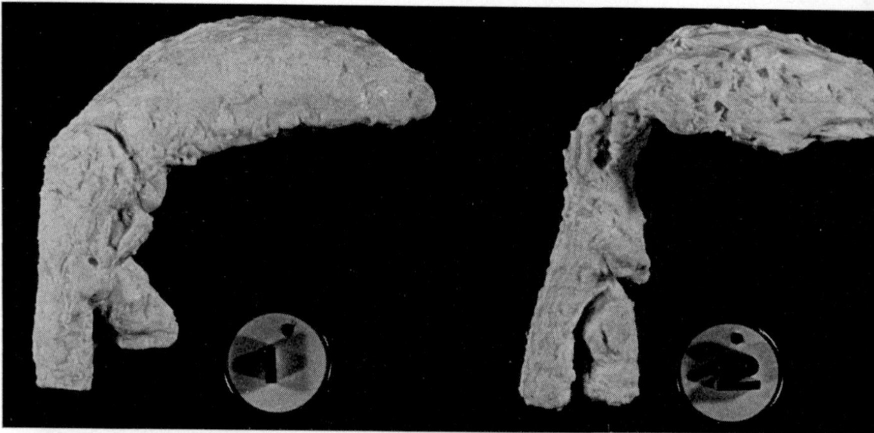

Plate 5. Cast of the oral, pharyngeal, and laryngeal cavities of the (1) Broken Hill reconstruction and (2) adult *Homo sapiens* (refer back to the key on Figure 1 for anatomical details). Note that the fossil reconstruction's supralaryngeal airway is an intermediate form. It has a right-angle bend, but has a pharyngeal cavity smaller than that of adult, modern *Homo sapiens*

Index of Names

Index of Subjects